Memorial Book of Kremenets
(Kremenets', Ukraine)

Translation of
Pinkas Kremenits; Sefer Zikaron

Original Yizkor Book Edited by: Abraham Samuel Stein

Published in Tel Aviv 1954

Published by JewishGen

**An Affiliate of the Museum of Jewish Heritage—A Living Memorial to the Holocaust
New York**

Memorial Book of Kremenets
(Kremenets', Ukraine)
Translation of: *Pinkas Kremenits; Sefer Zikaron*

Copyright © 2020 by JewishGen, Inc.
All rights reserved.
First Printing: December 2020, Kislev 5781

Editor of the original Yizkor Book: Abraham Samuel Stein
Published in Tel-Aviv, 1954
Translation Project Coordinator: Dr. Ronald D. Doctor
English Translation Editors: Dr. Ronald D. Doctor and Ellen F. Garshick
Layout: Jonathan Wind
Cover Design: Rachel Kolokoff-Hoper
Name Indexing: Bena Shklyanoy

Published by JewishGen, Inc.
An Affiliate of the Museum of Jewish Heritage
A Living Memorial to the Holocaust
36 Battery Place, New York, NY 10280

JewishGen, Inc. is not responsible for inaccuracies or omissions in the original work and makes no representations regarding the accuracy of this translation. Digital images of the original book's contents can be seen online at the New York Public Library website.

The mission of the JewishGen organization is to produce a translation of the original work, and we cannot verify the accuracy of statements or alter facts cited.

Printed in the United States of America by Lightning Source, Inc.

Library of Congress Control Number (LCCN): 2020949673

ISBN: 978-1-939561-97-8 (hard cover: 564 pages, alk. paper)

Cover Credits:

Front Cover:

Background photo by Rachel Kolokoff Hopper
Background image, map of Kremenets from the book page 8
Illustration from the book "Near the High School" page (334) 397

Back Cover:

Background photo by Rachel Kolokoff Hopper
Background image, map of Kremenets from the book page 8
Illustrations from the book:
      Top of page, right: "Old Style House" page (351) 413
      Bottom right: "Street and Homes Scene" page (273) 355
Upper left photo from the book: R' Tsvi Menachem Rokhel page 271
Text from the editors page 7

JewishGen and the Yizkor Books in Print Project

This book has been published by the **Yizkor Books in Print Project**, as part of the **Yizkor Book Project** of JewishGen, Inc.

JewishGen, Inc. is a non-profit organization founded in 1987 as a resource for Jewish genealogy. Its website [www.jewishgen.org] serves as an international clearinghouse and resource center to assist individuals who are researching the history of their Jewish families and the places where they lived. JewishGen provides databases, facilitates discussion groups, and coordinates projects relating to Jewish genealogy and the history of the Jewish people. In 2003, JewishGen became an affiliate of the **Museum of Jewish Heritage—A Living Memorial to the Holocaust** in New York.

The **JewishGen Yizkor Book Project** was organized to make more widely known the existence of Yizkor (Memorial) Books written by survivors and former residents of various Jewish communities throughout the world. Later, volunteers connected to the different destroyed communities began cooperating to have these books translated from the original language—usually Hebrew or Yiddish—into English, thus enabling a wider audience to have access to the valuable information contained within them. As each chapter of these books was translated, it was posted on the JewishGen website and made available to the general public.

The **Yizkor Books in Print Project** began in 2011 as an initiative to print and publish Yizkor Books that had been fully translated, so that hard copies would be available for purchase by the descendants of these communities and also by scholars, universities, synagogues, libraries, and museums.

These Yizkor books have been produced almost entirely through the volunteer effort of researchers from around the world, assisted by donations from private individuals. The books are printed and sold at near cost, so as to make them as affordable as possible. Our goal is to make this important genre of Jewish literature and history available in English in book form, so that people can have the personal histories of their ancestral towns on their bookshelves for themselves and for their children and grandchildren.

A list of all published translated Yizkor Books in the project with prices and ordering information can be found at:
http://www.jewishgen.org/Yizkor/ybip.html

Lance Ackerfeld, Yizkor Book Project Manager
Joel Alpert, Yizkor-Book-in-Print Project Coordinator
Susan Rosin, Yizkor-Book-in-Print Project Associate Coordinator

JewishGen
Yizkor Book Project

This book is presented by the
Yizkor-Books-In-Print Project
Project Coordinator: Joel Alpert

Part of the Yizkor Books Project of JewishGen. Inc.
Project Manager: Lance Ackerfeld

These books have been produced solely through efforts of volunteers
from around the world. The books are printed using the Print-on-Demand technology and sold at
near cost, to make them as affordable as possible.

Our goal is to make this intimate history of the destroyed Jewish shtetls
of Eastern Europe available in book form in English, so that people can
experience the near-personal histories of their ancestral town on their
bookshelves and those of their children and grandchildren.

All donations to the Yizkor Books Project, which translated the books,
are sincerely appreciated.

Please send donations to:

Yizkor Book Project
JewishGen, Inc.
36 Battery Place
New York, NY, 10280

JewishGen, Inc. is an affiliate of the
Museum of Jewish Heritage
A Living Memorial to the Holocaust

Notes to the Reader:

We apologize ahead of time for the poor quality of images in the book. Often these images had been scanned from the original Yizkor books which were of poor quality to begin with, being copies of old photographs. Each transfer results in loss of quality. We have done the best we could, given the original material and the resources and technology at hand. Even though images often appear of higher quality on computer screens, that does not transfer to high quality images in print. A reader can view the original scans on the web sites listed below.

Within the text the reader will note "{34}" standing ahead of a paragraph. This indicates that the material translated below was on page 34 of the original book. However, when a paragraph was split between two pages in the original book, the marker is placed in this book after the end of the paragraph for ease of reading.

Also please note that all references within the text of the book to page numbers, refer to the page numbers of the original Yizkor Book.

The original book can be seen online at the New York Public Library site:

https://digitalcollections.nypl.org/items/d248b860-7a84-0133-2519-00505686a51c

or at the Yiddish Book Center web site:

https://www.yiddishbookcenter.org/collections/yizkor-books/yzk-nybc313839/shtain-a-sh-pinkas-kremnits-sefer-zikharon

In order to obtain a list of all Shoah victims from Kremenets, the reader should access the Yad Vashem web site listed below; one can also search for specific family names using family name option. These lists are continually updated by Yad Vashem, so it is worthwhile to periodically search these lists.

There is much valuable information available on this web site, including the Pages of Testimony, etc.
http://yvng.yadvashem.org

A list of this book and all books available in the Yizkor-Book-In-Print Project along with prices is available at:
http://www.jewishgen.org/Yizkor/ybip.html

Geopolitical Information:

Kremenets, Ukraine

The town is located at 50°06' N, 25°43' E and 213 miles W of Kyyiv

Period	Town	District	Province	Country
Before WWI (c. 1900):	Kremenets	Kremenets	Volhynia	Russian Empire
Between the wars (c. 1930):	Krzemieniec	Krzemieniec	Wołyń	Poland
After WWII (c. 1950):	Kremenets			Soviet Union
Today (c. 2000):	Kremenets'			Ukraine

Alternate names for the town: Kremenets [Rus, Ukr], Krzemieniec [Pol], Kremenitz [Yid], Kremenez [Ger], Kremenits, Kremenec', Kshemyenyets

Nearby Jewish Communities:

- Velikiye Berezhtsy 4 miles W
- Podlesnoye 5 miles SE
- Katerynivka 10 miles SE
- Pochayev 12 miles WSW
- Verba 13 miles NNW
- Vishnevets 14 miles S
- Kozin 16 miles NW
- Rakhmanov 17 miles E
- Shumsk 18 miles E
- Novyy Oleksinets 21 miles SSW
- Radyvyliv 21 miles W
- Pidkamin 21 miles WSW
- Dubno 22 miles N
- Lanivtsi 23 miles SE
- Brody 25 miles W
- Yampil 25 miles ESE
- Vyshhorodok 26 miles SSE
- Zaliztsi 27 miles SW
- Varkovychi 28 miles NNE
- Demydivka 28 miles NW
- Mlyniv 28 miles N
- Mizoch 28 miles NE
- Ozeryany 29 miles NNE
- Muravytsi 29 miles NNW
- Leshniv 30 miles WNW
- Zbarazh 30 miles S

Jewish Population: 6,539 (in 1897), 7,256 (in 1931)

MAP OF UKRAINE IN 2014

Map of Ukraine with Krements'

Hebrew Title Page of Original Hebrew/Yiddish Book

פנקס קרמניץ
ספר זכרון

PINKAS KREMENIEC
A MEMORIAL

המערכת:

מרדכי אוטיקר, מנוס גולדנברג, טוביה טרושינסקי, יצחק רוכל

העורך: א. ש. שטיין

הוצאת ארגון עולי קרמניץ בישראל

תל־אביב, תשי״ד / שתים עשרה שנה לשואה

Translation of the Title Page of the Original Hebrew Book

PINKAS KREMENIEC

A MEMORIAL

Editorial Board:
Mordechai Otiker, Manus Goldenberg, Tovye Troshinski, Yitschak Rokhel

Editor: A. S. Stein

Published by the Former Residents of Kremenets in Israel

Tel-Aviv 1954 – 5744/Twelve Years After the Shoah

PINKAS KREMENETS: A MEMORIAL

EDITORIAL BOARD

Mordekhay Otiker, Manus Goldenberg, Tovye Troshinski, Yitschak Rokhel

EDITOR

Avraham Samuel Stein

**Published by the Organization of Kremenets Emigrants in Israel
1954 / 12 years after the Holocaust**

TRANSLATION PROJECT COORDINATOR

Dr. Ronald D. Doctor

ENGLISH TRANSLATION EDITORS

Dr. Ronald D. Doctor and Ellen F. Garshick

This is a translation of *Pinkas Kremeniec: A Memorial,* published by the Organization of Kremenets Emigrants in Israel, 1954 (453 pages; Hebrew, Yiddish, Latin, and Polish).

TABLE OF CONTENTS

HEBREW SECTION

YIDDISH SECTION

TRANSLATION EDITORS' NOTE

This yizkor book has two major sections: one in Hebrew, beginning on page i, and one in Yiddish, beginning on page 274. Each section has a short table of contents, without page indicators. A detailed table of contents (including page indicators) for the entire book begins on page 451 of the book, but for convenience, we have moved it to the beginning of this translation.

It was not possible to maintain pagination as it appears in the book. The page numbers in the actual book appear in square brackets just *before* the first line of text that appears on each physical page of the book. In some cases, placement of the page numbers is not be exact because we also tried to maintain continuity of text. So we caution you to examine contiguous pages for the text you seek. Images of photos and line sketches from the Yizkor Book appear on or near the appropriate pages. In addition, we have added a List of Illustrations and a Name Index.

In translating Hebrew and Yiddish, we followed the guidelines used for all Kremenets-area translation projects, which are based generally on the ANSI Z39.25-1975 General Purpose Standard for Hebrew, YIVO's transliteration schema for Yiddish, and Alexander Beider's *Ashkenazic Given Names*.

There are no guarantees that the "rules" we have applied in this translation are "correct," but we have tried to be consistent in applying them, and we have tried to apply them in a way that allows the reader to work backwards to the original Hebrew or Yiddish (whoops, make that Yiddish) spelling. As Editor, I take full responsibility for changes I have made to our translators' work. And, I welcome any comments, criticism, and suggestions for improving this work.

If you identify any errors in the translation, or if you take issue with the way we have transliterated specific names, please advise me of them so that we can get them corrected. You can contact me at rddpdx@gmail.com.

Ellen Garshick
Ronald D. Doctor
Co-coordinators, Kremenets Shtetl CO-OP/Jewish Records Indexing—Poland
An activity of the Kremenets District Research Group
https://kehilalinks.jewishgen.org/Kremenets/web-pages/index.html

TRANSLATION ACKNOWLEDGMENTS

We are thankful to the volunteers who have generously contributed their time to this project. We especially thank Yocheved Klausner, who translated most of the Yiddish section, and Thia Persoff, who did the bulk of the Hebrew translation. Other volunteers who contributed translations and proofreading include Aya Betensky, Ite Toybe Doktorski, David Dubin, Howard Freedman, Rob Goldstein, Michael Hirschfeld, Jack Horbal, Lynne Tolman, and Steve Wien. Aya Betensky translated the Latin text and Jack Horbal translated the Polish text in the History chapter of Part One. The project also has benefited from expert assistance on particularly difficult translations. We particularly acknowledge the help we received from David Wilk of Bar-Ilan University Central Library in Israel and Ema Horovitz from Portland Jewish Academy and Portland State University, as well as Shalom Bronstein, Jules Feldman, Nathen Gabriel, David Goldman, Alan Hirshfeld, and Sara Mages. In addition, Steve Wien secured the services of professional translators, Sari Havis (for Hebrew), Aviv Tzur (for Hebrew), and Rabbi and Mrs. Ben Friedman (for Yiddish). Grzegorz Gembala of Krakow, Poland, translated much of the new material that appears in the Supplement.

We all are indebted to all of them for their devoted work on the project. We take full responsibility for changes made and any damage done to the work of our translators.

Ellen Garshick
Ronald D. Doctor
Co-coordinators, Kremenets Shtetl CO-OP/JRI-Poland
An activity of the Kremenets District Research Group
https://kehilalinks.jewishgen.org/Kremenets/web-pages/index.html

TABLE OF CONTENTS

This is the Table of Contents for the English Translation

R' Yitschak Ber Levinzon (the RYB"L)   A. Ben-Or (Orinovski)

Public Life

Zionism, Pioneering, Immigration

Kremenets Exiles in Israel

The Destruction of Kremenets

Remembrances and Customs

[ii]

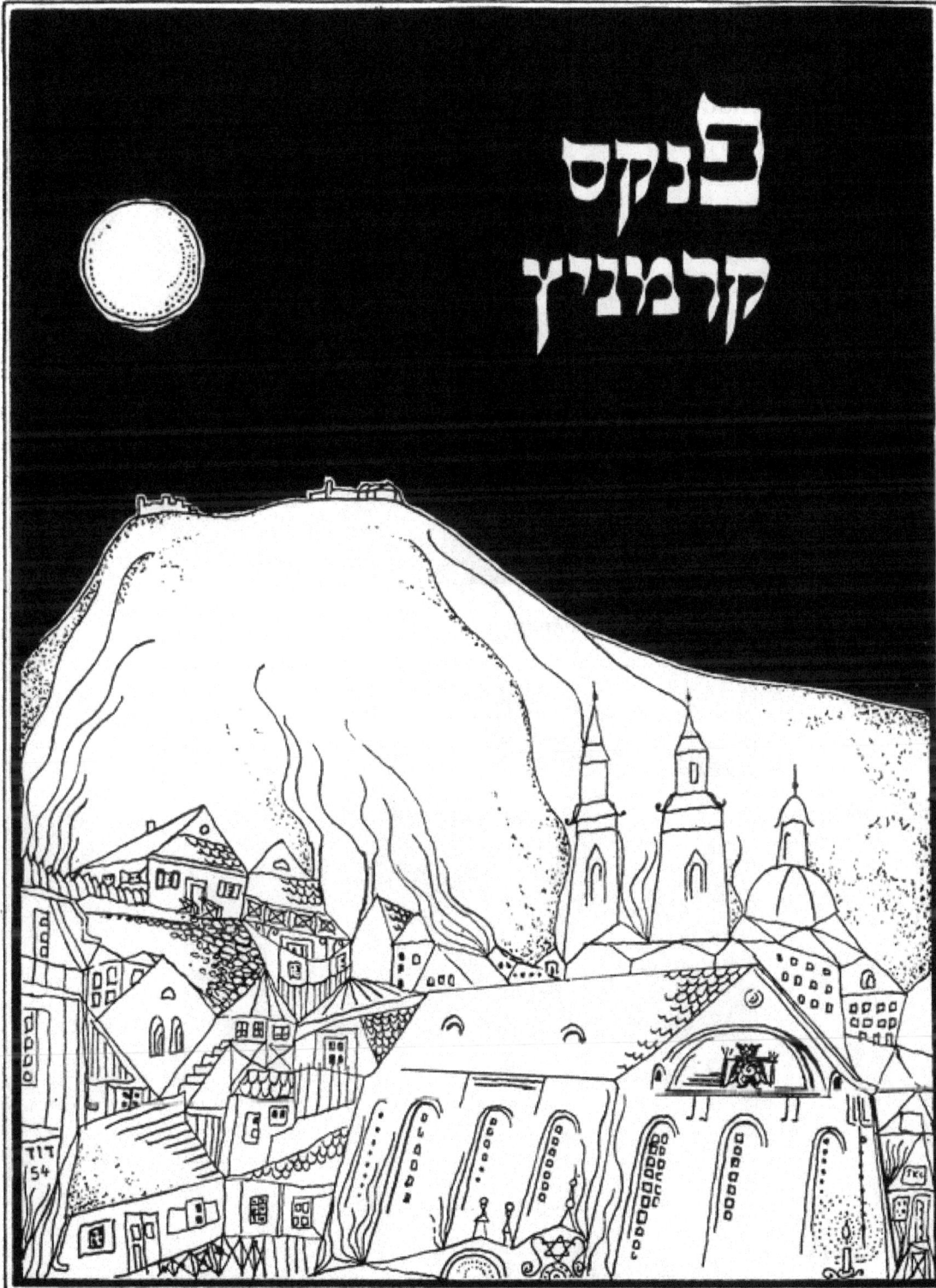

Kremenets and Mount Bona

[iii]

Cover—Duvid Tushinski, Paris
Graphics—Moshe Kagan, Kibbutz Shamir
Engravings—HaTsinkografiut HaMeuchadit, Tel Aviv
Printing Cooperative Achdut Inc., Tel Aviv

Kremenets, panoramic View

ביה הכנסת הגדול (צילום אלתר קציזנה)
„בית קדשנו ותפארתנו"
(הכתובת שהתנוססה בחזית בית הכנסת)

The Great Synagogue

Photograph by Alter Katsizne.
The inscription in the caption, "House of Our Holiness and Glory," appears on the façade of the synagogue.

PINKAS KREMENETS

PART ONE

Within the Book
History of Jewish Settlement in Kremenets
Chapters in the History of Kremenets Jewry
The RYB"L
Public Life
Zionism, Pioneering, Immigration
Education and Culture
Memories and Lifestyles
Characters and Personalities
Kremenets Exiles in Israel
The Destruction of Kremenets
Supplement

[4]

Contour Map of Kremenets and Surrounding Area

PLAN SYTUACYJNY

srodkowej części

MIASTA

KRZEMIEŃCA

Podziałka

G. Wołowica.

G. Przereza.

Objaśnienia:

1. Liceum.
2. Kościoł parafjalny rz. *
3. " bazonianbonski
4. " parafjanski względnie pobazyjanski/filowy/
5. Cerkiew Prawosławna Kaplica
6. " rzymska
7. Synagoga
8. Cmentarz katolicki
9. " pobazyjanski
10. " ruński
11. " żydowski
12. Starostwo
13. Sejmik
14. Magistrat
15. Poczta
16. Pow. Komenda Policji
17. Szpital powiatowy
18. Gimnazjum samorządowe
19. Kopalnia kredy

Park Licealny

G. Bony.

Boisko sportowe

G. Krzyżowa.

Kremenets Street Plan

LEGEND

1. Lyceum
2. Roman Catholic Church
3. Post-Franciscan Church
4. Reformed Church [unintelligible]
5. Orthodox Church of the Ascension of the Cross
6. Orthodox Church [unintelligible]
7. Synagogue
8. Catholic Cemetery
9. [unintelligible] Cemetery
10. [unintelligible] Cemetery
11. Jewish Cemetery
12. County Offices
13. Regional Council
14. City Hall
15. Post Office
16. District Police Headquarters
17. District Hospital
18. High School of Commerce
19. Chalk Mine

[**Translator's Notes:** The main north/south street is Sheroka, which means "broad." Four hills surround the town; for example, *G. Wolowica*, where *G.* stands for hill/mountain.]

WITHIN THE BOOK (INTRODUCTION)

The Editors (Tel Aviv)
English translation by Thia Persoff

The Jewish community of Kremenets was completely annihilated by the Nazi enemy along with the rest of the Jewish communities of Poland and Ukraine. Between 1 and 10 Elul 5702 [1942 CE], nearly 14,000 of the town's Jews were slaughtered. Only 14, who hid in caves and among the rocky crags, managed to escape. The extermination was accomplished with a satanic cunning: the first to be slaughtered were the heads of the community, its leaders and intellectuals. Then the young people were deported, never to return, killed in "labor detachments." The rest were locked in the ghetto, tortured, humiliated, and oppressed pitilessly. Stripped of strength of spirit and the ability to carry on, their national and human pride fell prey to unimaginable tortures—and when the bitter day arrived, they were defeated and slaughtered without even trying to mount an active, organized defense. Jewish young people, brave and proud, were plundered by the hands of evildoers.

So was destroyed and exterminated a magnificent community, capable and devoted, that wove its thread of existence for 500 years in an area that was a land of contention among Tatars, Lithuanians, Ukrainians, Poles, and Russians. Amid all the political perversities, the Jewish community persevered, shaped and strengthened its way of life, lived through times of highs and lows, wrote brilliant pages in the history of Jewish Volhynia, and produced leaders and Torah greats, writers and intellectuals.

But maybe its main greatness and value is in its spirited, folksy life—in the character of the laboring Jew who is content in spirit and soul, and full of the joy of life; who has deep emotional ties to Judaism and all its vivid creative forces, the campaigners and builders among them: Hasidim and *Mitnagdim*, Orthodox and intellectuals, pioneers of Love of Zion and Zionism, advocates of Hebrew and Yiddish culture, of socialism and the movement of those who work the Land of Israel, of pioneering and immigration—in all of those, the Jews of Kremenets took an active part, in body and soul and devotion.

> [**Translator's Notes:** *Mitnagdim*, meaning "opponents," were Orthodox Jews who were opposed to Hasidism. Love of Zion (in Hebrew, *Chibat Tsion*) was a 19th-century Zionist movement to rebuild the homeland of Israel.]

One day, this kind of life was cut down.

Fate left a remnant of fugitives from the town—people who had left it at different times—in Israel and the USA, in Argentina, and in small communities in other lands. In their hearts they carry the memories of their birthplace and their youth. These people have come together to commemorate it. Though the community was cut down, its name and remembrance will be perpetuated in a book. The difficult mission of publishing *Pinkas Kremenets* was taken up by the people who left Kremenets and now are living in Israel, with help and contributions from those living in other countries.

After four years of labor, we present this book as a small contribution to Holocaust literature and to Jewish historiography in general.

****

The book is the result of a collective effort by dozens of writers and the editors; each one told his memories and thoughts, and the chapters intertwine and form a true mirror.

Some of the articles were dictated to members of the editorial board. Some material was translated. We also used important material about times past from the newspaper *Kremenitser Shtime* to memorialize those who have passed away. Blessed are the young scientists, Sh. Etinger and Ch. Shmeruk of the University in Jerusalem, who wrote the historical monograph of the history of the Kremenets Jewish community—a work based on original sources.

[8]

Valuable material about Jewish daily life was contributed in tales from our comrades in America, particularly Chanokh Gilernt and others. Two Holocaust survivors, Betsalel Shvarts and Tova Teper, each contributed a chapter on the annihilation. We thankfully acknowledge all of them.

A son of our town living in the USA, Mr. Yitschak Vakman, helped us materially and spiritually. Our thanks are given to him here.

The material was collected according to a plan. We wanted the book to reflect and encompass the town's daily life and all its colorful variety of public, social, and intellectual activities. To our disappointment, we did not fully achieve our goal. And the book may be lacking. For example, surveys of Jewish merchant associations, the Joint's activities, the cooperative movement, cemeteries and their ancient gravestones, and even the Zionist movement and all its factions were not described properly (missing are descriptions of the Mizrachi, Betar, and others).

> [**Translation Editor's Note:** "The Joint" is a nickname for the Joint Distribution Committee, a worldwide Jewish relief organization. Mizrachi is a religious Zionist movement. *Betar,* which stands for *Brit* (covenant of) Yosef Trumpeldor, is the educational youth movement of the Revisionist Zionist Organization.]

But we did not want to postpone publication of the book for another year in an effort to complete it, and we decided—under pressure from many of our members—to publish it without any more delay and not to endanger its appearance.

Also, it was decided to publish the book in Yiddish, too, for our brethren in foreign countries and new immigrants in Israel. This has spread its readership but damaged its completeness a bit, increasing our budgetary struggles. For this reason, except for the opening historical chapter, the book was not translated from the Hebrew to Yiddish, and vice versa. The reader who reads both parts of the book will get a complete picture of Jewish Kremenets and life there. Much effort was invested in collecting the photographs, some of which have historical and artistic value.

Finally, we give our thanks to the editor, the writer A. Sh. Stein, who helped, led, and directed our work and designed the appearance of the book.

In the 12th year since the annihilation of the Kremenets community—1 Elul 5714 (1953/1954)—we present to you, the reader, *Pinkas Kremenets*, as a memorial to the last   generation.

[9]

HISTORY OF JEWISH SETTLEMENT IN KREMENETS

Sh. Etinger and Ch. Shmeruk (Jerusalem)

A. THE TOWN OF KREMENETS AND EARLY JEWISH SETTLEMENT THERE

English translation by Thia Persoff

Kremenets is one of the ancient towns of Volhynia. Its location on the highway between "Red Russia," Galicia, and Lithuania made it an important geographical crossroads. In addition, the mountains surrounding the town provided a favorable environment for erecting the castle around which the town developed. Some say that the town has existed since the 11th century and even before then, but documents show the date as the 12th century. In a Russian chronicle from 1226, the town is mentioned in connection with a Hungarian king's war against the principalities of Halych and Volhynia: "and the king went to Trembowla and conquered Trembowla. Then he went to Tikhomel, from there he went to Kremenets and fought near Kremenets. (The Russian prince Mstislav the Brave) killed and wounded many Hungarians."[1]

> [**Translation Editor's Note:** The numbered notes are footnotes in the original book. In this translation, they appear as endnotes.]

In the early 1240s, the armies of the Tatar commander Batu-Chan fought but failed to conquer the fortified castle of Kremenets. Nor did they succeed during their next try in the fifties. In the 1260s, at the demand of the Tatars, the Halych princes managed to destroy the town's fortifications. In spite of the Tatar invasion, the Halych-Volhynia principalities continued self-rule throughout the 13th and into the first half of the 14th century. Accelerating pressure by the Lithuanian princes began to have an impact in the middle of the 14th century. The Polish king, Kasimir the Great, took advantage of the weakening principalities and tried to conquer parts of them. He succeeded in annexing only the Halych lands to his domain. He was forced to give the Volhynia lands to the Lithuanian princes. In 1366, Prince Aleksander Koriatovich, a vassal of Kasimir the Great,[2] received the towns of Vladimir and Kremenets. After his death, the Hungarians took Kremenets, but by 1382 the town was back in the hands of the Lithuanian prince Liubart and was included in the Lithuanian principality.

---

[1] *Chronicles, Year 1226; ....* Moscow 1915, pp. 29-31.

[2] Lyubavski, M., *Historical Essay on the Lithuanian-Russian State System of the Lithuanian-Russian Union.*

In the late 14th and early 15th centuries, the lands of Volhynia were divided among three principalities: Lutsk, Kremenets, and Vladimir. After the Lithuanian Archduke Vitold (Vitovt) dissolved the principalities, the town of Kremenets and its district were governed by the archduke's appointee.[3]

[10]

Internal struggles and constant pressure by the Teutonic order paved the way for stronger relations between Lithuania and Poland at the close of the 14th century. Solving the difficult question of the Polish royal crown contributed to a process that concluded with a treaty in 1385, although a large segment of the Lithuanian aristocracy was opposed to it. The struggle surrounding the treaty greatly influenced the fate of all the Lithuanian archdukedoms. In 1430, after the death of Vitold, the tension reached its peak. The princes, together with the Russian Boyars, who had always been against a Polish-Lithuanian treaty, supported Svidrigaillo as archduke. A struggle for dominion ensued between Svidrigaillo and Prince Sigismund, who was supported by Polish King Jagiello, and ended with a crushing defeat for Svidrigaillo at the hands of his opponents. All the Lithuanian archduchies were now under the rule of Sigismund, except for Kremenets (thanks to its special geographical situation) and the eastern part of Podolia, which remained in the hands of Svidrigaillo until the mid-forties. During his rule over those small areas, Svidrigaillo wanted to make Kremenets his capital. This may explain the privileges, similar to those of the Magdeburg Law, granted to the townspeople of Kremenets in 1438 (e.g., approval of self-organization by the townspeople in the manner of German cities). These privileges gave the German Mayor Yorka the right to judge the "Russian, German, Volokhy, Armenian, Jew, and Tatar."[4] However, this does not prove that there was a permanent Jewish settlement in the town of Kremenets at that time. The document was apparently worded to attract new settlers to the town, which was destined to be Svidrigaillo's capital, by giving them favorable conditions. Jews, who were well known as an important factor in the economy, would have been among these settlers. Until the Jews were expelled from Lithuania in 1495, we have no document that in any way mentions the presence of Jews in Kremenets.[5]

One can assume that the settlement of Jews in Kremenets began with their return in 1503. Still, although the documents of special privileges decreed by Sigismund I in 1514 state that Jews are exempt from military service, Kremenets is not mentioned as

---

[3] Ibid., pp. 166-167. The governor of Kremenets carried the title *dyerzhavtsa* [prefect]. In the 1420s, the title was changed to *starosta* [elder].

[4] *Archives of Southwestern Russia*, part 5, vol. 1, p. 3 (hereafter *ASR*).

[5] Relying on Svidrigaillo's privilege-document, it was thought to date the onset of Jewish settlement in Kremenets as 1438. See E. Ringelblum, "The Jews in Kremenets before the End of the 18th Century," *Landkentnish* [Geography], 1934, p. 68, also reprinted in the Yiddish collection *Kapitalen Geshikhte*, Buenos Aires 1952, p. 146; also see Shatski, *The Decrees of 1648-1649*, Vilna 1938, p. 159. A thorough study of the documents from that period does not justify this assumption.

one of Lithuania's main communities.[6] However, by 1536, a significant Jewish settlement existed there. At that time, King Sigismund gave the Kremenets district to Queen Bona (Bona Sporza), and on that occasion he gave the district the privileges of the Magdeburg Law and freed them from taxes. Still, the same document says, ". . . but the Jews who live in the town of Kremenets will not benefit from the privileges, and they are not allowed in any way to disturb or harm commerce, by way of opposition to the privileges (of the townspeople)."[7]

[11]

In general, the kings of Poland-Lithuania valued, even encouraged, the Jews' economic activity in that period, and it is clear that this paragraph was inserted in the document of privileges on the demand of the townspeople. That they demanded the inclusion of a paragraph that is clearly directed against the Jews shows that the Jews were already having an effect on life in the town and that there was concern about competition from them. Characteristically, this document, the first to deal clearly with the Jews in the town of Kremenets, hints at the townspeople's conflict with the Jews. This conflict would be like a thread woven through the history of the Jewish settlement in this town for hundreds of years.

Jewish settlement in Kremenets is mentioned among other Jewish settlements in Lithuania for the first time in 1551.[8]

B. THE PROSPEROUS ERA (MID-16TH TO MID-17TH CENTURY)

English translation by Thia Persoff

The 100 years between the mid-16th century and the persecution decrees of the mid-17th century were a period of continual development and prosperity for the Jewish residents of the town of Kremenets.

How many Jews were in Kremenets in that period, and what were the goals of the development, quantitatively?

Royal Lithuanian documents are one of the most important sources of help in answering this question. During the reign of Sigismund Augustus II, a registration system was established for the royal lands in an effort to organize the administration of the Lithuanian archdukedom. The resulting lists were called *lustrations*.

---

[6] In this document, *Acts of Western Russia*, vol. 3, pp. 111-112, only the Jews of Truk, Horodna, Brisk, Lutsk, Vladimir, Pinsk, and Kobrin are mentioned.

[7] "... the Jews living in the city of Kremenets partake of these freedoms, but in spite of these freedoms, should not and will not disturb or interrupt commerce or trade by whatever means." *Archiwum XX Lubartowiczów*, vol. IV, p. 26, *Źródła dziejowe*: vol. V, p. 172. Also *ASR*, part 5, vol. I, p. 42.

[8] *Acts of Southern and Western Russia*, vol. 1, pp. 133-134; *Reading v. Social History in Ancient Russia from Moscow University*, vol. 199, p. 46.

[**Translation Editor's Note:** The word lustration derives from *lustrum*, which in ancient Rome was a purification of the people through ceremonies held every five years, after the census. Hence lustration, in the sense used here, has to do with a periodic census or registration.]

According to the 1552 lustration, there were 48 Jewish houses in the town of Kremenets.[9] In the 1563 lustration, the number of Jewish houses increased to at least 63.[10] The next lustration is from 1629, when there were 169 Jewish "smoke" (houses).[11] In addition, it is possible to get an idea of the number of Jews living in Kremenets from the taxes they paid, particularly since a "head tax" on the Jews was established in 1578. According to the list of taxpaying Jewish communities of that year, 100 gold coins were received from Kremenets.[12] Figuring one gold coin per "head" (head of household), the Jewish population was about 100 households in 1578.[13] Relying on all the information given in the lustrations and the head-tax lists, one can estimate the number of Jews in the town:

Year	No. of Units	No. of Jews	% Increase since 1552
1552	48 houses	240	—
1563	63 houses	315	52%
1578	100 "head"	500	102%
1629	169 "smoke"	845	252%

[12]

It is assumed that the town's population continued expanding until the mid-17th century decrees.

What percentage of the town's total population consisted of Jews?

In 1552, the total number of houses in the town of Kremenets was about 450. In 1629, the number was 1,119. From this, we calculate that the percentage of Jews was only 10.6% in 1552 and about 15% in 1629.

We should also mention the increasingly important socioeconomic status of the Kremenets Jewish community among the Jewish communities of Volhynia. In the breakdown of taxes, the percentage of overall taxes from Volhynia that came from Kremenets was as follows:

---

[9] *ASR*, part 7, vol. 2, p. 30.

[10] Ibid., pp. 42-63.

[11] *Kiyev Central Archive of Ancient Acts*, Book 1516.

[12] Baranovich, O., *Population of Ukraine*, Kiev 1930, p. 36; *Źródła dziejowe*, vol. XIX, p. 64.

[13] According to the Polish historian Yablonovsky, the estimate for a "house" or a "head" (family) is at least five people; p. 67.

Year	Percentage
1563	7.8[14]
1566	10.3[15]
1578	17.0[16]

The overall amount, we believe, tended to decrease. But the increases in the Kremenets Jewish population and in the community's importance in Volhynia are very apparent. The numbers above demonstrate that this was an era of prosperity for the Kremenets community.

During that period, the main livelihood of the Kremenets Jews came from business and assorted leases. As mentioned, Kremenets was situated on an ancient crossroads of commerce; of special importance was trade from south to north. The town is mentioned as a passageway for the salt trade. The privilege document of Sigismund I releases all the subjects of the Prince of Ostrog from paying taxes, no matter their origin, nationality, or religion.[17] From the 1430s onward, we have proof of business dealings between the Jews of Kremenets and Greater Poland. We see this in the city of Posen's council books.[18] In 1544, three Jews, the brothers Yitschak, Yosef, and Avigdor received a two-year certificate of protection.[18a] There is information about Jews from Kremenets who dealt in fattening and selling oxen on a large scale.[19] The increasing number of complaints by the townspeople and of royal orders forbidding Jews to disrupt the townspeople's businesses indicates the expansion of Jewish businesses.[20]

[13]

The information that we have about the assorted leases is greater than what we have about trade; Jews from Kremenets leased taverns in 1554–1557, and the development of Kremenets attracted Jews from other communities. Thus, in 1559, a Jew from Brest

---

[14] According to *Russian-Jewish Acts (RJA)*, vol. 2, p. 119.

[15] Ibid., pp. 184-185.

[16] *Źródła dziejowe*, vol. XIX, pp. 64-67.

[17] "... we have pronounced that all—subjects of whatever origin, nation, or religion, who are taking white Ruthenian salt by the ancient and customary routes through our military camp of Krzemyenyecz—will be free and exempt from all tax payments ...." *Archiwum XX Lubartowiczów-Sahguszków*, vol. III, p. 312.

[18] Litterae a dominis consulibus civitatis Posnaniae scriptae, 1535-1545, 40. L. Koczy, Handel Poznania do połowy wieku XVI, Poznań 1930, p. 274.

[18a] Wierzbowski, *Matriculum Regni Poloniae Summaria*. Warsaw 1905, IV 3, 225.

[19] *RJA*, vol. II, pp. 58-61.

[20] Since 1542, we have known of Queen Bona's edict that forbade Jews and people in the suburbs to manufacture alcoholic beverages (Ringelblum, op. cit.); similar forbidding edicts were given by Sigismund August II in 1564 (Balinski-Lipinski, *Starożytna Polska*, vol. II, p. 897; *Źródła dziejowe*, vol. V, p. 180), 1569 (*Źródła*, ibid., p. 173), 1571 (Balinski-Lipinski ... op. cit.), and 1572 (*Źródła ...* op. cit., 173).

took over the lease of the taverns, mills, and distilleries in Kremenets. In 1560, it went to a Jew from Vilna, the son of Feliks, who was in charge of the coin foundry in Vilna.[21] In 1561, this same Yakov, son of Feliks, succeeded in obtaining a special privilege from the king: a permit to build distilleries in Kremenets.[22] The lustration from 1563 notes that this Jew paid 750 large *shuk* (groszy), a very large sum in those days, to the king's treasury for all of his leases. Also, Jews from Kremenets, in partnership with a Jew from Vladimir, leased the collection of various taxes for the upkeep of the castle, such as the moat, as well as the business fee, the store fee, fees for horses and other livestock, and leases on taverns in neighboring villages.[23] It seems that there were also some Jews in charge of the Kremenets customs house.[24] In addition, we have some information about Jews from Kremenets who rented flourmills and water reservoirs in different villages, and some even owned them.[25]

Little information about the kind of work that the Jews did in that period has survived, although we do have information about the struggle of Jewish butchers in Kremenets against the Christian butchers' guild. According to the latter, the Jewish butchers refused to join the guild, so they had to pay taxes directly into the castle treasury.[26] The Jews, like the Christian townspeople, cultivated the land and had vegetable gardens and fruit orchards in town and in the suburbs.[27] According to the 1563 lustration, a Jew named Sore had more than 10 frants of land (1 frant = 56 square yards) in different areas of the town, as well as 6 frants of vegetable gardens and 16 frants of fruit orchards. A Jew named Avraham owned 8 frants in different areas of the town and 9 frants of vegetable gardens.

Additional evidence of the stable economic condition of the Jews of Kremenets is the employment of Christians by Jews in spite of the high taxes that this incurred.

Direct information about the economic activities of the Jews of Kremenets in that period is very limited, but the information we have corroborates the conclusions we derived from reviewing the numerical growth of the community: the Jews' economic worth increased. The community became more and more established in various economic sectors. Competition from the townspeople was unsuccessful in blocking growth in various sectors, and Jews from other towns were attracted to Kremenets. And so it was that Kremenets became an important town for the Jews, one of the leading communities in Volhynia province and all of eastern Poland.

---

[21] *RJA*, vol. II, pp. 62, 69, 79, 156.

[22] Kiev Central Archive, Book 1479, Act 56.

[23] *RJA*, vol. II, pp. 79-80.

[24] Ibid., pp. 138-139; Bersohn, *Dyplomataryusz*, No. 544.

[25] Ibid., p. 133.

[26] *ASR*, part 7, vol. II, p. 74.

[27] Ibid., pp. 51-55.

Until 1569, Volhynia belonged to the Lithuanian archdukedom, and its Jewish residents were bound to the Lithuanian rulers in all legalities and tax burdens. The basis for their legal standing in Lithuania was the privilege granted to the Jews of Brest by Lithuanian Archduke Vitold in 1388. According to that, the Jews were under his rule and that of his representative, the *starosta*. Eventually, Jewish self-rule was established in Lithuania, as it was in Poland, and the authorities recognized this self-rule.

[14]

The Lithuanian Jews, returning after the expulsion in 1503, were forced to recruit and pay for 1,000 horsemen to guard the country. Shortly after, this obligation was changed to regular monetary payment. In the mid-16th century (1563), Lithuanian Jews were compelled to pay 4,000 large *shuk* (groszy). Of this amount, Kremenets Jews had to pay 150 large *shuk*.[28] In addition to special taxes on Jews, they had to contribute, as non-Jews did, to the upkeep of the castle (its walls and towers as well as a cannoneer and his helpers) and to other community works (such the upkeep of the bridge over the river). For this purpose, a 2.5 percent tax per house was collected from all inhabitants of the town, Jews and Christians. Added to those were special taxes on stores and parcels of land, as well as other taxes.[29] Until 1556, residents had to contribute labor, but that year the king, Sigismund August II, released them from most labor and substituted special payments. In addition, Jews and non-Jewish townspeople had to pay *servashchizna* (money tax), which was levied irregularly from time to time as a tax for defense purposes.

The Lublin Confederation of 1569 severed Volhynia from Lithuania and added it to the Polish crown. The principles of Polish law began to penetrate Volhynia. Immediately after the declaration of unification, Volhynia's military governor, Aleksander Chartoriski, requested the right of jurisdiction over the Jews from King Sigismund II, as Volhynia was in Poland. The king granted his request, and on August 9, 1569, gave him jurisdiction over the Jews of Lutsk, Vladimir, and Kremenets, adding that no one was to dare to contest this privilege.[30] The annexation of Volhynia to Poland created a great deal of friction, as royal bureaucrats tried to take advantage of the unclear status of those territories and particularly that of Volhynia's Jews. In 1576, this resulted in a direct appeal by the rabbis and Jews in general to King Stephen Báthory for a clear declaration that Volhynia Jews had rights equal to those of Polish Jews and that Lithuanian jurisdiction over them had been abolished. On December 1, 1576, the king granted the petition and added the sentence, "In the future, the deputies of the military governors are not to judge [the Jews of Volhynia] differently or in different places, but together with two leaders of the Jews, in their house of worship."[30a] This

---

[28] Bersohn, *Dyplomataryusz*, No. 120; *RJA*, vol. II, pp. 119, 184.

[29] *ASR*, part 7, vol. II, p. 71.

[30] *RJA*, vol. II, p. 259.

[30a] Bersohn, op. cit., no. 152.

paragraph was a first for Volhynia's Jews, as there was nothing like it in the privileges given to Lithuania's Jews.

Polish King Báthory's new system for levying taxes included a special head tax on the Jews (*pogłówne żydowskie*). In 1578, Jews of Volhynia paid 587 gold coins, of which 100 gold coins[31] were the portion from Kremenets. The special tax was to be paid by Jews who employed non-Jews (as mentioned above). In 1583 the tax was raised to 15 gold coins only for the Jews of Kremenets.[32]

[15]

What was the character of the Jewish community in Kremenets during this period?

We have no information about the Kremenets Jewish community's internal organization in the first half of the 16th century. The abovementioned lustration of 1563 gave us a glimpse the Kremenets Jewish community, with all its assets and institutions. The lustration includes registrations for two lots for the house of worship. These may be a synagogue and a study hall. Added to this were a hospital (Hekdesh—Jewish Hospital) and a Jewish cemetery. In the town, there was also a rabbi or a head of a study hall by the name of Shmuel and a beadle named Yosko (Yosef). A Jewish physician is also mentioned.

In "1573, in the days of the MHRSh"L (R' Shlome Luria), the head of the Kremenets yeshiva, R' Yitschak Ha-Kohen, was teaching Torah." This R' Yitschak was the son of R' Duvid Shapira, who later was a rabbi in Krakow, and the son-in-law of the MHR"M of Lublin. The latter was very proud of his son-in-law and used to sign most of his responsa "the in-law of the royal genius, our teacher the rabbi, R' Yitschak, righteous Kohen." R' Yitschak Shapira's responsum is cited along with those of the other great ones of that generation, the supporters of the MHRSh"L, in the famous case of the release from wedding vows of a woman whose husband was killed in battle by Muscovites in the city of Polotsk in 1563.[33]

Until 1587, R' Mordekhay Yafe, *Ba'al Halevushim,* held the Kremenets rabbinical chair and was the head of the yeshiva there. "He is the distinguished scholarly rabbi, the notable elder who carries the flag of the Jewish nation, etc., who was rabbi and head of yeshiva for as many as 20 years in the holy communities of Gorodno, Lublin, and

---

[31] *Źródła dziejowe*, vol. XIX, p. 64. Even before that, there is information (*Archiwum Skarbowe, Dz. I pobocowy*, 112) that 106 gold coins were received from the Jews of Kremenets as a tax. We thank Mr. A. Feldman, who gave us a copy of this information as well as the information in Note 18a. It is interesting to point out that in 1576, King Stephen Báthory released the rabbi, cantor, house of worship, and Kremenets cemetery from the *protowszczyzna* tax (Bersohn, ibid., no. 149). According to Shipper, this tax was collected from all Jewish communities for the privilege of having a house of worship and a cemetery, and from all the magnificent holy places because of the bureaucrats in the community. See *History of the Jewish People*, vol. 9, p. 307.

[32] *Źródła dziejowe*, op. cit., p. 148.

[33] *David's Offspring*, 1573; Fridberg, *Memorial Tablets*, p. 9. His answer is found in New Responsum 28, note on the women's gallery.

Kremenets. He has educated many students and is a leader among the great heads of yeshiva and judges of the three lands."[34]

> [**Translation Editor's Notes:** MHRSh"L is an abbreviation for "our teacher the rabbi R' Shlome Luria." MHR"M is an abbreviation for "our teacher the rabbi, R' Meir." Responsa (*teshuvot*) are written decisions and rulings on Jewish law.]

In 1587, the head of the rabbinical court in Kremenets was R' Shimshon, son of R' Betsalel, the brother of the MHR"L of Prague. That year his signature was on a document signed by 30 rabbis prohibiting and banning the purchase of rabbinical degrees. In 1597, at the Jaroslaw fair, these decrees were renewed, and the first signature again is that of R' Shimshon, son of R' Betsalel of Kremenets. Apparently, he was the rabbi there until the end of the 16th century.[35]

> [**Translation Editor's Note:** MHR"L is an abbreviation for "our teacher the rabbi, R' Liva."]

From this list of rabbis, we can see that Kremenets was already one of the leading Jewish communities in Volhynia province and an honored one in Poland in the 16th century. We learn this from the character of the rabbis and from the role of R' Shimshon, son of R' Betsalel, in reforming the regulations by the Council of Four Lands. In 1596, too, one of the two judges of the "land of Volhynia" was R' Avraham of Kremenets.[36]

In the early years of the 17th century, the head of the rabbinical court of Kremenets was R' Yehuda, son of R' Naftali.[37]

The last head before the decrees of 1648 was R' Chayim, son of R' Shmuel Ashkenazi Ish Tsvi. It appears that he represented Kremenets at the conventions of Volhynia's communities, which were initiated by R' Yom Tov Lipman Heler, as he writes in *Scroll of Hate*:

> [**Translation Editor's Note:** *Scroll of Hate (Megilat Eivah)* was R' Yom Tov Lipman Heler's autobiography.]

[16]

> And lowly me, in the holy community of Vladimir, with principals and leaders of that region, we confirmed my original words and added to them, as they were only about those who receive money; but these leaders and I have added prohibitions and ostracisms on top of the accepted ones. Because of this, I

---

[34] *David's Offspring*, 1592; Fridberg, *The History of Hebrew Printing in Poland*, Tel Aviv 1939, p. 145. R' Mordekhay Yafe was called *Ba'al haLevushim* [master of clothing] after his articles and many books about clothing, Jewish law, the Rambam's philosophy, and the Kabbalah. He was admired by rabbis but had opposition, too. See, for example, *Masat Binyamin* and others.

[35] Y. Halperin, *Register of the Council of Four Lands; Memorial Tablets*, p. 16.

[36] Halperin.

[37] Fridberg, *Hebrew Printing*.

acquired enemies and much hostility, without good reason, and they spread fiendish accusations about me. In spite of all that, I did not retreat. I joined the convention in the holy community of Vishnevets (Wisniowiec, near Kremenets) in the region of Lutsk, where the leaders of the four holy communities of Volhynia—Vladimir, Ostrog, Kremenets, and Lutsk—got together. On 18 Adar, all of us—the heads of the four communities' yeshivas, along with the emissaries of the heads of other lands, as is the custom—reconfirmed the prohibitions and ostracisms. In addition, we announced those decisions most efficiently, in a large public meeting.[38]

This was in reference to the ban against buying a rabbinical degree.

About half a year after the Vishnevets convention, a major dispute broke out between the leaders of the Volhynia communities and the writer of "The Additions of Yom Tov" on the matter of the Lokachi community's rabbinate. The Ostrog community approached the leaders of the Vladimir community (where Yom Tov Lipman Heler lived) with a request to restrain their rabbi's extreme opposition to R' Yozl of Lokachi. A similar letter, signed by the rabbi and leaders of the Kremenets community, did the same.[39]

The abovementioned Rabbi Chayim kept his rabbinical chair until the 1648 decrees and witnessed the demise of his community. He passed away in 1649 and was eulogized by R' Avraham, son of Yisrael Yechiel Rapaport, the Rabbi of Lvov, who called him "my in-law."[40]

In 1644, as the representative of Kremenets at the Four Lands convention during the Jaroslaw fair, R' Yakov of Kremenets signed an approbation on book publishing.[41]

---

[38] *Scroll of Hate*, by R' Yom Tov Lipman Heler, Braslav 1817.

[39] M. Brann, "Additions à l'autobiographie de Lipman Heler," *Revue des Etudes Juives* [Review of Jewish Studies], vol. 21, p. 274.
The signatures on the letter are:

"Chayim, son of my master, my father, our teacher Shmuel Ish Tsvi

Eliezer son of my master, my father, our teacher Barukh, may his memory be for a blessing in the world to come

Shlome son of my master, my father, Rabbi Yisrael Isarel, may his Rock preserve him and keep him alive

Yosef, son of my master, my father, Rabbi Aharon

Moshe and Yitschak, son of my master, my father, our teacher Shmuel, may he live a long and happy life, amen

Avraham son of my master, my father, my honored teacher Tsvi Hirsh, righteous Kohen, may he live a long and happy life, amen"

R' Yitschak, son of Shmuel, whose signature is on this letter, may be the same R' Yitschak of the holy community of Kremenets who was eulogized by the one of the "Citizen Eytan." See *Responsa Citizen Eytan*, last pamphlet, Nitsavim portion, p. 58.

[40] Yitro portion, p. 48.

[41] Y. Halperin, *Register of the Council of Four Lands*, 198.

Kremenets was established as an important center of Jewish learning not only because some of the generation's greatest rabbis held the rabbinical chair there, but also because sages from outside the town settled there. In the early 17th century in Kremenets, we find important scholars whose writings are widely read. R' Yosef, son of the holy R' Moshe of Kremenets, wrote a commentary on *The Great Book of Commandments* by R' Moshe of Kotsi and received "the acceptance of the sages and heads of Poland's and Volhynia's *yeshivot.*" Among them were *Ba'al Halevushim* R' Mordekhay Yafe and R' Shmuel Eliezer, son of R' Yehuda.[42] This R' Yosef also wrote other books.[43]

[17]

Also of the Kremenets community was R' Aharon Shmuel, son of R' Moshe Shalom, author of the book *Man's Soul,* which was published in 1617 in Hanau, with the approbation of R' Yeshayahu Horovits, author of *Two Tablets of the Covenant.* The reasons for R' Aharon Shmuel's leaving Kremenets had to do with some unexplained persecution.[44] After wandering for a long period, he accepted the rabbinical chair in the town of Fulda, Germany.[45]

> [**Translation Editor's Note:** In Hebrew, *Man's Soul* is *Neshamot Adam,* and *Two Tablets of the Covenant* is *Shney Lukhot Habrit.*]

Other proof that Kremenets was an important religious center is that R' Shimshon, head of the holy community in the town of Brest, copied an "extremely old" book found in Kremenets.[46]

We also know that the Kremenets community had ties to Israel. It is well known that emissaries from Israel visited the Jewish communities of Poland with the purpose of collecting donations to help in the resettlement of Israel. In 1645 and 1646, R' Yitschak Binga Ashkenazi of Jerusalem toured Poland's main communities, and he mentions Kremenets in the list of towns he visited.[47]

Thus the general picture of social and religious life in the Kremenets Jewish community parallels some of the lovely passages in R' Natan Neta Hanover's book, *Abyss of Despair,* describing the life of Polish Jewry before the great destruction. In

---

[42] Y. Halperin, ibid.

[43] Ben-Yakov, *The Book Treasury,* p. 63, #121-2.

[44] "and me … Aharon Shmuel the small, son of my master, my teacher, the pious one, our teacher, Rabbi Moshe Shlome, the holy, righteous one of blessed memory, from the holy community of Kremenets, in the country of Russia, may God keep it forever, as God led me astray from the home of my father, my teacher, the righteous one of blessed memory, and from my native land, my country. From diaspora to diaspora I was expelled, from vessel to vessel emptied. Insecure, no rest or peace did I have because of certain bad things that were visited upon me … ." *Man's Soul,* Introduction.

[45] *Epilogue,* by Olma Zelikman.

[46] *Responsa Citizen Eytan,* last pamphlet, Vayeshev portion, p. 42, side A.

[47] A. Yaari, *Israel's Emissaries,* p. 271.

spite of all the exaggeration in the mourner's words, we can definitely agree with him: "The famous ones do not require proof that there was not as much learning in the Diaspora as in the land of Poland"—and among the important communities in Poland was the holy community of Kremenets.

[**Translator's Note:** In Hebrew, *Abyss of Despair* is *Yeven Metsula*, and *The Suffering of Many* is *Tsar Bat Rabim*.]

C. THE DECREES OF 1648 AND 1649

English translation by Thia Persoff and David Dubin

The great events that shook Poland in the middle of the 17th century resulted in widespread disaster for all of its Jewish residents, and particularly those in the eastern districts. There were many reasons for the Cossack rebellion, led by Bogdan Chmielnitski ("Chmil the Evil," as he was called by our people), which most Ukrainians joined within a short time. There was a sharp socioeconomic contrast between the oppressed Ukrainians and the ruling Polish nation, between serf and landowner, and between the Ukrainian Pravoslavic farmers and the Polish Catholic nobility. At the core of the enormous force of the eruption was the fact that Ukrainians were mostly Pravoslavic farmers while Poles were mainly Catholic nobles. The Jews in Ukraine were tied economically to the Polish nobility, but this did not make them an independent factor in this struggle.

The rebellion began on the Dnieper River. But before Chmielnitski had the opportunity to organize the Cossacks into an army, the indentured farmers rose up in all the areas east of the San. Banding together in gangs, they attacked farms and towns, murdering and pillaging. Led by Maksim Krivonos, the gangs acted with frenzied violence, especially in Volhynia and Podolia, until Chmil and his army arrived. They acted with excessive brutality and cruelty.

[18]

The surge of riots arrived in Volhynia with dizzying speed: the Polish army was attacked on May 26, 1648, near Korsun, and by June 10 the besieged Nemirov had already fallen, and its Jews were slaughtered. In June and July, Tulchin, Bar, and Polonnoye fell. After a meeting between the Polish representative, Jeremi Wisniowiecki, and Krivonos in the vicinity of Konstantynow, the Polish army retreated westward, and all of eastern Volhynia was given over to gangs, who were joined at the end of July by Chmil's Cossacks.

Kremenets was not damaged by the gangs until the end of July, since the area was used as a staging area for the Polish army.[48] Despite a great deal of harassment in the area, the gangs did not bother Kremenets during September and October. Only after

---

[48] W. Tomkiewicz, *Jeremi Wiśniwiecki*, Warsaw 1933, p. 215. See app. A and *Abyss of Despair*, Venice 1653, p. 6.

Chmil's armies laid siege to Lvov and began to send gangs in different directions did Chmil send Dzhidzhaly, a famous gang leader, to set siege to and capture the town and its defenses. He began on October 20, continued until December 13, and finally captured the town and its defenses and completely destroyed it.[49] It is likely that some Kremenets Jews managed to escape before the siege, but the descriptions of the community's destruction found in Jewish chronologies are apparently tied to this siege and capture of the town.

There is no doubt that the descriptions of contemporaries, Jews and non-Jews alike, require investigation. A witness to the destruction of communities and the mass murder of fellow citizens is not inclined to investigate specific events and the exact numbers killed. By quoting the records, he seeks to emphasize the magnitude of the destruction. In his thoughts, the frightening sights and terrifying reports combine into a single catastrophic vision. From this approach, we evaluate the stories of the events in Kremenets as they appear in the chronicles of the events of 1648–1649.

No eyewitness accounts exist of the decrees in the holy community of Kremenets. Testimonies were written down from hearsay. In *Stressful Times,* R' Meir of Szczebrzeszyn mentions the killing in the community when Chmil's armies laid siege to Lvov:

> [**Translator's Note:** In Hebrew, *Stressful Times* is *Tsuk Haltim.*]

> For several miles around Lvov,
> Greece dwelled with all the armies
> and killed among the Jews with death as their aim,
> leaving the provinces of Volhynia empty.
> They flew lighter than eagles and were braver than lions;
> the province is destroyed, arise, arise.
> Kremenets, the holy and great community,
> they destroyed her and left her at the bottom of the sea,
> and they killed Jews without mercy.
> The cruel one slaughtered 100 children,
> a holy seed pleasantly planted,
> the blossom of Israel, Levites and priests.
> When the evil one killed them in anger,
> he told the cruel ones standing with him:
> throw all the prey to the dogs.

[19]

> And the evil one slaughtered the others
> and exposed the area to be cut as if they were cows,
> laughing and saying, these are kosher.

---

[49] N. Kostomarov, *Bogdan Chmielnitski*, St. Petersburg 1884, vol. 1, p. 341, and the comment in *Stressful Times* connect the fall of Kremenets with this siege on Lvov, which began in early October 1648.

> And they killed in every corner of the cities,
> the fleshy along with the dainty;
> they gave them no mercy.[50]

In describing the destruction of the large community of Kremenets, the author specifically emphasizes the slaughter of "100 children" and the desecration of their bodies, which reminds him of the traditional connection with nonkosher meat.

Other chronicles return to this motif. In *Abyss of Despair*, R' Natan Neta Hanover, after mentioning "also in the province of Volhynia, in the holy community of Vladimir, the holy community of Lyuboml, the holy community of Lutsk, the holy community of Kremenets, and their outskirts, they carried out great massacres of several thousand Jews," continues in the manner of *Stressful Times*: "And in the holy community of Kremenets, one evildoer took a ritual slaughtering knife and slaughtered several hundred Hebrew children, asked if this was kosher or nonkosher, and threw them to the dogs. Afterward, he took one corpse, uncovered the place of the cut, said, 'This is kosher,' and examined it as one does kids and lambs. They carried the corpse on a stake through all the streets of the town, and he announced, 'Who wants to buy kids and lambs?' May God avenge their blood."[51] In *The Suffering of Many*, R' Avraham Ashkenazi says, "No evil like this calamity had ever befallen the holy community of Kremenets or the holy community of Bar. The enemy fell upon the small children, sharpened the knife, and slaughtered them in a complete carnage. Afterward, they hung them by their feet above, as it is done. They opened their throats, examined them, and asked, is it nonkosher or kosher?"[52]

[**Translator's Note:** In Hebrew, *The Suffering of Many* is *Tsar Bat Rabim*.]

This unique occurrence in the description of the Kremenets massacre was elaborated on further in the retelling: R' Natan Neta Hanover transformed R' Meir of

---

[50] *Stressful Times*, by R' Meir of Szczebrzeszyn, Venice 1655, p. 8, col. 2. This source, of utmost importance, was left out of the bibliography on Kremenets during the decrees of 1648 found in Y. Shatski's introduction to the Yiddish edition of *Abyss of Despair* (*The Decrees of 1648*, YIVO, Vilna, 1938, p. 195). Note that this list is faulty and is missing many details.

[51] *Abyss of Despair*, pp. 8-9.

[52] Quoted from *The Suffering of Many*, Fridberg edition, Lvov 1906, p. 11. In the British Museum manuscript (p. 103), the city is called "Kremnik." Gurland (*The Occurrence of the Decrees*, booklet, p. 16) corrects this to "Kresnik," but this correction has no basis, since the story of the children's slaughter agrees with the one about Kremenets in *Stressful Times* and *Abyss of Despair*. There is no doubt that this quotation is also about Kremenets. Our thanks go to the administration of the Central Archives for the History of the Jewish People, which made the abovementioned manuscript available to us.

[52a] This story is also mentioned by N. Kostomarov, *Russian History in Biographies*, St. Petersburg 1874, vol. II, pp. 243-244. It is interesting to note the connection between the sanctification of God's name and kosher slaughtering ("anyone with a sharp knife should inspect its blade to see that it does not have any deficiencies and should slaughter in the name of the Holy, Eternal One"; *Decrees of Germany and France*, Jerusalem, 1946, p. 31, and similar descriptions elsewhere in the same source) in the stories about the decrees of 1196. The chroniclers of the 1648 decrees regarded the entrusting of this holy task to gentiles and the differentiation between kosher and nonkosher as a mockery.

Szczebrzeszyn's sentences into another frightful incident of mockery: the "slaughterer's knife," the examination for kosher status, and the traditions of the Jews in general. And according to R' Avraham Ashkenazi, there was also a desecration of the slaughterhouse, in which the bodies were hung up on hooks.[52a]

A later chronicle, *Deep Mire,* states, "From there Chmil went to the holy community of Kremenets, where there were 800 householders, and nearly all were killed."[53]

[20]

Apparently, refugees from the community who went to Germany expressed a similar impression of hundreds slaughtered, as is also mentioned in the Memorial Book of the community of Worms: "The innocent and holy, several hundred souls of Israel, who were killed and burned and gave their lives into water, sanctifying the Holy Name in the holy community of Kremenets in 1649. May their souls be bound up in the bonds of eternal life."[54]

Without pursuing the question of the numbers and particulars of the slaughter, it is clear from all of the above that the Kremenets community was destroyed in 1649. The refugees left in various directions. Information on one of the refugees has been preserved for us in a letter from R' Yochanen, son of R' Meir, head of the rabbinical court of Markisch Friedland (in the Posen district): ". . . my renowned father, our rabbi and teacher Meir Kremenetser, who escaped in the decrees of 1649 to Kalisz; he was the son of the Kabbalist Rabbi Yitschak."[55]

The sentiment of the descendants of that generation and their assessment of general and personal destruction are genuinely described by R' Moshe Naral, a native of Kremenets,[56] in his heartfelt eulogies for all the children of Israel in Poland:

---

[53] *Deep Mire,* by R' Shmuel Fayvish, son of the sage, our teacher, Rabbi Natan Faydel of Vienna (*The Occurrence of the Decrees,* booklet 6, p. 22).

[54] Handwritten collection III, p. 30. Also, the martyrs of Kremenets are mentioned in the Memorial Book of the holy community of Furth; *Jahrbuch der jüdisch-litararischen Gesellschaft,* Frankfurt am Main, XVI, p. 246.

[55] Y. Halperin, *Register of the Council of Four Lands,* p. 462.

[56] R' Moshe Naral was the son of R' Eliezer Velshim, who arrived in Poland in his youth and finally settled in Kremenets as a doctor. R' Moshe was apparently born in 1598 in Kremenets and was a student of our teacher the rabbi Shmuel Eydels. During the decrees he was the head of the rabbinical court in the holy community of Naral. From there he escaped westward and was chosen as a rabbi in the holy community of Metz (Gurland, *The Occurrence of the Decrees,* booklet 3, pp. 8-9, and the literature cited there in note 4).

Along with R' Moshe Naral, other rabbis grew up in Kremenets: his brother, R' Yisrael Kohen Naral, whose insights on the Torah are cited in *Good Blessings* by his brother R' Moshe, and R' Yakov, son of R' Pinchas of Kremenets, head of the rabbinical court of the holy community of Pinczow, who is mentioned several times in *Good Blessings*. He was killed during the decrees (Girondi, *History of the Scholars of Israel and Sages of Italy,* Trieste 1853, p. 156). R' Moshe Naral's son was R' Tovye the Doctor, who is famous for his book *Tovye's Deeds* (Tsinberg, vol. V, pp. 169-173).

Those who wait for death and search for it in the depths,
the leaders of thousands of the wise and intelligent of Israel,
we are for God, and to God our eyes are looking,
and they died for the holiness of the Lord of the first and the last.
I turned from hearing, I despaired of seeing and was overcome by trembling,
how could holy stones be spilled in every street,
and the holy seed be intermingled with the nations of the world,
and the small temples be like scattered limestone blocks.
In noble Poland, ancient seat of Torah and renown
since the days when Efraim split from Yehuda,
the Torah was learned and sealed,
and now is exiled and removed, desolate and forsaken.[57]

D. THE ERA OF CONSOLIDATION

English translation by David Dubin

We do not know exactly when the community of Kremenets was reestablished after the decrees of 1648. There are even traditions that the Council of Four Lands amended its ban "not to live in the province of Ukraine" after the decrees.[58] But we know that a few years after 1648, Volhynia's Jews had already begun to return to their places.

[21]

And as early as 9 Nisan 1656, the emissary of the Kremenets community, "Yitschak son of Rabbi Ozer of blessed memory of Kremenets," appears among the signatories to the judicial ruling by the supreme leaders of the Lands at the *Gromnits* fair in Lublin.[59] One can infer from this that the Kremenets community suffered at most a six-year hiatus. Although the community was reestablished, it did not return to its former glory for many years, until 1793, during the second partition of Poland, when all of Volhynia was annexed to the Russian state.

> [**Translation Editor's Note:** *Gromnits* refers to the Catholic holiday *Gromnice* (Candlemas Day, in February).]

As mentioned, before the events of 1648–1649, the Kremenets community comprised more than 800 people. In the Jewish census of the Kremenets vicinity on January 2, 1765, 649 Jews were counted in Kremenets proper, and together with its environs, there were 1,029.[60] Even if we allow for a certain percentage who were not counted (the census was performed for the purpose of assessing per capita taxes), even considering

---

[57] *The Occurrence of the Decrees,* booklet 3, p. 15.

[58] Halperin, *Register of the Council of Four Lands,* pp. 79-80.

[59] Ibid., p. 87.

[60] *ASR,* part 5, vol. II, p. 109.

that one-third were not counted,[61] the number of community members in 1765, more than 100 years after the events, does not exceed the number before the events. Comparing this static condition with the continual increase before the 1648 decrees, and especially comparing the state of Kremenets in 1765 with that of other communities in Volhynia, even nearby communities, such as Starokonstantinov and Lakhovtsy, one can argue that the weakening of the Kremenets community is quite apparent.

	1629	1765	% gain or loss
Kremenets	845	649	−23
Lutsk	440	1,112	+153
Kovel	400	825	+106
Dubno	290	1,923	+663
Starokonstantinov	650	1,394	+114
Lakhovtsy	185	589	+218

Moreover, in the towns and villages in the Kremenets district where communities had not previously existed, the number of Jews also increased, while the number in the central town did not. Before the decrees of 1648, Jews were known to live only in 13 cities and towns in the Kremenets district, and in 1765, Jews lived in 40 cities there, in addition to the large number of settlers in the surrounding villages. In 1765, 20,085 Jews were counted in the Kremenets district,[62] which constituted the second-largest

---

[61] Dov of Bolikhov notes in his memoirs that in his city, one-third of the Jews were not counted in this census. Published by M. Vishnitser, p. 89.

[62] The following are the populations of the Kremenets district Jewish communities in 1765 (the numbers include the community and its vicinity). Communities marked with an asterisk were known to have a Jewish settlement before 1648. We do not list towns without an independent community separately.

*Starokonstantinov	1,801	Yampol	476	Vishgrodek	668
*Vishnevets	664	*Zbarazh	910	*Kozin	332
Verba	181	Krupets	114	Lanovtsy	85
*Pticha	112	Teofipol	516	Kuzmin	232
*Polonnoye Stare	897	Shumsk	170	Kulchiny	288
Polonnoye Nove and *Ostropol	544	Rokhmanov	170	*Bazaliya	240
Sudilkov	397	Lyubar	467	Krasilov	273
*Zaslav	3,891	Shchepetovka	390	Kremenets	1,029
*Lakhovtsy and *Kornitsa	860	Slavuta	246	Kunev	325
*Radzivilov	298	Labun	678	*Gritsev	86
Leszniow	494	Oleksinets	317	Ozhigovtsy	317
Gorinka	203	Volochisk	774	Zalozce	644
					20,085

Jewish population in Volhynia after the Lutsk district—23,289 Jews—many more than the Vladimir district's 7,421.[63]

[22]

How can we explain the stagnation of the Kremenets community during this period?

We have seen that in the same era in which the Kremenets community did not flourish, other communities in Volhynia and even in the Kremenets district itself did so. Therefore, we cannot ascribe the situation to the destruction resulting from the decrees of 1648–1649.

Events after 1648 changed the entire complexion of the Polish state and even its method of governance. The monarchy, which had been weak beforehand, was even weaker after the disturbances. The nobility, particularly the large landowners, had more and more influence over the management of the state, and the existing administrative order teetered. This phenomenon is best appreciated with regard to cities that were under the direct influence and rule of the king's administration or, as they were called, "royal cities." The functionaries stationed in these cities were interested in amassing the maximum benefit for themselves. Often, the cities were administered by low-level officials, and they were obviously that much less reliable. Especially in this era, these cities found themselves increasingly in competition with cities located on noblemen's land and under their rule and guidance or, as they were called, "private cities." The owner of the private city, interested in its expansion, used all his influence to protect residents' rights, including those of Jewish residents. Moreover, royal cities were by and large administered under the Magdeburg Law, which gave townspeople great power, and they tried to use the law against the Jews, as these cities had no incentive for restraint. On the other hand, in private cities the owners determined the character of relations between the Jews and the citizenry. Thus the Jews fled royal cities like Kremenets to privately owned settlements in the area. Practically speaking, it seems that the Jewish population of Kremenets was greater than that counted in the census, but in some counts Jews may have been included as residents of private cities.

Moreover, the Kremenets Jews' situation was worse than in many other royal cities. The frequent wars and their attendant terror also left a mark on community life. Relations with Kremenets townspeople were strained during the entire era under discussion.

[23]

The priesthood joined these enemies of the Jews of Kremenets, and the severe blood libels of the mid-18th century were promulgated from this camp of persecutors.

---

[63] All numbers and calculations are based on *ASR*, part 5, vol. II; O. Baranovich, *Population of Ukraine. Archiwum Komisji Historycznej AU w Krakowie*, vol. VIII; J. Kleczynski and F. Kloczycki, *Liczba glow zydowskich w Koronie z Taryf roku* 1765.

As far as we can determine, the era of persecution began in 1687, when the local Franciscans complained about the Jews, saying that the city manager had sided with them. They complained that the Jews were allowed to build houses close to the church or encroaching on the Uniate Cemetery and made other, similar accusations. Their complaints were transferred to the tribunal in Lublin.[64]

The 18th century in Volhynia began with the ominous appearance of Cossack attacks and wars. In 1702, a Cossack rebellion broke out under the leadership of Samus Weflay. They enlisted the villagers in revolt against Polish rule and particularly against Polish officers and Jews. After capturing 20 cities west of the Dnieper River, several bands advanced into Podolia and Volhynia to the Bug River.[65] We have information about severe attacks on Jewish settlements in the Kremenets district: In 1703, the Jews and townspeople of Starokonstantinov entered in the annals of the siege a declaration of a week of destruction in Kremenets in 1702 by the Cossacks.[66] A similar declaration was entered in the annals of the Jews of Lyubar, also in the Kremenets district. In this declaration, the Jews complain not only about the rebelling Cossacks of 1702, but also about the Polish army and its Mazfa Cossack allies, who came to Volhynia to quash the rebellion, looted them, and refused to allow them to return to their homes.[67] Presumably, the Kremenets community also suffered from these armies. The Polish army and the Russian Cossack army from Mazfa, which had participated in the northern war against Sweden, entered Volhynia. We have testimony of the Jews' complaints about these armies' actions. In 1706, the Swedish army invaded Volhynia, decreed a heavy tax, and looted every location that came into their hands. After the Swedes retreated, the Russian armies entered and repeated their enemies' actions. In 1707, the Polish army came in place of the Russians, and it also demanded money and provisions from the impoverished population and attacked it, especially the Jews. In the annals of the siege of Kremenets, two declarations of the inhabitants report their inability to continue to pay the required contribution due to the destruction of the preceding years.[68] Similar statements are recorded by residents of most towns in the Kremenets district.[69] The Haidamaks also apparently attacked the Jews in the Kremenets district.[70] After the Haidamak revolt of 1768 and the beginning of the war between Russia and Turkey, "the plague increased (in 1770), and the fire spread in many districts in innumerable cities and villages, to the point where the Jews fled their land, left their houses and property, and escaped to be hamlets and fields. The panic also increased in the region of Volhynia." An eyewitness, an inhabitant of

---

[64] Ringelblum, *Kapitalen Geshikhte*, pp. 147-148.

[65] A. Zaluski, *Epistolae historico-familiares,* vol. III, p. 333.

[66] *ASR,* part 3, vol. I, pp. 599-601.

[67] Ibid, pp. 681-682.

[68] *ASR,* part 5, vol. I, p. 236, in the editor's notes.

[69] Ibid. The following cities are mentioned: Lakhovtsy, Zalozce, Yampol, Stary and Novy Zaslav, Polonne, Vyshgorodok, Kunev, Zbarazh, Leszniow, Slavuta, Labun, and Sudilkov.

[70] *Documents and Inscriptions,* vol. III, no. 2176.

[70a] *A Bundle of Hyssop,* by R' Yakov Yisrael of Kremenets, part 2, p. 22, col. 1.

Kremenets, describes the situation in his town as follows: "I fled to Berestechko and stayed there desolately, fearful and trembling, expecting to hear what had happened in my town. During the week of the *Shoftim* portion, a refugee came to say that the town had been conquered and all its inhabitants were also fleeing, dwelling together in the dust. The people observed Sukkot, trembling from the plague, the rains, the bread no longer in their vessels, and the sustenance and provisions cut out of their mouths and out of those of many villages near and far...."[70a]

> [**Translation Editor's Note:** "The week of the *Shoftim* portion" refers to the portion of the Torah read each week. *Shoftim,* in the book of Deuteronomy, would be read in August or September.]

[24]

The 18th century is famous in Polish Jewish history for its cycles of blood libels. The popularity of libels was rooted in the economic bitterness between the townspeople and the young nobility on one side and the Jews on the other. There is no question that directions for libels were given by the Catholic priesthood, which was always and forever notable for its hatred of the Jews. Also, the upsurge in the struggle of the Orthodox priesthood, which was supported by the Russian government, had no small part in the blossoming of libels. Several libels took place on Volhynian soil, and Kremenets in particular was a forum for several libel trials.

In 1747, in Zaslav, the fate of several Jews who were accused of killing a Christian found frozen in the snow was decided before the governor and the citizen-prosecutors of Kremenets. As a result of this judgment, four Jews were taken for execution.[71]

Several years later, an attempt at a blood libel was made in Kremenets itself. In 1753, one of the Christian residents of the town attacked his three-year-old daughter and stabbed her through the heart in a stable belonging to a Jew. Luckily for the Jews of Kremenets, the girl did not die of her wounds and testified against her father. The Jews registered a complaint in the Kremenets castle court regarding this event.[72]

In 1756, a blood libel case from Yampol was heard in Kremenets. R' Elyakum son of Asher Zelig, one of the accused of Yampol, escaped from prison in Kremenets to nearby Starokonstantinov, where the Council of the Lands sat in those days. There it was decided to send a special emissary to Rome, and R' Elyakum volunteered "out of personal responsibility to include himself in the troubles of Israel."[73] As a result of his efforts, the Pope decided to investigate the affair and delegated responsibility to Cardinal Ganganelli (later Pope Clement XIV). The Cardinal assembled a great deal of material about the history of blood libels and in 1758 presented a memorandum that

---

[71] I. Galant ... 1747. *Jewish Past,* vol. 5(1912), pp. 202-218.

[72] See Addendum 2. It is interesting to note that a similar attempt in the same year near Zhitomir ended tragically for the accused Jews.

[73] M. Balaban, *History of the Frankist Movement,* vol. 1, pp. 105-106; Halperin, op. cit., pp. 418-424, 428.

acquitted the Jews of these accusations. One of the major proofs in his memorandum regards the abovementioned incident of the Kremenets blood libel.[74]

It is worth mentioning that the area surrounding Kremenets never ceased to be a center for the blood libel phenomenon: In 1772, at Pochayev Lavra near Kremenets, a Russian translation of the anti-Semitic text called "Fables of the Talmud" was published;[75] it had originally appeared in Polish in 1758, during the famous dispute with the Frankists in Lvov. Among other matters, this book discusses the blood libel. The Russian translation was published a second time in the same place in 1794, with the annexation of Volhynia to the Russian state.[76]

> [**Translation Editor's Note:** Pochayev Lavra is a monastery of Orthodox Christian denominations in Pochayev.]

[25]

We should not assume that these incidents in the vicinity of Kremenets are mere coincidence. We have already noted that relations between the townspeople and the Jews were especially strained. We can imagine that this tension is what led directly to this anomaly, and there is no question that this affair further weakened the Jews' status in the town.

Relations between the townspeople and the Jews of Kremenets, which were strained during this entire era, were especially so in the second half of the 18th century. The townspeople maintained that the Jews had no right to lease the town's taverns. In 1777 and 1778 they brought their complaint to the authorities, and the affair reached its peak in 1778, when it was dealt with at length. As a result, relations became more and more strained.[77] Furthermore, the townspeople complained about the Jews' right to retain houses that had been built on town land many years before and attempted to forbid the Jews to rebuild their homes after fires during those years. In 1781 the affair reached the courts, which ruled against the Jews, despite the intervention of the governor, Prince Sangoszko.[78] The municipal record of 1789 shows that the verdict was not enforced. The townspeople complained about Sangoszko, who "does not allow the judges' verdicts between the townspeople and Jews to be carried out and protects the Jews with his soldiers from the enforcements of these verdicts, etc.; the Jews do not want to come to agreement; they refuse to billet the soldiers; they occupy trades and occupations and services without licenses from the town; they do not want to pay taxes on their businesses to the town coffers; they do not participate in paying fees for the upkeep of roads and bridges; they build on thoroughfares and in places where they are not allowed; they do not pay taxes to support town services and the students

---

[74] A. Berliner, "Gutachten Ganganellis (Clemens XIV)," in *Angelengenheit der Blut Beschuldigung der Juden,* Berlin 1888, p. 47; C. Roth, *The Ritual-Murder Libel and the Jew,* London 1935.

[75] Talmudic Fables ....

[76] Yu. Gessen, *History of the Jewish People in Russia,* Leningrad 1925, vol. I, pp. 98-99.

[77] Ringelblum, op. cit., pp. 149-150.

[78] Mentioned by A. N. Frank, *The Townspeople and the Jews in Poland,* Warsaw 1921, p. 57.

sent to school in Krakow."[79] These words show the sharpness of the struggle between the two sides, a struggle that was especially difficult for the Jews because of the contemporary parliamentary policy of inciting the cities. The Jews had been exempted from taxes until then because of founding privileges bestowed by the municipalities and their councils. New rulings of the Sejm provided an opening for the townspeople to ask for judicial limitations on and taxes from the Jews. Since Kremenets was a royal city, the Jews were at a disadvantage, despite the governor's support. At the end of that municipal record, we hear the recordkeepers' opinion of the town's status. They state that the townspeople's complaints and actions regarding the Jews were destroying the town and that many of the Jews had left. Despite this, a new Christian population had not materialized, so the town's income was not ensured. The town found itself in decline.[80]

[**Translator's Note:** The Sejm is the lower house of the Polish parliament.]

[26]

E. INTERNAL LIFE (FROM 1648 TO THE SECOND PARTITION OF POLAND)

English translation by David Dubin

What is known about the internal life of the Jews of Kremenets between the decrees of 1648–1649 and the entry of Kremenets into the Russian realm?

We have already mentioned that the community was reestablished soon after the decrees, and in 1655 we find R' Yitschak son of Ozer's signature on a judicial ruling of the Council of Four Lands. This same R' Yitschak of Kremenets continued his public service not only in the Kremenets community and the Volhynia District Council, but also in the Council of Four Lands. In 1661, he signed a judicial ruling of the Four Lands regarding a refugee from Posen. [81] He was chosen as one of the two representatives of the Volhynia district to the Council of Four Lands meetings to be held in Przeworsk. At the request of the Vladimir community, his election was recorded in the municipal archives there.[82] Around 1687, we meet him again as one of

---

[79] T. Korzon, *Internal Events of Poland*, Warsaw 1897, vol. I, p. 221. "X. The city elders do not allow the execution of decrees drawn in soviet or communal courts, specifically preventing Jews from executing such decrees by military force, etc. The Jews are not willing to forgive the contractual obligations, are resisting feeding the soldiers, engage in trading prohibited goods and commerce without authorization from the city, refuse to pay taxes to the city coffers, do not pay taxes for road and bridge repair, obstruct city streets with their buildings and build in prohibited areas, do not pay taxes for city workers and students sent to Krakow schools...."

[80] Ringelblum, op. cit., p. 151.

[81] Halperin, op. cit., pp. 93-94.

[82] Ibid., p. 105, XXII.

the leaders of the "Volhynia district" in the distribution of the tax burden among the various districts during the celebrations of the Four Lands.[83]

The ancient principal communities of the council of Volhynia jealously guarded their positions; the strength of this stand is shown by the fact that only two additional communities—Dubno and Kovel—managed to become principal communities. Kremenets continued in its status as a principal community. One document reveals a bit of the Volhynia District Council's internal workings and procedures. This is the document appointing R' Fishil son of Leyb as district leader beginning in 1705. R' Fishil was a well-known community worker from Vladimir who had worked for many years as a trustee and leader of the Four Lands and the district. Apparently, the leaders of the autonomous Jewish institutions in Poland were already heavily embroiled in difficulties by that time, and few were willing to jump into these situations. The representatives of the principal communities, among them R' Leyb son of Menashe and R' Leyzer son of Moshe of Kremenets, implored R' Fishil to take on the district leadership again, and they obligated themselves to lighten his load: "He will not have to arrange the division (of taxes) for the surroundings (settlements subordinated to the principal communities and the district), only for the principal districts along with their settlements and for the cities of our district, Volhynia."[84] Kremenets also dominated a broad surrounding area, including several settlements larger than itself.

In 1720, the Volhynia District Council met in Kozin. The town's rabbi at that time, R' Shmuel son of Efraim of Vladimir, and R' Moshe son of Menachem Mendil Margalit participated as emissaries of Kremenets.[85]

At that time, the problem of old debts owed to the Kremenets community and several of its inhabitants arose among the leaders of the Four Lands. At that time, "R' Mikhel (of Kremenets) lent to all of the lands." Of this amount, the leaders of the lands were obligated to pay a set sum to the Kremenets community (325 złoty per year) and to the donor's heirs (72 złoty). The 1724 Jaroslaw council expresses the view that "this debt is operative permanently, and the abovementioned payment will be assessed yearly and paid to the holy community of Kremenets without any delay or interference, and with an eternal obligation on our trustees of the Four Lands, and this judgment in the hands of the holy community of Kremenets empowers it as if it had a lien from the trustees of the lands worth 397 zloty yearly."[86] Apparently, the R' Mikhel who is mentioned in this document is identical to "Officer Merkil," who later traveled with his wife to the Land of Israel, and soon after the decrees of 1648 he opened a *kloyz* in Kremenets.

---

[83] Ibid., p. 469.

[84] *ASR*, part 5, vol. I, pp. 221-223.

[85] Halperin, op. cit., p. 277.

[86] Ibid., p. 300, XLVIII-XLIX; according to the list of obligations and Kremenets city records.

[**Translator's Note:** *Kloyz* (plural: *kloyzelakh*) is Yiddish for small study hall or synagogue.]

[27]

It was said, "He lent an enormous amount to the officers, the leaders of the Four Lands, to provide for the relatives of the poor and students, first to those nearer, and he also stipulated that they should give a yearly specified sum to the poor of Jerusalem."[87]

The Volhynia District Council protected the Jews' affairs in the district not only in the narrow range of the district itself and in relation to the Council of the Lands; it also helped the merchants of Volhynia in their business outside the country. In 1733 a representative specifically for the district sat in Braslav. Kremenets appears as one of the cities he represented. Its Jewish merchants apparently reached Silesia. On the power of attorney granted this representative in 1734 is the signature of "R' Barukh (apparently this should be R' Arye) Leyb the rabbi in Kremenets and the district trustee of Volhynia."[88] R' Arye Leyb served as the Volhynia representative at meetings of the Council of Four Lands for the purposes of dividing the tax burden in 1739.[89] He apparently was very rich, and the community owed him substantial amounts. In 1750 he acquired from King August III the privilege of serving as rabbi in Kremenets and its surroundings and as district trustee and trustee of the House of Israel in the Four Lands.[90]

In 1735 and 1758, the aforementioned R' Moshe son of Menachem Margalit served as leader of the Volhynia district.[91]

In 1750, "Bner (Avner?) of Kremenets" signed an invitation to the community of Chernobyl along with other leaders of the Volhynia district.[92]

In 1758, the municipal records of Kremenets record a protest by the Volhynia district trustees (the rabbi of Kremenets, R' Arye Leyb, and the rabbi of Vladimir, R' Shaul) against the communities of Ostrog and Lutsk. The trustees claimed that the Ostrog community, "the first and the greatest of the communities of Volhynia," refused to pay the expenses, which approached 38,000 gold pieces, incurred by the district trustees while they attended to the Jews' affairs in the aforementioned community. A District Council convened in Rokhmanov to deal with these expenses certified their justice, but

---

[87] Ibid., p. 462.

[88] D. Weinryb, *Studies In the Economic and Social History of the Jews in Poland,* Jerusalem 1939, pp. 40, 62. It is known that during this time the rabbi of Kremenets was R' Arye Leyb son of Shmuel, who was also a Volhynia district trustee.

[89] Halperin, op. cit., p. 313; *Greater Dubno,* p. 47.

[90] M. Bersohn, *Dyplomataryusz* etc., No. 305.

[91] Ibid.

[92] Documents and Inscriptions, vol. III, no. 1973.

the community of Ostrog did not pay even the amount that it acknowledged.[93] In that same convocation in Rokhmanov, the district leader, R' Moshe son of Menachem Mendil, and the other district leaders gave power of attorney over their own affairs and the settlement of the district accounts to the abovementioned trustees. This power of attorney arranged tax collection and debt coverage for 10 years. Besides the district leader, other signatories were three other representatives from Kremenets: R' Duvid son of Yakov, Eli son of Moshe, and Leyb son of Leyb.[94] In the same year (March 25), the District Council convened in Korets and, among other things, decided that several satellites of the Kremenets community would be transferred to the community of Teofipol. Among those signing were other delegates from Kremenets: Chanokh son of Chayim, Eli son of Moshe, and Zelig of Yampol.[95]

The Council of Four Lands was disbanded in 1764, but the District Councils continued to function even afterward.

[28]

In 1774, we find the rabbis of Kremenets and Dubno arranging the tax burden of the Ovruch community. They voided a previous decision by the rabbis of Kremenets and Polonnoye.[96]

From these small amounts of information, a picture forms of the Kremenets community as active in the District Council and sometimes appointed by its members to the positions of district leader and trustee. Nevertheless, we also see the decline of Kremenets: settlements previously subordinated to its authority freed themselves and were transferred to other communities of greater note.

The first rabbi known to us after the decrees (of 1648–1649) is Nachman son of Meir Katz Rapaport, also known as Lifshits (his mother's name). He was a judge—the head of the rabbinical court in Lvov—and from there was appointed head of the rabbinical court and head of the seminary in the holy community of Kremenets. His approbation of the book *Gates of Zion,* by R' Natan Neta Hanover, was given in Kremenets on 17 Kislev 1662. However, the next year we find that he had already become the rabbi of the holy community of Dubno.[97]

> [**Translator's Note:** In Hebrew, *Gates of Zion* is *Sha'arei Tsion.*]

After R' Nachman, we know that the Kremenets rabbi was the renowned Rabbi Yakov son of Eliezer Temerils of Vermayza. When he left Germany, he went to Lublin "and

---

[93] Ibid., no. 2058.

[94] Ibid., no. 2060.

[95] Ibid., no. 2059.

[96] Ibid., no. 2229.

[97] His signature at the Jaroslaw fair in 1663 shows him already as the rabbi of Dubno. Afterward he served as the rabbi of Belz. He died in 1674. On him, see Halperin, pp. 98, 126; Pesis, *The City of Dubno,* pp. 15-17; *Knowledge of the Holy Ones,* p. 152; *Men of Renown,* pp. 172, 239.

from there he pitched his tent, the tent of Torah, in Kremenets in the Volhynia district and settled there for many years and disseminated Torah in Israel overtly and covertly...and as he disseminated Torah in Kremenets, his name had already become well known by all of the exiles of Israel as a holy man of God, to the point where many of the great men of Israel would appear early at his door to bathe in the light, the dear light, and to hear enervations and discoveries about things open and hidden. Because R' Yakov was a simple man besides being a true sage in the Talmud and the rabbinical decision makers, and because his name was known in all the great gates of Jewish law for his Responsa, which he sent to those requesting his opinion on matters of Jewish law, he was also the rabbi of the entire Diaspora in the wisdom of Kabbalah, as is written in the frontispiece of his *Book of Jacob's Humility*, which he wrote in keeping with the ways of Kabbalah according to the writings of the ARI, of blessed memory...."[98] At the end of his life, he settled in Vienna.[99]

> [**Translator's Note:** In Hebrew, *Book of Jacob's Humility* is *Sifra Detseniuta de Yakov.* ARI is an abbreviation for the name of Rabbi Yitschak Luria.]

In the 1671 Council of the Lands during the Jaroslaw fair, R' Meir son of Yitschak, "who dwells in the holy community of Kremenets," signed approbations for books. Apparently, he is the R' Meir Kremenetser, mentioned above, who escaped to Kalisz during the 1648 decrees.[100]

Rabbi Yehoshie Heshil, son of R' Tsvi Hirsh, head of the rabbinical council of the holy community of Lvov, was a leader of the Lvov community and the district of Russia and a director of the Four Lands, as his father was.[101] He served as rabbi of the Kremenets community during the 1680s and 1690s. There he gave approbations for several books between 1688 and 1695.[102]

After him, apparently, "Yakov son of my master, my father, the sage, the great teacher, Rabbi Yitschak" served in the rabbinate of Kremenets and the district.

---

[98] *Perfect Beauty*, 117. His book was published after he died in 1669.

[99] Ibid.; Girondi, p. 210.

[100] Halperin, ibid., pp. 121, 462; Fridberg, op. cit., p. 145.

[101] His signature appears in the Council of Four Lands at the Lublin fair in 1678 with those of his father and the rest of the leaders of the Lands on an approbation of the publication of a Bible with a Yiddish translation, published by R' Yosef Atiash, Amsterdam 1678, and on an approbation of the Lands of the holy community of Tykocin's request for a permanent representative at the "table of Four Lands." Halperin, ibid., pp. 163, 165; *Men of Renown*, p. 85; *Perfect Beauty*, section 1, 85; section 2, 95.

[102] Loewinstein, *Key to Approbations*, Frankfort am Main 1923, no. 1864; Halperin, ibid., pp. 213-214; Fridberg, op. cit.

[29]

We know of his approval of the books *City of Benjamin* in 1698 and *Book of Horns* in 1709.[103]

> [**Translator's Note:** In Hebrew, these book titles are *Ir Binyamin* and *Sefer Karnayim*, respectively.]

During the Council of Four Lands at the Jaroslaw fair in 1718, one of the signatories on a judicial ruling was "R' Shmuel the Insignificant of Vladimir, who dwells in the holy community of Kremenets and the district [?], who is mentioned above.[104] During the same council, he signed a ban on the publication of the book *The Face of Moses*.[105] We know that his approbation of the book *Living Torah* was given in Kremenets in 1711.[106]

> [**Translator's Note:** In Hebrew, these book titles are *Pnei Moshe* and *Torat Chayim*, respectively.]

We know that beginning in 1742, the rabbi in Kremenets was R' Arye Leyb son of R' Shmuel. As mentioned above, he served as trustee of the Volhynia district and participated in the Council of Four Lands' apportioning of taxes in 1739. In 1740, he received a letter of standing from August III, in which the king places him under his aegis and guards his rights to the rabbinate of Kremenets, where he had been serving for quite a while. As was the case for any rabbi of a principal town, any revenues that came to the rabbi of Kremenets would belong to him, even if he left the town. The same decree includes his appointment as trustee of the district and the Four Lands, as we have already mentioned, and a promise to appoint his son after him, if he is worthy of such. The king commands that the rabbi be paid all debts owed to him and places the responsibility for this on the heads of the community. The rabbi is also declared exempt from paying taxes and from responsibility for the community's debts.[107] It can be assumed that this privilege was given in return for a substantial payment—and to the discomfort of the community. These rabbis were generally appointed for a short time (three years) by community leaders, but some of the more helpful rabbis tried to ensure their standing by involving the ruler. One year after receiving the privilege, R' Arye Leyb, along with the rest of the leaders of the Four Lands, signed an approbation of the Amsterdam edition of the Talmud and, in 1752, of the responsum *House of Abraham*.[108] He was also involved in the famous dispute

---

[103] Loewinstein, ibid., no. 1603; Fridberg, ibid. *Book of Horns* is a book of Kabbalah published with a commentary by the famous Kabbalist R' Shimshon of Ostropol, who was killed in 1648.

[104] Halperin, ibid., pp. 277, 279, 280, 528.

[105] Ibid., p. 500.

[106] Fridberg, op. cit.

[107] Bersohn, op. cit., no. 305.

[108] "The insignificant Arye Leyb, son of the rabbi, the illustrious great light, my great teacher and rabbi Shmuel, the pious one, of blessed memory, who dwells in the holy community of Kremenets and the

between R' Yakov Emden and R' Yonatan Eybeshuts in Poland.[109] We also know of his approbations of 1746 and 1775, and it turns out that he served in the Kremenets rabbinate for over 30 years. His son R' Shmuel served in the Ostrog rabbinate.[110] After him, R' Arye Leyb son of R' Shmuel of Pinczow held the rabbinate. One of his approbations, given in Kremenets in 1782, has been preserved.[111]

> [**Translator's Note:** In Hebrew, *House of Abraham* is *Bet Avraham*.

Apparently, after him the rabbinate was occupied by R' Mordekhay son of Yisrael Halperin, who previously had been in Zaslav. He was the son-in-law of R' Yakovke of Brody. At the end of his life, he immigrated to the Land of Israel.[112]

At the end of the 18th century, we find in the community of Kremenets the *magid* R' Yakov Yisrael Halevi son of Tsvi, famous in his time, who authored the following books: *A Tribe of Israel,* a commentary on Psalms (Zulkva, 1772); *A Bundle of Hyssop,* a commentary on the Five Scrolls (Zulkva, 1782); and *True Voice,* a commentary on Proverbs (Lemberg, 1788).

> [**Translator's Note:** A *magid* is a preacher or narrator. In Hebrew, these book titles are *Shevet MeYisrael, Agudat Ezov,* and *Sfat Emet,* respectively.]

[30]

These books depict the social and ideological upheaval that characterized the Jews of Poland in the 18th century, and it appears that in his words we can hear an echo of the local conflicts.[113] Also known to us is the Torah scholar R' Meshulam Fayvish HaLevi Horovits of the community of Kremenets, who wrote *Teachings of the Sages* on the Six Orders of the Mishna,[114] which was published by his son shortly after his death (Ostrog, 1796), with the approbation of the "Famous One in Judea"—R' Yechezkel Landa and others.

> [**Translator's Note:** In Hebrew, *Teachings of the Sages* is *Mishnat Chachamim*. Six Orders (*ShA"S,* or *shisha sedarim*) refers to the six divisions of the Mishna (the Oral Law), which with the commentaries make up the Talmud.]

---

district and is trustee of the House of Israel, may his Rock preserve him and keep him alive." Halperin, ibid., pp. 360, 373.

[109] R' Yakov Emden, *Torat ha-Kenaot,* p. 64.

[110] Remembrance of the Great Ones of Ostrog, p. 169.

[111] Fridberg, op. cit.; Loewinstein, op. cit., no. 241.

[112] Remembrance of the Great Ones of Ostrog, p. 98.

[113] See Addendum 3.

[114] R' Meshulam Fayvish and R' Dov Ber, *magid* of Mezherichi (who was the head of the Hasidim after the Ba'al Shem Tov's death) were the respective fathers of a married couple. R' Avraham Malakh, the *magid*'s son, married R' Meshulam Fayvish's daughter. See *Praises of the Ba'al Shem Tov,* Horodetsky Publishers, Tel Aviv 1947, p. 88.

We can thus see that even in this era characterized by a lack of advancement and even relative decline, Kremenets continued to hold its central standing in the district, its community workers worked in external affairs, and its rabbis were renowned and were Torah scholars.

F. KREMENETS UNDER RUSSIAN DOMINION (1793–1917)

English translation by David Dubin

The second partition of Poland in 1793 brought Kremenets under Russian dominion. Practically speaking, this change did not affect the basic appearance of the social framework or the Jews' standing in the annexed territories. The Russian government adopted the Poles' organizational structure and traditional relationship with the Jews along with their problems. Furthermore, the Polish delegation of responsibility in Jewish affairs was such that the Russians gave a recognizable legal standing to the regional and district councils, even though the Polish authorities did not recognize any core Jewish leadership for a few years before the partition—after the dissolution of the Council of Four Lands (1764). Thus the Russian approach was established, especially after the ascension of Aleksander I (1801), because the government had no desire to become involved in the previously Polish territories' internal affairs or make any serious changes. In many ways, this worked to the Jews' detriment. The Russian government did not wish to shield the Jews from the landowners' accusations, which were increasing at the end of the 18th century, or from the townspeople's demands, even when they contradicted Russian law. The change in the Jews' political conditions in these territories began with the Polish uprising of 1830. The Russian authorities began to fight Polish nationalist aspirations by instituting specifically Russian structures in the territories annexed to Russia. This also left its mark on the lives of the Jews.

Immediately after the Russian annexation, Jews were required to register in one of two categories: townspeople or merchants. However, they were doubly taxed relative to the taxes imposed on members of the same categories in other religions. According to the law of 1804, Jews were condemned to ejection from the villages, but the authorities were unable to enforce this decree. Nevertheless, this symbolizes the new legal standing and the trend at that time: a loss of traditional trades and an increase in the percentage of Jews involved in specifically local finance.

After the partition of 1793, Kremenets found itself on the Russian-Austrian border. The town and its surroundings were separated from its previous economic base, which had been annexed to Austria, and, on the other hand, the proximity to the state's borders opened new financial opportunities, especially in the smuggling of people across the border. It is noteworthy that Kremenets was near Brody, the major trading city in Galicia, whose economic rise can predominantly be ascribed to its trade with Russia.

[31]

Illegal trade between Jews in Volhynia and those on the other side of the border drew the Russian government's attention in the first years after annexation. In 1812, the district governor of Volhynia suggested removing the Jews from the border region because of their smuggling of people, and the suggestion received royal approval. Similar decrees were published again in 1816 and 1821, and in 1825 they received the status of a general law, according to which Jews were only allowed to live within 50 *versts* of the border if they were with their belongings or in a settlement with an established community. [115] After this legal action did not bring about the results expected by the government—and apparently the smuggling continued—the government took an even more radical approach on April 28, 1843. It was decided "to remove to the interior wall Jews living within 50 *versts* along the entire border with Prussia and Austria, giving those with private houses the opportunity to sell them within two years and to fulfill this decree with no exceptions." [116] It is clear that, inevitably, this decision would completely destroy the Jewish settlement on the border, including the entire Kremenets community. Although the Russian authorities were hasty in promulgating cruel decrees, it was not in their power to enforce them.

> [**Translation Editor's Note:** A *verst* is a Russian measure of length containing 3,500 English feet. It is equivalent to 1.067 km, about two thirds of a mile.]

One can assume that the Jews immediately instituted great efforts to abolish the evil decree. Already in January 1844, the Senate had convened to clarify the issue and received the Czar's agreement to lighten several of the decree's clauses, among them a lengthening of the time to liquidate assets and special treatment of factory owners. [117] Also, the important roles that the Jews played for the government in the economy, especially their well-established involvement in leasing the right to sell alcohol (known as an "excise" tax), had a great influence in easing the decree in practice. For example, at the end of 1849, the rules for tenders for the abovementioned excise taxes explicitly mention that Jews in the border areas were allowed to participate. [118] In early 1850, Ginsberg and Landsberg, holders of the alcoholic beverage lease in Kremenets, Vladimir, and Lutsk, complained before the Senate [119] about the prohibition against border Jews selling alcoholic beverages. The Senate, however, did not accept the complaint but allowed alcoholic beverages to be sold in taverns belonging to Jews. The

---

[115] V. Levanda, *The Complete Chronological Collection of Laws and Legal Positions Concerning the Jews*, Petersburg 1874, no. 124.

[116] Ibid., no. 475.

[117] Ibid., no. 484.

[118] Ibid., no. 608; also 618, 716.

[119] This Landsberg was apparently Duvid Ayzik Landsberg, who published articles in *Hamelits* [a newspaper] and who is mentioned by Aleksander Tsederboym-Erez as being one of the city's enlightened during the disagreement that broke out in 1865. Regarding that, see below.

Senate mentions in its opinion the fact that the exile of the Jews from the border region had not been completed and, in another place, that "it has not even begun."[120]

Despite all this, this proclamation caused the Jews to suffer, and the decree hung over their heads until 1858, when it was repealed for Jews who were already "written" (listed in the community register) in the communities in the border region or who owned real estate in these areas. However, the settlement of Jews and new ownership of material in that region was entirely prohibited.[121] Even though this repealed the worst part of the decree for Jewish settlement in general, there were many Jews in various cities, including Kremenets, who for long periods were not listed among the communities. For them the ban was in force, even though the government apparently was not particular about it during the relatively liberal era of Aleksander II.

[32]

The changes resulting from Aleksander III's ascension brought about a shift in this matter. The idea remained, such that at the end of 1881 by the regional governor published a decree exiling approximately 2,000 Jews from Kremenets who were not "listed" in the area.[122]

Kremenets' burden as a town on the border took other forms as well, and its culmination came during World War I, when residents suffered not only from the hostilities in its vicinity but because the intergovernmental agreement of 1915 meant that they had to wander further inside Russia.

Nevertheless, the Jewish population of Kremenets and its vicinity grew during this period.

Population Growth				Percentage Growth			
Year	Town	Region	Volhynia [123]	Year	Town	Region	Volhynia
1765	1,029	4,676[124]	50,799	176	100	100	100

---

[120] Levanda, op. cit., no. 619.

[121] Ibid., no. 816.

[122] See Addendum 4.

[123] The area of the Polish province of Volhynia was larger than that of the Russian province (*gubernia*) of Volhynia, so the increase was that much greater. However, we must remember that the percentage undercounted in the 1765 census was certainly much greater than that in the general population census of 1897.

[124] The area of the district (*powiat*) of Kremenets in 1765 was much greater than the area of the district (*uyezd*) of Kremenets under the Russian government. A portion of the district of Polish Kremenets passed to Austria, and in another portion, two new districts were added: Zaslav and Konstantin Yashan. We compare the Jewish settlement in the district during Russian rule with that of 1765 only for the communities included in the Kremenets district during the Russian era. Following are the populations of the various district communities:

				5			
1847	3,791	18,264	—	184 7	270	293	—
1897	6,539	26,965	395,782	189 7	545	477	680

The greater increase in Jewish settlement in Kremenets relative to that in the region in general may be explained by the exile of Jews from the villages and their banishment from travelers' inns, as well as by the banishment of tenants from the border itself. The even greater increase in Volhynia as a whole in relation to Kremenets and its vicinity illustrates the upheavals that led these new communities to flourish because of the limitation on settlement within 50 *versts* of the border.

[33]

Despite the enormous growth in the Jewish population of Kremenets, the town still had the lowest percentage of Jews of any town in the Volhynia district. According to the 1897 census, the town had 17,704 residents, with Jews constituting 37 percent. The mean among other cities in the district was 50.77 percent, with the high in Ostrog, with 62.4 percent. It is clear that the situation in Kremenets resulted from the constraints placed on border cities by the Russian government and from the abovementioned traditional hostility of the townspeople toward the Jews.

We have already mentioned several occupations held by Jews. At the beginning of the era under discussion, their occupation was basically tenancy. Most Jews had little means. In 1800, 2,400 Jewish townspeople were listed in Kremenets, and only 33 were merchants.[125] It is worth mentioning that a net worth of 500 rubles was necessary to be listed as a merchant. Some economic encouragement was injected by the famous Polish Lyceum, which was located in Kremenets from the beginning of the century until after the 1831 Polish rebellion. Although we happen upon rich Jews in the middle of the century, such as the alcoholic beverage tax lessor Landsberg, the general

	1765	1847	1897		1765	1847	1897
Aleksinets	317	613	1,515	Krupets	114	103	-
Berezhtsy	-	627	428	Lakhovtsy	860	523	1,174
Belozirka	-	360	1,070	Pochayev	-	401	1,371
Vishnevets	664	3,178	3,294	Radzivilov	298	3,054	4,322
Vyshgorodok	668	1,018	1,078	Rokhmanov	170	306	93
Katerburg	-	1,465	693	Shumsk	170	1,101	1,962
Kremenets	1,029	3,791	6,539	Yampol	476	1,724	1,482
					4,766	18,264	26,965

Totals include villages that are not listed. Regarding the numbers for 1765, see note 62. For those of 1847 and 1897, see *Jewish Encyclopedia*, vol. IX, p. 832; vol. V, pp. 739-743.

[125] Yu. Gessen, *History of the Jewish People in Russia*, Leningrad 1925, vol. I, p. 84.

situation apparently can be summed up in the words of RYB"L: "Heads of families were generally indigent and downtrodden." The reason for this, according to him, was that the town "sits in a desolate corner (see Isaiah 5:6) and far from the King's Way, without discussion or involvement with the world's large cities, and from long ago subsists with difficulty by trading tobacco, which grows surrounding the town, with the Christian inhabitants, or by selling whiskey and the like, or by trading forged documents or worthless engravings, etc.; one large part are tailors and simple craftsmen, who are the only ones who subsist on their own handiwork."[126]

This situation and RYB"L's preaching among the inhabitants of Kremenets led 52 Jewish families living there to move inland in 1843 and request an agricultural homestead in the Kherson district. The minister gave the applicants permission to settle, but as became clear later on, for one reason or another not a single one of the families reached its goal.[127] Even so, at the end of the century, in 1897, the occupation of the Jews of Kremenets in agricultural work was notable, likely because of the influence of Zionist preaching. At that time, an agricultural school was set to open in a village near Kremenets, and several Jewish inhabitants wanted to apply to the agriculture minister to allow the children to live in the village during their studies (as Jews had not been allowed to live in villages since 1882).[128] The great momentum given to the country's economy by the farmers' liberation and the liberal policies of the 1860s led to far-reaching changes in the economic structure of the Jewish population. Although we have no numbers for Kremenets itself, the trend toward impoverishment of the masses due to the loss of their traditional occupations can be seen in the Volhynia district. The number of Jews opening manufacturing businesses rose. In 1881, 118 of the 123 factories in the district belonged to Jews, as did 60 of 82 other manufacturing businesses; of the merchants, 3,533 of 3,650 were Jews, as were 496 of 559 taverners.[129]

[34]

According to the 1897 census, 40 percent of Volhynia's Jews were in commerce; 25 percent, in manual work; 10 percent, in manufacturing; 25 percent, in services and public service; 3.7 percent, in transportation; and 2.3 percent, in agriculture.[130]

Kremenets under Russian rule was challenged by all the afflictions imposed on the House of Israel in the territories that passed from Poland (not to mention exile, the Pale of Settlement, the draft, and pogroms) and was especially challenged by the burden of being a Jewish border town, whose poor inhabitants were forced into difficult and dangerous occupations and were particularly affected by the gentiles' hatred of them. In these conditions of impoverishment and struggle, RYB"L's

---

[126] *Pages of History*, Warsaw, vol. III.

[127] See the article by Hasan in *Experience*, vol. III, pp. 15-16.

[128] *Hamelits*, June 12, 1897.

[129] *Materials for a History of Anti-Jewish Pogroms in Russia*, vol. II, p. xxi.

[130] *Jewish Encyclopedia*, vol. V, pp. 739-743.

exhortations highlighted the Enlightenment's specific outlook and, to some extent, objective reality.

G. BETWEEN HASIDISM AND ENLIGHTENMENT: LOVE OF ZION*

English translation by David Dubin

*Because of the vast amounts of historical and contemporary material on the modern era discussed in the rest of the book, this is summarized very briefly.

The great excitement brought by Hasidism did not bypass Kremenets. Already in the expositions of R' Yakov Yisrael of Kremenets, we hear, apparently, echoes of its infiltration of the town. And this is no surprise, as Kremenets was a neighbor of Brody, the center of this excitement over a long period: beginning in the *kloyz* of the Brody Kabbalists and ending in the well-known center of Enlightenment in this large town of finance.

We have little clear information on the relationship between the rabbis who held the seat of the rabbinate in Kremenets and Hasidism. The rabbis at those times were R' Duvid Tsvi son of Arye Leyb Averbakh[131] and R' Tsvi son of Naftali Hirts Rokeach.[132] However, in the early 19th century, Kremenets already had its own Hasidic master—R' Mordekhay of Kremenets. He was one of five sons of R' Yechiel Mikhel, the *magid* of Zloczow. R' Mordekhay was R' Meir of Przemysl's teacher and R' Nachum of Chernobyl's father-in-law. We see from this that he was connected to the most famous spiritual masters. He was renowned in the area, and his disciples even settled across the border in the villages of Galicia.[133] R' Mordekhay's great influence is shown by the fact that a large, important city like Tarnopol turned to him when it required an additional slaughterer: ". . . in his opinion (of the head of the rabbinical court of the holy community of Tarnopol) and by the agreement of the special leadership of the prominent members of this community, I write to his holiness (R' Mordekhay of Kremenets) and ask to him to let us know his opinion, as a wise man is more important than a prophet, and if he will agree to accept this slaughterer, all is good, and if he does not agree, then woe unto us if we accept him...."[134] R' Mordekhay died in 1817. His influence was felt in the town even after his death, and he was a target of mockery for Enlightenment Jews like Yosef Perl and RYB"L.[135]

---

[131] Fridberg, op. cit., p. 146; *The New Names of the Greats*, Warsaw 1889, p. 36.

[132] Fridberg, ibid.; *Knowledge of the Holy Ones*, p. 185.

[133] *The New Order of the Generations*, Lvov 1858, p. 24, col. 1; *The New Names of the Greats*, p. 97. On him, also see *Glory of the Righteous One*, Warsaw 1909, p. 49.

[134] *Exposer of the Hidden*, Vienna 1819, p. 39: 2. There is no question that this letter is authentic and that the aliases mentioned in the body of the letter are meant to be discerned using gematria (codes). R' Nechuri of Reketsits is R' Mordekhay of Kremenets, and the Judge Rekme son of Tan Yetz of Greater Tsidon is Judge Moshe, son of Yechiel Mikhel of Tarnopol.

[135] Ibid., p. 40, col. 2: "I also received information that in the holy community of Reketsits (= Kremenets) the Mitnagdim took one heavy man and dressed him up like the rabbi, and just as our kind

[35]

R' Mordekhay's synagogue was named for him until the end and was the central synagogue for the town's Hasidim.

The first flower of the Enlightenment in the town was the plan of Tadeusz Czacki, founder of the Polish Lyceum in Kremenets and Polish Jewish historian, to found a Jewish nationalist teachers' school next to the Lyceum. In 1821, RYB"L returned to Kremenets from Galicia and settled there until his death in 1860. However, RYB"L was not immersed in community life, and he similarly testifies about himself: ". . . I escaped to settle far from the town, once I came to live after I left the dear city of Brody; I sit alone outside the encampment and I have no involvement with anyone, and because of my illness, I cannot tolerate walking or traveling and have not been inside the town these 35 years."[136] Nevertheless, he had a great influence on town life, which can be seen from his writings. In his satires *Topsy-Turvy World* and *The Story of the Evil Mr. X,* he undertakes a formidable investigation of the community and its leaders, and there is no doubt that RYB"L also used Kremenets as a background for his description of the situation. He vehemently protests the heavy burden placed on the impoverished community members by its leaders and notables.[137] We can also assume that the prototype of the corrupt public servants described in *The Story of the Evil Mr. X* is based on life in the community in which the author lived.[138]

> [**Translator's Note:** The original book titles are *Hefker Velt* and *Toldot Ploni Almoni Hakazbi,* respectively.]

RYB"L's presence succeeded in bringing together a group of Enlightened Jews, who were financed by their esteemed neighbor's estate until the end of the 19th century. Thus, we know the names of the Landsbergs, L. Etinger, and Hirsh Hirshfeld (Noach

---

takes the local rabbi to the bathhouse every Friday, they also take their rabbi, and since they saw that the real local rabbi has a special skullcap with which he goes to the bathhouse on Friday, they bought their own rabbi a special skullcap just like it, and they brought him to the bathhouse with this skullcap; every Sabbath they eat three meals with their rabbi, and they gather there, and he tells them words of Torah called Hasidic Torah, and everything the local people do for the local rabbi, those clowns also do for their local rabbi, and no one protests, and one can imagine the spectacle this causes." The reference here is to R' Mordekhay, because *Exposer of the Hidden* was written and even submitted to the Austrian censor before 1817 (R' Y. Weinles: *Yosef Perl, His Life and Times, Yosef Perl's Yiddish Writings,* Vilna 1937, p. XXVII.

In RYB"L's "Valley of Giants," the second section of his renowned Yiddish composition in *Topsy-Turvy World,* which investigates the community's routines, a character named R' M... is tested in hell for acts of "subterfuge" ("Valley of Giants," in *RYB"L Anthology,* Warsaw 1878, p. 128). It is clear that R' M... is R' Mordekhay of Kremenets, and the proof is that in the Yiddish edition of "Valley of Giants" the city is called "Ketsar Enayim," an anagram of Kremenets.

[136] Quoted by D. B. Nathanson, *Memorial Book,* Warsaw 1881, p. 11.

[137] *Topsy-Turvy World,* quoted by Z. Reisen, *From Mendelssohn to Mendele,* p. 260.

[138] As he writes, "several partners from our community." *RYB"L Anthology,* p. 14.

Prilutski's teacher).[139] A second source of Enlightenment influence in Kremenets was Avraham Ber Gotlober's presence as a teacher there during the 1930s.[140] During his stay in the town, Yeshayahu Gutman studied with him, and he later wrote several expositions in Yiddish.[141]

In the 1860s a bitter dispute broke out between the town's Enlightened Jews and its Hasidim regarding Mendelssohn's (Bible) translation.

[36]

One of the Enlightened youth dared to bring the book to the study hall, the Hasidim chased him away, and a bitter fight ensued, which involved the leaders of the community; eventually the editor of *Hamelits*, Aleksander Tsederboym, also became involved.

The following are worthy of mention among the town's institutions in the first half of the 19th century: the Hebrew press, which was operative only for a short time,[142] the charitable Free Loan Society,[143] and the Pursuers of Justice, of which RYB"L was a founder.[144] During the 1930s, the Great Synagogue was built with the active support of workers and peasants in town.[145] Regarding this synagogue's unique style, RYB"L wrote, "In general, the tailors, shoemakers, bakers, butchers, and similar workers pray there, and also some householders, mostly worthy and believing, but also simple men who are not learned," although students of Torah and the Enlightened gathered in the study halls.[146]

The "southern storms" of 1881, which strongly affected southern Russia's important Jewish center, did not directly affect the Volhynia district and Kremenets. However, one of its major outcomes—the awakening of the Love of Zion movement—made its mark here, too. However, its blossoming in Kremenets was somewhat delayed, and only in the late 1880s and early 1890s were activities established here.[147] The breath of life for the movement in Kremenets was Tsvi Prilutski, who later served as editor of *Moment* in Warsaw. During his stay in Kremenets at the end of the 19th century, he maintained ties with the Odyssey Committee, the Yeshurun office in Warsaw, and various personalities in Lovers of Zion. Ts. Prilutski was involved in the movement's

---

[139] *Hamelits,* March 23, 1865, the list of Erez; Reisen, *Lexicon,* vol. 2, p. 954.

[140] Tsinberg, in *YIVO Pages,* vol. 11, p. 325.

[141] Tsinberg, ibid., and M. Weinreich, *Archives of the History of Yiddish Theater,* pp. 175-238.

[142] From 1808. Fridberg, ibid., p. 145.

[143] From 1827; see below.

[144] From 1846. *Memory Book,* p. 78.

[145] Manus Goldberg, in *Gazit,* year 8, vol. 9, p. 2.

[146] *RYB"L Anthology,* p. 15.

[147] See the correspondence from Kremenets in *HaMagid,* 10 Tevet 1890, vol. 1; *Hamelits,* 1891, vol. 69; 1893, vol. 13.

central problems, made various suggestions (that is, he was one of the first to emphasize the importance of members settling in the Land of Israel), and participated in the fight that erupted in the movement after the appearance of Achad Ha'am's article "Truth from the Land of Israel," and so on.[148] Working alongside Prilutski was Dr. Tovye Hindes, who settled in Jerusalem in 1893, but he maintained ties with the people of Kremenets and with the brother of Yechiel Mikhel Pines, Dr. Arye Leyb Pines, who replaced Hindes.[149]

> [**Translator's Note:** In Hebrew, Lovers of Zion is *Chovevey Tsion,* a 19th-century movement focused on settling Jews in the land of Israel. The original title of "Truth from the Land of Israel" is "Emet MeErets Yisrael."]

In the early 20th century, the community's social life expanded in every avenue, and Zionist organizations appeared in their various forms in Kremenets, including the Federation of Workers, the Bund, etc. This activity continued even during World War I, and when an attempt was made to arrange attacks on the Jews of Kremenets on December 15, 1917, a Jewish self-defense was immediately organized in the town.[150]

[37]

The spiritual life of these years in the town and life under the difficult conditions in the Jewish border region of Russia demonstrate the awakening of feelings of inclusion and influence, whether the ideas came from Brody, from the camp of those fighting for the Enlightenment lurking in the corners like RYB"L, or from those who latched onto general notions of Jewish society, such as Zionism and the Bund. The town was blessed with a number of outstanding personalities, such as R' Mordekhay of Kremenets, RYB"L, and Tsvi Prilutski, who managed to gather groups of community workers around them and who founded organizations in order to mold the community in their image.

ADDENDA

ADDENDUM 1: ANNOUNCEMENT OF THE KREMENETS CITY SECRETARY ON THE DESTRUCTION OF THE TOWN'S DEFENSES BY THE COSSACKS IN 1648

> [**Translation Editor's Note:** In the yizkor book, this addendum is in Russian (pp. 37–38), followed by a Hebrew translation (pp. 39–40). The following is an English translation of the Hebrew.]

---

[148] In the Sons of Moshe files in the Central Zionist Archives in Jerusalem are the preserved letters of L. Pinsker, M. L. Lilienblum, Z. Opshteyn, and others to Tsvi Prilutski as well as an interesting letter from Prilutski to the Yeshurun office in Warsaw on the second day of Hanukah 1883. These letters deal with suggestions to advance the settlement of workers in the Land of Israel, among others, and an anonymous donor from Kremenets who gave 100 rubles for this purpose.

[149] See Prilutski's abovementioned letter to Warsaw.

[150] Tcherikover, *Anti-Semitism and Pogroms in Ukraine*, Berlin, 1923, p. 198; M. Goldenberg in *Gazit*, year 8, vol. 10, p. 13.

[39]

TRANSLATION OF THE ANNOUNCEMENT

April 17, 1649

The prominent personality, the honored Lord Jan-Casimir Mesirchkov Ruzhinski, holder of specified lands found in the village of Tulichuv and Klusk in our Volhynia district in the Vladimir region, and the scribe of this town appeared before the officials and record keepers of the castle of Kremenets who were present before the *starosta* and before Stanislav Kaminski, who is responsible for the castle of Kremenets, since we have managed some free time for everyone to approach the public books: [Ruzhinski demanded] in his name and the name of this town that they must guard them [the town's books] as part of the scribe's responsibilities, so that they will not be damaged by the warrior Bogdan Chmil or Chmielnitski, formerly a registered Cossack who swore allegiance to the [Polish] state and is now a leader [of the transgressors]. He must guard the books against all the rest of [Chmielnitski's] allies, whether partners or aides, and especially against those acting on his orders and guidance who spent a prolonged time here in Kremenets during the disturbances that came upon the entire state. These allies include Vasili Tripals, officer of hundreds, his unit from the Krivonos Brigade, and also Dzhadzhili, head of the Brigade, who came with 7,000 [men], and Seve Semchenko, head of hundreds, and Peter, head of hundreds of the Brigade of Chmielnitski himself.

And he [Ruzhinski] decreed that the abovementioned Chmil or Chmielnitski, along with other registered Cossacks who swore allegiance, who last year, in 1648, intentionally disregarded their oath of allegiance to all [the lands of] the Polish crown and the late Polish monarch, may he rest in peace, immediately after the tragic death of Wladislaw IV, may he rest in peace, the Polish king. And for their conspiracy, evil, injustice, and bloodthirst, as he discarded behind his back all who were created with the love of God, as he forgot the love of his homeland, which nurtured him and made him into a man; and after he showed strong defiance of all taboos, [he assembled] a large crowd of various farmers; he sinned without fear of punishment and drew them to him with bribes from the looting of the nobles' property. And he showed himself as the preeminent enemy of the state, as he called the chief enemies of the state Tatars and other heathens, several tens of thousands of people, in order to destroy the status of the knights, to strangle and devastate and ruin the freedoms of the landed nobility, with the power of arms; and with all these he invaded the country, and first and foremost he attacked the houses of the landed nobility with his rebels, destroyed various holdings and people by the sword and by fire, [and his people] killed noblemen and various people wherever they went, first and foremost torturing them in various ways; they desecrated the churches and various holy places, attacking them in order to incur the wrath of the most Exalted and Supreme Judge; they looted the treasures of the churches; they did not allow the dead to rest in peace in their graves, looting them without mercy; they cruelly cut off people's arms, legs, and heads throughout the Polish kingdom and in the end threw the dead out of their coffins for the dogs and animals of prey to eat, and prohibited the living from burying the dead on pain of decapitation, contravening divine and historical law.

[40]

And as they did these things, their great and fearsome members, the abovementioned leaders of the brigades and of the hundreds, came to Kremenets last year, on October 30, 1648, and remained there cruelly until December 13. They attacked the welfare of many innocent Christians, spilling the innocent blood of many children and priests with their cruel swords; they tortured many until their souls desired to leave their bodies from the great pain. And finally, although now it is spoken about most prominently, they attacked the stronghold of Kremenets with fierceness and cruelty, breaking into the locked and bound cabinets in which the nation's and town's well-preserved and protected books were kept, looking for money. Some of these books, lists, and protocols had their covers looted. Others were completely torn, a third group were cut to shreds, and a fourth group of books—after they were ruined—were thrown to the wind and landed in the snow and later in the rain, where they stayed until the following April. Only a few them were found here and there, and even these were ruined.

Given that the complainant [Ruzhinski] is particular about his reputation remaining spotless, he registered a proclamation and declaration in order to assure himself of such by complaining of this well-known and infamous crime before all the inhabitants, and he requested that this be entered into the books, which I approved.

ADDENDUM 2: THE TRIAL FOR BLOOD LIBEL IN KREMENETS*

English translation by Thia Persoff and Aya Betensky

> [**Translator's Note**: In Addendum 1, the author notes that the priest wanted to make sure that the account of this case was preserved as a warning.—AB]

> *Recorded from a copy in the Vatican's Polish-Russian collection. Our thanks to the administration of the Central Archives for the History of the Jewish People, which gave us access to this document. Translated by D. Ploser.

Summary No. 3. Extract from the books of the castle of Kremenets in the Year of Our Lord 1753, the 16th day in the month of April.

In my official presence under the currently constituted Acts (Laws) of the castle of Kremenets, and with Antonio Michael Ceceniowski, the hunter and tenant of Ciechanovie Burgrabiatus of Kremenets, appearing in person in front of me: the well-known Joannes Pawłowicz, Pro-Consul, and Michael Jurkiewicz as witnesses for themselves and for the whole court of Magdeburg and court of justice of Kremenets, and also the Hebrew infidel Wolf Laybowicz Cantor as witness for himself and in the name of the whole synagogue of Kremenets, for the sake of taking note of an undeserved trouble, an unlawful attack, and an abuse against this state, in the presence of the defendant named by the Noble Court of Justice mentioned above, in which for the sake of winning a conviction and obtaining complete official exoneration, they are diligently making a complaint against the noble Borscowski of whatever name he may have and are bringing to bear evidence against him. They claim that this noble Borscowski, wanting to make constant trouble for the above-said State, and wanting even more to bring final destruction to the Jews, in order to cause great harm, in the depth of night, while outside of the villa Piszczatyniec, falling upon his own baby, a girl called Maryam Anna, he attacked her, thrusting a knife once under her eye and twice in both feet, wounding her. Then, wanting to hide this baby daughter so that the infidel head of the household Leyzerowicz would not see her dead, he tied her in a sack, put her into [Leyzerowicz's?] stable, and left. The wounded girl, making no sound throughout the night, spent the whole night in the stable. But her father, when he got up at the height of the morning, being hungry to kill his baby girl, took her from the stable and placed her under the Xenodochum Religious Fathers' Reformatory and then immediately left Kremenets.

[41]

The well-known Wasgh Kochan, citizen of Teofipol, will testify about this. He saw this baby lying like this in the stable with his own eyes and saw the same father take his own baby daughter from there, carry her, and say in the presence of this citizen, "I am carrying her to the doctor," but, in fact, took her out of the aforementioned stable and put her under the Xenodochum Religious Fathers' Reformatory.

> [**Translator's Note**: Evidently the intent was to blame the girl's injury and eventual death on the Jewish family that owned the stable. But then why take her to the reformatory?—AB]

Wanting to counter such a troubling insult and deceit, the whole synagogue of Kremenets presented this daughter in the court of Magdeburg and in the Kremenets castle court, accusing this man of unlawful and abusive actions and strongly urging that this discovery be made public, which was granted. Joannes Pawlowicz, Pro-Consul; Michael Jurkiewitz, the lawyer, stamped the seal of the holy cross; Wolf Laybowicz.

> [**Translator's Note**: These may represent signatures.—AB]

And in a restrained manner Palatinus Woshynik agreed personally for the Minister General and the others, the prudent Stephanus Papayuck, who firmly acknowledged his true and faithful report openly, publicly, and freely; that he himself on April 16 in the present year of 1753, in judicial examination of the well-known citizens of Kremenets, of the whole court, of the court of Magdeburg, of the whole synagogue of Hebrew infidel citizens, and of inhabitants of Kremenets standing by the faith of the worthy noble people, Francisci Kobecki and Jacobi Piotrowski, thanks to good and clear testimony, these people came up to him as witnesses to this act in the civic praetorship of Magdeburg, and there prominently with the abovementioned nobles, he saw and observed the baby, clearly laid out and placed by the hands of this very father himself at the Xenodochum Religious Fathers' Reformatory. This baby called Maryam Anna, more than three years old, was wounded by her own father once beneath her left eye with a small knife and also on her feet, to which the girl testified against her own father that she had this scar from him, speaking in her own infant voice and showing how miserable she was, with terrible consumption. I saw this and explained it clearly to the abovementioned nobles participating in the trial. Returning from there, in my official presence he [Stephanus Papayuck] gave his true eyewitness account of this matter and authenticated it.

With the same Minister General presiding, he [the witness], not knowing how to write, stamped the seal of the cross on this report, and from these books and Acts that extract was narrated and written under the seal of the castle of Kremenets.

[The place of the seal]

Authority having been granted to me in the castle of Kremenets as Apostolic Notary Public, I hereby witness that the whole original document, safe and undamaged, with no suspicious sign, has been presented to me, and it agrees word for word. Leopol Day 22 January AD 1754. So witnessed, Joseph Augustinowicz, Doctor of both Law and Philosophy, Public Notary with Holy Apostolic authority.

[42]

TRANSLATION OF THE DOCUMENT
"FROM THE KREMENETS CASTLE BOOKS OF APRIL 16, 1753"

English translation by Thia Persoff

> [**Translation Editor's Note:** In the Yizkor Book, this section is a Hebrew translation of the Latin section that appears on pp. 40–41. There appear to be minor differences, especially in names.]

Appearing before me in the presence of the hunter Antonius Mikhael Checheniovski of Chekhnov, who is substituting for the one in charge of the Kremenets castle, and the current Kremenets castle office and its record books, are the well-known Yohanes Pavlovits, the vice president of the council, and Mikhael Yorkevits, the town mayor, representing themselves and all the Magdeburg Council members of Kremenets and its judges, and the nonbeliever, the Jew Volf son of Leyb Chazan, representing himself and all the members of the Kremenets Jewish community. They came to protest the unseemly, and false, accusation and the unlawful, vilifying slander that was cast upon the town by the accused honorable monastery, to be mentioned here; they removed themselves from it and declared themselves pure of heart, accusing instead the aristocrat Borshkovski. They declared that this nobleman, Borshkovski, wanted to deliver a final blow on the town and cause the complete destruction of the Jews. In the village of Pishchatintsy, when the night was at its darkest, he grabbed his daughter, Maria Anna, diapered and wrapped in a cloth, then stabbed her with a knife, once under her eye and twice in her two legs. He hid her—this girl who is his own daughter—in the stable so that the owner, Leyzerovits the nonbeliever, would not see her dead, and left her there tied in a sack. But the injured child did not make a sound and slept throughout the rest of the night. In the morning, this father who wanted to kill his daughter through starvation took her from the stable and laid her on the doorstep of the Reformed monks' monastery, and proceeded to the town of Kremenets. There, the man Vasek Kukhen, a known resident of Teofipol, will witness that he saw the girl lying in the stable and the father taking her, telling that man that he was taking her to the doctor. But what he did was to take her out of her sleeping place in the stable and throw her on the monastery steps. To contradict and demolish such a libel, the defamation and the fraud, the community of Kremenets presented the said daughter to the City Council, the Magdeburg Court, and the Kremenets castle. They repeated their rational arguments against him and his unlawful, defaming accusation and in declaration requested that their statements be accepted. This was granted.

[**Translator's Note:** The Magdeburg Court was an autonomous city council.]

It was signed by the vice consul, Yohanes Pavlovits; the mayor, Mikhael Yorkevits, who signed with the sign of the cross; and Volf Leybovits.

After those words, Military Governor Voznik agreed personally on behalf of the Minister General, and Stefan Papayuk, the sexton of the communities in charge of checking complaints, appeared to testify—in public, of his free will, declaring truly and honestly: He was personally present on April 16, 1753, during the court's inquiry and investigation of the known Kremenets citizens, as were all the members of the Magdeburg Court and its judges, all the community, and also the nonbelieving Jews of Kremenets and its residents. In the presence of noble personages who are trustworthy, the noble Frantsiskus Kuvetski and Yakov Piotrovski were added to the town's Magdeburg Court at this trial for the purpose of strengthening the evidence. When he was there, together with the additional noblemen mentioned above, he saw the girl thrown and then put with the hands of her very own father on the steps of the reformed monks' monastery. The girl's name is Maria Anna, and she is just over three years old. She was injured at the hand of her father, who used a small knife, once under her left eye and also on her legs.

[43]

That girl testified in a childish voice against her father and explained that the wounds were made by him. I saw that poor child was very weak and sick. With the said attending noblemen, I examined her and affirmed it. Then, after returning, he, the clerk, testified before me to what he truly saw and examined, and the current general sexton affixed the sign of the cross to this document, because he does not know how to write.

This section, taken from the books and documents, has the seal of Kremenets castle and was written in Kremenets.

[The place of the seal.]

This copy of the declaration that was made in Kremenets castle was compared by the Apostolic Notary Public whose signature is at the bottom with the true and correct, complete and unfragmented original that was presented and given to me. There is no reason for worry or suspicion, as it is equal to the original word for word, and to this I testify. In Lvov, January 22, 1754

So it is. Yosef Avgustinovits, Doctor of both Law and Philosophy, public notary under the authority of the Holy Apostolic, in his own hand.

ADDENDUM 3: THE MAGID OF KREMENETS, R' YAKOV YISRAEL SON OF TSVI HALEVI

English translation by Thia Persoff

The *Magid* R' Yakov Yisrael of Kremenets is one of those people who do not receive sufficient attention. It is known that the sermons of the *magidim* and ethics literature in general in large part reflect the society's way of life during different eras. A contemporary of the *Magid* of Kremenets was the *Magid* of Dubno, R' Yakov Krants, whose name was famous in the Jewish world. Although R' Yakov Yisrael was not proficient in composing folk parables, as the *Magid* of Dubno was, there is no doubt that echoes of the events around him are heard in his sermons, so it is worthwhile to pay special attention to them.

R' Yakov Yisrael was a student of "the Gaon Kabbalist Rabbi Yitschak, head in the court of the holy community of Belz" (*A Tribe of Israel,* paragraph 64, verse 6, and elsewhere). His writings are evidence of this—one can see that the *Magid* of Kremenets was proficient in the Six Orders of the Mishna, the Midrash, and the Zohar. He often quotes the ShL"H and the Talmudist R' Shmuel Eydels, and also the book *The Tribe of Judah.* Even in 1758/1759, he was preaching to the people, as we learn from his quotation: "I gave this parable at my sermon during the burning of the Mishna, heaven save us, in 1758/1759." He mentions the official edicts against the Talmud in connection with the debates against the Frankists in Kamenitsa and Lvov. He was a witness to the dread engulfing the eastern regions of Poland when "in 1768, the depraved nation called the Cossacks rebelled against the Polish nation, murdered the people and the Jews living in eastern Ukraine, and looted and pillaged their properties. Then there was destruction and desolation in the cities of Uman, Tetiev, and countless other towns and villages. Of the two curses, there was not one that did not come true at that time...through His anger, blessed be His name, He remembered mercy as He promised us and made the rulers of Moscow and Poland have pity on Israel, favoring them by catching the rebel leaders and punishing them severely. Then the people of Israel had some help in their stumbling; from the far places the refugees returned to their masters, each person to his town and his country; and not much time had passed, but the wrath of the 'crocodiles' had not abated; that very winter, thousands were slaughtered, and those who escaped were deported again, owing to our great sins, and Yakov was very scared and troubled. A new war then began between the Ishmaelites and the large, strong nation of Moskovi. It was a whirling storm on the rebels and a balm for the aforementioned" (*Bundle of Moss,* part 2, p. 22, side 1. See also *A Tribe of Israel,* 56, sentence a). Afterward, the affair passed through these districts, and the *magid* was forced to flee Kremenets and stayed for some time in Berestechko.

[**Translator's Notes:** In Hebrew, *A Tribe of Israel* is *Shevet MeYisrael*. The Zohar is the book of Jewish mysticism. *ShL"H* stands for *Shney Lukhot Habrit* (*Two Tablets of the Covenant*), a book of morals. In Hebrew, *The Tribe of Judah* is *Shevet Yehuda*. *Yakov* is another name for the people of Israel, and the "nation of Moskovi" refers to Russia. In Hebrew, *Bundle of Moss* is *Agudat Ezov*.]

[44]

Concerning an epidemic in Kremenets, he remarks, "And Israel had made a vow: God, if you save this town in which I dwell, grant mercy on the town in the morning, in the morning this thing will awaken awe, love, and worship toward you, and God's wish will be successful by my hands."

R' Yakov Yisrael provides a lively response to general political events, and especially interesting is his reaction to the first partition of Poland: "And it came to pass in 1772, when my book *A Tribe of Israel* was published, that the land of our birth was partitioned and split to the four winds of the heavens, and from then on God's people were in decline, and an activity (the printing of religious books) that had been increasing before then began to decrease more and more" (*Bundle of Moss,* part 3, p. 1, side 1).

He was still a *magid* in Kremenets in 1787.

R' Yakov Yisrael lived in the era when the Hasidic movement was spreading. It is possible that these words against the study of the Zohar and separate minyanim were said in connection to that and the well-known 1772 ban in Brody: ". . . and so we should consider why such a thing happened in our time. Know for certain that this wickedness came upon us because there is much disease among our people; because the young, who have not yet reached their twenties, busy themselves with matters that are of worldly importance and delve into the depth of the secrets. Even the uneducated among the people, whose bags are empty of bread or a piece of clothing, who are shaken out and empty of any knowledge, will forge toward the Lord to seek the knowledge of the Kabbalah...And now, because of our many sins, the fence of the world has broken open, the sealed book is now with the uneducated ignorant, and our faces turned sickly; because of this, they left the straight and narrow and fell into bad ways and heresy...." (*A Tribe of Israel* 64, 9). "People who were sword makers came from nearby to the world to come, and each of them was deemed worthy—because they had prayed in a minyan. Therefore, I said, I will uncover their ears to find fault with those who pray at home but not with those who pray in a synagogue" (*Words of Truth,* p. 6, side 2, and p. 7, side 1).

[**Translation Editor's Notes:** In Hebrew, *Words of Truth* is *Sfat Emet.*]

R' Yakov Yisrael speaks against the modern innovations of the time, too. He speaks of theaters in which people do amazing things with fiery flames and all sorts of inscrutable tricks that fools think are nearly miraculous deeds, and they rush to these games on the Sabbath and the holy days. "I said, fool, what is this merriment, that you violate the Sabbath and forget the time for praying, as I saw, because of our many sins" (*A Tribe of Israel,* p. 2, side 1).

But R' Yakov Yisrael did not preach only about fear of heaven. His sermons contain a deep social message. The following parable depicts the social relations prevalent in the Jewish community of that time quite realistically: "And we knew, as we sensed from the morals of the royal court and the ministers, that they would renew harsh decrees not only for the poor and destitute, but that they would spread their claws, saying that the decrees are on the wealthy, too, for the benefit of saving the poor. In the end, the poor are trapped while the rich escape. It is like when a net is cast on the water. Since it is the nature of the small ones to dwell on the bottom, where their food is, the small fish get caught, even though the one who casts the net claims to have aimed for the large ones. Yet the large ones who swim on the water's surface escape, for when the net is cast, they swim down to the bottom, causing the small ones to get scared and swim away from their [bottom] place upward, where they are then caught. The parable is about a villain who says he is doing this to the wealthy, and it ends with the wealthy ones demeaning themselves, taking the poor's livelihood into their own hands and claiming that they are the ones who carry all the burdens. Now all the small ones are caught, and they [the large ones] escape. It is clear to anyone who is well aware of the ways of the world that ten different interpretations may be found for this parable" (*A Tribe of Israel,* p. 7, side 1). The *magid* opposes all those who, while claiming reforms and protection of the poor, suggest to the rulers plans that will undermine the socioeconomic bases of Jewish society. Whatever their aims may be, the end result will worsen the conditions of the lower economic classes. In truth, given the tense background of the community of his time, it is possible to interpret his parable in "ten different ways," each of which reflects a reality of the time.

Additional articles are said to be written by R' Yakov Yisrael. Yosef Perl tells in *Bochen Tsadik* (Prague, 1838, p. 70): "Surely you remember that, after the death of one ritual slaughterer who lived in a village near Przemysl, they found books that he composed, filled with Kabbalah and devotion, and that during his life no one knew if he had even a spark of holiness."

[45]

"Some heretics among them [from Galicia] even said that it was the *magid* of Kremenets who had authored the book under the name of said ritual slaughterer; and only because he [the *magid*] was not considered important by our sect did he put out the word that those treatises had been left behind by this ritual slaughterer." He also refers here to the *magid* R' Yakov Yisrael (1803): "I searched in the bags of my late father, my master, my teacher and light, the great rabbi and famous *magid,* whose name was well known and recognized in all the Diaspora of Israel, our teacher and rabbi, R' Yakov Yisrael HaLevi, of blessed memory, who was a *magid* in the holy community of Kremenets, where he excelled in the Torah; his fame had spread throughout the Jewish communities, and I found one book and saw that it was clearly written by one of the wisest Kabbalists of our time, the Holy Light, our teacher Yitschak Ayzik, who was a ritual slaughterer in the village of Zurawica about a half-mile from the holy community of Przemysl, whose fame had already spread as a righteous one unique in his generation with his book *Trustworthy Mysteries.*" From the foreword to R' Yitschak's book, it appears that R' Yakov Yisrael also had published a book called *Trustworthy Mysteries*. The details in Perl's story are similar to those of R' Yitschak Ayzik, the ritual slaughterer from Zurawica, and to those of R' Yakov Yisrael. We did not succeed in getting the book *Trustworthy Mysteries* in Jerusalem (according to ben Yakov: Lvov, 1790), so we have no means of verifying Perl's references.

[**Translation Editor's Note:** In Hebrew, *Trustworthy Mysteries* is *Raza Mehemna*.]

It is worth mentioning here that he was not considered "important" by the Hasidim, a fact that was known many years after R' Yakov Yisrael's death, and in that connection it is interesting to note the rumors that R' Yakov Yisrael had used the name of an obscure ritual slaughterer so that the Kabbalistic book that he authored would have readers.

We have given just a few signs here that the *Magid* of Kremenets and his writings are surely worthy of attention and even some special research.

ADDENDUM 4: THE TROUBLES OF THE "UNREGISTERED" IN KREMENETS

Hamelits, January 12, 1881
English translation by Thia Persoff

Kremenets, November 20. As is well known, the law decreed long ago that Jews who were not registered as residents of the towns within 50 *versts* of the Russian border would be deported from there. The authorities, though, ignored the law and did not bother to check carefully. They did not pay attention to honest and forthright people who settled here and in the other towns in this area, because they had compassion for those heads of families and did not want to take away their livelihood. But malicious people rose from among us, and out of jealousy or vicious hatred, they wrote letters to the district governor accusing some people who had recently come and settled among us and stating that according to the ancient law, which is current, those people were not permitted to settle here. That resulted in a rapid reply from the governor with an order to deport from the Russian border all Jews who were not lawfully registered residents of towns within 50 *versts* of the border. This order caused a great panic in our town, as there were about 2,000 people in that situation, including well-to-do merchants, craftsmen, and laborers. This is the way of our people: wanting to take revenge on the offenders, they did not bother to think of what it might lead to—that it could harm many and in that way reawaken and bring back harsh decrees that have long been forgotten.—Anonymous

CHAPTERS IN THE HISTORY OF KREMENETS JEWRY

English translation by Thia Persoff

CHANGING ERAS

Manus Goldenberg (Givat HaShlosha)

In my mind's eye, my birthplace Kremenets survives: here is the long, main street—the shops throughout its length are shut and locked, since it is a summer Sabbath morning; Jews clothed in finery are flocking to the many synagogues; peace and tranquility are all around. On the evening of the departure of a Sabbath or holiday, this street is very crowded; celebrating people, old and young, men and women, flood the street, escorting Queen Sabbath. But the church bells announce the coming of workdays filled with worries....

The Jewish holiday comes in privacy, and in privacy it exits.

The next day is the Christian holiday: noise and raucousness accompany it; there are thousands of wagons, myriad colors, and ringing bells; endless numbers of farmers flood the streets, stores, and workshops. Smells of tar and resin penetrate everywhere; Jews' and Christians' voices commingle with curses and blessings, laughter and anger—there are negotiations and deals in the shops, streets, and wagons. The crowding is intense. Great strength is stored in this flood of people, and if it flows peacefully, it brings much good, but when it becomes unruly and riotous, much destruction and ruination results.

You never can tell what path it will take, as any market day or fair may turn out to be a day of loss and misfortune for the Jews. And so, at the end of the weary day, the town takes a breath of relief: the wagons disappear; the farmers disappear like locusts that swoop in and suddenly disappear. Straw and trash are left in the streets and markets...the Jews are left alone with ample profits, peace and tranquility return to the town, and the main street is filled with strolling people conversing warmly in their mother tongue of juicy Volhynia Yiddish. The town's Jewish appearance has returned.

THE LANDSCAPE

The town and its surroundings are beautiful. It was called "the Switzerland of Volhynia" for good reason. Its houses, most of which were ancient, were constructed from wood in the old Polish picturesque style. The houses stood crowded in the center, attached to each other, filled with busy Jews, craftsmen, and fair merchants whose entire lives were toil and weariness. Mountains and forests, at which each and every street and alley ends, surround the town. There are many gardens in town, and it seems to be embedded in greenery. On the eastern side, towering in its full glory, is the tall Mount Bona, on which the ruins of an old castle stand. Its steep slopes are green in summer and sparkling white with snow in winter. From its summit the whole town can be seen as if it is spread on the palm of a hand, and from every window, even a small one in an attic or a cellar, the summit can be seen and brings a sense of joy. Kremenets had a special charm on Sabbath eves, when candles were lit. It was good then in the Jews' homes, with all those thousands of lights in the glory of the night's stillness.

[47]

Mountain of the Virgins

Kremenets, Gary Dziewicze

Throughout the generations, the people wove many legends around the mountains. Each stone, each cross, and every surviving remnant had a wondrous story attached to it. The townspeople enjoyed frequent hikes in the mountains, resting in the shade of the groves and the gardens growing on them. There was a sort of tradition to those hikes. Each mountain had its own hiking season. Each holiday had the appropriate mountain. One of the groves, the prettiest of them, was called "the forest of the Hasidim." The story was told that, years ago, the Hasidim used to stroll there on the Sabbath and even hold a community afternoon service there. In the summer, many people would rent a summer cottage in the mountains from the farmers. The fresh mountain air and beautiful scenery even attracted vacationers from nearby towns. Those unique properties influenced the temperament of the townspeople and made them easygoing, happy, and imaginative. Jewish folklore was very rich here. The people favored funny stories and jokes that were retold from generation to generation.

RYB"L AND HIS ERA

In 1821, R' Yitschak Ber Levinzon returned to Kremenets and settled there permanently. His small, modest house at the edge of town had one room and a cellar that was flooded most of the year (the house stood there until recently). For 35 years, this "Russian Mendelssohn," who favored enlightenment, worked and labored there. In those years it was difficult to get to his house, as a swamp lay between it and the town, and it was so deep that wagons got mired in it even during the hottest summer days.

[48]

As soon as he settled in Kremenets, Levinzon got involved in community life. After his book *Testimony in Israel* was published, the local Hasidim began to persecute him, and he was forced to seclude himself. Any Jew who kept in touch with him was bound to be treated roughly. To them his name was shame, and they nicknamed him "Teud'ke"....

[**Translator's Note**: In Hebrew, *Testimony in Israel* is *Teuda BeYisrael*. The nickname "Teud'ke" is based on this book title.]

RYB"L's private letters from that time, written in bitterness, bear witness in great part to the Kremenets Jews' socioeconomic conditions in his time. In one of them, he writes about the people of his town: "The intellectuals are not intellectual, and the learners are not learning. Most laymen are poor and destitute. What they all have in common is that they are enveloped in darkness under the Hasidic banner. Some spew nonsense, some are money grabbers, and some tyrannize the population. They scarcely make a living by dealing in locally grown tobacco or selling hard liquor. A large number are tailors and simple craftsmen, who are the only ones making a living through their own labor. Their poverty is great. A Jew who manages to earn 2,000 rubles considers himself a wealthy man and feels entitled to honor and an important position."

At that time, apparently, the Kremenets Jews situation had taken a deep decline, as at the end of his letter Levinzon adds, "And all this has occurred only in the past 40 years."

His bitterness toward the residents is expressed in a second letter, which reveals his hostility toward the Hasidim. He writes, ". . . every day I hear around me the groans of the wretched poor, exploited by those who tyrannize the people, our brothers, the policemen and their commanders. And I hear behind me loud noises rising against angels, drinkers of hard liquor, and herds of Hasidim who dance in the streets and make a loud noise. Many new rabbis driving in carriages make it a habit to visit my town; one arrives, and one leaves, and in contrast with them, the angels get drunk and say *kadosh* ...."

[**Translator's Note:** *Kadosh* (holy) refers to the prayer that starts "Holy, holy, holy ...."]

For his extensive and in-depth works, Levinzon needed books on science and the wisdom of Israel, which were not available to him in the libraries of the local laymen, and he complained bitterly about this. The Lyceum library and Tadeusz Czacki's private one were a big help to him. The teachers' libraries were also open to his use. A few principals and teachers at the Lyceum kept in personal touch with Levinzon and encouraged him in his efforts at productivization among the Jews. There is no doubt that in spite of his ostracism, Levinzon's years of activity in Kremenets left their stamp on the life of the Jewish community and many of its citizens.

In due course, to honor him, important visitors—enlightened Jews and Christians—gathered in Kremenets to meet with the RYB"L. Even representatives of the government came. All around him were the enlightened intellectuals of the town, also including Gotlober, who settled in Kremenets to be near him.

As a result of Levinzon's call for people to change to a life of farming and crafts, 52 families declared their desire to move to one of the farming settlements in the Kherson region. Levinzon corresponded at length with the Interior Minister and Governor of Vilna, and eventually those Jews received land in the Kherson region and settled there. The families mentioned in this correspondence include some of Kremenets' largest, for example, Basis, Fishman, Barshap, Raykis, etc.

The government's attitude toward Levinzon and the gifts he received from it increased his honor in the eyes of the common folk, and the legends embroidered against this background remained in their hearts for generations.

In 1856, while Levinzon lay sick, masked robbers attacked his house and stole, among other things, the letterbox in which he stored his important, valuable letters, including one from Czar Nikolas I about his newly published book, *Testimony in Israel*. The identities of the robbers were not known, but it was suspected that the Hasidim meant to destroy his writings.

[49]

Remains of the Castle on Mount Bona

In 1860, Levinzon passed away. An atmosphere of heavy mourning descended on the town. All the stores were closed, and all the town's citizens attended his funeral. His works were carried in front of his casket.

Levinzon's students, the town's intellectuals, were the activists in the town's population, and the local Lovers of Zion and Society of Lovers of the Hebrew Language movement grew out of them. The house of Nachman Prilutski, a close friend of Levinzon, was the meeting place for the Hebrew language group. His son, Tsvi Prilutski, along with Dr. Tovye Hindes and Dr. Pines, established the Love of Zion movement in town. Many of the Talmud school's young people were attracted to the movement.

[**Translator's Note**: In Hebrew, the Society of Lovers of the Hebrew Language is *Agudat Chovevey Sefat Ever*. Love of Zion is *Chibat Tsion,* a movement to rebuild the Land of Israel.]

In the late 19th century, the *Hamelits* newspaper printed Tsvi Prilutski's correspondence, and later that of Moshe Eydelman, on Zionist goings-on around the town, the enlightened people of Kremenets, "who were numerous because of Levinzon's influence," enlightened young women, their national pride in the company of Christians, etc.

When Dr. Hindes immigrated to Israel, Prilutski published Hindes's private letters in *Hamelits*; those letters are rich with information, and there is much to be learned from them about the first steps in establishing the settlements and in the fields of labor and education. Tsvi Prilutski moved from Kremenets to Warsaw, where he published the newspaper *Dos Leybn* and then *Moment*. For many years, from its establishment to its final day, *Moment* was one of the most popular newspapers among Polish Jews. His son, Noach, a writer and community affairs worker, was educated in Kremenets. His teacher was a student of Levinzon. Tsvi Prilutski never severed his connection to Kremenets. His large, extended family, all of them devoted Zionists, were there. In the early 20th century Dr. Pines also left Kremenets, moving to Bialystok, where he opened an eye clinic whose reputation gained renown throughout Russia and Poland.

[**Translator's Note**: *Dos Leybn* means *Life.*]

The group came apart, but its place on the social stage was filled by the young and energetic, who continued Zionist activities enthusiastically and diligently. The most active were Moshe Eydelman, Dr. Meir Litvak, Dr. Landsberg, Munye Dobromil, Getsi Klurfayn, and others.

[50]

IN THE EARLY 20TH CENTURY

In the last half of the 19th century, the Kremenets Jews' economic situation was not very good. Lumber merchants did not get rich; manufacturers hardly existed. Their main livelihood was business with local farmers and the production of some crafts and home products. Some Jews were suppliers to the Pravoslavic seminary for priests, which took the place of the Lyceum. The army's two regiments, which were stationed near the town, added a bit to the residents' income.

By the early 20th century, echoes of the political happenings in Russia had reached Kremenets. A few townspeople were sent to the Far East but did not reach their destination, as the hostilities had ceased. Only Dr. Litvak spent a long time at the front, and he returned as a high-ranking officer. He published a very interesting pamphlet about his life and adventures at the front. Dr. Litvak, who came from a middle-class background, maintained allegiance to it all his life, which for many years was tied to Kremenets community life. The Christian population accepted him. He was an enlightened intellectual and a champion of the Russian language in town as well as a physician and lecturer on hygiene in the secondary schools. Along with this, he was an ardent Zionist, met with people in the synagogue and at funerals (he was very active in the Burial Society), and saw to people's education and health. He planned on erecting a monument as a memorial to RYB"L and devoted much time to it. In 1914 he was drafted into the army and returned in 1917 with the rank of general. After his return, he devoted himself to public works with extra energy.

On the eve of the 1905 revolution, a strong Bund organization was formed, functioning vigorously "underground." Meetings were held in the mountains. More than once, the police ambushed them and beat up some of the workers. Young people from the best of the local Jewish intelligentsia joined the revolutionary movement. Some who immigrated to America had important roles in the labor movement there.

At that time, the Labor Zionist Party was established, attracting to its ranks some people from the revolutionary movement. As activists in the Bund, some of them joined the Communist Party after the October Revolution.

> [**Translation Editor's Note:** In Hebrew, the Labor Zionist Party was *Poaley Tsion* (literally, Workers of Zion).]

After the 1905 tribulations, life in town flowed peacefully; on the surface, the country seemed to be at peace. Hopeful springs gave way to long summers, with a sleepy town and empty streets. The army regiments went to their training, schools were out, and many of the town's residents left on vacation. The farmers were busy in their fields, and only the grocer stayed, guarding his store and yawning into the vacant street. On Tailors' Street, young and old sat at sewing machines in small, sparse rooms, relieving their long and gloomy days with folk songs. The machines clicked in a rapid cadence, producing thousands of fall-season warm coats for farmers. In the fall, with its days of markets and fairs, Jewish residents earned their livelihood for the year.

Before World War I, Kremenets had cheders and a Talmud Torah. A yeshiva was established in 1910; most of its students came from far away. Many children studied in the public Jewish-Russian primary school. In 1906, the High School of Commerce, financed mostly by Jews, was established. According to the school charter, which was liberal for its time, studies could proceed as soon as enrollment consisted of 60% non-Jews and 40% Jews. To achieve this, Jews had to beg non-Jewish citizens, who were mostly poor craftsmen, to send their children to the school. Each Jew who wanted his child to be accepted had to bring a non-Jewish child, give him a uniform and all necessary school supplies, and make sure he continued to attend. That chore had to be achieved by encouraging the child's father, with the help of an occasional serious drinking session.

[51]

In 1907, two teachers, Mr. Burshteyn and Mr. Sirayski, opened a Hebrew school in Kremenets—a "progressive cheder" in which boys and girls could enroll. Later, most of these students were active members of the local Zionist movement.

In the years before the war, Zionist activity was quite slow—selling *shekalim,* distributing shares in the bank, passing a "bowl" on Yom Kippur eve, etc. A Zionist library contained a few dozen books and pamphlets, and sometimes a *magid* lectured in the study hall.

[**Translation Editor's Note:** *Shekalim* were tokens of membership in the Zionist Organization.]

The Bund and the Labor Zionists ran a large cultural program at that time. Jewish literature penetrated into all strata of the population. The writer Anski, who toured the border towns and villages collecting material and Jewish folklore, stopped in Kremenets for an extended period. The best of the young students who had not alienated themselves from their people and their language gathered around him.

This was the calm before the storm .... In 1913, a regiment of the artillery corps came to town for maneuvers in the mountains, from which they later bombed Austrian positions. At that time, the first casualty of the coming war fell: one of the participants in the maneuvers and his horse rolled down the mountainside and were killed.

DURING WORLD WAR I

At the height of the summer of 1914, on a stifling night when the town's streets were empty, the gallop of a horse suddenly was heard. As the horse and its rider passed through in a flash, someone said, "General conscription!" Immediately, people gathered in the streets, full of worry. The next morning, one could already see crying women and families accompanying departing fathers, some of whom would never return. A few days later, the town's inhabitants saw the first injured soldiers; after the first battle, they were brought from Zbarazh on the Austrian border on farmers' wagons, dusty and wrapped in bloody bandages. Seeing this blood was terrifying; all the townspeople ran to the wagons, and women cried bitterly. As time went by, they became used to seeing a great deal of blood.

From then on, the streets were noisy day and night from long convoys and marching soldiers—the pride of the Russian army marching toward Brody after its successful attack on Galicia. But a year later the tide had turned, and endless convoys of the retreating army galloped in panic in the opposite direction. The large retreating forces stopped about two kilometers from our town. For ten months, this was the front. Cannons thundered above the heads of the inhabitants, and machine guns rumbled. Government institutions and schools abandoned the town, part of the population fled, and people from other towns that had been destroyed took their place. Economic and community life was completely destroyed. Large amounts of money flowed into the pockets of those who knew how to serve the army. Corruption and licentiousness spread. The town was flooded with deserters from all the Ukrainian towns, who had escaped from the hated Czar's army in the hope of rapid salvation by the Austrian army that fought to conquer the town. But being protected by mountains on all sides, the town was not conquered or damaged. On the second day of the Shavuot holiday in 1916, the Austro-Germans were repelled, the command headquarters of the famous

Eleventh Army Corps moved into town, and the town started to live life on the home front.

DURING THE REVOLUTION AND THE CIVIL WAR

Many laborers—active members of the revolutionary movement—from Petersburg and Moscow were members of the engineering corps and drivers who accompanied command headquarters.

When the October Revolution began, they were the first to organize demonstrations, which in our town took the form of celebrations. The soldiers' council of the corps included notables from the Social Democrats and the Socialist Revolutionaries. A veteran member of the Communist Party, Lieutenant Krilenko, who organized the Bolshevist propaganda in our town, represented the Bolsheviks. In the fervor and excitement of the revolution's first days, the pulse of community life in town began to beat strongly again. The Bund, Labor Zionists, and Zionist Organization were reestablished—this time they were legal and free—and they all attracted a large membership. There were elections to the City Council, the Jewish Community Council (which won with a Labor majority and was called "the Red Community"), the all-Russia Founding Assembly, the Ukrainian Jewish Convention, etc.

[52]

Zionist leaders, those who raised the national flag and stayed true to it even in the darkest days of the period, worked with devotion and much energy. Representing the Zionists with great success in stormy discussions were Dr. B. Landsberg, easygoing, logical lecturer and honest public worker; Meir Goldring, full of energy and a fearless fighter; Y. Shafir, who is now in Israel; Gorengut, the first head of the town's militia (now a resident of Pardes Chana, Israel), and others.

The intoxication of victory and freedom had not yet dissipated when the dark clouds of civil war covered the sky. The army began to disintegrate, and wagons filled with weapons and ammunition appeared in the market for sale to anyone. In December 1917, gangs from the army stationed in town started riots, robbed stores, and burned homes. Two Jews were killed. The next day, soldiers returning from the front with their weapons formed a Jewish defense squadron. The defense did not last long, though. The Germans, who had begun to move into Ukraine, entered the town. The defense was dismantled, order was restored, and the Jews began to trade and speculate. At first, the town did not much feel the hand of the Germans, but with pressure from the Bolsheviks at the Ukraine border, a period of persecution and arrests began. Dr. Landsberg and others were arrested. They were released after a few months by Ukrainian rebels, who stormed and conquered the town after street fights with the Hetman officers' platoon. At the head of these rebels were two local young Jewish men.

> [**Translator's Note**: "Hetman" is a historical military title used in Poland, Lithuania, and Ukraine.]

It was the start of the period of independent Ukraine, which was soaked with Jewish blood. Kremenets suffered little from the slaughter, but the tension and dread of death did not leave for many months. Once, during the change in regime, the town faced a large slaughter; this was in 1920, when the Bolsheviks retreated after killing a few dozen locals who had previously been officers. Rebellious farmers, who burst into town like animals of prey, were ready to take out their anger on the Jews, but then they heard from one of the officers who had miraculously survived that the Jewish officer Chachkis was one of the officers who had been killed. The Cheka people wanted to release the officer, but he refused, choosing to share in his friends' fate. The rebel commander used this information to calm the farmers, who then limited themselves to looting and robbing. Under Dr. Litvak's initiative, a yearly memorial day for Chachkis was established in Kremenets.

[**Translator's Note**: The Cheka (the "political police"), which later became the NKVD, initially fought counter-Soviet activity. The acronym stands for *Extraordinary Commission to Combat Counterrevolution, Sabotage, and Speculation*.]

UNDER POLISH RULE

The conquering and retreating Poles also cost the town a great deal of robbery and rape, as well as arrests of Jewish community workers who were moved from one concentration camp to another. With the signing of the Peace of Riga, Kremenets was assigned to Poland. At the beginning of Polish rule, all political activity was forbidden. Later, as a result of strengthened links with Warsaw and other centers, an awakening of community and economic life took place. In that period, in 1922, the first election to the Sejm was held, for which the Jewish-Ukrainian bloc began a wide-ranging battle. (See the memoirs of A. Levinson in this book.)

In the first decade of Polish governance, the town spread and enlarged, and commerce and industry flourished. New institutions were established, and old ones were enlarged and improved. The Zionist Organization, with all its branches, grew and was housed in a nice building, along with its library—the largest in the town. The revenue of the national foundations climbed. A Tarbut School was opened and flourished. In 1926, the ORT School was built, and the building of the orphanage, which was the favorite charity of L. Rozental and Mrs. Kremenitski, was completed. The Burial Society, which had a great deal of money, generously supported charitable institutions.

[**Translation Editor's Note:** ORT stands for *Obshestvo Remeslenofo Zemledelcheskofo Truda* (Society for Trades and Agricultural Labor), which provided education and employable skills.]

[53]

The hospital and the Home for the Aged were enlarged and improved. TOZ expanded its public health activities. New banks were established to serve the people by supporting young merchants and craftsmen with loans. The Charity Fund was established. Professional guilds (left-wing) were established, for the main purpose of protecting workers' salaries and improving working conditions and cultural activities. The Lyceum, which reopened after the Polish conquest, abandoned the tradition of its founders; with very few exceptions, its doors were now locked to Jewish young people. Admission to the agricultural school, which was annexed to it, was based on notions of racial purity.

[**Translation Editor's Note:** TOZ stands for *Towarzystwo Ochrony Zdrowia*, Polish for Association for the Protection of Health.]

The days of revolution and freedom left deep memories within our people, and we would not accept the Polish tyrant who tried to break us with cruelty and maltreatment. We thwarted every effort of his "darling sons," who came from far away to study in Kremenets, to abuse the Jews.

During the 1930s, the ruling party, Senatsya, also began its corrupt politics in Kremenets, which was based on threats and oppression. Government authorities began to intervene in Jewish community life, supporting aggressive public workers of their choice and creating dissent among the Jewish population. All those who opposed this policy were doomed to persecution—loss of livelihood, etc. With political oppression came economic oppression. The Jews collapsed under the weight of taxes, and their sources of livelihood were closed to them. Young men, forced into idleness, were in decline. Under the influence of the authorities, an atmosphere of *pshitik* penetrated our area.

[**Translation Editor's Note:** The word *pshitik* refers to the township of Przytyk in the Radom district, Poland. On March 9, 1936, there was a pogrom in the township, but it met Jewish resistance. There were casualties on both sides, but the Polish court found the Jews guilty of starting the so-called trouble. The one-sided system of Polish justice was supported by the Polish government and became its policy toward the Jewish minority. The atmosphere created by the trial spread throughout Poland and was referred to as the "*przytyk* atmosphere." Thanks to Bill Leibner, and many others, for this explanation.]

A Jew walking alone at night in a street far from the center of town was not safe anymore, a worry that the Jews of Kremenets had not had for many generations. Nevertheless, the Kremenets Jewish community workers and Zionist leaders persevered. The attorney Dr. B. Landsberg, whose license to appear in court could have been revoked any moment, continued to fight in the community and City Council against the authorities' schemes. Goldring, Zeydi Perlmuter, and others fought relentlessly against the powerful members of the community who put their trust in and reliance on the authorities.

At that time, a new Yiddish weekly paper was established in Kremenets, with the main participants being Zionist activists from all branches. The paper fought strongly against the forces of evil and encouraged community work with a consistently Zionist direction. The paper, put out by volunteers, was published for few years and had a great influence on the population.

DURING WORLD WAR II

With the start of World War II, the Polish government and diplomatic corps moved to Kremenets. The gigantic Lyceum buildings accommodated all of them. The Germans discovered this, and the town was attacked heavily from the air. The Soviets protected the town for two years. Young people received them with much enthusiasm. They remembered well the Polish oppressor's whip and the disgrace of idleness. Government institutions, where a Jewish foot had not stepped for so long, were opened wide to them. Although the national movement was ordered to fold its flag and cease all functions, the Zionist leaders were not harmed this time. The Russians left town suddenly, and with them went the young people who were close to their regime.

The Nazi darkness descended. They established a ghetto, which existed for a year, and in 1942 the annihilation of the tortured community began. At the Nuremberg Trials, a German engineer testified that he had witnessed the great tragedy: 15,000 Kremenets Jews were slaughtered within two days and buried in a common grave across from the train station.

A small group under the leadership of Yonye Bernshteyn successfully escaped into the forests, where they conducted a partisan war along with others who joined them. The Germans offered a large sum of money for Yonye's head.

[54]

BEFORE WORLD WAR I

Yitschak Rokhel (Tel Aviv)

Who will uncover your ruins, Kremenets, my hometown?

After the Holocaust that befell us, I decided to write a few lines about life in our town during my childhood in memoriam.

A VIEW OF THE TOWN AND ITS SURROUNDINGS

Kremenets lies in the southwestern part of Volhynia province, in a valley surrounded by mountains that are a part of the Carpathians. Being the district's center, the town oversaw the many villages and townships in its district. Before the war, the population numbered about 30,0000 people, 10,000–12,000 of them being Jews, but the non-Jewish residents—Ukrainian, Russian, and Polish—lived mostly on the outskirts of town and in the mountains, while the Jews lived in town and in two suburbs—the Dubno suburb and the Vishnevets suburb. So when a visitor came to town, he received the impression that the majority of the residents were Jewish. And in fact, in the town's central streets lived a never-ending, congested Jewish population, while the houses were ethnically mixed in the side streets: a Jewish one next to a Russian or Polish one.

> [**Translation Editor's Note:** The Dubno and Vishnevets suburbs refer to two neighborhoods in Kremenets located on roads that lead to the towns of Dubno and Vishnevets, respectively.]

A large area of town was taken up by the seminary for priests, its gigantic buildings and large grove reaching the foot of Mount Vidomka. To a certain extent, this institution had vested the town with a Christian-religious quality. The second educational institution, which was also in a large grove at the foot of the mountain, was the High School of Commerce, where more than half the students were Jews.

The town itself was long and narrow, with one long street dividing it from one edge to the other from the Vishnevets suburb through the center of town and the Dubno suburb, all the way to the railroad station. Although the street was quite narrow, it was called "Sheroka [Broad] Street." Side streets and alleys stretching from it twisted and interwove all the way into and through the mountains. Mount Bona, the highest of the mountains surrounding the town, afforded a panoramic view of the whole town. Its history was cloaked in assorted folktales about the castle that had been built there and the deep pit at its summit. The Jews called it "the Pit of the Condemned to Death," where, according to traditional tales, castle soldiers who had committed a crime and been sentenced to death were buried. During our time, this mountain was used as a lookout for fires; a scout walked day and night on the turret at its peak, and if he spotted a fire, he would blow the trumpet to alert the firefighters.

The mountain was connected to the town by a paved road, which was used for leisurely walks on the Sabbath and holidays. Across from it Mount Vidomka spread wide, with its groves and with vacation cottages built on its slopes and in its crevices. Zionist young people used to assemble in those groves on the Sabbath, and during the revolution it sheltered most of their illegal meetings. Other famous mountains were the Mountain of the Cross (Krestova), because of the cross at its peak, and the Mountain of the Virgins. This mountainous area left its stamp on the town's life and the residents' character.

There was no river in town, but a narrow and turbid stream, which wound its way to the foot of Mount Bona, flowed full of water in winter and dried up in summer. The residents called it Potok, and the Jews called it Potik. When a divorce decree was issued, it would read, "issued in the town on the River Potik."

[55]

There were 12 subdistricts in the Kremenets District: (1) Radzivilov, (2) Berezhtsy, (3) Belaya Krinitsa, (4) Pochayev, (5) Vishnevets, (6) Shumsk, (7) Vyshgorodok, (8) Lanovtsy, (9) Belozirka, (10) Yampol, (11) Katerburg, and (12) Oleksinets.

ECONOMIC LIFE

How did the Jews of Kremenets earn their living? No statistical research has been done on this, so this review is general.

The area was mostly agricultural and had a market day (fair) every Sunday, when many of area's non-Jewish farmers would come to barter and shop with the townspeople. Most commerce at every stage (retail, wholesale, stores, and peddlers) and in all sorts of products (grain, lumber, iron, cloth, groceries, cattle, horses, etc.) was in Jewish hands. About half of the town's Jews were involved in business, about 20% as professional craftsmen and laborers. They were in only certain kinds of crafts, and no Jews practiced others; there were no Jewish stonemasons or builders, or even plasterers. In contrast, there were many Jewish tailors, shoemakers, carpenters, woodcarvers, tinsmiths, seamstresses, and bakers, and Jews supplied all the town's transportation for people and merchandise as well as porters.

Except for one large foundry, owned by Jews and employing non-Jewish laborers, industry in Kremenets was not modern. A match factory lasted only a few years, and near the town, by the village of Belaya Krinitsa, a factory for fired bricks was owned by Jews, but the laborers were non-Jews; it was originally built to accommodate the construction of the army barracks in the vicinity.

Ours was not a large commercial town. It served only the area within the district and its needs. We did not have people with great wealth in Kremenets, but neither did we have extreme poverty. It was a town where people made a living, and generally the Jews had an economic base in it. The district did not have industrial plants either, except for those directly tied to agriculture, such as flourmills and distilleries. These were owned by the estates and leased to Jews, as were the fishing rights for the rivers.

PUBLIC LIFE

How did Jewish community life in Kremenets look in the pre-World War I period? The community was not well ordered and organized, but it did have a few public institutions with hardworking and devoted community workers. The following are worth mentioning:

A. Care for the Sick (also called Hekdesh)—a public hospital intended for the poor, containing about 30 beds. Physicians volunteered their services, and the needy were treated for a minimal fee or none at all. In the last few years, this institution received a building of its own, and the two Jewish physicians in town, Drs. Landsberg and Litvak, worked there. Mikhael Shumski, Yisrael Margalit, and others were active in that institution for a very long time.

[56]

B. Talmud Torah—This Orthodox school, intended for the children of the poor only, had its up and down periods. For a long time, it was run by R' Duvid Leyb Segal, the son-in-law of the previous rabbi, R' Velvele. R' Moshe Rokhel, a wealthy Orthodox merchant, invested much effort in this institution and succeeded in strengthening it economically.

The affairs of the rabbis, ritual slaughterers, synagogues, and Burial Society occupied an important place in community life. The same was true of vigorous public activity in various public arenas, such as charitable concerns, acts of lovingkindness, anonymous donations, supporting the sick, the Free Lodging Society, hospitality, and the like.

The atmosphere of volunteerism among the townspeople when it came to community affairs and charities should be noted. A "rebbe" ("a good Jew") who came to town for a few days would never leave empty-handed. He was given donations generously.

VOLUNTEERISM AND COMMUNITY WORKERS

Emissaries from distant yeshivas in Lithuania used to come to town to collect donations. At times, a particular public project would excite the town and bring a wave of volunteering with it. I remember when the new bathhouse was to be built; a few donations were for the sum of 1,000 rubles each. During the dispute over the rabbis, each side made sure his rabbi was well taken care of. Here is an episode that illustrates the spirit that lived within the hearts of the best community workers. One day, a new district governor, known to be impeccably honest, was installed in our town. When two community workers of his acquaintance mentioned during a conversation that he was dishonoring the town by driving an old carriage, he explained to them that a government employee who does not accept bribes and cannot afford a stately carriage cannot purchase one. Daringly, they offered to buy him a new carriage as a gift. After vacillating, he finally agreed to accept the carriage as a token of the Jewish community's friendship. But, he added, from then on, he would not veer from his habit and would not take bribes. When the two community representatives left him, one suggested taking up a collection from the wealthy members to buy the carriage, but the other said, "God forbid! You and I will give him the carriage out of our own money." They did so, and without publicity, so as not to cause problems, they presented the carriage in the name of the community. This helped establish good relations between the governor and the town's Jews.

The community representatives chosen to deal with the authorities came mainly from assimilated circles, whose language was Russian, and in everyday life they associated with Russian society and the government office staff. Of these representatives, Mikhael Shumski and Yisrael Margalit stood out. They usually functioned together, so much so that the townspeople tended to mention their names in one breath. Both were City Council members and were generally considered expert Jewish representatives in dealing with the authorities, though no one could tell for sure if or when they had been elected for this task or whether circumstances had put them there. They were also among the founders of the High School of Commerce and members of its supervisory committee for many years. Those connections took the character of intercession in personal matters and communal affairs through the use of personal influence and gifts. From time to time, certain religious circle members whose personal standing, strong character, and wealth had trained them for it would join the negotiations with the authorities.

THE STORY OF THE DISPUTE

A bitter dispute about the rabbis in our town lasted for nearly ten years. Rabbi Velvele (his family name was Mishne) from the town of Novograd Volynskiy held the Kremenets community's rabbinical chair for 25 years—from 1880 until his death in 1905.

[57]

Group from the Young Zion Society, 1912

(Right to left) sitting: (1) Avraham Biberman, (2) Yeshayahu Bilohuz, (3) ... (4) Moshe Biberman, (5) Chanokh Hokhgelernter. Standing: (1) Yeshayahu Katz, (2) Yakov Broytman, (3) Goldenberg, (4) Aleksander Rozental, (5) Okun, (6) Yitschak Rokhel, (7) Yisrael Biberman, (8) Chanokh Kesler, (9) Moshe Yampol.

He was a learned and God-fearing man, but hot-tempered and quick to anger. He never showed favoritism to people of important standing in the community, and because of that, he was unpopular among community workers. When his son-in-law, R' Duvid Leyb Segal, settled in our town, he made an effort to remove pivotal institutions—Care for the Sick, Talmud Torah, and others—from the influence of the town's community workers and put them under the rabbi's sphere of influence. As long as R' Velvele was alive, the opposition remained restrained, but the community's workers kept their resentment inside. After his death, a group of his close associates brought Rabbi Senderovits from Petrikov to town. With this choice, they intended to continue the rabbi's influence on the town's affairs. Another group of influential community workers, who were opposed to this choice, brought a rabbi of their own choice to town, R' Yitschak Heler from the town of Kurilovtsy. For about ten years, the discord between each rabbi's supporters continued. With it came many negative side effects: defamation of the opposite rabbi, his expertise in the Torah, and his authority, subversion, slander, disruptions in the reading on the Sabbath, divisions in the synagogue, the establishment of new synagogues, and even fights. But to their credit, it should be noted that talebearing and slander were never brought to the authorities, though in general our town's hands were not clean of this offense.

The discordant chapter is a sorry one in the late period of our town's life. It brought on a deep division and unwarranted hatred, as a result detracting attention from the community's essential affairs. It is fair to assume that the ones to suffer most from the discord were the two rabbis, and it is possible that they did not even get involved in it at all, even if they could not stop it.

Both were great scholars; one of them, Rabbi Heler, had authored few books of Responsa: *Isaac Acceded, The Offering of Isaac*, and others.

> [**Translator's Note:** In Hebrew, *Isaac Acceded* is *Vayater Yitschak*, and *The Offering of Isaac* is *Minchat Yitschak*.]

[58]

I still remember today the sermon given by the rabbi from Kurilovtsy at my bar mitzvah. The subject was "Tefillin for the Head and Tefillin That Is in the Head."

At the head of the opposing factions were Aba Tsukerman, supporter of the rabbi from Petrikov, and Hirsh Mendil Rokhel, supporter of the rabbi from Kurilovtsy. During the war years, the discord dissipated. The rabbi from Kurilovtsy left town with the flow of refugees and settled in Odessa.

TORAH AND FEAR OF GOD

Was our town a place of distinguished scholars who were erudite in the Torah? Not particularly. It could be said that the town was graced with an "average character": it had no extremely wealthy people and no wretchedly poor ones, but was a town consisting of people who earned a living. There were no fanatic Hasidim and no sharp *Mitnagdim,* but mutual tolerance between them. There were neither extremely religious people nor converts. The same thing was true in relation to "scholarship": there were not many distinguished, erudite scholars, but complete ignoramuses and illiterates were almost nonexistent. Most Jews knew the Torah—how to read portions of the Pentateuch with Rashi's commentaries. Between the afternoon and evening prayers, they would study a chapter in the Mishna and sometimes a page of Gemara. In the synagogues and study hall, permanent study groups mainly studied the Mishna and *Ein Yakov.* From time to time, in honor of finishing a section, they would celebrate with a glass of brandy and cakes. True, there were a few distinguished scholars like the venerable R' Shlome Alinkis the Gemara teacher, R' Chayim Leyb Volf, and the sharpest of them, R' Moshe Velis, who served as a permanent arbitrator in money problems because of his great astuteness. There was no yeshiva in our town, so those few who desired to do yeshiva study had to travel to other towns—to yeshivas in Lithuania. For a few years, a small yeshiva existed in our town, run by a head of yeshiva who had moved to our town from Novograd Volynskiy. One of the prodigies that he brought with him was Avraham Ikar, a member of the Second Immigration and the Haganah.

[**Translation Editor's Note:** *Ein Yakov* is a compilation of stories from the Talmud.]

Most of our people were religious, and few were freethinkers. The general atmosphere in town was imbued with devotion to tradition; during the Sabbath, all the stores were closed, work stopped, and the synagogues were filled with worshipers, and the effect of the holidays was very obvious. People did not drive on the Sabbath, and those who breached the rules did so out of sight, not daring to enter the town in a vehicle. Most old and middle-aged men wore *kapotas*, especially on the Sabbath and holidays. Most men of the young generation shaved their beards and walked in public with their heads uncovered, and some spoke Russian. But as the saying goes, "Even the sinners of Israel are full of good deeds, like a pomegranate," for the truth is that members of the young generation were deeply embedded in Jewish traditions, and to "honor thy father" they would come to the synagogue on the Sabbath and holidays, keep kosher, and follow the other ways of Judaism. The High School of Commerce had a destructive influence on traditional ways, as its students had profaned the Sabbath since their youth and instilled this habit in their parents' homes and everyone around them. A second reason for breaking rules and traditions was the revolutionary movement, which swept up a considerable number of the town's young people. The World War speeded up the process of secularization.

[**Translator's Note**: The *kapota* is a long coat, generally black.]

RELATIONS BETWEEN PEOPLES

Because the law forbade Jews to settle in villages, few settled in the villages in the vicinity of Kremenets. In the townships and the town itself, Jews were a considerable part of the population, and their effect was bigger than their numbers. It should be noted that the Jew did not see himself as a "temporary visitor" but as a citizen involved and rooted in a country with an ethnically mixed population. And this was also how the other ethnic peoples saw the Jews. Certainly, anti-Semitic propaganda was carried out, and here and there it also bore fruit, but in day-to-day life, hatred of the Jews was not seen. In daily life, their treatment was completely proper. Our town and its surrounding area did not experience pogroms (though during the days of Petliura, there were some isolated cases of murders of village Jews).

[59]

As opposed to this, the Jews were discriminated against when it came to the law, and they had no part in town and government administration. For that reason, every government action was received as a decree that had to be overcome through lobbying, bribery, and such.

Reciprocal contacts among different ethnic groups occurred mainly for work and business purposes, and they were only minimally ties for mutual cultural and public activities. Wealthy merchants and members of the intelligentsia, who spoke Russian, saw it as an honor to be members of the public club called "the high-society salon," where they enjoyed their evenings playing cards and dominos in the company of Russian intelligentsia and officials. There were other means of cultural association and close relations, but in general it has to be stated (that is, for the period before World War I) that the Kremenets Jewish community formed a tightly knit, unified, independent entity—it had a way of life of its own, including a pronounced national folklore with all its light and shadows. And Jews were largely immune from assimilation into the other ethnic groups that formed the majority in the area. The fact is, mixed marriages or conversions were very rare.

STATUS OF THE ZIONIST MOVEMENT

What was the status of the Zionist movement in our town? The attitude of most people from our town was one of indifference and dismissal, while a considerable number were openly opposed to it. The average person—a merchant and craftsman who saw himself as a wise and practical man—looked at the handful of adolescent and adult Zionists and saw a bunch of impractical idlers. In the days of public awakening, as in the 1917 revolution or during general elections, public sympathy seemed to be with the Zionist movement, but as soon as the wave of excitement dissipated, the Zionist Organization was pushed back into a corner, and the practical man went back to his business.

From time to time, a Zionist preacher would visit our town (Preacher Berker, father of Kariti of Kiryat Anavim, is remembered favorably) to preach to the public in the study halls between the afternoon and evening services. And it would seem that he had awakened dormant sentiments toward Zion and its new life. Community leaders, whether they were religious or freethinking, were not Zionist adherents. The religious ones opposed the basic idea because of *dechikat hakets*, and some did not approve of meetings where men and women attended together, sat with their heads uncovered, and spoke Russian. It is true that, in the early period, many of the talks during Zionist meetings were in Russian, even though most Zionists were members of the middle classes. In the eyes of the religious ones, the Zionist movement equaled heresy. Later, the situation changed. In 1920, in addition to the veteran Zionists, the Young Zionists and Labor Zionists were active in Kremenets, and a group of pioneers immigrated to Israel. Early 1921 saw the Zionist Organization fighting to gain a leading position in the town's public institutions. Gathered around them were young people—mostly children of community notables and some from different circles—and a few adults. At that time, there was no clear difference between the Zionist factions; the Young Zionists, a fellowship without a clear program, were an active and lively part of the Zionist Organization, a sort of "youth guard." As for the adults, although they were few in number, they were deeply rooted in their belief in Zionism and steadfast in their ideas. Each of them had an influential personality and was well known in the community: Dr. B. Landsberg, Yakov Shafir, Meir Goldring, Aharon-Shimon Shpal, Moshe Eydelman, Getsi Klurfayn, Aharon Fridman, Munye Dobromil, Meshulam Katz, and some other personalities—community workers who paved the way for widespread cultural and Zionist activity in the period between the two wars and prepared for a large-scale pioneer immigration.

[**Translator's Notes:** *Dechikat hakets* refers to the concept of forcing the issue of the messiah's arrival by returning and rebuilding the homeland of Israel before the messiah's arrival. Young Zionists is *Tseirey Tsion* in Hebrew.]

[60]

EDUCATION

Where in our town were Jewish children educated? Here, too, precise numbers are missing. It is reasonable to assume that about half the boys were educated in the cheders, and the rest in other schools. Also, when they grew up, those who studied in a cheder for few years went to a Jewish or mixed school. It should be noted that Kremenets had dozens of cheders, each with 20–40 pupils. There were three schools in town where the language of instruction was Russian: a Jewish primary school, a town (primary) school for Jews and non-Jews, and the High School of Commerce. For some time, there was a private high school for Jewish and non-Jewish girls that belonged to Mrs. Aleksina. It is estimated that about 500–600 children were educated in those institutions. The two primary schools drew middle-class children, and the children of the wealthy attended the High School of Commerce, due to the high tuition and long years of study. A good number of this school's graduates went away to large cities for higher education: to Kiev, Odessa, Petersburg, and Moscow. When they graduated, some became physicians and settled in different towns, but only a few returned and found a place in their hometown.

HOW KREMENETS WAS SAVED FROM THE RIOTS

Akiva Zeyger (Haifa)

It was right after World War I. Russia was still embroiled in the revolution. From day to day, whole regions found themselves under different governments. This happened to Kremenets, too. Here Petliura's gangs ruled, and the roads to Kremenets were already overflowing with the Polish army. Petliura's men abandoned the town, which was left without rule of law or government protection, and immediately gangs of farmers from the area got together with insurgent townspeople and schemed to slaughter the Jewish population. The Polish estate owner Visotski, who was in town, heard about this and immediately joined the gangs as a leader and commander, telling them to get ready to land a mortal blow on the "Zhids." He assembled all of them in the Lyceum and told them that the following morning they would sweep throughout the town and destroy it completely. In the dark of night, Visotski went to the Dubno road, where the Polish army was awaiting him. Secretly, he led them in, and thus the murderers' scheme was thwarted. My father, of blessed memory, told me later that Kremenets had been saved thanks to the blessing received from a visiting rabbi. The fact is that Kremenets came out of World War I without damage. But this time, even the rabbi's blessing did not help … annihilation came upon it, together with the rest of the holy communities.

HELP FOR REFUGEES DURING WORLD WAR I

Menachem Goldgart (Tel Aviv)

Close to the beginning of the war, the Russian-Austrian front stretched near the shores of the River Ikva, about six kilometers from Kremenets, for a long period. But in the summer of 1915, General Brusilov opened a big offensive on Galicia, and within a few days the front shifted westward. During this move, quite a few cities and towns in the area were completely destroyed, and a stream of Jewish refugees began to flow into Kremenets from Radzivilov, Kozin, Pochayev, and other places. The wealthy families had left town earlier. But the poor came walking into Kremenets emptyhanded; all their property and houses had gone up in flames. They had escaped to save themselves after many were killed during the battles, and many injured people came with them. It was only 35 kilometers from Radzivilov to Kremenets, but it took the refugees weeks to arrive, hiding in the forests during the day and walking at night.

As soon as the community heard the news about the approaching refugees, community workers set up a committee to help them (Aleksander Frishberg, Dr. Arye Landsberg, Yitschak Poltorak, Mrs. Perlmuter, and others), and young people from the refugees joined them. The main concern was feeding the people, even before their arrival in town. The committee appealed to the Red Cross, which sent field kitchens to the forests where the refugees were roaming. The provisions were handed over to the committee, which oversaw the distribution of kosher food. About 3,000 refugees came from Radzivilov alone, and with those from other towns, the number swelled to about 5,000. Meanwhile, the need for shelter was being taken care of. As soon as the refugees arrived in town, they were placed in the buildings of assorted community institutions, private homes, with relatives, and other places. The main shelter was the Talmud Torah building, which had previously been used as horse stables by the Russian army and was a semi-ruin by now. It was very crowded, with 10 people per windowless, doorless room. The Christian seminary buildings could easily have housed most of the refugees, but the buildings stayed empty, as they were not offered for use. The Red Cross kitchen, however, was allowed to set up in the seminary's spacious yard.

A few dozen of the town's young people, mainly from Zionist movements, established a group to help the refugees, for some reason calling itself the Market Statistics Council, and at its head stood the young and enthusiastic Bozye Landsberg. In reality, this council took on the responsibility of caring for the refugees, developing effective, extensive activities in many fields, and thanks to their devotion, physical and emotional degeneration was avoided. The first thing they did was to create a detailed list of the refugees according to Red Cross regulations (the name of the council came from this task). They set up real legal aid, seeing to identity documents and the like. Financing for the assistance came from three large organizations that worked in the field in Russia at that time: the Red Cross, the United Councils of Cities, and the United Zemstvos. An oversight board made up of representatives from the three organizations was formed, and the youth council worked with them as their implementation group.

> [**Translator's Note:** *Zemstvos* refers to an elective council responsible for the local administration of a provincial district in czarist Russia.]

The kitchen that opened for the refugees in the seminary yard, which was run by the young volunteers, supplied three meals a day for more than 3,000 people. As the products received from the Red Cross were insufficient, the volunteers solicited money from other sources and improved on the food given to the needy.

[62]

Youth Committee for Refugee Aid, 1916

Sitting, right to left: (1) Vayser, (2) ...?, (3) M. Goldgart, (4) ...?, (5) Sonye Landsberg-Poltorak. *Standing, first row:* (1) Balter, (2) ...?, (3) ...?, (4) Zamberg, (5) Sonye Perlmuter, (6) ...? *Standing, second row:* (1) Yitschak Eydelman, (2) Dr. Binyamin Landsberg, (3) Bazdizhski, (4) ...?

The towns from which the refugees came were almost completely destroyed, but some had saved a few possessions in underground cellars. After much effort and persuasion, we rented 100 wagons from local farmers and, in a large caravan, went to Radzivilov to collect what was left of the possessions. At that time, the czarist regime suspected that Jews were spies for the enemy, so they allowed only two Jews to accompany the caravan: Mr. Barats and this writer.

Endangering their lives, they managed to rescue the possessions that had not been burned, particularly clothing, and bring them to town. They were put in communal storage, from which they were distributed among the refugees.

Because of the general situation in the town, it was not possible to provide jobs for the refugees, so some of them eventually moved to other places in Ukraine and Russia. However, the majority stayed in our town and needed public support and care for a long period.

A special chapter of the youth council made sure the refugees' children received an education. Temporary schools were formed in which some of the young volunteers served as teachers. Eventually, those temporary institutions became permanent, regular schools, where children from the town were educated together with the refugees' children. Much effort, enthusiasm, and endless devotion were invested in this generous and blessed project. Thousands were saved from starvation. Many young people, who with the fervor of youth were carried away with this work, found that it was the way to reach the nation's masses. Later, some of them became good social workers, educators, and community workers.

[63]

AT THE BEGINNING OF THE REVOLUTION

M. Kornits (Jerusalem)

It is February 27, 1917, an ordinary winter day with no discernible changes. Life continues in its routine tracks as in days past. The train has not arrived, nor have the newspapers. Even when they arrive in an hour or two, will you find the echoes of today's happenings in them? They were published in Kiev or Moscow or Petersburg two days ago. Suddenly, an unusual movement is felt in town. Here and there a group of people forms in the streets, excited discussions begin, and in moments the whole town knows that a revolution has begun in Petersburg, the czar has abdicated, and a temporary government has been elected under Kerensky's leadership.

Is that believable? Finally, even we, the Jews, would not be singled out for discrimination, but we would be citizens with equal rights like the rest of Russia's nations. Joy and merriment! Every face is radiant. The masses streamed to the Great Synagogue for a public meeting. Young members of the freedom movement came out with exciting speeches. The thousands who gathered decided to elect a Jewish Community Council, and on the spot the young people elected young Fritz Eydis as head of the community. Later it was seen that this was a hasty move ... the era demanded the injection of young blood into community life. After some time, a Community Council of representatives from different political factions was elected, and I was chosen as the council secretary. The members worked on a voluntary basis, each willingly donating his time and efforts on behalf of our town's Jewish community.

Until that time, the authorities had appointed the members of the City Council, and under the czarist regime the council had included Christians and only one Jew. This was M. D. Shumski. As it happened, the town fathers never considered the Jewish population's needs, and more than once Mr. Shumski had to take on the battle singlehanded. Although he fought his war with wisdom and dedication, he never succeeded. Jews constituted about 40% of the 30,000 residents of our town. We then decided to bring about a drastic change in the ratio of power and representation on the City Council. When a new law governing elections to the City Council was announced, we started a fierce campaign and successfully elected a City Council of which 50% of the members were Jews from different circles and factions. These were M. D. Shumski, Avraham Verthaym, Meir Goldring, Moshe Eydis, M. Storozh, Konya Segal, Sh. Fingerhut, Krozman, and this writer.

After a new mayor, the City Council, and its assorted committees were elected, we set a goal for ourselves: to improve the poor conditions of our public institutions, such as the hospital, the Home for the Aged, the Talmud Torah, etc., as soon as possible. Municipal offices, which had not previously employed Jewish clerks—even though about 75% of the levied taxes came from the Jewish population—now employed quite a few. The situation with regard to supplies in the town was quite serious; these were days of shortage and scarcity of flour, sugar, salt, fuel, soap, etc. At one of the City Council meetings, it was decided to establish a supply department, with Meir Goldring at its head and me as his assistant. After many negotiations and much travel to the county seat of Zhitomir, we managed to acquire essential consumer goods. Town stores were opened and supplies were distributed according to ration cards. Slowly, day by day, matters were brought up to acceptable levels, but then the political situation worsened and, with it, economic conditions. A separatism movement began in Ukraine, and thanks to encouragement by the Germans, it yielded fruit in a short time. Ukraine declared itself an independent country, and Skoropadski was declared the head of free Ukraine.

[64]

The regime's "fist-and-whip" policy was felt most strongly among the Jews. The beating and arrest of the progressive members of city councils and public institutions began. In our town, Bozye Landsberg, Fritz Eydis, the Ukrainian socialist Koval, the pitiable Tsiperfin (the poor man was so depressed by his arrest that he died shortly after his release), and I were arrested and jailed. Meir Goldring managed to escape arrest at the last minute. We were kept in jail without investigation or trial for 99 days until our release. A few days before that, we had declared a hunger strike and demanded that each of us be given a notice of charges. This was denied, and instead, the warden in charge, a veteran clerk from the czarist days, came to our cell (we were all incarcerated in the same cell), and addressed us as follows:

"Gentlemen, please stop this hunger strike. Tell me what you want for the evening meal, and I'll order a samovar heated for you immediately and send someone to buy fresh sausage and white bread. This jailhouse is the best place for you; if you were free now, who knows how many of you would still be alive ...." Indeed, his words were almost true; waves of rioters ran all over Ukraine rampaging against the Jews. But we did not stop our hunger strike until the next day, after we received a secret note from a young Jew not to worry, that on the next day he would be arriving at the head of a detachment from Petliura's army and would free the town. And so it was. The young man came riding on a white horse, conquered the town, and sent his soldiers to release us. When the gate opened and we saw who was releasing us, we preferred to stay in our jail cell, so terrible did our saviors seem to us. Eventually, we left the jail and dispersed, each to his home.

We had spent hardly a few days at home when new trouble arrived: the Petliurans had been chased away, and new rulers arrived. More correctly, chaos reigned and there was no rule. The Bolsheviks came, stayed a few days in town, "purified" the bourgeois a little, and went away. Rumors spread that the Polish armies were nearing the town, but until they did, our town suffered a few hours of horror.

Farmers from Shumsk and nearby villages found out that the town of Kremenets had been left abandoned without anyone in charge, and they decided to "take the law into their own hands." The gang arrived in town with sacks on their backs, because their leaders had promised them that they would be given permission to ransack and loot the Jewish population to their heart's content. Vysotsky, who had previously been an officer in the czarist army and was in town at that time, saved the community from a total pogrom. He succeeded in approaching the Polish army posts and getting them to hasten their entrance to the town. On their arrival, the Shumsk gang escaped with their lives. This reign, too, was short-lived; the Poles retreated under pressure from Marshal Budyonny's troops. Again the authorities changed, and our town went from hand to hand until the Bolshevist army retreated from the Warsaw vicinity, and the Poles recaptured our town and ruled it until September 1939.

Many hardships were visited on Kremenets in 1917–1918, but the town's Jewish representatives guarded the interests of its residents in spite of all the vagaries of the time.

[65]

DURING THE CHANGES OF 1917–1920

Azriel Goren (Gorengut, Pardes-Chana)

When the Kerensky government was established, I moved from my hometown, Yampol, to Kremenets, where I served as a rabbi. This was a short honeymoon period for the Russian intelligentsia in general and Jews in particular. With the declaration of equal rights for all minorities in Russia and abolition of the special restrictive laws that had oppressed the Jews for generations, a wave of excitement flooded the Jewish section of Kremenets, too. In national and communal work, our national intelligentsia in particular excelled. At its head stood the distinguished B. Landsberg, a high school classmate of the president of the Knesset, Yosef Shprintsak, may he live long.

This activity focused on three aspects: (1) preparation for immigration to Israel, (2) cultural activities, and (3) attainment of equal rights for Jews in law and in practice.

The first immigration group was established in those days, but because of all the political entanglements, immigration was postponed for a year and a half. In the town's two high schools, for boys and for girls, the study of Bible and the history of Israel (which I was teaching) were added to the curriculum. Lectures on the history of Zionism and the culture of Israel deepened our young people's national consciousness.

Five representatives of the Kremenets Jewish community were elected to the Kremenets City Council, headed by the liberal and likeable Judge Pokrovski. For the first time, the Jewish community became organized into an intrinsically autonomous national framework, which kept a constant link with the Center for Jewish Communities in Petersburg.

The excitement and elation lasted just a few months; our achievements in the life of the country's renewal and in local authority were large and important—and then heavy blows landed on our heads from the national movement led by Petliura. The situation worsened with the disintegration of the Russian army. Every day Ukrainian and Russian deserters showed up in town, extorting, robbing, and terrorizing. How could the police use weapons against hungry and embittered soldiers? The atmosphere was permeated with dread and horror, particularly in the Jewish section. In one of the alleys, a young Jew was killed after refusing to take off his shoes and hand them over to an extorting deserter.

It is hard to bring up memories from our youth; our feelings seem to be similar to those of an amputee who feels pain in an amputated foot ....

> **Editor's Note:** The era of Polish governance, 1920–1939, is covered extensively in the next sections: Public Life, Education and Culture, and Zionism and Immigration.

[66]

TWENTY-ONE MONTHS UNDER SOVIET RULE

Ayzik Hofman (Tel Aviv)
English translation by David Dubin

On September 10, 1939, the Polish government and its diplomatic corps escaped from Warsaw through Kremenets-Zbarazh-Zaleszczyki on their way to Romania. On their way, they stopped in Kremenets for three or four days and stayed in the Lyceum and hotels. The town had never witnessed such regal pomp, fancy cars, and consular representatives of foreign countries with their flags and symbols as were seen in those few days. Of all the countries' representatives, apparently only the Italian and USSR delegates been forewarned of the coming bombardment, and they left in time, while the rest of the diplomats stayed.

The next morning, the town was bombed; it was market day, and hundreds of people were killed in this surprise attack, which was aimed at striking the government and causing confusion among the citizenry. Many people left their homes to hide in the mountains and forests. Some returned at night, while others stayed and slept in the open. This one shelling was sufficient to paralyze the life of the town.

On September 17, the citizens listened to Radio Moscow announce the agreement between Russia and Nazi Germany. People left their hiding places and awaited the arrival of the Russians. Some wealthy people and landowners escaped to Poland and Germany, but none of the Jews left. When the Red Army arrived on the 22nd, it was received cheerfully.

The mayor and the Polish police were ready to help the new regime keep order; a "temporary administration" was formed immediately—under the authority of the Russian army and politicians—to which were added some local clerks from the Jewish intelligentsia and Communists who had been released from jail and returned to Kremenets.

In general, the new regime showed a tendency to favor the Jews, who were an intellectual and devoted element, while many of the Poles were members of nationalist movements. During the early months of Soviet rule, the Jewish population swelled by 5,000–8,000, including refugees from western Galicia and Congress Poland, escapees from the Nazis, returning students, and those from the town who had been living out of town temporarily. The tendency for families to reunite was growing stronger. Some newcomers were absorbed into the government administration, and others, young Jews with a technical education, who had been denied the opportunity to work in their profession because of the Polish oppression and had been forced to go into commerce, were now able to pursue their professions.

Rapidly, all the economic institutions prevalent in Russia were established: a national commerce network, including national companies to utilize forests and buy agricultural products and supplies. Industrial cooperatives, such as a large one for shoes, were formed. Coal and peat mines that had not operated during the Polish regime were rehabilitated and employed many workers and clerks. In those enterprises, refugees who did not know Russian found work as laborers.

In those days, the saying was that all three nations living in Volhynia were satisfied during the Soviet regime: Jews received jobs in offices, Poles were permitted to deal in secondhand clothes (before then, they were jealous of the Jews, who had a monopoly in this), and Ukrainians were permitted to have signs in Ukrainian (the official language in the government offices was Russian only).

[67]

Until January 1940, economic life continued in an orderly fashion; commerce was free, and products were sold in stores according to the ruble-gulden exchange. Quite soon it became evident that stocks would not be replenished, resulting in rising prices. The delivery of supplies was irregular, and when sugar or manufactured goods arrived in the government stores, long lines formed in front of them.

At the end of November 1939, any inventory of goods in wholesalers' stores was gone, and their keys and all their goods were confiscated without any compensation, although retailers were left alone. This harmed lumber and iron merchants most of all.

After a while, flourmills and bakeries were confiscated. Step by step, systematically and consistently, all commerce and industry were taken from the town's Jews.

At the end of 1939, residents were ordered to vote for or against annexing the town to the Ukrainian-Soviet republic. Obviously, the Jews voted for annexation. For fear of the authorities, or because they had no choice—as when the choice was Hitler or the Soviets—they chose the Soviets.

In spring 1940, an order arrived for all refugees to register and declare their choice to stay in Russia or return to Nazi-held Poland. Many felt that living under Soviet authority was too difficult and, believing that they would be given permission to leave, declared their wish to return. The result was not what they expected. One night, a squadron of the NKVD took them and their families and sent them to work camps in the Urals and Siberia. (The Polish citizens who had been settled in the vicinity of the town during the 1930s to give it a Polish character were taken away in the same manner.)

The Jews felt very miserable, but later realized that they had been saved while the others perished.

****

National Jewish life came to an end without the need for the authorities to act. The Jews understood that public activities were not acceptable under Soviet rule and that they had better concern themselves only with their personal needs. The most outstanding public personality in our town was Dr. Binyamin Landsberg, leader of the Zionist movement. He resigned all his public positions, moved to Lvov (where he was not known as a Zionist), and got a job as a Russian teacher. Then many other Zionist activists and members of the bourgeoisie moved to Lvov and other towns, which saved them from being deported (many people in the town of Dubno were deported). Fear had done its job.

All Zionist and other types of organizations ceased to exist. Everyone devoted himself to adapting to the new way of life. The head of the NKVD in Kremenets was Kovalenko. While he hesitated when Ukrainians and Poles questioned why he did not destroy the Zionist movement's resources, he replied that even if he simply wanted to ban Zionist activities, he would have to imprison the majority of the Jews of Kremenets in the jailhouse, yet the Zionist Hebrews are useful and faithful subjects to the Soviet regime. And, indeed, the Jews adapted themselves quickly to life under the new regime.

Use of language in public life soon changed. Without being forced, the Yiddish that was used during trade union meetings gave way to Russian and Ukrainian.

[68]

The Jews' public and cultural life was completely cut off. Ended were meetings and conventions; organizations were terminated; even the Dramakrayz, the trade union organizations' amateur theater group, ceased to exist. The movie house continued to function, of course, but showed only Russian movies.

Key positions generally were given to party members who came from eastern Russia and were "Easterners" ("*Vastatshniki*"), and they were assisted by some local Communists. For example, Meir Pinchuk (a former member of the Youth Guard turned Communist) was appointed to be in charge of the Lyceum, and his wife, in charge of other schools. The Tarbut School existed, but in a physical way only; it used the same building, furniture, and teachers, but the languages used were Russian and Ukrainian, and the teaching system and content were completely changed.

> [**Translation Editor's Note:** The Youth Guard (in Hebrew, *Hashomer Hatsair*) was a socialist-Zionist youth movement.]

It is interesting to note that some Jewish laborers who were leaning toward communism thought that now they would be relieved from labor and given positions in government institutions, but the new authorities preferred to choose from the intelligentsia, and rejected them completely or gave them a minor job, like being in charge of a storage plant. Because of they lacked knowledge of business management, they often got in trouble in their new jobs and later were accused by inspectors of wasting public property. Then they were arrested or exiled. True, in the long run these actions benefited the exiled, as it saved their lives. Note, also, that the Communist Party was a "closed shop"; for 21 months not one new member was accepted: "Slowly, first you have to adjust to us, prove your allegiance, then your time will come to join" .... But the time never arrived.

****

Taking us by surprise, the war between the USSR and Germany erupted on June 22, 1941; four days later, the Germans were close to the town. The residents were inclined to move east, deep into Russia, but an order soon came that no one was to leave his job or he would be considered a deserter. Most people accepted the edict and stayed in town. Only a minority, a few hundred young people, took a chance and left town for the east on June 26–27, while the sound of shots echoed behind them. At the former border, near Yampol, Lakhovtsy, and other places, they got into arguments with the border guard, but eventually were let through into the depths of Russia and thus were saved. Why did many not leave but, instead, stay to be annihilated? There were several reasons for this. First, there was a strong belief that the Germans would win and overtake the escapees, so it was preferable to await them at home and not break up the family. Second, although the Nazi's cruelties were known by then, the atrocities of the extermination were not yet known. Third, many hesitated to endanger themselves by acting against the authorities, who had forbidden them to leave town.

After a while, Stalin's famous order commanding loyal residents to leave their locations, burn and destroy everything, and leave behind only scorched land changed the policy. Many Jewish settlements, such as towns in Bessarabia and others, obeyed the order, moved east, and were saved. For the Jews of Kremenets, the order arrived too late; by the time it was announced, their fate was set for annihilation.

[69]

COURAGEOUS SPIRIT

Brigadier General Y. Avidar (Jerusalem)
English translation by David Dubin

The bravery and courage of my town's Jews are engraved deep in my memory. They proudly stood up against all foes and attackers, defending their life and honor. From the oldest to the youngest, they were imbued with heroic spirit, and when the time came, they were ready to fight back. Here are some episodes from my youth.

When news about the pogroms in Proskurov reached our town, the School of Commerce, which was attended by Jews and gentiles, was engulfed in an atmosphere of hostility toward the Jews. Provocative writing appeared on the walls, proclaiming "We'll do to you as was done in Proskurov" and similar sentiments. The Jewish students, a minority in the class, were attacked by hoodlums. A fight in the third grade (13-year-olds) between the two nationalities lasted about an hour, and the non-Jews were beaten badly. The teachers could not stop the fight until the trusted and well-liked school principal, Yefim Konstantinovits Domanski, intervened. He was finally able to stop the fight.

When I was just a small boy in preschool, a Russian student, the son of the police commissioner, insulted me and called me "Zhid." I did not let him get away with this; I followed him home, hitting him all the way from school to his home. The commissioner complained, and the principal called me and informed me, officially, that a complaint had been filed against me. I replied that it was true, I did hit the boy, but that he deserved it as he had insulted my people. The principal accepted my explanation and did not punish me. More than once, during games, a fight would ensue when a group of Jewish children felt insulted by their gentile friends. And though fewer, they did not shrink back, and they won more often than not.

Brigadier General Moshe Carmel told me his impressions after visiting our town and meeting its young people. In the different towns that he visited as a representative of Young Pioneer, he witnessed incidents of cowardice by Jewish young people when intimidated by hoodlums. In Kremenets, the situation was completely different. When groups of boys were walking out of town near the Ikva River or in the mountains, gentile boys often attacked them. After seeing the reaction of the boys from other towns, they expected this group to run away and were surprised to see them immediately marshal themselves for a "defensive battle," fighting and hitting their foes until they ran away.

> [**Translation Editor's Note:** Young Pioneer (in Hebrew, *Hechaluts Hatsair*) was a Zionist organization aimed at preparing young people for immigration to Israel.]

Such were our town's children, such were our young people, and this was the spirit of the adults.

In a later period, during Polish rule, I remember soccer tournaments between Jews and Poles. When the Polish group was going to lose, the Polish audience would start to provoke the Jewish audience, but the gentiles ended up being the losers.

Pogroms were not perpetrated on Jews in Kremenets. This was not a matter of the gentiles of our town and its surroundings, but mainly because the Jewish Kremenets was courageous and knew how to stand and defend itself in times of trouble.

Over the years, in times of civil war and with frequent changes of government, the Jews had established "self-defense" groups of different forms or names. Sometimes they were joined by the gentiles and other times not, according to the situation. However, the initiative and instruction of these groups came from the Jews. In the interval between governments—and sometimes that lasted for days—authority was in the hands of the "Defense." When the new government was established, the commanders of the Defense presented themselves to the government and handed over the authority and part of the armaments and ammunition.

[70]

Most of the time, the new authorities acknowledged the Defense as a semiofficial civilian force. In this form, it continued until the new "revolution."

The existence of the Haganah imbued the townspeople with a feeling of security and pride. I can still recall the strong effect on me, a young boy, watching the Haganah's guard platoon striding confidently, guns in hand, in the center of the street, guarding the town's peace. My heart was full of pride, because my brother, Chanokh Rokhel, and my cousin, Avraham Biberman, were two of the guards, erect and confident, their guns bayoneted. I remember well a Polish man, Mr. Visotski, who was a big help to the Haganah organization.

In 1917, all of Russia was raging in the throes of the revolution. On the eve of the Bolsheviks' takeover, hooligans began to erupt. These were not just "underworld" people but also some decent citizens who felt it to be an opportune time for reckoning with the Jews. Near Mr. Goldenberg's store on Sheroka Street, a pogrom was organized under the leadership of an officer in the motorcycle troupe stationed in the area. The Jewish *druzhina* showed up immediately and dispersed the hooligans. Their evil plot was thwarted.

[**Translation Editor's Note:** *Druzhina* is Russian for a select detachment of troops.]

I remember another aborted pogrom in our town. During a change in government, a sort of authority vacuum was created in the town. The gentiles in the suburbs "smelled" the odor of lawlessness; tempted by the army's supplies, which were housed in the large seminary buildings, they started to ransack and loot them. The farmers from the area rushed into town to join them in robbing and looting. A bloody storm was at the town gates. There was no doubt that as soon as the lawless crowd was done there, it would proceed to the Jewish areas of town and start looting and murdering. A pogrom was sensed in the air. Rapidly, the defense groups organized, appeared at the entrance to the center of the town, prevented the gangs of hooligans from entering the town limits, and put an end to the looting.

The self-defense of the Jews of Kremenets was not a passing episode; it existed for many years under different names and forms: *druzhina,* Home Defense, Self-Defense, and Civil Militia. I remember Mr. Azriel Gorengut, the active Zionist and "government-appointed rabbi" who was a longtime leader of the Civil Militia. The young members of the Haganah trained themselves in the use of weapons. There was a constant concern for the acquisition of weapons and ammunition, as most were acquired from those abandoned during changes of government. Although they were required to relinquish their weapons to the new authorities, they made sure not to be left emptyhanded. Most of the time, they owned a few hundred guns. The Defense's ability to organize should be noted. In general, good order prevailed, as well as responsibility, protection of property, chain of command, patrols, passwords, weapons assignment, messenger boys, and even an information bureau to find out ahead of time about impending changes of authority so as to be ready and well organized.

Who were the members of that self-defense? They included mostly Zionist youth and students, but also adults and many ordinary people.

The existence of the self-defense organization in Kremenets was well known in the area, near and far, and maybe that was the reason our town was spared the bloodbaths that visited many towns in Volhynia and Podolia during the years after World War I.

Some attribute the heroic character of our town's Jews the fact that they lived in a mountainous area. But the Zionist idea, which permeated Jewish hearts more and more, strengthened its spirit and awakened feelings of personal and national pride and honor.

****

Courageous youth, a proud Jewish settlement—how you were pillaged!

[71]

R' YITSCHAK BER LEVINZON (THE RYB"L)

RYB"L: HIS LIFE AND PERSONALITY

A. Ben-Or (Orinovski)
From the book *Chapters in the History of New Hebrew Literature*
English translation by David Dubin

In his personality and his community and literary activities, the RYB"L symbolized the cultural movement that began among the Jews of southern Russia during his lifetime. He devoted his life to fulfilling the demands of the time and essential public needs and duties while abandoning his personal affairs and needs. For 40 years (1820–1860), he lived a life of loneliness, poverty, and poor health in his native town Kremenets, in Volhynia, his house standing at the edge of town. The poet A. B. Gotlober describes him as follows:

> The house is small and narrow, consisting of only one room built of wood and reeds and plastered with mud inside and out. The furniture consists of a rickety table, a small simple chair, and a bed like that of the poorest of poor in Israel, and upon it lies the man I was seeking—the great, wise rabbi, RYB"L, the one after whom we start counting the new era in the Jewish annals in Russia.

In this house, RYB"L was bedridden, his nerves weak and his body emaciated and weak, unable to take even a few steps. He lived like a hermit secluded from the world around him, but from his poor dwelling removed from life's noises and in spite of his weakness, he sent his messages to his people and the Russian government, courageously and tirelessly battling on two fronts—the inner and the outer—and scored victories. In this house, he wrote many books and penned memoranda to the government. He never veered from his self-assigned life duties. In this house, Jewish intellectuals and gentile government officials often visited him. One of them was the Russian government minister Graf D. A. Tolstoy, who described him as a monk and a holy man.

RYB"L was the first Hebrew intellectual in Russia who was well versed in Russian and advanced Russian culture and not German. His father, R' Yehuda Levin, a wealthy Kremenets merchant and Jewish scholar and intellectual, taught him Jewish studies and Russian and instilled patriotic feelings toward Russia in him. From this came his belief that "what the government wants for us is peace and our best." This brought the turning point in the intellectual movement from German to the country's native language. He also wrote the first Russian grammar book in Hebrew, called *The Basics of the Russian Language*. During the Napoleonic wars, the young RYB"L and his wife lived in the border town of Radzivilov (1812), and he worked in the Russian army as an official translator and garnered distinctions. When the war was over, he composed a poem, "Sounds of Heroism," to honor the victorious Russia.

The defense minister sent the poem to the government as a proof of the love of the motherland in the hearts of the Russian Jews. From then on, RYB"L was honored by the government, received with prizes for his books, and was listened to attentively for his advice on regulations for the Jews. Legends circulated among the Jews about his great influence in government minister circles. Thanks to this influence, he succeeded to some degree in achieving his ideas in education. What were his ideas?

[72]

First, *reform the educational system*: "Establish schools to teach Jewish children Torah, religion, and the commandments; ethics and integrity toward the sovereignty and the nation in which they live; learn their language, arithmetic, and the sciences. Teach young girls and boys a profession or skill, because idleness and unemployment are the roots of sin; it is not necessary for all to be rabbis, all smart, all proficient in a few languages, all physicians, philosophers, poets."

Second, *reform the rabbinical organization and community leaders*: "A national head rabbi should be elected, an eminent scholar, judicious and wise, with a large assembly of wise and scientific-minded scholars to serve as his law court. Wise, honored wealthy citizens should be elected to oversee and tend to community members' needs." Also, "there should be *magidim* who do not talk of hints and Kabbalah but of the duties of the heart and such."

Third, *correct economic conditions*: The government should give land for farming and raising cattle and sheep to at least *a third of the people*, as was done by our ancestors.... And all the people of the Jewish nation should be forbidden by order of the rabbis to wear expensive and silken clothes, silver, gold, and precious stones, use silver and gold vessels and utensils, or ride in fancy carriages. In principle: *they should not live in luxury*, as is the custom today, when even the poorest of the poor dresses his sons and daughters as one of the wealthy. The truth is that all those luxuries are at the root of all the corruption resulting from our sins. The people of Israel, and particularly our brothers, the children of Israel, who dedicate themselves to working the land, should make every effort to distance themselves from any luxury—*to live a simple life, to wear inexpensive, plain, but clean clothes*."

Collage of the Life of R' Yitschak Ber Levinzon

[73]

These ideals came from the general Enlightenment movement, and the RYB"L's ideas were *in a practical formulation*: he was the first of our scholars to draft a clear, definite, detailed plan for all the needed reforms in our lives for the Hebrew population. His belief and trust in the Russian government and in the importance of instilling a patriotic foundation in the nation was another of his new ideas. In the early 19th century, the RYB"L was able to proclaim proudly that the Russians "never lifted a hand against a Jewish soul," as opposed to the Poles and the Ukrainians and all the other Western nations.... Obviously he did not see the future, as the Enlightenment blinded his vision, but at least some of his ideas came into fruition: under his influence, special schools were opened for Jewish children, rabbinical colleges opened in Vilna and Zhitomir, a review board for Hebrew books was formed, and settlements for Jewish farmers were established in southern Russia.

Although on the outside he saw reforms begin for the benefit of the Jews, on the inside things were not good. Jewish life in Volhynia was deeply mired in ignorance and extreme fanaticism, and his goal was "to open blind eyes" .... Spiritually, he was close to the enlightened scholars of Galicia, and he maintained friendly ties with them and followed their path. When he was young, he lived in Galicia for about 12 years (1813–1824) and was inspired by the satirists Perl and Arter. He wrote the satire *Words of the Righteous,* which is a sort of an epilogue to the book *Revealer of Secrets,* and *Valley of the Giants,* as in "lower hell," where souls of the righteous and all the sinners of Israel were taken. (The "valley of the giants" preceded the "transmigration of souls" and is where the soul told its troubles.) But RYB"L's grandeur came not by way of satire but from his work as a *writer on current scientific affairs.* From the Galician School, he inherited the notion of the importance of *history* as a basic principle for understanding Judaism and its needs. He was not a philosopher like RN"K or a scholarly researcher like ShY"R. For that reason, there is no scientific value to his many books, which contain long articles dealing with current problems that he solves from a so-called

89

scientific-historical perspective. RYB"L was expert in all the secrets of our ancient literature and highly knowledgeable in languages and sciences. He was diligent in his studies even when ill. In faraway Kremenets, he found the historian Czacki's large library and studied scientific books day and night. He acquired a basic knowledge of Arabic, Syrian, Aramaic, Greek, and Roman (Latin) as well as in the new philosophy and other sciences. All his scholarly learning was his means to achieve his life's goal: to reform the life of the Jews, to rejuvenate and establish it on solid ground, and to blend Judaism with Humanism and the laws of Israel with the culture of the nations. Having great talent as an author, he knew how to use his knowledge for basic, theoretical, convincing propaganda.

> [**Translation Editor's Notes:** In Hebrew, *Words of the Righteous* is *Divrei Tsadikim,* and *Uncovering the Hidden* is *Megilah Temirin.* RN"K stands for R' Nachman Krochmal, and ShY"R stands for Shlome Yehuda Rapaport.]

In his scientific-current affairs books, there is no stormy war on religion but peaceful words of explanation. RYB"L was a pious, Orthodox Jew, follower of all the religious laws and Jewish customs. He did not change the way he dressed, always wore a hat, and was as careful with all the light as he was with the serious commandments. His behavior gave the Hasidim no room to find fault in him, a fact that irked them a great deal, because the young generation, who saw in him living proof that general education does not negate the validity of religion, looked up to him .... In truth, in his many books he continually emphasized that "observance of the Torah's laws is vital to the existence of the nation, because only those laws link all Jews as one, friends all. If not for them, our people would have been lost, assimilated, absorbed by the other nations. Anyone not following the Torah's laws is betraying the people. Jewish customs should be dear to any Jew who wants his people to continue its existence, unless he is an abhorrent offshoot, planted among us from without—in all our laws is logic and mystery unknown to us, and it behooves us to follow them according to God's edict without reason or argument." He was extremely angry to read of the Bible's critics, who write openly and through innuendo against prophesies, denying the truth of the miracles told within and God's protection of His people Israel, etc." In his will, he is revealed as a highly moral and ethical person; the will includes 13 cautionary notes:

[74]

> You must trust God in every place and time; refrain from anger, hostility, and holding a grudge; speak truthfully; have your words reflect what is in your heart; not slander others; not have sinful thoughts; speak gently with all people; admit the truth; consider people to be innocent; prefer to be insulted than to insult others; refrain from chasing after honors; not swear even on the truth or ask God to be brought to the test, because you do not know if you will be able to resist.

The RYB"L was a religious, ethical person, devoted to his people and looking out for its betterment as he saw it. Because he was well received by government officials and was an interceder for his people, even those who envied him did not harm him. He worked with tremendous diligence and wrote many great books.

RYB"L'S BOOKS

As mentioned, he began his literary work with words of satire, but sometimes he showed "weakness" and composed poems and rhetoric, epigrams and riddles. Those were published in his pamphlets *RYB"L's Pouch* and *The Writer's Scholarly Collection;* nevertheless, their writer cautioned that "these are not worthy to be called 'poems.'" He also published linguistic research papers: *Lebanon's Roots, Shem's Tents,* and others. Being shallow, these are not valuable, for the author lacked knowledge of modern linguistic research methods. More important were his books *Zrubavel, Bloodless,* and *Achiya the Shilonite.* In those he defended Judaism in general and the Talmud in particular against accusers and hate-mongers "among allies and adversaries" who attacked them with insults and defamations. He fought fiercely against all vicious, false charges, particularly the blood libel that our enemies accused us of. Those books show us his deep love of the people and his bravery in talking openly with anti-Semites, declaring his favor for Judaism over Christianity.... The Talmud was hated by the Russian government and by the extreme enlightened among us, but RYB"L was an adoring admirer of Judaism and all its holiness, and especially of the people who wove their lifestyle in accordance with Talmudic Judaism. Defending Judaism and its values against the anti-Semites who ruled ruthlessly in Russia and the heretics who "defile and degrade all that is holy to us" is how the people fights for its culture and existence among the other nations. This was RYB"L's goal, and he dedicated himself to this more than to preaching for scholarly enlightenment, for craftsmanship, and for farming the land.

> [**Translation Editor's Note:** In Hebrew, the book titles are as follows: *RYB"L's Pouch—Yalkut RYB"L; The Author's Scholarly Collection—Eshkol HaSofer; Lebanon's Roots—Shorshey Levanon; Shem's Tents—Ohaley Shem; Bloodless—Efes Damim;* and *Achiya the Shilonite—Achiya HaShiloni.*]

With all those, his main greatness is in his Enlightenment propaganda books: *Testimony in Israel* and *House of Judah.*

> [**Translator's Note:** In Hebrew, *House of Judah* is *Bet Yehuda.*]

TESTIMONY IN ISRAEL

In his preface to this book, RYB"L says that "pastors and friends, despisers of falsehood and lies" asked him to explain to them what the studies are necessary "for the perfection of humanity in general and Jewish perfection in particular" besides the Talmud and the commentaries. From their words, five main questions stood out: (a) Is it a duty for the Jew to study the holy tongue according to the rules of grammar, or is the translation of the words that are in the holy writings and the Talmud to the spoken language sufficient, as is customary in cheder? (b) Is he permitted to study foreign languages? (c) Is he permitted to study the sciences and literature of other nations? (d) What is the usefulness of learning languages and sciences? (e) Would not their usefulness end up causing a loss of religion and faith?

[75]

RYB"L answers those questions in the four chapters of his book. In the first he brings evidence from the Talmud, commentaries, and rabbinical literature for the knowledge of the Hebrew language and an understanding of the holy books—first by understanding the words based on their grammatical construction. With this, he also emphasizes the national rationale: "Nations are recognized and distinct from each other by their tongues." Not in vain does our ancient literature identify the concepts of "people and tongue." "All the nations and tongues," so how can a man be called a "Hebrew when he does not know Hebrew?" Besides that, the Hebrew language "became the religion's link to the existence of the people; the central pillar to latch together all our exiled brothers who are spread among different nations, from one corner of the universe to the other. How would they express their ideas to each other in distant lands if not by using the holy tongue that is common to all Jews?"

In the second chapter, he gives proof that the Jews always knew and spoke Aramaic, Greek, Arabic, etc. and that "there is no holiness or defilement in writing and speaking different languages," a book in Hebrew is not "kosher and pure," and a book in a foreign language is not "unfit and profane." He talks bitterly about Jews who speak "not in their holy tongue and not in a pure and clear tongue of the local language like German or Russian" .... As a practical man, he points to the economic benefits for the Jews of knowing the country's language, which will afford them business contacts with local inhabitants and government officials.

In essence, his third chapter's main idea is this: "Know, dear reader, that any and all knowledge, small or large, is very essential for a person; therefore, he has to study and know it, as there is no wisdom and knowledge that will not benefit us—and only simpletons whose intelligence God has destroyed and contaminated fools will undermine this wisdom."

To strengthen this opinion, the RYB"L cites a long, chronological list of Jewish sages, from ancient times to the Vilna Gaon, who were outstanding in knowledge and erudite in all fields of wisdom. But "all the knowledge and sciences in their time, compared to those of our time, were lacking. So when we say that our ancients were eminent scholars, the meaning is as far as knowledge was available in those days."

The RYB"L knew, though, that Israel's salvation does not lie in education alone, and he dedicates the final chapters of his book to the idea that "the duty of a Jewish man is to learn a profession or a craft so that he can support himself." Again, he relies on Talmudic scholars, citing as an example their writings that praise labor and condemn idleness, as in "Anyone who does not teach his son a craft, it is as if he teaches him thievery," and he lists a long line of teachers and sages who were shoemakers, tinsmiths, woodcutters, porters, tanners, etc. After much deliberation, he comes to the conclusion that (a) Jews lived in their country and in other countries as an agrarian people for long periods; (b) the Jewish religion admires all forms of work, especially agriculture; (c) the Jewish people is capable even now of revolutionizing its way of life and turning from commerce to become an agrarian nation; (d) the time when Jews had to grasp business as a way of life was during the Middle Ages, when Jews were restricted and dispossessed of all economic positions but commerce and money lending; and (e) now, when the sun of general education and love of one's fellow man "is shining in the world," it behooves us to follow the Russian government's advice to abandon the life of business, which is full of lying and cheating, and start working in agriculture, which brings true happiness to men. And in this "we will gain respect in the eyes of His Majesty the King, who wants us to be happy and successful...."

A few months after the book's publication (1828), the RYB"L received 1,000 rubles from Czar Nikolas I "for a book in the Hebrew language whose purpose is the correction of the morals of the Jewish people." The book made a great impression on Enlightenment scholars but caused great anger among the Hasidim.

[76]

HOUSE OF JUDAH

This is RYB"L's most scientific book. It is a kind of historiography on the history of Judaism, the aim of which is to prove that study of Hebrew scholasticism is not new and "heretical" but stems from historical Judaism. The book closes with a lecture on the practical reforms that are necessary in Jews' lives. This book, too, has left a great impression on our world.

RYB"L AMONG CHILDREN

Dictated by L. Rozental
(Presented for publication by M. D.-N. From *My World,* a Newspaper for Young People)
English translation by Thia Persoff

In the days of RYB"L, Jewish children were educated in cheders and yeshivas, which taught only holy studies and Jewish religion; the children did not receive a general education there. What is more, in those days Orthodox Hasidim prohibited their children from reading history books or mathematics, etc. Anyone who wanted to read such books was forced to do it in secret.

One summer, the government issued a command to open special schools throughout the country where Jewish children would be taught general learning and knowledge.

The Orthodox Jews were sorry, as it seemed to them as if their children were being led into apostasy.

Y. B. Levinzon was the single Jewish person in Kremenets who liked this edict. He lived on Gorna Street, which was named Tyrants' Street by the locals. Because of his grave illness, he could not live in his house on the heavily trafficked, noisy Sheroka

Street. He stayed in his house, alone on quiet Tyrants' Street, and each day he was carried outside to enjoy the sun's healing warmth and light. Once, while sitting on his bed wrapped in a heavy robe and smoking his long pipe, he was disturbed from his rest by a Jewish man running and screaming that his son had been registered for school by the authorities. He raised his arms to the heavens, howling that his son was being taken to "apostasy" .... Many children followed him, perplexed and frightened. The RYB"L called the children to him and softly explained to them that the government had done them a favor by opening schools for them where they would learn Torah and knowledge, the country's tongue, and the history of nations; then they would not be ignorant as before. The children, who had liked him for a long time, accepted his words with affection and lost their fear.

A day will come—predicted old RYB"L—when fathers will feel sorry when their children are "secondary" in school. One of those children was my mother, who remembers the words of RYB"L to this day.

[77]

ON THE VALUE OF CRAFTS AND AGRICULTURE
(A COLLECTION OF IDEAS FROM THE WRITINGS OF RYB"L)

English translation by Thia Persoff

We have already been ordered to teach our children crafts, as our sages said: the father is obligated to teach his son a craft. R' Yehuda said, "Anyone who does not teach his son a craft, it is as if he is teaching him thievery."

And R' Nehorai's words, "I disregard all the crafts in the world and teach my son the Torah only," were explained by the MHRSh"A, of blessed memory. He does not mean for a person not to teach any craft altogether but to teach it to him casually, because the teaching of a craft is a firm charge on every father.

> [**Translator's Note**: MHRSh"A stands for our teacher the rabbi R' Shmuel Eydels.]

And it was written in *Avot*: "Any knowledge without a craft is bound to end in idleness followed by sin." The Rambam, of blessed memory, said, "Anyone who deliberately occupies himself with studying the Torah and does not work but lives on charity profanes the Lord, shames the Torah, puts out the light of religion, brings evil on himself, and forfeits the world to come, for it is forbidden to derive any temporal advantage from the words of the Torah."

> [**Translation Editor's Notes:** *Avot* refers to *Pirkey Avot (Ethics of the Fathers)*, a compilation of ethical teachings. Rambam is an abbreviation for the name of the philosopher R' Moshe Ben Maimon.]

From now on, I will not keep my lips sealed but will alert my brethren and my people to another ill that has taken deep root among us, and this is it: Why have we—men and women, small and big, rich and poor—made commerce our goal? Why do we not follow in the steps of our ancient forefathers and work the land, too? Why did we despise it, distance ourselves from it; and today none of us is a farmer or rancher. The people loathed this work, but it is unjustified; unfairly, they held it in contempt; this occupation was never contemptible or degrading but the opposite: since days gone by, it has been considered honorable and glorified and has received top praise, for out of it comes life, and not only the poor but also nobles and the gentry did this. Princes and kings also plowed their land and harrowed their fields.

And in fact, we will see when we explain that supreme wisdom lies in teaching the people of Israel to be a realm of only farmers, not businessmen. First: each person in Israel received as his property a plot of land to cultivate so he could provide food and all the necessities, for himself and his family. Second: in all the promises for the future that are written in the Torah, the blessings and the curses, for riches and for privation, you will not find anything but mentions of field, vineyard, and livestock.

Out of all these we conclude that (a) the main occupation of the Israelite man in making a living in ancient days was working the land, which was desirable and honorable in his eyes, (b) that the law of our holy Torah not only is not against working the land but commands it, (c) that a Jewish man is as capable of doing this kind of work today as any other person from another faith, which is in opposition to what our antagonists say: that the law of our Torah is against it and that it is not in the Jew's nature to be able to do this kind of work, and (d) that commerce was foreign to the ancient Israeli man, and he did not know of it or its name. Their sons who came after them and intermingled with the gentiles slowly learned from them. As was explained, a few hundred years ago we acquired a higher opinion of the occupation of commerce, and we became so accustomed to it that today it has become second nature to the Jew.

[78]

THE STUDENT TRAVELING TO HIS TEACHER
(A CHAPTER FROM THE BOOK *THE VIRGIN FROM VLADIMIR*)

Yochanen Tverski
English translation by Thia Persoff

... Mountains surround Kremenets; mountains related to the Carpathians, drawn and extended from them, make it seem as if it is sitting in hiding. The distance nearly nullifies the mountains into a suspension of blue that is caught at first glance and is barely perceptible. Mount Bona rises up and overlooks the whole town, the center of the region.

"Do you see the castle over there, on the mountain?" says the cantor from Zaslav, who travels for his earnings and is eager to find listeners for his tales.

For a moment, Binyamin concentrates on the tall, strong buildings; on the cannons lying in wait, taking aim at the valley; on a tower on whose top you can stand and see everything going on in the area.

And there, my dear people, at the top of the mountain, is a deep pit called the "Pit of the Condemned to Death." The story is told that soldiers who have done wrong to the King are punished and then lowered and concealed in it. Yes, that hollow, they say, is full of bones.

The horses are raising dust; an incline drags a wagon down to the town. In the mountains and the outskirts of Kremenets are speckles of Ukrainians, Russians, and Poles; gardens and orchards surround their houses. Only Jews live in the town and its two suburbs.

Binyamin descends, rummaging in his money pouch and paying the wagoner. Suddenly a feeling of complete freedom assails him, as always happens in a foreign place. He enters an inn in the Dubno suburb. In the room sit a few merchants who came to the fair and some passengers who happened to stop by. The landlady places bowls of food in front of them.

"I heard," says one of the guests, while slicing bread on the table, "that some of your townspeople have petitioned the government for land!"

"Yes, fifty-two families!" answers the landlady.

"Give me some good brandy, from the best!" The man moves the edges of his coat a bit to prevent wrinkling. In truth, how odd that Jewish people would take it upon themselves, willingly, to be gentiles ... farmers working the land!

"Is this the influence of the *Testimony* by the upcoming rising leader?"

> [**Translator's Note:** This refers to RYB"L's book, *Testimony in Israel.*]

Binyamin exits the room.

On the small veranda stands a young woman, the sun gilding her yellow eyelashes. She rubs and buffs a large samovar while humming a song to herself, pronouncing the words in a Volhynia dialect: A soldier's bride is not worth a quarter/like a calf he'll be led to the slaughter!

"Excuse me, could you be so good as to tell me where Yitschak Ber Levinzon lives?"

Her face took on a blush. "Who?"

"Yitschak Ber Levinzon, the famous sage."

"Oh, you probably mean Itsik-Berl Yidel's!" she says, happy that she realizes whom he means, and starts rubbing and shining the copper again, ambidextrously. "He is not liked in our town."

"No? Why? He is a great man and a wonderful scholar."

"A seducer and an instigator, it's been said."

[79]

"Heaven forbid!"

"And he is eloquent. He always has assertions and arguments. And he is very close to the 'movers and shakers' in the government."

"No, everyone seeks his company because he is one of our people's scholars."

The young woman realizes now that disreputable words about the old man are somehow insulting to the young man. She does not want to upset him. After all, he is not speaking to her as to a servant, the way all the others do. But why does he champion the man? She raises her head.

"Are you two related? Are you an actual relative of his?"

"Yes, in spirit."

The young woman unrolls her sleeves. The samovar is ready, buffed all over, and its copper shines like a mirror, but she stays. It is clear that she is happy to continue conversing with the tall, open-faced young man, even though she is puzzled by his words.

"And they say more in town. You should know, here in Kremenets they can drown a man in a spoon of water. He always cries that he is in dire poverty—and he has a servant at home. She is waiting, they say, for him to leave her an inheritance of his money. But what nasty tongues and scoundrels say here in Kremenets should befall the trees and stones! But he is sick—this is true. Did you come to visit him?"

"Sick?"

"Yes. Didn't you know? And you said that you are related to him. He hated his wife, and before they were divorced, she put a little poison, deadly poison, in his soup. She was a bad-tempered one. Since then he has been sick with some sort of a fever."

"Are those words true?" Binyamin asks himself, or are they imaginary suppositions of his enemies?

"And where does he live?"

From behind the door the voice of the fat landlady, thin and sharp, is heard:

"Shifre?! What happened to you there? Where is the samovar?"

The young woman lowers her voice, "At the edge of the town ... go straight from here, then turn left."

Binyamin turns, walking through the long stretching town. Here is the school for priests, called the "seminary"; crosses covering the domes, inner and outer buildings, front and back yards connected to each other ... its grove thick with trees, climbing up to Mount Vidomka. The street is named Sheroka [Broad] Street, probably in jest, as it is narrow and tight. Pathways twist and turn toward the Bona ....

At the edge of town, far from its tumult and noise, Binyamin stops in front of a small house. People who go to the homes of the famous, in their own town or in others, come to this clay cottage. There is power in him, the writer of the *Testimony,* to debate with the world's scholars!

Binyamin's heart is beating hard and fast. After a cautious knock, an old woman who is all bones and tendons appears. The servant? Following her, he enters, eyes taking in the room and its contents.

By the square, crisscrossed single window stands a rickety table, tottering from old age. Across from the entrance is a bed with raised sides, haphazardly made. As in every sickroom, it seems, the center is the sick person among the few pieces of furniture. And in the center of the center: him.

His head is crowned with long, wispy, messy hair, thickening near his earlobes, maybe side locks, maybe curls. This is the head of a man whose correct age is hard to tell—his rounded beard looks youthful here and snowy there.

[80]

Binyamin wants to rush to his master and teacher and shake his hand, but realizes that the other is not at all aware of his existence.

"Well, did you go to him?" Levinzon asks the woman in a meek voice, as if she is the lady of the house.

"I certainly did," she answers.

"And he sent you back emptyhanded?"

"No. He sent you a different book. Here! He said, 'What is the difference? The essence is learning!'"

Yitschak Ber Levinzon's face turned greenish white. "There is no such sorrow as when you request something you want and receive something you do not want. And this from a man who is an important member of the community, supposedly intelligent."

"And did you send the letters I gave you?" Levinzon continued.

"I sent. What do you think, I did not send? But what good is it? You write and write—and nothing!"

Levinzon, focused on their talk, does not see the stranger. However, his presence in the room makes him feel self-conscious, embarrassed, and angry. Because of that, he boasts,

"Nothing, you said? His Majesty the Czar awarded me his support. His Honor, the Czar himself! And the Deputy Minister of Enlightenment in Lodov wrote that the prize given to me is 'for a book in the Hebrew language, about moral reform for the people of Israel.' No, I am not wasting my time! You will see. All the philanthropists in the world will answer and grant my request."

The old woman exits quietly. Now Levinzon focuses his attention on the stranger. Was it not, really, to him that he directed his last words? But now he looks at him with distrust, as if searching him inside and out. He feels that the young man's looks, which radiate health, have a calming influence on his nerves. There are times when a person has a strong need for the closeness of strangers, as they help calm his spirit.

"Enter, please!" he says softly, as if contrite for his previous suspicion. "Why are you standing by the door? Please remove the papers and sit down!"

Binyamin removes the sheets of paper from the small chair made of white wood, which stands by the bed and serves, apparently, as a sort of table.

"Forgive me, my young friend, for receiving you while lying down. For many years now I have been in pain, but any man that I find truly singular and good is like having grapes in the desert."

For a moment Levinzon gets lost in memories of his years of residences and roamings in Galicia. Maybe it is not a good idea for a writer always to associate with his colleagues if he wants to avoid competition and jealousy. But also, that is where he met wonderful people, and at the top of the list is R' Nachman Krochmal, the "unique superior one," a person of powerful new achievements. Each day at sundown, the two of them would walk up and down the hills and mountains surrounding Zolkiew, each conversation an exchange of ideas and influences.

"Here, my young friend, I sit alone outside the encampment. Yes, in my native town I am in exile: there is no writer, no book. No one tells the news, and there are no new pages to be seen. And those who scorn knowledge are so many."

Only now does Binyamin notice that the shelves attached to the wall behind the bed are empty. So where does he collect the large amounts of material for his writing? He probably copies all the material he needs from the books that happen to come his way by chance. Mainly, his memory must be excellent.

"But, sir, are not even a few of the town's citizens supporters of the Enlightenment movement?"

"Yes." The old man's voice enlivens and his face lights up: "I thank the Lord for the gift of a few just and righteous people, who were educated by me."

[81]

"Beside people passing by from near and far from time to time, Jews and Christians, big and small, visit me. Nevertheless ...." He looks again at the young man as if searching his mind. "And what brings you to me?"

"Sir, acquiring knowledge is the joy of my life, but it is very hard for a person to open the road for truth without teachers or friends!"

Levinzon gathers strength and sits up in the bed, his knees covered by the blanket. His head is that of a grandfather, and his narrow shoulders are those of a grandson.

"My dream, from my youth until old age, has been to form an assembly of intellectuals—with the condition that they be honest and righteous men—to be named "Zion," which would strive for the betterment of scholars and seekers of knowledge and for the development of the sciences.

"For how long," his voice takes on some self-pity, "will we see the Hasidim holding on to each other tightly, helping each other and winning, while our people totter and decline?"

"Have you realized your dream, Sir?"

Suddenly Levinzon inhales a sharp, hoarse, breath. "The schism, my enlightened friend, the schism of the hearts! Not all scholars are truly working for the good of all, to find favor in the eyes of God and men and the nation we live in. Particularly in the eyes of the great King, may his honor increase, and his governors."

"But sir, the decrees against us ...."

The clock ticks with his quick, even movements.

"My enlightened friend, are you also asking: why all those changes? Don't you understand that those reforms are good and beneficial, that they are the privileges of the country? Yes, our Lord the King, may his honor increase, has done great kindness to us, so Jews will be like the rest of the citizens, wearing army uniforms and civilian clothes. This is a great change!"

"But sir, the hatred."

Levinzon's face turns chalky, but his eyes, feverish eyes, sparkle, and his breath is hot. Is his fever causing all this nervous excitement?

"Yes. It happens that clerks do trample the government's good orders, but even they are not to blame. It is the foolish Hasidim, through their bad and perverse behavior, who cause the country's hatred for no reason! Their rabbis live a life of success, happiness, and the pursuit of luxury. They do not understand that in our time, the time of Enlightenment, the period of restrictive laws is over, and they incite our people against loyalty to our ruler and well-wishing government. Is not she the one who is opening the way for us to enter the garden of knowledge—the country's schools?"

Now Levinzon's face expresses a mixture of softness and importance.

"On October 16, 1836, I set myself to write to His Royal Majesty, our Czar Nikolas I, about reforms for my brethren. God supported me and rewarded me with a reply from His Royal Majesty. And indeed, the government wants to open new ways for earning a living to us, too. Did you hear that many families have already settled in villages and are working their land? With God's help, and the King's, I have caused this!"

The room is in stillness now, the silence deepening and strengthening; you can almost hear it. Suddenly, from outside, faint steps on the pebbled, sloping walk are heard. Binyamin wants to get up. How can the one who goes to the head of the nation, carrying the torch of Enlightenment, find even a morsel of goodness in this wicked kingship?

The old servant enters the room.

[82]

PUBLIC LIFE

THE KREMENETS COMMUNITY UNDER POLISH RULE

Munye Katz (Haifa)
English translation by David Dubin

After the establishment of Polish rule in Kremenets in 1920, various agencies, assemblies, and committees became active in town. Only in 1928, however, under the law governing the autonomy of religious minorities, did an organized Jewish community develop in Kremenets, as it did in other towns.

The first Community Council was elected in 1928 to a four-year term. The election was by secret, direct ballot of male voters age 21 and older. The first head of the community was Avraham Vaynberg, a Zionist, one of the honored elders of the town. The council was an official institution with specific authority under the law. Among its duties was dealing with Jewish issues and education. Beyond those responsibilities, the council also dealt with practical issues such as social services, health, and vocational training, because it saw the vital importance of alleviating poverty. From the 1932 budget published in full in the *Kremenitser Shtime,* we see that the community was directly involved in (1) the slaughterhouse, (2) the bathhouse, (3) the cemetery, (4) the hospital, (5) the rabbinate, (6) the Talmud Torah, (7) the Home for the Aged, (8) hospitality, (9) registration of the Jewish population (births, deaths, marriages, etc.), (10) care for Jewish soldiers on leave, (11) care for Jewish captives, and (12) occasional social work as required.

Moreover, the Community Council supported other organizations, such as TOZ; the ORT School; the Charity Fund; Chashmonaim, the sports organization; and others.

To cover its budget expenses the Community Council used fees from the enterprises it controlled (fees for ritual slaughter, cemetery fees, registration fees, and the like). Thus direct taxes were charged to the Jews of the town. There were over 1,000 items in the 1932 budget.

The Community Council worked on various projects without undue publicity. In its meetings, it would decide on the issues of the day, and its personnel would carry out the decisions.

Unusual problems, such as distributing wood during the winter or distributing matzot (the *maot chitin* campaign) and potatoes for Passover, would provoke great behind-the-scenes wrangling. This was also true when it came to choosing a new rabbi or ritual slaughterer. The Community Council would also call public informational meetings in the Great Synagogue or the new Kozatski Study Hall, where stormy, protracted arguments would take place. Decisions, sometimes contradictory ones, were reached. The decisions were not binding on the council, which always retained its own authority by virtue of its elected status, but it would generally consider the decisions made by the voting public during these meetings.

> [**Translation Editor's Note:** *Maot chitin* (literally, "money for wheat") is the custom of providing for the Passover needs of the poor.]

[83]

Undoubtedly, the Community Council was very influential in the town's public life. It was natural for political organizations in town to try to influence the Community Council and even rein in its power. There was no shortage of struggles for power by powerful individuals. Moreover, the community was quite accustomed to bitter political battles especially between the Zionist representatives, with M. Goldring and Perlmuter, and the apolitical citizens under Sh. Brodski and his colleagues, whose opponents saw them as tools of the government. The strife within the community was even reported by the local media.

After the death of Avraham Vaynberg in 1930, a second Community Council election was held, and Moshe Kapuza, Meir Goldring, Dr. Zalman Sheynberg, Tsvi Barshap, Avigdor Perlmuter, Rabbi Mendiuk, Sh. Brodski, and the representative of the neighboring village Pochayev were elected. The second head of the council was Avigdor (Zeydi) Perlmuter.

In the next elections in 1934, the third head of the council, Sh. Brodski, was elected. He served in this capacity until 1937.

From the council's official inception, the Polish authorities inspected its actions and knew well how to use internal struggles to its advantage. The climax came in 1937, when a struggle broke out between the sides and the rabbis of the town took an active part (Rabbi Mendiuk on the side of the Zionists, and the religious Judge Lerner on the side of Brodski et al.). The regional government official suspended the elected Community Council under the rationale that internal struggles were endangering the community's normal functioning and the council's activities. The government appointed Fred Rozin, the engineer (son-in-law of the old industrialist Yisrael Margalit), to the office of "commissar" of the community, with several advisors at his side. The most active and dedicated of them was Ratsenfeld, formerly a government-appointed rabbi in the village of Shchepetovka.

Rozin the engineer was distant from religious life, had been brought up in an assimilationist environment, was a reserve officer in the Polish forces, and was trusted by the authorities. Moreover, the government entrusted the community's authority to him. It must be noted that Rozin fulfilled his duties dutifully and with understanding, establishing community institutions and even managing to promote peace between the warring factions. As a result, in the elections of 1938, a united list of candidates appeared.

In the fourth council, Getsi Klorfayn, Tsvi Barshap, L. Krivin, Y. Gintsburg, A. Maystelman, Yisrael Margalit, Rabbi Mendiuk, and the representative of the village of

Pochayev served. The fourth head of the council was Yisrael Margalit. This council functioned until World War II—until the arrival of the Russians in Kremenets on September 20, 1939.

The secretary of the Community Council was Duvid Leviton, and after his death in 1934, his son Arye Leviton took his place.

Light and shadows appeared in the Kremenets community's workings and daily activity, but during all the years of its existence, it served as a true advocate and powerful castle for the Jews' autonomy in Poland and succeeded in going beyond the bounds set by the authorities.

[84]

THE JEWS IN THE TOWN

Zev Shumski (Tel Aviv)
English translation by David Dubin

The Jews of Kremenets always took an active role in the town, whether in its administration or its organization. During changes in regime, the various governments could not ignore the Jewish population, and they incorporated the community's notables into the town's administration. In the years before World War I, three Jews served on the City Council: Yosef Bitiker, Yisrael Margalit, and Mikhael Shumski. The friendly relations assured the people that the general atmosphere in town was more liberal than in previous administrations under the czar, and anti-Semitism was not prevalent in town. Jews paid town taxes and benefited in one way or another from town services as citizens, merchants, and businessmen. However, attaining public office was not even a dream ....

During World War I, the mayors of the town were the Catholic priest Bilatski and, after him, the Ukrainian Tsayts. At that time, Azriel Kremenetski arrived in town, and he served as assistant mayor and, after a time, as mayor. In the struggles between the Russians, Poles, and Ukrainians for influence in the town and bitter changes in government authority, the Jews were a neutral and steadying force, and it was natural that a Jew would rise to the rank of mayor.

The Foot of Mount Bona

Under Polish rule, Reyveski, Bartok, Zelevski, and Jan Beaupré served as mayors in succession—the latter for many years, until the Soviets captured the town. During this period, 12 representatives from various circles served on the City Council on behalf of the Jews. Every few years, new elections would be held, but, notably, very few personnel changes were made between one election and the next. The following served on the council (with minor changes from one council to the next):

Meir Goldring—from the Zionists
Dr. Zalman Sheynberg—from the Zionists
Zeydi Perlmuter—from the Zionists
Chayim Rozenberg (1927–1930)—from the trade union
Aba Lisi—from the trade union
Duvid Goldenberg—from the craftsmen
Yitschak Yosef Alterman—from the craftsmen
Maystelman—from the craftsmen
Chayim Bakimer—from the merchants
Shaul Brodski—from the merchants
Moshe Gershteyn—from small business
Mikhael Shumski—independent

These men served in the seven-member town administration under Polish rule:

Azriel Kremenetski
Shlome Fingerhut

[85]

In spite of the variety of factions, the Jews in the town formed a united coalition, voting as a bloc except on matters of importance to a particular class, when trade union delegates from Jewish trade unions sometimes voted with Polish and Ukrainian delegates against delegates from other Jewish factions.

Jewish officials were not appointed in town even under the Poles, other than one Jewish tax collector and in the town power plant, where Jews served as engineers, fee collectors, and specialized workers because the plant was originally under Jewish ownership and had been transferred to the town with its workforce intact. Jews did serve the town as suppliers and middlemen. Also, the town had no choice in several special services, which could only be provided by Jews: dyers, tinsmiths, builders, plumbers, electricians, locksmiths, carpenters, coachmen, and even street repairers. Especially notable was Chayim Leyzer Lampel, a street subcontractor, who would deal only with Jewish workers, relatives, and others who were expert at paving roads and paths.

The City Council meetings were held in public and sometimes drew large crowds, especially on matters of monetary allotments, which aroused great public controversy and sometimes were even debated in the Jewish newspapers. The town allocated sums for Jewish public institutions, such as the Home for the Aged, the Jewish Hospital, the ORT School, the bathhouse, the orphanage, and others, and the allocations engendered widespread public struggles. In the final years before the Holocaust, an anti-Semitic spirit entered Kremenets, and from 1930 on, the deprivation of rights, alienation, and clashes grew.

[86]

I could not complete my overview of the Jewish role in the town without mentioning the town secretary, Strumchinski, a Pole who held the position for decades, first under Russian rule and later under the Poles. He did not love the Jews, but he loved their money and was known as a bribe taker. The Jews appreciated this and "took care" of him so that he would take care of their municipal issues. This "honored" arrangement held strong under the different regimes. He was also an officer in the fire brigade (in which there were many Jews), loved his uniform, and was thus called "General Strumchinski."

Town Hall

With the Russian conquest of the town (September 22, 1939), a Jew, Moshe Sugan, a local Communist, was appointed mayor, and soon thereafter his successor, the Ukrainian Kustriuva, who was not a town resident, was appointed. In that period a Jew, Avraham Rayz, was appointed chief of police; he had previously spent many years in prison on the charge of being a Communist.

[87]

SYNAGOGUES AND STUDY HALLS

A. Gluzman (Afula)
English translation by David Dubin

Synagogues and study halls held a highly honored place in the lives of Kremenets Jewry, and they played many roles in different situations. First and foremost, of course, they were places for prayer. Jews came there to pray three times daily, not to mention on Sabbaths and holidays. Secondly, they were used as venues for celebrations. They were the news centers of the town, places to discuss politics. Each class and social group had its own prayer hall. One's class could be distinguished by the synagogue one frequented. Groups without their own synagogue building would at least have their own minyan.

During the workweek, the Jews engaged in a battle for their very sustenance. But when the Sabbath or holidays arrived, all the stress and troubles were forgotten. Then all were partners in the day's restfulness and joy and in hope and celebration, sharing the "honors" of the liturgy and Torah readings, and peace and tranquility reigned throughout the community. If there was an occasional disagreement, it was only for the sake of heaven.

The scene was unforgettable on a Sabbath morning, when the entire length of Sheroka Street began to fill with streams of distinguished community notables, craftsmen, and merchants in Sabbath garb, holding their children's hands on their way to Sabbath prayers. All the stores were closed. Each person went to his own synagogue, to his own permanent place. At around noon, people left the synagogue and held their secular conversations and discussions about synagogue goings-on, giving reviews of the cantor's or *magid*'s performance, and they would part with the "Good Sabbath" greeting, go home to recite the Kiddush, and enjoy the restfulness of "the day more honored than all others."

The Great Synagogue was the most important synagogue. It was actually considered one of the most beautiful in Poland. It was housed in a grand and lofty building adorned by a surrounding stone-paved courtyard. The architecture was beautiful. There was no real intimacy of unity. The congregation was varied and not always the same. Distinguished householders did not pray there, but *nouveaux riches,* young married men, craftsmen, and travelers did; cantors and famous singers would lead the services on Saturdays. There were also regular cantors like Cantor Sherman and the famous Koussevitsky's brother. Cantor Sherman was a fine-looking, tall man, wearing modern clothing with an aristocratic air. He had a fine tenor voice. When he appeared wrapped in his prayer shawl and began the prayer "How goodly are your tents, Jacob" in his powerful voice, silence fell upon the crowd of congregants. He would descend the stairs at his own slow pace and cross the synagogue between the aisles of congregants to his place next to the Holy Ark, which itself was a work of fine art.

The synagogue was full of glory during Hanukah, when, according to custom, the first candle was lit, accompanied by song and instrumental music. Great crowds streamed in to hear the celebration and the performance of the family musical ensemble Hatskele and Anzele the violinists and their sons the flutists, and the singers Fingerhut and company, who would sing "These Candles" and "My Rock of Salvation." Then the large menorah was lit, and immediately a multitude of electric menorahs would light the area.

> [**Translator's Note:** In Hebrew, these song titles are *Hanerot Halalu* and *Maoz Tsur*, respectively.]

Beautiful experiences and cherished memories of childhood were associated with this synagogue.

How wonderful was the tradition of escorting a bride to the Sabbath services during her first week of marriage!

[88]

For this auspicious occasion, a special dress and headdress were prepared for the bride. When all the congregants had assembled in the synagogue, a stream of marchers left the bride's home accompanied by her in-laws, her friends, and others, all dressed in especially fine clothing—and in the center was the bride's shiny countenance, happy and serene. The young matron was accompanied by love and good wishes from all the surrounding houses in honor of her first visit to the synagogue. In the synagogue, she was brought to the eastern wall of the women's section, and hundreds of women raised their eyes admiringly to the beautiful and graceful bride and thus welcomed her to the bosom of the holy community.

The Great Synagogue also served as a meeting hall for public assemblies, celebrations, and the greeting of important guests.

The Kozatski Study Hall. This study hall was completely different; it was the second largest of the Kremenets synagogues. Several hundred congregants came on the Sabbath and during the week. The main hall was large, as were its windows. On the walls were drawings of animals and birds in shiny colors, which inspired a distinctive frame of mind. Many explanations of the origin of the synagogue's name were common among the populace, one of them being the thought that people rushed through their prayers there like Cossacks .... The congregation was multifaceted: working men and young merchants, peddlers, porters, people without specific occupations, and some travelers. The women's section divided the hall into two, taking the form of a roof-covered balcony in one third of the hall. There was always noise there: people coming and going. Many minyanim prayed there in succession, and if one tarried, there was a second and a third minyan waiting. Prayers were recited aloud, with voices heard from one end of the synagogue to the other. Large tables were arranged along the length of the hall, each serving as a meeting place for a specific group. At the first table, people read newspapers, while the Zionists of the town ruled at the second, where Torah study was not pursued, but instead Zionists spoke and *magidim* gave their sermons, as worshipers at this study hall were among the most excellent listeners.

On winter nights, storekeepers and workers who had frozen during the day came to the study hall, quickly washed their hands, wiped them on the moist, long towel, and rushed to warm their bodies and souls, and especially to enjoy the camaraderie of their fellow Jews, hear a good word or some news, or read the synagogue bulletin.

The most interesting figure in that synagogue was the cantor R' Yisrael, a tall Jew with a beautiful, dark beard flowing over his shirt, who was always dressed in a clean suit. He was the cantor Moshe-Chayim's assistant. He could always be found at the synagogue involved in spiritual matters. He was beloved and respected by all. His sprightly step and kind demeanor toward all engendered honor and respect in those who encountered him.

The women's section during the High Holidays was a special experience. Next to the long tables sat the poorest women, who could not read from the prayer book. A woman who knew the prayers would sit at the head of the table, and she would read the prayers and supplications aloud, show the words to the assembled women, and indicate when to cry .... More than one would begin to cry before the right time, at which point cries and wailing would come forth from hundreds of women. The men below would pound angrily on the tables and scream upward, "Women, women, not yet ...." The cries would then die down slowly. Innocent, dear souls—this is how they spent their holidays. Later at night, they would go at their own pace through the alleyways of the marketplace to their homes, where their families would be waiting patiently for their dinner.

The Old Study Hall. Those who prayed in the Old Study Hall were peaceful and patient. The owners of nicer homes, wood merchants, and wholesalers, such as the Bokimer, Lastsuver, Kapuzer, and Katz families, as well as the ritual slaughterer Leyb, prayed here.

[89]

Elijah's Chair [for Circumcisions] in the Great Synagogue

Dr. Landsberg was one of the members of the Jewish intelligentsia who prayed here. The congregation comprised approximately 150 people. It was the only study hall on Sheroka Street without a women's section and the only one with a rabbi, the elderly rabbi from Kurilovtsy. Young workers prayed here also, and each Sabbath they read the Torah portion themselves, usually in Eliezer Vakman's home. They divided up the honors of being called to the Torah there, and after the additional service they made Kiddush over wine. "Sabbath and holiday Jews ...." The study hall sexton, a wood merchant, saw it as his special privilege to underwrite all the synagogue's expenses.

Glory and honor were showered on the synagogue on Yom Kippur eve, Kol Nidre night. Large wax candles were set up in boxes of soil laid out in the hallway. The congregants were in their places. A deathly silence took hold of the small synagogue, each person silently praying *Tefilah Zakah*. The old rabbi ascended the platform and quietly began his sermon, including words of rebuke appropriate to the time and ending with a "happy new year" blessing to the congregation. The congregation listened to the rabbi's words with respect and an uplifted soul.

> [**Translation Editor's Note:** *Tefilah Zakah* ("pure prayer"), recited individually before the Kol Nidre prayer, states that the individual forgives anyone who may have sinned against him or her in any way.]

The priestly blessing in the Old Study Hall was beautiful. It was pronounced in a special way by the Kohen R' Itsi Shkurnik, a merchant from Nofketora, and his sons. He was a fine-looking Jew with a long beard, wrapped in a prayer shawl with a large collar-piece. He and his five sons stood for the washing of their hands before the priestly blessing. Three Levites with special cups in their hands poured water on the priests' hand, and when R' Itsi—a textile merchant the rest of the year—stood among them surrounded by his five sons and intoned the special tune to bless the holy congregation, he was wrapped in glory and splendor like a High Priest ....

[90]

After services, the congregation would surround the elderly Dr. Landsberg to hear from his lips about the Land of Israel, which he had seen in his travels. Like an ever-strengthening fountain, his stories streamed forth, and the congregation never tired or wearied of hearing the man who had had the privilege of seeing the wondrous sights in our glorious Zion with his own eyes....

House of Prayer. Continue on Synagogue Row to find the second merchants' synagogue—the House of Prayer. The Kitay, Landsberg, and similar families prayed here. The House of Prayer was always full wall to wall with worshipers. It was also the town's news center. People wrapped in prayer shawls stood outside in the hallway and the narrow alleyway; groups of people would talk about secular topics and goings-on in town. For many years, the sexton was Kitay, the iron merchant, who also had a traditional hold on reciting the "You Have Learned" prayer on the night of Simchas Torah. In fact, the younger members once tried to change this tradition, and one of the wealthy merchants even paid a large sum for the honor, but at that moment some important members got up, took the elder Kitay firmly, and brought him to the lectern. Thus the "putsch" failed ... and the younger generation was utterly defeated; apparently great rebellions were not Kremenets' forte....

> [**Translation Editor's Note:** "You Have Learned" (*Ata Horeisa*) is the beginning of the set of verses recited on Simchas Torah (Rejoicing in the Law), when the reading of the Torah is finished and begun again.]

Huge throngs streamed to the House of Prayer on the night of *Selichos*. Here the *Selichos* were chanted in a particular tune, and the echo of the prayers with their haunting melody resounded a great distance.

> [**Translation Editor's Note:** *Selichos* are penitential prayers recited in the period leading up to Rosh Hashanah and culminating in a service the Saturday evening before Rosh Hashanah.]

Itsi Bedrik's *Kloyz*. Why this synagogue was called a *kloyz* and who Itsi Bedrik was— no one in this generation had any idea. It was only known that after it burnt down, it was built anew as a synagogue for young merchants and craftsmen. Berl Royv, a textile merchant, served as sexton. The atmosphere was light. The members were lighthearted and appreciated a good joke. More than once they tried to derail the cantor in his Sabbath eve tune toward the holiday prayer tune. The elders naturally objected, but they could not hide their smiles over the cantor's exasperation in his attempts to return to the Sabbath eve tune.

The Porters' Small Synagogue. Along one of the long corridors in the Great Synagogue's courtyard was the Small Synagogue of the town's porters. Each weekday they would assemble a minyan with difficulty, but on the Sabbath all the laborers in town gathered there. They comprised two groups. On one hand were the young laborers, who formed a type of cooperative consisting of owners of large wagons that transported goods from trains to town. They did not deal in small contracts or the transport of packages and bags; the elder porters did this work. Both groups included powerful, strong-shouldered men with warm, Jewish hearts, always ready to help a fellow Jew. Of course, the leaders of the synagogue came from the elder group, from which were chosen the four sextons to whom all paid heed. After the six-day workweek, the porters came to their small synagogue. Their boots were cleaned and polished, their trousers were folded above their boots, and they were dressed in their wedding *kapotas*. Early Sabbath morning they said Psalms here, and the finest readings took place here. People would stream to the Porters' Synagogue from all over town to recite psalms before prayers. With a pleasant tune and extra intention, even without understanding the meaning of the words, the simple folk would repeat Psalm after Psalm for each day of the week. Also, on Sabbath afternoons after naptime, people would listen to the teacher Hirsh Itsik give an explanation of the Torah portion of the week. An elderly Jew with a gray beard, he tried to perform the special good deed of educating simple folk about the Torah by using books of legends from the midrash *Ein Yakov*. For them this was a true Sabbath joy, a recompense for and lessening of the burden of their hard work during the previous six-day week.

[91]

Thus they would sit until nightfall, and only then did they pray the afternoon prayer and eat their third Sabbath meal as prescribed, drinking a mouthful of good whiskey and washing it down with challah and salted, pickled fish. After singing and the evening prayer, everyone would return to his home and his burdens.

The Tailors' Small Synagogue. The tailors and furriers who worked for the area farmers prayed here on Sabbaths and holidays. Every weekday, sewing machines rattled in the small factories while they traveled between "markets" in the towns and cities to sell their wares. On the Sabbath, after their meandering journeys through snow and rain, they congregated in their miniature temple, telling each other their adventures and news, and after prayers they would go together to recite Kiddush over a cup of wine. Some of them also knew how to sing. At to their machines, they would sing folk songs and the most beautiful cantorial pieces; they were actually considered some of the most knowledgeable people in the town regarding the cantorial arts.

The Butchers' Small Synagogue. Its location was Butchers' Street, next to the large slaughterhouses. The butchers, and the ritual slaughterers who worked with them, powerful and strong like cedars, prayed here. On the Sabbath, they came all dressed up with the wealthy Leybchi in the lead. Frequently, arguments erupted over issues as the "jurisdiction" of a ritual slaughterer, community elections, etc. The arguments were for the sake of heaven, however, and the synagogue united them all.

There is no describing the happiness that prevailed on Simchat Torah. Drinking was the order of the day, and more whiskey was consumed here than anywhere else.

The Hasidic Synagogue. Several generations before, the Grand Rabbi of Kremenets, R' Mordekhay'le, prayed here, and since then it has been called the Hasidic Synagogue. In the last several decades, this was the synagogue of the rabbi from Petrikov, who lived right next door. The rabbi would sometimes come to learn Torah in the synagogue, and this was the only location in the town where nightly learning took place. Also, during the day a stray Jew might come in to "grab" a page of Gemara. The tables were full of books. Along the walls were stands for individual learners.

The Nesvizh Synagogue. This synagogue, which also stood in the courtyard of the aforementioned, reportedly had been associated with the followers of the Rabbi of Nesvizh. It was even said that among the fringes of the Nesvizhers was a string of blue, of which only the Rabbi of Nesvizh knew the secret of dyeing. All this was in the distant past, however. In modern times, the Nesvizh Synagogue's congregants did not differ from the other synagogues in town in their liturgy or customs.

There was one Hasidic rabbi in town, Rabbi Moshke'le, but he did not have a "Hasidic table" or take "contributions." He lived in a fine apartment and had a personal synagogue where his sons and close relatives prayed.

R' Hirsh Mendil Rokhel, a well-to-do merchant and head of a many-branched family, also had a private synagogue such as this. Most of his family members were Zionists, while the remainder wanted to hear nothing of Zionism. R' Hirsh Mendil erected a synagogue in this courtyard for the prodigal family members, who, to honor him, would come inside with him to pray on the Sabbath and holidays.

****

This is a summary of the synagogues and study halls of the Kremenets community. Our ancestors spent their sad and happy occasions inside these walls of their miniature temples for many generations; here they wove the tapestries of their lives, which were viciously torn by the murderers.

[92]

EIGHTEEN SYNAGOGUES

Yonatan Kucher (Tel Aviv)
English translation by David Dubin and Thia Persoff

These I shall remember, and for them my soul shall be desolate: the synagogues and study halls in our town, Kremenets, where the voice of prayer never ceased, whether on a Sabbath, holiday, or simple weekday; with the destruction of the community, they are now destroyed and desolate.

I said that I would erect a monument to them—that I would inscribe in a book the synagogues that existed in our town in the last few years before the Holocaust. They numbered 18:

> The Vishnevets suburb synagogue, in Fayvel Feldman's home.
>
> Judge Yisrael'ikl (Lerner)'s Synagogue in Moshe Kapuzer's home.
>
> Hirsh Mendil Rokhel's Synagogue on Slovatski Street.
>
> The New Study Hall (Kozatske Study Hall) on Sheroka Street.
>
> Yankele's *Kloyz* on Kladkova Street.
>
> Bedrik's *Kloyz* on Kravatska Street.
>
> The Tailors' Little Synagogue (*Shnayder Shulkhel*) on Kravatska Street.
>
> The House of Prayer on Kladkova Street.
>
> The Old Study Hall on Sheroka Street.
>
> The Butchers' Synagogue (*Katsavim Shtibl*) on Butchers' Street.

The Ruzhin Hasidim's Little Synagogue (*Nesvizh Shulkhel*) in Yitschak Bat's home.

The Hasidic Little Synagogue (*Chasidish Shulkhel*).

The *Magid*'s Little Synagogue (*Magid Shulkhel*) in the Great Synagogue courtyard.

The Great Synagogue.

The Community Little Synagogue (*Kahal Shulkhel*) next to the Great Synagogue.

The Tailors' Little Synagogue (*Shnayder Shulkhel*) next to the Great Synagogue.

The Dubno suburb synagogue.

R' Moshke'le's Synagogue.

The list is arranged by street, from one end of town to the other, and includes semiprivate places of prayer.

THE ECONOMIC SITUATION BETWEEN THE TWO WORLD WARS

Leon Hokhberg and Zev Shumski
English translation by David Dubin and Thia Persoff

With the end of World War I, after the era of Petliura and Soviet rule, the town of Kremenets fell under Polish governance. The Jewish population, which had been devastated during the war, entered a new stage in its economic life. The economic framework of the Jewish population in the Czarist era—with the majority occupied in commerce, a substantial minority in crafts or manufacturing, and a minority in free professions—did not change much at the beginning of Polish rule. Small businesses and wholesalers' warehouses reopened, as did the craftsmen's workshops. Some factories reopened, and new ones were begun.

[93]

In 1919–1925, there was a great demand for merchandise. The Jews of Kremenets were the main suppliers then, so they directed the economic life of the area. They also imported goods from the western regions of Poland and exported agricultural products. The inflation of the Polish currency caused a brisk turnover of merchandise; it could be said that this was a period of prosperity for the Jews of Kremenets. But it did not last long.

In 1922, the Polish currency began to stabilize, which brought stability in commerce, too. The business cycle normalized, and the need for financial credit grew. At that time, two Jewish-owned banks opened in Kremenets: (1) the Bank of Mutual Credit, under Ruven Goldenberg's direction, which drew its resources from its members' deposits, membership dues, and loans from the Warsaw Central Bank of Mutual Credit, and (2) an interest-free loan fund (Charity Fund) for those who needed credit assistance. This fund was also supported by the center in Warsaw and money from the Joint, though even those two organizations could not supply enough credit for the business cycle.

In spite of the difficulty in adjusting to the new conditions, the period of 1919–1925 seems to have been the most normal economywise for Polish Jews, Kremenets included. The Jews of the town and the surrounding area drew closer to the land and merchandised its products. During the Czar's reign, Jews had not been permitted to own land or live in villages. Now that this edict had been rescinded, some Kremenets Jews (such as the Blit brothers and others) purchased farms, and some leased them. The grain business, for local sale and export, was entirely in the hands of the Jews until 1933, when Polish cooperatives were established to sell agricultural products and most of the grain-selling business went to them. Jews were involved in utilizing the natural resources of forests. Most forests in the area belonged to the Lyceum, which employed many Jews as experts, business managers, and lumber salesmen. The same was true of privately owned forests; there, too, many Jews were involved in utilizing parts of the forests and as owners or leasers of lumber mills (a large and well-known lumber mill in Verba was owned by Jews and was used for a long time as a base for Kibbutz Pioneer in Verba). Most of the leather and linen business was in Jewish hands, as were the industrial plants, most of which employed Jewish laborers: the flourmills in the area were leased by Jews, including the two in town (owned by Ovadis and by Brodski), the peat production plant, Chayim Grinberg's chalk factory, Vaysman's brick factory, Frishberg's and Grinberg's two large shoe-manufacturing plants, a confection factory, printing presses, etc. Some of the factories employed dozens of workers. Quite a few were building contractors, some very large and prominent. Most crafts were in Jewish hands: carpentry, metalsmithing, tinsmithing, tailoring, shoe repairs, teamsters, barbers, and confectioners. Those businesses, too, hired employees. Most hotels were in Jewish hands, as was transportation in all its modes in town and between towns: porters, teamsters, drivers, porters, and water-carriers, as it used to be in the old days. As a result of the increased numbers of laborers and hired workers in industry, crafts, and commerce, craft guilds were formed, as was a municipal committee that developed a range of professional and cultural activities and even established its own sports club. The craft guilds were mostly under the influence of the Communist Party, but Pioneer also tried to establish influence over them. Later, under Niunye Shtern's initiative and management, the carpentry shops (dozens of them with hundreds of workers) organized into a cooperative for the purpose of buying raw materials and selling finished products, mainly furniture.

[**Translation Editor's Note:** The Pioneer movement (in Hebrew, *Hechaluts*) was aimed at training Jews and bringing them to Israel.]

[94]

Reception for Pilsudski at the Great Synagogue, 1922

Jews could not penetrate the town bureaucracies or national governments. The Polish authorities prevented Jews from obtaining those positions. The only exception was the electric power station, because Jews had previously owned it, and when it was taken over by the town government, its workers went with it.

In 1925, signs pointed toward currency deflation in Poland. The government began to confiscate the means of circulation from the population's hands by levying heavy taxes on goods and property, and particularly on businesses, as they were mostly in Jews' hands. Nothing was easier than loading a wagon with the merchandise of a grocer who was delinquent in paying his taxes (and in many cases it filled only one carriage) so the rest of the storeowners would see and beware. That time was known as Gravski's Era. Most Kremenets Jews, who made their living from commerce, were ruined. Even our banks could not help, in spite of the assistance they received from their centers in Warsaw. The resources of the Polish bank in Kremenets were much greater, but it did not deal much with Jewish residents.

This was the situation when the Polish authorities began an open war against Jewish businesses. The authorities supported the establishment of Polish cooperatives in the villages and cities as a means of confiscating all trade from Jews. This move to cleanse their commerce of Jews began in 1933 and strengthened greatly from 1936 until World War II. Craftsmen were affected, too, as they were part of that population.

[95]

Because of the economic depression, many of the town's Jews could not earn a living. The nutrition level of their food declined, and with this came a decline in the population's health. Despair increased, as did pressure on the community's social institutions, but they could not give sufficient help to all the needy. Many were helped by relatives in America, and even public institutions were in need of this support. The extent of impoverishment in those years is evident from the fact that when monthly help from the *landsmanschaft* in America arrived (generally a minute sum: $100–$120 a month), it was typically announced it in the local newspaper, along with the amounts given to each institution: $5 to this one, $10 to another one, and so on.

This was the economic situation of most of the Jewish population in Kremenets at the start of World War II.

THE JEWISH BANKS

Moshe Shnayder (Rechovot)
English translation by Thia Persoff

After World War I, economic conditions among the Jewish population of Kremenets were very poor: unemployment was high, many had no means of earning a living, and others had a very low income. With the stabilization of the political situation in this area, which was annexed to Poland, there were signs of economic recovery. Business contacts with villages were renewed; the area abounded with a variety of agricultural products for local consumption and export. It was natural, then, that this development increased the need for bank credit. There was a branch of the Bank of Poland in town, but its main dealings were with the estate owners; it had only very scant dealings with Jewish merchants and craftsmen.

At that time, two Jewish banks were established in Kremenets: a merchants' bank, headed by Ruven Goldenberg (the director of the Society of Mutual Credit that had existed before the war), and the Povshekhni Bank (People's Bank), headed by Shimon Gendler. Both were enterprising and responsible, knowledgeable about banking, and practical in their economic activities. Knowledgeable volunteers were found in the community, and they formed the management boards and examiner boards. Very soon, those cooperative institutions earned the public's trust. Many new members joined, and the two banks developed into large, modern, well-organized banks. They had an influence on economic life; merchants and craftsmen received the credit they needed. Stores and workshops were reestablished, and new enterprises were added. The new, relative economic prosperity brought on an increase in building; new houses were built, and old ones were renovated. The town wore a new look. New factories and grocery stores were opened, as some of the clerks who had previously worked for the merchants Moshe Rokhel, the Bakimer brothers, the Landsberg brothers, and others opened their own stores, established a position, and even exploited their previous employers. The grain merchants and wholesalers, who always needed a great deal of credit for their large businesses and could not get help from the Bank of Poland, benefited from the Jewish banks. In this way, these two banks held most of the businesses, small factories, and craft shops in their hands and boosted the economic status of the town's Jews.

[96]

These banks also maintained high standards in their relationship with the public. As cooperatives, they held a yearly general meeting, which members would attend; they listened to reports and took an active part in the discussions. Sometimes they would voice strong criticism, and in some instances it was not free of personal reasons. Nevertheless, the members proved savvy in the banking business, were concerned about keeping the banks functioning, and chose the management wisely, from the most capable people in town, those who had proved themselves by volunteering for public activities with great dedication. More than once, walking on Sheroka Street late at night, I saw lights in the windows of the two banks; members of the management boards or boards of examiners were still dealing with matters that the community had entrusted to them.

Managing Committee of the Small Business Association (1934)

Sitting (right to left): (1) ..., (2) Shaul Brodski, (3) Fayvish Rozenblit, (4) Krivin. *Standing (left to right):* (1) ..., (2) ..., (3) Yakov Tsmokun, (4) ....

[The Yiddish handwriting on the photo reads: "Central Management of the Small Business Association in Kremenets Patl. Blushteyn—25 November 1934"]

Among the active members of the Merchants' Bank, the names of Avraham Vaynberg; Perlmuter, a cloth merchant; and Olshnitski are worth mentioning. Notable active members of the People's Bank were Yone Zeyger; Shmuel Gendelman; the executive secretary; and Buts; head of accounting.

Both banks were connected to national associations: one bank to the Jewish Merchants of Poland, and the second to the Jewish Credit Cooperatives Association of Poland.

Besides those banks, our town had a Charity Fund managed by Gershteyn and Shtern, which developed a wide range of activities among the community's middle class. There is more about this institution in another article.

With the destruction of the Kremenets Jewish community came the end of those two fine enterprises, which served as an expression of Jewish creative force in the field of the economy. Let us remember with appreciation all those who are not with us anymore, who worked and labored to bring about and strengthen those two enterprises, which evidenced Jewish wisdom and strength as well as a stubborn struggle for existence and mutual aid.

[97]

TOZ BRANCH—HEALTH CARE ORGANIZATION

Y. Port-Noy (Haifa)
English translation by Thia Persoff

From its inception, the TOZ branch in Kremenets was viewed with fondness, and many people used its clinics when they needed of help. Because of the warm, friendly attitude of the clinic staff and the patients' inability to pay a private physician, the waiting rooms were full on the days when it was open to patients, and the number of patients continued to increase.

A regular supervisor visited the homes of pregnant women and young mothers.

Mrs. Dr. Golander provided general medical treatment in the clinic; Dr. Yosef Landsberg treated gynecology and obstetrics cases.

Because of a shortage of funds, the TOZ in Kremenets concentrated on only three areas: general clinics, an infant wellness center, and sports medicine for young people and adults.

TOZ was supported by donations from Jewish organizations in other countries, the organization's monthly membership dues, and moneys raised through plays, parties, flower days, and so on.

The branch management was elected once a year. For many of those years, Dr. Zalman Sheynberg, the dentist, was a dedicated chairman who fulfilled his obligations faithfully. The rest of the board members, such as Yechezkel Opshteyn, Fanye Baytler, and Moshe Shnayder, were also known for their dedication to the institution. I must say that the officers and staff (Chayim Gibelbenk, the secretary, and Niusye Baytler-Katz, the nurse) carried out their duties mostly as volunteers.

The newspaper *Kremenitser Shtime* mentions other TOZ board members' names from different periods: Ch. Zigelboym and M. Vitels. May their names be blessed along with those of the other TOZ workers who perished in the Holocaust.

THE JEWISH WORKERS' STRUGGLE

Netanel Kagan (Petach Tikvah)
English translation by Thia Persoff

My review of the history of the community of Jewish workers in Kremenets encompasses a period starting with the takeover by Polish authorities after World War I until the invasion of the Nazis in 1939.

Kremenets was not an industrial town. Its main livelihood came from commerce and crafts. Many residents were craftsmen running small businesses, but in time a large hired workforce developed, such as tailors, shoemakers, carpenters, bakers, barbers, salesmen, and clerks.

Eventually, as the worker population grew, the need arose to organize the labor force to help solve essential problems for workers, improve working conditions, and provide protection from exploitation, such as an eight-hour workday, raises in salary, compensation, and so on. Under the guidance of the central labor institutions, various guilds were established in Kremenets. From time to time an official supervisor would come and help develop them. When occasionally a conflict arose between labor and management, most of the time it was settled by arbitration. Only seldom was a strike called, which lasted weeks, during which the workers had to support themselves.

[98]

The first workers to use the strike as a weapon were garment workers. They labored in unsanitary conditions 14–16 hours a day, received minimal pay, and had to work under a contract system. These conditions caused great bitterness among the workers; meetings were called, and the workers demanded an eight-hour workday, the abolition of the work-by-contract system, and so on. Obviously, the employers, who generally persecuted workers who joined the guilds, reacted to this with rancor, and more than a few workers who had families to support backed out under the employers' pressure. Nevertheless, the organizers of the strike succeeded, overcoming the many difficulties as well as the hunger and privation suffered by the strikers and their families. Only after long and arduous negotiations, when the better work conditions were achieved, was the strike called off.

With the increase in the worker population, cultural activity began. A library, which purchased many books in Yiddish and other languages, was established. The library attracted a large patronage among young people from the high schools and others, and many patrons of the municipal library left it to join the new guild library, which had an attached reading room containing newspapers and other assorted periodicals.

At that time, an amateur theater was established. The writings of Peretz, Shalom Aleichem, Hirshbein, and so on were performed, acquainting the workers with their creations. The theater grew in popularity, and it performed in the surrounding towns, too. A string orchestra was also established, with young people joining; it performed for the public occasionally.

Evening classes were offered for extension and advanced studies, particularly for young people who had to quit school and start working to help their parents support their families.

The guilds even played an important role in sports. In a sports club named Morgenshtern (Star of Dawn), trained coaches worked on developing skills in soccer, handball, and track and field. They also held rousing sports competitions, which were popular among the citizens. In time, our town had good young athletes in spite of the difficult economic conditions. The sports club offered them a place for education and training. When the cultural and sports activities became highly successful, obstacles arose. Agents of the Polish government, which did not look kindly on the working population, and particularly on Jewish workers, began to interfere. From time to time they would search the library, confiscate books, and arrest members. It was obvious that their purpose was to destroy the working population's achievements.

With May 1 getting close, we were ready for clashes and arrests, but the workers' holiday was celebrated as planned, although under the watchful eyes of plainclothes policemen. The next day, certain members were called in for interrogation at the police station. This procedure was repeated year after year. Members were arrested, taken to court on charges of supposedly Communist activities, and sentenced to years in jail. Two members were incarcerated in the infamous Bereza Kartuska concentration camp. You could already see then that Poland was following in Hitler's footsteps, and this is why the great Jewish Holocaust was able to start precisely within her borders. After those arrests, the unions resumed their activities as before. On February 27, 1937, the authorities arrested all active union members, as well as other young members from the ranks, 36 people in all, accusing them of being members of the Ukrainian Communist Party. This was the final blow for the unions.

After ten months, one member was released from the concentration camp due to a complete breakdown of his health. Four months later, the second member was released. Both of them met with us, the group of 36, in prison.

[99]

Before we were moved into the prison, we were held for three days in the police station, where we were tortured in many ways so we would admit to the charges we were accused of. They hit our feet with clubs, stuck our fingertips between doors and their frames, tied us upside down and poured water into our nostrils (a person feels as if he is drowning), stuck needles under our nails—all with the purpose of forcing us to declare that we were members of the Communist Party. But none of us admitted to it. Then they tried something else: they released two young people and made them into provocateurs who agreed to sign the papers, as the fear of torture broke their bodies and spirits.

Using those confessions, the authorities sentenced hundreds of people to jail. It is important to say here that one prisoner who had done a great deal for the betterment of workers had a serious heart condition. Nevertheless, he was taken to prison. When all our pleas to have him moved to a hospital went unanswered, we declared a hunger strike. By the third day of the strike, we managed to notify the rest of the members, and when it threatened to spread into a general strike, the sick friend was secretly taken to a hospital, where he died immediately. All of us were very weak by the third day of the hunger strike, so the prison doctor gave orders to force-feed us. By chance, we found out from one of the criminal prisoners that our sick friend had been hospitalized, so we stopped the strike. The prison administration could not understand how we discovered their secret.

In the meantime, monotonous prison life continued. The brutal regime, restrictions, and inadequate nutrition, which were meant to break our spirits, achieved the opposite results. After two years of interrogations, the trial began. Chained two by two, we were led to the court. A heavy guard was stationed at the courthouse. A large crowd of people milled around. From the start of the trial, the provocateur nature of the prosecution witnesses was revealed. Although the defense attorneys, headed by Dr. Landau, had proved very quickly that the accused were innocent of the charges, they were sentenced to 4 to 12 years in prison.

None of us completed the full prison term. Soon afterward, the Poland-Germany war began and the Polish army fell apart, and when the Russian Red Army entered, we were released. Many of us who were in other jails were also released and returned home. When we came back, we found out that the Russian authorities had arrested the two traitors, together with the agents of the Polish police. We do not know what happened to them.

[100]

JEWISH SPORTS

Chayim Taytsher (Tel Aviv)
Translated from Russian and Prepared for Print by Munye Katz, Haifa
English translation by Thia Persoff and by Steven Wien and Sari Havis

The Jewish young people of Kremenets were already active in gymnastics, the first branch of athletics, during the final days of World War I. The first students were high school students in town. Later, other types of sports were established: soccer and track and field. Among the first athletes in our town were Binyamin Vaynberg, Nolik Sofer, Avrashe Rozenfeld, the brothers Liove and Manus Goldenberg, Azriel Gorinshteyn, Shonye Rish, Moshe'ki Margalit, Yisrael Grinberg, and M. Chirga. They also founded the Maccabee sports organization, out of which the successful Chashmonaim organization developed and continued as long as the Jewish community in Kremenets existed. They invested most of their time in organizing and developing sports and informing the public of the importance of physical training and development in the nation's life.

The mountainous terrain in our area and transportation difficulties restricted the development of sports; during the summer it was difficult to find a suitable field close to town. In 1922, thanks to the lobbying of Sonye Baytler—a Maccabee Odessa trainee who settled in Kremenets—the High School of Commerce students gave a public gymnastics exhibition in the gymnasium. Yosef Torchin, a Maccabee trainee in Bialatserkov, Russia, stood out among S. Baytler's helpers. He was a lively source of inspiration for our athletes for many years. The sports "headquarters" was in Manus Goldenberg's apartment, and our few pieces of equipment were kept there, too.

It began like this: in 1918, Duvid Klurfayn (Getsi Klurfayn's son) rounded up a group of young men from among the students, and he began training them in Swedish gymnastics in the Tivoli Garden.

Group of Skiers from the Chashmoni Club (1932)

[101]

Chashmoni Military Fitness Division

The acceptance of physical fitness as a valuable asset was still unfamiliar to the young people, and more so to their parents. The organization, the primitive "equipment," and the poor language of the orders (in Hebrew!) prompted laughs. But Duvid Klurfayn did his work with great enthusiasm and succeeded in winning over his group of trainees, who would show up every evening to exercise on the small field in front of curious watchers. After a while, other types of sports were established: soccer, and track and field.

By 1928, gymnastics and track and field were very well developed and popular, attracting a large number of Jewish young people. During this period, a notable member was Braver (a Maccabee Grodno trainee), who worked in our town as a coach in the ORT vocational school. In time, girls joined the ranks of our athletes. Some of the first ones were R. Zeyger, M. Gorinfeld, P. Borevits, Bela Pintsberg, and others.

The sports pioneers did not neglect soccer, a game that won a special place of honor. The members of the first team, established in 1922, were M. Chirga, Sh. Rish, B. Vaynberg, N. Ovadis, N. Sofer, M. Port, Y. Kroyt, A. Gorinshteyn, M. Goldenberg, L. Goldberg, Y. Goldenberg, A. Rozenfeld, Y. Rabinovits, Y. Grinberg, Mandelker, and Shnayder. With their limited means, they acquired a ball but were unable to purchase shoes and uniforms. Their first training ground was the deserted yard of the old Talmud Torah, and only after much effort were they able to rent a plot of land that was unsuited to their purpose, as it was in a mountainous area an hour's walk from the town center.

Soccer games were very popular among the town residents. Two years later, in 1924, the team's permit to use their primitive plot was taken away. Then, with the support of the public, a plot called Klinovka was rented near the town and prepared for soccer, gymnastics, and track.

The soccer team lost its first games, so when an amateur coach came to town, he was asked to help. The team began to compete with other teams in the area, and the level of play increased. These were the district's first experiences with soccer. The practice sessions and the games with non-Jewish teams from inside and outside the town aroused great interest among the Kremenets Jew. The community's connection to the sports organization was now a matter of honor—winning or losing a game was winning or losing for all of local Jewry.

[102]

Soccer—expensive game. The games did not bring in enough income to cover the costs of keeping the teams going, and only through the financial support of the fans did the organization manage to exist and balance its budget. Some of the main contributors were Yechezkel Opshteyn, Ayzik Shteyner, Muzya Barats, Simche Gintsburg, Yisrael Grinberg, Asher Kagan (Buzek), and others.

For many years, the authorities refused to legitimize the single Jewish sports organization, which changed its name many times in the hope of earning the requested approval: from Maccabee, to Chashmonaim, to Sports Fans, then to TOZ Physical Culture Section. In 1928, it finally received official approval as the TOZ Department of Physical Culture. A board was chosen, and membership was opened with an official announcement. The first board consisted of Yechezkel Opshteyn, the chairman, and members Chayim Fishman, Moshe'ki Margalit, Mikhael Gintsburg, Sonye Baytler, Munye Katz, and Avrake Zilberg. The board members understood the job relegated to them and spared nothing in their efforts to develop Jewish sports in Kremenets. After that, different Chashmonaim teams began to compete for town, district, and county championships.

A few of the teams' best members were sent to take coaching courses. Among those finishing and excelling in the courses were Avrashe Trakhtenberg and Nisye Segal in gymnastics and A. Benderski in swimming.

The number of members kept increasing. Practices, training, meetings, and lectures were held each day and evening— on the sports field during the summer and in an indoor hall during the winter. Many young people who had not been involved so far and who spent their leisure time in billiard halls and coffeehouses began to join the sports organization, where they found a place to develop their bodies and minds.

In the final years before World War II, sports in the schools were of a high caliber. These institutions' Jewish trainees were the main source of the increased number of sports coaches. Most of our members were also members of Zionist organizations, and with every wave of immigration to Israel, the sports teams got smaller. We tried to eliminate this "deficit" by drafting additional members from the next generation of young people.

Indeed, the organizers' ability, the coaches' dedication, and the members' efforts did not disappoint—already in 1931/1932, several of our teams had won respectable positions in the county and district championships.

The C League soccer team was moved to the A League after its decisive victories. Among the track and field champions were Pesach Mandelblit, Shayke Gliklis, and Lolik Yahalom. Soccer and volleyball teams reached the district finals. Swimmers Moshe Modrik and Munye Katz won first place in the 50- and 100-meter events.

Skiing, the king of winter sports, occupied a special place in the ranks of Kremenets sports. In our area, we knew very little about this sport until 1928/1929. The mountainous terrain that restricted the development of summer sports played a very positive role here; our athletes adapted well to it and soon dominated the field. Excellent surface conditions (even in the town's steep streets) and dedicated, experienced coaches (Chashmonaim graduates) made skiing a popular sport. Every day of the week, and particularly on the Sabbath and holidays, skiers covered the slopes. In the mountains, a ski jump, the third largest and third best in Poland, was built according to specifications for P.I.S. (International Ski Federation) competitions.

[103]

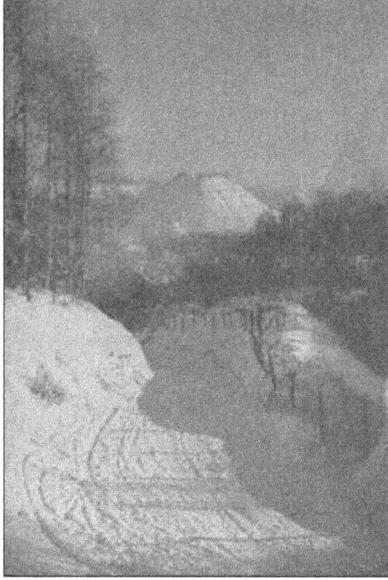

Ski Run

Our people reached the championship and set various records in this beautiful sport. The athletes' names were known all over Poland: Berl Kuter jumped 78 meters (the national record was 84 meters, and the international record, by a Norwegian, was 91 meters). In the 18- and 24-km races, our members were always in the top ten, the best being Melekh Efrat, Babe Fingerhut, Shayke Gliklis, Keytelmakher, Chayim Taytsher, and others. Among the girls, Ize Ovadis and T. Fridman were the best.

Our athletes' achievements and the board's efforts had turned Kremenets into the ski center of Polish Jewry. Under the leadership of M. Katz and Sh. Gliklis, ski workshops were held annually, in which representatives of most Jewish sports organizations in Poland—particularly from the northern, central, and eastern regions—participated. The leadership of Poland's Maccabee ski division was delivered to Chashmonaim of Kremenets.

Seeing the achievements of our athletes, the Polish sports authorities supplied us with all necessary equipment, discounts for train travel, and free lodging in hostels.

We should mention that within the framework of sports, athletes were given military training, too. In 1932, when the sports organization was renamed under TOZ and received official approval, Manus Goldenberg got in touch with the military authorities in an effort to give the members military training. The officer in charge of military training for Polish youth agreed to send one of his subordinates as a coach. The organization received a few dozen rifles, and basic training began. This was an important opportunity to train Jewish youth in use of firearms, considering the relations between Polish and Jewish residents at that time. The members of the organization who saw the future of the youth in Israel particularly were interested in this.

[104]

Guidance was provided by an army commander, Mr. Munye Katz (who resides in Haifa today). At the time, he was a reserve officer in the Polish army. Of the various physical education proponents among Jewish Kremenetsers, we will mention the names of Manus Goldenberg, Sonye Baytler, Y. Opshteyn, M. Barats, Chayim Fishman, Moshe'ki Margolis, Simche Gintsburg, Mikhael Gintsburg, Dr. Landsberg, A. Zeyger, Munye Katz, and Shonye Rish. Some of the best students were Niunye Yoklov, Berl Kuter, Moshe'ke Reznik, Dani Gurevits, and Pesach Mandelblit.

Sports Enthusiasts, 1931

The sports organizations were a large movement, and even with the growth of immigration to Israel, the number of our people participating in various sports organizations never diminished. In its last years, the number of people involved in various organizations came close to 500 young people. Before the eruption of World War II, anti-Semitism intensified in the Christian population of Kremenets, and as a result, attempts at provocation and conflict grew on the part of Polish young people. But our athletes always stood on guard, overcame the instigators, and upheld Israel's honor.

[105]

INSTITUTIONS AND ORGANIZATIONS

English translation by Steven Wien and Sari Havis

The following is a list of public institutions and organizations that were active in our town during the final years before the annihilation. The list, which may be incomplete, includes only Jewish public figures in Kremenets. Please keep in mind that every institution and organization was centered on a group of activists and a large number of members. The following list includes the principal activists.

Community Council	Avigdor Perlmuter
Secretary	Duvid Leviton
Municipality	Azriel Kremenetski (vice-mayor)
Rabbinate	Rabbi Mendiuk
Jewish Hospital	Moshe Kapuzer
Orphanage	Sofie Kremenetski
Home for the Aged	Yisrael Landsberg
Talmud Torah	Simche Yakov Blumenfeld
Burial Society	Chayim Zigelboym

Hospitality	Ayzik Hindes
TOZ	Dr. Z. Sheynberg
ORT	Chayim Ovadies
Tarbut	Aba Taytelman
Zionist Organization	Dr. Meir Litvak and Dr. Binyamin Landsberg
Mizrachi Movement	
The Union	
Betar	Sh. Morjik
Pioneer	Hershel Bernshteyn (now in Argentina)
Young Pioneer	M. Ditun (now in Argentina)
Youth Guard	
Youth Organization	P. Holtsman
Chashmonaim, sports club of various organizations	Yechezkel Opshteyn
Dramakrayz—drama society of various organizations	
Merchants Bank	Hirsh Gilrant
People's Bank	Shimon Gendler
Charity Fund	M. Gershteyn
Charity Fund in the Dubno suburb	Duvid Basis
Merchants' Association	Meir Goldring
Small Business Association	Duvid Goldenberg
Craftsmen's Association	Shlome Fingerhut (member of the town administration)
Municipal Guild Committee	
Clerks' Association	M. Rabinovits

[**Translation Editor's Note:** The Union (*Hitachdut*) is the short name for the Union of Young Worker (*Hapoel Hatsair*)–Young Zionists (*Tseirey Tsion*).]

[106]

Tailors' Association	M. Goldsher
Barbers' Association	Y. Taytsher
Synagogues	
Great Synagogue	Yisrael Margalit
Old Study Hall	A. T. Katraborski
House of Prayer	Yechezkel Opshteyn
New Study Hall	Dov Kremenchutski
Hasidic Synagogue	Shalom Gibelbank
Aleksanderski Synagogue	Duvid Shvartsblat
Shapoval *Kloyz*	Dov Rom
Tailors' Synagogue	Avraham Shtivelman
Butchers' Synagogue	Yerachmiel Bezpoyasnik
Izbitser Synagogue	Asher Kahana
Community Synagogue	Pinchas Baltsh

New Study Hall in the Dubno   Eli Fishman
   Old Study Hall in the Dubno   Shlome Matler

Mount Bona and Surroundings

[107]

ZIONISM, PIONEERING, IMMIGRATION

THE EVOLUTION OF THE "ORGANIZATION"

Yisrael Biberman (Jerusalem)
English translation by Steven Wien and Sari Havis

The "Organization" was very well known in our town. There was no need to translate and say the "Zionist Club" or the "Zionist Organization chapter." It was very common to say briefly the "Organization," and everyone understood what was implied.

True, the Organization experienced many ups and downs. At times, it expanded; at times, it shrank. It knew times of ebb and flow. But it always served as the center for Zionist life in the town and even the surrounding area. It served as a center for Zionist thought and activity in every manifestation. The elderly, the young, men, women, and speakers of Yiddish, Russian, or Polish all received their Zionist education and their general preparation for public life within the Organization's walls. Here, it had a lasting effect on community affairs, the municipality, and political life. There, it had a formative influence on immigration to Israel, various movements, and cultural activities.

I was fortunate enough to accompany the Organization in its various activities for over two decades. I said I would write about some of its events and evolution as I experienced them.

The Organization began as a small, illegal library in a book cabinet that traveled from one house to another to avoid searches. In my collection, I have a picture of the "Library of the Zionist Organization of Kremenets"; the dates on it are 1902–1928. [See the photograph on p. 111.] Although the library was formed in 1911, I have strong recollections of the library only beginning in 1911. I recall that for some time the library found a home in the of Gutye Aksel's apartment, close to the Vishnevets suburb. Afterward, it wandered to Biberman's apartment on Kaznacheyskia Street. The cabinet traveled from house to house. The contact with the police with regard to the library was Benderski. The officer of the gendarmerie would notify Benderski in advance about any search that was to take place. The same day or night, the books would be shifted to another house, so that by the time the search took place, the library could not be found. Often the books were divided among several members' houses. After the danger passed, they would be collected in one house again, and the library would continue to exist. Naturally, the collection of money for the library and other practical activities (for the Jewish National Fund and at synagogues on Yom Kippur eve, the distribution of *shekalim*, etc.) was taken care of by young people. They were a very tightly knit group. They called themselves Young Zionists, not in the sense of the known party, which had its own program and agenda, but because they were young and very Zionist.

[**Translation Editor's Note:** In Hebrew, Jewish National Fund is *Keren Kayemet LeYisrael*.]

This group had no permanent headquarters, and so they met from time to time in a private apartment.

[108]

Whether in this or that apartment, the meetings provided an opportunity for conversation, lectures, and meetings. On the Sabbath there would often be a lecture on one of the mountains. Usually it was Mount Vidomka, in a hiding place between the rocks. The gathering, the trip, the enjoyment of open country, the drinking of fresh milk—were all interwoven, one with the other. The young people would lie down by a spruce tree and travel in their imaginations, dreaming about village life and open country in the Land of Israel.

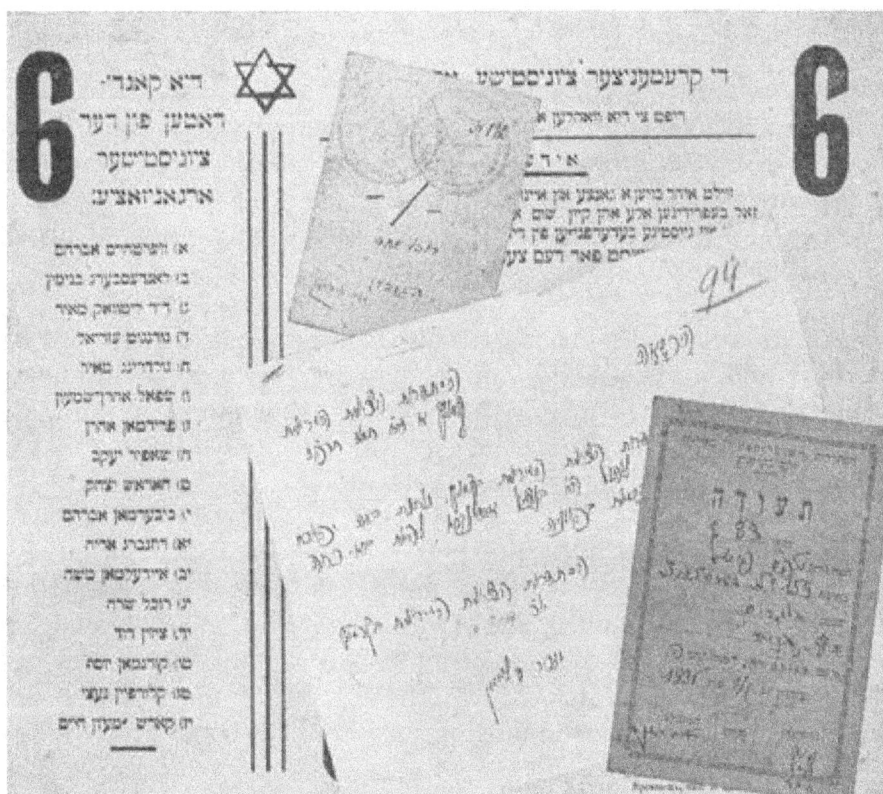

Zionist Documents

[Translation Editor's Note: This is a collage with a caption in Yiddish and Hebrew. The background document is a ballot with names for the Zionist elections of 1917 (top to bottom): (1) Avraham Verthaym, (2) Binyamin Landesberg, (3) Dr. Meir Litvak, (4) Azriel Gorengut, (5) Meir Goldring, (6) Aharon Shimon Shpal, (7) Aharon Fridman, (8) Yakov Shafir, (9) Yitschak Charash, (10) Avraham Biberman, (11) Arye Rachenberg, (12) Moshe Eydelman, (13) Sore Rokhel, (14) Duvid Tsivin, (15) Yosef Kornman, (16) Getsi Klurfayn, (17) Shimon Chayim Karsh. The top image is "Zionist" money. The middle document is an authorization to attend the Zionist Organization's 1927 national convention in Poland. The bottom-right document is a 1935 Youth Guard membership booklet.]

This is how things went until the Revolution. Then, in 1917, the library was transferred to a rented room in Getsi Klurfayn's house. In early 1918, they rented a four-room apartment for the Zionist Club on Aba Tsukerman's property; this included a library and a reading room. They ordered some furniture and added many more books in three languages: Yiddish, Hebrew, and Russian. The Organization stayed there for about two years, until the Poles entered the town and forbade the existence of the Zionist Organization. The club was closed, and the library was transferred to the children's home of the Joint, which was at Komervits's house next to the fire department.

[109]

For about two years, the Organization existed illegally, although its activity did not diminish. In 1920, it held a very large Purim carnival with dancing, food, and music. At about one o'clock in the morning, knocks were heard at the door, and a window opened. Two Polish detectives entered through it with revolvers in their hands. Because I was the one responsible for this carnival, I was arrested on the charge of organizing an illegal gathering. But I was released after one day.

In 1922, the Polish authorities legalized the Zionist Federation, and therefore the Zionist Club remained in the same house, which served as a kindergarten in the morning and as the Zionist Club and library in the evening. In 1923, the morning kindergarten was closed. The whole house was devoted to the Organization, and Tarbut activities were also developed there.

While the Organization resided in Tsukerman's house, Mikhael Barshap, who lived in the kitchen with his wife, was accepted as the house custodian. He would bake cookies to sell to visitors to the club. Barshap belonged to one of the leftist parties and was always engaged in political discussions. He was a nonbeliever, yet he grew a long beard .... The Organization's kitchen, which was his home, served as a place of assembly for leftist young people, including various Bundists, and there were always stormy arguments there.

Most of the readers were young people. More books were acquired and requested in Yiddish than in other languages. In the final years, the library also acquired books in Polish. In its peak years, the library consisted of about 3,000 volumes.

Due to financial trouble, the Organization had to abandon its spacious apartment in 1925, and it moved to a one-room apartment. After a while, it recovered a bit financially and again rented a four-room apartment. Naturally, the financial trouble reflected a decline in Zionist activity. Then another group of proponents got organized, and the Zionist Club was revived. Around the time of my immigration to Israel (1934), the club was set up in Dr. Sheynberg's house. He was a dentist and well-known Zionist activist.

In the first phase, there was only one Zionist Organization in the town, which included Zionist adults and youth in all their diversity who had not yet formed a unified movement. Of course, there were debates between the young people and adults, and between pioneering members and the general membership, but everyone was incorporated under a single Zionist Organization. Around 1922, there was a division into organized factions and defined parties. These included Pioneer itself, the Union Party, the Youth Guard movement, and others. After this division, the Organization served as more of a center for general Zionists. But at various times, other Zionist parties also joined and used the club. The largest movement based on numbers was Youth Guard, which at times included up to 200 young people.

Here are the names of people who chaired the Zionist Organization in our town at different times: Binyamin Landsberg, Moshe Eydelman, Dr. Litvak, Avigdor Perlmuter, and Meir Goldring. Members of the various Zionist committees were Aharon Fridman, Getsi Klurfayn, Dr. Zalman Sheynberg, Arke Rozenberg, and Chane Broyner. And still alive are Frume Vaynshtok (now in Jerusalem), Henye Lukatsher (now in Binyamina), Avraham Fisherman (now in Nachalat Yitschak), and others.

[110]

Zionist Activists, 1929

Sitting, right to left: (1) Chayim Grinberg, (2) Meir Goldring, (3) Dr. Meir Litvak, (4) Moshe Eydelman, (5) Dr. Arye Landsberg, (6) Avigdor (Zeydi) Perlmuter, (7) Duvid Leviton. *Standing, right to left:* (1) Getsi Klurfayn, (2) Vayner, (3) Dov Kremenchutski, (4) Muni Dobromiler, (5) Kutsher, (6) Yitschak Katz, (7) Shmerel Rishnivker, (8) Eliyahu Reznik.

Movie Day for the Jewish National Fund, 1929

[**Translator's Note:** This photograph may depict a show of which the proceeds went to the Jewish National Fund. In the center is Yisrael Biberman, the author of this article.]

[111]

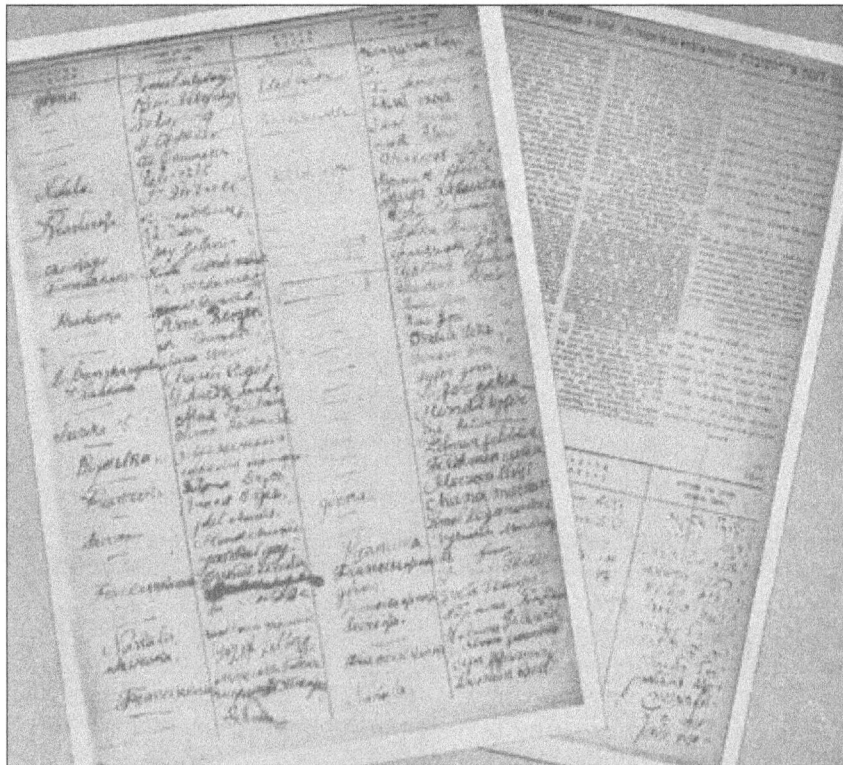

*Petition of the League for a Working Israel
against Closing Immigration*

Zionist Library

[**Translator's Note:** The text in the photo reads, "Library of the Zionist Organization of Kremenets, 1902–1928."]

[112]

THE PIONEER MOVEMENT

Yisrael Otiker (Na'an)
English translation by Steven Wien and Sari Havis

Our town's ties to the Land of Israel were many and deep. Kremenets was a Zionist town. The Lovers of Zion movement arrived in Kremenets almost at its inception. The town's intellectuals joined and later took part in the first Zionist Congresses. From then until the final days of Jewish Kremenets, staunch, dedicated activity for Israel did not cease, nor did the Zionist and Pioneer movements.

Between the two World Wars, many of our town's young people immigrated to Israel, so ties were of a personal kind, too, through sons and daughters, brothers and sisters, with a general awareness of and interest in everything that happened there. Many people lived vicariously, treating events there as if they were close and personal. A letter that arrived from Israel would be shared, moving from hand to hand; Israeli newspapers would be read at different circles and meetings. When an Israeli emissary happened to come to town, he would be "wrung dry" through all possible means and taken to the top of Mount Bona and the Vidomka to be treated to Kremenets' wondrous panoramic view; anything so he would tell.... Young people wanted to know about kibbutzim and the "conquest of labor," the Arabs, protection and defense, and so on.

[**Translator's Note**: "Conquest of labor" describes the efforts of the early Jewish immigrants to Israel to reclaim the right of building and tilling the land with their own hands. At that time, physical labor by Diaspora Jews was so unusual that it was not done by the early newcomers but by hired Arabs. The pioneers who wished to fulfill the dream of rebuilding the country and working its land were not accepted as laborers by the previous immigrants who owned farms and orchards.]

I particularly remember the tension as we waited for news and newspapers during the riots in Israel. Our concern for the future of the Land stayed with us day and night. Young pioneers followed every detail of the events and searched for ways to join the defenders.

Young Kremenetsers stood out for their idealism and devotion, animatedly involving themselves in the nation's and the world's problems. Most were members of youth movements. Many were among those who, in the era of Israel's "locked gates," penetrated them. But there were also many who despaired, gave up in the hour of crisis; they joined other, non-Zionist movements and devoted their lives to fighting the Polish government's policies. Dozens were sentenced to long years in jail, and some lost their lives in concentration camps and jails; some fell on the battlegrounds of Spain, in border smuggling, and the like.

[**Translator's Note**: "Locked gates" is a term used to describe the British government's refusal to permit Jewish immigration to Israel. This was combated by what was called "illegal immigration."]

A refusal to accept the current reality and aspirations for a different kind of life blazed in the young people and pushed them to attempt daring and hopeless deeds.

At the end of World War I, when the third wave of immigration began, young Kremenetsers broke loose and joined the first of those immigrants. Pioneers had left even before the local chapter of the movement was established. In Israel, they were found among those paving the roads, establishing work battalions, and joining the first kibbutzim. As the community life of Poland's Jews became organized, chapters of national organizations opened in our town, such as Zionist parties, youth movements, and Pioneer.

Pioneer's level of activity and membership, though, fluctuated from time to time depending on the situation in Israel and immigration there.

As the time for the first group to immigrate drew near, an official chapter of Pioneer formed, and a few years later a chapter of Young Pioneer as well. (Separate chapters formed in the Dubno suburb, and for years parallel chapters of Pioneer and Young Pioneer existed there.)

The chapters held extensive, structured cultural activities.

[113]

The members learned Hebrew, the geography of Israel, and, in separate classes, Hebrew literature, the history of the workers' movement in Israel, the kibbutz movement, the Federation, and other subjects. In 1926, the first central seminar of Pioneer in Poland was held, and two members from Kremenets took part.

[**Translator's Note**: The Federation (in Hebrew, *Histadrut*) was a union of the assorted Labor factions. Young Worker (in Hebrew, *Hapoel Hatsair*) and Unity of Labor (in Hebrew, *Achdut HaAvoda*) were socialist Zionist parties.]

In the years after the war, a group of members of the Zionist-Socialist Federation's Liberty movement passed through on their way to Poland from the USSR. In their opinion, the most important task was to build the Pioneer movement, and they devoted their best efforts to that end, establishing chapters and training centers. They made their way to Poland through Volhynia, where they stayed for some time, organizing the district council and helping to strengthen chapters and establish training centers.

[**Translator's Notes:** In Hebrew, the Liberty movement was called *Dror*. Training centers (in Hebrew, *hakhsharot*) were farms where young people learned handicrafts and agricultural skills before immigrating to Israel.]

At that time, Kibbutz Klesov, a stonecutting kibbutz named after Yosef Trumpeldor, was established, marking a turning point in the forms and functions of pioneer training in Poland. The kibbutz was situated in north Volhynia, in the Sarny area. A large group of members from Kremenets went there and stayed for many years while immigration was closed. Having already adapted to a life of communal work, the Kibbutz Klesov members determined that they would wait there until immigration was possible. When that time came and the gates were opened, the first to go included a good number of members from Kremenets, who joined Yagur and Givat HaShlosha in Israel.

Klesov was a symbol and example to the Zionist movement in Poland. Among the younger set, many stories were told about the kibbutz's approach and stability. Klesov, being close to our town, had quite an influence on it, and for years it was a driving educational force for the pioneer movement.

Training Chapter of Pioneer of Kremenets (1933),
Kibbutz Klesov Chapter

The 1929 riots caused a great awakening. The movements called for volunteers to register, and hundreds of young people answered, wishing to immigrate immediately and join the ranks of the defenders.

[114]

In the years following the riots, the years of the Passfield decrees, came days of heavy crises for the Zionist movement. It looked as if any hope for immigration to Israel would be postponed for a long time, causing despair and depression among the young. Dozens withdrew and joined the non-Zionist Left, severing their link with Zionism and the Land of Israel. A very few kept the faith.

In spring 1932, the first breach appeared in the "locked gates." Many young people came as tourists to a Maccabiah held in Israel but never left, and dozens of people from Kremenets used the same method. In fall 1932, authorization for 1,500 certificates was issued, and most of the training center members immigrated. The path had reopened to pioneering immigrants!

> [**Translator's Note:** A Maccabiah is a large sporting event, named for the national heroes of old, the Maccabees.]

Early 1933 marked a turning point for the movement. Hundreds of young people joined and registered in the Pioneer chapters, and training kibbutzim sprang up in Poland's towns. A "conquering detachment" from the nearby training kibbutz in Verba, which numbered more than a hundred members who worked in the local sawmill, arrived in Kremenets and settled in one of the houses in the Dubno suburb. The pioneers—men and women—would show up in town carrying saws and axes, looking for jobs: chopping wood, drawing water, or doing any kind of unskilled labor. Kremenets Jews received them well. Zionist activists and Pioneer members made an effort to help them find living quarters and work. Later, as their kibbutz enlarged and increased in numbers, they moved to a larger house in the north of town.

During 1933 and 1934, the pioneer movement in Poland grew to include many thousands of members, and thousands were in training centers. Youth groups far removed from Zionism and pioneering had joined Pioneer. The movement included members of the middle classes, laborers, and students, a very colorful mixture. The Pioneer movement occupied a central spot in Jewish community life. "Certificate" came to be a magic word for young people and many thousands of Jews. The war between parents and children was no more—now they came together, asking to be sent to a training kibbutz. In their hearts, hope was kindled that, in time, the children would get their parents to immigrate, because here, you see, everything was being undermined and falling apart—

That was the situation in most Jewish settlements in Poland, and so it was in our town. In 1933–1934, the Pioneer chapter in town had about 300 members, and the chapter in the Dubno suburb numbered a few dozen. Together with the youth movements and the League, they numbered about 1,000, a fact that became evident during elections to the Zionist Congresses (the 17th in 1933 and the 18th in 1935), in conventions, and at conferences. The town was often bustling with large pioneer conventions—public assemblies, colonies, and summer camps—all of which aroused much interest among the town's Jews.

In 1932–1938, many people emigrated from Kremenets, and they are spread all over the country: in kibbutzim, villages, cities, and other place. But a larger number were not lucky enough to emigrate. At the beginning of the war, there were dozens, maybe hundreds, of pioneers from Kremenets in the training kibbutzim, some of whom had been waiting for their turn to immigrate for five or more years. Some wandered east to the USSR during the war, and after repatriation at the end of the war, they returned and immigrated to Israel. But many perished on the roads, having been murdered— annihilated—and no one knows what happened to them.

[115]

THE FIRST GROUP OF PIONEERS

Chanokh Rokhel and Yitschak Biberman
English translation by Steven Wien and Sari Havis

In early 1921, 12 pioneers, the first group from Kremenets, immigrated to Israel. With that, sporadic, organized immigration of pioneers from our town began, including hundreds of young people and lasting until World War II. The members of the first group were (1) Avraham Biberman, (2) Yitschak Biberman, (3) Shlome Poltorak, (4) Dina Krivin, (5) Yakov Tsizin, (6) Yitschak Eydelman, (7) Bunim Bakimer, (8) Aharonov, a driver, (9) Aharonov's wife, (10) Chanokh Rokhel, (11) Yakov Raykhman, and (12) Yitschak Rokhel.

The first nine arrived on the ship *Avetsia* on February 8, 1921, and the next two on the ship *Marno* on February 20, 1921. The last to arrive was Yitschak Rokhel on April 4, 1921. Azriel Gorengut and his family arrived with the first group. Three members of the group stayed in Kremenets: (1) Katye, Dr. Meir Litvak's daughter; (2) Sime Raykhman, who got "cold feet" at the last moment; and (3) Pesach Litvak, who immigrated in 1929.

A certain number of young Zionists in Kremenets felt dissatisfied with their Zionist and community activities in the Diaspora, even though they took a very active part in them. They wanted to fulfill personally what they demanded from others: immigrate to Israel and live a life of working the land there. A few members of this group did immigrate before World War II (Moshe Biberman and Yakov Tsizin). Some were sent by their parents to study in Israel (Yitschak Eydelman to the Herzliya High School, and Avraham Rokhel to the agricultural school in Petach Tikvah). When the war ended, a large number of young people decided to immigrate at the first opportunity. Fifteen of these dozens of young people had formed a group that had decided to leave immediately, and they began preparations. A small group forced the issue: in 1919, five decided to take a chance and make their way on foot, using any possible means to get there. The town was under Bolshevik rule at that time and changed hands every so often. The group planned to walk to Bessarabia, cross the Dniester to Romania, and from there pass through Turkey to Israel. A small stream of immigrants used this path in those days; some of them were killed, some got lost, and some arrived at their destination. But in the meantime, with the final conquest by the Polish forces, the government had been stabilized, so the plan reverted to preparing for the whole group to immigrate legally.

Most of the group's meetings took place in the Biberman family's large garden. The discussions centered on the future in Israel and practical preparations for immigration. In those days, there were no separate Zionist factions in our town yet; we all belonged to the Young Zionists, and in 1918 a Young Zionist regional convention was held in our town, with Avraham Biberman as an active participant. Willingly and enthusiastically, we took on the fulfillment of Zionist ideals as something that was obvious for young, true Zionists—pioneers of immigration. That is why we called ourselves pioneers; we did not indulge much in ideological discussions of Zionism or socialism, although we had socialist tendencies and looked forward to a working life.

In Israel, most members of the first group adopted the kibbutz lifestyle, which motivated and excited us and in which we saw the pinnacle of Zionist fulfillment. This is not to say that we aimed for this lifestyle even in the Diaspora, as at that time Pioneer was just being established and its emissaries had not yet arrived in Kremenets. Our group was established on our own initiative, and we did not even name it Pioneer but rather called ourselves a group of pioneers.

[116]

What was the composition of our group? We have mentioned the names of the 15 members. Most were children of householders who had received a traditional education, so they knew Hebrew, but most had also received a general secondary education. At that time, the Zionist Organization included circles of intellectuals and householders, and the members of our group came from those. We admired the laborers and craftsmen; we aspired to form a basic, ordinary class of people in Israel. We were anxious to have real working people join us, but at that time those people were not in the area of Zionist influence. When the driver Aharonov and his wife joined us, we were very happy—we saw him as right kind of person for immigration and were sorry that he was the only laborer among us.

At our meetings, we spoke in Yiddish and Russian, but some of us were Hebrew zealots and insisted on speaking Hebrew, which then took its rightful place in our meetings and private conversations. We were greatly influenced in that matter by Yitschak Eydelman, a Herzliya High School student who had returned to Kremenets for summer vacation in 1914 and did not return because the war had started; but when we immigrated, he joined us. Our group also included most of the young community activists who gathered around the first Hebrew kindergarten in our town and other general Tarbut projects. In Israel we did not encounter difficulties in adjusting where the Hebrew language was concerned.

There was a sort of selection or a discussion about each member's fitness to join the first group and immigrate or to postpone his or her turn.

At that time, training operations were not yet established, but in the summer of 1920, two members of the group (Chanokh Rokhel and Yitschak Biberman) went on their own initiative to receive agricultural training at the Jewish farmer Itsi Kotitshiner's farm in a village about 30 kilometers from our town. They trained there for about three months. At first, it seemed peculiar to the farmer that he should employ Hirsh Mendil Rokhel's grandchildren on his farm, though he finally agreed to do it. They slept in the granary, where the non-Jewish laborers also slept. They worked at harvesting and threshing and in the cow barn, and did other work on the farm. At the end of the season, they returned home full of self-assurance, happy and "trained."

Preparations for immigration were starting. At a distance of 50 kilometers from our town is the town of Berestechko, which was famous as a Zionist town from which some people had immigrated before World War I and as soon as the war was over. Other people from there were the first in our area to immigrate. We sent our friend Yitschak Rokhel to find out what the procedure for immigration was, and he brought us encouraging information. After that, in August 1920, we sent two of our members, Chanokh Rokhel and Pesach Litvak, to Warsaw to explore the possibility of immigration. After a few weeks, they returned and told us that the Zionist Directorate had announced the suspension of mass immigration, but that there was a chance that permits would soon be given to craftsmen. Immediately, we began to acquire documents certifying that we all were craftsmen: metalsmiths, carpenters, farmers, and the like. We received letters of verification from different craftsmen, which we had notarized according to law. A second delegation, Avraham Biberman and Chanokh Rokhel, was sent to Warsaw with the documents. This made a big impression on the Palestine Bureau: a group with members who are all professional craftsmen! All our members were approved for immigration, and we started the process of obtaining passports.

[117]

At that time, this was a very complicated task, as our region was not considered part of Poland, yet was still a conquered area, so we had to obtain special assurances of our proper political standing from the police. The second hardship was obtaining visas: first a British one for entry to Israel, and then those for border crossings. A young person coming from the east was suspected of Bolshevism…. We divided the chores among us: Avraham Biberman returned to Kremenets to obtain the needed visas, organize the group, and see to financial means. Pesach Litvak and Chanokh Rokhel continued their efforts in Warsaw. We had to wait there for many months to overcome all the difficulties.

While there, we met delegates from pioneer groups from different cities and towns. At that time, Pioneer and its headquarters were being set up. With others, we participated in establishing pioneer houses at 5 Dzika Street and 10 Tverda Street, whose tenants were arrested numerous times by the Polish police. Another serious worry was subsistence for pioneers who were waiting there to immigrate. We also participated in the Palestine Bureau's work, and they demanded that we join their staff for a prolonged period and postpone our immigration. Pesach Litvak gave in to the pressure, stayed in Warsaw, and worked in that office until 1929; the other two refused, and when they had obtained the documents, they returned to Kremenets and immigrated to Israel with the group.

In connection with the first group to immigrate, a local Palestine Bureau was established in Kremenets, headed by Azriel Gorengut, with Yitschak Rokhel as his secretary. There, requests for immigration by the townspeople and others from the area were checked and approved, which the Warsaw office used as a sort of recommendation.

Raising the financial means to immigrate caused quite a few problems, as the town was poor then, and families had a hard time raising the amount needed. Nevertheless, the parents of most members helped them: one had a few gold coins left, and another took a few dollars or pounds out of his savings and gave it to his immigrating son. Some of us had saved money from our salaries, and others sold some of their belongings, but all of these were insufficient.

Then an emissary arrived from New York Kremenets Relief with money for community institutions. When he and the representatives of the institutions were negotiating the distribution of the funds, we joined the debate, and having no other way, demanded that they budget a portion for the necessities of immigration. As far as we remember, the result was that each person would receive $10—and with that, the last obstacle to our immigration was removed.

The authorities' attitude changed frequently. First, we received papers clearing us politically. Then they began suspecting and provoking us. So we left town quietly, sneaking out one January night in 1921. We took the train to Lvov and stayed there one day, exchanged our money for dollars, and continued on our way to Vienna, where we spent about 10 days until the date of the ship's departure from Trieste.

In Vienna, we found out that we had insufficient funds to purchase tickets, but we were helped by the local Palestine Bureau, and we—70 pioneers—left on the freighter *Avetsia*. We arrived on the shores of Jaffa after a 17-day voyage down the entire eastern Mediterranean coast. No food was served, and hygienic conditions were sordid, but morale was high, and there was constant singing and dancing; local Jews brought us food at the different stops along the way.

The ship stopped in Alexandria for two days. At that time, Chayim Weitzmann and Alfred Mond were there, and learning that they were to give a speech in one of the Zionist clubs, all 70 of us pioneers went to hear them. Mond spoke in English, and Weitzmann in Hebrew. He even blessed us. The Sephardic Jews of Alexandria fawned over us, showed us the town, and supplied us with food.

[118]

Then we truly arrived in Israel. On February 8, 1921, nine group members and the Gorengut family disembarked on the shore of Jaffa. We were taken to the immigrants' house in the Ajami neighborhood, and from there we moved to the immigrants' house in Tel Aviv. We stayed in Jaffa and Tel Aviv for 10 days—we were delirious.

The Federation was newly formed, and its impact was not yet felt. Most influence was in the hands of the Young Worker and Unity of Labor parties. The manager of the employment office for the Young Worker at that time was Tsvi Liberman of Nahalal, and he was the one to see that we got jobs and to arrange for us to get meals in the Young Worker restaurant on Nachalat-Binyamin Street, which was known as "Chane Mayzel's kitchen." By then we were out of money, and we needed some so we could buy stamps and laundry soap. We went to Jaffa harbor under Yakov Tsizin's advice, to the place where lumber was unloaded, and after a long argument with the Arab porters, who were strongly against us, we succeeded in "capturing" one boat loaded with lumber, unloaded it, and earned 90 cents in hard cash. We were nine men, so each one's share was 10 cents. Joyfully, we returned to the immigrant house, bought stamps and soap, and quickly wrote letters home. This was the first money we earned in Israel.

Soon after, Yehuda Kopelevits and Yisrael Shochet came to the immigrant house and told us about the work battalion named for Yosef Trumpeldor, which had just then negotiated with the British authorities to build railroad tracks on the Rosh HaAyin—Petach Tikvah line. For that purpose, the battalion formed a new detachment: the Railroad-Track-Building Detachment. They suggested that our group and the Shavli group also living in the immigrant house form this new battalion detachment. After a few discussions, we agreed to do it. A few members of our group and the Shavli group rode in freight cars by way of Lod to Rosh HaAyin with a load of tents, beds, and work tools, and on their arrival, they unloaded and set up the detachment's tent camp at the Antipatris Castle near Rosh HaAyin. A few days later, the rest of the members arrived in camp, and the paving work began. By day we worked, and at night we danced. When the last three members of our group arrived (Chanokh Rokhel, Yakov Raykhman, and Yitschak Rokhel), they joined the work battalion. Also accompanying us on the ship was Yeshayahu Fishman from Kremenets, who had immigrated from Gorokhov, where he had been living for the past few years, and with a couple of other members (Fayvishis and Tsvik), the Kremenets group—group 6 in the work battalion— then numbered 12 men. The detachment took in new members daily as singles and in groups, and soon we numbered 150. The Kremenets group made a noticeable impression in the Rosh HaAyin detachment; it was known as a group of good, disciplined workers, and its members were assigned to public roles in the detachment. Our comrade Avraham Biberman was chosen as work organizer, Chanokh Rokhel was a member of the detachment's board, and Yitschak Rokhel founded the battalion's bulletin, *MiChayeinu,* which still runs today as the bulletin of Kibbutz Tel Yosef. Not everyone in our group joined the work battalion; Aharonov settled in Jaffa and opened a metalsmith shop (after a time, he left the country), and three settled in Tel Aviv:

Yitschak Eydelman, Dine Krivin, and Yakov Tsizin. The Gorengut family settled in Haifa but later moved to Pardes Hanna and settled there as farmers.

> [**Translation Editor's Note:** The name *MiChayeinu* means "from our life."]

Our absorption into the Land was easy and rapid. We made sure to speak only Hebrew and set an example for the other groups in the battalion. We were happy in our lot and our new life in the country; it may have been the finest period in our lives.

But the days of glory did not last. A few weeks after our arrival in the Land, the May 1921 riots began.

[119]

Most members of the detachment had gone to Tel Aviv for the May 1 celebration, and with the outbreak of the riots, they were attached to Haganah troops in the Jewish neighborhoods of Jaffa. They were given pick handles as weapons. The wounded and fallen were brought to Herzliya High School, and some of our members were given the task of caring of them. It fell to Yitschak Biberman to receive the body of Y. Ch. Brener, and even today he has not overcome the shock it gave him. A few of us who stayed in Rosh HaAyin participated in the defense of Petach Tikvah.

About six or seven months after we joined the work battalion, the first split took place. The Young Worker members fell out and left, and most of the Kremenets members went with them. Some joined the building group in Tel Aviv; others went to Jenin to work in the building trade for the British army and later founded the builders' group Basalt in the city of Tiberius. The members who stayed in Rosh HaAyin were later among the founders of Kibbutz Tel Yosef.

Within a short time, the *ba'al habatishe kinder* group from Kremenets turned into good builders, plasterers, scaffolding erectors, farmers, road pavers, and layers of train tracks. But the group had disintegrated as a united entity by then, and its members had gone their own separate ways.

> [**Translator's Note:** *Ba'al habatishe kinder* is Yiddish for "householders' pampered children."]

Besides the Aharonov family, three more members of the first group left the Land in the following years: Dine Krivin, Yakov Tsizin, and Bunim Bakimer. All the rest are deeply rooted in the life of the country and have prospered. They became integrated into and completely involved in the country's bustling life and did not take the time to maintain regular ties with friends in the Diaspora. But there is no doubt that the existence of an established group that had put down roots in the country influenced the continued immigration of pioneers from our town. And, indeed, immigration continued constantly, in singles and in groups. They numbered in the hundreds, and most of them adapted well.

Such was the beginning of the immigration of pioneers from Kremenets.

THE SECOND WAVE OF PIONEERS (1921–1925)

A. Yosef
English translation by Steven Wien and Sari Havis

The first group of pioneers from our town immigrated in early 1921. Soon afterward, other members of that same group came singly. It seemed as if the town had been emptied of pioneer forces, community activists, and educators, but the pioneer movement did not stop with their immigration; it strengthened, spread, and became more cohesive. The first group's immigration had served as an example for young members who stayed home. Even though the members who had immigrated did not keep in regular contact with them, letters received by parents, siblings, and friends circulated among many others who read them, and caused waves of excitement.

In mid-1921, an official chapter of the national Pioneer organization in Poland was established in our town. It was in existence there until I immigrated in 1925 and continued to exist after that. During those years, its membership was 100–150, mostly between the ages of 17 and 20, and about a third of the members were girls. They came from all strata of the community: high school students, young laborers, craftsmen's apprentices, and businessmen's assistants. The parents of the householders were not happy to have their children associate with young people from poor families, which often caused friction between parents and children.

Local training sites did not exist in Kremenets at that time, and in 1924 members were sent to training camps in the towns of Rokitno and Klesov, where they worked in the lumber industry felling trees and in the lumber mills. As the sites could not accommodate sufficient numbers of trainees, the Kremenets chapter began to organize training in the local area in and near town. In the village of Sapanuv, they experimented with manufacturing peat in a primitive way, and they attempted other ventures, too.

[120]

During the summer, members went to Folwarki Wielkie near our town, where a few Jewish families had farms and were glad to take in the pioneers for agricultural training. During those years, about 10–15 of our members at a time were in out-of-town training kibbutzim. Here is an example: in 1922, a group of 30 students from Krakow came to our town for training. They settled in the Dubno suburb and worked in the lime-burning factory, in the brick factory, in tree cutting, and at other jobs. They stayed the summer and then left. What else did the Pioneer chapter do besides training? First of all, they recruited members to our movement, prepared them spiritually for a life of labor in Israel, and taught them the lay of the land. A few times a week there were meetings as well as lectures—based on material from Israeli and local newspapers, books, and pamphlets—on current problems in Israel, the conquest of labor, and the kibbutz way of life. Generally, the lectures were in Yiddish, but since quite a few members knew Hebrew, lectures were given in that language, too. Members who did not know Hebrew had to learn it through lessons held jointly with the Zionist Organization and given in its clubhouse. At that time, in an effort to prepare a reserve from the young, Young Pioneer was established.

Pioneers from our town immigrated in a stream of about 15–20 a year, not including people from other circles. The local chapter board would deliberate and choose candidates for immigration. The main consideration was whether the candidate had the potential to acclimate to Israel and the kibbutz. The second consideration was the candidate's character—whether he would be able to adjust and adhere to a life of labor in Israel. There were also personal considerations: seniority in Pioneer, obligation to register for the army, and others.

Group of Young Zionists, 1921

[121]

Union Party Chapter, 1925

Pioneer Board Members

[122]

The results obviously proved that the decision makers made many serious mistakes.

Deliberations on candidates for immigration were always bound up with much tension, almost as much as a matter of life and death, so, not satisfied with the immigration quota allocated to them by the center, the chapter did not sit on its hands, but looked for additional ways for members to immigrate. The chapter even attempted illegal immigration, not as an organized entity but as individuals or small groups from Pioneer.

In that period, families from Kremenets who were not pioneers also immigrated. These were middle-class families from the Dubno and Vishnevets suburbs.

What was Zionist life like in our town at that time? Besides the official Zionist Organization, a strong, active chapter of the Union Party had 100 members. They participated actively in the Sejm election and all manifestations of community life. There was also a small chapter of Labor Zionists—Left and the beginnings of the Liberty party. The Youth Guard movement had not yet made its mark. The different outlooks of the assorted Zionist factions were not sharply defined then; their members took part in many spheres of activity together, and Zionist Organization veterans helped with Pioneer activities.

YOUNG PIONEER AND PIONEER (1923–1934)

Arye Shochet, Tsvi Zeira, and Sore Bat (Yagur)
English translation by Steven Wien and Sari Havis

In 1923, Young Pioneer was established in our town to attract youngsters to the ranks of Pioneer and prevent the movement's depletion after the emigration of the adults. This came about at the initiative of Pioneer's adult members. For years, the driving force in organizing the movement's activities was comrade Manye Gurevits (now living in Haifa). At that time, the Youth Guard movement was also being established in our town, but while its members were mainly high school students—mostly children of wealthy families or the intelligentsia—most Young Pioneer members were young workers.

Young Pioneer, Kremenets, 1925

[123]

Young Pioneer, Kremenets, 1926

At its formation, the chapter already numbered about 60 boys and girls, and as time went by, its numbers reached 100 and more. Activities focused on hikes, marches, exercises, discussions, and lectures. Study groups to learn Hebrew were formed. For a while, they had their own clubhouse, where members would congregate every evening. Cultural activities included learning the geography of the Land of Israel, Zionism, Jewish history, and, most of all, about the movement and its goals, the Labor movement in Israel, and the kibbutz movement. Many adult members of the local Pioneer chapter (Eliezer Gluzman, Yisrael Otiker, and others) were a great help in these activities. Many emissaries visited us from Israel and the Pioneer center. They expressed their admiration of the pioneering spirit and liveliness of the young people in our town, and each visit brought a wave of renewed excitement. Training activities generally took place in Pioneer, but a few experiments in teaching professional crafts took place within the frame of Young Pioneer: dozens of boys were put into Frishberg's and Grinberg's factories to learn the crafts of stitching and sewing. But, generally, Young Pioneer dealt with the ideas and spiritual aspects of training.

As the young ones matured, most of them would move on to Pioneer in groups of 40–50. Parents did not object to their children joining Young Pioneer. On the contrary: they were glad to have them play, hike, sing, spend time in the fresh air, read, and develop. But when they matured and their turn came to join Pioneer and go to a training kibbutz, they encountered fierce objections from their parents. In particular, the parents objected to daughters going to training. Indeed, many sons and daughters could not withstand the parental pressure; their "pioneering" ended in Young Pioneer, and they never arrived at Pioneer. And then, with a "diploma" from the youth group, our group graduated to Pioneer. Pioneer's main concern at that time was where and how to get enough places for training.

[124]

Many were sent to Kibbutz Klesov (about 20 members from Kremenets went there, and when the kibbutz in Verba was established, about 10 members from Kremenets went there). The members of those kibbutzim endured great hardship. They experienced deprivation and hunger, but ended up stronger and ready for immigration.

In 1932–1933, there was a training kibbutz in Kremenets itself, with about 30–40 people. Few members were local; most were from out of town. The kibbutz in Kremenets enriched the pioneering look of the town. To begin with, the members lived in the Dubno suburb, but later they moved close to Ovadis's flourmill, where most of them worked. The others worked at woodcutting and any job they could get. The women also worked at housekeeping. Local members had left their parents' homes and refused to live there even on the Sabbath. They severed their ties completely from that way of life and immersed themselves in kibbutz life. Sometimes, a townswoman would be seen standing by a young man, crying and lamenting for someone from a good family who had gone to work at hard jobs befitting "the gentiles."

In those years, the Zionist movements in our town functioned under a mutual understanding. This was not the case with the Brit Trumpeldor movement, which was established in our town in 1925. Quarrels and clashes broke out from time to time between them and the Land of Israel's workers' movements. Some Pioneer members belonged to the Union Party, and others belonged to the Liberty Party. The Pioneer chapter in Kremenets was one of the most active in Poland. Standing out among the activists in the local Pioneer movement in the final years were A. Ditun in Young Pioneer (now living in Argentina), and Shayke Kapuzer and Hershil Bernshteyn in Pioneer (now living in Argentina).

Members of Pioneer of Kremenets

VERBA—A SPARK OF KLESOV

M. Belizhovski (Givat HaShlosha)
From _Book of the Pioneers_
English translation by Steven Wien and Sari Havis

In Verba, there was a spark of the former Klesov. Verba built on Klesov's "pedigree," keeping the benefits of the old tradition. It was not in vain that she was crowned with the nickname "Verba the Educator." It had a sometimes indefinable quality. True, the kibbutz in Verba was naive when it came to economics, but in contrast it possessed something like extra inspiration, a sort of modesty, and a nice way of hospitality— valuable pioneering characteristics. Singing was also essential: "Verba is a branch of the Song of Songs," as one member put it. In her singing, she was spiritually uplifting. In the winter, through the wet walls of the low, small house, and in the summer, from the yard under the blossoming cherry trees, songs were heard in the surrounding fields, and from them came consolation, hope, and elation.

Verba's members were known for being learned in Hebrew. And the members were proud of that, for they had acquired their knowledge of Hebrew after hard days of labor in the kibbutz. Anyone who did not attend classes or come to the reading room— the "mini-temple of Verba"—was looked on with shame and disgrace.

Verba struggled with the angel in charge of making a living for five years and did not give up. A few times it was abandoned, but then would return to the way it had been. Members used to mark the years by the number of times the kibbutz had been abandoned. In good days, veteran members would sit and leisurely recall the first abandonment.

Ownership of the factory also changed hands, and various farmers from nearby villages challenged the members' right to work. Nevertheless, the kibbutz continued to fight bravely and honorably for its right to work, and eventually it was given the responsibility for executing even the most important jobs. An economic crisis arose in the country and did not spare the kibbutz in Verba. There were times without work and days of unemployment. Some types of work were completely eliminated. The kibbutz membership grew smaller. It was a difficult time, but the members withstood it bravely and devoted themselves to working in the garden and with the cows and chickens, and became attached to each green stalk. Alas, in the end they were forced to see things as they really were: on the one hand, they could disperse again, with the danger of losing the land because of the imminent factory closure, and on the other hand were new possibilities, new jobs ... and plain logic said: find more secure places and better living conditions. The result was a decision to merge Verba with Bedzin.

Verba overcame its sadness and, fortified, set off on its long way.

THE KIBBUTZ IN VERBA

Sh. Zaromov
From *Book of the Pioneers*
English translation by Steven Wien and Sari Havis

A short road crossing the railroad tracks led to the kibbutz, which was housed in a Volhynia-style farmhouse. It was whitewashed and had a wooden tiled roof and small, single windows overlooking the garden. The members planted two rows of acacia trees to make the kibbutz stand out from the rest of the farmhouses on the roadside. On summer days when the trees were in bloom, it was a pleasure to feast your eyes on the sight of the green garden, the willows greening both sides of the road, and the wide fields stretching in wavelike fashion in all directions, silent and serene but for the train from Lvov, which crossed them with a harsh whistle.

[126]

Training Kibbutz in Verba, 1933

But during the fall, when the rains were bothersome, you had no choice but to tramp in the deep mud, and the women became weary of scrubbing the floors every day.

The walls were simply whitewashed. There were two long tables made of unplaned lumber with two long benches, as in the old study hall in the town, and there was a small, dark compartment for washing and shaving. The kitchen was long, dim, and uncomfortable. The member working in the kitchen had to go frequently to the well in the yard for pails of water, and in the summer, she would stumble into a fellow washing his face or his hands by the well, or drinking or reading a book. This was a real well with a bucket tied to the end of a long chain. The chain would jingle when it was used, which brought a bit of a down-home feeling to kibbutz life.

Large pumpkins grew in the well-tended garden, peeping out from between the large leaves. The cows in the barn gave enough milk. The horses, coats shining and heads held high, were neither skinny from hunger nor exhausted from hard labor. At nine in the evening, the members departed from the kibbutz: the 12 groups called out a joyful "Shalom!" to each other and left for their apartments, which were spread throughout the village.

The town of Verba sits between two large cities: Dubno and Kremenets. But Verba does not attach itself to Dubno or to the kibbutz in Kremenets, in spite of its elegant house with many rooms, veranda, and large balcony overlooking the mountains—this glorious kibbutz in Kremenets was nothing but a group whose administration squad and life came from Verba. Verba itself had a true and beautiful pioneering culture.

[127]

THE YOUTH GUARD MOVEMENT

Ayzik Hofman (Tel Aviv)
English translation by Steven Wien and Sari Havis

In 1921, Kremenets was emptied of mature Zionist youth. In two pioneer groups, one after the other, Zionist activists had left for the Land of Israel, and the younger generation remained without leadership. At the same time, rumors reached us that various Jewish youth organizations with more of a scouting nature had been established in other cities in Volhynia. And thus, on the initiative of the brothers Goldenberg, Avraham Rozenfeld, and others, an organization named Youth Guard was established in Kremenets, in which the idea of scouting and sports took a central role.

The first groups included mostly middle-class students, with a minority from the poor and blue-collar classes. The groups included young people from the ages of 8 to 15–16, and only the guides were older; among them were Avrashe Trakhtenberg, Shifris, and others. Another founder of the core of this movement was a youth from Rovno named Bushl, who was an outstanding athlete. The nucleus of this movement participated in activities for the national funds as well as various cultural performances. During that time, an instructor named Chane Horovits, who had come to our town from Russia, joined Youth Guard. After that, the movement became more ideological, and local headquarters contacted the national Youth Guard center in Warsaw. Various classes were offered in Hebrew history, Zionism, Hebrew and Yiddish literature, the geography of the Land, and the like. On every Hebrew holiday, parties and dances took place. Gradually, Youth Guard in our town was transformed from a scouting movement to one with more ideological, national, and humanist content. The energy attracted young people in Kremenets, and they began joining the ranks of Youth Guard. Within the first few years of the movement's existence, the local leaders in Kremenets had already initiated several regional conventions.

Unlike other youth movements, Youth Guard included young people from a very young age; even eight-year-olds were drawn to intensive activities, and thus they were somewhat distanced from the influence of the family and non-Jewish school. This movement departed from its counterparts culturally in that it was more religious about the acquisition of Hebrew. Activities were conducted in Yiddish or Russian, and later in Polish, but nonetheless, the guides paid attention to teaching Hebrew. They purchased and read Hebrew newspapers from the Land, and some movement members were active in our town's Hebrew Corner.

At the legislative conference in Warsaw in 1926, Youth Guard was officially transformed from a scouting movement like Baden-Powell's to a program of immigration, personal fulfillment, and establishment of communes in the Land. The Kremenets representatives were quite involved in that convention. At the same time, the following members participated in leading the home chapter: Meir Pinchuk (who later became active in the Communist movement and was killed in the Caucasus), Moshe Krementsutski (who now lives in Ramat Gan), Yonye Bernshteyn (who also joined the Communists and was killed as a partisan near Kremenets), Duvid Vinokur (who was killed in Kremenets in the Holocaust), and the writer of these lines. The movement's national leadership regarded the Kremenets chapter with great respect and gave it a great deal of attention. Messengers from the national center, as well as from the Land, used to visit it quite often. Among them were Y. Chazan, Y. Guthelf, Ts. Luria, M. Shenhavi, and others. Y. Riftin stayed in Kremenets for almost a month and conducted extensive cultural activities.

In 1926, the first group left the Youth Guard chapter for training in Dubrovitsa, near Semiatyche. The group included five people: Krementsutski, Hofman, Yonye Bernshteyn, Avraham Margalit, and Sunye Keselman. (The latter two immigrated to the Land, then fought in the international brigade in Spain and were killed there.)

[128]

Group of Young People from the Youth Guard Chapter, 1928

This marked a very important turning point toward personal fulfillment. The members were in training for almost a year. After that, almost yearly, groups would leave for training, mostly in lumber mills near Stolin, Rokitno, and other locations using a specific framework established by the Youth Guard movement.

The movement's members were also active in the town's public life. The group kept a certain distance from other "working" Land of Israel youth groups in the town (such as

Pioneer, Young Pioneer, the Union Party, and Liberty). But there was no sense of animosity among them. Whenever members of any youth group immigrated to Israel, members of all the groups accompanied them to the train station, and this was a festive event for all Zionist youth regardless of their movement. Cultural activity centered mostly on the Zionist library; Youth Guard members formed part of its main clientele. At its peak, the movement consisted of 200 boys and girls.

Most parents objected to their children joining Youth Guard because it interfered with their studies. But mostly the parents became upset when a young person graduated from Youth Guard and the movement asked him to interrupt his high school studies for training.

A competing wave of communism attacked the movement's centers beginning in 1925, reaching our town only between 1929 and 1931. The limited chances of immigration, the White Paper decree, and other factors made some members of the movement desperate. Also, ideological training began to lean more toward the Soviet Union. All these factors led several members to join the Communist Party. Many dropped the movement, but some Youth Guard members remained even after joining the communist movement, with the clear intention of spreading propaganda for communism (one of them was Tonye Grinshpun, who later immigrated to Israel. From there she went to the USSR and was killed in one of Stalin's purges in 1937). This defection affected mostly the older generation and instructors. Some who went to Israel joined the Communist Party there. Some left Israel. Of those who remained in Kremenets, some became leaders of the town's Communist Party, as well as active in trade unions. Several were arrested by the Polish authorities.

[129]

Group of Youth Guard Members, 1930

Bottom row, right to left: (1) Meir Pinchuk, (2) Rachel (Koka) Otiker**Error! Bookmark not defined.**, (3) Moshe Kremenchutski, (4) Polye Bernshteyn, (5) Efraim Teper. Middle row: (1) Sunye Keselman, (2) Perel, (3) Munye Mandelblat, (4) Rosye Sudak, (5) Ayzik Hofman, (6) Rachel Otiker, (7) Ite .... Top row: (1) Yonye Bernshteyn, (2) Duvid Vinokur, (3) Sonye Landsberg, (4) Avraham Landsberg.

Group of Youth Guard Members, 1934

[13]

In a long trial against the communists in 1936, quite a few of the defendants were Youth Guard graduates. Indeed, the chapter's younger set was mainly spared this digression toward communism. But when their instructors left for Israel, the movement's center was careful to bring in a new class of instructors who had been inducted at the center's training kibbutz in Czestochowa.

The club was used as the movement's permanent location only during the winter months; in the summer, all activities and meetings took place outdoors.

In 1936–1937, the movement continued to dwindle in numbers. There was a rise in anti-Semitism, desperation settled on everyone, immigration to Israel was almost completely closed off, and there was a sense of reaching a dead end. All this affected Youth Guard, and it declined from year to year in quantity and quality. In 1938–1939, the movement consisted of only a few dozen members. Even then, there were ten members from the Kremenets group in the Czestochowa training group.

With the capture of the town by the Russians in 1939, the end of the Youth Guard movement arrived, and it ceased to exist.

ACADEMIC PIONEER

Sh. Taytelman (Jaffa)
English translation by Steven Wien and Sari Havis

Side by side with the large, flowing rivers of the Pioneer and Young Pioneer movements in our town trickled the small stream of Academic Pioneer. It included only a few dozen young people, but, still, it fulfilled a certain role in the Zionist life of Kremenets.

[**Translator's Note:** In Hebrew, Academic Pioneer is *Hechaluts haAkademi.*]

A group of friends who, for assorted reasons, did not find a place in Pioneer established a chapter of Academic Pioneer in 1932. To begin with, there were only about 15 members, but in time the membership grew to 40. Their goal in particular was to bring in the town's assimilated youth and familiarize them with Zionism and the Land of Israel. And, indeed, their efforts had quite a bit of success, as dozens returned and rejoined their people. Academic Pioneer existed in Poland as a national movement, with a center in Warsaw, a publication in Polish, and a training site in Czestochowa.

The chapter dealt with intellectual preparation and dissemination of the Hebrew language.

Considering the circle's composition, you would have expected it to prepare members for "white-collar" and clerical professions in Israel, but that was not the case. Just like regular Pioneer, Academic Pioneer's goal was to train members to work the land and for kibbutz life. Some members were sent to the training ranch in Czestochowa, and some of the girls, to the Girls' Agricultural Training Farm in Nahalal, Israel. More than two thirds of the chapter members immigrated and settled in Israel.

The chapter was active in local community life, too: in elections, work on behalf of funds, the Zionist club, and the library. It helped with the trusteeship of the orphanage and was active in all Zionist and community work. The chapter had its own clubhouse, where it held cultural activities.

Of the active members, I will mention Shmuel Gendelman, Yone Frenkel (both were murdered in the Holocaust), Yehoshue Goldberg (now in Poland), Yakov Shats, Charash, and the writer of these lines (the latter three are in Israel).

Academic Pioneer existed in our town until World War II began.

[131]

EDUCATION AND CULTURE

MASTERS AND RABBIS

Tovye Troshinski (Tel Aviv)
English translation by Thia Persoff

> A memorial candle to my sisters Chaye and Chane, their husbands Shlome Tsipes and
> Yakov Barshap, and their children Hershele, Gutele, and Niunile, who perished in
> Kremenets, killed by the Nazis.

Kremenets was not the town of my birth.

The storm of blood and death that passed through Ukrainian towns during 1919 and 1920 uprooted our family from a small, remote town in the outer reaches of Volhynia. There were hard times when vigilante troops of Ottomans, "Batkas," and plain marauding brigands descended on us. After our house was burned and our meager property destroyed, my father found a job in Kremenets and moved our family there. I was then ten years old.

I did not live in Kremenets for very many years. In 1928 I left, and since then I have visited only once, in the final days of winter in 1940, for a short, hasty two-day visit ... eager to continue my wanderings through the towns and villages of Russia, the steppes of Uzbekistan, and the Caucasus. When the flood of bloodshed ceased, after many hard journeys through the foul murderers' lands, I reached my longed-for shore.

I lived in Kremenets for only seven years. I met her in my childhood and left her in my youth. It was the first station on the road of my life, seven years blessed with childhood memories and experiences of my youth. They were good years that never lost their value and charm! I do not see myself as a transient guest there, but as bone of the bone and flesh of the flesh of the holy community of Kremenets. Seven souls, so dear to me, perished in Kremenets at the hand of the foul murderer. As one of your sons, I carry your sacred memory in my heart. Here I will unearth some of my buried memories of the town of my youth.

A. ESTABLISHMENT OF THE FIRST HEBREW SCHOOL

I will relate here the struggles of Hebrew education devotees to establish a Hebrew school in Kremenets. The fact is, for almost ten years, the Hebrew school fought hard to exist, having no proper housing or necessary tools for learning. It had to move from one place to another almost every year. For a few years, it resided in the Zionist Organization's clubhouse, near the post office building on Sheroka Street. This house had four average-sized rooms and was a sort of a "spiritual center" for Kremenets Jews. The library and reading room and the kindergarten were here, and this was where meetings and gatherings of youth groups and Zionist organizations took place.

[132]

In time of need, that is where the Hebrew school found shelter. Since the number of rooms could not accommodate all the classes, the school had to operate in two sessions.

Only in 1928 was the school moved to a permanent home—one built specifically for it on the Dilovoy-Dvor lot in Kremenets. The official school principal who was responsible to the authorities was Mr. Barats, who served as government-appointed rabbi in Kremenets. In actuality, Mr. Yakov Shafir, who lives here with us, took care of and responsibility for the continued functioning of the school. I see it as my duty to mention with blessing the Hebrew and Jewish studies teacher, Yakov Vayner, a learned, genial and humble man. He immigrated to Israel and he passed away there.

About 200 pupils were educated in that Hebrew school.

B. TALMUD TORAH AND SMALL YESHIVA

This institution, which so shaped our spiritual-moral character throughout our Diaspora lands that one can hardly describe the Jewish communities in Lithuania, Poland, and Ukraine without it, obviously existed in Kremenets, too. I cannot estimate the number of children who studied there during the 1920s, the time I write about here. I do know for certain, though, that the number was higher than the number attending the Hebrew school. Not only did Orthodox parents, followers of the Torah laws and traditions, send their children to the Talmud Torah, but all the children of poor families who went to the free Polish public schools also attended because of the compulsory education law. Also, many Hebrew school students whose parents did not deem the religious studies in the public school sufficient went there in the afternoon to study and increase their knowledge. In the Talmud Torah, students were divided into classes according to their knowledge, each class having its own regular teacher, starting with the teacher of the youngest to the one who taught Gemara and commentaries. When you walked in the street close to the Talmud Torah, you would hear the loud voices of the younger children from afar as they read in unison from the prayer book, diligently pronouncing each syllable, and the teacher even louder, leading them; or the pleasant melodies of the 11- and 12-year-old Gemara boys as they repeated the lessons they learned from their teacher. Sometimes your ear would catch a single voice singing a commentary or reading verses from the Book of Proverbs, once from the book and then translating it into Yiddish. I do not know what happened to the Talmud Torah after I left Kremenets. I was told that this institution became a highly important pedagogical instrument when Arye Feldman, of blessed memory, the dearest of men, began teaching there and greatly elevated the level of study and the school's prestige.

C. TEACHERS

I learned Torah from three teachers in the Talmud Torah in Kremenets: Rabbi Shmuel "the Small," Rabbi Shmuel "the Big," and Rabbi Yosl Berger.

Rabbi Shmuel "the Small" taught Pentateuch and Rashi. He was short and black-bearded, and his face reflected goodness. He described the sad stories in the Torah to us so well, in a musical voice, half words, half sighs and groans: the death of Rachel, Joseph confessing his identity to his brothers, the death of Moses. His voice was heartwarming when he described Rachel's crying and weeping for her children in the Diaspora. His eyebrows twisted in a frown when describing Judah speaking harshly to Joseph for framing and falsely charging Benjamin, as Rashi explained it. Together with his pupils, he rejoiced when the tragic episode ended happily; a heavy weight was lifted from our hearts; we were relieved, and so was he ....

> [**Translator's Note:** Rashi is an abbreviation for Rabbi Shlome Yitschak, a leading Bible and Talmud commentator of the 11th century.]

[133]

Rabbi Shmuel, the Gemara teacher, was called "the Big" not just because he was tall, but because he was an expert in Talmud and a *posek*. This was told to us by Rabbi Damta Senderovits, of blessed memory, who came twice a month on Thursdays to test us in Gemara studies. He was the complete opposite of the Pentateuch and Rashi teacher: slim, tall, and white-bearded, with bright, sharp eyes. In a dry voice, he would explain a complicated problem in the Gemara, and like a hard taskmaster, would not leave you but would demand exacting answers to the statements of the dissenting teachers and sages. He called the best students "goyim"—"Goyim"! What will become of you? Just "goyim" and not more ....

> [**Translation Editor's Note:** *Posek* means "arbiter" or "decider," especially a rabbinical scholar who pronounces in disputes and questions of Jewish law.]

Rabbi Yosef Berger, the Bible, penmanship (in Yiddish, obviously), and arithmetic teacher, was a handsome man with a round, short beard, elegant dress, and meticulous conduct. We liked his Bible lessons very much. His voice was pleasant, and he had a separate melody to fit each of the holy books; a melody for the Book of Proverbs was not right for the Book of Ecclesiastes, and the trilling of Psalm verses did not fit the polemic chapters in the Book of Job. What is more, he had a different melody for each prophet in the Books of the Prophets. The verses he read were clear and well pronounced; it was a pleasure to sit and listen to God's living words rising in chants and melodies.

Old Rabbi Senderovits, who came to test our Torah knowledge, was not healthy in his older years and would have coughing attacks. I remember that one Thursday, being in a good mood after testing a few pupils, he asked me what was being taught in Hebrew school. One subject I mentioned was Jewish history (*Short Chronicles of Israel*, by Dubnov). "Well, tell me something from this history—let's hear it," said the rabbi. I stood in front of him and recited, verbatim, a chapter from the history of the Jewish people. When I came to a section that quoted a few sentences from the Bible, which started, as usual, with the words "The Torah tells us ...," the rabbi stopped me with a forceful hand movement, spitefully repeated "the Torah tells ... the Torah tells ...," and began to cough harshly. I did not know what I had said to cause this anger in the old rabbi and stood there as if I had been rebuked. After the rabbi left, uttering, "the Torah tells ... the Torah tells ...," the good "small" Rabbi Shmuel came to me, held my chin, and said, "Our Torah does not tell, my son! Torah you study. Remember my son, Torah—it is a *torah*, and she needs to be studied.

[**Translator's Note:** The Hebrew word *torah* means "doctrine," "laws," or "dogma."]

The old rabbi died in the 1920s. May this righteous man's memory be blessed.

The institutions of the Talmud Torah and small yeshiva existed until the Holocaust arrived. What happened to our teachers? Who passed from this earth in peace, and who died a martyr at the hand of the German beasts of prey? I do not know.

May the memory of our Jewish shepherds and teachers be sanctified and blessed!

[134]

JEWISH PRIMARY SCHOOL

Motye Kornits (Jerusalem)
English translation by Thia Persoff

At the end of the 1890s, there still was no school of commerce or high school in Kremenets. The town had two schools established by the government: one was a Russian primary school, meant mainly for Christian children and a limited number of Jewish children. The other one was meant for Jewish boys only, according to a yearly quota set by the Volhynia provincial ministry in Zhitomir.

The classes in this school were not called classes, for reasons unknown to me, but groups and grades. In all there were two groups and three grades in the Jewish school, which meant five years of schooling. As many as 150 pupils attended. The teaching staff consisted of three men, and the school principal was Moisey Borisovits Goldfarb, who served for many years and was highly respected by the students. The school was free, but this does not mean that the czar's government was benevolent to its Jewish citizens; the school was supported by taxes on kosher meat, which were levied only on Jews. Thanks to the teachers, the standard of learning in the school was very high. During my time, the first and second groups were taught by the goodhearted and calm Mr. Boym.

M. B. Goldfarb served as the Russian language teacher for all three grades. He was an excellent man and a good pedagogue. The students feared but also respected him. He was known for his love of the Russian tongue and its literature.

Government Primary School for Jews

Teaching mathematics, geography, history, and calligraphy was Mr. Shklovin. He was an excellent pedagogue and mathematician. His pupils were filled with awe for him. Mr. Shklovin was a music teacher, too, and instilled the love of music in the pupils.

[135]

I remember when he auditioned two groups and three departments to form a 20-member choir. I was one of the blissful ones chosen for the choir, which began performing just a few weeks later. Shklovin taught us to sing only popular Russian songs. Some of the choir members, such as Polye Shkurnik and Asher Manusovits, had very good voices.

Near the school was a library with about 1,000 books—quite large for those days—mostly books by Russian authors, but also some classical literature translated from other languages. The pupils showed interest in the books and read with ardor.

Each year, a new class graduated. Of them, I will mention Meir Goldring, Bozye Landsberg, my dear brother Ayzik, Zanvil Batler, Leyb Rozental, Volodye Shvartsman (who committed suicide in 1901), Shlome Fishman, Grishe Milshteyn, Yitschak Barbak, and many more; they were great young people, the pride of the school and the teachers.

SCHOOL OF COMMERCE

Moshe Shnayder (Rechovot)
English translation by Thia Persoff

The memory of Kremenets' School of Commerce is strongly tied to the names of two community activists: Mikhael son of Duvid Shumski, a member of the City Council, and Yisrael Margalit, who founded it in 1906.

162

Until that time, the Jewish primary school was the only institution disseminating a general education to Jewish young people in the town. Each year, most of the students in the graduating class wanted to continue their education, but at that time, who would dare leave town, even for the nearest town, to continue his studies? For one thing, it was financially prohibitive; also, the "numbers quota" did not permit it. Getting a degree as an assistant pharmacist was a bold dream. Only a few students, the most talented and industrious, dared to do it. And occasionally they earned a diploma externally.

To begin with, the founders set themselves two objectives: (1) to create a financial reserve and (2) to purchase a suitable building. Their energy and devotion helped them achieve their goal; by charging an "entrance donation" for students of well-to-do families in our town and others, they accumulated a large reserve fund. This enabled them to accept a number of poor Jewish and Russian students and to purchase a nice building with an original turret projecting between the mountains and surrounded by a lovely grove. Before two years had gone by, this modest building was transformed into a large one with two stories housing corresponding classes, physics and chemistry laboratories, a library, a concert hall, and all the equipment necessary for a well-appointed, modern high school.

Special attention was paid to assembling a teaching staff with high pedagogic standards, particularly among liberals and progressives. Yakov Vasilyevits Yarotski, a talented and experienced pedagogue, was appointed to head the teaching staff as school principal. His assistant was the art teacher, the artist Timofey Alekseyevits Safonov, who devoted his time and being to the schoolchildren; he was like a father to them, unifying them into one family regardless of differences in nationality or race, Jewish, Russian, or Polish. I do not remember even one complaint about being called "Zhid," while in the public school, for example, the term was in widespread use.

[136]

The program of study had high standards. Could any student who attended that school ever forget Yakov Yarotski's wonderful lessons in history and political economics? And Nikolay Nivirovits's chemistry lessons and lessons about the Mendeleyev system, and the work in the chemistry lab under his guidance? These people transformed their admiring students' spirits, encouraged their desire to learn, enlivened the subjects of study, and widened their listeners' horizons. The founders and supervisors (from the parents' council), Mr. Shumski and Mr. Margalit, who ensured cooperation with the school's pedagogic board and did all they could to balance the budget, will also remain in our memories. Many young people from poor homes acquired an education at this institution.

The first and second graduating classes brought much praise: a generation of young members of the intelligentsia who continued their studies and earned degrees as engineers, physicians, economists, mathematicians, and the like.

HOW A HEBREW SHELTER FOR THE NEEDY WAS ESTABLISHED OVERNIGHT

Pesach Litvak (Tel Aviv)
English translation by Thia Persoff

In 1919 or early 1920, after Kremenets had been cut off from the world and undergone a change of government, two American Jews, emissaries from the Joint organization, came to Kremenets wearing uniforms and carrying a pouch filled with money to help needy Jews in our town. Mr. Moshe Eydis, a well-known pharmacist and community activist, was put in charge of the money, a community committee was established, and widespread Joint activities immediately began.

At that time, there was a shelter for children in town that had been established by the Bund organization, and obviously it was on the list of institutions to benefit from the Joint's support in money, clothes, and food. At that time, there was also a Hebrew kindergarten in town run by the teacher Mrs. Verthaym, which was morally supported by a group of young people from the Young Zionists, who were dedicated to Hebrew education. We, too, approached the Joint's board, requesting a budget for the Hebrew kindergarten so that we could enlarge it and attract the children of the poor, who could not afford to pay the high tuition. Our request was denied, saying that the children in our school came from wealthy families that did not need financial support and that the Joint did not open new institutions. We immediately announced that a Hebrew shelter for poor children existed beside the kindergarten and that we had come to request financial support for it. The board accepted this, and a date was set for them to visit the shelter; then they would decide in the form and the amount of the support.

We left the meeting encouraged, but where was this shelter? We had no choice but to set it up within two to three days, no matter what! We divided the tasks among us. That day, we managed to acquire some money and rented an apartment. We moved in some furniture that we took from the kindergarten—here was a shelter.

The next day we began to register children. I was charged with finding teachers. I went to the district's Tarbut center in the city of Rovno and demanded two kindergarten teachers for Kremenets immediately. Eventually, I received an address for one teacher, named, Rachel Kit from Lutsk, who "surely will not go, as she was promised to another place; besides, she does not want a job, etc., etc. ...." After much effort, I located her and began coaxing her, demanding that she come immediately to save Zionism, the new generation, and the Hebrew language. After a long discussion and many arguments, she accepted and packed her belongings, and we left directly from her room to take the train to Kremenets. We arrived at night, and having no choice, I brought her to the home of Mrs. Verthaym, our kindergarten teacher, and introduced the new teacher who was moving to our town.

[137]

The next morning, our board met, and the new teacher came with us. We were all very young then (including Avraham Biberman, Chanokh Rokhel, and others), and I announced the success of my mission to them. In the meantime, the apartment for shelter was secured, a second teacher was "borrowed" temporarily from the "wealthy" kindergarten, and ... the shelter was established! The Joint acknowledged the shelter and found it deserving of its support. Our happiness was boundless.

A short time later, I left Kremenets, went to Warsaw, and from there immigrated to Israel. But the institution that we established with such enthusiasm lasted a long time, and generations of poor youngsters from our people were educated there in Zionism and Hebrew.

This was the spirit that permeated and moved the Zionist youth society, which was zealous about and devoted to the Hebrew culture. Today most of the members are with us in Israel.

TARBUT SCHOOL

Yehuda Kenif (Tel Aviv)
English translation by Thia Persoff

Modern Hebrew education in Kremenets did not start with the establishment of the Tarbut Primary School in 1928 or the Tarbut High School in 1922. Private and semipublic Hebrew educational institutions existed in town many years before then. Two teachers, Mr. Burshteyn and Mr. Sirayski, established a Hebrew school that existed continuously until World War I. Even before this, there was a progressive cheder, possibly the first educational institution in town where the study of the Hebrew language had an important place in the curriculum at a time when study of holy books took precedence over all others. For few years, the author Asher Beylin taught at the progressive cheder in Kremenets. He was the first to introduce the "Hebrew-in-Hebrew" teaching method and truly to teach the grammar and syntax of the language. At that time, some other teachers of Hebrew taught individuals and small groups, mainly in well-to-do households. Among them was Aharon Shimon Shpal, whose home was the first Hebrew-speaking home.

During World War I, many refugees from surrounding towns poured into Kremenets. For them and for the local poor, in 1916 the Joint established two primary schools, where the students also were served hot meals. One school had the teacher Mr. Shpal as principal, and the other had the government-appointed rabbi Sh. Barats as principal. Russian and Yiddish were the languages used in both schools, but Hebrew was taught, too. At that time, no community body existed to demand or take on the burden of maintaining it.

After Mr. Shpal immigrated to the USA, Mr. Gibelbank was appointed principal. He was an active member of the Bund organization and a staunch Yiddishist. Under his influence, Hebrew language studies were completely eliminated, and all lessons were in Yiddish only. From then on, the school began to lose its worth and value to the Jewish community, the number of students increasingly diminished, and in 1922 it was closed. The second school, under Sh. Barats, was basically Zionist and was already called Tarbut by the community, even though it was not a branch of the Tarbut School network. The teachers in this school were Y. Shafir, Dr. B. Landsberg, Chanokh Rokhel (until he immigrated to Israel), Azriel Gorengut, Y. Vayner, Finkelshteyn, and others. All were active members of the Zionist Organization in town. This school was the nucleus for the Tarbut Hebrew High School that was established in 1922.

[138]

The Kremenets Hebrew kindergarten, which existed for years, should be mentioned here, too. It was established during World War I on the initiative of few Zionist women and a group of Zionist youth, and was run and taught by the teacher Yente Verthaym.

All these are mentioned as background to the establishment of the Tarbut School. I am unable to give a full report on the history of Hebrew education in Kremenets, as I lived there for only 12 years, from 1922 until I immigrated to Israel in 1934. For that reason, I will write only about the Tarbut Primary School and the Hebrew movement in general at that time.

Tarbut Board Members and Faculty (1930)

Bottom right—school building; *bottom center*—students. *Top row*—committee members: (1) Y. Vayner, (2) Y. Kenif, (3) Dr. Z. Sheynberg, (4) Ts. Gilrant, (5) Dr. Landsberg, (6) Z. Barshap, (7) M. Karsh. *Middle row*—faculty: (1) Sh. Germarnik, (2) Z. Baytler, (3) F. Baytler, (4) A. Katsner, (5) M. Zelinger, (6) R. Fishman, (7) Ch. Shpigl, (8) Y. Otiker (school secretary).

When I came to Kremenets in 1922, the Tarbut Hebrew High School had four preparatory grades and two classes. The principal was Dr. Ben-Tsion Katz (son of R' Meshulam Katz, one of the original Lovers of Zion members).

Throughout its existence, the high school suffered from a tight budget; from a lack of teachers, textbooks, and other tools of learning; and mostly from persecution by the Polish government, which schemed and devised obstacles to its growth and existence in general. Tarbut activists in the town, knowing that before long they would not be able to withstand the heavy pressure and keep the high school open under those conditions, tried to get a permit for a primary school that would impart a Hebrew education while drawing from a larger portion of the population. Their efforts met with success, and in 1928 the high school was closed, and in its place the Tarbut Hebrew Primary School opened.

[139]

Tarbut School Students

[**Translator's Note:** The inscription on the photo reads "Tarbut School of Kremenets."]

The branch of the town's Tarbut organization officially owned the school. It had dozens of members—sometimes a hundred and more—paying monthly dues. It held general meetings, elections to the board, and so on. Truthfully, it was a very loose-knit organization, and in practice the weight of the Hebrew educational project was shouldered by a group of dedicated workers and parents, who elected representatives to the Tarbut administration. Since the Tarbut chapter did not run other activities except to support the school, there was actually unity between the school administration and the Tarbut chapter.

Undoubtedly, the general tendency among the intellectuals and common people in town was clearly Zionist. Nevertheless, most parents preferred to send their children to Polish schools, reasoning that, for one, a Polish education would ensure a good future.

For another, the Polish public schools were tuition free. The Tarbut proponents had to go against the tide and recruit students for a Hebrew education. For that purpose, they started a broad publicity campaign, but eventually the school itself was its own source of publicity. The Hanukah and Purim parties held in the school, which were considered a festive cultural happening in town, attracted big crowds and brought additional groups into the circle of Hebrew education.

The school opened in a four-room house built specifically for that purpose by Moshe Shnayder (a Tarbut activists). Two years later, a second building to house the whole school was added at the same location.

[140]

Three classes were offered first, with 12–15 pupils per class. Later, as the number of students increased, more classes were added, until there were seven. In peak years more than 200 students were enrolled.

Throughout its existence, the school was blessed with good, dedicated teachers. Its first principal was Dr. Mordekhay Zelinger (at the time of writing, he is principal of a school in Givatayim, Israel). After him, Mr. Goldberg served as principal (he now teaches in Kibbutz Yagur, Israel). Mr. Zaytsik was the last principal (he perished in Kremenets). Of the teachers, I will mention Mr. Katsner, Yakov Shafir (he is now principal of a school in Tel Aviv), Mr. Zanvil Betler and Fanye Betler, Mrs. Holander, Mrs. Farber, and others. Most of the teachers instilled a spirit of devotion to Zion and Hebrew in their students. In addition to their regular work at school, the teachers volunteered their free time to organize traditional Hanukah and Purim parties, which were mostly held in the Lyceum's auditorium. Most devoted to the task was the teacher Fanye Betler, who was gifted with a strong sense of organization and public spirit. It was she who established the Women's Tarbut Society and was active in other areas of Zionist community life in town (such as the annual bazaar for the National Fund and the like). She was a prominent figure in the school—a born pedagogue who was beloved by her young students. In 1935, she visited Israel. While there, she tried to raise money for the Tarbut School among Kremenetsers there but was not successful.

Generally, the teaching faculty worked with the administration/governing body of the school—the Tarbut organization—in harmony and with mutual respect, but sometimes there was friction. One day in 1932, a teachers' strike began, but with the intervention of the supervisor from the Tarbut center, it was settled, and peace returned. Both sides resumed functioning in cooperation and dedication. It should be said that in spite of the constant financial hardship, the school administration understood the need to pay the teachers a decent salary.

Throughout its existence, the school struggled with budget problems. Tuition could not cover expenses unless it was raised to a very high 5 guldens per month, a sum that was beyond the ability of many parents to pay. It should be noted, though, that some parents who were devotees of Tarbut committed to paying five times the tuition. Other sources of income were the monthly dues of Tarbut chapter members and the budget allotted by the City Council, which was received after solicitation by the Jewish City Council members. Plays and celebrations brought in some money, as did a $50-a-month donation by Mr. William Zaltsman and Mr. Yitschak Gilman from Tarbut supporters in the USA. Mr. W. Zaltsman visited Kremenets in 1927 on family business, and when he was told about the school's budget troubles, he took it upon himself to ensure a monthly endowment, which he continued for 12 years until the outbreak of World War II. Both are deserving of blessings.

From time to time, the local newspaper announced a call for volunteers to help the school.

Who were the community activists who took on the Tarbut education project? Until 1927, it was Mr. Gilirant, chairman of the Tarbut chapter. After him, this role was given to me, and after I immigrated to Israel, Mr. Aba Taytelman took over. Some of the devoted proponents were Dr. Zalman Sheynberg, Dr. Binyamin Landsberg, Zeydi Perlmuter, Meir Goldring, Yakov Vayner, Aleksander Frishberg, and Moshe Shnayder. Later they were joined by Mr. Tsvi Barshap, and from the young, Yisrael Otiker (today he is a member of Kibbutz Na'an, Israel), who later worked as the school secretary. I would like to point out the blessed work of Tsvi Barshap from the Dubno suburb, a man of the people with a gentle soul and a serious, sympathetic attitude toward Hebrew education.

[141]

He functioned in a very difficult area: among the suburb's people, most of whom had little interest in Hebrew culture. Nevertheless, he succeeded in instilling a positive attitude toward Hebrew education in the neighborhood and brought dozens—maybe hundreds—of students under the wings of the national education program. Out of his own pocket, he paid tuition for many students whose parents could not afford it. May his memory be blessed. Favorably remembered, too, is Mr. Yakov Vayner, one of the top people among the Tarbut proponents. He immigrated to Israel and passed away after some time there.

From time to time, representatives chosen by the parents joined this group of activists, which bore responsibility for the school. The members of this group worked hard, but they saw fine results: a multitude of young people received spiritual and practical training in Zionism and the Land of Israel, and later they formed the core of the town's youth groups and Pioneer organization.

Tarbut School Board and Faculty Members with Benjamin Weinberg, Representative of Relief from America

We had strong organizational and educational ties to the Tarbut center in Warsaw. From time to time, the center sent representatives and supervisors to visit us: Tsvi Zohar, Moshe Gordon, Rozenhek (the three of them are now in Israel), and others. They gave lectures, which were open to the public, on Tarbut and instructed members and teachers in their work. We received a great deal of help particularly from Rozenhek, the educational supervisor, who knew how to arbitrate between the administration and the teachers. He helped raise public awareness, encouraging and advancing the project.

****

Despite all these efforts, only some of the town's Jewish children attended the Tarbut School. Where were all the rest of them—the majority—educated? Two hundred children studied at the Talmud Torah, which was strictly for boys and offered a religious education. It was supported by the Jewish Community Council and assorted donations and was supervised and influenced by the town's rabbis, who taught there. It had good teachers and high standards. The ORT vocational school had many young students—boys and girls—who received vocational training in assorted fields.

[142]

This school was considered a stronghold of the town's Yiddishists. There were a few cheders, too, but their imprint was not seen in the young generation's education.

Actually, most Jewish children in town went to the Polish primary schools, where tuition was free. For Jewish pupils, a few hours a week were allotted to religious studies. In those lessons, they learned something about Judaism and a bit of Hebrew. Children from religious homes attended the Talmud Torah in the afternoon, and some received private lessons in Hebrew. But the majority grew up without a real knowledge of Judaism or Hebrew. There were three high schools in town, all using the Polish language: the Lyceum, which accepted a small number of Jewish students; a Polish high school, in which there were considerable numbers of Jews; and a Jewish-Polish high school. This institution was supported by a particular group of Jewish activists and came to replace the High School of Commerce that had existed during the Russian regime, even being housed in the same building.

This is the general background on the education received by the town's Jewish children. From this, one can understand why the Zionist organizations were so anxious to create and develop the Tarbut School.

Hebrew kindergartens did not exist continuously in those days. Every now and then, a private kindergarten would open, but it would close after a while, until the next effort. Mrs. Chane Horovits-Goldenberg ran one of those kindergartens for a short time. In 1930, the local Tarbut chapter opened a Hebrew kindergarten and brought an experienced teacher from the city of Rovno, but this effort did not succeed either, mainly for lack of money.

In 1938, the Tarbut proponents decided to work for a higher level of Hebrew education and to reopen a Tarbut high school as well as a primary school, and announced plans for a new building for that purpose. Those plans never materialized—in the meantime, World War II began.

The Tarbut proponents immersed themselves in maintaining the school and did not take time for other Hebrew language and cultural activities, such as encouraging people to speak Hebrew, providing adult education and enrichment, disseminating Hebrew books and newspapers, and so on. All those activities were taken on by the Union Party, Youth Guard, and Pioneer. Those groups as well as the general Zionist Organization held Hebrew and advanced studies courses. They instilled knowledge and speaking of the Hebrew language among their members. Lectures in Hebrew were common in youth organizations. I have to say again that many of them were Tarbut graduates, and they were the ones to keep the flame of the Hebrew language alive. The Tarbut chapter helped young people by letting them use the school's rooms for cultural functions and parties.

The Tarbut people in town did fine, dedicated educational work. According to all signs, it would have broadened and reached a higher level, but fate decreed differently.

[143]

THE HEBREW CORNER

Yisrael Otiker
English translation by Thia Persoff

Even as children, we grew up in a communal and educational atmosphere that stimulated us to be involved in political activities. Echoes of the Russian Revolution had penetrated our world and filled the air with the great hope of returning to Zion and rebuilding our land. Even we, the children, saw ourselves obligated to do something ....

I remember well the experimental "sagas" of local youth organizations even before we knew of the national movements and their approach. So, for example, we established a youth movement for boys and girls in the Jewish-Polish school. It was named Flowers of Zion (later, the name was changed to Children of Zion) and had its own articles of association and program (based on three principles: Zionism, socialism, and Jewish religious ethics). This organization included about 150 children, mainly from the upper grades of the primary school. It had groups and their commanders, regiments and their commanders, the supreme command, etc. After school, we marched in order to the activity area, Mount Krestova (our regular club ...). There we would read about the courageous history of Israel, the wars of Bar Kokhba and the Maccabees, the renewed Land of Israel, the Guard, the pioneers, and more. We organized and managed the activities ourselves until one day we caught the attention of the school's administration and were called in front of them for an explanation. This resulted in our having to go "underground." Not long after, our movement dissolved anyway with the establishment of a Youth Guard cell and Young Pioneer chapter in our town. The development of the other kind of youth group—for extension courses and discussion of ideas, what we called in Russian *kruzshak*—did not go so well.

> [**Translator's Notes:** In Hebrew, Flowers of Zion is *Pirchei Tsion,* and Children of Zion is *Bnei Tsion.* The Guard (in Hebrew, *Hashomer*) was a group dedicated to guarding the life and property of Jewish settlements.]

During Passover 1924, a few of us boys of the age before bar mitzvah established a club that we named the Cornerstone. Its main aims were to establish the use of the Hebrew language in everyday speaking, study of Hebrew literature and history, the geography of Israel, the development of friendship and brotherhood, and the observance of good manners. We invited Libchik Feldman to be our advisor and worked intensively for a few months, getting together during every free period we had to read and converse in Hebrew. Our group included Shmuel Pozner, Matityahu Pundik, Yone Frenkel, Yosef Handelman, Tovye Troshinski, the writer of this chapter (these last two are in Israel now), and possibly someone else. The activities lasted only half a year and stopped in the fall, when most of the members left for out-of-town schools.

> [**Translator's Note:** Cornerstone is *Even HaPina* in Hebrew.]

A much larger and more basic activity took place in the fall of that year (1924), when 20 boys and girls got together to found the Hebrew Corner, a movement that continued intermittently for a few years and left its mark on the life of the town's young people.

This time, the members were older, their ages 16 and 17 (and one or two who were much younger), and the organization had a more serious character. The first meeting was held at the home of Miryam Horovits (Manya, who is now in Haifa, Israel), in an atmosphere of earnestness and commitment to do what was necessary. A board of three was elected: Tsvi Fisherman (chairman), Yisrael Otiker (secretary), and Miryam Horovits. (Fisherman left the country after a while. Today he is in Israel. Manya and I carried on with the group's activities until the end.) Some of the most active members were Ayzik Hofman (Zunya, now in Israel), Duvid Vinokur (who perished in Kremenets), Kopel Korn (now in Israel), Rachel Otiker-Feldman (who perished in Kremenets), Rachel Koka-Otiker (now in Israel), Malke Feldman (Maliusia, who perished in the Diaspora), Rivke Feldman, the sisters Pole and Chayke Kucher, the sisters Beyle and Rachel Senderovich (all these are in Israel), and a list of other young people. About 30 people were in the group, and the number of steady attendees was 10–15.

Most of the participants were active members of Youth Guard, Young Pioneer, and Pioneer. Others were not affiliated with any movement. An atmosphere of intimate friendship and camaraderie prevailed within the group's framework. (A group of friends who later left the Youth Guard movement to join the Communist Party and were active in the region and the vocational guilds temporarily participated in our organization's activities.

[144]

But note that even they did not succeed in ridding themselves completely of Hebrew and Zionist influence and would sometimes come to borrow a Hebrew book or newspaper ....) At first, we met almost every evening, then three or four times a week. We did not have a permanent clubhouse but met in three different places: at Miryam Horovits' home in Frantsishkanska Street (mostly outside on the veranda, in the moonlight); in a corner room at our home, near the Lyceum in Tshatskiego Street (and again, mostly outside on benches at the foot of the giant Lyceum buildings); and the third, a spacious place, Mount Bona, at the Dzievitsa Rock, with the forests at their feet. When pressed, we met at the nearby Vidomka and Krestova [mountains].

One person who guided us and great influenced our work was Libchik—Arye Feldman (who perished in Kremenets). Some of us who had known him previously and knew him to be very knowledgeable and a deep thinker immediately suggested that we invite him to be our mentor. He worked with us with strong dedication all through the years.

Libchik was a man with a religious-Jewish outlook and an idealistic worldview, but he had a respect for the Hebrew workers' movement, recognizing its place in the struggle for the nation's revival. Uppermost in his outlook on life were the search for sparks of beauty and morality and constant striving for spiritual and moral elevation.

With his large treasury of knowledge, Libchik prepared us for spiritual struggles in Judaism, opened the gates to universal thinking for us, and brought us into a labyrinth of philosophical questions.

How did we occupy ourselves in those evenings at the Hebrew Corner? With Kabbalah and Schopenhauer, Nietzsche and Hasidism, the Rambam and Rabbi Saadia Gaon, and Carlyle and Bukharin. Those discussions were accompanied by reading and study. We delved deeply into general and modern Hebrew literature. I cannot forget our discussion of Bialik's "The Pool," which lasted a whole night and into daybreak .... (More than once, it happened that daylight surprised us in the midst of discussion and, disappointed, we had to leave, each one to his workplace, questions left unresolved and unsolved ....)

In the early period, the Corner held parties that were open to all young people, published a wall-newspaper called *Echo from the Corner,* and worked to disseminate Hebrew language and literature. In the later years, we were involved more with functions within the framework of the club.

[**Translator's Note:** In Hebrew, *Echo from the Corner* is *Hed Hapina.*]

Also, the number of regular members decreased. As it happens, "crises" visited the life of our club, ideological and social crises; in some periods, there was a noticeable slowdown in activities, though the club picked up and renewed its functions and continued so for five years, from fall 1924 to early 1929. For many of us, this club was not only a precious corner for young people, but also a serious school in which to learn the problems of society and the world.

THE ORT SCHOOL

Munye Katz (Haifa)
English translation by Thia Persoff

Kremenets was always a craftsmen's town, a center for the small townships and villages in her vicinity. Assorted craftsmen worked there: tailors, shoemakers, hatters, metalsmiths, tinsmiths, barrel makers, tile makers, bookbinders, glaziers, jewelers, watch repairers, barbers, butchers, water carriers, porters, and road workers. Topping them off were producers of cigarette holders. Their products were distributed and used throughout Russia.

Craftsmen worked in a primitive system. The craft was family property and was passed from father to son. But with the general advance of industry, there arose a need for advanced vocational education.

[145]

The ORT organization, which was formed to aid the productivization of Jewish young people, found itself in Kremenets, a town where Jews were usually seen as workmen— a fertile area for its activities. With the active support of Chayim Ovadis, Fishel Perlmuter, Kroyt, Yisrael Margalit, Meir Goldring, the architect Rozin, Moshe Trakhtenberg, Ratshiner, Vaynshtok, and others, ORT was a center for community activity.

Chayim Ovadis was the mover and shaker behind the project. As the owner of an industrial plant (a large foundry, later turned into a flourmill), he recognized the importance of manual labor. Out of allegiance to his people, he saw the plant as his life's work.

In the early days of its existence, the ORT vocational school was housed in a small, unfit building on Vishniovtska Street. In spite of the difficulties, the number of students was large, and to the first two classes—metalsmith work and lathe turning— were added classes for mechanics and welders, and a sewing class for girls.

The administration, under the leadership of the engineer Dekelboym, received supplies and tools from the center in Warsaw. Institutions such as the City Council, the Community Council, the Lyceum, and the vocational education board of the Polish Cultural Bureau were also supporters. That much help made it possible to offer education to poor young people, but the school was supported in part by tuition and even more so by the sale of the products of the students' work, which became well known in the area.

Group of ORT Students

[146]

THE KREMENETS NEWSPAPER

Yisrael Otiker (Kibbutz Na'an)
English translation by Steven Wien and Sari Havis

As we recount the story of the weekly newspaper *Kremenitser Shtime*, we must look to the past for the circumstances that preceded its establishment and publication.

We were young at the time, and the atmosphere of the time did not allow us to be sheltered in the beautiful worlds that are part of youth; it required action from us on behalf of the Jewish masses.

The Jewish population in Poland suffered tremendously in those days. The tax system was especially aimed at forcing the Jews from their positions and destroying their sources of income. Vicious competition was often accompanied by assaults and pogroms, which took place with the support and encouragement of the country's official institutions. We rebelled with all our being against the essence of exile and life in the Diaspora, but we loved those wretched, persecuted Jews and saw ourselves, the younger generation, as responsible for their fate and as mandated to support and encourage them.

[**Translator's Note:** In the original text, the following quotations from *Kremenitser Shtime* are in both Yiddish and Hebrew, with the Hebrew in parentheses following the Yiddish.]

In its opening article, the *Kremenitser Shtime* wrote:

"The way of Jewish life is full of obstacles. Desperation and indifference prevail among all the people. Many find themselves helpless, and the slope of our life descends and drops very fast. We return to the same position and situation where we stood hundreds of years ago, in the darkest of the Middle Ages.

"We, the members of the more enlightened people, without any bias of camp or party, see it as our holy obligation to preserve the correct path of the Jewish masses and to fight in the war against desperation and degeneration that has spread among us.

"Life in the provincial town has its own unique problems. Newspaper publications in the capital cannot depict and describe the various hues and shades of life in provincial towns. Therefore, we come forward to try to establish a platform whose role will be to serve as a spokesman, to describe various public, cultural, and economic problems of Jews in our places, a platform that will reflect life and will call for action and activity."

[147]

Newspaper Clippings from Kremenitser Shtime

[**Translator's Note:** Headlines include "Life in Kremenets and Environs," "Lyceum Auditorium—B. Bakst—'Bar Kokhba,'" "The Levant Fair in Tel Aviv," "Lyceum Auditorium—Friday—Kol Nidre," and an obituary for "Nachum Sokolov, of blessed memory."]

[148]

These lines, which we copied from the editorial board's opening article in the first edition, relate the various causes and motivating factors that brought us, as inexperienced young people, to such a venture as the publication of a local newspaper.

The first attempt to publish the newspaper in our town was by Moshe Gershteyn, of blessed memory, who was a community activist. He was formerly a Bund member. In

February 1929, he published a newspaper of four pages with the help of Neta Shtern, Leyb Rozental, Yakov Shafir, and the writer of these lines.

Afterward, there were repeated trials and experiments with single publications, dedicated mainly to mutual and social help in the community and other social institutions. Thus, in April 1930, a very diverse newspaper with six large pages was published with the support of the Charity Fund. Another newspaper published in November 1930 was dedicated to the problem of abandoned children and the orphanage.

Two editions were also published in 1931, on January 4 and November 11, again with the Charity Fund's support.

The participants in these ventures were the same group of people. They also participated regularly in the newspapers published periodically in Rovno and Lutsk. These newspapers were available in town and were welcomed because they reflected mostly local life.

But one day, we decided that those alone were not enough and that there was a need for a more permanent platform that would speak directly to our townspeople and describe specifically local phenomena that required some clarity and reaction. The "deciders" were three young men: Neta Shtern, the writer of these lines, and another member who from the beginning opposed and gave up on the whole matter. Since then, we have reminded ourselves more than once that our "final hour of decision" was on one of those long nightly trips to Mount Bona in autumn 1931, when we talked a lot about the lives of Jews and their problems. We saw the newspaper as a very important instrument, an opportunity to reach every Jew in the town, and we were determined to execute this decision even if the older businesspeople in the town mocked our "inventions."

We approached one of the veteran printer owners in town, Volf Tsvik, a Jew who was prudent in business matters. He took to our ideas and suggestions and, in fact, expressed his willingness to join our venture as a partner, with the condition that we share any losses evenly with him. We drafted a very detailed contract, and we signed it as the "second party." We sat in V. Tsvik's house, pragmatic and serious, as was appropriate for people who were going to open a corporate business. But once we left, we both laughed and began shouting, struck by the realization that we had finally established a foundation for publishing the newspaper.

We decided to draft a group of staffers and participants. First, brothers Leybke and Aleksander Rozental joined; both were veteran writers for other newspapers. Leybke Rozental, who lived in the center of town, provided a room in his apartment for the newspaper. That room served as the center for a long time and was always crowded with people writing, editing, proofreading, and so on, and with people who just came to find out what was happening with the newspaper.

Meir Goldring, who was the head of the Zionist Organization and one of the most prominent people in town, accepted official responsibility for the newspaper and helped in its editing and organization. Other regular participants joined us: Yakov Shafir, Shlome Fingerut, Libchik Feldman, Dr. Meir Litvak, Dr. B. Landsberg, and others. A short time later, Manus Goldenberg joined us and contributed his dynamic editing to the newspaper until he immigrated to Israel. My sister, Rachel Otiker, and Yehudit Rozental (L. Rozental's daughter, who married N. Shtern and today is in Poland) worked with us on the editorial board and in the newspaper's administrative department.

Hadasah Rubin's poems received special attention. (Today she is in Poland, and not long ago her poems were published in a Yiddish book called *Mein gas iz in Pener* [*My Street Is in Pener.*]) She was a talented poet with the promise of a bright future. She later belonged to a group of young authors called Young Vilna. Her poems, which were published in various literary publications in Warsaw and Vilna, received many accolades. But she was first published in the *Kremenitser Shtime*.

[149]

Editorial Board of Kremenitser Lebn [Kremenets Life], 1934

Sitting (from right to left): (1) Yisrael Otiker, (2) Manus Goldenberg, (3) Chane Goldenberg-Horovits, (4) Meir Goldring, (5) Dr. Binyamin Landsberg. *Standing:* (1) Shlome Fingerhut, (2) Leyb Rozental, (3) Aleksander Rozental, (4) Moshe Gershteyn, (5) Goldberg, (6) Neta Shtern.

The newspaper also served as the first means of publication for other young people who engaged in literary or scientific work. Its various editions contained literary works as well as memoirs, sad documentaries and historical works mainly about the past, and daily articles about everyday life. Much of the material that was published in the newspaper was later picked up by other publications.

Ideologically, the newspaper expressed the labor Zionist spirit and aimed to be a progressive publication, but it had a generic tone and aimed to be an open platform for anyone. Those who flip through the newspaper will find the words of Communists, revisionists, religious Jews, etc., and polemics on pivotal political issues, etc., because it was the sole platform in town.

Our mailbox was always full of correspondence, and writers, both young and old, suddenly discovered their writing skills and wanted to be published. More than once, people came on foot to the center and demanded their "right," but more than a few of these pieces were published in the famous "basket." But we frequently encountered expressions of great interest and persevered in publishing them.

We had no lack of worthless material that sometimes hurt the newspaper's image. For instance, following the example of other principal newspapers, we were forced to publish sensational serial romances to "pull in" readers, and it happened that we published a serial romance called "The Secrets of Mount Bona."

[150]

The content of the romance was local, complicated, and convoluted. It was "suspenseful," as romances are, and its merit ... was like that of other romances. After a short while, we decided to stop publishing the romance in the middle pf the story (even though many readers scolded us and demanded to know the outcome of the romance ...). Most of the editorial board members were of the opinion that such material should not be published. Other incidents raised a bit of argument, but generally the atmosphere in the editorial board reflected a responsible, serious attitude toward the publication of news and articles. A group of about 10 to 15 people coalesced around the newspaper, the best of the best people in the areas of community and culture, who persevered in caring for the newspaper throughout its existence.

The newspaper had correspondents in most of the neighboring towns, and it was commonplace there. (The newspaper usually printed 1,000 copies.) Once there was an attempt to establish a chapter of the newspaper in neighboring Rovno, a town with a large Jewish population. But the experiment was not successful, and the newspaper continued to be prevalent mainly in Kremenets and its vicinity.

The first edition of *Kremenitser Shtime* appeared on October 2, 1931. From August 1932 until February 1933, two weekly newspapers appeared: *Kremenitser Shtime* and *Kremenitser Vochenblatt* (with the cooperation of the Yiddish newspaper in Rovno). Internal arguments and disagreements among the editors were the cause of the appearance of these two newspapers. They split for a short while, but after a few months, the newspapers merged and continued as one local newspaper named *Kremenitser Lebn*. The newspaper continued to appear weekly until the war began. It held a prominent place in the community and cultural life of the town's Jews.

> [**Translator's Note:** *Kremenitser Vochenblatt* means *Kremenets Weekly*, and *Kremenitser Lebn* means *Kremenets Life*.]

Finally, a friend who is currently editing the "Book of Kremenets" told me that, while looking for material about the town, he went to the National Library. The librarian there informed him that he had some very interesting material and handed him several issues of the *Kremenitser Shtime*. The friend became agitated and, for hours, paged through those issues that the newspaper staff worked so hard to bring to the National Library of Israel.

And today, when we flip through the archived copies that we have, bitterness takes hold of us. Was there any way to know then, while editing the newspaper, that in such a vast, lively and Jewish community the day would come when these issues would serve not only as archival material but also as a memorial to the entire Jewish congregation?

[151]

MEMORIES AND LIFESTYLES

KREMENETS—ELECTION HEADQUARTERS

(From *The Volhynia Collection*, Book 1, 4 Tevet 5706 (December 8, 1945)
Avraham Levinson (Tel Aviv)
English translation by Thia Persoff

The following words are but a bundle of memories, my recollections of the elections for the first Polish Sejm in Volhynia.

It was 1922. Jewish politics consisted of a "bloc" of minorities organized by Yitschak Grinboym. I remember that under his leadership, the foundation for the minority political bloc was laid at endless meetings in Warsaw. Apparently, the government didn't appreciate all its minorities' quantitative and qualitative value and clung to a policy of wait-and-see-how-things-develop. In the Jewish camp, too, national-patriotic awareness was underdeveloped among the members of the Union and the merchants, and they supported the bloc. The one group that did not join was the Folksists (founded by Noach Prilutski), which united with the Craftsmen Folksists (founded by craftsmen's guild chairman Chayim Rasner), but the Zionists among them supported the bloc. With all the nation's forces joined, victory in the election was assured, though no one had envisioned its extent—55 Jewish representatives in the Sejm and Senate.

I remember that one day, in Lodz, my hometown, I received a telegram from the Central Election Bureau in Warsaw, ordering me to go to Volhynia for a month to manage propaganda for block 18, my election district, where I was put forward as a candidate. This district comprised the towns of Kremenets, Dubno, and Ostrog, including the small towns between them: Radzivilov, Berestechko, Gorokhov, and others. My chances to be elected were none, as there were five candidates for the Sejm; I was in last place after four Ukrainians. And besides ours, there was a government slate, too. In the midst of the election eve's warlike atmosphere, I did not dare defy the bureau's order, and I left for Volhynia.

Election headquarters was in Kremenets, a lovely town framed by trees and high mountains. The chairman of the Kremenets election board was the attorney Binyamin Landsberg, a staunch Zionist, son of the old physician Dr. Arye Landsberg, also a Zionist.

[152]

I can see the old man in my mind's eye as if he were alive: goodhearted, pleasant to his fellow men, and knowledgeable in ancient Hebrew literature, too. Even today I still have in my bookcase the gift that he gave me for a souvenir—*Living Soul*, by Menashe ben Yisrael. During the short recesses between the propaganda speeches, he would tell me about an eminent and respected honored Jew of the town named R' Yitschak Ber Levinson, who secluded himself in an attic, dreaming of Hebrew Enlightenment and of popularizing agriculture and crafts in Israel. He wrote also his books there, on one hand *Zrubavel* and *House of Judah* and on the other, *Bloodless*. Until recently, the house where RYB"L lived in Kremenets was still standing. Among other people of merit who came from Kremenets, Landsberg recalled his memories of an active Lovers of Zion member and one of the first Zionists in Poland, Dr. Tovye Hindes, whom I knew well from his years of participation in Warsaw's Lovers of the Hebrew Language movement. In contrast to Dr. Landsberg, who still practiced medicine in spite of his advanced years but lived mainly in the world of his memories, his son Binyamin was young, alert, and very active; although busy with his law practice, he was devoted heart and soul to the needs of the community and Zionism. His dainty wife, Sonye, was at his right hand during the difficult periods of his life. Besides Landsberg, Frishberg, Goldring, Dr. Litvak, and others, all devoted Zionists, participated in the activities at that time.

[**Translator's Notes:** In Hebrew, *Living Soul* is *Nishmat Chayim,* and Lovers of the Hebrew Language is *Chovevey Sfat Ever.*]

Working on the election in Kremenets and its vicinity was not easy. In spite of the large amount of publicity in those areas, the notion of the Minority Bloc had awakened in the Jewish population painful, sad memories of the pogroms the Ukrainians had inflicted on them during their civil wars. As a result, it was difficult for the Jews of eastern Poland to accept the political coupling of the Jews and the hated Ukrainians. My political rival, N. Prilutski, who remained sheltered under the wings of the Polish *starosta*, took advantage of these feelings, saying that his job was to save his district from the Ukrainian *Iridenta*.

[**Translator's Note:** *Iridenta* was the political party working to recover local Ukrainian regions that were under "foreign" control.]

But by chance the *starosta* was from my hometown, Lodz, and a friend of my brother-in-law, so he refrained from standing in the way of my activities. Another psychological difficulty that worried me greatly was this: my political foe, Prilutski, who was known for his literary scientific work and well known to the public, was—my bad luck—a Kremenets native, and his whole family was living there at the time of the election. Not long afterward, it became clear that I had worried for no reason; the Minority Bloc, which had been established as a result of the Jewish fight against the reactionary Polish government, was so popular that all of Prilutski's close family members supported us. It came to the point where Prilutski avoided visiting his family when was in Kremenets and stayed in a private hotel.

I recall one of the mass gatherings held in the Kremenets synagogue close to election day: it was organized by the members of the Folksist Party, featuring Prilutski. Before he began his speech, the people demanded that he give me a chance to reply after he finished. He refused their request, and they reacted by heckling and making so much noise throughout the synagogue that he could not be heard. Having no choice, he agreed to allow me a half hour to reply. Prilutski's speech was generally cautious and polite. His first words proclaimed his good deeds for the betterment of the Jewish population and his scientific activities. The beginning of his speech made an unpleasant impression on me, as each sentence began with the word "I." A large part of his speech was devoted to comparing the Folksist candidate in my district, the folk writer Hirshhorn, who already had made a name for himself in the Jewish-Polish newspapers, to the almost unknown Minority Bloc candidate, who had returned to Poland from Ukraine just two years ago. This, obviously, was not pleasant for me to hear.

[153]

This demagogic maneuver, which was meant to degrade and belittle the minority candidate, forced me to use the same maneuver, which I had always detested. At the end of his speech, my friends raised me above the heads of the assembly and put me on the pulpit (it was not possible to reach it otherwise because of the huge crowds). I was insulted by the speech. I climbed above the ocean of heads on every side onto the pulpit, where the carved, handsome Holy Ark stood high, and on it, the two holy tablets. The "I" of the first commandment spurred my first words. I negated the personal, boastful, and arrogant "I" compared with the carved "I" on the tablets. I pointed to the contrast between the Folksists' subjective program, which lacked a foundation of ideas, and the bloc's national, objective one. All votes for Zionism, I said, are votes for the establishment of the nation's immortality, a contribution of conscience and soul to the validation of the national freedom movement. All votes for a temporary party of individuals contribute to *keren hatsvi*—a doubtful enterprise, meaning to Hirshhorn .... The rest of my words were lost in the loud cheers of the crowd. When Prilutski came up to reply, he was met with a tremendous, resounding rendition of *Hatikva*, deciding the outcome of the election.

> [**Translator's Note:** *Keren hatsvi* means "horn of the stag." Putting your money or wares on the horns of a stag may cause it to get lost when the stag runs. This is a play on words, as the name Hirshhorn means "stag's horn."]

... The election campaign took about a month. The results were splendid: in this district, the bloc came away with a complete victory. All five candidates were elected to the Polish Sejm. This was achieved thanks to the national solidarity of the Jewish population of Volhynia.

I must point out that an instinctive love of Zion, Hebrew, and national freedom nested in the hearts of all the simple Jews in the Volhynia townships, the awkward and often jobless *horopashniks*, who were burdened with large numbers of children to support. This period in the Diaspora was a period of passage for them. I saw masses of Jews at the rallies in Kovel, Lutsk, Rozishche, Rovno, Korets, Ludvipol, and other small towns, I visited their nearly empty stores and poor workshops, and I was always amazed at their spiritual awareness of what was holy and at their financial contributions. Once I visited Berestechko, an amazing town where all the Jews spoke Hebrew and most of their children immigrated to Israel at various times. One of the propaganda meetings, under the chairmanship of Dr. Forman, was dedicated to the Foundation Fund. After his lecture, the assembly requested a recess, and as soon as I agreed, they disappeared, but soon returned and immediately piled a large mound of gold and silver coins, jewelry, religious articles, etc., on a table. That evening, a special envoy came from Gorokhov to Berestechko and brought me an anonymous donation—a sack filled with jewelry for the fund. And there is much more to tell about Berestechko.

> [**Translation Editor's Note:** *Horopashnik* has not yet been translated. In Hebrew, the Foundation Fund is *Keren Hayesod.*]

More than 20 years have passed since my visits to the towns of Volhynia, and they still stand as large as life in my mind's eye: kindly Jews who invested in the rebuilding of Israel the best of its strength and wealth, the choice of her children—her builders. My heart aches with the knowledge that we will never see them again.

May these pages be accepted as a memorial to this glorious Jewish community, which knew how to love, fight, build, and create, and assure it an honored place in the national creation for all eternity.

[154]

IN THE TOWN OF R' YITSCHAK BER LEVINSON (RYB"L)

(From *My Travels in Poland's Cities and Towns in 1928*)
Rachel Amari (Tel Aviv)
(In the Diaspora—Rachel Faygenberg)
English translation by Thia Persoff

This time I went to the country's eastern border district. I wanted to see Volhynia. I reached the border and longed to visit Kremenets.

This town that dwells among mountains is like an enchanted, faraway corner somewhere in Switzerland. Each neglected, dilapidated Jewish shack here is stamped with a romantic quality. Each Jew here has a long pedigree and is a neighbor and relative of all the illustrious personalities who were in Kremenets, the pride and glory of its natives.

The crowning glory of Kremenets is R' Yitschak Ber Levinson (RYB"L). In this town, there was "Mendilzon the Vohliner," a veteran resident and property owner. Still alive then was a woman in Kremenets who remembered how the RYB"L himself had talked to her. One morning, when she was a little girl about ten years old, he asked her as he sat by his door whether she was earning something from the tailor who was teaching her the craft of sewing.

This old woman, whose parents used to live on the same street as the RYB"L, would often see him sitting on the stoop of his house, bent over an open book. She also remembered that on the Sabbath, the Jews of the town would lift their curious eyes to his roof, checking his chimney for smoke, because they suspected that he lit a fire in his stove. Once a prominent squire came to visit him in a carriage. People in town said that he was an important minister from Petersburg, the capital. She also knew that the RYB"L lived in poverty, but that later the enlightened people of Kremenets who were rich got together and arranged a monthly allowance for him, thereby assuring him a decent living. As far as she remembers, he always had a Christian manservant in his house.

The RYB"L's house, small and painted blue, stands in the center of town. The partially blocked windows and reddish, rust-eaten door, which face the noisy, main street, make it look like a kind, pretty old lady, puzzled and astonished at the sight of all the innovations that have come about in this new world. But as soon as you approach the house, you see that the crooked, old building is squeezed between roofs and wooden poles, as if it is getting ready to walk with crutches under its arms ....

You enter through a narrow path, from which you see that R' Yitschak Ber Levinson's old nest is completely destroyed inside and out. The ceiling is bent out of shape, doorways are broken, and the wooden floor is full of holes. The house is full of broken household items and junk that used to be furniture.

The widow who sits in this blue-painted ruin, with windows that are white inside and look like a blind person's eyes from the outside, is bent and bored. But this miserable tenant, too, has an honorable pedigree. Besides the importance of being the tenant of the RYB"L's property for years without paying rent to the Kremenets Community Council, she has another great privilege on her husband's side. He was a porter by trade, carrying heavy loads on his back all his life. At the same time, he was an educated man and an avid reader of *Hatsefira*. Their sons were highly educated, too, and although their father lived in poverty and hardship, he took extra care of his *Hatsefira*. He saw to the children's education in the Torah and sciences, and sent them to high schools and universities. Their son stayed in Russia, and their daughters are looking for jobs in Polish towns, their proud mother tells me. Everything in her humble home shows her pride in her educated children; it is full of their intellectual spirit.

> [**Translator's Note:** *Hatsefira (The Siren)* was one of the first Hebrew newspapers of the 19th century.]

Among the cobwebs on the walls hang photographs of Ch. N. Bialik and Maxim Gorky.

[155]

Here and there are lines of drawing and painting made by the skillful hands of an art lover. A great number of books—the new creations of young Polish and Ukrainian authors—are strewn among the junk and dusty rags.

These are the kinds of neighbors that R' Yitschak Levinzon had. Learning and knowledge have not ceased in his old corner. Nor is his memory forgotten in town. On the hill, in the center of the Jewish community's cemetery, the gravestone of RYB"L stands out. A poem in Hebrew is etched on it, the one he wrote for that very purpose many years before his death. In it he tells future generations of his fight for the ideas and opinions that were precious to him during his life.

This town flows with the romantic glamour of generations past. Its market street lies in the shadow of a mountain, which is crowned by a royal legend inspired by the ruins of a palace on its peak. The Jews of Kremenets have legends of their own—they are kept modestly, and their contents are paved with spirituality and suffering for the sanctification of God's name. Culture and history are like heirlooms for them, to be passed down from generation to generation. In the Great Synagogue, on "the stand," the ancient community journals and prayer books rest, beautifully handwritten in the artistic calligraphy practiced by students and writers in Kremenets and Dubno since the 16th and 17th centuries. In the open, for all to see, are the town's historical documents and those of Jews from the surrounding area. It has never occurred to the leaders of the community that such precious things need to be well guarded and locked up, safe from rough and irresponsible hands. The late Mr. Anski noticed this while researching Jewish folklore during his travels through Volhynia's towns and villages. While he stayed in Kremenets for many weeks, copying the handsomely written old notebooks, he advised the people to guard their old journals, but they did not listen to his advice and continued to leave them exposed on the lectern. Among the people of Kremenets, they said, "antiques" do not disappear, nor do people consider them very valuable. Take a look at the bookcase of any decent, learned Jew, and you are likely to see a book that has been in the family for 200 or 300 years, sometimes even longer.

Indeed, the Jews of Kremenets have honored their people's history and it held dear. During World War I and the Great Russian Revolution, a group of soldiers formed a Communist Council. They wanted to remove the decoration in the synagogue of a crown with two lions, which they considered to be like the symbols of the nation they had just conquered. The Jews explained to them that they were ancient symbols originating in King Solomon's time, and the soldiers backed down and decided not to touch them. In Kremenets, this story used to be told during a relaxed conversation among the town's Jews, and, while enjoying a glass of tea in a nice house, the host would entertain his guest with a page from local community history, such as the free-loan ledger of the Charity Fund, which the upstanding citizens formed about 200 years ago to lend money interest-free to the poor for mortgages.

In that ledger, some other very interesting information was recorded for posterity, including a detailed list of the menu for the fund's yearly dinner, which consisted of 13 different kinds of food, among them stuffed chicken necks and gizzards. In the charter, an important paragraph about the members' social class states that membership is closed to professional craftsmen and their descendants.

During World War I, the fund lost its monies and had to rely on American philanthropists. The old members planned to write to the townspeople and say that even though they were American now, they should still remember their enchanted nights on Mount Bona. But the young members were not enthusiastic about the suggestion. The bourgeois laws were ignored as if they had been abolished, even to the point where the children of fund members who had rejected the working class filled the ORT School of professional crafts, seeking to learn smithing and carpentry.

[156]

THE GOLDEN KEY OF KREMENETS JEWRY

(From *My Travels in Poland's Cities and Towns in 1931*)
Rachel Amari (Tel Aviv)
English translation by Thia Persoff

... Again my travels took me to Kremenets, and again I took walks among her green-covered mountains. In the valley, the town shines white inside the ancient splendor of her arching town walls, built by generations past—God-fearing Orthodox Jews and Christians.

In the center of the town rises the castle on Catholic Lyceum grounds, one of my local companions explains to me. The church and its many adjacent seminary buildings, containing schools with classrooms for various courses, are like a gated town that is locked away from the noise of the streets around it.

And here, a bit down and to the right, are the outer walls of the old synagogue. This, too, is a grand building, built in the old style to last for coming generations. Among Kremenets Jews, there is an old man whose seat in the place of honor by the eastern wall of this ancient synagogue is as assured, as he had personally inherited it from his father, according to the tradition maintained by the townspeople for generations. According to this tradition, the old man's father, who was a carpenter and one of the builders of the synagogue, received his salary of 3 pennies a day for five days only. The sixth day he worked for free, and that granted him the privilege of the honored seat by the eastern wall, a right of ownership for him and his descendants forever.

The sanctuary in the synagogue had windows with iron bars, left over from the "kidnapping" days when young Jewish boys were grabbed and taken to serve in Czar Nicholas I's army. The parents of the wealthy Jewish boys, as you know, bought their freedom, so only the poor suffered from the severity of the decree. People hired from the community would abduct the sons of the poor from their parents' low-class homes and hand them over to government agents. In that dark period, the Kremenets community was forced to make a prison for poor children in the sanctuary so that their desperate family members could not rescue them. In that room, there is still some evidence of how the confined children were chained to tables and benches to prevent them from escaping when the door was opened.

Indeed, there is much that the walls of the old synagogue of Kremenets can tell about the past.

Here, in an alley shaded by trees behind the fortified walls of the Catholic Lyceum, lived the parents of Yuliush Slovatski, the great Polish poet, and his mother was laid to rest in the local Christian cemetery. Many visitors of all ages from all over the country come to visit her grave, with its freshly painted stone and a long inscription describing the life of the woman who gave birth to the Polish nation's renowned lyrical poet.

I lay the two white roses that are in my hand at the head of her stone, and we continue on our way.

We walk up the mountain to the ruins of the castle, which is adorned with a legend about an ancient queen who built a castle from which to reign on the top of this enchanted mountain in Kremenets.

Even today, young people and lovers favor the mountain's slopes for hikes and secret rendezvous. In summer, the air here is saturated with aromas of fresh hay and apple blossoms from the nearby orchards. Soft, aromatic grasses cover the mountaintop. According to the legend, the princess still guards the royal palace ruins on the mountaintop; at midnight, she appears in the palace ruins, mounted on a horse and wearing a royal crown, a golden key in her hand.

[157]

The legend goes on to say that whoever takes the golden key away from the princess will find the abundant treasure that was hidden in that spot thousands of years before. To take the key, the person must be there alone exactly at midnight. So far, in the whole town, not one brave person has been willing to dare to make the midnight visit to the ruins, when the princess appears with the golden key in her hand.

They also say that, indeed, once a Jew in Kremenets risked his life to get the golden key, climbing up to the ruins at midnight. The next morning, his body was discovered at the foot of the broken wall. His coattail had become entangled with his cane when he stuck it in the ground as a marker that he had arrived there.

My touring companions give me all this information as we walk. We descend among gardens, orchards, and whitewashed farmhouses, which lean on the mountain slopes, and we reach the highway leading directly into town. From one of the tour participants, who is the current Jewish representative on the Kremenets City Council, I learn that Jews did most of the work of paving those excellent roads. He and his colleagues on the council have invested a great deal of energy in accomplishing the goal of repairing the roads to help the residents of this mountain-dwelling town in their commerce with the outside world.

He, the Jewish representative on the Kremenets City Council, worried about the health of all residents, Jews and non-Jews. His great hope was to bring about order and comfort in the narrow, neglected alleys in the neighborhood near the old synagogue. But his hands were tied by the City Council's financial difficulties and mainly by the local Jews' declining economic situation.

"Maybe you should try to take the golden key from the palace princess again?" I asked him.

But he replied in very seriously, "The golden key in this town used to be in the hands of the Jewish carpenters—their excellent products were a source of generous income for local Jews. Kremenets was the furniture supplier for all of Volhynia's cities and towns. People made jokes about the pride Kremenets Jews took in their carpenters, and we made fun of ourselves, too, saying: "Happy is the mother who is blessed with a son who is a carpenter."

It turns out that all this is history from the past, and the reason is well known. The lauded Kremenets carpenters have no one to produce for, as the impoverished Jews cannot afford to buy furniture and decorate their homes, and the non-Jews are openly boycotting Jewish products.

On a humorous note, at the same time, the economic leader of the local Jews adds some interesting information about his people. "Once the Kremenets Jews and their families went on vacation in the local mountains. They did so for two lifesaving reasons: first, to save money, as the food was extremely inexpensive in the mountain villages, and the other, to eat their fill during the summer and gather strength for the great scarcity in the winter."

Smiling, he concludes, "When you return to the Land of Israel, tell them that the revisions in Zionism are in the hands of eight-year-old children here, in our town. And, another important thing: because of unemployment and scarcity, our young people, too, are seeking education in the Polish government high schools, so that they can get diplomas ...."

Indeed, the Jews of Kremenets have a strong desire for government diplomas. They are desired by sons, fathers, and everyone else.

The children in the orphanage also dream of education in Polish government high schools and of diplomas.

Besides the tragedy of being orphans, those children have nothing to complain about regarding their lot in the institution called the Kremenets Orphanage.

[158]

They are not deprived of food, clothing, housing, or Jewish and general education, and they have excellent workshops in which to learn professional trades. Many children in this town who are blessed to live with their parents do not enjoy all the privileges of the wards of the community.

Nor does the Kremenets community itself have any complaints about the children who grow up in the orphanage. Everyone knows that they are good children who study hard. The drama troupe they established has made a name for itself in the town through its success on the stage and is well known now among the area's small towns. From time to time, the troupe goes to the Jewish neighborhoods in the vicinity to perform plays about the people's lives, earn a little money, and acquire some fame.

But in spite of all that, the wards of the Kremenets orphanage are not satisfied. In their opinion, to achieve equality in the community, they need an education in the Polish government's high school and the resulting diploma.

And the young people, boys and girls, charming and capable in the general and professional studies in the institution, look with suspicion at anyone who tries to tell them that this country's official high school diploma is not very valuable. The poor children are afraid that this "happiness" is denied to them because they are orphans.

Only the comedian among them jests about the *Matura* illness of the middle-class children, all of them wanting to be doctors so that they can snatch the golden key from the mountain-dwelling princess's hand. But they will not snatch the desired key. They will go from house to house looking for patients so they can earn a living, and in every house, they will be told that they already have their own physician, as all young Jews will be doctors ....

> [**Translator's Note:** *Matura* refers to the exam taken at the end of secondary school.]

The town's comedians will tell you that the key to the treasure in the Kremenets mountains is already in the hands of Reyze the Whiner, as every season she—just like the management of the orphanage—receives dollars from people who used to live in Kremenets.

NAMES AND NICKNAMES

K. L.
English translation by Thia Persoff

Only a few of our townspeople were called by their given and family names. Most had nicknames. Generally, a man was called by his own and his father's name.

For example, Shaye Shilem's (Yehoshue son of R' Meshulam), Chayim Leyb Volf's, Duvid Pesach-Yosi's, Chayim Leyzer's, or Eli Chaykel's. Sometimes he was called by his mother's or mother-in-law's name, as in Moshe Velis, Motye Chaves, or Yosi Henales. At times his lineage would reach back to the third and fourth generation: Motel Moshe Velis (Mordekhay, son of Moshe, son of Velye) or Berish Beyle Berkis (that is, Berish, son-in-law of Beyle, daughter of Berke). And even Avraham Berish Beyle Berkis. This Avraham's daughter was called Chayusi Avraham Berish Beyle Berkis, namely, Chaye, daughter of Avraham, son of Berish, son-in-law of Beyle, daughter of Berke. You see, five generations were commemorated in one mouthful and one breath, so the girl's usual nickname was Chaye'le.

Sometimes a man was called by his wife's name, usually if she was the boss in his home, as it was for Moshe Chaye-Temis (Moshe husband of Chaye-Teme), Gedalye Tsimels, and Fayvush Chaye-Rikel's.

Other people were called by their or their father's profession:

[159]

Leyb Shochet (ritual slaughterer), Nachman Chazan (cantor), Shimon Melamed (teacher), Ayzikel Shlisale (Ayzik the middleman), Chayim Gershon Shnayder (tailor), Pesye di Milkhike (dairywoman), Barukh Katsav (butcher), Mordekhay Stolyer (carpenter), Shlome Beker (baker), Yoel fun der Leyveent (from the linen—a cloth seller), Chaykel Bayder (bath attendant), Rachel fun di Gendz (from the geese), Babtse fun der Puter (from the butter), Menashe Shuster (shoemaker), Freyde di Miltshnitshke (flour seller), Mordekhay der Damske Shnayder (ladies' tailor), Pesach Kadushke (water carrier, or transporter of water in barrels. This was a many-branched family called "di Kadushkes," or the barrels), Moshe der Agent (the agent), Nachman Zeygermakher (watchmaker), and also Heynikh dem Shochet's (the ritual slaughterer's son) and Moshe dem Rav's (the rabbi's son-in-law).

Some people were called by the name of the area where they lived or worked, in town or in their birth town. For example, Mendil funem Mark (from the market), Yosl funem Plats (from the plaza), Chayim Duvid funem Potok, Leybish fun unter der Bad (from below the bathhouse), Leyzer funem Dielavay Davar (from Business Matter Courtyard), Moshe Lanevitser, Duvid Shumsker (from the town of Shumsk), Berl fun der Vishnevetser Ragatke (from the Vishnevets suburb), Chaye Kokerover (from Kuchurov village), Shlome Katerburger (from the town of Katerburg), Ezra Podkaminer (from the town of Podkamien).

The two rival rabbis also were called by the names of the towns they came from: the Kurilovtsy Rabbi and the Petrikover Rabbi. Their family names were known to very few in town—only to the people closest to them.

There were two sisters-in-law in town with the same name. To differentiate them, one was called Shprintse di Grobe, and the other was called Shprintse di Groyse (Shprintse the Fat and Shprintse the Tall).

A whole list of Jews were called by animal names, some in jest and some affectionately, like Ayzi di Kie (the cow), Fayvush Kelvales (heifer's), Shmuel Oks (bull), Yisrael Telitse (calf), Yankel di Shof (Yakov the sheep).

Some names also were funny, and some were insulting: Leyb Atiets (the priest), Avraham Shpring-in-Bet (jump-in-bed), Duvid Parkh (scab), Hirsh Leyb Pipik (bellybutton), Yoel Kishke (gut), Moshe Tate (Father), Kalman di Mame (Mommy), Moshe Hipsh (nice), Hirsh Mendil Amalek, and Yashke Ponimayesh (who always added a word to his sentences: "Ponimayesh (Understand)?").

> [**Translation Editor's Note:** *Amalek* refers to a descendant of Amalek, grandson of Esau and enemy of the Israelites."]

Diminutives were also used for some people in our town, some affectionately, and some disrespectfully: R' Velvele (the rabbi), R' Hertsele (the judge), R' Moshke'le (grandson of the righteous). And to differentiate him from them, the famous robber whose name spelled horror to young and old was called "Lep'ki" ....

A person who didn't have any particular nickname was called by his first name (which was usually a combination of two names), without adding his family name. When you said Hirsh Itsik, or Hirsh Mendil, or Duvid Leyb, or Moshe Chayim, it was perfectly clear whom you meant. If you mentioned the family name, you only caused confusion and doubt about his identity. Truly, who needed to know the family name of Duvid Leyb the rabbi's son-in-law, Moshe Chayim the cantor and matchmaker, Shimon Chayim the builder and whitewasher, or Hirsh Itsik the hymn singer (his famous "Today You Strengthen Us" is honey sweet!).

> [**Translator's Note:** In Hebrew, this hymn is *HaYom Te'amtsenu*, sung on Rosh Hashanah and Yom Kippur.]

A special way of life was reflected in the townspeople's nicknames, which added a personal touch. The nicknames are one example of the local color of the town that was and is no more.

[160]

THE HEROES OF THE VILLAGE OF FOLWARKI WIELKIE

Sore Bat (Yagur)
English translation by Howard Freedman and Michael Hirschfeld

There once was a village named Folwarki Wielkie halfway between the towns of Kremenets and Katerburg.

It was a village like all the other gentile villages in Volhynia, the only difference being that 20 Jewish farm families lived there. They were not tenants or grain or cattle merchants, but true farmers—owners of farms that they cultivated with their own hands. This was unusual in the entire area. I do not know when they settled there or by what right their ancestors had settled there in spite of the prohibition against Jews living in villages, but it was a fact that they had lived there for many generations. The families had many children—children who associated with the gentiles of the village but kept the Jewish flame alive. Furthermore, the younger generation was infected with Zionism and attracted to the Pioneer movement, and many immigrated to Israel. When the Pioneer movement spread to Kremenets and its environs and searched for places to train its members, Folwarki Wielkie was chosen as a training site for scores of pioneers. They arrived for three to four months in the summer and were well received by the local Jews, who felt honored to train pioneers for the Land of Israel. The parents also yearned for Zion, and many made plans to join their children. But they did not have the heart to abandon their farms and native villages. When the persecutions came, the axe also fell on the small, innocent community of Folwarki Wielkie. Some of the Jews refused to go to the Kremenets ghetto as ordered, but they were overpowered and murdered in their homes. The rest, with their women and children, were exiled to the Kremenets ghetto and killed with the rest of the local Jews.

I wish to commemorate my father and his family, who were murdered in their home village. The older children—my two sisters and I—had joined Pioneer and spent some years in several training kibbutzim until they immigrated to Israel. I remember that when I was in the training kibbutz in Verba, my father (of blessed memory) came to visit me. After examining the functions of the kibbutz, he expressed his astonishment that I had wandered off to Verba to whitewash houses—was not his farm in Folwarki Wielkie a more suitable place to train for agricultural work in the Land of Israel? Indeed, Father was right. But we were attracted to the Pioneer community and the training atmosphere. We left our quiet village and went to work in sawmills and quarries. After three of his daughters immigrated to Israel, Father decided to immigrate, too, along with my mother and the remaining three children. He began preparations but was too late.

The gentiles in the village were wary of Avraham Bat, because on past occasions he had shown them his strength. When the end came, he decided to defend himself. In spite of his advanced age of 60, with a rifle in his hand, he and my brother Aharon fought the Ukrainian policemen who came to deport them to the Kremenets ghetto. My father killed one of the policemen. Then he and my brother Aharon were killed on the spot—their heads cut off. The rest of the family was deported to the ghetto and killed on the day of the great murder: my mother, Chane-Rachel née Akerman, my brother Efraim, and my sister Etye. May their memory be blessed.

If there is a consolation for their deaths, it is that they fought and died in battle, and died a hero's death.

[161]

CONSTRUCTION STYLE

Zev Shumski (Tel Aviv)
English translation by Thia Persoff

For generations, the power struggle for rule over the town of Kremenets (as for all of Volhynia) continued between Russia and Poland. It was a political, religious, and cultural struggle. Throughout the generations, the town was shifted from one ruling government to another; each tried to make its own imprint on her while erasing the previous one. The area of architecture—the style of the buildings, courtyards, and streets—was not exempt from this struggle. There is no doubt that the basic motif in the town's houses was the old Polish style, which was preserved even during Russian rule. With the renewal of Polish rule in 1920, the Poles tried to preserve the old national construction style as much as possible.

Did the original, old style follow set architectural prescriptions? No, not at all. This style just happened. It was apparently anarchic, and even so, it showed signs of uniformity.

Typical Old House in Kremenets

In the late 18th and early 19th century, dozens of courtyard houses (*dwarik* in Polish) were built in the vicinity of the Lyceum in town, with its Baroque style, for the Polish aristocracy. Those courtyards were mostly on Slovatski Street, Directorska Street, and others; the houses, which had one or two stories, were located in the center of a large courtyard and surrounded by a large garden. Each had a protruding balcony with an outdoor staircase, a solid fence made of stone or wooden planks, a handsome gate, and, sometimes, a horse stable in the corner.

Although these typical houses had a definite style, they were not the ones that gave the town its general character. The many hundreds of houses belonging to the common people that were scattered all over the town's streets were what molded its shape. There is no doubt that those houses, which belonged mostly to Jews, were influenced by the "courtyard" style.

[162]

Typical Multifronted House

The houses were mostly small to begin with, but as the children grew and married, they enlarged the house by adding to it or building a second story. Sometimes one of the children would leave and sell his section to a different person. By then, the house had had more than one owner. Each one repaired, added, and made changes that were not consistent with the rest of the house. The result was a mosaic of many protrusions, balconies, "sectioned" roofs, secondary roofs, and varied covers to the roofs: wooden shingles, burned clay shingles. With the different sections painted in assorted colors, the houses took on a "polychromatic" look. None of this was planned; it was a natural development. Nevertheless, the town maintained a uniform construction style, as everyone built the way his neighbor did, and everyone saw the design of the courtyards around the Lyceum. The balconies were supported by a couple of wooden pillars and had low wooden banisters. Most of the roofs extended out to the street, and a few steps led from the street up to the entrance to the house. There was a complete lack of symmetry. Windows and doors under the same sharply slanting and sectioned roof were placed at different levels. These motifs and their "artistic disorganization" gave the town its uniqueness—an original style that developed in a period that had no "architectural ambitions" as yet but had simple, intimate construction with good proportions and favorable a relationship to nearby houses, resulting in a healthy feel and a sense of natural beauty and comfort at the same time. When you stood on Mount Bona and looked down over the town, you immediately sensed its special character: its great beauty, its profusion of gardens, and the inner harmony of its diversities. The multiple soft colors brightened the eye but were not harsh or bothersome.

In addition, one could find uniformity in the town's elegant buildings, the large public ones. The Great Synagogue building was identical to the church by the Lyceum. This is easy to understand, as the same architect built both of them at about the same time.

True, the town's houses were not "modern," and when the "new time" came, during Russian rule, people began building differently: large, square houses of straight lines with no protrusions, which were comfortable to live in but tasteless on the outside, reminiscent of barracks. The roofs were made of green-painted tin, and the fences were iron. In time, wealthy Jews purchased most of the "courtyards," and when they added to them, they built according to the "modern" Russian style. Sometimes a person built an addition to his old house in a different style—two styles remote from and foreign to each other in the same house.

[163]

Old Houses in the Lyceum Neighborhood

After that, houses with different styles would meet in the same courtyard, and the "Polish-Russian War" would appear within the boundaries of one courtyard. At that time, large, multifamily buildings were being built as rentals, for which no one was concerned about style. It is noteworthy that in the poor section of town, the old style was preserved, since people there did not make many basic changes. If they did change or add, they did not wander far from the original style.

When Poland took over the town in 1920, the government immediately appointed a special "conservator" to ensure the preservation of the old construction style. Polish architects were gnashing their teeth about the modern houses built in the past ten years, which were "spoiling" the town's tastefulness and beauty and the original style of its buildings. Zealously, the conservator tried to bring the old glory back to the town. If he had been given the permit he needed, he certainly would have razed many of those beauties—"destroying" new buildings without pity. Since he did not receive the permit, he began by at least saving the remaining old-style buildings. Each change in a door or window, a banister or cornice, required a special permit from the conservator, who was more concerned about the old shape and style than the comfort of the people living in the house.

[164]

At any rate, the Polish architects thought that the town of Kremenets contained more well-preserved original old-style buildings than any other town did, so much so that town's general character retained its own original style. The architects made the town a sort of center for disseminating the original Polish construction style. Each year an incursion of dozens of artists and painters spread all over the town's streets and its surroundings, painting the views and old buildings. The authorities supported this project, and the visiting artists received stipends and boarded in the Lyceum's buildings.

What was the Jews' role in this "war"? They were a completely passive element. They liked the Russian style of simple, straight lines and inexpensive construction. The Polish opinion was that the Jews, and particularly the wealthy among them, had "destroyed" the town's style, and so the Poles were very angry with them. As a result, the Jews saw the conservator's demands as a senseless edict. They were unsympathetic to his reasons and tried to circumvent him and his oppressive demands. This was another cause for friction, and here, too, the Jews were the "third side" whom each rival saw as his enemy.

Pravoslavic Church

Catholic Church

[165]

ALTERMAN'S COURTYARD

Manus Goldenberg (Givat HaShlosha)
English translation by Thia Persoff

ABOVE THE STAIRCASE OF GRANDFATHER'S HOUSE

Many cloudy days were visited on our town. For weeks on end, a dense mass of clouds would hang over our heads beyond Mount Vidomka, which is on the west side of Mount Bona in the east. But in my memory, I always see it awash with sunlight and the bright glow of childhood.

I remember a clear summer morning. The east side of the street rests in the shade, while the west side is dipped in the sun's radiance. On the stone steps leading to the entrance of my grandfather's house, in the center of the street, are the distinguished wagon drivers, some sitting and some lying down. Their strapping young sons, who already enjoy an important position in the profession, surround them. Drunk on sun and the scent of acacia, the elders are enjoying their conversation and reminisce about bygone days. Their language is flowery, spiced with folk sayings and proverbs.

I had witnessed their talks since early childhood. Hour upon hour, I used to sit in a corner and listen. This was my first window on the wide world. With those still-hearty old men, I traversed—in my imagination—the steppes of Ukraine in a two-horse carriage. I met other travelers, generous squires and Jewish contractors, builders of railroad tracks and roads through the vastness of Mother Russia all the way to Kiev and Odessa.

With the young cart drivers, I enjoyed hearing about the quantities of roasted goose they ate and the wineglasses they emptied when they brought their passengers to blessed Bessarabia.

I was a partner to their life and adventures in the early 20th century, which we spent together on the steps. I still think about them.

FROM THE STORM'S ECHO

I recall a fresh morning during the harvest season, when the wagon drivers arrived from the train station with information about a shocking incident that had taken place there: two young Russians who were waiting on the platform for the train to arrive looked suspicious to the policemen. The Russians were ushered into a separate room to be checked out, and soon shots were heard. When people burst into the room, the two policemen and the two Russians were dead. The young Russians had shot the policemen first, then shot themselves. Leaflets from the revolutionary underground were found next to their bodies. The policemen were buried with a grand ceremony, but the young revolutionaries were buried in the sand at the foot of the Mount Krestova. The residents there, who held the young men close to their hearts, remembered their burial place. When the right time came, the Bolsheviks dug out their bones and buried them with proper honor.

Here, on the steps, this incident was discussed in whispers and linked to ... a comet that is approaching the earth and is liable to destroy it with one sweep of its tail. They told of bloodstains on the moon, too, in which they saw bad omens for the future—and, indeed, evil times came.

Those sitting on the steps could see colorful sights. Each horse passing by led to a discussion, as the bloodlines of all the horses in the district were well known to them. When the mood came upon the youngsters, they entertained the older men with shenanigans: sneaking up behind a Pravoslavic priest and sticking a paper tail on his long cassock or stringing a rope across the street. Then young and old would burst into thunderous laughter when a young couple walking by tripped and fell to the ground. They had many pranks up their sleeves, with particular shenanigans for each season.

[166]

The century's first decade passed slowly, but by the second, events began to tailspin. In 1912, we viewed the grand parade of the Czar's army celebrating the 100th anniversary of the victory over Napoleon. Soon after were the parade and even grander celebration of the Romanov dynasty's 300th anniversary. Had our town ever seen such a display of grandeur and glory, and had anyone ever admired the czars and fully believed in their victorious might as the wagoners did? From these steps in 1915, we followed with wonder as convoys of the Russian army's service corps, heavy artillery corps, and infantry, all supplied with the best equipment, flowed endlessly from the center of Russia toward Galicia.

Fascinated, they sat and watched for days as division after division galloped lightly in front of them with their many marching bands. Troops of Cossacks from the Ural, Kuben, and the Don, as well as Cherkasian and Kirghizian horsemen, all moved north, north toward the breach in the front that General Brusilov had opened. "Mr. Thief," some of them mutter, excited by the splendid-looking horses passing by. Their eyes lit up with a powerful desire at the sight of the bearded brigadiers' and generals' valiant stallions. But in my childish imagination, I had a nightmare that they had been trampled under the horses' hoofs, their beards stained with blood ....

WITH THE COLLAPSE OF THE TYRANT

Returning, the convoys again flowed steadily, this time in a panic, the wagons, horses, and soldiers looking wretched. This was Czar Nikolas's retreating, defeated army.

The world of the inhabitants of the steps collapsed on them. The revolution's stormy days skipped over them and passed on. They were only passive onlookers, and they seemed to continually resent it. Now that the broom of the revolution had swept away the squires and officers, who had scattered their money generously, no one called to them in a lordly way, "Wagoner!" Now their providers were grocers and peddlers, enriched by the war, who sometimes would walk to the train station to save a coin. Their world became gray and narrow ....

Years have passed since then. Their carts stand in a long line near the stone fence of the Pravoslavic church. The street is empty. When someone approaches, the drivers run toward him, each trying to pull him to his cart. Pandemonium reigns. But soon they find out that he is just passing through ....

I remember their days of glory, and I witnessed their shocking deterioration. With a pounding heart, I walk up the street to the sharp left turn. Where did the gully disappear to, the one into which the rainwater flowed mightily? Each big rainfall turned it into a roaring river, carrying thousands of tons of mountain silt and heavy stones with it. Once, a farmer who dared to cross the flooding water was washed away into that gully with his wagon, right in front of some people, who stood by helplessly. The gully was filled with dirt, and in place of that Kremenets "Niagara," the public toilets stand, the crowning achievement of the Polish mayor ....

TOVYE SHAYKOVSKI

The first house at the end of the street was ancient. In the front it had one story, but in the back, facing the Potik, it had two.

[167]

A high fence made of planks surrounded the lower one, concealing its secrets. Now and then, hysterical sounds accompanied by hair-raising curses erupted from there. When that "storm" calmed down, we, the children, would peek through the narrow crack in the fence and see a green fruit orchard and a cow barn. The house and courtyard belonged to a widow and her slightly mad daughter. Only the boldest of the boys dared to sneak into the orchard, and woe to the one who was caught. Only once did I succeed in penetrating this mysterious world. One evening, my grandmother, who liked drinking fresh cow's milk, took me there with her. A cheerful view met my eyes: in a pastoral courtyard full of plants and flowers wafted a mixture of lilac fragrance and the odor of fertilizer. All this was only a few steps from the center of the town, which was crowded with stores and workshops.

At that moment, animosity toward the courtyard's occupants dissipated. The milking mother and daughter were a remnant of a family that had lived on its land in a village but had been deported as a result of Czar Alexander's edict.

In the apartment facing the front lived Tovye Shpigl, called Shaykovski, with his family. In the only room except for a small kitchen, he sat bent over a machine, sewing shoe uppers for the shoemakers who surrounded him on all sides: non-Jews from the nearby mountains. They all understood Yiddish, and Tovye spoke with them mostly in his mother tongue. The floorboards shook and squeaked, and through their cracks you could see a dark chasm, but the atmosphere was jolly. Ukrainian and witty Jewish jokes followed one after the other. The shoemakers waited patiently, sometimes from morning to evening, as Tovye was busy with community needs most of the time.

The Burial Society—the poor survivor of Jewish autonomy in our town—was to Tovye like clay in the potter's hands. Even the town's dignitaries went along with his decisions. Ordinary citizens followed him like after a revered leader. On Simchat Torah, he showed up in full splendor, accompanied by his devoted adjutants, as the conductor of the Burial Society members' circuits. The next day I saw him again, wearing a uniform. A reserve soldier, he was called to serve in the army the year the war began. With his divided red beard, he looked like a knight out of a folktale. I can still hear the voices of his family members accompanying him on his way to the front. When he returned safely after many years, he had his hands full. It was a troubled time for Jews. On one of the fateful days, when the lives of countless Jews were hanging in the balance, Tovye risked his life to save them. There was an uprising of angry farmers the vicinity, and the Jews stayed hidden in their homes, awaiting their fate in great fear. I heard the echo of heavy steps. I peeped through a crack in the shutter. Tovye and his adjutant Sender Shepsel, weighed down with heavy sacks, were walking in the empty street. As we found out later, the sacks were filled with food from the residents for the rebels, to appease their anger. A high-ranking czarist officer who headed the rebels and had had ties to some Jewish families in the past helped them in this endeavor. This was a deed of great self-sacrifice, as death was lurking at every step. After the rebels ate their fill, peace returned. And except for a few cases of robbery, there were no casualties. The rabbis, who had been taken out of town at gunpoint, were rescued at the last moment.

> [**Translator's Note:** Simchay Torah (Rejoicing in the Torah) is a holiday whose celebration includes *hakafot* (circuits), in which the Torah is carried around the house of worship.]

During Polish rule, Tovye again took community affairs into his own hands. His humble apartment turned into a "high command center," where his secret allies attended him all day. Through them, he negotiated with the miserly, wealthy relatives of those who had passed away and demanded large sums of money from them. On the other hand, he generously supported poor families and took it upon himself to contribute to poor brides' weddings, charity associations, the hospital, the Home for the Aged, synagogues, and so on.

He was firm, loved by the poor, and accepted by non-Jewish craftsmen.

The period of his "reign" came to an end with the *Senatsya* clerks' interference in community affairs.

> [**Translation Editor's Note:** *Senatsya* was a Polish political movement that came to power in 1926.]

[168]

ALTERMAN'S COURTYARD

A few steps from the house where Tovye lived stands a partially destroyed fence. This is Alterman's Courtyard. Here is where I spent my childhood. The courtyard was built on a slope that continues up to the Potik. The back fence is at the foot of Mount Bona. During my childhood, I used to feel apprehensive about this close proximity, because the rabbi's assistant liked to ask himself, in front of us, "What would happen if the Bona collapsed during the night?" and immediately give the answer: "It would cover the whole town." Since our house in the courtyard was the closest to the mountain, I was scared of the impending avalanche and the large rocks peeking through our windows. The rabbi's assistant said that if one of them were dislodged, a tremendous flood of water would burst out of the mountain .... I was about five years old when we came to live in this courtyard, whose owner was no longer living. His old widow lived in one of the courtyard houses, surrounded by her sons and daughters. She was then in her declining years and was treated with the honor reserved for a wife of a high-ranking officer—her husband being a supplier to the army troops lodged in the many buildings in the courtyard. Even today, the women are jealous of her ... on account of her glamorous past.

Tsukerman's Courtyard, Next to Alterman's Courtyard

The *Nagid* R' Duvid Leyb, a person of great dignity from one of the town's aristocratic families, lived in one of the houses in the courtyard. People used to talk with great admiration about his philanthropy and the fine manners in his home. The elder son, although he dressed traditionally, became caught up in *tarbut ra'ah* and ran away to the university in Petersburg. The family moved away from Kremenets.

[**Translator's Notes:** A *Nagid* is a prince or leader, or a ruler. *Tarbut ra'ah* (bad culture or manners) refers to an interest in secular education.]

R' MOSHKE'LE

Into the white house moved Rabbi Moshke'le, one of the many great-grandsons of the Ba'al Shem Tov, who lived on his great reputation and witnessed its decline. He did not perform miracles or distribute amulets. He had a small study hall in one of his rooms. My father was one of the regulars who prayed there. Jews of all classes would come to his house and give him a donation; they enjoyed being his guests at Sabbath and holiday dinners and discussing daily events. He was not a scholar, and his regular visitors were simple people. But at the close of the Passover holiday and on Simchat Torah, a spark of the Hasidic excitement was lit here; Hasidim would gather around his table and "grab a couple of songs," singing and dancing until dawn.

[**Translator's Note:** The Ba'al Shem Tov was Rabbi Yisrael ben Eliezer, an 18th-century mystical rabbi who is considered the founder of Hasidic Judaism.]

For many years, the citizens of Kremenets remembered his eldest daughter's marriage to the son of the rabbi from Radzivilov. For about a week preceding the wedding, the town bustled with preparations.

Section of Sheroka Street / Photo by Alter Katsizne

A giant tent was erected near the house, where a meal was served to the poor the evening before the wedding. We, the children, watched the assorted cripples, some of whom stayed in town to collect alms.

On the wedding day, all work stopped in the town. The main street was flooded with people, Jews and non-Jews. A troupe of "Cossacks"—Jews in Cossack costumes—rode on horses out of town to receive the groom. For hours the crowds waited on the sidewalks, and then a colorful procession arrived. The groom was sitting in a four-horse carriage followed by many other carriages and wagons, which were greeted with cheers. The policemen in charge of maintaining order were already tipsy from the brandy they had "tasted" until it was time to collect payment for their services ....

For years, all the "young rabbi's" time was devoted to study, while R' Moshke'le supported him. In the evening, when my father's workday was done, he would study some difficult passages with the young rabbi. He praised the young rabbi highly but did not hide his sadness over his expending all his energy on one small section of *Halakha*. After the revolution, the family immigrated to America, where they were supported generously by the Kremenetsers there.

[**Translator's Note:** *Halakha* is Jewish religious law.]

The rabbi's house, which stood at the entrance to the courtyard, was drenched in peace and tranquility. In the courtyard, under the canopy of an ancient chestnut tree that shaded the rabbi's house, noise and tumult reigned. The children of the courtyard played there all day long with their friends from nearby and faraway streets. In that place grew up a generation devoted to public movements that shook up the Jewish street.

A MEETING PLACE FOR REVOLUTIONARY YOUTH

Very close to the rabbi's home stood a small house. At the same time that the rabbi would formally receive the district governor in his splendidly lit home, the best of the young generation would meet in a neighboring house to heatedly discuss human rights, freedom, and ways to topple the regime of oppression and slavery.

The house belonged to the widow Chave Hirsh Aba, a seamstress to high-society Russian ladies. Her clients, attracted by her pleasant personality and dignity, would come to her salon with their best manners.

[170]

Her home served as a meeting place for the best of the Jewish young people in our town: university students, students from the upper grades of the High School of Commerce, leaders of the Bund organization and Labor Zionists, etc. The owner and her family received everyone in a pleasant, friendly way. The atmosphere was always saturated with the joy of youth. The laughter of the students from the high school for girls, the owner's daughters and their friends, would accompany the lively discussions.

During the summer nights, many of them would leave the rooms and arguments to sit on the benches under the chestnut tree and express their love for their nation in lyrical songs.

The courtyard's tenants would gather around them, joining the singing and playing the guitar and mandolin. Their only competitor was the chorus of Ukrainian young people hidden among the mountains, whose soul-capturing singing would penetrate all corners of the town.

Among the frequenters of the house were members of the Manusovits family, educated left-wing activists who were talented in the arts. It was they who nurtured the love of literature and Jewish folklore in our town. Under their guidance, parties and celebrations were arranged in honor of current Jewish writers.

Preparations for celebrating the anniversary of the writer Mendile in Chave's house lasted for months. The rehearsals drew us in. We listened to readings, recitations, and songs. A big celebration held in the spacious second-floor apartment of Vitser, an army supplier, topped off the preparations. Here it was safe to enjoy ourselves without causing suspicion. It was an important event, as the law did not permit Jews to hold plays, parties, or meetings.

When Anski came to Kremenets, he was the guest of the young people in Chave's house. With their help, he got in touch with townspeople who could enrich his collection. And in Kremenets, he enriched it greatly.

He would spend his resting hours under the chestnut tree in the company of young people, and to entertain the women and children, he would play folk records. Close to the beginning of World War I, all the members of the Manusovits family immigrated to America, where they were very active in Jewish education and arts.

A few years later, Chave's only son, the student Hirsh Aba, also began preparations to leave. It took a long time, and on the day of his departure, his mother gave in to the unexpressed pain of the coming separation, and she had a stroke. The son did not leave. Her limbs paralyzed, the mother spent the rest of her life in a wheelchair. When the war and general conscription began, a few of the town's young people continued to come over. This center was completely destroyed when Chave passed away, her son Hirsh Aba left for Petersburg the capital, and two of her daughters enlisted as nurses.

ARTS AND CRAFTS IN THE COURTYARD

The courtyard bustled with creation and labor. In three large carpentry workshops there, the town's best cabinetmakers, Fingerut and Alterman, produced the most elegant furniture in the whole area, each piece a lovingly created work of art.

We, the courtyard's young children, loved watching their faces radiating with the joy of creation. A tall pile of lumber was stacked near each workshop, each board and plank cared for and tended by its owner. A piece of lumber that had not fully aged would not be used. In that period, furniture would be kept in a family from one generation to the next, and each item carried a tag identifying its maker.

During the summer, work stopped at day's end.

[171]

The workers laid their tools down and hurried to their homes, then went for a stroll on Sheroka Street. The carpenters and cabinetmakers would come out with their wives to breathe the fresh air and sit on the piles of lumber. We liked to sit with them at that hour and take in the aroma of the forest emanating from the wood.

As darkness slowly fell and the shadows lengthened, the music of a violin accompanied by piano poured from the windows across from us. Now and then, a song sung in a subdued bass accompanied them: the voice of Sioma Kaplan, the tailor's son, who had succeeded in enrolling in the High School of Commerce, sang Russian romantic songs with feeling ....

Night fell, and all was silence. Everyone listened to the melancholy notes coming from the Rozenblits' apartment. This family of storekeepers was preoccupied with making a living, but their apartment was clean and comfortable. The family members were blessed with talent and beauty, and the children studied music and painting, which attracted many young people to this enlightened household. Kremenets is the hometown of the father of the Russian Enlightenment, and not without reason was the nickname "Kremenets Philistines" pinned to its residents. Many of the elders in town still spat and showered curses on Levinson when they passed his hut ....

Levinzon Street

This courtyard was a miniature world: a cross section of the society's life and its classes and characters. Here was the army supplier, Vitser, a member of the preeminent class in town, and here were storekeepers, brokers, and craftsmen. In one of the far corners was a shoemaker, and in the basement of the house was a machine for baking matzot, called "the big machine" to differentiate it from the other two machines in town.

The week after the Purim holiday, the scrubbed and whitewashed basement was turned into a factory that hummed from early morning to late at night. It was here that we first witnessed "sweatshop" work: the thin line of dough moved rapidly out of the machine onto a long table, next to which sweat-drenched boys stood holding knives and slicing the dough, trying to keep up with the speed of the machine. The bakers worked quickly next to the blazing-hot ovens. The baker near the machine urged the boys to speed up, his mouth flowing curses. You felt as if you had been thrown into Hell ....

[172]

The hardest work was done in the dark areas in the far corners of the basement. There, laborers—only non-Jews did this work—toiled 12–14 hours a day, kneading huge lumps of dough with iron bars attached to tables covered by metal sheets. Their breath was labored, and their sweat ran into the dough. Two of them had an earring in one ear, and I saw them as submissive slaves and was full of pity for them. During the 1930s, this work, too, was "conquered" by pioneers from the training kibbutzim, to the puzzlement of the local Jews.

> [**Translator's Note:** Submissive slaves, according to the laws of the Torah, are slaves who do not accept freedom at the end of their service. They were marked by piercing, a mark of shame.]

The status of the wagon drivers there was represented by their chosen sons.

In the far reaches of the courtyard were stables left from its days as an army barracks. The wagon drivers who owned several pairs of horses were the "leviathans" of the profession, big, strong Jews followed by legends of their heroic deeds. Jews and non-Jews called "whippers" worked for them for a daily salary. For the few coins they earned, they manned their vehicles all day. Their status was considered the lowest on the social ladder.

More than once, we awakened at night to the screechy wailing of a "whipper." We knew that this was the hour of reckoning between the boss and his employees and that punishment for assumed incorrect billing was being meted out. We thought it odd that grown men would cry like little children, yet they were known to be strong-armed men. Like stricken dogs, they would hide in a dark corner of the stable, sobbing for a long time.

On other days, when the owners set out for an official reception, the stables could be seen in a completely different light. From the dark opening of the stable, one could hear the joyful laughter of Jewish women in colorful outfits, who were known in town to be prostitutes. Here they were honored, and they seemed like elegant ladies with lapdogs. The rough, boorish drivers were gentle and polite in their company, and all the scorn and contempt they received throughout the year were forgotten here. Their self-esteem rose. This was not so hard to understand, as the drivers were their knights and protectors. Sometimes, as a result of those visits, quarrels would start in different parts of town as the protectors retaliated against those who had insulted the women. Blood was spilled on the streets of Kremenets, and no one dared interfere, not even the police. The heavy hand of the czarist police was very soft when it came to the forces of the underworld, which terrorized even non-Jews. They always had the upper hand.

With the revolution, the drivers' economic standing was destroyed, and civil war put an end to their arbitrariness.

Between the two carpentry workshops across from the stables was the first Hebrew school in our town, which was established in 1909. For two reasons, the school was given the modest name of *Cheder Metukan*. One was to prevent the devout traditionalists from getting angry. The other was to prevent the czarist authorities from refusing to give a permit for a Hebrew school. This was the first school in our town where boys and girls attended and studied together. Some of those students continued their studies in the Herzliya High School in Tel Aviv-Jaffa and in the school for agriculture in Mikve Yisrael. There, the founders, teachers Burshteyn and Sirayski, knew how to awaken a longing for Zion and love of the Hebrew tongue in us.

[**Translator's Note:** A *Cheder Metukan* is a progressive Hebrew school.]

It was while we were in school that we first felt the heavy hand of the czarist authority. For a long time, we had been preparing for a Purim celebration by learning to recite long sections from I. L. Gordon's writings, and we were nervous at the prospect of this gathering, at which our parents would be the audience.

[173]

The celebration was held at the spacious home of a parent, R' Mordekhay Chasid, in a room lit by large kerosene lamps. Slowly the parents arrived. Spirits were high. A screen sewn from bed sheets was raised. The first to perform were four children, including me, reciting together; after us, it was students Brak and Shnayder's turn. While they were reciting and the parents were admiring them, policemen burst into the room—and the boys stopped as if they were frozen in place. After an extended interrogation, the policemen wrote down the names of all the attendees, ordered them to disperse, and arrested Chasid.

BOYS WHO ROSE HIGH

What happened to those two from the upper grade?

One of them, Brak, deviated from our ways some years later. Dark forces among the Christian residents had influenced him to convert. At a crucial moment in the civil war in our town, he appeared on a horse at the head of a Ukrainian rebel regiment of local farmers. The regiment attacked the town, which supported the Hetmans and their German lords. Among the Hetmans' supporters were some students from the Ukrainian high school and some Jews who had given in to the principal's coaxing. After a bitter battle, the rebels were victorious. One of the rebel commanders who led the negotiation for the German surrender and leaving the town was our Jewish-school friend Brak. He was also one of the people who punished residents who helped the Germans—former officers and policemen who excelled in cruelty toward farmers and hatred of Jews.

The young life of Brak's partner in the recital, Shnayder, was rich in deeds.

Well built, he showed up one night wearing an army uniform and a gun in his belt, while we, a group of his previous school friends, were on civilian guard duty on Voskrasanskaya Street near our courtyard. He was then on assignment as an officer representing the revolutionary board.

The meeting was very friendly. In the peaceful, deeply sleeping street, we felt the ties from the days of our childhood in spite of the distance between us, which was very great by that time. We were still involved in the world of youth, while he, who was two years older than we were, had already taken an active role among the makers of that period's history.

We were told that during the Bolsheviks' temporary retreat from our area, Shnayder was left as one of the revolution's underground organizers in the rear of Petliura's army in the Dubno area. There were many stories of his daring adventures during the brave partisans' war against Petliura's army in the district.

In the Bolsheviks' great attack on this unruly army, which began with the conquest of Kiev, their capital, Shnayder was one of the first commanders who entered as victors. The Jewish residents, who had been saved from a bloody massacre, hugged the young fighter. The painful insult inflicted by the czarist police at Mordekhay Chasid's had probably made a lasting impression on these two heroes.

The courtyard's neighbors to the north—the czarist policemen—contributed to its color and oddness. Here, in a large hall, was the barracks of the town police force, numbering about 20. These policemen, with whom Jewish mothers threatened their children, walked around in embroidered shirts like simple farmers. Most could not recognize a letter when they saw one, but they liked to joke with us. Only the weapons, swords, and guns we saw on the walls through the open windows kept us from getting too close to the place. Their ignorance made even the children laugh. To show how ignorant they were, we tried more than once to sing revolutionary songs under their windows, but they did not understand them and simply asked us not to disturb their rest.

[174]

Across from their windows was the apartment of Tody Shvarts, a bespectacled Jewish clerk in the chicken slaughterhouses. All the members of his large family, young and old, were laborers. Everyone respected this family, as it was crowned with courage.

The eldest son had shot himself to death. Such a death inspired the Jews of that era; there was something in it that aroused young people's respect, particularly when we heard from the adults that the reason was disappointment over the failure of the 1905 revolution. He had been active in the revolutionary underground and, with his comrade in the movement, Y. Kremenetski, had been arrested, jailed for a long time, and beaten by the police.

Tody's sons taught us the revolutionary songs and encouraged us to sing them in front of the policemen. Once, one of the sons dared us to get a real bayonet from the police—an "expropriation" that we successfully achieved. We were suspects in the theft and were interrogated for days, but not one of us squealed on the others.

THE YESHIVA

About two or three years before World War I, the police left the courtyard, and in their place came the Yeshiva. Young men of different ages arrived from villages near and far, with each one known by the name of his village. By day they studied in those rooms, and at night they slept there. We heard them chanting day and night. Even then, we saw that some of them occupied themselves with books from the outside, and the neighbors in the courtyard, most of whom were progressives—adherents of the Bund or Zionism—were willing to help them get those books.

The head of the Yeshiva, who came from the town of Novograd Volynskiy, is worth mentioning.

His beard disheveled, he walked bent over, with his eyes lowered to the ground so as not to meet a woman's eye. He never smiled at his children or his wife, and he never called his wife by name.

The Yeshiva existed on donations from the town residents. The students went hungry often, as did the family of the head of the yeshiva. A slice of bread dipped in oil was his main food, and the oil was used as a remedy, too, for any ailments in his family ....

He never raised his voice to his students. He could calm any storm with his gaze, and they treated him with indescribable respect and love. But the ones who were caught with books from the outside paid a bitter price, as then the head of the Yeshiva showed himself to be a vengeful, vindictive zealot. Only a few of the students became rabbis. Some left after a few years and went to national schools, and nearly all of them were swallowed up by life's whirlpool when the revolution began. They all ended up in one political movement or another. Across from this Yeshiva full of noisy and vibrant students, the humble, poor Hebrew school stood in a corner, leaning on skinny, sickly Burshteyn's shoulders.

THE COURTYARD DURING THE WAR

About a year after World War I began, the front was approaching our town. Great changes took place in the courtyard. The Yeshiva closed its doors, and the students dispersed to their hometowns, most of which had been destroyed.

New residents moved into the courtyard. Some were families that had been evacuated from border towns, and some were young men from Odessa and Kharkov who came to hide until the Austrian forces arrived and freed them from the threat of forced conscription into the Czar's army. They brought some big-city glamour, new songs, new etiquette, and new behavior with them. The army took over the stables, storage facilities, cellar, and Yeshiva. Outdoor field cooks raised smoke and steam all day long, and the smell of coarse whole-wheat bread being baked for the soldiers in the matzot-baking cellar permeated the area .... The schools were evacuated, the children went idle, and their parents lost any influence over them. Armies marched to and from the front, transporting wounded and prisoners, and officers paid generously for any service rendered ....

[175]

The distance from the front to the town shortened until the line of Austrian trenches was only 6 kilometers from the Dubno suburb. All government and community institutions were evacuated, and a Cossack commander with the rank of captain took over the rule of the town. The town's entire economic structure collapsed, as farmers from the unconquered side hardly ever came to market, and many stores closed. For the first time, the town's residents faced a curfew, and every infraction of the commander's rules was punished by flogging. The echoes of machine gun and rifle fire were constant, and the sky was red with the reflections of burning villages. The oppressive terror of war struck fear into the hearts of the residents.

On those evenings, a lively social life continued in the courtyard more than in the rest of the homes. Was it because of the soldiers and officers who lived there, or the young men and women in student uniforms? In their loneliness, friendships and relationships formed among the courtyard residents. During the dark evenings, the young residents still sat under the canopy of the chestnut tree and carried on discussions as before. The main speakers were fugitives, who were integrated into the courtyard's free, genial atmosphere ....

As the Austrians' chances for victory increased, the residents drew even more closely together, and we were like one large family united in its fate.

The situation completely turned around with the partial victory of the Russians' great counterattack. The front retreated 20 miles. The headquarters of the famous Eleventh Army Corps, which included many units with all sorts of armaments, came to Kremenets.

The town and the surrounding area were flooded with soldiers and with those directly or indirectly in the service of headquarters; there was no other way of making a living. For those seeking to make a profit, money was flowing. Every other home was turned into a coffeehouse. Grocers profited, beggars multiplied, and their pockets swelled. Licentiousness reigned. At the same time, the families of the conscripted and those whose heads of household had run away to avoid conscription were even more destitute. There was a sharp contrast between the starving and freezing and those who were getting richer.

Life in the courtyard declined decisively during this period. Some of the young people were conscripted, some left to study in Odessa and Kiev, and the escapees and refugees returned to their homes and towns. People from headquarters penetrated every corner. The atmosphere in the courtyard was influenced by gold fever in the army's rear. Even the carpenters and drivers were forced to trade and speculate—in wartime, who needed furniture or a ride to the train? Until the war began, only very seldom did a single car, belonging to the president of the noblemen's society, pass by on Kremenets' main street, and it drew a large crowd. Now the army's elegant cars and trucks passed through day and night.

THE REVOLUTION ARRIVES IN THE COURTYARD

The February revolution erupted. Large demonstrations organized by the headquarters' drivers and mechanics added to the wave of joy and excitement that permeated the Jewish community. The laborers from Petersburg and Moscow had a great deal of experience in such operations …. From them, the residents of Kremenets heard revolutionary marching songs for the first time. They were the first to wave red flags by the hundreds, and they cautioned us about provocation by the headquarters' military police. The streets of Kremenets lived the life of revolution to its fullest. Endless demonstrations and meetings attracted everyone, including the young residents of the courtyard, some of whom had returned from the large cities where they had studied and threw themselves enthusiastically into the arms of the stormy revolutionary life all around them. The easy rhythm and tranquility of life in the courtyard did not fit the new era.

[176]

Its young residents had left. Members of the underground surfaced and moved into the open to function in assorted institutions and cultural centers. In the courtyard next door, the second-largest to ours in the town, events of historical importance were taking place. This courtyard had also been used as an army barracks at one time. The house in the center of that courtyard was built in the Polish aristocratic style of the 18th century, one that Polish architects and painters often photographed and painted.

The soldiers' council of the Eleventh Army Corps was headquartered in this house. At meetings there, Russia's destiny was discussed: there were arguments about how to continue the war or whether to stop it, the kind of government to have in Russia, etc. Among the council members were well-known leaders of the Socialist Revolutionaries and Social Democrats and speakers from the liberal royalist party Constitutional Democrats.

Every day, large delegations of soldiers would arrive from different areas of the front with marching bands and flags. In the wide-open space of the courtyard, their spokesmen would present their demands to the council and, through stirring patriotic speeches, persuade them to accept a decision to continue the war.

In a corner of the council hall sat a delegate wearing a czarist lieutenant's uniform, who from time to time asked permission to speak. He expressed the opposite of the other delegates: a demand to stop the war and divide the estate lands among the farmers. At first, his words were like a voice calling out in the wilderness, and he was dubbed a follower of the traitor party. Nevertheless, he drew more and more sympathizers. In addition to his talks in the council hall, he appeared in a series of lectures in the Lyceum auditorium and talked with groups of soldiers in the streets. His influence became stronger, and by the end of the summer, he had surrounded himself with many supporters who helped him promote his ideas. Among his adherents were few Jewish students from Kremenets. This young lieutenant was the famous Krilenko, who stood at the head of the Red Army at its inception and was later the Soviet Union's public prosecutor for many years.

THE ZIONIST CLUB IN TSUKERMAN'S COURTYARD

In the entrance to that courtyard, called Tsukerman's Courtyard, stood a large house. Its wings were decorated with white and blue flags, and extensive Zionist activity began there. It was the center for a national movement, and for young people who had studied in Odessa and Kiev and devoted themselves with the passion of youth to disseminating information and culture. Committees were established for the National Fund, Hebrew classes, Zionism, the expansion of the library, the formation of Hebrew education institutions, etc., and the first Hebrew kindergarten was housed here, too. The conference of the district's Young Zionist movement, which was infused with an atmosphere of newly acquired power, was held here. During elections for Jewish Russian or Jewish Ukrainian institutions and for the first community governing council in our town, this house was turned into a war zone. In Jewish neighborhoods, it was necessary to break the lobbyists' rule.

Those forces were attacked from another opposing side, that of the Bund organization, which was very powerful in those days. Bund members considered themselves the best men of the revolution, and the workers of Kremenets followed them enthusiastically.

Two strong, opposing factions struggled for this first community government: the Zionist Organization, and the Bund with the Labor Zionists. The latter faction won the election, and the first organized community in Kremenets was declared with much ado as a "Red Community" and celebrated with victory parades.

The "Red Community" did not last very long, just as all sorts of other public institutions at those unstable times did not.

[177]

But I'll never forget that community's stormy board meetings, whose debates took place under the slogan of liberty, equality, and fraternity. People sat listening until the late hours of the night and sometimes participated in the discussions.

From the balcony of the Zionist Organization house, we watched the progress of the events that decided the fate of the Russian revolution. There were more and more delegations of soldiers from the front, and their appearance was increasingly stormy. Spring was over, and summer came to an end. Every day we heard news of murdered estate owners, burned mansions, and lynching in our area. The "October" winds were blowing.

I moved to the city of Rovno to attend the School of Commerce. During my six months there, the glamour of the February Revolution faded, and in the midst of the turbulence and confusion of the time the election for Greater Russia's constitutional assembly began. A few factions campaigned for the Jewish vote, and one of the first candidates on the Zionist Organization's ballot in Volhynia province was M. Gindes, from Kremenets. He campaigned in Rovno and Kremenets against Goldshteyn, the famous attorney, who represented an independent slate. In Kremenets, Dr. B. Landsberg argued heatedly with the rivals of the Zionist slate who had turned away from the center.

News from Kremenets seldom arrived. The town was used as a transition stop for soldiers who had left the front to move east and south with large stores of weapons and supplies. The year 1917 came to a close, and October was a long way behind us. At the end of December, my sister and I took the train—which was crowded with soldiers—to Kremenets for Christmas vacation. The train dragged on its way all night, and we were impatient to see our family, which by then had moved from Alterman's Courtyard to Grandfather's house in the center of Sheroka.

GRANDFATHER'S HOUSE GOES UP IN FLAMES

It was a gray, wintry morning at the station. The drivers, who had known us since our childhood, met us with an odd indifference, and only one dared to take our luggage and asked us to his sleigh. We approached the town center. Frishberg's house was already behind us, and there was the Grand Hotel, but where was our house? The sleigh stopped in front of an empty lot. In place of our house and the Vitels' house were smoking embers in which a few people were rummaging .... Our parents, their cries restrained, hugged us. We learned the whole story: the house that our grandfather had inherited had burned. On the ground, the metal sign announcing

"Watch repairs, gold and silver articles for sale. Margolis. Established in 1861," was like a single witness to the old house that had stood there. Each corner had been like a museum. The house went up in flames when a rabble of soldiers who had stopped in Kremenets on their way from the front attacked, murdered, and looted. During the robbery, the owner of the adjacent store, Mr. Vitels, was shot.

Four of the Vitels' little children were asleep in the house at the time. The rioters, who were busy looting, did not harm them. When the attackers left the house for a few moments, my mother, accompanied by my young uncle, ran out under a shower of shots to bring help. It was a daring and dangerous act in a lifetime of suffering and sacrifice. They succeeded in rescuing the children and some of the jewelry from the safe, which enabled my parents to rebuild the house and continue their business.

Only the stone steps on which the cart and wagon drivers had sat for so many years were left. For a while afterward, they refrained from sitting on them, discouraged by the empty space behind them ... the looting and murder, and our destroyed house. This was the only pogrom in our town during the entire civil war, in which all of Ukraine's Jewish settlements experienced an abundance of riots and slaughter.

The next day, self-defense began in Kremenets. About 50 Jewish soldiers who had returned from the front with their weapons volunteered to be the organizers.

[178]

On the first day of the defense's existence, groups in uniform and full combat equipment were already holding watch in the town's streets. For the groups' maintenance, well-to-do people were taxed heavily. Those who refused were denied permission to open their businesses, and guards were posted at their doors. A sense of peace and security returned to the town's residents.

After a few months, my parents were able to rebuild their home, the house that had been a meeting place for the town's notables during the life of my grandfather, R' Nachman the watchmaker, as well as for pious Hasidim who dined at his table during the holidays. Now big changes were taking place in it. Most visitors were young students and people from all social strata in town. Every important occurrence in the Jewish world or our town was discussed there. Initiatives for projects to help the national funds came more than once from there; stormy discussions were held here among the Zionist movement's members and opponents. The local storeowners went there to warm their frozen bodies by the stove on freezing cold days, and they found help there during the summer when they needed to pay a note at the bank .... Some went there to read the newspaper or seek advice and encouragement from my mother or help from my father, who, as a representative of the government's social services, was a custodian to the town's poor Jews and Christians in addition to his official community jobs. The large samovar was steaming, and everyone was welcome to a glass of tea and cookies .... When a labor emissary from the Land of Israel came to our town, he found a warm atmosphere and a place to stay in our house. This was one of the houses in the countryside that the writer Sholem Asch immortalized in his book *The House.*

215

As soon as the house was rebuilt, the inhabitants of the steps, the cart and wagon drivers, returned to them. One fall day, their curious eyes saw long convoys of military vehicles, artillery batteries, and foot soldiers marching in line on the main street. The army uniform, marching style, and language of the commands were different from what they had been used to all those years. This was the German army that burst with tremendous force into Ukraine in 1918. A period of peace had begun, the calm before the great storm—the civil war.

It seemed as if the events that took place between the two world wars, until the Holocaust, had chosen this house to put their stamp on. The house was partially destroyed by a German bomb at the beginning of the World War II. During Nazi rule, it was destroyed again along with all the other Jewish homes.

The Old Market

Photo by Alter Katsizne

[179]

CHARACTERS AND PERSONALITIES

RABBIS AND SLAUGHTERERS

Yonatan Kucher (Tel Aviv)
English translation by Thia Persoff

Kremenets was known as a cultured and enlightened town, but each generation had its geniuses—distinguished, great sages learned in the Torah. There were many Trisk, Chertkov, Sadigora, Ostraa, and other types of Hasidim. Their regular place of study and prayer was R' Mordekhay'le Mishne's synagogue, also called the Hasidic Synagogue, where the sounds of Torah study were heard day and night. Anyone who graduated from cheder studies and had a thirst for learning the Torah could find fulfillment there. Well-known scholars in the last generation were R' Shlome Sambar (Shlome Alinkis), R' Shlome Ditun (Shlome'le Avraham Leyb), R' Yisrael Mordekhay Yosi, and R' Shmuel Leyb Muchnik. Even though teaching was their profession, they did not discriminate between those who paid tuition and those who could not afford to do so, and taught their lessons for the sake of learning.

The rabbis and slaughterer-inspectors in our town were some of the most excellent ones of their time. A few generations back, R' Yochanen, son of Meir, held the town's rabbinical chair; he was the author of the book *Path of Righteousness*, about the *Nazir* tractate of the Talmud. At the same time, there was a famous *magid*, after whom the synagogue was named the *Magid's* Synagogue. The great rabbi R' Yitschak son of Moshe Leyb Maler, who was a rabbi in Holgrad, New Bessarabia (Romania), was born and raised in Kremenets. He wrote many new interpretations of the Torah and a wonderful one on Eben Ezra, which he called *To Understand Ezra*, and one on the book *Light of Life*, called *Hidden Light*.

> [**Translator's Notes:** In Hebrew, *Path of Righteousness* is *Orach Mishor*, *Light of Life* is *Or HaChayim*, and *Hidden Light* is *Or HaGanuz*. *Nazir* means abstinent.]

Our parents said that R' "Avraham Ozer Shabtay" was the rabbi in their day and that there was never another one like him. Before he came to Kremenets, he was a rabbi in the town of Pochayev, and it took a great deal of work to persuade him to agree to take the rabbinical chair in our town, as he was a modest man. For years after his death, people spoke about him with praise.

After him, R' Zev Mishne of Novograd Volynskiy, or, as they called him, R' Velvele the emissary of R' Mordekhay'le Mishne, held the rabbinical chair. He was a famous scholar and an expert in negotiation. He and his friend, Rabbi Alter of Starokonstantinov, would be asked to sit in Torah court by people from far and wide to judge or arbitrate, and their good names preceded them. R' Velvele served in his rabbinical chair with pride but without favoritism, and not once did he bring the anger of the community's leaders on himself. When he was out of town on a court assignment, his son-in-law, R' Duvid Leyb Segal, a man of learning and greatness, substituted for him.

The town's judge at that time was R' Hertsele Bronshteyn, who was respected for his honesty and righteousness.

When R' Velvele died, it was hard to find a replacement for him. Then, for the first time in the history of Kremenets, the town was split in two.

[180]

Rabbi Yakov Chayim Senderovits (the Rabbi from Petrikov)

The householders, headed by one of the most prominent men in town, R' Hirsh Mendil Rokhel, appointed Rabbi R' Yitschak Heler of Kurilovtsy, a great scholar and author of some books: *Isaac Acceded*, *The Offering of Isaac,* and others. The other side, which was the Hasidic side, appointed Rabbi R' Yakov Chayim Senderovits, who was known as the "prodigy from Petrikov," young in years but rich in Torah knowledge and wisdom. And he won the support of a significant majority in our town. For about ten years, the two rabbis served in the same capacity. Then, when the frontier of World War II reached the Ikva River near our town, most wealthy people and all who could save their life and property escaped. Rabbi Heler left his congregation at that time, too. Rabbi Senderovits stayed in town with the poor throughout the war years and led them with his wisdom.

[**Translation Editor's Note:** In Hebrew, *The Offering of Isaac* is *Minchat Yitschak.*]

One day during the change in regime, the rabbi, along with Judge R' Hertsele Bronshteyn and R' Moshke'le (Yunger Leyb), was arrested by the Bolsheviks. They stayed in prison for eight days and were released when the Bolsheviks retreated, but they were rearrested by a gang of Ukrainian insurgents who captured the town under the leadership of the officer Visotski. Rabbi Senderovits and R' Moshke'le were going to be killed, but miraculously they were saved.*

During Polish rule, an organized Jewish community was established, and Rabbi Senderovits was its rabbi. He died of an illness at age 52 after serving the town for 20 years, from 1906 to 1927. The townspeople, who worshiped him, mourned him sorrowfully.

After him, the town appointed R' Yechiel Yitschak Rapaport of Lutsk, a learned man and an active member of the *Mizrachi* organization, who was received favorably by the entire town. When he arrived at the train station, he was greeted by a delegation of the

---

* See the article by A. Zeyger, "How the Town Was Saved from Pogroms in 1920."

community's representatives: Mikhael Shumski, Zeydi Perlmuter, and Sh. Brodski. He was a gentle person who was easy to get along with and well liked by everyone—Orthodox, intellectuals, and householders.[†] But before long, he, like his predecessor, was taken ill with a heart condition from which he did not recover. He was 35 years old when he died in 1930. The town of Kremenets was bewildered, as if the people felt that because of their sins, those two "lights" had been extinguished ....

[**Translation Editor's Note:** Mizrachi is a religious Zionist movement.]

While traveling to give tests to yeshiva students, Rabbi Rapaport had noticed a student, Mordekhay Mendiuk, and planned to give him his daughter in marriage and bequeath him the rabbinical chair after his death.

[181]

His close friends and admirers used their influence to fulfill his will, and the young rabbi was elected to the post. They also arranged for an elaborate marriage celebration. Although some people in town opposed this choice of a rabbi, they were defeated by his supporters. In a short time, he learned Polish and received a governmental license for his appointment. Judging by his talents and scholarship, it was hoped that in time he would be a great rabbi, but he perished with the whole community at the hand of the Nazis, may their names be erased.

"Rabbi" Moshke'le was not one of the congregation's rabbis, but he was from a good family, being the son of Rabbi Aleksander Shuel "Yunger Leyb" of Vishnevets. His father's followers as well as other circles supported him, and he had a synagogue of his own. After his experience (as told before), he immigrated to America, and some years later, he died there peacefully.

****

Kremenets was noted for its ritual slaughterers and inspectors (*Sh&B*), who were men of integrity and mostly scholars. In out day, old men R' Duvid *Sh&B* and his friend R' Mendile *Sh&B* (Hokhgelernter) were the heads of the ritual slaughterers. R' Duvid was a simple and just man, a Stolin Hasid who never bothered with useless talk, and on the Sabbath, he never spoke Yiddish but conversed only in the holy tongue. R' Mendile was a Ruzhin Hasid. They were in charge of the slaughterhouse, and the young slaughterers/inspectors received their ordination from them. They were also expert circumcisers. The third member of this group of four friends was R' Shlome *Sh&B*, a great scholar who constantly studied the holy books. He knew all the books of the Bible and the six books of the Mishna by heart, and although he was blind in his old age, during the High Holy Days he would stand at the Holy Ark and recite the prayers. The fourth friend in the group was R' Tsadok HaKohen Yashpe, a God-fearing and hospitable Kutsk Hasid; he would not enjoy his meal unless he had arranged for all guests (and soldiers) to have Sabbath and holiday meals, each one according to his station in life, and never sat at the table without having a guest join him.

[†] See a special article about Rabbi Rapaport (in Yiddish).

[**Translator's Note:** *Sh&B* stands for *Shochet Uvodek* (slaughterer and inspector).]

After them came the second generation of slaughterers and inspectors. R' Dov Kliger took over from his father-in-law, R' Duvid *Sh&B*. He was a scholar, an Ostraa Hasid, and an expert in his profession. All his life he wished to immigrate to Zion, and his wish was fulfilled when family members living there sent for him. He was happy there and continued to work in his profession. Some years later, he passed away in Haifa. After R' Mendile Hokhgelernter, his son R' Leybele took over the post. He was an outstanding person in every way and was liked by everyone. Both men, like their fathers, were head slaughterers and expert circumcisers. R' Shlome *Sh&B*'s post went to his son, R' Yukil, and son-in-law, R' Chana, who did their jobs faithfully. R' Tsadok's sons did not follow in their father's profession but went into the world of commerce.

****

When R' Hertsele Bronshteyn was very old, the community chose a new judge for the town: a young rabbi, R' Yisrael Lerner, son of R' Mordekhay'le of Shumsk, who was learned and scholarly. So as not to diminish the honor due to R' Hertsele, they called Rabbi Lerner the judge from the Vishnevets suburb. During the split between the rabbis after Rabbi Rapaport's death, the Dubno suburb congregation on the other side of town, where the population was larger, took advantage of the situation and chose a separate rabbi. This was R' Fayvish-Leyb, who used to be a rabbi in Katerburg, an experienced man and an expert teacher. The Dubno congregation also brought in its own slaughterer, R' Aharon Fayngloz, who used to be a slaughterer in the town of Berezhtsy and was a scholar and the author of the book *Sons of Aharon*. Now he lives in Tel Aviv and serves as an inspector at the *kashrut* bureau. When the Kremenets community was organized during the Polish regime, the Dubno suburb congregation wanted to split and form its own community, but it did not succeed and remained subordinate to the Kremenets community.

****

The continuity ended there. Hasidic Kremenets was exterminated in the Holocaust with the rest of the Jewish people.

[182]

TEACHERS AND CHEDERS

English translation by Thia Persoff

In memory of the teachers R' Simche Ayzik and R' Shakhna Buts, from whom I learned the Torah.

R' SIMCHE AYZIK

Zev Kligman (Jerusalem)

He was faithful and true in all his ways, pouring all his efforts into instilling the knowledge of the Torah and Rashi's commentaries in his pupils. He had a helper whose job was to bring the children to cheder and return them home. In the evening during Heshvan, Kislev, and Tevet, he used to bring the children home with lanterns in their hands. There was no bigger pleasure for a child than to walk home holding a lantern. The only thing about the cheder that remains in my memory is the melody of the verse "And me, when I came from Padan Aram." His wife used to sew for the wealthy. He and his wife were childless, and running a cheder brought the joy of children into their home. They worked to earn a living and were content with their lot.

> [**Translator's Note:** Heshvan, Kislev, and Tevet are Hebrew months, corresponding approximately to October through December.]

R' SHAKHNA BUTS

Zev Kligman (Jerusalem)

When Simche Ayzik's cheder closed down, my father moved me to the cheder of R' Shakhna Buts, who was considered to be one of the best teachers in town. Everyone respected R' Shakhna, who was short with wide shoulders and a bright, intelligent face.

He was a wise and learned man, and was full of life in spite of his age. His only wish was for his students to be brought up to do good deeds. He always kept two sticks next to him—one long and thin, with which he spanked the naughty, and a thicker one that was meant for those who did not know their Pentateuch and Rashi .... He would mark mistakes with a black pencil the first time, in blue the next time, and in red the third time. We would anxiously wait for Passover eve, when we would start to learn the Song of Songs, etc. R' Shakhna would explain and interpret a verse, and the pleasing melody would flow and fill the cheder. We treated him with respect and honor, and we will never forget him. His wife, Toyve, was given to anger and more than once took it out on the children. Because we honored R' Shakhna, we never dared to disobey her.

THREE CHEDERS WITH AN EMPTY LOT IN BETWEEN

Bunya Shniftman (Pardesiya)

Three cheders were concentrated in a certain section of town: the teacher R' Hirsh-Leyb Pipik's, where I studied, R' Yoel Kishke's, and Leyb Rochele's. The three were separated by an empty lot, which pupils from all the cheders in the area used as a playground. The pupils were mostly boys, with very few girls. The teachers were not very scholarly, but their "helpers" were complete ignoramuses and caused the children a great deal of misery. Their job was to bring the children to the cheder and return them home at the end of the day and, during the lessons, not to teach but to keep order. They achieved this by hitting, cursing, and insulting the children. In the morning, the "helper" would carry the child on his shoulder to the cheder, where he stayed till late in the evening. During the summer, the children spent most of the time in the empty lot playing the button game. A child would tear buttons from any clothes he could find, even his own pants, and groups of children would sit around a small hole in the ground, playing eagerly with the buttons. As they sat, deeply involved in their favorite game, the "helper" from one cheder or another would sneak up on them and, whipping a leather belt right and left, break up the group and chase the children to the cheder to be greeted by a cross and angry "rabbi" .... First, they were given a reading lesson by the helper, and then, one by one, they moved to the "rabbi" himself to learn "Pentateuch with Rashi."

> [**Translator's Note:** *Pipik* means navel (bellybutton). *Kishke* means gut.]

R' HIRSH-LEYB "PIPIK"

Bunya Shniftman (Pardesiya)

R' Hirsh-Leyb had a large belly, which is why he was nicknamed Pipik. He wore a sleeveless black coat with the shirtsleeves showing through. On top of the coat he wore a ritual-fringed garment large enough to cover his whole belly. He wore high boots to which the garment's fringes reached ....

[183]

"*Vayomer—hot gizogt, Adonay—Got, El—tsu, Moshe—Moshe, lemor—azoy tsu zogn.*" The teacher read, and the child was to recite after him word by word. But when the child blundered and distorted the words because his mind was still on the button game from which he had been torn by force, the belt would appear in the rabbi's hand, and he would be whipped: "*Mamzer!*" "*Sheygets!*" From the cooking area, his wife—a small, skinny woman with constantly tearing eyes—appeared with a wooden spoon in her hand, and a storm of curses rained down on the head of the poor "*sheygets*" from her mouth, too ....

[**Translator's Notes:** *Vayomer—hot gizogt, Adonay—Got, El—tsu, Moshe—Moshe, lemor—azoy tsu zogn:* a sentence from the Torah in Hebrew, with each word translated into Yiddish: "Said, God, to, Moses, saying." *Mamzer* means bastard, and *sheygets* is a derogatory term for a young (male) gentile.]

That is how cheders were in those days. Nevertheless, learned people and scholars, even geniuses, emerged from them.

WATER CARRIERS AND PORTERS

Akiva Zeyger (Haifa)
English translation by Thia Persoff

Like every city and town where Jews live, Kremenets was blessed with assorted and odd characters. The town was set in the bosom of mountains and crowned with nature's glory, but it was a town of crowded streets and alleys. There was no running water in the houses; in each house stood a barrel into which the water carriers would pour a portion of water daily, according to the household's needs. The water carriers worked from early morning until night but made only a meager living. The king of the water carriers was R' Pinchas, who was called Pinchas Kadushke. From early morning on, he and his son carried water pails on their shoulders. When he walked with his large, quick steps, no one could pass him....

[**Translation Editor's Note:** *Kadushke* means "barrelmaker," or transporter of water in barrels.]

When the Sabbath came, R' Pinchas wanted to be like one of the distinguished householders. He walked to Sheroka Street (which meant Broad Street, though in actuality it was quite narrow), dressed in his Sabbath clothes; he wore two watches in a conspicuous place, one for daily use and one for the Sabbath, and above them a shiny copper chain. Those watches were not his, God forbid—how could a water carrier achieve such a thing?—he borrowed the watches from the watchmaker. When he was asked for the time, he would reply with great pride, "According to which watch, the daily one or the Sabbath one?"

As I said, he worked with his son, but he still had to walk in front of his son with water pails. Sometime later his son got married, and each worked for himself. In spite of that, the father continued to carry water pails ahead of his son.

The porters in Kremenets seemed to me to be different from those in other towns. Could anyone forget the porter Moshe, who was called Moshe Hipsh (Nice)? He used to announce, "Fresh fish, *hipsh* fish! Come, women, *hipsh* women! Buy fish, *hipsh* fish, good fish!" Which is how he got his name. Besides carrying sacks on his old shoulders, he was forced to supplement his income by working as a town crier. This was an old custom: instead of posting written notices, criers were used to announce events loudly in the street. Moshe Hipsh knew his job well and did it in his own special way, with "*hipsh*" words. For example, when a cantor came to pray the afternoon and evening services, Moshe would announce it like this: "A *hipsh* cantor came to us to pray a *hipsh* afternoon and evening service." When the fishermen wanted to sell their catch, they hired Moshe, who announced, "*Hipsh* fish for sale! *Hipsh*—woman! Buy *hipsh*—carp!" and because of this they called him "Moshe *Hipsh*"....

Such were the characters among the people, who were completely uprooted. We carry their memory in our hearts along with those of the rest of the murdered.

[184]

TWO OUT OF THOUSANDS

Mordekhay Otiker (Tel Aviv)
English translation by Thia Persoff

> My son, where is your soul?—
> Roam the world, seek it, my angel!
> In the world, there is a tranquil village, surrounded by a wall of forests,
> And that village has a blue sky, a sky without limits,
> And that blue sky has a single daughter in its center:
> A solitary cloud, small and white.
> And at noon on a summer day, a boy played there alone,
> A boy left on his own, tender, alone, and dreaming—
> And I am that boy, my angel.
>
> ("And If the Angel Will Ask," Ch. N. Bialik)

There are so many cities, towns, and tranquil villages where our soul was left, a sorrowful soul, on "a wall of forests" and "blue sky," which did not fly into a rage when our dear ones were herded like sheep to the slaughter. Is it possible to think that all that was there is still as it was? Walls of forests and mountains all around, tranquil brooks, black soil that produced wheat, vegetable gardens, and fruit orchards, etc.— all as it used to be?

When was this? It seems like 20 years, according to the calendar, and maybe dozens of years ago, or was it just a fantasy? Then, when I walked in your streets, Kremenets, my town, not even one of us could have imagined you, your sky, your mountains, and your streets without Jews—without those tens of thousands of people looking alike yet so completely different from one another. But woe—it is a bitter reality. The few remnants who miraculously escaped saw your streets—your ruins—Kremenets, with not a living Jewish soul left in them. Only in the depths of the earth, where the foul hand of the desecrators has not touched the memory of our martyred holy ones, may some bones of innocent and holy Jews still be hidden, the final witnesses that we were born, lived, and died here until no Jew was left to walk those streets ....

Kremenets, the town of my birth, rises up in my memory like a mixture of fantasy and reality without a definable line of separation between them. There I was born and lived my first 14 years. Although the memories are fragmented and disjointed, I remember the names of people and streets. More than once I have confused one sex with the other and found myself embarrassed when conversing with a person from my town. Many images from my childhood float through my memory without a definite shape: hazy facial images of Jews—men and their wives and children, many of whom were my childhood friends. I see them passing and slipping away among the town streets: women working at home, men rushing from the synagogues and *kloyzelakh* after the first minyan so as not to be late for their businesses.

[185]

And those "businesses" were in stores, shabby alcoves, and elegant shops. There is a very wealthy Jew's store, and next to it are stalls selling penny notions; this next to that, and these across from those. Most of the time, the work of earning a living was noisy and tumultuous, and some was done in secret, in private, in whispers, all according to the deal's and the person's requirements.

The Jews in Kremenets were neither very rich nor very poor. If I am not mistaken, the same was true of their righteousness and scholarship: they were neither terribly righteous or world-renowned scholars, nor evil villains either. In general, they were good people whose sins and meritorious deeds were not too weighty to bear.... Kremenets' Jews were renowned. They were not "killers," God forbid, or something equally terrible, but at the same time, they would not forgive an insult to their honor, no matter what. They did not fear or cringe before non-Jews who lived among them or in the surrounding area—and the villages and towns and the army barracks near the town were teeming with them.

The rumors—among the non-Jews in town and the surrounding area—that our town's Jews were not fearful weaklings helped guard, to some extent, against our neighbors' assorted attempts at provocation. But this weapon was not a sufficient shield against the evil schemes concocted by the people in the surrounding area. Our town's protection rested on the shoulders of its Jews, particularly the young ones. Some were warriors who knew how to organize a protective arm and detecting eye against the attempts at provocation, which were firmly repelled. Here I will tell about two such warriors who were very different from each other.

****

M. M. was not a professional brawler or a "sword-for-hire" that anyone interested in his services could pay for. But before revealing his qualities and ways, I will offer some words about his background: his father, a coal merchant whose business dealings went awry, ended up committing suicide. The son was blessed with traits that the father's bad dealings did not influence. For one thing, he was strong, as you will see. And he was brought up in a family of noble ancestry. A high school graduate, he loved sports and was partial to the Young Pioneer movement. He was handsome and tall, as it is written, "head and shoulders above," etc. Polite and friendly to all, he did not talk down to people and was not rude or aggressive. He was like this throughout the year— except when our Christian neighbors celebrated their holidays and when the "spirit moved them" in all the excitement of merrymaking and revelry. At that time, his world was turned upside down, primeval forces burst out of him, and he was ready to

225

prepare to act or to act according to the demands of the hour and his knowledge of war strategy. Here is one of the many deeds that are still fresh in my memory.

[**Translator's Note:** Quotations are from Samuel I, 9:2, describing the future King Saul.]

It was the time when the students from the Ukrainian upper school of agriculture near our town decided to have a good time celebrating their graduation. Husky, bloodthirsty fellows, they came into the town armed with an assortment of "cold instruments" and a decision to break the pride and strength of our town's Jews. Our hero M. knew that the heroism that comes from an individual person's bravery is not sufficient. Ahead of time, he and his people were watching, aware of the gentiles' every move. To tell the truth, for quite a while M. had been anxious for an opportunity to "get together" with the students, who from time to time showed their "love" for the Jews. Now that the opportunity had arrived, he was sure not to miss it.

[186]

Without delay, he summoned his well-organized and disciplined men, and like a leader in battle, assigned each man to his place and struck with full force at just the right moment. M.'s name became well known among the area's gentiles, and they tried hard not to clash with him on the battlefield. M., though, would choose the "choicest cut" for himself, one who would do him honor, and give him a proper beating, while never neglecting his command post. He gave orders, rushed to weak spots, organized a false retreat, and then charged with a new assault, giving each of the attacking students a healthy beating—God forbid that one should be overlooked.... I will not describe that particular "good time" and the "glorious retreat" of the students, who begged for mercy, many of them wounded, torn, and filthy with dirt and mud. But I will tell you that at the end of this battle, our group held a celebration to honor our headman and leader, and for a long time afterward, the area's gentiles went around mourning and shamefaced because of the Jews' limitless audacity.

****

Our second hero, Chayim K., may have been the only one with the strength to wrestle with M. in a serious way and possibly even win. While M.'s body strength was seen only when used to defend the Jewish community and was not used for personal gain, this was not the case with Chayim—as you will see as I continue.

He was of average height, with protruding jaws that were unshaven, although he was not growing a beard. His feet were large, like a camel's; when he walked, his body swayed from side to side as if he were going to fall, but he did not; he did not like falling unless someone else did the falling. Indeed, anyone who got in his way had to worry about falling.... I am not an expert in Ch.'s pedigree, but I suspect that his father was not a learned man ... and if I am wrong and he was a scholar, none of that scholarship was inherited by his son Ch. If a serious fight erupted in the market, he was the main "star" in it. As a matter of fact, a fight without Ch. was not feasible. If one started, he popped up immediately, as if he had come from under the ground, and the "celebration" then continued in full force: beatings flew left and right, and the air filled with assorted curses. When Ch. was pleased and estimated the situation to be satisfactory, he would let fly with a declaration such as "Enough! Dogs, horses born of pigs, your children's parents be blasted, what are you fighting about?" Hugging and shaking hands, they would "wet their whistle" with some "bitter drops" after the "dry" beatings. I forgot to say who was considered worthy enough to be counted among Ch.'s company and what their "spiritual nourishment" was. I suspect that the historians of Kremenets, our little town, who labeled this Chayim as a pimp, were doing him an injustice—not because he was not involved in this profession, as in general he rejected no repugnant occupation that could keep him in generous profits—but the truth is that this was just a sideline for him, as his main profession was the use of his great strength. If someone tried to sabotage your livelihood, if you got embroiled in bad dealings and you were afraid of being beaten up, if you needed a strong and ready arm, being a Jew or a gentile made no difference. "In the cause of justice and money," Ch. was always ready to stand by you and fight the battle of the wronged....

In conclusion, I want to tell you about an incident that was related to me by a reliable source. As I said, our hero M. was a peaceful person, not eager to fight, particularly among Jews, while Ch. was a man of strife and contention, as if he were in a rush to fulfill a commandment to "beat thy neighbor." There were some good Jews who did not participate in the game of heroism but were nevertheless eager to watch such things. Many efforts were made to get those two together for a "power contest," but they did not have the opportunity.

[187]

The ways of fate are amazing, and what those people tried to do but did not succeed at, fate did in a simple way. A large sporting event was arranged in town to raise money for a certain public institution. Kremenets Jews had a peculiar impassioned love of sports but for some reason liked to watch them for free. Some held on to the fences and went under them, some climbed on trees, and others used endless cunning and sly tricks on the security guards. Chayim, who was a regular attendee, self-assuredly and with insolent audacity climbed over the fence in no time, and he was in. At this event, though, M. was in charge of the security guards. When he noticed Chayim, he leapt to the fence, and in a commanding voice he roared, "Chayim, come back!" Something like a shudder went through Ch.'s body—the moment had arrived! He waited a few seconds as if considering the matter, his face twisted with anger, but in the end he returned to the fence without delay, climbed up, and like a boy who has done wrong and tries to justify himself to his teacher, twisted his face in a little half-smile, or maybe a worried look, and said, "Forgive me, Sir M., I did not know you were here."

I am not sure that this story really happened this way, but the land and sky are my witnesses that this is how I heard it from people, and so I am relating it.

IMAGES (YOUTH GUARD MEMBERS)

Rachel Otiker-Nadir (Tel Aviv)
English translation by Thia Persoff

Most of the time, we—the young members of Youth Guard—would gather in the bosom of nature, in the shade of the trees in the mountain cliffs. It is there that we wove our dreams of immigration and community life in our homeland.

The Hebrew Corner, under the guiding hands of Leybchik Feldman, will never be forgotten. It included about 10–12 people who were anxious to deepen their knowledge of the Hebrew language. Leybchik was the kind of person to whom anything that even bordered on evil or falsehood was foreign. He was our teacher, connector, and moving spirit. He taught us to believe in goodness, and he discovered talents and potential in each of us.

His lifetime mate was Rachel Otiker (my cousin), who was an innocent, upright Jewish woman. In their soul lay the sorrow of Diaspora life and the yearning for rebirth and renewal. But they were not privileged to live and fulfill it.

Anyute Perel was an original and wonderful person, shy and retiring but with a powerful desire for knowledge. Conditions at home were difficult, but patiently and without complaining, she carried on unflinchingly. The most interesting discussions were held on the winter evenings in her house, near the warm stove. She understood and explained Max Nordow's work, "Paradoxes" so well, and we were so young then. And she had clever hands. Everything she made was in good taste—a dress, a hat, or an artificial flower. We did not know what was in her heart, as she refrained from talking about her own aspirations. It seemed that she had accepted her fate.

A completely different person, but close and dear to our heart, was Polye Bernshteyn. Together we were at the training kibbutz in Dubrovitsa. Her soul was as pure as her yielding and forgiving blue eyes. Responsible and disciplined, vivacious and full of encouragement, she gladly accomplished any job assigned to her.

And how difficult it is to think of extermination and death along with Yonye Bernshteyn, who was bubbling with life and energy. Thirsty for knowledge and action, he struggled and fought tirelessly all his life to achieve his dreams.

[188]

In every place and every situation, from the town of Kremenets to the training kibbutz and the army under the most dangerous conditions, he found a fertile field in which to spread his ideas. He was fearless and was loved and admired by his friends and acquaintances. Later, he joined the Communist Party and was an active member. During the Nazi occupation, he functioned as a partisan in the Kremenets area and apparently died in a battle.

MEIR PINTSHUK

He was blessed with talent, a sharp mind, and a significant aptitude for organization. As leader of a Youth Guard regiment, he fulfilled his role with devotion and strictness, demanding discipline and devotion from himself and his trainees. He was diligent in study and work, and contemptuous of idlers.

While studying in Vilna (1928–1930), he became an active member of the Communist Party. At first, it was hard to accept the fact that Meir had changed his ideas. He had seemed so firm and steadfast. But, together with his friend Rozhke Holander, he stayed true to this path till the end of his days. Both with gifted personalities, they studied and succeeded together and devoted themselves with fervor to propaganda and party activity.

This was a difficult period for the national movement. Many of its best veered from their ways and turned away from its aspirations. Too late! When the Nazi slaughtering knife was on their necks, they realized their mistake. Some of them took part in ghetto rebellions, and some in the partisans, and many (like Rozhke) suffered in jail for years.

SUNYE KESELMAN

The first time I met him was at a meeting of Youth Guard in our town. He was a continual attendee and presented social and literary questions for discussion, in which he participated. Indeed, it was as if he were in the shadows, keeping silent, but his earnestness and pointed remarks drew attention.

We left for training in different places, and to my surprise I received a letter from him, which was followed by others. His letters were short but filled with feeling and belief in the kibbutz lifestyle.

After some time, he decided to continue his studies and entered the technology institute in Vilna. Together, we were somewhat like a commune with a limited circle, and he serve as an example in all matters. A person of rare character, he was prepared to yield much, but not his beliefs or his happiness.

Like many young people in those days, he deviated from the Zionist way and devoted himself wholeheartedly to the new one, and he easily handled the most dangerous assignments in the Communist Party. Suddenly, he decided to immigrate to Israel, and a new chapter opened in his life.

Though there, too, he stayed true to his beliefs—when the civil war in Spain began, he volunteered for the Republican Army, where he was killed in action.

It was said that at the end of the battles he was alive, keeping vigil by his wounded friend. The friend asked him to leave and save himself, but then he was shot in an ambush.

TSVI PRILUTSKI (1862–1942)

Yosef Heftman
English translation by Thia Persoff

Tsvi Prilutski

For many years we worked together at the *Moment* newspaper. These were years of many changes in the life of the Jewish people in general and Polish Jews in particular. R' Tsvi Prilutski was the founder and chief editor of the paper, even in the days of czarist rule, when Poland was only a section of Russia called "the Visle region" (*"Privislanski Kraj"*). He also edited the paper in the era of an independent Poland, after World War I. For a man who had been educated in the Russian political and public atmosphere, soaked in its literature and culture, and lived most of his life in its capital, Petersburg, in the final years of the 19th century, adjusting to the new conditions caused an emotional upheaval. In one day, he had become a citizen of a new country, the likes of independent Poland, which was limited not only in area but also in nationalistic zeal, and which was scrupulously and meticulously ridding itself of all vestiges of the previous rulers' language. Obviously, this was difficult for a man like Tsvi Prilutski, who stood at the head of a large newspaper that fought daily for the Jewish minority's privileges and standing in the new country. Tsvi Prilutski not only was a talented editor, but also had a distinctive sense of politics, understood the atmosphere of the time, and knew what the limits were. Others derisively call this ability "adjustment," but the truth is that it is a talent not for adjusting but for looking at events and evaluating them without getting caught in the empty doctrines and leftovers of a bygone era.

I should make a special point of talking about his talent as an editor. Although he never authored a fine literary portfolio of stories and poetry, he knew how to attract talented writers and newspapermen; he wisely rejected the accumulation of emotionality in the publications and emphasized the essence. As a result, the tone of *Moment* was not stormy and loud but tempered and logical. Because of that, he was accused by his competitors of being a compromiser and even with having a tendency to give way in the face of problems.

[190]

The truth is that he always avoided anything that smacked of demagoguery. It was difficult then to swim against that current, but Prilutski nevertheless proved his ability to influence *Moment*'s style with his temperate, logical ways. And here is the proof: the majority actually made their trust in the moderate *Moment* obvious, and it became the most widely read paper in Poland. After all, deep in its heart, the Jewish community preferred moderation, and this inner sense led it to distinguish words that made public sensations from those of the moderate paper, which were instructive about reality.

Tsvi Prilutski himself was not only one of the original Lovers of Zion and a member of the Sons of Moses organization founded by Achad Ha'am, but also a devoted nationalistic Zionist, whose whole being was steeped in strong feelings for the Land of Israel. He belonged to the enlightened and educated generation of the second half of the 19th century, which had woven A. Mapu's novel *Love of Zion* into the golden dreams of their youth. Continuing into their old age, the charming book's romantic notes beat in their hearts. The Land of Israel was like a never-ending song in their soul. Zion was a celebratory corner of their hearts, like a bit of a Sabbath in the ordinary weekday. Whatever had to do with Zion's resurrection and settlement was the holy of holies for them. During his free hours, in private, Prilutski would "swallow" all the literature that dealt with the work done to settle the land, and he would confiscate all the Israeli newspapers that arrived at the office. In his mind's eye, he saw the map of the Land of Israel and remembered all old and new settlements well. When a staff member traveled to Israel for a visit, the editor would explain at length the directions on the roads he would travel and the settlements he would pass. He even knew how to enumerate the distances between one place and another. Whenever he spoke about the country and its landscape, towns, and settlements, he seemed to be renewed and refreshed, as if he himself were passing through all those places with the traveler.

> [**Translation Editor's Note:** Sons of Moses (in Hebrew, *Bnei Moshe*) was a secret Zionist society.]

He himself was not privileged to visit the country because of a physician's advice that an ocean voyage would be hazardous to his health, but it was as if he lived there in spirit. Every article or telegram that arrived pertaining to the Land of Israel, a policy of the Mandate government, or occurrences in the international Zionist movement had to go to him, even if it was long past midnight. The night-shift editor and crew were well aware that the "old man" was adamant that this sort of information should reach him first so that he could attach explanatory notes if needed.

I have not seen him since my last visit to Poland in early 1938, but we corresponded until the beginning of World War II. Obviously, his letters were written in Hebrew, as was everything he wrote about Zionism and Israel outside the paper's office; he had been and remained a Hebrew scholar since the time when a circle of writers and activists gathered around the Zionist idea even before the first Congress. His last letters were full of worry about Zion and its Jewish settlements, although the storm was approaching Poland first. In spite of his advanced age, he continued working diligently every day with the same youthful enthusiasm and devotion that I see as typical for the people of Kremenets in Volhynia, as if it were isolated among its mountains and traditional in its fight for education and the national spirit. The memory of him as a newspaperman, instructor, and guide, a close friend to all his acquaintances, and an idealistic Zionist who was anxious for any information from Israel, is like David's harp in the murmur of the wind—he will stay inscribed forever in the hearts of all who knew him.

> **Editor's Note:** There is an additional article about Tsvi Prilutski's life and scholarly works in the Yiddish section of the book.

[191]

EXCERPTS FROM TSVI PRILUTSKI'S LETTER TO THE SONS OF MOSES YESHURUN LODGE IN WARSAW, 1894

(From the Zionist Archive in Jerusalem, Israel)

Kremenets, Second Day of Hanukah 1824*
*Since the destruction.

> [**Translation Editor's Note:** The meaning here is probably "1,824 years since the destruction of the Second Temple," in 70 CE. (1,824 + 70 = 1894, the year in which Prilutski was writing).]

Honorable Yeshurun Lodge—shalom and blessing!

First of all, I beg your forgiveness for keeping silent so long—there were different reasons that I cannot get into. Some are mine and some are our association's, which was napping....

Second, I congratulate our association on the adjustments it has made and the new officers in their fitting positions, who will usher in a new era in our association's activity; may we be granted, and, even though its beginning may be small, it will end in greatness! The main thing is not to keep the association's work a secret ... all members should know its goals and needs in every phase, etc. This will increase its membership and the number and spirit of its activities.

I cannot increase my donation to the cause of settlement, since throughout the year I donate to assorted national causes, such as the league for "perspicacious language" in our town, which distributes free books written with a nationalist spirit to the people. It supports Hebrew teachers here, who converse with their students in the Hebrew language during class and who often organize national celebrations (Hanukah, Purim, and the other Jewish holidays, and last year—on the 15th of the month of Av—the 10th anniversary of the establishment of the Rishon LeTsion settlement). In addition, I donate to the upkeep of the periodical *Self-Emancipation* (in addition to my subscription fees). I donate for the purpose of bringing patriotic lecturers here. I donate six rubles a year to the society in Odessa and the same amount per year to our association—in addition to those, I am willing and ready to donate (special donations) for our association's occasional needs.

[**Translator's Note:** "The cause of settlement" refers to the settlement of the Land of Israel.]

As a representative of the Odessa board here, it is my duty to send my donation directly to the board, and in addition I am supposed to send them the moneys collected by others.

I was told by my acquaintances who returned from the Holy Land about the lack of unity in the Jaffa communities and other towns in the Holy Land. I'd like to suggest that the Yeshurun Lodge talk with the main lodge in Jaffa and see about establishing an Israeli meeting house there, where locals and visitors from other areas can gather for literary discussions and lectures in Hebrew and arrange celebrations during the holidays, festivals, and other occasions (such as an anniversary, etc.). A meeting place like this could have a great spiritual influence on the Jaffa community and, as such, be a model for other communities. With the efforts of our brethren, I hope that my words will bear fruit and that the Yeshurun Lodge will make the effort to put these ideas into practice.

According to what I have read, the Torah Flag association in the Land of Israel runs a lottery that provides some income. I was thinking of bringing up the idea of starting one like it at our Jaffa chapter, with the prizes being cash, not a parcel of land in the Holy Land (as many have suggested). This will make it easy to distribute the tickets to our brethren in the various towns and also to good members of Lovers of Zion here and in other countries. It would provide a large income (up to 50% of the collected amount), and then our organization could really do things. As you know, our brethren even bought tickets for the Antislavery Lottery in Germany in large numbers (because their situation led them to look for happiness even by chance), as with the lottery that the Russian government runs to help the hungry (although out of 6 million rubles, only 20% was awarded, that is, 1.2 million rubles). Our brethren bought those tickets with great enthusiasm, and the same is true of the lotteries in Braunschweig and Leipzig, which are selling large numbers of tickets. Why shouldn't we, too, use a lottery for the good of our holy cause instead of letting our property go to other peoples and their causes? Will Israel's redemption really come from the collection of small coins or donations from generous types who have grown apart from our people, who do not understand their aspirations, and whose generosity is as thin as cobwebs?

[192]

Attached here is my donation for last year	6 rubles
Also, our brother Dr. Tovye Hindes's donation, may his light shine, for half of last year, which he left with me before leaving for the Holy Land	4 rubles
Also for HaSharon:	2.50 "
Total	12.50 "

I request that a receipt be sent from the Yeshurun Lodge to Dr. Hindes in Jerusalem. With this, I will leave the honored lodge and say shalom to all our brethren.

Your devoted servant,
Tsvi Prilutski

P.S.

In a few days I will suggest that the organization accept a new member from here. He is Dr. Arye Leyb Pines (R' Yechiel Mikhel Pines' nephew) of Children of Zion of Moscow, who has settled here, and he would take Dr. Hindes's place.

It is very important to renew HaSharon in order to influence the young generation with our aspirations.

I send regards to our dear brother, my soulmate, my teacher, Rabbi Eliyahu Zev Opshteyn, may his light shine. Dear friend, in a separate letter I will argue with you about your idea to terminate jobs for daily farm workers in the colonies of the Land of Israel. No, no, my brother, those workers are beloved material for building our farmers' party in the Land of Israel (institutes in the future Israel), and we should see to it that they establish themselves on the land according to cooperative self-help and build "cooperative associations" from them with funds collected at least from single people, who can afford to save!

Cordially, Tsvi

Lately, in my free time from the business, I keep reading literature that discusses the principle of cooperative self-help, in particular Schulze-Delitzsch's books and the yearbook of Hautefeuille, the agent for the Land Worker's Association in France. When I get the necessary material, I will draw up a complete plan concerning the matter. Because how long are we to be eager "beggars" and "collectors" instead of using the abovementioned principal that has had worthy results in Western countries?!

I remembered this, and so I am urging our brethren in Warsaw to make an effort and distribute the periodical *Self-Emancipation,* which, according to the letter I received from Dr. Birenboym, is on the brink of failure for lack of subscribers. Ah! How miserable are those Lovers of Zion who could not support a single national periodical in a language that is understood by most of our brethren. Let us, my brothers, support it! Its price is 4 rubles per year.

We wrote a letter about this subject to Usishkin, and our words have brought good results in Yekaterinaslav.

[193]

DR. TOVYE HINDES (1852–1920)

Avraham Zamir

Translated by Thia Persoff and David Dubin

Dr. Tovye Hindes

Dr. Tovye Hindes was born in Kremenets in 1852 to a respected, wealthy merchant family. Although he left town as a young man, seeking the "light of science" in the wider world, he maintained his ties to Kremenets until the end of his life. Both he and Kremenets were devoted to each other. Kremenets was the symbol of fine tradition, magnificent scenery, and eternal romanticism. From time to time, Dr. Hindes and his whole family would spend the summer months there in old Mr. Keytelmakher's country house on Mount Vidomka or with one of the Ukrainian farmers in the area. Kremenets always welcomed him with honor; young and old would come to greet him, and the doors of his pharmacist brother's house (where he always stayed on the first night) hardly closed for a moment. During Polish rule, even the gentiles honored him. After Dr. Hindes's death, the Polish mayor complained that the democratic City Council had named some of the streets after foreign Jews but none after "two Jewish Kremenets natives who were famous all over the country: Hindes and Prilutski...."

In his childhood, he was sent to study Torah with a well-known rabbi in the area, in keeping with his Orthodox mother's wish. A few years later, he had become famous as a prodigy. The rabbi sent him back home, saying that the boy did not need to learn anymore but could teach others now. But the boy was anxious for knowledge, and against his parents' wishes, he left home and entered the Rabbinical College in Zhitomir. From there he went to study in Petersburg, Kazan, and Dorpat. His vibrant and justice-seeking soul pushed him toward the Russian revolutionary movement, and he joined the People's Will party. While a student in Kazan, in the far north, he endangered his life by going to the most distant and desolate Russian and Tatar villages in the winter to save the many villagers from a cholera epidemic. For being "a friend of the people" and a revolutionary, he was expelled from the university in Kazan and arrested. A few years later, he received permission to continue his studies in the German university in Dorpat (now part of Estonia).

During his stay in Dorpat, his basic point of view and general outlook underwent a major change. The pogroms of the 1880s shocked Russian Jewry, and this young revolutionary's heart started beating with a sense of Jewish national pride. He was one of the founders of the famous Students' Association in Dorpat, which, like the one in

Berlin, trained a generation of Zionist activists in Russia. When he finished his university studies, he decided to immigrate to the Land of Israel, and he settled there as a physician. In his personal life, he always followed his religious beliefs. He traveled to Constantinople to be retested for his physician's credentials. From there, he went to the Land of Israel as a "spy" and was offered a job as one of the heads of a Jewish hospital. Later he returned to Europe, and in Warsaw he married a woman from the noble Gezundhayt family and moved with her to Jerusalem. Life was very hard in Jerusalem in those days. Dr. Hindes and his wife belonged to a close-knit group that included Eliezer Ben-Yehuda, Duvid Yelin, and Efraim Kohen and their families, as well as some foreign consuls in Jerusalem.

[194]

Despite the difficulties, he did not want to leave Jerusalem, but an unremitting fever, which had previously affected him and, later, his wife, broke his spirit and compelled him to leave. Two years after his arrival in the Land, he was forced to depart with a dejected spirit.

Two stories, both of which sound like fables, are told about his immigration to and departure from the Land of Israel:

When he disembarked from the ship in the port of Jaffa, when he placed his foot on the sand, he bowed [according to the first story] and, placing his face on the ground, kissed its soil, and then took from his coat a sword he had secretly brought from Europe and cried fervently: "A sword for God and my land!"....

And when he boarded the ship on his departure from the Land of Israel, he entered a cabin, closed the door after him, made a small wound in his left hand, and, using his right hand, wrote with the blood on a small piece of paper: "If I forget thee, O Jerusalem, let my right hand forget its cunning".... He showed the handwritten note to his son many years later on his bar mitzvah day and told him of the vow he had made as he left the land of his fathers, which he kept faithfully until the end of his days.

On his return to Europe, he lived in Warsaw, his wife's birthplace, and soon became renowned as a physician involved in national affairs and an ardent Zionist. His home became a meeting place for everyone who helped in the national awakening—whether with a pen, statements, or toil. An illegal meeting of the Warsaw Zionist Committee (1898) took place in his home. He was host to Achad Ha'am, Sokolov, Mandelshtam, and Usishkin when they came to Warsaw. Dr. Hindes worked hard in Warsaw: he began to discuss Zionism in secular intelligentsia circles and to the Orthodox in Sha'arei Tsion Synagogue (which he and others had built on Pavia Street). His lectures were attended by large crowds of young men and women who came to find answers to their doubts and a basis for their outlook, for he was a fine speaker, with broad knowledge and a pleasing style. He fought for the use of Hebrew and fiercely dedicated himself to its dissemination: he founded the Lovers of the Hebrew Language in Warsaw, donated money to establish schools and publish Hebrew books, and occupied himself with teaching natural sciences and physics in the town's Hebrew schools. His drive and dedication drew throngs of followers and believers; his absolute integrity won over the hearts of his detractors among the assimilationists and even among Polish anti-Semites.

Two of his followers were the renowned physicians Dr. Henrik Nusboym, a leading assimilationist, and Professor Bronovski, a leader of the Polish National Democratic Party. When the Jews of Warsaw won a majority of the votes for the 1912 Russian Duma, many people (and much of the Jewish press) requested that Hindes be chosen the first Jewish representative in the Russian Parliament, the Duma in St. Petersburg. The masses, which loved and respected him, supported this. However, after consultations, and also because of "what the gentiles would say," it was decided to elect a gentile Polish Socialist Party member, Yagallo, the worker.

A special chapter in his activities was his role in the Jewish Cooperative Movement. Not because of simplistic notions, but rather as a result of day-to-day involvement with the indigent (in his capacity as physician and national figure), he decided to help Jewish workers establish manufacturers' cooperatives. With his friend and assistant Mr. Lederer and with the help of the well-known cooperative activist Batko (Aba) Levitski, a Ukrainian Christian, he founded shoemakers', waiters', and bookbinders' unions, and his home became a workers' club. Even though the movement failed to take root, many appreciated his role and were faithful to him until his final hour.

In 1914, with the outbreak of the war, a catastrophe occurred that affected him deeply. His young son, Moshe-Maksimilian, a mathematics student at the University of Warsaw, traveled to the Land of Israel, and when he reached Jaffa, he was stricken with dysentery and died. He was never again at peace. His only dream became to return to the Land of Israel and work there as a physician or teacher. "My oldest son was born there, and my youngest son died there; how can I stay in the Diaspora?" he would say to motivate himself in those days.

[195]

This thought, which had taken hold deep in his soul, led him to look for ways to bring it about. As he prepared to leave (during the war), he left Warsaw for a short time to go to agricultural towns, left medicine for two years to complete teacher training, and looked for new ways and means of reaching his goal....

Suddenly, before he could achieve his goal, his fragile life was taken, and he died in Warsaw in 1920. The whole community mourned him bitterly. His family realized his dream. One by one, his family members left (sooner or later) for the Land of Israel, and they brought with them the memory of his unblemished name, a true Zionist from the pioneers of the generation, and one of the first members of the reawakening movement.

He was a great man, a son of Volhynia, and he left a good name in Kremenets and in various Warsaw circles. His name is etched on the hearts of Jewish workers, who were close to his heart. Everyone recalls his image as one of integrity, honesty, trustworthiness, and self-sacrifice to his people, his land, and his culture.

DR. BINYAMIN LANDSBERG (1890–1942)

Tovye Troshinski (Tel Aviv)   English translation by David Dubin

He was the image of a popular aristocrat. He was known in the town and its environs by his nickname, Bozye, and everyone simply called him that, whether in his presence or his absence. Son of an ancient and prominent family—his grandfather, R' Chayim'l, was related to RYB"L—he was a cultured man and a community activist, in the contemporary sense. His father, the physician Dr. Arye Landsberg, who was one of the first Zionists in Kremenets, a community activist and populist, a keeper of tradition, and beloved by all, would come to the study hall daily for communal prayers, and he did not neglect communal matters for his entire life. (He lived to an exceptionally old age.)

B. L. was born in Kremenets in 1890. He was his father's only son. (His mother died in his early childhood.) He acquired his early education at the primary school in Kremenets and later in the Kishinev Gymnasium, from which he graduated with distinction.

[196]

He received his Jewish and Zionist education in the home of his uncle, Dr. Sh. Etinger, who served in Kishinev as a government-appointed rabbi. While he was still a gymnasium student, aged 14, an article of his was published in the Russian newspaper *Kievskaya Otkliki*; this article was worthy enough to be the editorial. Then he began his Zionist work in earnest, organizing and leading groups of students. This worked to his disadvantage when he sought admission to university. B. L. left Kishinev and went to Switzerland, studied law in Geneva, and on the eve of World War I returned to Kremenets as a Doctor of Laws.

During World War I, Dr. B. L. volunteered in organizations to help Jewish war refugees. The central committee in Petersburg noticed his work and extraordinary organizational ability and appointed him head of the committee in the city of Nezhny Novgorod, which was then a central station in the wanderings of the Jews of the Pale of Settlement.

Dr. Binyamin Landsberg and Family

After the February Revolution, B. L. returned to Kremenets and began feverishly engaging in Zionist activity. Those were the days of elections to Jewish and general organizations in Russian centers and in the town itself. In those stormy days, B. L. acted as a national captain who moved many with his words and won their loyalty. In public debates with representatives sent from the headquarters of the various parties, which were arranged because of the elections, B. L.'s power of persuasion and sharp intellect drew interest. He was chosen for the first Congress and as a member of the town administration standing election for the education party. B. L.'s enthusiasm and fiery nature are revealed in his formation of organizations for Hebrew and Jewish education and culture. The leaders of the Christian Reactionaries looked askance at his work in the town, and at the first opportunity, when the Ukrainian Hetman took control with the help of the Germans, B. L. was imprisoned with several other prominent town leaders. He was released after eight months when insurgent farmers broke into the town and opened the prison gates. The era of changing governments began. Public Zionist activity went underground and became sporadic. When the Polish army captured the town, B. L. was imprisoned a second time, along with other Jewish leaders, and was accused of Communist Party membership. After a long investigation by the Polish authorities, he was released for lack of evidence.

In the 1920s and 1930s, under Polish rule, there was a great public awakening in Kremenets. This awakening came from two directions: from Congress Poland and from eastern and western Galicia. It arrived from different sources: through Yiddish newspapers and personally through messengers, business relationships, and cultural sources. These days were full of triumph and failure, with Jews fighting government authorities for their legal rights even in rural villages. Kremenets supplied plenty of the disputants, the most powerful and stubborn being B. L., who was a follower of Y. Grinboym. Like his mentor, he was fearless and vigorous, and as a proud, self-respecting Jewish citizen he wasted no opportunity with the local authorities, tirelessly working for all the rights to which Jewish citizens were entitled.

In the election battle for the first Polish Sejm in 1922, Kremenets was one of the major centers of the Minority Bloc. B. L. gave himself completely to the fight, appearing at many gatherings and encouraging the masses to struggle for victory. He traveled to towns and villages in the area and spoke in Ukrainian before Christian voters, and thanks to him, the Minority Bloc won a great victory in the Kremenets area, and A. Levinson was chosen as representative to the Sejm. During transition periods and during relatively calm times between elections, B. L. dedicated himself to day-to-day Zionist activity. For many years, he would gather the Foundation Fund contributions from the town and its environs. This role required a great deal of effort, and it was not uncommon for him to make several visits in a single day to "difficult" donors, whose better judgment to contribute only he, with his personal magic, could appeal to. His hard work and selflessness came out of a sense of duty to the cause. The party platform, which he accepted upon himself, became second nature and to a great extent determined his way of life.

[197]

He also expended great effort for the Tarbut School Foundation in the town, and along with a small group of philanthropists, he accepted the burden of its upkeep. In general, he worked in all areas of public life. As one of the founders of the local newspaper *Kremenitser Shtime* and a member of the editorial board, B. L. tried to raise the paper's level of cultural and political standing as an organ for ideas and guidance for the region's Jewish public. His newspaper articles covered Zionist topics, national contributions, cases and rulings of local government institutions, community matters, taxes, etc., and their influence was substantial.

B. L. stopped his public good works for only about two short years, while he was preparing for his legal examinations, as was usual for lawyers with foreign diplomas. (The local authorities found their chance to retaliate against him for his public-political activities and did not allow him to take his exams in the courthouse in Kremenets, his hometown, so B. L. traveled to the village of Radzivilov, where he stayed for a long time.) But immediately after his acceptance as an attorney, he returned to all his former activities for the movement.

When the authorities began to threaten the Jewish community's security and institutions, B. L. acted as a shield against those acting under the "persecutor's" orders, and even the "persecutor" himself was not spared.... As a City Council member, he led the Jewish faction and undertook a fierce battle (which only a select few could undertake in those dangerous days) against the gentile council members who, with the government's encouragement, had banded together to void the economic and cultural rights of the Jewish citizenry. Often, he was reminded from "on high" that he was jeopardizing not only his livelihood but even his life, and on the other hand the government knew how to reward its supporters. However, B. L. was not swayed, and he stood fast in his resolve to continue his fight even outside the town.

As an attorney, B. L. excelled from his first appearance in court. His colleagues predicted a shining future for him. Praise of his propriety and uprightness brought him many clients from the town and surrounding areas. It is noteworthy that at home, the language used was Yiddish even though he was brought up speaking Russian, and his Polish speaking style impressed even the Polish judges.

Not many know that B. L. tried to move to the Land of Israel in 1921. He completed all his local affairs and traveled with his family to arrange a British visa, which was never granted, so he remained with his people in his town. He worked and struggled and was killed among his relatives and friends. B. Landsberg was one of the members of the Jewish intelligentsia who were shot behind Tivoli Garden, long before the destruction of the ghetto. (According to another story, he took his own life.)

MOSHE EYDELMAN (1864–1942)

Yitschak Rokhel
English translation by David Dubin

He was all fire, all movement. He had nothing, if not Zionism and the Land of Israel. All the rest—economic matters, family matters—was secondary. And what did his Zionism consist of? Only immigration to the Land of Israel. Certainly, selling *shekalim*, distribution for the Colonial Bank, Congress elections, conquering the hearts of the community—these were important, too, but they were merely a means to an end: the

Moshe Eydelman

Land of Israel. "Prepare yourself in the anteroom in order to enter the palace," but do not tarry in the anteroom so as not to lose sight of the goal. The fateful hour arrived in March 1925, when Moshe Eydelman arrived in the Land and settled in Tel Aviv. For decades a battle raged in the family. His wife, a storeowner, did not want to uproot her business and follow her husband to a "desolate land," and only when the children grew up and became independent did Moshe Eydelman leave. He left alone and lived alone here until he died. Previously he had visited the Land several times, and when the Herzliya High School was founded in Jaffa, he sent his son, Yitschak, to complete his studies there, and each year he would accompany him back from his vacation in Kremenets to Jaffa.

[198]

When he returned from his visits to the Land, "his breath ignites coals." Despite his age, he was youthful and kept company with young people. He would gather his "group," the young people, and tell them of his travels in the land—about the settlements, farmers, and workers, about the gymnasium and Moriah schools, about the Arabs and their doings, the Guard and nights in Canaan. The young people would listen silently with sparkling eyes, rapt and inspired by love and longing for Zion.

[**Translation Editor's Note:** The quotation is from Job 41:13.]

He was born to his father Yakov on Hanukah 1864, lost his father in childhood, was raised by his mother, a storeowner, and received a traditional education. He befriended his contemporaries Tsvi Prilutski, Tovye Hindes, and others, entered the "garden," and began to read Enlightenment literature. He joined the Lovers of Zion at its inception and later joined the Zionist Movement, and dedicated his whole being to its mission, coming into conflict with the opponents of Zionism and even with members of his family. He bought a tract in Ein Zeitim in the days of the "Association of 1,000."

[**Translation Editor's Note:** The Association of 1,000 was founded in Minsk in 1891 with the idea that 1,000 members would raise 40 rubles per year for five years, buy land in Israel, and plant vineyards on it. After eight years, each member would receive land and a house there. After initial success, the vineyards failed, and the project was abandoned.]

He was a founder of the first modernized cheder in town, under the late Asher Beylin's leadership. He did not neglect community activism: during World War I, he devoted himself to helping refugees. With the outbreak of the revolution, he was chosen as a member of the Community Council and served as vice chairman. His son moved to the Land of Israel in 1921, with the first pioneers. Later, his daughter also went, and then came his turn to go.

In the Land, he did not seek greatness. He did not request priority. He did not knock on the doors of charities. But he found a lowly job as a tax collector, which he fulfilled faithfully, and supported himself to his final days. The very fact of living in the Land, among the builders and realizers of the dream, filled his heart with happiness. Every building that was built, every new place, brings us closer to the ultimate goal. He hoped and believed that the redemption would arrive soon, paving the way for the Kingdom of Israel.

While here, he kept his strong connection with the Diaspora and worked with all his might to bring individuals and groups of Jews from Kremenets. He worked and labored for any residents of his hometown to get a visa to come, whether as a purported businessman or as a cantor or rabbi. Any Kremenets Jew who arrived would be visited by Moshe Eydelman, brought to his apartment, guided in his first steps in the Land, and asked about all the little details of the news in Kremenets. Many years ago, he had already suggested establishing a society of Kremenets expatriates in order to spur mass emigration from the town. He never complained, was happy with his share, and was satisfied to see Zion being rebuilt.

He died at age 78 in 1942. He was laid to rest in Nachalat Yitschak Cemetery near Tel Aviv, and the following is inscribed on his tombstone:

> Love of our land
> and our people
> was a candle for his steps
> all the days of his life.

[199]

DUVID GOLDENBERG (1880–1934)

Manus Goldenberg
English translation by David Dubin

The house of my grandfather, R' Nachman Margolis, the watchmaker, was not a place for young people. There, his friends, Chabad Hasidim, the elite of the yeshiva, ruled in an ambiance of the Jerusalem Talmud, the Babylonian Talmud, and books on

Hasidism. On matters of Torah, there were learned discussions, sharp wit, and more. We, the young grandchildren, their playthings, did not even know another way, and we felt the influence of our own parents only when they moved to their own apartment in Alterman's Courtyard. These steps resonated "with noises and thunder," for they immediately traveled a radically different path when they removed us from a religious teacher and placed us in the Hebrew school that had just been established. This move was an open rebuff of tradition, and they never reconciled with their elders.

Duvid Goldenberg

My first memories here are connected with the magical world of the Hasidic legends, Andersen and Grimm, which our father read to us from the pamphlets *Nitsanim* and *Prachim,* published by the Tushia House in Warsaw. After them came the booklets *Hashiloah* and the volumes of *Hatsefira*. Eventually his whole worldview became clear:

[**Translator's Note:** *Nitsanim* means shoots, and *Prachim* means flowers.]

Two of our children had already been born before he left his studies in the religious study hall with his young friend, Getsi Klurfayn. Under the latter's influence, he became caught up in Enlightenment literature. With him, he read Mapu and Smolenskin, and joined the Love of Zion movement and Lovers of the Hebrew Language. However, his whole life he knew how to synthesize his traditional leanings with the idea of a return to Zion.

While he was busy with his livelihood and affairs and involved with his large family, he found time to study a page of Gemara and read books and newspapers.

He served for years as treasurer of the Charity Fund and as an active member of the Burial Society. After the Sabbath, our home would become a national bank, to which Jews would come for loans in the presence of the committee. For several years, the Burial Society's traditional meals were held in our house.

My father spent many nights next to the beds of the ill as a member of the Righteous Slumber society, and more than once he returned late at night from the distant cemetery, escorting an old man or woman to his or her final resting place.

[**Translator's Note:** In Hebrew, *Righteous Slumber* is *Linat HaTsedek*.]

Shortly after the establishment of the workers' union in Kremenets, he was chosen as president, and he kept this position to his final day. He took on a heavy burden with his appointment by the authorities as a member of the tax assessors' committee. He had to fight hard to limit the taxes on every Jew. These meetings lasted months, and the merchants and laborers exerted considerable pressure. He suffered greatly, defending against a reduction of the Jews' standing. But there was one bright spot in his life: the Land of Israel, where he longed to follow his children.

The deep darkness of Jewish poverty was also clearly revealed to him in his visits to shelters for the poor, both Jew and Christian, when he was appointed guardian by the Social Service Office. His peace was disturbed at his desk, as he was surrounded by people asking for help and telling him their troubles.

Approximately two years before he died, he was elected to the City Council, and he involved himself in the fight for Jewish rights, joining the Jewish faction led by Binyamin Landsberg.

His simple manner, modesty, and gentle ways endeared him to all ranks of society. He was a man of the people who lived among the people and for them. Our mother also stood with him during his short life by being his partner in managing his affairs.

[200]

He was 54 years old when he passed away in the winter of 1934 because of the incorrect removal of the cast from a broken leg. The news about his unexpected end shocked the town's Jews. Businesses and workshops closed, and many people came to his funeral. The love of the people accompanied him on his final way.

On the day he died, only few of his family members were present, as three of his sons were in Israel, and one was in America.

He never fulfilled his dream of immigrating to the land of his dreams.

R' BEN-TSION HOFMAN

Ayzik Hofman
English translation by Thia Persoff

R' Ben-Tsion Hofman

One of Kremenets' personalities—a nonpolitical one, but one of Torah and good deeds—was R' Ben-Tsion Hofman. His "base" was the Hasidic *kloyz*, where the regulars were Hasidim from all social levels who were steeped in Jewish warmth and religious devotion, and in giving material aid to the needy. In spite of his zealous Orthodoxy, he would quote the words of I. L. Gordon: "If you do not seek God in your heart, you will not find Him anywhere else in the world." He would invite the poor, laborers, craftsmen, small merchants, and peddlers to his Gemara lessons, which were open to congregants.

His best pupil was the young prodigy Leybchik Feldman, who regularly mentioned his teacher's high morals and influence on him. It was in his nature to befriend people, so he was said to be one of the disciples of Bet Hillel.

> [**Translator's Note:** Bet-Hillel refers to the school of Rabbi Hillel, a Jewish religious leader of the first century CE, who was famous for his good nature, patience, friendliness, and scholarship.]

When he was wealthy and owned much property, he used to keep precise accounts so that he could figure out the correct amount equaling 10 percent of his income—his share to donate, according to the law in the Torah—and he collected material donations for people, such as a horse for a peddler, a cow for a milkman who made his living from supplying "Jewish milk," or a sewing machine for a tailor. He constantly repeated the saying, "It is deeds that count, not words."

After World War I, when he lost his property and wealth, he did not abandon his traditional activities and continued his good deeds in the framework of the American Committee, serving as its head treasurer throughout the Joint's existence in

Kremenets, 1920–1923. He was also active in ransoming captives, and thanks to his handsome appearance and pleasant personality, he was the savior of dozens of Russian Jewish families who crossed the border near Kremenets in the hope of reaching their relatives across the ocean.

In this way he continued his life, studying the Torah and fulfilling the commandments, until World War II broke out. In the Holocaust year of 1942, at the age of 76, he perished with his entire family and our town's martyred people.

May his memory be blessed.

R' MESHULAM KATZ (1850–1908)

Moshe Katz (Haifa)
English translation by Thia Persoff

His literary nickname was Maze ben Maze, taken from his name and his father's name: Meshulam Zev HaKohen, son of Mordekhay Zalman HaKohen. The founder of the famous Katz dynasty, he was born in the small township of Belozirka, near Kremenets, in 1850. His father had three sons and three daughters, of which Meshulam was the firstborn. R' Mordekhay Katz amassed great riches during his life from forest merchandising and leasing estates and hard liquor factories from the local squires.

[201]

Although he was a miser, he did not stint on expenses for arranging marriages with aristocratic families of teachers and rabbis. He was a God-fearing Jew, the wealthiest and most powerful in his township and in the area.

R' Meshulam Katz paved his own road in life. Although he grew up in the path of Hasidism, he had been attracted to philosophy books since his youth. He was proficient in the writings of the Rambam, Eben Ezra, and others. He knew Russian, Polish, and German very well and read books, mainly on philosophy, in those languages, too. He was one of the intellectuals of his generation and studied Enlightenment literature. He was proficient in Hebrew, and his style was clear and brilliant.

In 1899 he moved to Kremenets, where his home served as a meeting place for intellectuals and writers. From his youth he favored Zion and, during the period of Herzl, he joined the Zionist movement and advocated for it in speeches and writing. He was elected as a representative to the Sixth and Seventh Zionist Congresses.

His writings were published in the press of his day, *Hamelits* and *Hatsefira*, under his penname, Maze ben Maze. Like the rest of his family members, he dealt in forest merchandising. He was in partnership with his brother (my father, of blessed memory), Mikhel Katz, and in business, too, he was considered sharp. He served as an expert arbitrator of complicated business deals, and people would come to him from far away for this.

He was smart, with clear logic, and was noted for speaking to the point, sometimes caustically. While living in Kremenets, he had great influence on the townspeople, in particular on Zionist and intellectual circles. Many members were frequent visitors, enjoying his wisdom and guidance. One of them was a distinguished chess player.

He saw that his sons were educated in Jewish wisdom and European teachings. He sent his eldest son, Ben-Tsion Katz, to study in Switzerland and Germany, where he graduated from university physics and mathematics departments. In those days, this was a very daring achievement.

R' Meshulam suffered from heart disease all his life; he died of this in 1908 at the age of 58. He left four sons and daughters. His son-in-law, Zeydi Perlmuter, of blessed memory, was a well-known Zionist who stood at the head of the Kremenets community for many years. His grandson, Meir Katz (Ben-Tsion's son), is a mathematics professor at a university in the United States. It seems that R' Meshulam endowed his descendants with his brainpower.

Quite a few of his grandchildren live in Israel.

Most people of our generation did not know him and may never even have heard of him, but he was one of the original members in the Zionist group, the "heralding" generation of enlightenment and Zionism.

BORIS LIAKH

Manus Goldenberg
English translation by Thia Persoff

Some of the pages from the *Kremenitser Shtime* newspaper that were left to us include tender stories about Jewish life. The writer shows compassion and sympathy for his heroes, the wretched townspeople. Those stories are by Boris Liakh, son of Russian aristocrats.

I first met him when he returned from the front, wearing a captain's uniform. In his uniform, he came to our school, to which he had returned after the disintegration of the czarist army. He stood out because of his acrobatic maneuvers and wasteful ways, which were those of the wealthy landed gentry. His noble and very rich family lived on one of its properties, a township in our district, which was founded, apparently, by one of their ancestors, and was named after them: Lakhovtsy. His brothers and sisters, some of them writers and artists, lived in the capital but returned home after the October Revolution. The family members belonged to the Russian liberal intelligentsia and became friendly with members of the Jewish intelligentsia, particularly the Kremenetski family.

When rebelling farmers captured our town from the Bolsheviks and the residents were in danger of destruction, he was one of the "White" officers and estate owners who took it upon themselves to untangle the mess they had caused. He was a member of the delegation that went to the old Austrian border to ask the Polish army to save them. He was sorry for this move for the rest of his life, and his hatred of the Poles grew stronger.

[202]

When we began to develop a Jewish sports team, Liakh established a Russian sports team, with most of its members being Jews from assimilated families. At first there was tension between the two groups, but when the Poles came with their team, which was supported by the authorities, Liakh began to support our organization.

By then his family had lost its wealth as a result of land reform and squandering, and Boris was in financial straits. One day he invited my friend, Azriel Gorinshteyn, and me over, and to our astonishment he presented us with a packet containing 50 gold rubles to purchase athletic equipment for our Maccabee group. Knowing his financial situation, we hesitated to accept the money, but he became very offended, so we asked forgiveness for our behavior.... Later we discovered that he had sold a plot of land out of the small amount that had been left to him, and that is where the gold came from. He derived great pleasure from seeing our soccer team in their new uniforms and the athletes using the equipment—things we never had before.

But one unforgettable incident in our town shows Liakh in his essence. It was on a summer Sabbath, at a soccer tournament between the Maccabee and Polish teams, with Maccabee as the winners. I was a soldier in the Polish army at that time and on my annual leave. Together with the Jewish spectators, I rejoiced for the victors. Then we saw a group of young Poles shouting, "Beat the Jews and save Russia!" These were some of the Poles who had escaped from Russia and inherited this call from the "White" Russians, Denikin's men.

The Revolution was still fresh in our minds. Only two years of Polish occupation separated us from it. We had not forgotten how it felt; the sense of human dignity and of being free Jews was powerful in us. I could not contain myself, and when the large gathering of people streamed into the narrow alley that led to the center of the Vidomka through the orchards and gardens, I approached the group and punched the most vocal of them. A big fistfight erupted, and some of the young Jewish men joined in to help me. In the excitement that reigned for about a kilometer, this fight was like a spark in a barrel of gunpowder.

Jews and Poles lit into each other with a great fury; screams and curses filled the air, and posts were uprooted from fences and waved in the air. Throughout all this wrestling, the multitudes streamed forward, while each of the opposing sides struggled to be the first to extract themselves from the alley.

I was at the head of the stream, surrounded by that group of vile Poles. My army uniform caught their attention. We burst out or, more correctly, we were pushed out, first to the square in front of the Jew-hater Bikovski's farm. I was in great danger, surrounded by enemies. At that moment I heard a shout: "Hey, you, rotten Poles!" It was Boris Liakh with his group of Russian friends, who had preceded us, and instantly I found myself behind a safe wall of Russians. By making themselves a partition between the Poles and me, they took the worst of the beatings. In the meantime, the rest of the people flooded the square. Liakh ordered me to clear out before the military police showed up, and he and his group covered my retreat. The fight in the square continued until dark. From the town came reinforcements of butchers and porters, headed by Miron Gindes, and for the Poles from the Lyceum. Liakh and Gindes led the fight, which ended in victory for the Jews. Many wounded Poles filled the hospital. The police came much later, and the inquiries into the event continued for many months. Liakh, thanks to his connections, was cleared, while I suffered a pack of trouble from the army command.

In the 1930s, Liakh suffered great losses. The degenerate atmosphere brought about by the society of immigrants depressed him, and he frequented the billiard halls. At that time, he wrote his stories and was a regular contributor to the *Kremenitser Shtime*. His Jewish friends did not abandon him in his hard times, and as always, he was a welcome guest in their homes.

What was his stand during the Holocaust—did he keep his noble spirit, and was he one of the few Christians in our town who, even then, did not lose their humanity?

[203]

YISRAEL MARGALIT (1865–1942)

Zev Shumski (Tel Aviv)
English translation by Thia Persoff

Yisrael son of Lipa Margalit (Izrail Filipovich) was my father's close friend for many years. Active together in many fields of public interest, the townspeople would say—in one breath—"Shumski and Margalit." They had similar educations and opinions about life around them, and they worked together with compatibility and understanding.

Yisrael was a wealthy forest trader. Not finding satisfaction in business, he invested most of his energies in public affairs. He was a member of the intelligentsia and was well versed in the Russian language. He was not religious in his private life, remaining distant from Zionism and the national movements, but he was dedicated with all his heart to Jewish causes and served as their representative to the government.

He saw the future of the Jews in the places where they lived and did much to promote general education and crafts among Jewish youth. He was a founder of the High School of Commerce and a member of its governing board for many years. When the ORT School for professional crafts was opened, he immediately joined the group of activists who took responsibility for it and did much to strengthen and enlarge it. An admirer of Yitschak Ber Levinzon, he saw himself as his student and worked to fulfill his ideas by spreading education and crafts. The house where Levinzon used to live was then a tavern, and Margalit saw this as an insult to the great teacher's memory. He convened a community committee and succeeded in rescuing the house for public use by establishing a library and reading room there. (See the article on this subject in the Yiddish section of the book.) He was the son-in-law of government-appointed Rabbi Kunin. After some time, he was elected head treasurer of the synagogue and did much to upgrade it and take care of its maintenance. He invited well-known cantors there and made it into a community meeting place, deserving of its name. Even before World War I, he founded the Bank of Mutual Credit with his friend Ruven Goldenberg; later, during Polish rule, the name was changed to the Bank of Commerce.

[**Translator's Note:** "Deserving of its name": in Hebrew, synagogue is *bet kneset,* or house of assembly.]

He had a special affinity for helping organizations and not only collected from others, but also donated his own money generously. He was a goodhearted, generous person, and so was his wife.

He adjusted to the new conditions on the Jewish street after 1917 without difficulty; he drew closer to the common people, began to speak their language, and continued to work for the community. Later he was elected head of the Jewish community—the fourth and last in Kremenets—and perished with the rest of the Jewish people.

SHLOME FINGERUT (1888–1942)

Yisrael Otiker (Na'an)
English translation by Thia Persoff

Shlome Fingerut

One of the town's prominent community activists, he was born in Kremenets in 1888. At home he absorbed the atmosphere of devotion to all things that had to do with the Jewish people, and he was brought up to be aware of and true to his community's needs. His father, R' Mordekhay Leyb Fingerut, who was highly ethical and learned as well as modest and humble, tried to instill those qualities in his children.

On the eve of the 1905 revolution, when new trends and political parties formed in Jewish communities and stormy discussions filled the air, the Fingerut family, too, was split; the older children leaned toward Zionism and Israel, while Shlome, the youngest, joined the Bund. He went to the workers, taught himself carpentry, and was an active worker and laborer in town for many years. Later, he opened a workshop and was an independent craftsman. From that time until his death, he organized the town's craftsmen and artists, took care of their professional needs, helped establish mutual aid institutions, and was active in many other areas of public interest, such as leading the community and its institutions, and so on.

[204]

When a self-governing City Council was elected (including a Polish mayor, a Russian vice mayor, and two Jews), he was elected as one of the two Jewish members and successfully represented Jewish interests.

During the Holocaust, he was murdered by the Nazis under very tragic circumstances. Two of his sons have survived—one in Poland, and one who immigrated to Israel, fought in the War for Independence, and established a cavalry force.

When the *Kremenitser Shtime* newspaper was founded, Shlome—as was his way—lent a helping hand to establish it. On different occasions he published articles on public affairs, memoirs from the days of his youth and the stormy period of 1905, and some poems. We show some of those poems here (in the Yiddish section of the book); they describe the life of workers and are typical of the style of that time.

ARYE FELDMAN (1900–1942)

Yisrael Otiker (Na'an)
English translation by Thia Persoff

Arye Feldman, called Libchik by his friends, was one of the more interesting people of the younger Jewish generation in Kremenets. Humble and shy by nature, he disliked publicity. At the same time, he was one of the people who greatly influenced the youth group, which was a core of awareness and activity in the town's pioneer organizations and community.

He is especially remembered for the role he played as leader of the Hebrew Corner—a youth group that existed from 1924 to 1929. His trainees and pupils later joined different organizations, such as Pioneer, Young Pioneer, Youth Guard, and so on, most of which were in the Labor movement, but some had no political affiliation and were nonpartisan. There was even a group that eventually distanced itself from the Zionist movement altogether. All of those recall the man Libchik with appreciation and admiration—as a person who knew how to teach them knowledge and information and instill Jewish and personal values in them, in spite of the occasional differences and distances that stretched between their varied outlooks and opinions.

He was born in 1900 and received a traditional religious education. His father, a secretary of the Jewish community, saw to the education of his son, who exhibited wondrous talents from early childhood. After a short time, he left his teachers and started to study by himself, amassing knowledge in many areas, particularly Jewish ones. He was proficient in the Bible, the Mishna, the Talmud, rabbinical and Hasidic literature, Sephardic poetry, the Rambam, Kabbalah and the Zohar, and so on. He was well versed in the commentaries, delved deeply into the study of Jewish history, and followed new Hebrew literature, world literature, and modern European ideas.

Those who were close to him knew that this shy, retiring young man was a treasury brimming with knowledge and serious thought.

When some of us young people wanted to organize an advanced Hebrew study group, Libchik was at the top of their list of people with the expertise and capability to promote their learning and advanced study. For half a year, he tutored the Cornerstone group, and when invited, he led the educational program for the Hebrew Corner. (On the Hebrew Corner and A. Feldman, see the article in the Education and Culture section.) He accepted this gladly, with his typical dedication, and devoted most evenings and all his free time to the group members. He infused meaning and a certain spirit into the sessions and continued to do so for years, even as many changes took place in the group itself.

****

In the 1930s, he went to Vilna to take supplementary courses in teaching. He graduated from the Teachers' Seminary and also gave lectures in the Mizrachi movement's courses. He absorbed the atmosphere of the Jerusalem of Lithuania, met with circles of writers and Yiddish activists, and spent much time in the Strashun and Institute for Jewish Research libraries.

> [**Translation Editor's Note:** Vilna, a center of Jewish culture and learning, was known as "Jerusalem of Lithuania."]

[205]

When he lived in Warsaw, he was a frequent visitor of Hilel Tsitlin, to whom he was very close and with whom he later corresponded and exchanged ideas with for years.

On returning to Kremenets, he began to work as a schoolteacher. In the spring of 1933, he married a student, an active member of the Hebrew Corner—Rachel Otiker. Their ties of love and deep friendship lasted for many years.

Absorbed in the daily routine of life as a Hebrew teacher, he taught in the Tarbut and Yavne schools in the districts of Lublin, Volhynia, and Congress Poland. He dreamed of immigrating to Israel, but with the difficulties of immigrating in those days, it was a farfetched dream.

In 1939, the onset of World War II found him with his wife Rachel and young daughter in Makow near Warsaw, where he worked as a teacher in the Hebrew school. Miraculously, they managed to escape and reach Kremenets, which at that time was under Soviet control. There they stayed until they were caught by the Nazi invasion in 1941. On that bitter, infamous day of the annihilation of Kremenets' Jews, they perished with the rest of their families.

****

Libchik was a man who imparted a sense of proportion and inner culture, one of the best. He carried within him and practiced the high standards of the Jew. He sampled those of many others, but neither his spiritual perfection nor his constant reaching for the good and lofty was ever blemished. He was a man of faith, believing in the future and the goodness hidden in the depth of men's souls. He believed that the time would come when humanity would experience spiritual greatness.

In a postcard sent on one of those faraway Rosh Hashanah eves, he wrote, "There is a glorious and radiant world, and its spark is the soul; the spark is longing for its world, longing and sparkling—"

In his final days, L. Feldman saw the darkest, most sinister side of humanity. The man fell; his inner spark went out. But the remnants of light and the things he believed in and spread around him were certainly carried on in those who knew him.

AVIGDOR (ZEYDI) PERLMUTER (1876–1942)

Ayzik Hofman (Tel Aviv)
English translation by Thia Persoff

Avigdor was born in the small township of Vyshgorodok in Kremenets district. Family relations linked him to our town (he was the son-in-law of R' Meshulam Katz, one of the original members of Lovers of Zion in our town), and in 1922 he moved to Kremenets. An energetic man with a well-developed sense of community, he soon occupied an honored place in Kremenets' community activities. He made a living from his large textile store. Being childless, he devoted his interest to community work.

Though a religious man, he did not belong to any of the religious factions, only to the general Zionist Organization. Learned, pleasant, fair, and honest, he had a wise and sharp mind and was admired by many. Because of his deep patriotic feelings, he made a dignified and proud impression when representing the community in front of the authorities.

There was hardly a project or public institution in which Zeydi Perlmuter did not take an active part. He was a dedicated worker for the Zionist Organization, and he was in charge of the Palestine Bureau as well as active in the Merchants' Association, the Bank of Commerce, Tarbut, and assorted charities. Still, he did not hold himself apart when it came to publicly fighting all the circles that ingratiated themselves to the authorities and acted against the interests of the Jewish community. Within this stormy war, in 1931 he was elected head of the Jewish community (after the death of A. Vaynberg, the first to hold that post) and conducted its business with talent and dedication for years. He was staunch and daring in his stand when it came to the public interest, and he did not get involved in personal intrigues. He was a community activist of high standing.

He perished with his community.

[206]

MOSHE (MISHE) FRENKEL (1902–1944)

English translation by Thia Persoff

Moshe (Mishe) Frenkel

Born in Kremenets, Moshe was the son of R' Shlome Frenkel, a scholar and enlightened man who owned a grocery store. From his childhood, he grew up in an atmosphere of study and learning and developed into a significant mathematician. He graduated from high school in Kremenets and taught there and in other places. He was not content with this and wanted to study engineering. In 1924, he went to Belgium and entered the Technical Institute in Ghent. During the week he studied, and on the weekends, he worked in a factory to earn a living. There was no Jewish community in Ghent, but the Jewish students made an effort not to lose touch with Judaism. Sometimes Moshe Frenkel would lead the prayers when the students held a minyan on the Jewish holidays.

After graduating with two degrees, he got a job as the lead engineer for the central electric laboratory of Belgium and settled in Ghent with his family (his wife, Vitye, was the daughter of Moshe Karshun of Rovno, an early Zionist and Tarbut proponent in that city). This assignment was much to his liking, as it afforded him the opportunity to do research and development. Nevertheless, he searched for ways to immigrate to Israel. In 1935 he met with Pinchas Rotenberg in Paris, in reference to a job offer in the electric company in Israel. The negotiations did not work out, so Frenkel continued his work in Ghent.

When the Nazis conquered Belgium in 1940, he escaped with his family to France and lived the life of a wanderer, hiding in villages. Each of his children found shelter in a different home while he roamed the forests to avoid the enemy. In 1944 he volunteered for the underground. A few days later he was killed, and he was buried in the village of Menville, near Toulouse. After France was liberated from the Nazis, his widow and their three children immigrated to Israel and settled in Tel Aviv.

One of our town's outstanding and talented natives, he wanted to go to Israel but did not have the opportunity.

R' GETSI KLURFAYN (1872–1942)

Leye Limonchik-Klurfayn (Tel-Aviv)
English translation by Thia Persoff

R' Getsi Klurfayn

If there were outstanding Zionist homes in our town, where Zionism, the Land of Israel, and Hebrew were like air in their lives—then the Klurfayn home was one of them. What names did Getsi Klurfayn give his children? Aminadav, Duvid, Leye, and Shulamit. He made sure his children had biblical and modern Hebrew names to emphasize a connection to the homeland and the breaking off of connections to the Diaspora.

[207]

Although burdened with the need to earn a living—he had a haberdashery—his interests were centered on community work and mainly on the Zionist Organization and institutions that cultivated Hebrew education. From his youth he was a member of Lovers of Zion, and as soon as the Zionist movement was established, he joined its ranks and was a devotee and activist. He knew Hebrew very well, but throughout his life he continued to study in order to become more proficient. He excelled in rhetorical style and was knowledgeable in the treasures of the Talmud.

He was a cheerful man with a pleasant personality, and he practiced what he preached. He was the first to donate, and generously, although he was not wealthy but was burdened all his life by the need to make a living. He also collected donations for Zionist funds. He helped the needy through the Charity Fund, too. Deeply rooted in community life, he was trusted and respected by the townspeople, who often came to him for arbitration in cases of quarrels and conflicts. He would mediate and make peace.

Getsi Klurfayn saw the source of the nation's resurrection in the pioneer movement and preached for its accomplishment by individuals. He waited for an opportune time to immigrate to Israel, but was not privileged to do so. Of his children, whom he had directed toward Israel since childhood, his daughter, Leye, immigrated to Israel in 1925 and is settled there with her family. His son Aminadav immigrated in 1926 and stayed for two years, working as a laborer in Nes-Tsiyona and other settlements. He returned to Kremenets for a short time but was conscripted into the Polish army and was not able to return. His son Duvid joined the Army of Budyoni to retaliate against Petliura's rioters. He hoped to cross the border during his wanderings and reach Israel, but he was captured and imprisoned by the Poles and died or was killed there. He, too, was not privileged.

May their memories be blessed.

HADASAH RUBIN

Yisrael Otiker
English translation by Thia Persoff

Hadasah was born in 1912. After World War I, her parents came to Kremenets as refugees from one of the small towns in the area and settled there. Her father, R' Duvid Rubin, was a man of ideas and aspirations. He was diligent about his daughters' education and made sure they received an extensive general and full Hebrew education. While studying in the well-known Polish Lyceum, Hadasah also studied (from her childhood) Hebrew language and literature with private teachers. She read a great deal and was influenced strongly by the poetry of Bialik, Tchernichowsky, and Schnaiur. She was partial to Rachel's poetry and liked the style of modern Russian and Polish poets—Mayakovsky, Yesenin, and Julian Tuwim.

From her childhood she exhibited a talent for writing and excelled in poetry, which was read mainly in the circle of her close friends. Only years later was she "discovered"; in spite of her strong objections, her friends took some of her poems and had them published in the *Kremenitser Shtime*. Her poems were very popular and were reprinted in the literary papers in Vilna and Warsaw. She was touted as an up-and-coming force among young Yiddish poets.

In her youth, during the events of 1929/1930, she was a member of Pioneer and Young Pioneer, but later, during the crisis, she left the movement with a group of friends and joined the Communist Party. She was arrested by the Polish authorities and sentenced to many years in prison, and, while serving her time, became gravely ill.

For some years she lived in Vilna, where she was in contact with and influenced by literary circles. There she joined a group of young writers called Young Vilna and took part in their activities. The proponents of Yiddish literature had many hopes for her, and today she lives in Poland.

After World War II she published poems in the Yiddish papers in Poland and in America. In 1953 a book of her poems was published in Warsaw. The poems in the Yiddish section of this book, which are reprinted from the *Kremenitser Shtime,* are among the first that she published.

[208]

R' TSVI MENACHEM ROKHEL (1835–1922)

K. L.
English translation by Thia Persoff

R' Tsvi Menachem son of Avraham was the name by which he was called to read from the Torah, but in town he was known as Hirsh Mendil.

In the memories of those alive today, life in town is remembered the way it was between the two world wars or, at the latest, in the early 20th century. But once there was a different Kremenets—patriarchal, without political parties, without democratic elections, and without desecration of the Sabbath. One of that town's staunch leaders and followers of its tradition was R' Hirsh Mendil Rokhel, descendant of an ancient, venerable merchant family and the patriarch of a widespread dynasty with branches all over the world.

During Polish rule, the street he lived on was named after Slovatski, but in Hirsh Mendil's day it was called Kaznatsheyskaya, after the government treasury house that stood at the top of the street. That street stretched from Sheroka at the bottom all the way up to Mount Vidomka. On the right was the wall of the Seminary for Priests, and on the left were the large courtyards of the town's wealthy people—Jews, Russians, and Poles. There was a saying: "If you want to breathe fresh air, go up Kaznatsheyskaya Street." This was the street that R' Hirsh Mendil chose to settle on, and it was there that his descendants and some of his relatives settled. This is the order of the properties, starting at the bottom of the street and going up: in the "red stores" at the corner of Sheroka Street was the haberdashery of Shimon Biberman, Hirsh Mendil's young son-in-law; on the left side of the street was the large Passage Hotel, which belonged to his grandson, Shmuel Kahaner; after that, on the left side, was the courtyard of Moshe Lis, his older son-in-law, and the residence of the family of Moshe Royt, Rokhel's relative. Next, also on the left, was the large courtyard of his son Moshe Rokhel, in which there were a few houses and a large textile store. Next on the left was the house of Berish Brik, a close relative. Next to his place was the house of another relative, named Meir Yampol. All those homes made for a continuous block of courtyards and houses. Across from them, in a two-story house on the right side, lived His Honor R' Hirsh Mendil himself; this place also housed a wholesale sugar and candle warehouse and his "private" synagogue. His son, Yehoshue Rokhel, lived in a house in the same courtyard. All these people, who were like a tribe unto themselves, were sheltered by Hirsh Mendil's patronage. Each of the grandsons (there were about 40) felt good in the "bosom" of the large family, and this feeling led to a kind of arrogance.

R' Hirsh Mendil was a man of erect bearing and elegant features, his white beard very long, his eyes sharp and penetrating, and his expression precise, sometimes biting. He was smart, vigorous, and influential among his people. It was usual to see him sitting surrounded by friends and acquaintances by the entrance to his courtyard, discussing business and community affairs. Generally, he did not tend to favor exceptions or concessions. In fact, he was not inclined to accept the opinions of others, but would force his on them. He was not dependent on others; he had his own street, his own synagogue, and his own bathhouse—even his own rabbi.

[209]

In his youth he worked in the sugar business. Even before there was a railroad, he would travel great distances for long months and return with a long caravan of wagons, loaded with blue-topped sacks of sugar. In the "new time," sugar started to arrive in railroad cars.

R' Tsvi Menachem Rokhel

After a time, he added candles and packing paper to the business. He made contact with the Lavre monastery in Pochayev and supplied its printing house with paper and other products. At that time, he contacted the German Heinrich Fokner, and from him leased a paper factory in Rudno, about 20 kilometers from town. Now he was a manufacturer, one of the first among the town's Jews. His son Yehoshue was his partner in the factory, and together they would leave on Sunday for the village, stay in the factory throughout the week, and return home for the Sabbath. In those days 20 kilometers was considered a long distance, and although a two-horse carriage was always at their disposal, it made no sense to waste horsepower and long hours traveling. It is true that even though they were "bourgeois" in their business and outlook on life, the 200 factory workers liked and respected their Jewish employers, who paid them decent wages on time. The attitude was one of mutual respect, and an injured worker and his family were cared for, which was completely the opposite of the way Polish landowners treated the workers who labored in their estates and distilleries.

Not far from there, in Verba, they built a factory to crush wood to make raw material for paper manufacturing. The area was rich with primeval forests, which were bought, section by section, to produce paper. Then it was discovered that the land in Verba contained a great treasury of peat, which was a good source of fuel for the factory. They purchased a large plot of land and developed a large-scale peat business. Hundreds of workers were employed in the plants, and hundreds of local farmers were kept busy transporting the goods. As a result of all this, the Jewish owners of the paper factory, Hirsh Mendil and his son Yehoshue, became the veritable rulers of the entire area. This was resented greatly by the owner of the estates in the area, the licentious Prince Tarnevski, who saw his losses and their gains, as he was forced to sell off his properties to pay his gambling debts from card playing while they got richer and stronger from year to year. The farmers hated him and liked the Jews. Angry, he started to find excuses to provoke them and instituted lawsuits against them. They defended themselves with pride and firmness, and even harmed him. There was an open, fierce war between the house of Tarnevski, father and son, and the house of Rokhel, father and son.

The different branches of Hirsh Mendil's business grew, but he never involved himself completely and exclusively in them; he was always involved in the community's needs, too. Parties did not exist yet, but there were factions: Hasidim and *Mitnagdim,* Orthodox and Enlightened. Hirsh Mendil was one of the extreme Orthodox all his life, without backing off or compromising. He was studious and very learned, with designated hours for study in the early morning, before dawn. His primary efforts went to strengthening religious institutions: synagogues, Torah schools, rabbis, and ritual slaughterers. Next came charity institutions and help for the poor. He demanded from others, firmly insisting on donations from those who could afford it, but first he fulfilled those demands himself. He donated to various projects willingly and with an open hand. When the old bathhouse burned down, he took steps to have a new one built; he was the first to donate a large sum and collected donations from others. In a short time, it was built. He did the same for other public institutions. He gave charity in private, too, directly to the needy, most of the time anonymously. On Passover eve he opened his potato-filled cellar and, according to his judgment, distributed portions to the poor of the town who came to him: "Go down to the cellar and fill up two sacks with potatoes." On the other hand, when asked to donate to the building of the High School of Commerce (in which the studies involved desecrating the Sabbath and distancing the pupils from Jewish studies), he replied to the activists who came to him: I will donate double the sum you request just for not building the school.

[210]

Despite his poor command of Russian, for a long period he was the Jewish community's liaison and representative to the government, a citizen of the town from the prior era. Because of his clear, sharp intellect and his proud manner and bearing, he was respected by the government, and his words were heard.

After R' Velvele's death, he became enmeshed in a bitter controversy when he refused to recognize the rabbi from Petrikov as the town rabbi. Although most of the town followed the rabbi from Petrikov, he brought Rabbi Yitschak Heler from Kurilovtsy and influenced a substantial number of the town's Jews to follow him. Thus the town split over a rabbi. No doubt, in his public activities he was quite forceful and possibly even arrogant, and on the heels of this battle, he and his entire family left the Hasidic Synagogue, whose congregation generally leaned toward the rabbi from Petrikov, and founded his own synagogue in his home, which lasted for several decades.

Then came a new age with new songs: love of Zion, Zionism, Hebrew literature, the Bund, and the like. Hirsh Mendil strongly resisted all these new trends and did not change his stand for the rest of his life. In his eyes, they were traitors to Israel. And Hebrew literature? Nonsense. He fought these vigorously and tirelessly, but without success. Even worse, a schism opened in his own home. He discovered that his daughter-in-law, Shprintse, Yehoshue's wife, leaned toward Zionism and read Enlightenment literature. His grandchildren were growing, and one by one they were being drawn to Zionism, Yiddishism and the Bund, Russian literature, and the Enlightenment in general. Moreover, his oldest grandson, Duvid Rokhel, began to shave his beard ... a family convocation was called, and R' Shimon Handelrafel, Hirsh Mendil's nephew, the family's advisor on important matters, was summoned from Kiev. The young rebel was called before him, and R' Shimon heard his regretful words. He mended his ways for some time, but afterward returned to his errant ways. Eventually he joined the Bund and got involved in secular literature in Yiddish and the like.

The siege was being broken from one direction or the other. Two families (Yehoshue Rokhel's and Biberman's) had gone completely over to Zionism and were some of the first in town to speak of the movement and leave for the Land of Israel. The remaining two branches (the Lis family and that of Moshe Rokhel) took different paths, but they, too, left the traditional ways.

Hirsh Mendil's final days were not pleasant. His descendants did not follow in his footsteps. In 5782 (1922), R' Tsvi Menachem Rokhel passed away, aged and old in days. With him, a proud, beautiful remnant of the old generation went to its grave.

MIKHAEL SHUMSKI (1857–1928)

Yitschak Rokhel
English translation by David Dubin

Mikhael Shumskl

Five sons and daughters were born to Duvid and Fride Shumski. Three lived in Kiev (Yitschak, Dvore Patin, and Rivke Greben), and only two remained in Kremenets: Leyb Shumski, the eldest, and Mikhael, the youngest. Strong ties grew between the Kremenets branch of the family and the great and enlightened city of Kiev, whether business connections or community and public connections.

[211]

The children received a mixed education, both traditionally Jewish and general, and the languages spoken at home were Yiddish and Russian. The mother, a woman of intellect and fashion, was known by her acquaintances as both Freyde Shumski and

Madame Borisovna. After her husband's death, she carried on the family's affairs in partnership with her two remaining sons in Kremenets, Leyb and Mikhael. They were careful to respect their mother. Weekly, the sons and their wives, as well as the grandchildren, would come to her home to light Sabbath candles and eat the Friday night meal at her table.

As a youngster, Mikhael Shumski was taught in a cheder. Afterward, he completed his education at the Rabbinical Seminary in Zhitomir—an institution that in those days served as a center for spreading general enlightenment among Jews and that trained a generation of rabbis for communities across Russia.

However, Mikhael did not enter the rabbinate, but rather public business in a general sense. In 1888 he married Nadia, daughter of Avraham Levit Midenski from Zaslav, and they had two children, Zev (Willie), now in Tel Aviv, and a daughter.

The Shumski family, which was quite wealthy, owned the town's southwest rail line station until 1914. The family also owned a private commercial bank and a sugar dealership, as well as tar pits near the railroad station. Most of their businesses were run in partnership.

At a young age, Mikhael, or as he was called by the townsfolk, Mikhail Duvidovich Shumski, entered public service and performed his duties faithfully for decades, as was his way, literally until his final day. He served every stratum of the Jewish public, but especially homeowners and the enlightened, and in those days was also in contact with the Russian and Polish communities. He established good relations with the government authorities.

His public service had many facets. There was no important community cause that did not enjoy his guidance and input. For decades, whether under the Czar, after the revolution, or under the Poles, he was one of the town's notables.

He generally served as the Jewish community's designated representative to the government, in all its upheavals and reincarnations. Under Polish rule, he represented the town in the regional Sejm (Seymik). It goes without saying that he was a firm believer in democracy. After the revolution, when young activists rose to public prominence, bringing a new public style, including assemblies, elections, votes, and other innovations, there was some friction between the new, democratic style and him, who represented the old-style merchant activists who led with their activities and personalities. But after a short time, he adopted the new style and seized a central role in public life under the various governments. His reliability in the eyes of the public, his self-sacrifice, and even his longstanding leadership methods concealed his faults and raised him to public prominence as a central figure.

In 1904, with his friend Yisrael Margalit, he conceived of and founded a vocational high school in town in order to raise the cultural level of Jewish young people. The language of instruction was, of course, Russian, and most of the students were even Russians, as was the law in those days. He spent a great deal of energy and zeal on founding the institution, and even afterward he gave the school a great deal of time and assisted in its administration.

As a token of thanks for his efforts, Minister of Trade Timiryaziv called him "a beloved citizen of his generation."

At that time, he worked hard to build a home for the Talmud Torah and was a sexton of the Great Synagogue as well as a founder of the Burial Society and funeral bier carriers. He took those positions in order to standardize procedures and to stop the shameful spectacle of extortion and deception when a death occurred.

With Ruven Goldenberg, he established the Society of Mutual Credit, the first attempt at a cooperative bank in Kremenets, which aided and supported young merchants and laborers. In partnership with the former judge Pokrovski and with Muzye Barats, Shumski developed a peat mine in near the town.

Tall, handsome, and well dressed with staff in hand was how the townspeople were accustomed to seeing him during the decades when he would travel on the public's behalf between institutions and offices, performing the noble and proud task of one who faithfully serves the public as the past generation's enlightened ones did.

[212]

Shumski was not at all affiliated, but he would visit the synagogue and faithfully deal with the community's religious needs. He was careful not to travel inside the town on the Sabbath, and if he happened to arrive by train on the Sabbath, he would travel from the station to the town on foot. He was also careful to say Kaddish when his mother died (1912).

On the eve of October 11, 1928, a great celebration was arranged to celebrate ten years of Polish independence. Obviously, Mikhail Duvidovich was one of the celebrants and even danced with the most beautiful woman there (an apostate Jewess, wife of a Polish police officer) when he was 71 years old. He still retained his power to lead the Jewish community, serve the public, and also be a man of the people. When he returned home at 3:00 a.m., he suffered a heart seizure and died soon after.

The townspeople and governmental representatives arranged a grand funeral for him. All the organizations, businesses, and factories closed out of mourning, and thousands followed his funeral bier.

It is fair to say that he was an assimilated Jew, but in truth, he was more Jew than assimilated, in his final years drawing closer to the masses. He was connected to the Jews of Kremenets with every fiber of his being and led the community with his intellect and dedication for decades.

Nevertheless, he was not a Zionist, and he trained his children in the Russian language and culture, although they also had a "Jewish spark." His son Willie immigrated to the Land of Israel after many stops elsewhere and settled in Tel Aviv as an engineer; he is active in the Organization of Kremenets Emigrants.

Shumski was fortunate: he died at the right time, and his eyes did not see the destruction of the Kremenets community, for which he had labored his whole life.

DR. ZALMAN SHEYNBERG

Sonye Radzinovits-Aksel (Mahane Yisrael)
English translation by David Dubin

Who among us, the remnant of the Kremenets community, does not remember this dear Jew, who for many years—especially the ten years before the Holocaust—held a central position in Kremenets Jewry? There was probably no field of public service in which Dr. Z. Sheynberg did not participate with all his heart. He was a creator of our town's social structure.

Dr. Zalman Sheynberg

I was fortunate to work in his presence for several years and got to know him up close. These few sentences should be a memorial lamp for his innocent soul. Dr. Z. Sheynberg completed his medical training in Vienna as a stomatologist and was known as an expert in his field. Many physicians from towns and villages in the area would come to consult him on cases that were difficult to manage, and he was always ready to give advice and guidance. His reputation preceded him, and he was accepted by both the Jewish and the Christian communities. Many government authorities, as well as regional notables and influential people from other cities, came to him for treatment, even though there was no shortage of local Christian physicians.

Of medium height, with bright, smiling eyes and a thick, blond mustache, he was brimming with life and enthusiasm and would dispense his goodwill to everyone who came to him. He set an example with his pleasant demeanor and good nature. Success in public activity was certain if Dr. Sheynberg was involved. Moreover, much of his time was devoted to communal affairs. As a long-standing Zionist, he devoted himself completely to practical and organizational work with the Zionist Organization.

[213]

He established a nonpartisan town advisory council for joint activities on behalf of the Jewish National Fund and the Foundation Fund, the Tarbut School, the library, the establishment of trusts, etc. For a few years, he was chairman of this group. When he was a member of the City Council, his presence signaled Jewish pride and wealth. As a faithful public servant, he fought with all his power against any restriction on the Jewish population's rights. He also worked hard for the TOZ organization and published many articles on hygiene and health issues. He often appeared before the public at symposia on various diseases and how to avoid them.

Dr. Zalman Sheynberg's work on behalf of the Jewish public in Kremenets was multifaceted and voluminous, and he will be remembered in the hearts of all who revered his reputation.

MEIR SAMSONS

Yisrael Otiker
English translation by David Dubin

This was the nickname of R' Meir Bernshteyn, a relative and student of RYB"L. As the story goes, he was anti-intellectual and a mocker and humorist by nature, and he wrote many satires of Jewish life and customs. In the town, he was the subject of many anecdotes and stories. He was known as a heretic who mocked the restrictions of the Orthodox. Clean-shaven, with a hoary, curly, uncovered head, he would enter and leave RYB"L's home. Tension and anger characterized the relations between him and the community. He earned his living in a liquor store.

His writings were saved by Mrs. Rivke Otiker, may her memory be blessed, and she passed on to her sons four compositions in verse written in his own hand, namely, (1) "A Command to the Empire and an Answer to the Four Questions," (2) "On the New Moon of Elul, a Fair in Heaven ...," (3) "The Jew with the Illustrious Family," and (4) "An Evil Woman Is More Bitter Than Death."

The late Aleksander Rozental copied the manuscripts and published them in the *Kremenitser Shtime*.

His previous writings were never published and would, it seems, travel from hand to hand. These copies are the only ones we have. His descriptions in these writings are most vivid on the Jewish way of life in contemporary Kremenets.

[214]

KREMENETS EXILES IN ISRAEL

English translation by David Dubin

KREMENETSERS' ROLE IN BUILDING THE LAND

Yitschak Rokhel

NUMBERS

The correspondents of the Organization of Kremenets Emigrants comprise 364 names, and, together with some unknown correspondents, the number of Kremenets natives in the Land of Israel is nearly 400. Including family members, this "*landsmanschaft*" consists of more than 1,000 people. They live in the following places:

Tel Aviv and suburbs	140
Greater Haifa	90
Jerusalem	25
Hadera	20
Afula	20
18 various kibbutzim	50
Collectives, absorption centers, and various other places	55
Total	400

There is no question that more than this number came to the Land—perhaps 600 families—but some eventually left, and some have died over the years, or fell in the War of Independence or acts of terrorism. It also should be noted that the number who wanted to come to the Land was greater than the actual number who came, but absorption quotas (put in place by the British Mandate of Palestine) cut short the possibility of immigration.

WAVES OF IMMIGRATION

We have no information on the part the Jews of Kremenets played in the Hasidic immigration 150 years ago. However, since the town served as a cradle of the Hasidic movement, one can assume that a few Kremenets Jews went along with those immigrants. As far as we know, Kremenets Jews did not take part in the First Immigration or the establishment of the oldest settlements. The one person who came to the land in that time, in 1893, was Dr. Tovye Hindes, who worked for several years as a doctor in Jerusalem, but illness forced him to return and settle in Warsaw.

Many of the towns surrounding Kremenets, including Berestechko, Boremel, and others, were swept up in the Second Immigration of workers between 1904 and 1914. These workers were labor pioneers in cooperative farms and founders of the first agricultural kibbutzim. However, only a few immigrated from Kremenets itself, some sent by their parents to study in the Land and some who came to the settlements as laborers. They corresponded with their friends and encouraged them to emigrate. After World War I and the Civil War, a group of pioneers immigrated as a unit in early 1921.

[215]

Gathering of Kremenets Natives in Tel Aviv

After them, individuals and small groups continued to immigrate as members of Pioneer or other nationalist groups. During Gravski's Era, there was an increase in the immigration of families, workers, and small shop owners, who saw no future for themselves in Poland. At that time, the Pioneer and Youth Guard movements broadened their scope to encompass hundreds of young people, some of whom dared to immigrate, and dozens arrived in the Land each year. They fought the rules, engaged in various forms of subterfuge, and reached their destination. Most of them had gone through training in Klesov and other places, and from the start they intended to join specific kibbutzim. Centers of attraction for pioneers from Kremenets tended to be primarily Kibbutz Yagur and Givat HaShlosha. At various times, each included 30–40 people from Kremenets. Some left later, but even today there are almost 20 people from the town in Kibbutz Yagur. In addition, several dozen families from Kremenets settled in Afula and were some of its founders. Several established farms for themselves in the town and its environs, and others took up trades or manual labor.

At the beginning of the Third Immigration, several agricultural centers were established in the land by immigrants from single cities (e.g., Kiryat Anavim by immigrants from Kamenets Podolskiy, Gevat by immigrants from Pinsk, etc.). The pioneers from Kremenets did not have the numbers or the organizational strength to found a specific center, and they had no desire to settle separately. Nevertheless, they played a strong role in several settlements and endeavors: in the Yosef Trumpeldor labor brigades in Rosh HaAyin in the early years; later in the founding of Tel Yosef, "the construction group," in Tel Aviv (this later became the Office of Public Works and Construction and was one of the constituents of Solel Boneh); in the founding of Herut, the sanitary installation cooperative; and others. As mentioned above, in the following years pioneer immigration was centered in Yagur and Givat HaShlosha, and its mark is still seen there today.

> [**Translation Editor's Note**: Solel Boneh is a construction and civil engineering company in Israel.]

[216]

After World War II, the remnants from Russia and other places began an endless stream toward the Land. Estimates are that as many as half the people from the town who live in the Land today are descended from those immigrants. They live mainly in the cities, with a portion living in immigrant settlements (Lod, Ramla) and cooperative farms. Some of them are from the pioneer movement, but those who did not immigrate before the war and arrived only after many twists and turns share a special attachment to the Land of Israel with the current crowds of immigrants.

THE ORGANIZATION OF KREMENETS EMIGRANTS

In 1947, a *landsmanschaft* called the Organization of Kremenets Emigrants in Israel was established in the Land of Israel. Before this, there was no such organization, and no one felt the need for one. Immigrants from Kremenets immersed themselves completely in their new lives. They were looking to the future more than to the past; they paid no attention to memories of bygone days or to communicating with their friends back in Kremenets in any organized way. This mindset changed when news of the town's destruction reached them and the first refugees from the town began to arrive in the Land. Their memories of the past began to strengthen, their nostalgia grew, and pain and sorrow tugged at their hearts. These feelings required redemption and expression. Several of our townspeople began to write their memories of the town, publishing them in several publications (*Volhynia Treasury*, *Gazit*, *Al Hamishmar*, etc.), and the connection among the town's natives in the Land of Israel strengthened. They began to meet to ask each other about the town's destruction and collect information about the survivors. They felt a visceral need to create an organized structure to bring together the old and recent remnants of the town and to facilitate as much as possible the new immigrants' social and economic absorption. A trailblazing group was established in Tel Aviv, with another group in Haifa, and in 1947 the organization was founded. Each year on August 14, the anniversary of the destruction, a memorial ceremony is held for the town's natives who were killed, and hundreds of people gather from the corners of the Land to meet and to mourn the destruction. Deep feelings emerge: some cry and some rejoice, some kiss and some commiserate.

Memories, names, streets, and houses all arise, one after the other. Even after the emotional memorial ceremony, the group stays together for a long time and disperses in distress.

> [**Translator's Note:** In Hebrew, *Volhynia Treasury* is *Yalkut Volin. Gazit* and *Al HaMishmar* (*On Guard*) are newspapers.]

The organization also sometimes arranges social gatherings—sometimes nationwide and sometimes each town separately—such as when there is a guest from the Diaspora. There is also some attempt at mutual aid: through the charity fund established by the organization, members in distress receive loans or support, and, with the help of various members, the organization also arranges work for new immigrants from our town.

The organization's establishment brought about a "meeting of the minds" among the town's natives in the Land as well as several kinds of mutual assistance. In particular, new immigrants find their way quickly to other town natives and do not feel alone. The organization charges a monthly fee to provide publicity and other material, but the collections themselves are not strictly organized.

During the past two years, the organization's main project, on which it has expended a great deal of effort, has been to publish *Pinkas Kremenets*. The planting of a grove in the Martyrs' Forest in memory of the Kremenets community is in the planning stages.

THE SOCIAL SITUATION

What are the 400 families of Kremenets immigrants in the Land doing—what is their financial situation and social standing? Approximately 60–70 work in agriculture: in kibbutzim, workers' settlements, and cooperative farms.

Party for Kremenets Natives in Tel Aviv

A large portion work in manufacturing, construction, and various other jobs. A significant number are self-employed or own small factories. A small minority work as merchants, and several dozen are officials and insurance professionals. Some individuals are without means of support. The vast majority have regular work, a significant portion being well off economically. Some have even become wealthy. For example, in Haifa, there are 80–90 families from Kremenets. Of them, 15 own their own businesses and factories, several work as officials, one as a merchant, and the rest in manufacturing, construction, and the railroad, most being workers in various occupations. Thus their socioeconomic conditions are favorable. In Jerusalem, on the other hand, a large proportion work in official capacities. In Tel Aviv, we find Kremenets natives working in health care and teaching, as well as a significant number of officials, but most work in manufacturing, manual labor, and construction, whether as workers or in ownership positions. If we remember the social situation of the Jews in Kremenets, we can see the blessed progress in productivization experienced by the hundreds of families that settled in the Land. Our friends in America occasionally send food packages to Kremenets natives in the Land, but the vast majority do not require the packages and refrains from benefiting from them. Some of the packages sent to Haifa are returned to Tel Aviv, since there are no Kremenets natives in Haifa who need them. Several town natives have become rich as contractors and factory owners. Other individuals have reached high positions in public administration.

In summary, we can say that the children of Kremenets answered the call to build the Land to the best of their ability. And this is not a small thing. It was natural that previously prominent people would fill the most prominent positions, but in terms of their material background, the new immigrants progressed further than their more established neighbors.

[218]

Get-Together with Guests from the United States,
Kremenets Natives Mr. and Mrs. Yitschak Vakman

DURING THE WAR OF INDEPENDENCE

During the War of Independence, Kremenets natives also contributed their share, fighting in various battles and having their blood shed on Israel's soil. The images of the two who fell at Yagur during the disturbances (Hinde Fishman and Shmuel Dishel); Eliezer Dobekirer, who died of fever in Givat HaShlosha; and Yisrael Goldenberg, who fell as a watchman at Tel Mond, are engraved in our memories.

IN POLITICAL LIFE

Nevertheless, our town's natives did not stay out of political life in the Land. Certainly, everyone is a member of a party or leans toward the views of a certain party (the vast majority toward the Labor parties). However, we find almost no party activists among Kremenetsers in the Land. It may be pertinent to mention that in Kremenets itself there were powerful Pioneer and Young Pioneer organizations, which were chapters of the Labor parties in the Land of Israel. They emphasized action more than ideological factors. We thus see a direct connection from the town in the Diaspora to the town's natives in the Land.

DISPERSION OF KREMENETS NATIVES OUTSIDE ISRAEL

Most Kremenets exiles are centered in three places: North America, Argentina, and Israel. The number of families that immigrated to America over the years is estimated at 1,000–1,500, and approximately 200 families immigrated to Argentina. Besides these, our townspeople are spread out in other lands, such as Soviet Russia and Poland, the Western countries of France and England, and other places as individuals or small groups. In the United States and Argentina, there are organizations of Kremenets natives, and the Israeli organization maintains connections with them in several ways: meetings with emissaries and guests visiting the Land, exchanges of letters, etc. During the past few years, these connections have been strengthened by the joint publication of *Pinkas Kremenets*.

[219]

GENERAL YOSEF AVIDAR (ROKHEL)

Dr. Duvid Lazar

General Yosef Avidar (Rokhel)

His office in the general staff of the Israeli Defense Forces shows the most severe economy, without contamination by outside influences and without adornment or furniture. The simplicity and sparseness follow the tradition of the days of the Haganah and Underground, being an escape from any attempt to "make waves" or distract the eyes. At headquarters as on the battlefield, in the Planning Department as at field headquarters, there are a temporary table, military blankets, folding chairs, and maps. And the pressure of work, focused concentration, and conquest of emotions—that is most important.

His path to the Planning Department at General Headquarters was a hazardous one. It progressed from Jerusalem to the "red house" in Tel Aviv, training grounds and leadership courses, the "fortresses" in the North, and the 11 settlements in the Negev, but the path began in Kremenets, Volhynia, a somewhat exceptional Diaspora town: the Jews there did not fear the gentiles. Even in the most difficult times, during the Revolution and the Civil War and during changes of governments and from one jurisdiction to another—from the "Reds" to the "Whites," from the Ukrainians to the Poles, during World War I and afterward—there were no pogroms in Kremenets. From her, our Jewish young people learned about Jewish independence and proud resistance against all enemies and adversaries. During the war the town found itself directly within the battleground: in the great offensive, General Brusilov's army made a stand in the Rokhel family's courtyard, with the battle passing directly by the house. Petliura's armies and the Hetman Skoropadski's bands were there; the Jews were armed, and they knew how to protect themselves from attackers.

270

Yosef Rokhel, the youngest of five sons, received military training when he was nine years old. In the same courtyard lived a sergeant in the Czar's army, who because of boredom after his discharge gave military training to the children in the area so as not to break his routine. He taught them military formations and even the use of firearms, and receiving this training while young did not fail to leave its influence on the young people. Another type of "education," which Diaspora Jews of the previous generation had accepted, was almost nonexistent: Yosef Rokhel never studied in a cheder and obviously never in a yeshiva. Hebrew was nearly his mother tongue—lullabies were recited in Hebrew, and the nanny—the Ukrainian *nyanye*—would say *El melekh ne'eman* with the children. The father was a well-to-do merchant and learned man, involved in the tradition but very liberal in his outlook, the mother knew Hebrew, and the school was a Hebrew school. At a young age, Yosef Rokhel learned to count in Hebrew with a decidedly Sephardic accent.

> [**Translator's Note:** *El melekh ne'eman* (trustworthy God) is a prayer said before going to sleep.]

[220]

It was a Zionist home, and when the time came, there was serious talk about immigrating to the land of Israel. "We must not stay here," was the final decision, and when the boy Yosef was asked what he would do in the Land of Israel and whether he would agree to become a goose farmer, he answered without having to think much that he would agree even to this. The story circulated around the family for a long time that it was as if the five brothers had signed a "compact" requiring each to immigrate as soon as he reached adulthood. And each did indeed come. The first to arrive was Avraham, who came before World War I, served in the Jewish Legion and the Haganah, and after contracting severe malaria returned for a short time to Kremenets and told stories of wonders and miracles about the Land—about the first settlements, the guards, and the farm workers—and this romanticism about the early days greatly influenced the rest of the family. They all decided to immigrate.

Yosef's first stop on reaching the Land in 1925 was Jerusalem, and one week after his integration, he was already in the Haganah as a member, leader, and officer. During the 1929 riots, he was an officer in the Old City of Jerusalem, with all that went with this position. Even then he served as a sort of barricade for the Jewish Quarter, and attacks were repulsed when the young officer walked before the defenders with his gun in hand. The headquarters were in the Yeshiva *Sha'ar Shamayim*—for the study of the visible and the mystical—and even today the General remembers the honor and fear he felt on seeing the visage of the mystic and Kabbalist Rabbi Horovits, a singular kind of image. There was great trembling on that hellish night inside the walls of the Old City when the first news about the massacre in Hebron arrived: the cries rose up to the heavens. The Jews of the Old City had familial ties with the Jews of Hebron, and the mourning was heartrending.

> [**Translator's Note:** *Sha'ar Shamayim* means Gate of Heaven.]

The Land quieted down, more or less. Approximately two years after the episode in the Old City, Yosef Rokhel went out one Saturday with a brigade of 50 men for exercises around the amphitheater of Hebrew University on Mount Scopus, on the eastern slope, in the direction of the Dead Sea. The exercises included throwing grenades, and the officer demonstrated the way to throw the *menachem* grenade, which was independently produced by the Haganah. This type of grenade needed to be "knocked" with the left hand before it was thrown, and during the "knocking," a grenade exploded in Rokhel's hand. Part of his right hand was cut off, and his left was crushed nearly to the point where it would require amputation. Very calmly under the circumstances, this seriously injured man took care to remove all evidence of the exercises before anything else so that they would not be exposed to the British police, gave over control to his second in command, Yakov Berger (who fell in the first days of the battle over Hanita), and only afterward agreed to be taken to the hospital. Since there was no stretcher, he was carried up the slope in sheets—a two-hour journey to the university—an Arab vehicle had to be "commandeered" to expedite the removal of the injured to Hadassah Hospital on HaNevi'im Street because he had lost a great deal of blood, and every minute was precious. Only afterward did Rachel Yanait—who is now the First Lady of the country and was then a Haganah staff member—arrive by car.

He needed emergency surgery, but no surgeon was available. Because there was no choice, a surgeon, a man known to be a dedicated Nazi, was called from the German hospital—it was 1931—and he performed the surgery. Very calmly and without complication or even a drop of "heroics," General Avidar recounts these events. His left hand healed completely, and it has a powerful grip, but by paying close attention one can see that the right hand is partially artificial—the general writes with it and operates a bicycle and car, and, what is more, he has adjusted enough that he can repair anything he needs to, whether a motor or just a broken shutter at home. He salutes with his left hand, just as another officer saluted in his time—he was also Yosef, hero of Port Arthur and Gallipoli—Trumpeldor.

[221]

Yet Yosef Rokhel, a high-ranking Haganah officer, never mentioned or even contemplated any such comparison between himself and the hero of Tel-Hai. He has a sense of proportion and does not engage in feelings of self-importance. He was Yosef Biberman, real estate agent. That was the simplest disguise to use in the days of the underground, with an official identity card—part stolen, part forged, but on first glance flawless—and a little makeup that, when necessary, changed his face to someone else's entirely, to the point where his two daughters, Rime and Dine (who when the time came gave their initials to their Hebrew surname, Avidar—father of Dina and Rima) would not recognize their father as he walked down the street. (But they knew to keep quiet wonderfully, and they knew the secret....) The way the hair was combed, with the "part" in it, the glasses, the mustache, the ostentatious, formal dress of a real estate agent—they did the job. The agent was registered with the appropriate housing and land office as required by law, and he even paid taxes according to the law so as not to bring any suspicion on himself. Once, he bought a shirt and used his identity card—that of Yosef Biberman—as identification in the store, as was customary in those days—all to have an "alibi" as a loyal and upstanding citizen.

The loyal citizen Biberman—who was also occasionally called Finkelshteyn and appeared occasionally with other names—traveled widely through the Land on business. He was an unusual real estate agent. He picked land for settlements in strategic areas during the state of emergency, he was always around when people staked their claims to the land, and he planned settlements from the viewpoint of security, with the possibility that the government might strongly oppose him if he set up these outposts in illegal areas. One of his better projects in this area was the establishment of 11 new settlements in the Negev in October 1946. The project was more successful than imagined, with the planner almost falling by the wayside. He appeared this time as a plumber from Solel Boneh Ltd. who had come to repair one of the pipes in a settlement, but after apparently arousing the suspicion of the nervous and irritable British police, he was detained on his return and brought to the police station in Gaza for questioning along with his friend Duvid Tuviyahu, now the mayor of Beersheba. The two were freed for lack of evidence, and the mysterious plumber demonstrated his almost "gentile" level-headedness. But there was another investigation in the office of the regional secret police in Gaza. Rokhel appeared without disguise, under his own name, and there was fear that his name was on a list of those wanted for arrest by the CID before Black Sabbath. The list had already been passed to the intelligence section of the Haganah, but only up to the letter M, and it was impossible to know if a National Headquarters member named Yosef Rokhel appeared on the list. The investigation went over well. Rokhel was not on the list.

Even before the United Nations decision in the summer of 1947, when it appeared that there was no doubt that war was on the way, Rokhel was charged with arranging the "instruments" needed by the army—from shoelaces to warplanes and tanks. General Avidar remembers well when he received from Duvid Ben-Gurion the full list of supplies required by each soldier. He needed to multiply the list by tens of thousands, and he arrived at a total of millions of supplies—which were not available. But when the day came, suddenly the first uniforms (still not those of the Israel Defense Forces, but rather of the Haganah, which was beginning to emerge from the underground with foreign-made rifles and homemade Sten guns) and rations appeared from secret warehouses, and the great expectation was that shipments of heavy armaments, ammunition, and heavy vehicles—artillery—would arrive from overseas. On seder night 1948, shortly before the declaration of the state, Rokhel boarded the ship that brought the first 20-millimeter artillery. There was great emotion, and after the unloading they shared a toast with the head of the Quartermaster Corps—the members of the staff and bystanders who had unloaded the ship in the Port of Tel Aviv.

[222]

Rokhel gave a short speech (he always gave short speeches): "All the Jews are reclining at the seder meal. You" (then facing the Salonican stevedores) "are also *beseder,*" and with that he finished. Afterward, several similar "shipments"—from the sea and from the sky—came one after the other in an atmosphere of drama and anxiety that one very dear package might fall into the wrong hands—the hands of the British.

[**Translation Editor's Note:** In this play on words, *seder* (meaning "order") is the ritual Passover meal, and *beseder* means "OK."]

Rokhel himself did not fall into the hands of the British. The unlucky kidnapping organized by LEHI as retribution for the imprisonment of several of its leaders was an "interesting" episode—on the border between drama and opera. The general, the one who was kidnapped, tells of the episode in a humorous tone. The kidnappers treated him with the utmost respect, and he held interesting discussions with them, from which came the happy promise that if the independence of the state were declared— something no one believed would happen—the boys would stand before the kidnapped officer as regular soldiers in the Israeli army. The day after the kidnapping, there was already a detailed plan for his escape. Even the armaments were secure. The prisoners were rescued even before the plan was carried out.

[**Translation Editor's Note:** LEHI is an acronym for *Lochamei Cherut Israel* (Fighters for the Freedom of Israel), a Zionist paramilitary group.]

Rokhel also organized the sending of supplies to besieged Jerusalem. Somewhere in an army camp in the south, female volunteers filled 16-kilogram bags of flour to load onto the shoulders of 600 mobilized citizens, who were taken straight from the factory, where they were taught how to tie the bags and carry them in the dark, under fire, before the Burma Road existed. The difficulties were not insignificant. Even here a great miracle occurred, involving the right words spoken at the right time in the right way. Rokhel calculated the daily requirement of bread for each resident of Jerusalem (160 grams) and turned to the carriers: "Each of you carries on his shoulders enough bread for 100 Jews in Jerusalem today ...," and the words had the desired effect. The carriers stood up and began to walk. The bread reached its destination. It was a great moment. Only then did the connection between *lechem* and *lechima* become clear.

[**Translator's Note:** In this play on words, *lechem* means "bread," and *lechima* means "warfare."]

General Rokhel concerned himself with the requirements of warfare, but his heart was always drawn to the battlefield itself, to the operations and command aspects of the war. He was chosen leader of the northern command, with all the intricate problems that involved: problems of shortage and military government, pressure on the borders, and skirmishes with the Syrians. The "man of Nazareth," Sholem Asch, was greatly moved by a discussion with him during his visit to Israel. The sentimental Asch said with Jewish emotion on leaving his meeting with Avidar, "For the first time in my life, I had the merit to see a true Jewish general ...."

From Nazareth, Avidar moved to the central command, later taking part in the military's "goodwill" mission to Yugoslavia, and made a great impression. He was sent to London for a military course for high-ranking officers. He completed the military training, and during the session met with many British officers who had served in the

Land and were nostalgic for it. At the end of the course, the officer, a British general, said about Avidar, "I'll never forget this outstanding personality."

The two prominent aspects of General Yosef Avidar were (1) an immense work ethic, immersion in his work, and particularly in what he required of others and especially of himself, and (2) the nobility of his soul, "uprightness that borders on the sick," as one of his closest aides described. He was extremely particular about impeccable measurement and economy—also in his private life—with hatred bordering on disgust for any evidence of waste, characteristics that in our environment are refreshing as dew from the heavens, as necessary as air to breathe. There is an old French saying about a military hero from the Middle Ages: "He was brave without fear and without stain." This saying describes exactly the brave, tall, and maimed Yosef Rokhel-Avidar, who would not presume, God forbid, to be Trumpeldor.

[223]

ELIEZER DOBEKIRER

Manus Goldenberg

Eliezer DobEkirer

Through the mists of the past his form appears: a child of about 11 (he was born in 1901) among children of his age in the Jewish Primary School, careful in his dress, well groomed, and beloved for his straightforwardness, behavior, and trustworthiness in defending the weak. He was one of the students who were ready to escape from the classroom to the nearby woods belonging to the old glassmaker Kveytel to catch the first snowflakes or the first breaths of spring, or to take a long trip on the paths of the Vidomka near the railroad station. Certainly, such behavior led to strong rebukes from Principal Goldfarb, but what poetic soul can resist the fragrant fields' siren song underneath the silent and proud snow?

In those same Kveytel's woods, the first student group in our town was established at the outset of the Revolution. E. Dobekirer, who was one of the organizers, surprised everyone with a fiery speech calling on the students to organize. This was the first time he had participated in such a meeting, and he showed such bravery at his age that contemporary events left deep impressions on his soul.

He was brought up in his father's house, a textile merchant who was careful to direct him toward becoming a man of means, concerned with providing for his family and his business. He therefore felt the pressure of his parents' strenuous objections when he joined a Zionist youth movement nearby.

When he finished high school, he enlisted in the Polish army. When I was drafted into the same artillery unit where he was serving, I heard from his superiors and colleagues that he was an excellent artilleryman. He then told me that he was paying close attention to his training so that he could become an expert artilleryman in the Land of Israel. Despite the anti-Semitic line taken by the Polish army officers and their desire not to give Jews access to training or courses in such materiel, he was sent to noncommissioned officers school, which he completed with distinction. He enjoyed his work with the 155-millimeter cannon, and more than once he said that eventually we would be able to use similar arms for defense in the Land of Israel.

On his discharge from the army, he joined Pioneer, which had just been formed. This alone brought him into vigorous conflict with his parents. When it came time for him to immigrate, his parents struggled with him bitterly, which led to a storm in the town. They disowned him and treated him as an apostate was treated in the old days.

After his immigration (in 1925), he joined the *Ma'avar* group in Petach Tikvah, founders of the kibbutz Givat HaShlosha. Conditions in the kibbutz were very harsh, but a pioneer spirit suffused their rickety tents. The letters we received from him were full of activity, but they suddenly stopped. Some thought that he had lost his spirit and succumbed to his parents' pressure, as well as the pressure of his wife and in-laws. An issue of the *Davar* newspaper that reached us several weeks later told us the fearful news: Eliezer Dobekirer had died in Hadassah Hospital in Tel Aviv, far from his relatives and friends. He had fallen ill with typhus, and for several days at his tent did not receive the medical attention he needed for his fever. Without a diagnosis, he was brought to the hospital, and he died there.

Even during his final days, he conquered his troubles, and his good sense of humor did not leave him until his final moment. In the old cemetery of Tel Aviv, his bones are buried beneath a modest tombstone: an unknown soldier in the battle for our revival.

[224]

THE TWO WHO FELL IN YAGUR

Ester Fidel (Meshek Yagur)

Hinde Fishman

Eleven young men and women, members of Meshek Yagur and the United Kibbutz Movement, and one from Kfar Chasidim, returned in the evening on Sunday, 19 Nisan 1931, from the Nesher neighborhood to Meshek Yagur, a 15-minute wagon ride. As they neared the farm, 100 meters along the road to Kfar Chasidim, they saw a few Arabs standing by the road. The Arabs allowed the wagon to pass, and once it had passed, they opened fire with a volley of shots. The first shots came from the left, and the first injured were those sitting on the left side of the wagon: Shmuel Dishel was killed immediately with a bullet to the heart and fell in the wagon, and the wagon driver, Yakov Zamir, a member of Meshek Yagur, was severely injured, fell from the wagon, and died several hours later. The donkeys panicked and ran toward the farm, and the shots that hit the wagon during its escape came from the right side. A member of the Movement, Hinde Fishman, who was sitting on the right side, was killed by a bullet through the heart, and she fell out of the wagon.

The three fatalities and the four wounded had previously been members of Kibbutz Klesov.

(*Davar* newspaper, April 7, 1931)

HINDE FISHMAN

She came from the Dubno suburb. Hinde did her pioneer training in the kibbutz known as Klesov in Poland. She immigrated in 1929 with the first wave of the Fifth Immigration, and she was sent near the farming kibbutz in Petach Tikvah. Quiet, nice to all creatures, and kindhearted, Hinde dedicated herself with love and purpose to labor. She worked in the orchards of Petach Tikvah and at the farm. After two years of training, she decided to make her permanent home in Meshek Yagur. There was already a group from Klesov there, and Mount Carmel reminded her of the hills of Kremenets, where she had spent her childhood.

In 1931, before Passover, Hinde came to Yagur. She was only with us for one week, because on the evening of Sunday, 18 Nisan 1931, a large group of us, mostly from Kremenets, traveled in the wagon to nearby Nesher (there were still no automobiles at the kibbutz). It was a very dark night, and as we returned, terrorists ambushed us. I will never forget how happy and satisfied Hinde was that evening, as if she suddenly and all at once felt the happiness she had not yet had in her short life. Poverty and an unhappy childhood did not give her much joy during her life, but that night she was very happy. Near her new home, full of dreams and hopes for working and creating her own homeland, she was cut down by an enemy bullet.

[225]

The horses were bewildered by the shooting and reared up, and Hinde, who was gravely wounded, fell from the wagon onto the road. We could hear her final screams of pain and protest at the attackers' unfairness and cruelty. This refugee screamed and then became quiet forever, at the young age of 26. When group members went to search for her, she was dead. Three were killed and five were wounded in the attack. One of the victims was another Kremenets native, Shmuel Dishel, who was killed by a bullet straight through his heart, and he fell without uttering a sound. They found him dead in the wagon. These three martyrs were laid to rest in a common grave underneath a massive stone expertly inscribed with sheaves blowing in the wind. They move (in the wind) but are not broken.

Nor were we broken. Our group of Kremenets natives, a sizable group at our farm, together with the other members, took the yoke of action on our young shoulders, and thereby we fulfill Hinde's aspirations.

Rest in peace, Hinde! You could not fulfill your life's dreams, but we will faithfully and happily continue to serve the homeland. We turned desolate land to fruitfulness, we did our part to create a refuge for our people, and we have built a home—about which you dreamed so eagerly—on behalf of those who wish to serve the people and the homeland.   Rest in peace, dearest one!

SHMUEL DISHEL

From *Davar,* May 5, 1931

Age 22. Native of Kremenets. Completed Jewish Primary School and immediately went on to work and pioneer activities. He joined Young Pioneer and learned the tailoring trade. After a while he became an active member—a member of the council—of the tailors' union in Kremenets. He was the only wage earner in his household, but his desire to immigrate prevailed. After two years in the Pioneer organization, he went to a training kibbutz. He spent one and a half years working in the factories of Klesov. He immigrated within a year, joined the Yagur group, and went to work in the factories in Atlit on behalf of the group.

From the time he left his student's desk, he never stopped working and toiling, and when he came home to the kibbutz to rest during the holiday, he fell at the hands of the oppressor.

Dishel's hands paved the road on which he was killed.

THE FUNERAL

From *Davar,* April 7, 1931

From the Haifa Workers' Council and Meshek Yagur, announcements were put up in Haifa inviting people to attend the funeral, and masses of people streamed to Hadassah Hospital. The funeral procession left there at 3:00 p.m., and at its head was a group of motorcycle riders from the Worker and an honor guard of British "foot-policemen" on horseback and in automobiles, led by Commander Flyer and then Deputy Petroz. After passing through the Technion courtyard, the procession turned to HeChalutz Street and stopped next to the Workers' House. From its balcony, Duvid Ben-Gurion eulogized the victims on behalf of the General Council of the Zionist Organization. From the factory, the procession went to Herzl Street, and next to the Central Synagogue, the cantor sang "God, Full of Compassion." Next to the Wadi Rushmie Bridge, across from the communal houses, the coffins were placed in hearses, and dozens of cars filled with passengers escorted them to Yagur.

> [**Translator's Note:** The Worker in Hebrew is *HaPoel,* an Israeli labor organization. "God, Full of Compassion" (*El Male Rachamim*) is a prayer for the dead.]

Next to the Nesher factory, inhabitants of the area and of Kfar Hasidim joined the funeral procession. The crowd at the cemetery in Yagur numbered 2,000. Members of the group, the farm, and Nesher placed wreaths on the coffins. At the graveside, Nachum Benari gave a short speech on behalf of the United Kibbutz.

[226]

YISRAEL GOLDENBERG

Manus Goldenberg

Yisrael Goldenberg

In memory of the members of the ranks of Maccabee of Kremenets who were killed in the Holocaust.

Above the storefront, an artistic billboard by Liora Gurvits announces with splashes of color a soccer match between the Kremenets Maccabee team and a Polish team from Dubno. The featured soccer player on the billboard, whose leg is raised high, preparing to kick, is an object of amusement for those who pass by. He is the crowd favorite, "the monkey," Yisrael Goldenberg of the Dubno suburb. With a few strokes of blue on paper, the 16-year-old artist has managed to capture his image, brimming with strength and eagerness.

The pitch, Harkov Field, sits in the shade of the trees that rise around it on descending slopes. The atmosphere is replete with the intoxicating aromas of wildflowers and grass. The match against the Polish team begins to the rhythm of melodies by the Gakman Band.

The Jewish spectators are very excited. The Polish team is strong, and the Maccabee team's victory is in doubt. The only hope is the runner on the left side. The distinctive darkness of his face contrasts with the white and azure of his jersey as he runs quickly from goal to goal. "*Kushi*, strike!" the hearty cheer is heard from the Jewish partisans. "*Molpe, gol!*" that is, "Monkey, goal!" comes the organized cheer from the crowd. Awe-inspiring kicks are directed toward the Polish goal, and every kick brings applause.

With his long limbs, hulking body, wide-open mouth, flared nostrils, and eyes bulging from their sockets, it was impossible not to compare him to a monkey; hence his nickname.

He did not fail in that game. The arms of the cheering crowd carried him high in victory.

A few years later, when a wave of anti-Semitism overtook Poland and our town, Yisrael appeared in a different light. With Moshe'ki Margolis and Dudek Barshap, he fought with Polish students who filled the streets of Kremenets, giving ten blows for every one they absorbed, and more than one of the injured ended up in the Jewish Hospital. A sense of loyalty to his people arose within him. He was blessed with a noble soul and a pure heart.

One day, we learned to our delight that Yisrael had joined Pioneer in Kremenets and had gone for training. We prayed that he would soon immigrate, because we knew how suited he was to working and protecting the Land. And again he did not fail. The story of his life and death on duty, guarding lives and property, was a natural extension of his life story in his hometown.

****

The guard Yisrael Goldenberg, who was wounded on duty next to Moshav Ein-Vered, died of his many abdominal wounds after four days of extreme suffering.

He was a native of Kremenets in Volhynia, a member of a typical Volhynian nationalist merchant family. He came to Zionism by way of Jewish sports youth groups in our town. In 1925 he immigrated to the Land. His years in the Land were a long chain of actions to conquer the Land and settle desolate areas. At first, he paved roads and cleared land in the hills of Mount Carmel; he then went to the Nahalal area near Kfar Yehoshue, where he drilled and installed wells. After Kfar Yehoshue he went to Migdal, near Tiberias; he helped lay the cornerstone of Tel Mond, and he worked there until his final days.

[227]

He injured his arm badly three years ago and could no longer to use it for meaningful work, so he became a full-time guard. He found his calling as a watchman in the field. He was brave and fearless. He had great confidence in his own strength, and he was always the first to answer the call whenever and wherever the need arose.

They called him "Johnny," a term of endearment, because he was loved by all his peers. He was devoted and trustworthy, and besides being strong, healthy, and vigorous, he was straightforward and full of youth, and he was therefore beloved by all.

In Tel Mond he was one of those most involved in security issues. When he died, there was no replacement in the entire region. He was one of the founders and first settlers of the workers' neighborhood in Tel Mond and a member of the Kfar Ziv neighborhood council. He built his home and family there. He left a wife and a one-year-old son.

He was 30 years old when he died. He was brought to burial in the pine forest between Tel Mond and Ein-Vered.

(From *Davar LaOleh*)

> [**Translator's Note:** *Davar LaOleh* means *Word for Immigrants*.]

SHMUEL KOYLER

M. O.

The road from Kremenets to Yad Mordekhay in the Negev—the road taken by Shmuel Koyler—is long. Shmuelik took his first steps toward the Land of Israel as a young man, almost still a boy, in Young Pioneer. Even in his childhood, he stood out because of his overwhelming skill, happiness, and kindheartedness. Who didn't know the happy boy, who sang as he went about his many activities? Shmuelik had "golden hands." While he was still a student at the Jewish Primary School, he was already an instructor of weaving, drawing, carpentry, and the like. When he completed his primary school studies, he practiced weaving in his desire to produce works of art. Before he immigrated, he did three years of training in Lublin, and he was anxiously looking forward to the day when his dream of living in the Land of Israel would be realized. And in the Land itself, he was the first to volunteer for anything: as watchman over the wearied and working and in many capacities as a soldier in the British Army until he joined the Jewish Brigades, with whom he fought on the front lines. When the enemy was beaten and the battles ended, Shmuel continued his dedication and personal bravery. He threw himself into rescuing the remnant of refugees wandering along the borders and illegally bringing them in. The final days of his life: he died in the home he loved, for which he fought, wandered, and toiled, Kibbutz Yad Mordekhay. Shmuelik fell as he attacked an enemy tank, and with his body, he stopped the Egyptian hordes from invading the heart of a country fighting for its survival.

He was 33 when he died, with a wife and two children mourning for their dear Shmuelik.

****

Sh.

During the battles it seemed that our hearts had turned to stone, but it is true that we are still given to fantasy and daydreams. Sometimes I imagine that I am in a dream, that I will wake up in a moment, rub my eyes, look out the window, and find everything in its place, and friends who are actually dead will be sitting on the grass, playing with their children as usual. However, the cruel, painful truth reminds us at every turn of the great losses we have suffered.

I shared a strong bond of friendship and brotherhood with Shmuelik for many years. We shared many common experiences in those years, and I will not soon forget him.

From the first moment I was drawn to him and loved him. In his appearance and manner, he was truly typical of a member of a Jewish nationalist family from Volhynia. The grace of a young Jewish man always shone on his face, and he exuded joy and lightheartedness until his final days. His infectious laugh, which came in wave after wave, could be heard from far away.

[228]

He inherited his beautiful voice and talent for poetry and music from his cantor father, R' Moshe Brechye of Kremenets. He would entertain us with Hasidic tunes and folk songs at every kibbutz and army gathering. Every song he sang would invite you, and you would be drawn to the music. The albums he gave to his friends are a testament to his talent for his job as a bookbinder. He also dabbled in carpentry, and without training, he produced first-rate work. He brought a nice children's cabinet—his handiwork—to his daughter, Mikhal, a gift from the camp in the desert.

When the Brigades were established, he failed his physical examination. Because of his longing for family and the kibbutz, he made sure to learn to be a driver, which allowed him to go to the front lines. Soon he was serving in the security patrol and "flew" along the streets of Italy, with its beautiful scenery. He returned from each sortie full of adventures and impressions. When he returned home, he became a carpenter. During the siege of our kibbutz, when driving on the dirt roads was a daily danger, Shmuelik stood up and announced his desire to sit behind the steering wheel again, as more drivers were needed. Aware of his eagerness and his driving ability, the kibbutz sent him to the Military Transport class. He took great pride in his "Tommy," his personal weapon. On the first day of battle, in the first hours, he was wounded by shrapnel, but he refused to lie down. He was simply bandaged and took it upon himself to bring ammunition and nourishment to the troops.

Despite his natural happiness, a feeling of foreboding stayed with him, a feeling that apparently came from despair, as if he realized his fate. When the news arrived that tanks had breached the farm's perimeter, he ran with everyone else to the danger zone and attacked a tank with a grenade in his hand. At that time, he had no fear of death—the danger to the farm was his single thought—as he went to destroy the tank. A volley of enemy bullets struck him, and he fell in a pool of his own blood. After the invasion was repulsed, we found him right beside the tracks of the tank.

The tears of our distress and grief over the loss of beloved Shmuelik will not stop. However, along with the pain we feel, we are proud of his outstanding bravery during his last few moments. Just as we learned from his tolerance and his songs, his self-sacrifice and bravery should serve as an example.

(From a booklet published by Kibbutz Yad Mordekhay in memory of its defenders who fell in battle: "Yad Mordekhay in Battle")

THE SPIRIT OF TWO FIGHTERS

Moshe Kremenchutski (Ramat Gan)
English translation by Aviv Tzur

Siunye Keselman and Avraham Margalit, who Fell in the Spanish War, 1937

Of all the blessed souls of our community, let us not forget the two freedom fighters who fell in 1937 Spain while fighting for the Spanish National Republic against the Franco regime.

Siunye (Yehoshue) Keselman and Avrasha (Avraham) Margalit were both members of Youth Guard in Kremenets. Both were honest and dedicated to their view and their life's purpose. Both were humble and followed their vision in life.

[229]

They were some of the first to do "pioneer studies," working in the forests of Poland during the bitter winters. Shortly after their return, they immigrated to the Land of Israel at the time of the 1929 pogroms. They joined the Youth Guard kibbutz in Binyamina and were among its builders. They never shirked hard labor despite their deteriorating health. They helped drain the swamps of Kabara and contracted malaria. Once they discovered the ideological contradiction between their position on the "Arab question" vis-à-vis that of the kibbutz, they felt that the honorable thing to do was to leave the kibbutz and move into the town, where they worked in construction and joined the Palestine Communist Party.

As the Spanish people began their war of independence, they were some of the first to join the International Brigade. From letters they sent to me, as well as from Siunye's memorial book, I learned that they volunteered to be in the front lines and perished as heroes in the fields of Guadalajara.

SHPRINTSE ROKHEL
1871–1952

A. Yosef

She was a native of the small town of Sudilkov, which was next to Shchepetovka, and came from the Heylprin family, which manufactured prayer shawls, as did most residents of the village.

The family had a love for the Land of Israel even long ago, and one of the family patriarchs, Bukhman, immigrated in his later years and settled in Safed. On her mother's side she was a scion of a rabbinic family that counted 23 generations of rabbis. She received a traditional education. Curious from childhood, she learned Bible and even Talmud with her brothers. At a young age she became attached to the Enlightenment and Love of Zion, reading in Russian and Hebrew, with her favorite poet being Frug. When she married Yehoshue Rokhel and lived in Kremenets, she found herself in a circle that had no love for the Enlightenment, Hebrew literature, or Zionism. As a person with strong convictions, she fought for her philosophy and way of life. Despite the opposition of everyone around her, especially her powerful father-in-law, Hirsh Mendil, she established a strongly Hebrew/Zionist home and taught her children (10 in number) in that manner. It was one of the few homes in the town where the children spoke Hebrew. One of the children was sent to study in the Land of Israel, and specifically not to the Herzliya High School but to an agricultural school in Petach Tikvah. As the children got older, they came one by one to the Land of Israel, and in 1930 the parents also immigrated.

She had a special interest in medical science. She read medical books, showed an understanding of illness, and served as a health consultant to many families. She taught her large family about Zionism and the Land of Israel. In addition, she always followed current events and Jewish politics. She literally read and studied until her final day.

During her first years in the Land, she lived in Kibbutz Tel Yosef with her son Chanokh. She fit in well with kibbutz life, but not with her position as one of the "parents." She ate in the communal dining room (she was not devout) and participated as much as possible in all the farming tasks. After that, they went to live in Tel Aviv. She was a member of the Society for Women's Equality. She went to lectures at Ohel Shem. She learned nutrition and improved her knowledge of Hebrew. She also took part in the Organization of Kremenets Emigrants.

[230]

During her final years, she lost three of her children, and her spirit was broken. The first of Elul was the anniversary of the death of her daughter Vitye in Kibbutz Ashdot Yakov. On returning from there to Haifa, her foot slipped on the steps. She fell and broke her ribs, and several days later died in a Haifa hospital. Her husband, Yehoshue, had predeceased her by several years. The two are buried in the cemetery at Nachalat Yitschak near Tel Aviv.

On her deathbed, she told her granddaughter her life story and concluded, "In my youth I recited the poems of Frug, and I longed to see the amazing cypress trees about which he wrote. And now I have had the fortune to see that two cypress trees stand outside my window, and my son Yosef lives on Frug Street, named for my favorite poet."

Thus she completed the circle of her life, which was full from beginning to end.

Shprintse Rokhel in Her Family Circle in Israel

THE DESTRUCTION OF KREMENETS

BURNING EMBERS ...

Manus Goldenberg
English translation by David Dubin

From *Al Hamishmar,* February 24, 1944

... Dubno and Zdolbunov were liberated. The thunder of the Red Army artillery already reaches my town, Kremenets. However, there is no longer a single living Jewish soul to joyously hear the echo that brings our salvation, as we heard back in 1919, when Petliura's sword was dangling over the town's head. The town, imprisoned behind shutters for many months, began to emerge, young and old, and filled its lungs with the air of freedom. And now the Red Army would find only smoking embers and mass graves.

Several days after war broke out in 1939, Kremenets received a great "honor": the Polish government, which had evacuated Warsaw, took up residence there with the diplomatic corps. A few days later, the German airplanes took note of the town and bombed it heavily.

And then Soviet tanks came and rescued her from loss and destruction. And again, town life began to flow normally.

My town, Kremenets, has truly fallen.

One day, Soviet tanks will again appear in its streets, but this time they will be met with the silence of death and the crowing of ravens from the branches of the trees in old, lush Lyceum Park, the center of Polish culture in the 18th century, where the great Polish poet Slovatski received his training.

On the slopes of a tall, steep mountain, the cemetery stretches between boulders and groves and near babbling brooks. The great, crowded stones look like a chaotic flock of sheep overlooking the town. A large congregation of many thousands is buried there today. They are silent witnesses to the enormous tragedy that befell their children and grandchildren.

And one day, if I come to you, beloved town of my birth, and climb the narrow paths to your cemetery, I will listen to the tombstones and absorb this story of terror and bravery in order to tell my children after me, until the end of the generations ....

THE FATE OF THE JEWS OF DUBNO AND KREMENETS

Telegram to *Davar* from the Jewish Antifascist Committee, Moscow, April 3, 1944
English translation by David Dubin

The first words that reached us from Dubno and Kremenets after their liberation described the Nazis' enormous cruelties. Not a single Jew survived in these two cities. The Jews who were imprisoned in the Dubno Ghetto held out much longer than in other places, since Ukrainian and Polish partisans brought them help and provisions. The Jews in Kremenets actively resisted the conquerors/murderers. With Comrade Bernshteyn at the helm, a large group of young Jews who had escaped from the Kremenets Ghetto assembled in the mountains. This was approximately one year ago. The German authorities posted a large reward for Bernshteyn's head. The Jewish partisans excelled in their actions against the Germans. After a while, they joined the Polish-Ukrainian partisans. Bernshteyn and his associates helped the Red Army with important intelligence and disruption of the enemy's supply lines.

Besides the Dubno and Kremenets Jews who joined the partisans—of whom many fell—Jews survived in the Soviet interior. A group of Jewish refugees from Kremenets found shelter in the village of Bogo-Yablonskaya near Tambov. Some of them, notably Rozental and Yosef Berkovits, a former officer, worked in the Caucasus. Some of the refugees now plan to return to Kremenets.

IN KREMENETS ONLY 11 JEWS REMAINED ...

Submitted by the Jewish Information Office in the USSR
"Letters from the Killing Fields," *Davar*, November 30, 1944
English translation by David Dubin

A refugee from Kremenets, a resident of Cheliabinsk, received the following letter from his Christian neighbor in Kremenets:

> I am very happy that at least you of your wonderful family survived. I will tell you about your family: when your countrymen went into the ghetto, your mother sold everything, including the furniture. I could not come to your house because I was sick, and your mother was mad at me for that. After that, she wanted to give us clothing to safeguard, but we were unable to because of the German edict that Christians who helped Jews were liable for capital punishment and loss of all their household goods. When the Jews were evacuated from the ghetto, your wife came to me and tossed me your blue suit and autumn coat. "I have someone to give these clothes to," your wife said, crying, "but I am afraid that they will not want to return them afterward. You will certainly watch over the clothing." She was separated from me and left. I did not see her again. They killed them all. Dashke, who served you in your

house, told me that she saw your wife as she was being taken by the Germans. Dashke yelled, "Tusye, where are Mother and the children?" She answered, "Mother's in prison, and I don't know about the children." About a month later they killed them. It is impossible to describe the murder because paper cannot contain the horror of it. Your house is still there, and Biduk, the shoemaker (a Christian), lives there. Your bricks and other things remain with the worker who worked for you. My Tusye wanted to buy the curtains from your mother, but she told her that the curtains were with the workman, and she gave Tusye a letter for him. He asked for an exorbitant price, and Tusye did not want to buy them.

Now, back to the house. I have your suit and coat, but nothing else is left. I will tell you everything when you return here. The horrible thing about your people (the Jews—Ed.) is that only 11 remain, and I do not know them.

Your faithful neighbor, P. S.

[233]

View of the Town before the Holocaust

View of the Town after the Holocaust

[234]

THE HOLOCAUST

Betsalel Shvarts (Tel Aviv)
English translation by David Dubin

The fearsome visions still confront passersby; the screams of our murdered brothers still ring out. Indeed, my eyes saw all these calamities, but even so it often seems to me that since such terrible things are unequaled in human history, these things could not really have happened. Is it possible that a father could leave his child alone, a brother could push his sister to the slaughter between his mother and father, and crowds of people could allow themselves to be led like sheep to the slaughter to be killed and cremated? Hale and healthy people stripped naked and lay in ditches to be shot and saw with their own eyes that their children had the same fate ... how can we not be ashamed, we the survivors, to continue to live after all this!

The world is indifferent to our suffering, even though the spilled blood continues to scream.

AND THUS THE HOLOCAUST BEGAN ...

Immediately after the outbreak of the German-Polish war (1939), Kremenets was bombed from the air. Of the 40 initial martyrs who died that day—not all Jews—the vast majority were not killed by the bombs but rather by the machine guns of the jets that strafed and cut down innocent passersby, including many children.

Not long afterward, the Soviet-German war began, and with it began the Holocaust. The area of Kremenets, which was known to have strategic importance, was again defended for a long time, and the Germans invaded our vicinity only on the 11th day of the war. Some inhabitants fled to the mountains in fear of the bombardment, and others escaped to various places. The flight was chaotic. Thousands held their walking sticks in their hands, but at first they were not allowed to cross the border and were forced back by the army—an action that weakened the stream of refugees.

German soldiers entered Kremenets around noon on June 4, 1941. No battle was fought, since the Soviet army had already retreated; only one military vehicle came by chance to get bread from the bakery, and meanwhile its inhabitants went to the restaurant (the Ras House). At that moment a German scouting battalion entered the town, and a grenade attack immediately began and decapitated a German sergeant. German forces arrived and began to pursue the Soviet soldiers, who in the meantime had taken refuge in Jewish homes. The Nazis shot into the inhabitants' homes, injuring some of them (among them Golde, Shlome the blacksmith's daughter). The dead German was buried in the courtyard of Pini Fridman, and the Jews who passed by were ordered to remove their head coverings. Many of them were viciously attacked and imprisoned for not obeying military orders ....

THE FIRST SLAUGHTER

The next morning, June 5, the looting of Jewish stores began, with the participation of the local population. There was an immediate bread shortage. The war had broken out suddenly, and no one had put aside provisions. Jews stood in long lines in front of bakeries to buy bread, but the recently established Ukrainian militia attacked them and forced them out of the lines. Suddenly, the militia began to kidnap Jews—women, the elderly, and children—stood them in groups, and chased them to the town jail in the Dubno neighborhood. They were beaten cruelly, drawing blood.

[235]

Eliyahu Resnik, who was rescued from the kidnapping, went mad; Potikhe died immediately thereafter. Gun was killed next to his home, in front of his family. Other martyrs died at the murderers' hands during organized outrages, with the active participation of many in the Ukrainian population, a few Poles, the SS, and the German gendarmes.

The unfortunate ones were brought to the jail, where political prisoners had been killed during the Russian administration, events for which the rioters blamed the Jews. With blows and gunfire, the Jews were forced to dig and exhume the executed prisoners' bodies from the mass graves and wash them. Some died from the violence of the blows. Bands of Ukrainian murderers assembled from the surrounding villages, clubs in hands. They ganged up on the Jews, forced them from their homes, and beat and killed them. About 75 percent of residents of the Dubno suburb were killed and thrown into mass graves at that time. Only a small number survived. The massacre continued on the fifth and sixth.

We thought that the end was near for all of us. It is hard to describe the outrages committed then on those in the jail. My wife told me that she had been kidnapped from the bread line. She survived because the corpses covering her stopped the bullets fired toward her. She fainted, sleeping until nightfall, and at night crawled out of the pit, almost unconscious, and returned home via back roads. Many escaped to the surrounding settlements, with some caught and tortured to death by farmers. Hirsh Barshap's son, who escaped toSapanuv village, was captured by villagers with barbed wire and drowned in the river. This was the fate of many who tried to flee wherever their eyes took them. They were attacked on the roads, tortured, and killed in all kinds of bizarre ways. Women were raped. After she was tortured, Dr. Groyzenberg's daughter gave birth to a child, who was given to the Jewish orphanage, and the mother went mad.

The next day the Jews went to the local officer, gifts in their hands and pleas in their mouths, to stop the slaughter. The officer seemed surprised that there had been riots for two days, and he knew nothing about them ... yet he got up, went alone to the rioters, and ended the massacre.

During the riots, about 800 people—men, women and children—were killed. Many homes were looted, and many Jews to whom the Ukrainians owed money were imprisoned. Also, the Nazis imprisoned Jews who were hiding in Ukrainians' homes and sent them to a place from which they did not return. Over several days, the Jews hid in their homes, overcome by fear, wailing over the dear souls who had been killed in the terrifying massacre, and fearful of the impending Holocaust that would overcome them all under the Nazi regime.

THE JEWISH COUNCIL (JUDENRAT)

A Jewish Council (Judenrat) was appointed by the town from the notable personalities in the community, some of them refugees from Western Europe who spoke German. The council offices were housed in Rokhel's courtyard on Slovatski Street. The council first organized slave labor, because until then any Jew who asked for food for his family would be captured in the street or even in his home and forced by threat of violence into slave labor; thus the council arranged bread rationing for the working Jews as well as a small amount for the poor.

These were days of riots in the entire region. The most violent were in Vishnevets, where most of the Jews were killed by the Christian inhabitants. This also occurred in Ostrog.

I do not have the exact Jewish population of Kremenets, which almost doubled during that time with the influx of refugees from Western Europe. I remember that there were 20,000 Jews until the Nazi invasion, but I am certain that 8,500 Jews were present in the ghetto in the summer of 1942.

[236]

DECREES AND COLLECTIVE PUNISHMENT

The founding of the Judenrat did not stop the cycle of collective punishment. Jews gave of themselves, or tried to give all they had, to pay the punitive tax inflicted on them. The government decreed that every Jew must wear a white band with a blue Star of David on the right arm; then Jews were forbidden to walk on the sidewalks, and Ukrainians would stand on the streets and cruelly punish those who disobeyed. With difficulty, the council managed to abolish this decree, and the Jews were again allowed to walk on the sidewalks. However, Ukrainians and Germans, who did not know or did not want to know about the repeal, continued to beat them. Commonly, a Christian inhabitant who had a German acquaintance would loot a Jewish home with his help. These things occurred every day. No Jew tried to complain to the authorities, because he knew full well that he was not protected by the law. The Jews were summarily evicted from their homes without being allowed to take any of their belongings, and German Nazis and even non-Germans settled in their apartments. Then a ruling was handed down that the Jews had to remove their head coverings before any German, but there were also instances where Germans attacked them for removing their head coverings, saying "Is the cursed Jew our friend, that he greets us? …" People looked fearfully into the eyes of any German passerby, not knowing whether to greet him or not. Ukrainian militiamen also attacked the Jews, also wanting them to remove their hats…. Torture and attacks were our lot every day and every hour. Frequently, you would see a young Nazi grab a Jew and force him to perform "tricks"— crawl on hands and knees, run, fall, etc. … Once, a German grabbed a Jewish child walking in the market and forced him to dance on the table; he spat on the child and on the table, and forced the child to lick the saliva, to the great enjoyment of the surrounding gentiles. Then Jews were prohibited from using the market. Those who disobeyed the prohibition paid dearly: the Ukrainian militia imprisoned and tortured them to death, and only a few survived. Nate Barshap told me that he was also imprisoned and tortured, and afterward, people's strength was a mere broken vessel ….

THE GESTAPO ARRIVES

Then the Gestapo arrived in the town and immediately imprisoned political and nonpolitical people and a large proportion of the Polish and Russian intelligentsia who were suspected of Soviet leanings.

The Judenrat was commanded to present a list of people of various trades, reputedly in order to employ them. I cannot tell you with certainty if the Jewish Council knew the fate of those sent to the Gestapo, but it is a fact that after the liberation, in the summer of 1945, they dug and found the bodies in a ditch known as "Pieskovozki" at the foot of Mount Krestova. One of those murdered was the engineer Rozen, an ORT activist, who was recognized by his clothing. The Soviet Historical Society excavated these pits to investigate the Nazis' crimes, and they also revealed a series of mass graves near the jail and in the defensive trenches remaining from World War I on the road to Podlisets.

People who worked near Tivoli saw and knew that these Jews had been kidnapped. The Jews were destroyed, but people did not talk about it. Nevertheless, the Jewish population did not believe it, or did not want to believe it, and the Judenrat encouraged the story that those sent to work were unharmed, that they survived, in order to avoid panic. On his return to this town, one Jew who had been rescued from the work camp said that with his own eyes he had seen the Nazis destroy Jews, some of whom were torn to pieces by the dog sent to attack them.

In the Gestapo's "action," most of the Jewish intelligentsia was destroyed, including rabbis, ritual slaughterers, and rabbinic judges.

[237]

It was a fearful sight when the relatives of the kidnapped would bring the Gestapo food packages for the unfortunate ones who were no longer living—and the murderers took the food from them and suggested that they "meet" their loved ones .... And we no longer saw them or their relatives. One of the fallen was Sheyne Shklovin, wife of B. Shnayder from Argentina, a citizen of a foreign country. She brought food for the old leader of the community, the engineer Ovadis. She left an orphan who died in misery from slow gas poisoning during the final destruction.

THE DESTRUCTION OF THE GREAT SYNAGOGUE

The Gestapo remained in Kremenets until the end of August, and its harvest of blood reaped 800 Jewish martyrs.

One night, we were awakened by a loud sound and a flood of light that overwhelmed the town. We did not understand what was going on. At first, we innocently thought that they were Soviet searchlights, and we were happy that we were about to be liberated. However, it quickly became clear that the Great Synagogue was going up in flames, which burned throughout the night. The Jews did not close their eyes, and they cried bitterly for the destruction of the burning temple. Others consoled themselves by saying that this would be atonement for our souls and that we would have the merit to build a new synagogue.

The next day we found out that the Gestapo had set fire to the synagogue, which had heavy stone walls, after bringing several barrels of benzene, hand grenades, and other explosives inside. Town firefighters stood by, not to put out the fire, but to prevent the Jews from doing so and to make sure that the fire would not burn anything but the synagogue. It became known that, the day before, the Gestapo had evicted the sexton from the synagogue and had looted many things from inside. After the fire, when only charred walls remained in memory of the destruction, the Gestapo came to the Jewish Council to "investigate" who had set fire to the synagogue. Afterward, they forced the council to sign a document prepared beforehand stating that the Jews themselves had set fire to the synagogue!

Several days before, German soldiers had caught Lipin and forced him to collect ten Jews for a prayer quorum in the synagogue. The soldiers forced them into the synagogue to don their prayer shawls and pray. Terrified, they prayed silently, but the soldiers were not satisfied, and forced them with verbal abuse and threats to pray aloud. The soldiers overturned prayer stands, and Lipin himself was forced to hit the worshipers to get them to dance around the central pulpit. After this ceremony, they kicked the Jews out and beat them some more.

THE GHETTO

In the spring of 1942, a decree was passed to imprison the Jews of Kremenets in a ghetto, and the area chosen worked out to one and a half square meters per person. The ghetto extended west of the town near the Jewish Cemetery up to Gogolevska Street, from there to Lyceum Street going up toward Sheroka Street, and from there eastward to the firehouse. I should add that the ghetto was crowded and stifling. Efforts were made to increase the area—unsuccessfully, due to the antagonism of the Christian population.

The ghetto was surrounded by a three-meter-tall wooden fence. Although the Jews were allowed to take all their belongings, they had to leave or liquidate a good amount because of the narrow confines of the ghetto. This overcrowding grew more intense with the influx of refugees over the course of the year, and against this background there were also scuffles that the Jewish police had to resolve.

At that time, the Judenrat received an order from Miler, the district commander, to dismantle the remains of the synagogue and leave no trace—to clean the area and plant it with grass.

[238]

They were given six weeks to complete the operation. The Jews were given a great deal of work to do on behalf of the German army—and few laborers were available. The Judenrat attempted to fulfill the order, which was difficult. Engineers, smiths, and others were organized, but the results were not satisfactory because the walls were exceptionally hard and fixed, and meanwhile day after day passed. They managed to increase the allotted time, but even after the second time period, not even half the work was complete. The officer then gave a final deadline accompanied by grave threats. The situation in the ghetto worsened, and terror increased. The Judenrat decreed that children aged 14 and over (who were exempted from work by the Germans) and men and women over 50–55 would work daily to dismantle the synagogue. It was a frightful sight—old men, exhausted from hunger, and children standing in long lines, working. As the deadline approached, the destruction of the synagogue was incomplete. The Jewish Council again decreed that every Jew who left the ghetto would need to work to dismantle the synagogue until nightfall after his return and in the morning before leaving for work.

Razing the synagogue was not without its fatalities. A wall collapsed in the darkness of evening and killed several people—and the unfortunate victims' voices shook the ghetto. The district commander, surveying the area on a white horse, allowed the firemen to assist the workers in the collapse. Even the German gendarmerie guarding the ghetto gates came to help. From beneath the collapse, injured and maimed men were removed, who were identified only with difficulty, including the son of Moshe Milman, a nice boy of 17, who had just returned from forced labor outside the ghetto.

DIFFICULT TIMES IN GHETTO LIFE

The Judenrat, which at first included several important members of the town's elite, broadened and branched out. At first, it tried to organize the persecuted population's life to solve the problems of forced labor, acquire bread, intervene with the government in instances of robbery and looting, collect taxes from the public, and the like. However, later, the Judenrat recorded some dismal chapters in the ghetto annals.

At first, the Judenrat was made up of local people who were appropriate and honorable and no doubt had their brothers' interests at heart. One example was Dr. Bozi Landsberg, the lawyer, who had already tried to commit suicide by cutting his throat with a razor at the beginning of the murderous regime, when he was beaten cruelly by the Nazis because he was against fulfilling the various degrees and paying the "contribution" tax, but he was rescued. His wife, Sonye, the daughter of Yitschak Poltorak, warned the Jews about observing the murderers' laws. Council members Dr. B. Katz and the lawyer Dr. Yonye Grinberg also withstood this incredible challenge. The first two were Zionists; the third was a Bund member. Dr. Katz was taken hostage when Jewish workers were late in cleaning up the barracks in Belaya Krinitsa. Only through the rapid deployment of many workers, who quickly finished the job, was he saved.

The Judenrat was forced to assemble a large staff to handle the increasing number of laws and edicts promulgated by the government. Several refugees from the west joined them, including Dr. Mandel from Krakow, who established a Jewish police force from the best people in the ghetto. The Judenrat had different bureaus, with the most important being finance, work, supplies, food, and others. A general kitchen in the ghetto was also established next to the firehouse.

Nevertheless, several of the Jewish refugees recorded an unfortunate and shameful chapter in the history of the ghetto, when, thanks to their facility in speaking German, they drew closer to the Nazis.

[239]

They came from various social spheres, and they showed cruelty toward the prisoners of the ghetto in that terrible situation. They were a disgrace to the ghetto. I will not spend much time talking about them; rather, I will give several practical details.

In the summer of 1942, Bronfeld, a Czech Jew, was appointed head of the Judenrat. He was the one who prepared the lists of those sent to the "work camp"—which included my brother-in-law, Lemberg, who refused—as others did—to go. After that, he extorted money from their relatives and promised to find the missing people, but did not do so. He aspired to leadership in the ghetto and got into a power struggle with Itsi Diamant from Lodz, who replaced him. He had an assistant named Nutin, and together they were connected to a group of international thieves and swindlers. Bronfeld and Diamant were killed with their families even before the liquidation of the ghetto, having denounced each other to the Nazi gendarmes.

A vast abyss of hatred existed between the natives and the refugees, who took every opportunity to establish themselves at the expense of the Kremenets Jews by seizing openings in organizations, work, etc. There were frightful moments in the struggle between the two council leaders. Bronfeld was able to ingratiate himself with Commandant Miler through large bribes. Afterward, Bronfeld's reputation sank rapidly among the populace, and reportedly Itsi Diamant then volunteered to be an intermediary between the Jews and the Germans. That is when the bitter battle between the two sides, including mutual denunciation and defamation, began. One day, Bronfeld was arrested and tried. A similar struggle took place between the Nazis Shuman, head of the gendarmes, and Commandant Miler, both of whom claimed "Jews of his own" .... As a result, Diamant and his people were jailed. When the Jewish ghetto police came to arrest him, Diamant jumped over a fence, spraining his leg, yet he was able to escape to Christian acquaintances. Nevertheless, when his family members were arrested, he presented himself. Prolonged mutual recriminations eventually ended with both Diamant and Bronfeld and many of their people being shot in the Kremenets castle. Of course, the Germans who were involved remained untouched. After these tribulations, which continued from autumn 1941 to summer 1942, Dr. Mandel of Krakow was appointed head of the Judenrat. He was well known to all for his honesty and his trustworthy service to the Jewish population until its destruction.

THE CRIMES OF COMMANDANT MILER

In the summer of 1941, Miler ruled that instead of an armband, Jews were required to sew gold patches on their backs, and I remember a Christian who cried seeing this humiliation .... At his orders, the Jewish population received 75 grams of bread per person per day, enough to worsen the famine to the point where 10–12 people died of starvation per day. The bread was made of barley flour. His commands worsened by the day. With his own hand, he signed the death warrants of 500 Jews arrested for various reasons. For example, ten young people who worked for Germans were arrested and shot for being suspected of stealing benzene. Every week, the fines imposed were more than the persecuted Jews' ability to pay. He also ordered them to surrender whites, furs, and winter clothing for the soldiers at the front, as well as food. At a time when dozens of people died of starvation daily in the ghetto and most walked around hungry, the ghetto was required to supply 25 tons of wheat! These forced contributions became hellish battles. The Jewish police and Judenrat members jointly raided the storerooms and secret, emergency warehouses in the bunkers in order to hand over the remaining food. The screams of those whose supplies had been looted reached the heavens. In practical terms, these supplies had been acquired outside the ghetto in return for merchandise hidden in the ghetto. During the autumn of 1941, an "action" of house-to-house looting took place, and then Miler, together with the German gendarmerie and the Ukrainian militia, loaded a caravan of wagons with Jewish property.

[240]

All men were forbidden to grow their hair, and women were also ordered to cut their hair. He ordered the destruction of the synagogue, and the Jewish cemetery was demolished. This work was also imposed on the Jews. Tombstones and the cemetery wall were preserved as construction materials, and only a small number of tombstones at the top of the hill were undamaged.

In autumn 1941, Miler ordered the Judenrat to build a brothel for young Jews aged 16–19 in order to degrade them and demoralize the Jews. In the order it was stated that every young Jew was required to visit it and to bring documentation of the fact. This order was repealed with the payment of a large "contribution" from the Jews.

Miler ordered the destruction of the remaining Jewish homes surviving outside the ghetto—and the materials were sold to Christian inhabitants or farmers in the area.

In August 1941 Miler extorted from the Kremenets Jews a heavy "contribution" of 11 kilos of gold and several dozen tons of silver, including religious holy articles from the synagogues and study halls.

THE JEWISH POLICE

In addition to regular police duties, the Jewish police dealt with special duties imposed by the government of the Nazi occupation. Before the establishment of the ghetto, it helped the work crews recruit workers, collect contributions, and especially act when Jews refused to go to work or pay the fees imposed by the Judenrat. In those situations, the Judenrat was compelled to command the police to bring people to work forcibly, and many were also forcibly recruited to the cruel Ukrainian militia. At first, three days per week of forced labor were required, and those who faltered were compelled to work six days. Their daily ration: a liter of soup and 250 grams of bread.

At first, the Jews refused to join the Jewish police. However, after the Jews were confined to the ghetto, the situation changed, as the German gendarmerie and the Ukrainian militia guarded them. The situation worsened. The Jewish police were given difficult tasks, the foremost being to oversee preparations for the starving and impoverished ghetto inhabitants to do forced labor. People died of starvation in the street. On the Nazis' order, the dead were placed on wagons and brought without funerals to their graves. Because of lack of nourishment, an epidemic of boils broke out. Even under these conditions, people were compelled to do forced labor—and the order to carry this out was placed on the police. Regardless of our judgment today, the heads of the Judenrat believed that arranging the work and obeying other orders would save the inhabitants of the ghetto from death.

It was a veritable miracle that in these terrible conditions no plague broke out in the ghetto, apparently thanks to the great care taken in sanitation and hygiene. In the ghetto, there were a total of three wells, where long lines stood at daybreak in order to receive the daily water ration. There was a severe water shortage. Lines even formed at lavatories. In general, cleanliness was carefully preserved in the ghetto. The police were careful to maintain order and cleanliness, including near the bakeries and grocery stores. The police also were careful to enforce the 7:00 p.m. curfew on walking in the ghetto and on speaking Yiddish, as requested by the Christian inhabitants.

Nevertheless, the most difficult job for the police was, as mentioned, recruiting people for work. Late at night or early in the morning, they would go from house to house, awakening the dejected people from their sleep and bringing them to the work office, where they were given weak soup from the public kitchen.

[241]

One-half liter of soup and, in particular, the one-quarter kilo of bread given by the Judenrat, on top of the meager ration of 75 grams, held the key for the hungry people. Fearsome battles took place during slave labor recruitment. Many volunteered for work despite their knowledge of the poor conditions but quickly lost their strength during the backbreaking labor. More than one used all sorts of devices to avoid the work. One of the responsibilities of the Jewish police was to bring the lines of workers to the workplaces and return them—only individuals were allowed to go without a guard.

A second reason for the public's disdain for the Jewish police was the strong measures taken to collect the large contributions that Commandant Miler demanded weekly. The finance office of the Judenrat determined each Jewish inhabitant's portion of the general levy, whether per capita or by the amount of property owned. But there were some who were unable to pay, and Germans were waiting for any opportunity to destroy the ghetto. On the Judenrat's order, the Jewish police held searches in the ghetto and confiscated everything they found. Thus, large storehouses of food were breached, and since not enough contraband was found to cover the punitive tax, these supplies were traded outside the ghetto for expensive items. By bribing the ghetto guards, people brought the goods into the ghetto and gave them to the government as a "contribution."

The Jewish police were given a laughable uniform: a hat with a golden covering and two gold stripes on the shoulders with a small cross between them.

The Jewish police caused the population a good deal of suffering, but from an objective standpoint, it appears to me that they preserved the ghetto until the general liquidation, when no concessions to the murderers prevailed. At night, in the dark, smuggling flourished—smuggling food from the outside, in order to sustain families. The Jewish policeman's benefit was that he was allowed to pass the German and Ukrainian ghetto guards without being searched and could therefore take care of his family by selling merchandise in the town. Of course, there were those in the police who excelled in cruelty, and the current catastrophe left its mark on them.

IN THE JAWS OF THE GHETTO

The good thing about life before the ghetto's establishment was that every Jew could maintain contact with the non-Jewish community and more easily acquire food for himself and his family. The Christians took full advantage of this opportunity, and in return for meager provisions, they acquired furniture, housewares, and expensive items from the Jews. In general, the relationship between the Christian inhabitants and the Jews was one of hostility and subjugation. Whenever the gentile wanted, he could easily loot the Jew of all he had and even cheat him out of his home. These things happened daily. Most of the killers of Jews were from the Ukrainian "underworld," but even members of the Ukrainian intelligentsia were not free of blood.

Already in the first week of the Nazi conquest, a group of Jews was forced to burn down the Jewish library. Between two lines of Nazis and under a storm of blows, they were forced to take out the books and throw them into the fire with their own hands.

In September 1941 we received word of the establishment of ghettos in cities, and soon the decree reached us, too. As mentioned above, the regional commander established a "living space" of one and a half square meters per person. Every effort to increase the size of the ghetto was rebuffed, and, coincidentally, the Christian population was also against the establishment of a large ghetto.

[242]

Enough time was allotted for the transfer, because the governor was interested in ensuring that the refugees would bring all their belongings into the ghetto. The Judenrat's residency office began apportioning apartments. People were given permission to choose appropriate neighbors. Various arguments in this environment were settled by the Jewish police. In December, the transfer to the ghetto began, using winter wagons harnessed to the people themselves, who dragged their meager belongings. The ghetto was surrounded by a fence, which negated the possibility of contact with the outside world. There was no sign of vegetation and no evidence of any trees in the ghetto, except for the garden next to the hospital, where children were taken during the summer to get fresh air.

People lived under stress and constant terror. Besides the backbreaking labor and struggle for survival, people were always subject to the fear of terrible news and evil decrees hanging in the air—so-and-so returned from work outside the ghetto and said that cars filled with SS men were approaching the town; another recounted that he heard a German say that tomorrow a new contribution of people for the work camps would be demanded or an "action" would be taken against the ill, children, and those unable to work, etc. etc. These gloomy reports gave no rest. During the day, people walked around feverishly. Only at night did a small amount of rest come, and people prayed that the night would last forever.

A TYPICAL DAY IN THE GHETTO

Life in the ghetto began early, at daybreak. First, the officers of the Judenrat's work office appeared, sometimes accompanied by policemen, to awaken the men for work outside the ghetto and to escort them there. Meanwhile, people rushed to the wells to get a place in line for water. Then the street cleaners began to sweep the roads. People rushed to the ghetto kitchen to get a little soup. Others went to the food storehouses to get bread since often there was not enough for everyone. Fierce battles would erupt between people, and the police were forced to intervene.

Meanwhile, the corpses of those who had died of starvation were collected for burial. This did not even make an impression on those living in poverty and the shadow of death; the opposite was true—people would say that they died a death of "luxury."

Next, lines of people congregated by the ghetto gates, among them the best of the young people, to go to forced labor and their places of work, and their hearts sank, knowing their fate. They stood group by group, and in front of each group would stand a Jewish policeman. One after another, the groups would leave through the gate. Outside stood the German gendarmes and the Ukrainian militia. The Jews were inspected, and if something was found on them, the murderers would take it for themselves, always hitting, hitting.

The situation was much worse when they returned from work: more inspections. Occasionally someone would have an onion or a potato that he had been given, and all would absorb the blows on account of one "criminal"; they also inspected women. Any woman bold enough to sneak an egg to her child would be beaten cruelly. She would enter the ghetto crying, even though it was miracle that she had not been arrested, because arrest meant certain death.

Occasionally, policemen who retained a remnant of human feeling stood by the gate, and then the Jews of the ghetto would say, "Today there was a good gate; we were able to take a little bit more with us." However, miracles like this happened very rarely. At these times, a Jewish policeman and a representative of the hospital stood by the gate collecting donations for the sick from those who entered. Most gave willingly, because the hospital did not receive food rations, and the ill were dying of starvation and lack of medication.

Near the gate, frightful sights were often seen, and cruel examples were made of those who smuggled even a small amount of food. Even so, people took their lives in their own hands in order to sustain themselves.

[243]

The ghetto had a shop where one could buy and sell. Although the store was forbidden by German decree, the Jewish policemen looked the other way. They themselves were among the buyers and sellers. When a warning that the Germans were coming arrived, they would immediately dismantle the store, but when the danger passed, people again congregated, and the trading continued.

On Levinzon Street, near the *kloyz*, exhausted and starving people would rest. They would warm themselves in the sun and wait for the death that would release them from their suffering. They would sleep in the *kloyz* on two-level bunk beds made of boards and covered with straw. Filth and insects were everywhere. Even after the burning of the filthy straw, bedbugs would crawl again. Here is where the impoverished lived. At the Grand Hotel, the picture was even bleaker, with people sleeping cramped and crowded on couches in the large and beautiful rooms, the most unfortunate being left alone and extinguished like candles. The fate of the ill lying in the hospital was no better. Some dragged themselves into holes like animals, entering them by crawling through caves or hollows in the ground or through attics. Every day, more and more poor people went house to house asking for bread, cuttings from vegetables, peels, etc.

"GOOD" GERMANS

Once, a drunken German entered the ghetto. He was on Gorna Street. People were shocked, and they began to run away. Only the children remained. The German distributed candies to them, hugged and kissed them, and burst into tears, crying, "Endangered Jewish children! What has that cursed Hitler done to you!"

The ghetto's inhabitants were extremely afraid of the consequences if this matter were to reach the governor of the ghetto. Generally, Germans entered the ghetto only rarely, and they showed humanitarian feelings toward the Jews. Even so, a saying appeared in the ghetto: "To a good German—a good death; to a bad German—a bad death." Every inhabitant of the ghetto was responsible for paying a per capita tax of 20 rubles to the Germans. The Germans also occasionally appeared at the gate guard station and for a bribe allowed wagons filled with supplies to enter the ghetto. In various ways, meat was also brought into the ghetto. As I mentioned, the smuggling was done only at night.

"BURIED IN THE SOIL"

When news about destruction of entire communities arrived, and as the Holocaust approached Kremenets, people in the ghetto began to look for salvation. Some escaped quietly from the ghetto and fled anywhere their eyes took them. Some died quickly at the hands of the murderers. Others left the ghetto to ease their situation, going to other cities, where the ghetto police were not as cruel as in Kremenets. Nevertheless, most stayed, building hiding places and digging "bunkers" in the ground. Because of overcrowding, the bunkers were very small, and when the Holocaust arrived, they were not large enough to hold all the members of the household. Besides themselves, people wanted to keep a minimal amount of property in the bunkers. It is easy to imagine the crowding in bunkers of 14 square meters containing 24 adults and small children. When the evil came, people could not stay hidden—and they placed their fates in the hands of the murderers. The inventiveness that people used in building the bunkers was indescribable. Some were built with incredible engineering, including electrical and sanitary fixtures. It was a veritable complete underground town, which required the executioners to burn the besieged ghetto in order to conquer it.

With the continued pressure, physical strength declined in the ghetto, and hopelessness and depression increased. Even the young people saw and felt the coming end, and despair led to acts of desperation ... people became inured to everything, including this. Jews from throughout the land—tried and true leaders, scientists, manufacturers, merchants, soldiers, and journalists, members of the intelligentsia and business professions on the one hand and members of the "underworld" on the other—were crammed into the ghetto.

[244]

Nevertheless, of all these people, there was not one person head and shoulders above the rest who could guide the confused and perplexed. And in everyone's heart lived the hope that perhaps he would merit freedom along with his family ....

Meanwhile, the famine became even worse. Stores of provisions were emptied in the form of "contributions." Food could no longer be smuggled in through the gate. New martyrs fell every day. Corpses were stripped of clothing and shoes. In their desperation, people tried to climb the high fence around the ghetto, and a few managed to sneak a small amount of food into the ghetto. Some were helped in their daring purchases by Christians, and many were imprisoned. Old and young endangered their lives. A 16-year-old girl who could no longer tolerate seeing the suffering of her family went to seek employment from a Christian acquaintance outside the ghetto, perhaps to ask for her life to be spared, or perhaps she was no longer in her right mind. One morning she took a small piece of bread with her and climbed the fence to escape, but before she was able to breathe the clean air, she was shot and killed. This was but one episode of many.

Some Jews left some of their property with Christian acquaintances outside the ghetto in the hope that after their liberation the property would be returned or they would be given provisions. However, only some of the Christians kept their promises; most waited expectantly for the end to come to the Jews so they could keep the goods. Only a few threw packages of food into the ghetto on behalf of their Jewish acquaintances.

TOIL AND TORTURE

Meanwhile, the ghetto's labor platoons continued to fill large work orders for the Germans under subhuman conditions. The ghetto was divided into seven work areas, with seven officers supervising the work orders. Most of the officers were not of a high intellectual caliber. They tried to lighten the load of the weak and impoverished. They exempted men of means from work in return for payment to workers who replaced them. There were instances where people refused with all their might to go to the most difficult jobs. When Tsiger, president of the Jewish work battalions—who knew the danger involved—began to investigate the reasons for this, he found out that the Ukrainians were viciously attacking anyone who did not fulfill the deadly work quota, which was beyond human capacity. Tsiger informed the German officer Hamershteyn about this, and when he found out the truth, he punished the Ukrainian overseers harshly and sent them to work in Germany.

Hamershteyn did what he did in return for frequent bribes given to him by Tsiger on behalf of the local Jews. This same Hamershteyn participated in the "action" in Rovno, only because the local Jews did not understand enough to get "attention in return for gifts."

In spite of the great need for men inside and outside the ghetto to work, it was difficult to find work for women. Work outside the ghetto was especially coveted because of the possibility of acquiring a small amount of food. Getting work for women required a great deal of "influence," often in the form of payment to the Christian who assigned the work. Every morning, as the workers went to their jobs, groups of women entered the Jewish work office and described their suffering and frustration that work was denied to them. There were women who sneaked into the groups of working men. The desire to smuggle a small amount of food into the starving ghetto is what forced them to do so.

[245]

TO WORK IN ROVNO

After the first "action" in Rovno and the resulting shortage of manual laborers there, the Rovno government imposed a contribution of manual laborers on the Jews of the nearby vicinity, including the Jews of Kremenets. On Hamershteyn's order, the Ukrainian and German police, as well as the Jewish policemen, began to gather people in farm wagons to be brought directly to the trains, after all forms of persuasion were unsuccessful. Hamershteyn himself orchestrated the work, and with violence forced the people to get into the wagons. The entire town felt the fear of God. The cries of women and children reached the heavens. Everyone thought that the hour of destruction had arrived, and many began to flee and hide. Some of the Aryan residents outside the ghetto looked upon the spectacle with amusement, and some saw themselves participating—and went on their way. Gripped with fear of their unknown, terrible fate, people went on their unknown ways. Some tried to jump from the wagons at the last moment. The Jewish police even helped several of them, who succeeded in escaping. They hid overnight in the fields and the hills, and the next day returned to the ghetto, to the delight of their relatives, who had held out no hope of seeing them again. The remainder traveled to Rovno.

And behold, all the Jews who had been taken returned to their homes! Very soon the answer became clear: their freedom had been achieved through the payment of ransom to Officer Hamershteyn. The story was that the hand of the Jewish overseer, Tsiger, was also involved. Over time the situation changed, because news came from Rovno that the condition of the men was good, the work was not difficult, and the food was good. Therefore, the second contingent saw men eager to work, and some scandalously paid money to be sent to work in Rovno. Meanwhile, Hamershteyn was transferred to oversee work in Dubno, and Tsiger lost his patron. The German officer Miler, who replaced Hamershteyn, now saw an opportunity to collect the debt from his enemy, Hamershteyn's protégé. This opportunity came to him when Tsiger sent a wagon filled with the corpses of starvation victims through the ghetto gate without permission from him. Miler imprisoned Tsiger, and he was killed in one of the "actions."

In August 1942, fearful news reached Kremenets regarding massacres in nearby Volhynia towns—Rovno and Radzivilov. All felt the approaching Holocaust but tried to console themselves by believing that Kremenets would be spared. The pressure was high. The feverish construction of bunkers began, starving people ran to work, and again people paid monthly contributions to the Nazis—and hoped for a miracle from the heavens. People took comfort from the secret news, gathered from radio sets of the Christian neighbors, of the Russian army's successes and the Germans' failures in battle.

THE HOLOCAUST APPROACHES

The Holocaust neared. One month before the "action," on a Sunday morning, the noise of megaphones in automobiles was heard in the streets outside the ghetto. The megaphones called on the townspeople to destroy the Jews. This was propaganda in preparation for the slaughter.

During the final week, the normal routine of the ghetto changed. On Sabbath eve, August 9, 1942, the Jewish work office received an order to send workers to the train station to unload grain after their labors. All the workers were laboring outside the ghetto at that moment. It was raining heavily, and the winds were violent. Jewish policemen gathered next to the ghetto gate and waited for the workers to return. When they came, broken, dejected, soaked through in the rain, and consumed by fear and terror, they were grabbed by the policemen and brought in columns to the train. A few tried to make a break for the ghetto gate, but the Ukrainian police beat them back into line. The Germans apparently already knew that the "action" would begin the next day, and they wanted to take advantage of the final night of those condemned to death.

[246]

The Jewish policemen brought the last group to work. The Ukrainian overseers prodded the Jews with curses to hurry to work. The unfortunate ones were brought back to the ghetto late, ignorant of the fate that awaited them the next day.

THE NIGHT OF TREMBLING

At night, the evening of August 10, the Jews of the ghetto were jarred awake from their sleep by the thunder of gunshots from every direction in the ghetto. At first the quiet of death reigned in the ghetto. People ran to hide in the darkness of night, expecting that the darkness would serve as cover for them. The rifle shots continued and increased moment by moment, bullets flying everywhere. Screams rose from Gorna Street and from the vicinity of the Great Synagogue.

The murderers were impatient. They tore down the ghetto fence and broke into Jewish homes to rob and loot. Meanwhile, they shot and attacked right and left, and the first victims died in the ghetto, causing terrible chaos. Babies were wailing bitterly, and there was no one to quiet them. Everyone was sneaking into the bunkers. Others climbed to the rooftops to see what was going on outside the ghetto. Gunshots broke out even there. People wandered aimlessly as if they were mad. Screaming and crying, people dragged linens, clothing, water, and provisions. Some risked their lives and went outside. From every direction, wailing erupted from people who had been separated from each other. Children were pressed close to their parents in an attempt to find refuge and protection. Even the youngest babies sensed the fear of the moment. On hearing their questions, the hearts of the adults shuddered. The young ones did not understand why the adults could not help them ....

Dawn broke. It was obvious to everyone that the dawn would bring destruction. The news came that 60 Nazi gendarmes had entered the ghetto with a Ukrainian SS detachment from Belaya Krinitsa. The Jewish policemen, whom they had chased away from the gate, told us that the enemy had purposely shot into the ghetto and claimed that the Jews were rebelling—and that this served as a pretext for the evacuation of the ghetto. Immediately, they requested that Jewish Council send all able-bodied men to the gate to report for work, reputedly. The Judenrat in turn called on the population, but only a very few responded to the call and proceeded to the gate. There stood a group of Germans, some in SS uniforms, performing a "selection." They delivered their judgment—whether to remove from the ghetto or not—according to workplace certificates. Over time, more and more people approached the gate, until they comprised most of the population, old and young, including people with children in their arms.

LIKE LAMBS TO THE SLAUGHTER ...

The line of people continued from the Great Synagogue along Levinzon Street to Tailors' Street. The second line extended from the great synagogue along Gorna Street. The Ukrainians stood on either side between the lines of Jews. Indeed, at that moment the Jews had a chance to attack the murderers and take their weapons. But, regrettably, there was no sign of rebellion. People had reached the final depths of hopelessness. No one reacted to the deathblows administered by the Ukrainians. People were pushed toward the gate, and everyone assumed that he would thus be saved. Even the ill and swollen crawled and came down from their beds. The selection continued. The fortunate ones were brought through the gate, and in groups of 400 they were taken under heavy guard to Belaya Krinitsa. Several tried to flee, and the Ukrainians chased them, killing them with bullets and stripping the corpses of their clothing. The murderers threatened that anyone who tried to escape would be killed. Along the way I recognized the indifferent faces of Christian passersby. Some of them were laughing .... I saw Sonye Goldenberg-Shpigl-Gurvits as she was pushed by the blows of the Ukrainian policeman's rifle butt. In her arms she carried her child, who looked into her mother's fearful eyes ....

[247]

ON THE ROAD TO DESTRUCTION

On the road, people try to calm each other. Some believe that they will allow us to survive; others say that they do not want to live without their families. The first column arrives. Everyone is pushed into stables. Outside, a strong chain of Ukrainian SS men is standing. Many of them are inhabitants of Kremenets, and they show not the slightest evidence of mercy. The thoughts of those condemned to death wander to their loved ones left in the ghetto, many crying bitterly. Others sit silently on the ground. Next to me sits the attorney Yonye Grinberg, covering his face with his hands—and crying. "I am a sinner," he tells me. "I left my wife and children in the ghetto." "How could we have behaved this way?" he asks me, and the question strikes my heart like an arrow, and there is no answer.

After the first day of selection in the ghetto, and after some of the men were removed to Belaya Krinitsa, the remainder searched for shelter in the bunkers. Of course, not everyone owned a bunker. Some of the first martyrs doomed to destruction were the inhabitants of the Grand Hotel and those lying in the hospital. The Ukrainian policemen and the German gendarmes chased them to the synagogue square, and from there were brought by automobile and even on foot to the barracks, where large excavations were left from World War I. The people were beaten and forced to undress and lie down in rows inside the pit.

The SS murderer, who was sitting at a table, fired volleys of bullets into them. Those who were not struck by bullets were killed by the Ukrainian policemen standing around the pit. The screams of adults and children were heard from far away. There was no lack of Christian neighbors who came from the town to see the spectacle of their Jewish neighbors' murder.

Every row of murder victims was covered with a few small shovels of earth and a layer of lime, through which some bodies protruded during their death throes, and their blood soaked through the earth and lime. On top of them came the new victims. The terrible spectacle was repeated over and over. Several tried to escape naked but were felled by the murderers' bullets. The survivors were forced to drag these victims into the trenches and lie down next to them.

After the mass murder, the German and Ukrainian policemen left to search for those hiding in the bunkers. It is clear that despite the utmost caution, people were unable

306

to control their crying children, whether they were crying from fear or hunger, and thus they were doomed by force of arms or otherwise to leave their hiding places and go to their deaths. In several bunkers, children were suffocated when their mouths were covered to stifle crying. Elsewhere, children were poisoned by injection. Others poisoned themselves and their families in order not to fall into the murderers' hands, but only a few had this cherished alternative. Some, for example, Dr. Shklovina, took too small a dose, which caused great suffering. In the deportation area, she begged the murderers to kill her, and a German did her the favor. Her granddaughter, age three, was brought to the pits desolate and consumed by crying, and was thrown onto the pile of corpses.

"SATAN HAS NOT YET INVENTED THE REVENGE FOR THE DEATH OF A SMALL CHILD ..."

During this selection, men, women, and children were strictly separated. When they found children among the men, they cruelly attacked the former. Two children stayed by their father. The older daughter begged the killers to allow her to say farewell to her mother. They gave permission.

[248]

After she had said farewell to her father, she went over and took leave of her mother, subsequently walking quiet and pale with the line of children who were being pushed into the trucks. Only the young son grasped his father, screaming with heartrending cries, "Father, I don't want to go!" One of the killers rushed forward, kicked the boy with his foot toward a second murderer, and the second kicked him to the third—and in this way the boy was thrown with harsh mule kicks on top of the heads of the children standing crowded in the truck.

THE MURDERERS' METHODS

To make it easier to find people hiding in bunkers, the Nazis spread a rumor that the remaining few people would not be taken out and killed but rather left alive to inventory the murdered Jews' property. Also, it was incumbent on them to remove the other people from their hiding places in the bunkers. Escorted by the Germans and Ukrainians, these people went before these homes and yelled aloud, "Jews, leave! No one else will be harmed! We only have to go to work now!"

Many who heard the Yiddish speakers or heard the voice of a Jewish acquaintance left the bunkers. They were brought together and transported to the prison. After they did their job of burying the masses of corpses exposed in the street, they were massacred in the prison yard. There were Jews who tried to save themselves by giving large bribes to the policemen, who promised to free them from the ghetto, but as soon as they escaped from the ghetto, the policemen opened fire and killed them.

Next to the ghetto gate, in the direction of Gogol Street, a woman with a child in her arms jumped outside the ghetto and was seen by a policeman. The woman yelled, "I surrender!" But the policemen shot her, and the woman and her child fell in place. The child was still alive when they threw them both onto the wagon with the dead.

The Christian inhabitants outside the ghetto continued their normal lives as if nothing had happened.

During the nights of the "action," people left the bunkers to find themselves a little food or water to sustain themselves or to meet their relatives and try to find a way to escape the ghetto—something fraught with double danger, because the Aryan population as well as the policemen and their families would enter the ghetto at night to loot the Jews' homes of everything inside.

THE MOUND OF DESTRUCTION

The evacuation of the ghetto continued for two weeks, and despite the murderers' exertions, there were still remnants left in the bunkers, and the murderers set fire to the ghetto from every direction. To prevent the fire from taking hold outside the ghetto, firemen were brought in from all the surrounding towns, and they were occupied not with putting out the fire but rather with preventing its spread. The unfortunate remnants were forced to leave their hiding places, which were consumed by flames, and the vast majority were murdered by the firemen or the German gendarmes and Ukrainian policemen.

The Nazis then spread the rumor that the remaining Jews themselves had set fire to the ghetto. This was contradicted by the Christian inhabitants, who saw with their own eyes that the Nazis had set fire to the ghetto in several places. It is a fact that the Germans did not allow the ghetto fire to be put out, but rather made sure to burn it down to its foundations in order to destroy the evidence of the crimes and kill anyone hiding in the bunkers. The burned bodies were collected by the Aryan inhabitants after the entire ghetto area had become a heap of ruins.

A long time after the fire, the murderers still found Jews living in a bunker in the cellar of the home of Milshteyn, brewer of the well-known Kremenets *kvass*.

> [**Translation Editor's Note:** *Kvass* is a fermented beverage made from black rye or rye bread.]

[249]

Live Jews were also found inside the bunker in the Fild house in the soda water factory. In this bunker were the Fild family, with a small child, and, and Shlome Basis the blacksmith's daughter, Golde, and their families and small children.

THE MURDER OF THE REST

Those left in the Kremenets prison suffered great torture after the "action" in the ghetto. Starving and filthy from the long stay in the bunkers, they were brought to the prison and awaited their death. The murderers waited until their number reached the hundreds. They were kept on the ground night and day, in the burning sun by day and in the cold by night, without food or water, as the children cried bitterly until the bitter end came. They were shot in pits prepared on the prison grounds. The pits were plowed over and turned into a garden so that even their place of burial is unknown.

Before their liquidation at the prison, the Jews awaiting death heard one of the Ukrainian murderers say that their judgment day had arrived and that they would no longer be able to suck the blood of the Aryans.

Despite this, many succeeded, through large bribes to the policemen, to leave the ghetto by ladder, but they were caught by the German policeman or Aryan villagers. In Veselivka village near Belaya Krinitsa, old farmers caught several such Jewish refugees and dragged them back to the prison. Others, appearing to give them sanctuary in their homes, later handed them over to Nazis or Ukrainian policemen. They took advantage of Jewish girls with the promise of saving their lives and betrayed them afterward. Gofman of the Yashpe-Gofman Company, who before the liquidation of the ghetto gave his property to a Christian inhabitant and during evacuation managed through various means to contact him, was handed over by him to the murderers, who in turn attacked him harshly and continued to beat him in the prison until he lost consciousness. A physician in the prison took mercy on him and ended his misery with a fatal injection.

OUR SPILLED BLOOD WILL YET BE AVENGED!

Next to the trenches at the barracks, one of those condemned to death provided words of comfort and encouragement that the innocent blood that was being spilled would eventually be avenged. Leybele the ritual slaughterer, Hokhgelernter's son-in-law, also provided words of comfort and vengeance to the ears of those going to their death.

During the final years before war broke out, a Jewish doctor named Meler settled in Kremenets. His daughter survived after her parents and all the Jews of the ghetto were destroyed. The girl spent a prolonged period in the prison under the protection of the policeman who worked there. She managed to calm down a bit and began to feel more comfortable with the policeman, who would frequently take her on walks in the prison yard. However, one day he received an order from his superiors to kill the one remaining survivor. The policeman took the girl on a walk in the garden, and as she was playing innocently near the flowers, he shot her with his pistol.

THE BEHAVIOR OF THE ARYAN POPULATION

There is no escaping historical speculation—from the outrages of 1648–1649 to the final destruction. Of the 14,000 people of the Kremenets community, only 13 survivors remained, and yet in Kremenets, surrounded by mountains, there were many possibilities for salvation! Besides these 13, 7 other Jews from various towns were saved, mostly with the help of individual Christians. Eight Jews found refuge with a Christian woman, and four with another Christian. The Christian population hardly lifted a finger to save the Jews.

[250]

The Killing Field (behind the Barracks)

It should be noted that the Christian who saved four Jews was later killed by the Ukrainian militia headed by Bandara in the Vishnevets suburb. In comparison with other nearby cities, such as Dubno, the Aryan inhabitants of Kremenets were particularly antagonistic toward the murdered Jews of the town.

CONCLUSION

Kremenets as a town of Israel was destroyed and has disappeared forever. The entire area is now alien to us. The ghetto area, which contains terrible secrets of torture and suffering, is a mound of destruction.

Kremenets, you and your inhabitants are cursed. We will eternally keep in our souls the memory of the holy tombs of those dear to us, and we will never, ever forget them.

[251]

THE STORY OF THE EXTERMINATION

Tova Teper-Kaplan (Jaffa)
Dictated by Tova Teper; Written and Prepared for Printing by Yitschak Rokhel
English translation by Thia Persoff

In memory of my parents, Nachman and Rachel-Feyge, and my sisters Lube and Sheyndil—all murdered by the Nazis.

BY CHANCE I RETURNED TO KREMENETS

I was born in 1920 to my parents, Nachman, son of Fishil Teper (1884), and Rachel Feyge, daughter of Mendil Leder (1884). We were five siblings. My eldest sister, Chane, trained in the Eastern Pioneer youth group and immigrated to Israel in 1936. My brother, Fishil, immigrated to America in 1939. Our parents and three daughters were left at home; of them, only one has survived—I, the tearful writer of the story of the extermination. My sister Lube, who is older I am (1918), and Sheyndil, the younger one (1925), were murdered with our parents.

> [**Translation Editor's Note:** In Hebrew, Eastern Pioneer (a religious Zionist group) is *Hechaluts Hamizrachi.*]

My brother and sisters and I were all members of Zionist youth groups. Our parents made an effort to see that we were in religious-oriented ones, and, indeed, my sister Chane was a member of Eastern Pioneer, and I was in the Religious Guard. In 1938 I graduated from the ORT School, and after the Russians conquered the town, I entered the technical-agricultural school in the small town of Zaleszczyki, where I studied for two years and even won a stipend. In June 1941, eight days before the onset of the Russian-German war, I returned home to visit my parents. My plan was to stay in Kremenets for a short time and then return to my studies, but fate had a different plan. I was with my family throughout the days of horror. Here I will relate what I saw and what I know.

> [**Translation Editor's Note:** In Hebrew, the Religious Guard is *Hashomer Hadati.*]

World War II erupted in September 1939, and Russia and Germany signed an agreement on the division of Poland. Our town, Kremenets, was given to the Russians, who ruled it for about two years. During that time, I was not in town. I know that in those years a great number of refugees flowed into the town from areas that had been conquered by the Germans, trying to save themselves. Jews from Warsaw, Lodz, Kalisz, Chelm, and towns near and far came to Kremenets. The number of refugees was estimated at 4,000, and together with the population when the Germans entered, there were about 14,000–15,000 Jews. During Russian rule, the organized Jewish community had disbanded, and the Nazis found a fragmented Jewish community. Earning a living was very hard, and there was a great deal of friction between the permanent residents and the refugees. Among the refugees were two who later played a most terrible role in the life of the ghetto: Diamant and Bronfeld. Even during Russian rule, Diamant once said that he would not rest until he had seen the blood of Kremenets' Jews flow like water. He was a base, cruel man, a swindler and a moneygrubber—a man of the "underworld." He had a mistress whose name—to be remembered with disgust—was Goldberg. She was contemptible, a thief known by the nickname "Golden Hand." Bronfeld, too, was a foul piece of human scum.

On June 22, 1941, the Russian-German war began, and on August 2 the Germans conquered the town. During those 40 days, many Kremenetsers rushed toward the borders, intending to cross into Russia. At that time the border was just few kilometers from the small town of Shumsk (20 kilometers from Kremenets). Those who worked for the Russians or had close ties to them crossed into Russia without a problem, but just plain citizens were not permitted to cross, and a multitude of refugees amassed at the border. Only during the final days, when the Germans were close to the town, did the Russians allow the residents to escape into Russia. Indeed, many saved their own lives by doing just that. The number of people from Kremenets who escaped to Russia is estimated to be in the 1,500s. Some of them later went to Israel, some immigrated to America and some to Poland, and a few even returned to Kremenets.

[252]

My two sisters and I left the town on foot and had to walk the 10 kilometers to the train station. By then rumors had started to spread about riots and murder at the borders and hunger in Russia, etc., so we decided to return: my two sisters, some other young people, and I. But many who had the courage continued to walk, boarded the train in one of the stations, and were saved.

THE FIRST SLAUGHTER

The day after the Germans conquered the town, rumors spread that the Russians had murdered 60 Ukrainian nationals in the jail and that they would therefore retaliate and take revenge on the Jews, who were, "as is well known," all Communists. And indeed, that very day a pogrom began. A gathering of gentiles from the area's villages entered the town through the Dubno suburb, armed with iron bars and assorted tools of destruction. They went from house to house, robbing and looting, and herded hundreds of people to the large jail, beating and wounding them without pity. Inside the jail, they were forced to wash the corpses of the murdered Ukrainians, then to dig pits near the jail and lie inside. German soldiers went from pit to pit and shot them to death. In this first "action," about 400–500 people were killed. The pogrom had been going on for three days when the order to stop the killing came. Those in the pits who were still alive were ordered to get out and return home. Among them was my friend Ronye Barshap, who had been shot in the pit; a few bullets had penetrated her body. She managed to crawl out and find her way to our house, black and blue from the beatings inflicted on her by the Ukrainians and scorched by the Germans' bullets. We nursed her and brought her to the Jewish Hospital, where she stayed for few weeks and recovered (later she was killed).

Our house was not harmed, because the Ukrainian who was living there would not let the rioters do so, but on the third day they attacked us, found my mother, and dragged her to jail. But a few hours later, when the "action" stopped, she returned unharmed.

After the riots, Miler, the district commissar, put out a "graceful" public announcement that it was forbidden to rob and kill Jews. Then the town quieted down for a while.

THE JUDENRAT

A few days after entering the town, the German authorities assembled a Jewish representative contingent, called the Judenrat. At its head they installed the notoriously corrupt Diamant and Bronfeld—two people known to be German agents and dealers in suspicious business with Commissar Miler and his lackeys—who were greedy to gain money and power by any means. The main function of the Judenrat was to execute the German authorities' orders concerning the Jews. The Judenrat office was on Slovatski Street, in Kopeyka's house and those across the street, in Moshe Rokhel's courtyard. As time went by, the Judenrat swelled into a large, wide-ranging office, with assorted sections and dozens of clerks. At first, some honorable public servants took part in the Judenrat, among them Dr. Binyamin Landsberg, Shimshek, Bruber, and others. After a short time, when the true character of the institution became clear to them, they resigned. Responsible roles in the Judenrat were filled by Mr. Tsigel, one of the refugees, who was in charge of the labor detachment, and Shmuel Barshap from the Dubno suburb, who was the commander of the Jewish police. He was arrested later and murdered, and Mr. Blit was appointed in his place.

[253]

OPPRESSION, OPPRESSION

The oppression began. From the beginning, Jews had to wear a white ribbon with a light blue Star of David on their left sleeve. A few months later, it was changed to a star on an eight-centimeter round yellow patch, one on the front and one on the back, so people could be identified as Jews from either side. Walking on the sidewalk was forbidden; Jews were permitted to walk only in the center of the road. Jews were not permitted to eat meat, fat, or eggs. All other residents were forbidden to sell them those items. Near the Judenrat, the authorities had established a special store to sell rationed foods: potatoes, bread, grains, etc. Forced labor was instituted: every adult had to register each morning in the Judenrat offices, and from there they were sent to work for the German authorities, receiving meager food in exchange but no salary. A few workshops were allowed to continue their work, but mainly for the Germans, for a miserly payment.

Week by week, the oppression became more severe. One day the Jews were ordered to give up all their furs. One day they were robbed of their blankets by the thousands, then all their silver and gold. A special collection place was opened for the confiscated possessions, and for weeks there were long lines of Jews, waiting to hand over possessions they had been collecting for years.

About a month after the Germans' arrival, the Gestapo came to town and opened an office in the building of Stshelets, the Polish sports association. Wearing army uniforms and a ribbon around their hats with a skeleton design on the visor, they roamed the town and spread fear among the Jews. Everyone understood that the end was near; the time for the total extermination of the Jewish population was approaching.

Their first deed was to burn down the Great Synagogue. First they lit the building on fire, and then they roused the people in the neighborhood, had them stand by the burning synagogue, and accused them of starting the fire. The entire interior of the synagogue burned completely that night, but the charred walls remained standing.

THE "ACTION" IN TIVOLI GARDEN

A few days after the burning of the synagogue, the Gestapo ordered all people in the liberal professions—physicians, attorneys, engineers, nurses, teachers, etc.—to congregate by the Tivoli Garden, near the Polish sports association's headquarters. Thus a few hundred people from the intelligentsia gathered there. They were called into the building for a meeting, supposedly, then the doors were shut on them, and no one was allowed to enter or exit. They were held there four or five days without water or food. This caused great fear among the detainees' families and the town in general. Relatives began to bring food but were not allowed entry. The food was put on tables standing outside. The relatives were sent back home, but the food was not given to the detainees. Then the Gestapo announced that anyone who volunteered to serve the food to the detainees would be permitted to enter. Ten of the people who brought the food over volunteered, among them Izye, Chayim Ovadies's daughter. They were let in, but never returned.

One of the assembled was Mrs. Galina Sorochinski, a Russian woman of German ancestry, who by chance happened to be there. She notified the Gestapo that she was not Jewish and was there in error. She showed documents proving that she had many generations of German ancestry, and after swearing not to reveal what she had seen inside, she was released. Nevertheless, people heard from her how the starving had been tortured there. They were forced to kneel for hours with their hands behind them and their heads between their knees, while the Gestapo walked among them and whipped them incessantly.

[254]

Eventually they were all killed and buried in the Tivoli grove. Among them were Dr. Tabak; Dr. Shklovin's daughter, who had come from Brazil to visit her family in Kremenets; Izye, Chayim Ovadies's daughter; Dr. Polonski's daughter; Yantsi (Yakov) Shrayer, a technical teacher in the ORT School, and his wife; Mikhel Chidis, a teacher in the Polish public school; Liusye Veksler, a graduate of the ORT School, and her sister; and many others.

That is how the intelligentsia of Jewish Kremenets was destroyed.

For few months after the "action" in Tivoli Garden, a relative peace settled on the town, although even then a soldier or German policeman would hit a Jew if he happened upon him, there were break-ins and looting, and Jews were thrown in jail for trifles. If a hungry Jew was caught taking a potato or a carrot from a Ukrainian's garden and the owner complained about him, he was thrown in jail immediately. The prisoner's fate was preordained: every now and then the Jewish prisoners were taken out and killed, no matter what their "crimes" were.

THE ANIMOSITY OF THE CHRISTIAN POPULATION

The non-Jewish population, particularly the Ukrainians, was hostile toward the Jewish residents. They joined in the looting and made libelous, false, and malicious accusations to the German authorities, harassing them and mocking their calamity. The first time I went out on the street wearing the yellow patch and ran into Ukrainian acquaintances, including the priest, they ridiculed me and laughed, saying, "Look what a lovely flower this one has adorned herself with ...."

One day, during the "peaceful" period, Ukrainian policemen burst into our house to conduct a search. They accused us of holding meetings of suspicious groups in our house and listening to radio broadcasts from Russia. We did not even have a radio, but using this opportunity, they discovered a live goose left from the old days, a forbidden thing, as Jews were not permitted to eat meat. Immediately a German policeman was called in, a thorough search was done, all the rest of our possessions were confiscated, and my mother was taken to jail. I understood what awaited her and could not rest. I turned to the Judenrat, to no avail. Then, through a Ukrainian policeman, we received a note from my mother telling us that if we paid a fine of 20,000 marks, she would be released. But we did not have a way to get such a sum. Although it was forbidden, I tried a direct approach to the Germans, but the vice-commissar told me simply that in a few days there would be a "cleansing," and all the Jewish prisoners would be killed. If I wanted to save my mother, I should hurry and bring in the money so as not to miss the deadline. He also added that, in his opinion, the Judenrat ought to pay this fine, as it had a great deal of money. I went back and approached Diamant. He agreed to pay the fine from the money that was in his keeping, on the condition that I disclosed to him the houses that had consumer goods or forbidden foods hidden. Obviously, I refused to be an informer. Then Shimshek, also of the Judenrat, said that the Judenrat would pay half the sum and that we should pay the other half. We sold everything we had left and brought the required amount. Together with Diamant and Bronfeld, we went directly to District Commissar Miler himself. I received a release note, rushed to the jail, and took my mother out. She had been incarcerated for two months.

[255]

A few days later all, the imprisoned Jews were murdered. These were regular events during the "peaceful" period.

THE GHETTO

At the end of January 1942, an edict stated that all the Jews were to move into only three streets, which would constitute the ghetto: Levinzon Street, Kravetska Street, and Gorna Street. In this zone were private homes and a few public institutions; these, too, were taken over to be used as living quarters: the ruins of the Great Synagogue, the government courthouse, the fire station, a few small synagogues, and others. The Jewish Hospital continued to exist even during the ghetto days and was not made into living quarters. One month was allowed for the move into the ghetto—and the "migration" began. Those who had acquaintances in the zone moved in with them, and others moved into the public buildings. In this way, the 14,000 Jews in Kremenets at that time were concentrated in this narrow area. A two-and-a-half-meter-high fence made of wooden planks surrounded the ghetto, with a single gate for entering and exiting near the Great Synagogue.

On March 1, 1942, Commissar Miler came to the ghetto, called on the Judenrat members, and fired three shots in the air, and the ghetto's gates were shut.

The ghetto existed for five and a half months, from March 1, 1942, to August 14, 1942—the day when the last "action"—the complete extermination—began.

Our family also moved into the ghetto, into Leviatin the dentist's apartment, on Levinzon Street.

The Judenrat was installed in Gorna Street. At its head were Diamant and Bronfeld. Next to the Judenrat, a Jewish police force was established under Shlome Blit's command. Only Jewish policemen were inside the ghetto, but the gate was guarded by German policemen, who were forbidden to enter the ghetto, supposedly to avoid causing riots. They made an effort to pretend to have no bad intentions toward the Jews. Relations with the Jewish policemen were good, generally, with some exceptions. They were assigned to guard duty but had the terrible role of handing over to the authorities people who were sent to other towns, supposedly for work, although they knew they would not return alive. And, indeed, only a few returned or survived.

A sanitation board under the guidance of a physician (I do not remember his name) functioned at the side of the Judenrat. They had public toilets built, where people had to stand in line, but they made sure it was kept clean. A public bathhouse was built in the fire station, where most people went to bathe and get disinfected, and the streets were kept clean. People were careful about cleanliness, knowing that if an epidemic began, the ghetto would immediately be exterminated.

Near the Judenrat, a kitchen was opened for the needy, who received food for a small fee, and the distribution of rationed bread—a starvation portion—was organized.

Young people had to work outside the ghetto. In the morning they were led to the gate, and in the evening, they were returned by the Jewish policemen. Many had signed up willingly for work because of the chance to buy food from gentile acquaintances and smuggle it into the ghetto for their families. In spite of the searches, some succeeded in concealing and bringing in a few food items, although in many cases people were caught with the forbidden food, sent to prison, and murdered there. In the final few weeks of the ghetto, the food situation worsened so much that in the public kitchen they were cooking all sorts of garbage.

[256]

There was a severe food shortage in the ghetto. Many went hungry, and 10–12 people died daily. First their feet swelled, and after a short time they died.

From time to time, people were sent to work in different towns, where most of them died. Some members of one group sent to the town of Vinnitsa survived by escaping to Russia.

A few hundred people were organized into a labor detachment called Artel. At its head was a Jewish refugee from Bialystok named Landoy. The Artel members were tailors, seamstresses, shoemakers, and other professionals, men and women. Their workplace was a large house outside the ghetto, but some of them were employed as helpers in gentiles' private workshops outside the ghetto. In the morning they were taken out, and in the evening, they were returned to the walled ghetto. The authorities treated these people better, and Artel existed until the very day of extermination.

At that time, the demolishing of Jewish houses on Sheroka Street and other streets outside the ghetto began. Jewish laborers did the work under the supervision of Ukrainians.

When the Jews entered the ghetto, they were not forbidden to take their possessions with them, so they took all they could. The result was dreadful crowding; several families had to share one room, but the greatest congestion was in the synagogues and courthouse.

From time to time, heavy taxes were demanded of the ghetto's residents, which were collected by the Judenrat with the help of the Jewish police. Later came a demand for a large amount of rye. As the amount was not available in the ghetto, the Jews had to sell their property for a pittance, buy the rye from area farmers, and hand it over to the authorities.

Depression, apathy, and helplessness permeated the ghetto residents. They had no initiative to find ways to save themselves: to escape, join the partisans, etc. They did not search for a means of escape either as a community or as individuals. Many worked outside, and none of those even tried to escape. For one thing, there was a worry that if such a thing were done, everyone in the ghetto would be slaughtered immediately. They still believed—in spite of all the signs and information that penetrated the ghetto—that thanks to their obedience, they would be allowed to live. There was no one who could stand up as a leader of the oppressed community and show them how to behave. The members of the Judenrat certainly did not think of that at all. They did not care about the community and its success. Both Diamant and Bronfeld were collaborating with the Germans, sharing with them the money that they extorted from the Jews in assorted ways; there was not a despicable thing that they would not do for the love of money. They hoped to escape from the country at the right time, but even they did not get to do that. Friction developed between Diamant and Bronfeld concerning the division of the loot, with the result that about a month and a half before the extermination, Diamant, his mistress, and some of his associates were arrested, brought to the jail, and killed there. Of what happened to Bronfeld, I have no knowledge.

The Rovno ghetto was annihilated, as is known, one month before the Kremenets ghetto. At the end of July, Pinchas Tseytag, a refugee from Rovno, arrived in our ghetto and spoke of the extermination in Rovno, saying he was the only one who had survived and escaped. He told the ghetto residents that this was what their end would be and called on them to dare to escape any way they could, as they had nothing to lose. They did not believe him and even ridiculed him. Even after this warning, no initiative to escape and survive surfaced in the ghetto residents. After a long period of oppression, hunger, and degradation, they were physically feeble and spiritually exhausted, incapable of acting to save themselves.

A few days before the extermination, Ukrainian policemen drove a truck through the streets outside the ghetto's boundary, announcing that very soon they would liquidate the Jews.

[257]

The ghetto residents saw and heard this and were worried, but even so would still not believe that, indeed, these were the final days. It was the Sabbath. On that day, many Jews, Artel members and others, were still working outside the ghetto. The gentiles who employed them had warned them that their liquidation was imminent and hinted that they should not return to the ghetto but escape. Nevertheless, they all returned to the ghetto to say goodbye to their families and escape the next day when they went to work. But they were not allowed out anymore.

On that same Sabbath, I was working outside the ghetto, in the house of Dr. Landsberg (a Jewish gynecologist), where German officers were now living. While I was washing dishes, a glass broke, and I cut my finger. Immediately, one of the German soldiers took care of my injury with courtesy and politeness—the same soldier who, no doubt, participated in murders the very next day.

On Saturday night, shots were heard coming from the mountaintops that surrounded the town. At the break of day, a detachment of German policemen entered the ghetto and ordered all those who had exit permits to go to the ghetto gate. About 1,500 people, they were organized into their work groups, lined up, and taken to Belaya Krinitsa, and the gates were closed.

That morning they hung a member of the Judenrat (I do not remember his name) and murdered a few people in the ghetto streets. And the ghetto was quiet the rest of that Sunday.

THE EXTERMINATION

The act of elimination began at early dawn on Monday. German policemen announced that the Kremenets ghetto residents would be moved to a different town. They were to enter the trucks waiting by the ghetto gate immediately; they were allowed to take only small packages with them. Wooden planks enclosed the truck beds. The first to get in were the old and the children. They did not show any resistance, and the rest of the ghetto residents got in after them. Whether they knew where they were being taken or not, or whether they pretended not to know, most followed the order to come to the gate, got into the trucks, and left on their final journey. Family after family they entered, each man and his family. Trucks went, and trucks came. The evacuation of the ghetto took two days, Monday and Tuesday. The trucks drove out of town in the direction of King's Bridge.

Half a kilometer from the train station, near the barracks, were army trenches from the days of World War I. Those trenches had been made not by digging but by pouring abutments above ground. This was the place the Germans had chosen for the mass extermination. They did not even bother to deepen or widen the trenches, but used them as they were. When a "shipment" of Jews arrived at the killing place from the ghetto, they were ordered to get down from truck. They were sorted into separate groups of men, women, and children, and ordered to undress and lie naked in the trenches. Ukrainian policemen guarded the area all around to prevent those destined for death from escaping. German policemen did the murdering; armed with machine guns, they walked the length of the trench, showering shots at those lying inside and murdering them down to the last one. After that, they poured a great deal of chlorine over them to prevent epidemics and obliterate the features of the murdered; that was covered by a thin layer of dirt. After a while, hundreds and thousands of skulls and human bones were scattered over this place. That is how the mass murder was carried out.

Not all the ghetto residents came to the trucks willingly. Some hid in attics, cellars, and bunkers, but the Ukrainian and German policemen conducted thorough searches of the houses and yards. Jews who were promised life in exchange for informing on others helped them. Hundreds of people were found daily, loaded on the trucks, and driven to the killing place. The searches for the hidden lasted about two weeks.

[258]

Each day the "shipments" got smaller. In early September 1942, the Germans burned the ghetto and all that was in it—and that was the end of Jewish Kremenets.

Yet there were some who did not join the "shipments" or hide in attics, but chose to commit suicide. Dr. Binyamin Landsberg, an attorney and well-known Zionist activist, and Dr. Chaskelberg committed suicide in the Jewish Hospital. All members of the family of Hindes, the pharmacist, put on black clothes, sat around the table, and met their death by swallowing poison. Brover, who used to own a yardage store and then worked for the Judenrat, hid for few days and then lost his mind.

What happened to the 1,500 workers who were transferred to Belaya Krinitsa the day before the last "action"? For some time, they were kept there and employed in assorted jobs; then the daily sorting began again. Those who (supposedly) had agreed to work in a different town were loaded on buses, brought directly to the mass-killing place, and murdered with the others there. In the end, only 200 remained, and they were put in jail. For a while they were kept there and even worked, until they, too, were murdered and buried in the jailhouse yard.

Such was the end of the Artel members, too. They were held in a special section of the jail, sent to work, and returned daily. The Germans told them that they would be allowed to live, and as odd as it seems, they believed it and did nothing to save themselves, though they had many opportunities to do so. Daily, the Artel sent my cousin, Moshe Teper, a stitcher by profession, to a Russian shoemaker outside the jail. Throughout the day he was not guarded, but nevertheless he returned to jail every evening. He kept his allegiance to his oppressors and murderers. Finally, the Germans informed the people of Artel that because the Jews themselves had burned the ghetto, there was no place for them to return to, so they would be liquidated, too. And indeed, a short time after that, they were murdered in the jailhouse yard and buried there. Of the Artel members who were murdered there, I remember the two Burbil sisters, Pozner, the two Rachiner sisters, the Teper family, and others.

The final "shipments"—the single few Jews who were the last ones to be caught, the Artel members, and others—were not brought to the trenches but to the jail, where they were murdered and buried in the yard. It has been estimated that about 2,000 people are buried there.

The clothes taken off the people's bodies before they were killed were collected by the Germans and brought to special warehouses in town. There they were cleaned and sorted, then sold to the Christian residents of the town, who bought them eagerly.

The attitude of ordinary Christian residents in those days was one of hostility. They assisted the Germans, investigated and searched out people who were hiding, handed them over to the murderers, and then rejoiced in the killings. But a few were out of the ordinary.

In our town there were a few families with mixed marriages. The Germans deemed them to be Jewish and murdered them, too.

Vaynberg, a German who had converted to Judaism and married a Jewish woman, lived in our town. When the Germans came, he was employed in a government office, and when the ghetto was formed, he and his family were allowed to live outside.

Eventually, they, too, were brought to the jail one day after the large "action" and were murdered there.

How many Jews were exterminated in Kremenets? We will never know an exact number, just as we will never know all their names. The estimate is that 14,000 people died in all the "actions," in individual murders, and from starvation.

[259]

Of them, 10,000 were murdered in the killing place, and the rest, in the jail, the Tivoli Garden, etc. Most of them were residents of Kremenets, and a few thousand were refugees who collected in our town during the Russian days.

THE SURVIVORS

Fourteen thousand were murdered, and 14 survived. One per thousand! I will tell briefly what the surviving remnants endured, how they saved themselves, how they hid in caves, and how they saw the sun again.

Here are their names, in order of their hiding places:

In Aleksandra Tarasova's house:

> Toyve Teper, from Kremenets, now in Jaffa, Israel, and her family is Kaplan.

> Sofie Kagarlitski, from Warsaw, now in Jaffa, Israel, and her family is Kohen.

> Pinchas Tseytag, from Warsaw, who was in Israel but immigrated to Italy.

> Avraham Chatski, from Kremenets, now in America.

> Vove Landsberg, from Kremenets, now in Poland, who converted and married the Polish woman who helped save him.

> Henrik Kot, from Lodz, now in France.

> Yakov Kot, from Kalisz, now in America.

> Miyotek Alerhent, from Chelm, now in Berlin.

In another hiding place:

> Niusye, daughter of Shmuel Kaner, from Kremenets, now in Kiev.

> Ronye Veldberg, from Kremenets, now in Haifa, Israel.

> Duvid Bilohuz, from Kremenets, who was drafted into the Russian army; I do not know his fate.

> Goltsman, from Kremenets, who was drafted into the Russian army; I do not know his fate.

In a cave in the Mountain of the Virgins:

> Mikhel Bankir, from Kremenets, now in America.

In a Christian's house on the Tonikis: I do not remember his name. He was not from Kremenets.

Among the survivors are eight from Kremenets and six refugees. Of them, one or two died later, three live in Israel, and the rest are dispersed in the world, America and Europe.

That is the sum of the town of Kremenets and its survivors.

SURVIVOR'S NOTES

My family and I—my parents and my sisters—hid in an attic. We were unaware of what was happening outside, but we felt the danger and escaped as well as we could. Through the cracks we saw that Christians had gathered outside the ghetto gate. One day, a boy, the son of Zitser the barber, ran to us and told us that he had been near the gate ready to go into the truck when he saw the Christians standing and looking joyfully at the loading of the Jews. He found out from them that the Jews were being killed, so he managed to escape from the gate and came to find shelter with us. After that, we all went down to the cellar and stayed there for two weeks; eventually we were found and taken to the jail.

[260]

And this is how it happened: one day in early September 1942, two Jews walked through the streets of the ghetto, announcing, "Jews, come out of your hiding places, there is nothing to fear anymore, they have stopped the killing. They are only taking people to work." In spite of everything that had happened to us, we were fooled into believing the announcers' words and came out of the cellar. Immediately, German and Ukrainian policemen appeared and took us to the ghetto gate, where a group of Jews was already waiting. We were organized into lines of four and marched to the jail in the Dubno suburb. There were about 50 people in our "shipment." In the jail we found 200 more. The jailyard was divided in two, one section for those intended to be killed, and the other for Artel members, who were still employed in assorted jobs. The first group was not given food. They crouched on the ground, and their strength slowly drained from them. Among them were the dead, whom the jail authorities would not remove. The Artel people received some food, though it was very poor: one slice of bread and a little soup. But they had a few possessions that they exchanged for some food brought from the outside by the Ukrainian policemen. The Artel members sneaked some of their food into the other section to revive the condemned. That was prohibited and put their lives in danger. The condemned were not allowed to get up from the ground, and if someone moved there, an immediate warning shot was fired into the air, and sometimes the person would be shot to death on the spot.

Among the jailers were a few acquaintances who used to shop in my parents' store. Following their advice, at night I escaped from the first section, crawled over to the Artel section, and was sent to work with them in the vegetable garden near the jail. At night I sneaked into a small shack by the fence, climbed onto the roof, and lay there without moving until midnight. Then I jumped over the fence into the garden, crawled to the outer fence, climbed up, and jumped outside. I crawled to a Ukrainian family's house not far away and hid there without their knowledge. Before morning, the woman of the house discovered me. I begged her to let me stay there until the next night, and she pretended to agree but immediately went and informed someone. Soon a Ukrainian policeman came and took me back to jail. This was how my first attempt to escape failed. When I was brought back to jail, my parents and sisters were still alive. They cried bitterly when they saw me back with them after believing that I had been saved. From the jailers I understood that our end was near and that I had nothing to lose. My friend Niusye Kaner was with me, and together we made plans to escape again. We decided to try to escape with my younger sister Sheyndele, but my mother advised me to go by myself and said my sister should be saved later in a different way.

On one of the nights soon after, I said goodbye to my family. I crawled barefoot up to the gate, climbed onto the wall, and from there climbed onto one of the outer guard shacks. I crossed to the next yard, climbed the outer fence, and dropped down. I crawled to a nearby semiruined house, hid for a while, and ran to the forest by the Christian cemetery. The whole time I thought I was being followed, so I continued to run—not being followed—until I found a hiding place beneath a boulder on the Mountain of the Virgins, where I lay for a few days. I got water and some vegetables from a garden in the area, and that is how I survived.

One night I heard the rumble of gunshots. I knew in my heart that the news was bad. And indeed, after a while I found out that on that night, all the Jews in the jail had been murdered, among them my parents and sisters. Death took them in the jailhouse yard. Of those in the jail, I still remember Gurevits, who used to own the flourmill; the Ratshiner family; Barats from the Dubno suburb, who owned a lumberyard; the Nudel family, who were tailors; Vaysbrod, Shchopak, Kopeyka, and many others. I assume that they all were murdered that night.

[261]

I also learned that the night of my escape, 30 more people ran away, but most of them were caught and then killed. Only four of the escapees were left: Niusye Kaner, Chatski, Alerhent, and I.

For five or six days I walked at night to Belaya Krinitsa village, where I found refuge with my parents' Ukrainian acquaintances. I stayed there eight days and then had to leave because of the Ukrainian police station in the village. My acquaintances suggested that I go to the Dubno ghetto, which had not yet been destroyed. Barefoot and dressed like a gentile, I started walking—this time during the day—and arrived at my destination without a mishap. Jews from the outside were not permitted to enter the ghetto, but I chanced to meet a group of Jews in the Dubno suburb working in road repair, and when they found out that I was a refugee from Kremenets, they hid me in a hut, and in the evening, I entered the ghetto with that group.

I stayed in the Dubno ghetto for three weeks. There I found the same attitude I had seen in the Kremenets ghetto: helplessness, discouragement, lack of will to save themselves. The Kremenets Jews did not believe the refugee from Rovno, and the Jews in Dubno did not believe the refugee from Kremenets. Only a few dared to save themselves, and some of them even succeeded.

I felt that the end was also drawing near in Dubno and searched for ways to save myself. There I met my friend Sofie Kagarlitski, and together we tried to negotiate with acquaintances, gentiles from Kremenets. They prepared a hiding place for us in the mountains, and one day between Rosh Hashanah and Yom Kippur, we both walked back to Kremenets, dressed like gentiles. On the way we happened upon some Germans, and to escape them we entered a nearby Catholic church and joined in the prayers, then continued on our way. That day the traffic on the main highway was stopped, as the Germans had already made preparations for the extermination of the Dubno ghetto. We made our way by using side paths and going through forests, and arrived in Kremenets the day after Yom Kippur. A day later, the Dubno ghetto was exterminated.

For 18 months—from the beginning of October 1942 to the end of March 1944—seven other Jews and I hid in Aleksandra Tarasova's house on Tonikis Mountain near Kremenets. By then, the town's Jewish population had been completely annihilated.

When I arrived at Aleksandra Tarasova's house, Yakov Kot was there, and later the others arrived. Altogether, eight Jews in hiding assembled there.

Tarasova's house was a solitary one in a large, parklike garden, some distance from the town, concealed among the mountains as if made for hiding. The owner, Aleksandra Tarasova, a good-hearted Russian woman, the adopted daughter of an important Russian official, was an enlightened, wealthy woman who had graduated from the Polish Lyceum in town. Living with her was her mother, a semi-insane person, who caused us a great deal of trouble and often endangered our lives, as she was liable to reveal our hiding place. At first, Tarasova took us in for money, but when our money ran out, she continued to keep us for free, and many times she endangered herself trying to hide and protect us.

Also living with her was her friend, the Russian Marye Dest, who did laundry for the Germans, so they used to come to the house regularly. Because of that, the house was never suspected or searched. Throughout the 18 months, even the gentiles who owned the yards nearby had no idea that Jews were hiding there. Because of the Germans visiting the house, such a suspicion never occurred to them.

All of us lived in one room. A few days after our arrival, we started to dig a bunker for all of us under the yard. It was 10 meters in length, 1 meter in width, and 1 meter in height. Support beams were installed inside to keep it from collapsing.

[262]

All the work was done during the night, and Chatski, who was an electrician, installed electric lights inside, and a code was established for blinking the lights: when the Germans came to the laundry, the lights would blink three times in the bunker so that we would keep quiet, and no sound would be heard. Sometimes we would dare to go up to the room above to get a breath of fresh air, and a few times the Germans arrived at the laundry just then. Immediately the light code was given, and we escaped into the bunker. Even with this excellent organization and all the precautions we took, I still cannot understand today how we managed not to be caught during the 18 months we were there. Indeed, it is a miracle.

Sometimes the insane mother would start mumbling about the Jews being down there, and then a great fear would assail us. One day Marye Dest, the laundress, asked us if we would be willing to accept a German soldier who wanted to desert into the bunker with us. Our reply was an absolute negative, and we told her that if he showed up, we would immediately shoot him to death with the single gun that we had. After that, she left us and never again brought up the subject.

WE WERE ALSO HELPED BY NON-JEWS FROM THE OUTSIDE

In town, the Russian Sorochinski family hid their Jewish friend Henrik Kot, a refugee from Lodz, in their house. When it was not possible to continue to hide him in town, they brought him to Tarasova's house, where he stayed until the Russians liberated the town. Mrs. Galina Sorochinski, a professional nurse, would come to the Tarasova house from time to time, bringing newspapers and encouraging the hidden as much as she could. Her husband joined us in digging the bunker and installed a camouflaged vent for air. After some time, she joined the Polish army, where she contracted typhus and died.

> [**Translation Editor's Note:** Although Galina Sorochinski enlisted in the Polish army as a medic, she did not die of typhus. As the army advanced toward Berlin, she was wounded and died on May 16, 1945. We thank her granddaughter, Anna Brune, for giving us this information and for allowing us to reprint Sorochinski's death notice in Supplement 3.]

Two of the men had Christian wives: Vove Landsberg's wife was Polish, and Yakov Kot, from Kalisz, had a German wife. They stayed in the town, outside the ghetto, and supplied food, newspapers, and money, not only to their husbands but also to all of us.

This is how we lived for 18 months and how we saved ourselves, the sole remnants of the thousands of Kremenets Jews.

The Russian army conquered the town on March 23, 1944. Because of fear and insecurity, we spent two more days in the bunker and emerged only on March 25, and went to see what was going on in the town. It was a horrific moment; the Russians were greeted joyfully by many residents, including Poles, Ukrainians, and Russians, but there were no more Jews. The impression was shocking. We did not recognize the town we had been born and grown up in. The ghetto was burned, the houses were destroyed, and everything was in ruins. Part of the area had already been cleared and leveled; we hardly recognized the town we knew.

We continued to live in Tarasova's house until June, and then we left for Rovno.

In May 1944, a Soviet committee from Moscow arrived in our town, including physicians and with them a troop of soldiers to investigate and determine the processes of extermination. My friend Sofie Kagarlitski and I approached the "killing place" while the committee was there. They threw hand grenades on the graves in order to open them, and immediately, like lava out of a volcano, the air was filled with flying skulls, bones, and parts of the murdered—those were our parents, brothers, and sisters. It was a horrifying sight. The dead were in hole after hole, the men, women, and children separated from each other. The committee members took photographs of the "killing place" together with the two survivors who were there. Afterward, we were ordered to come to the NKVD office in town (the office of the interior ministry), where they took down our testimony, in detail, on the extermination.

[263]

The Teper Family

In closing, may the three righteous women be blessed: Maria Dest, Galina Sorochinski and her husband, and last but not least, Aleksandra Tarasova. Thanks to them, all eight of us were saved, me, the writer, included. It took Tarasova patience and courage to keep eight people for 18 months. During that time, love developed between her and Pinchas Tseytag from Warsaw, and after the town's liberation from the Nazis, they were married. She sold her property in Tonikis for a pittance, and they moved to the small town of Reichenbach (Dzierzoniow in Polish) in Silesia. After a time, they were divorced. Tseytag left and immigrated to Israel and then to Italy. Tarasova serves as vice mayor of the town.

We will remember their charity toward us, and we will remember that what they did took place in an atmosphere of deep hatred toward Jews by the town's Christian population.

MIKHEL BANKIR—A ROBINSON CRUSOE

As mentioned, five more Jews were saved. They were hidden in two separate houses, one group not knowing about the other. But there was one more Jew who saved his life in his own unique way, and I will tell about him here.

Mikhel Bankir, a tinsmith from Kremenets, hid in a cellar during the extermination. Later he was caught but escaped on the way to jail. He began by making the rounds of the homes of his gentile acquaintances, but realized that taking refuge there was unsafe, so he escaped to the rocks in the Mountain of the Virgins. He lived in a cave for a long time, arranging a living area with some furniture, a bed, and a stove. Some nights he ventured out to the gentiles' houses in the area, requesting food, water, matches, etc., and returned immediately to his cave. He arranged the stove in such a way that the steam would dissipate among the rocks and not be seen outside. During the winter and snowstorms, he stayed inside for weeks at a time. Later he said that he craved the opportunity to talk, but there was no one there to talk with. When he knocked on the gentile's window at night to request food, he was careful that none of the family members were aware of it so he would not be betrayed and handed over to the Germans.

In March 1944, when he knocked on his acquaintance's window, as was his way, he was invited to come into the house (that was unusual) and was told that there was no more need to worry as the Russians were in town already. He did not believe it and thought that the man wanted to betray him.

[264]

He tried to escape, but the man came out to him and influenced him to wait, and showed him that Russians were already staying in the neighboring houses. After that, he agreed to stay. The next day, he came out of his cave and returned to his home in the town, which happened to escape destruction. His wife, his son, and all his family members had been killed. When he came out of the cave, he looked like a wild man, with a gigantic black beard and his hair grown wild. He stayed in Kremenets for a few days, then went to Rovno, where he led a more normal life and married again. After a time, he immigrated to America.

He has two brothers in the Land: Yakov and Shlome. They have a photograph of him with his hair grown wild.

Of the 14 survivors, not one was able to stay in town. They all roamed and traveled to different places. But out of the townspeople who did survive in spite of all the troubles in Russia at that time, few returned to Kremenets and settled there.

****

The nearby communities of Volhynia were annihilated in this order:

First the Jews of Rovno were murdered—about a month before Kremenets. After them, in Elul 1942, came Kremenets. About a month after Kremenets, in Tishrei 1942, came Dubno.

[264]

DESECRATED PARCHMENT

Tovye Troshinski (Tel Aviv)
English translation by Thia Persoff

> His students said: Rabbi, what do you see?
> He said to them: The parchment is burning, but the letters are floating free. (Sanhedrin)

A purse made of Torah scrolls.

The holy letters do not float ... gleaming in their blackness, they are set into the white parchment as if the nimble hand of an expert scribe has just engraved them. A black fire on top of a white fire ... the straight, black lines shine like strings of pearls from their case.

For many years, perhaps generations, this Torah scroll was kept safe in one of the many study halls in Kremenets. The Jew who had the honor of taking it out would approach the Holy Ark with awe and reverence, open it up, take the scroll, and carry it to the lectern. With awe and reverence, the person called to the Torah would move the corner of his prayer shawl over the open book, then kiss it and say the blessing "Who chose us ... and gave us His Torah." Lifting the Torah, rolling it, welcoming a new Torah—there are many ways to honor the Torah, and worshipers carried these out with sacred care throughout the generations until the reaper attacked our people.

Cut down, too, was Jewish Kremenets. The synagogues were smashed and demolished, and the Torah was booty in the hands of a filthy soldier who found the scrolls fit to be made into a woman's purse and sent to his wife in Bensheig, Germany, as a "victory souvenir."

A purse made of Torah scrolls.

In those days, when German industry found a unique source of raw material, "human" raw material for its products—Jewish women's hair to produce high-quality mattresses, laundry soap made from "pure Jewish fat," and Jewish scalps as decorative items—apparently it was the fashion to send souvenirs made of Torah scrolls.

[265]

This purse was in the German's contaminated possession for a few years until its deliverance by one of our townspeople, Mr. Binyamin Kornits. In a long, detailed letter, he describes the suffering and wandering that his family endured during the war years at labor camps in Siberia, the hardship they encountered on their way back to Poland after the war until their arrival at the refugee camp in Bensheig, and how he came to have the honor of rescuing the desecrated scroll:

Purse Made from a Desecrated Torah Scroll

"One day my daughter-in-law left the camp to buy some household supplies. A German woman she met on the way agreed to sell her what she needed in exchange for the food my daughter-in-law had received from the Joint, and the woman took her to her home to see the items. The German woman asked what her hometown was, and when she heard that it was Kremenets, she seemed to be in shock and could not speak. When she recovered, she said that her husband had been an officer in the German army and that, in 1942, he and his brigade had been stationed in Kremenets. From time to time, he would send her packages of war spoils from there, and in the last package was a modest present for her—a woman's purse made from a unique kind of leather. 'Although the purse is not particularly pretty, it is very dear to me, as it is the last souvenir from my husband, who was killed in the war,' said the German woman.

[266]

"'A purse made of a unique kind of leather'—a sudden suspicion stirred in the Jewish woman's heart, and she begged the German woman to show her the purse. The woman avoided doing so by giving various excuses and postponing it from day to day. Mrs. Kornits did not give up, and one day when she came to the house, she noticed a red object in one of the open cabinets. Her heart stopped: this was the purse! Before the German woman could notice, the purse was in her hand.

"Overcoming her agitation, she asked the woman if she would like to sell her the purse, but the woman refused to listen and took the purse out of her hand. All her requests at least to let her show it to her father were in vain, and she returned to the camp disappointed.

"From that day on—writes Mr. Kornits in his letter—I did not have a moment of peace; I could not sleep, and I walked around like a ghost. At that time, we received two months of food rations from the Joint, and I decided to give all of it in exchange for the purse. My daughter-in-law took the packages and went to try again with the German woman. After a short time, she returned and said that the woman had not agreed to sell the purse but was agreeable to giving it to her for a few hours so that I could see it, and then having it returned to her. I agreed to that ....

"... And now the purse was in my hands—continues Mr. Kornits in his letter. My hands were shaking. I opened it. Something inside me broke, I became dizzy, and I collapsed ....

"Sabbath morning prayers in the *Magid*'s Synagogue in Kremenets, Torah reading time. Chayim of Berezhtsy is reading the weekly portion. Chayim is a short, skinny Jew, but his voice is sweet and pleasant to the ears. Next to him stands Leyb Shrayer, the treasurer of the synagogue. He is so tall that his height almost entirely obscures the Torah and the reader. Since he was elected, it is hard to recognize the synagogue. Cleanliness and order are in every corner; indeed, the Divine Presence is in there. One of the worshipers is my childhood friend, Shlome Fingerut. We grew up and studied in the cheder together. Today he is a member of the City Council, busily devoted to the needs of the community, working for the good of everyone and particularly the craftsmen, whom he represents. R' Chayim is reading from the Torah, and the congregation listens. I hear my name called: I am called to come up to the Torah. I want to go, but I cannot move, and again my name is called.

"I woke up to my wife's screams. I had fainted."

Mr. Kornits did not return the purse. He left Bensheig and moved with his family to the refugee camp in Feldefing.

The purse, whose outside is dyed red, is made from three or four parchment sections of the Torah scroll. It has six compartments, three on each side, that fold inward. Now a third color is added to the white of the parchment and the black of the ink—the color of blood.

We open it and read, "Avraham looked up and saw the place from afar.... God will see to the sheep for his burnt offering, my son"—the portion on the binding of Yitschak.

Then, "Far be it from you! Shall not the Judge of all the earth deal justly .... And God said: If I find 50 righteous ones within the city of Sodom, I will forgive the whole place for their sake .... And he said: Please do not be angry, my Lord ... what if 10 are found there? And He answered: I will not destroy ...." —the Sodom affair.

And more: "You shall throw every boy that is born into the Nile ..."—Pharaoh's decrees. And the last one was Yakov's blessing: "Your brothers will praise you, Yehuda; your hand shall be on the back of your enemies' neck ...."

Astonished by the mystery—by the symbolism of the matter—we folded up the parchment.

****

Another "display" was added to the collection of horror in the cellar in Har Tsion. It is a mute outcry, testimony to one of the base abominations of the new Sodom that was not destroyed—a Sodom that is still standing to this day.

[267]

The Inside of the Purse (Sodom Text)

HEADS OF THE JUDENRAT IN KREMENETS

Ayzik Hofman (Tel Aviv)
English translation by Thia Persoff

From additional testimony that we collected, we learned that Diamant (about whom Shvarts and Tova Teper tell in some detail in their articles) was the third person to be head of the Judenrat. Before him, two others were in charge.

Dr. Ben-Tsion Katz was the first. He was appointed by the Nazis and agreed to accept the role. Having been educated in Germany in his youth, he was fluent in the German language and culture, and the Germans assumed they would find him a useful instrument in carrying out their base goals. They were very soon disappointed.

Born to a well-respected Zionist family, he was the son of Meshulam Katz, one of the first members of Lovers of Zion in town. He was a doctor of philosophy. From 1922 to 1928, he was the headmaster of the Tarbut Hebrew High School until its closure. He later served as the chairman of the local People's Bank (Povshekhni) and was well liked by the townspeople. When the Nazis came, the Jews were fooled into believing that the Judenrat would serve as their representative to the authorities and work for the Jewish community's benefit. And, indeed, a few community activists, such as Dr. Binyamin Landsberg and others, joined that first Judenrat. Even at the start of the Judenrat's activity, Dr. Katz received a demand to hand over a list of Jews who would be sent to (so-called) work outside the town. He handed over the list, and the first shipment went on its way. Soon after came a demand for a second shipment list. This seemed suspicious to him, so he notified the authorities that he would not hand over another list until the first shipment returned to town. The Nazi authorities saw it as a refusal to comply, and Dr. Katz was executed.

Yonye Grinberg was appointed after Dr. Katz's dismissal. He was an attorney, a talented man with a sharp mind, and a Bund member. In spite of his predecessor's bitter experience, he still believed that the Judenrat would be able to work for the good of the Jewish community and accepted the appointment. But before many days went by, he realized that the Nazis meant to use the Judenrat in the annihilation of the Jews. That knowledge caused him to sink into a deep psychological confusion, which led to a complete collapse, and he ended up becoming mentally ill.

Then that man Diamant, about whom much is told in this book—the man who was exactly the kind to suit the Germans but was despised and ostracized by the Jewish community—was appointed. He, too, ended up being shot by the Germans after he became embroiled in intrigues with the Nazi authorities.

[269]

HE DID NOT SUCCEED

Yisrael Otiker
English translation by Thia Persoff

Yosef Otiker

Davar, August 24, 1944: Kremenets refugees from Cheliabinsk have notified us that Yosef Otiker, who had been with them and later wandered to Central Asia, died in the town of Namangan (USSR) on September 7, 1943.

Our friend was a member of the Zionist movement in Kremenets. A few months before the Russian-German War, he was inducted into the Red Army with many of his fellow townspeople. He was at the front from the start of the war, in the vicinity of Kobi, and then was shipped to Cheliabinsk in the Urals. With the wandering and all the troubles he endured, he became ill and was released from his work in the army. He left for the south and died tormented by his illness, far from his friends, forsaken and lonely.

He strived to reach the Land, and even in the final months before his death, he believed that he would succeed. He had been a member of the Youth Guard and Pioneer movements since his childhood. He was 26 years old when he died. His brothers live on kibbutzim in the Land.

****

—About 30 refugees from Kremenets ended up in Cheliabinsk. Only Yosef Otiker separated from the group in order to make his way to Israel. He tried but never arrived. Death took him on the way. His friends say that he starved to death. Most of the remaining Kremenets refugees in Cheliabinsk came to Israel a few years later.

Indeed, fate treated him very bitterly. He was one of those who rushed toward fulfillment, but he did not succeed in reaching his goal. May his memory be blessed!

MY HEART, MY HEART ACHES FOR YOUR FALLEN

Duvid Shukhman (Buenos Aires)
English translation by Thia Persoff

My heart, my heart aches for your fallen, town of Kremenets—the old and the young, the men and the women, whose lives were cut short by beasts of men—bright as the sky, shining and sparkling. It was a precious and holy community, with its rabbis and generous public figures who erected institutions to be proud of—the large hospital and

Home for the Aged, the Talmud Torah and yeshiva, of which I was privileged to be an administrator—and especially officials and devotees of the Zionist movement and the young pioneer generation. They are no more, no more .... They were all extinguished in the fire set by the German Satan. Because of this, our hearts are filled with sorrow, and our eyes are dimmed. Was it not about this matter that the prophet cried, "Oh, that my head were water and my eyes a fount of tears; then I would weep day and night for my slain people." And the pain is great.

The sun rose and set. When the sun dimmed on the precious portion of the people of Israel that dwelled in Eastern Europe, a sun of righteousness rose for us in our Holy Land, bringing healing on its wings, and a voice of salvation sounded and announced: Return, children, to your homeland until the day of the ingathering of exiles and redemption.

[270]

NOTES

The Editors
English translation by Thia Persoff

The horror stories we heard from the two survivors are reproduced here in their entirety as they wrote and submitted them, with almost no changes, and it is as if they complete each other. Some details are the same in the articles, and some contradict each other, but we were not too scrupulous here: these were written after the deeds were done, and one fact or other may have blurred slightly in their memory. Indeed, the stories basically match, and they are true testimony from original sources.

To this section (and the one in Yiddish), we have added other details contributed by survivors who visited the town after the extermination.

In addition, we decided to put in this section the first reports about the destruction of Kremenets received by newspapers in Israel. We did this to preserve the initial reactions to the catastrophe, but they are different from the descriptions in the two foundational articles.

The Holocaust chapters published here give rise to the question: did the Jews of Kremenets resist their Nazi murderers? Both writers testify that an organized resistance movement did not exist. Anyone who reads the description of the extermination in all its stages will understand why it did not and could not. But there were definitely single cases of passive and active resistance in the town and its surrounding area, by individuals and by groups:

A. A group of partisans was active in the town's vicinity, and one of them was Yonye Bernshteyn of Kremenets. It is assumed that more young Jewish people from the town who were hiding in the mountains and forests joined the group and fought the Nazis.

B. The first two heads of the Judenrat, Ben-Tsion Katz and Yonye Grinberg, stood up honorably to the Nazis, did not follow their orders, and paid a high price for their actions: one was executed, and the other lost his mind.

C. The son of Peysi Kremen the barber refused to join an "extermination shipment," and when he was arrested, he shot the Nazi policeman with his pistol and killed him. In turn, he, too, was killed on the spot. People who visited the town after the extermination discovered this fact, and it is possible that this was not an isolated case.

D. A few families, mainly from the intelligentsia, committed planned suicide before the Nazis came to take them to the killing fields.

E. The Jews of Folwarki Wielkie village near Kremenets stood up to the enemy, fought them, and killed some of them (see the list on page 160). It is possible that there were similar cases in other corners of the town and its surroundings, but we were not informed of it.

F. There were hundreds of escapees and hundreds of attempts to escape. People also tried to save themselves and their families through various sorts of subterfuge, and some even succeeded. Indeed, even in the midst of the horror, many did not give up.

****

An organized resistance movement? It did not exist. But there were definitely pockets of resistance, although there is no way to know how much.

THE MOUNTAIN

From *The Hidden Light,* by Martin Buber, part 1, page 122
English translation by Thia Persoff

When Rabbi Avraham * came to the house of his father-in-law, the genius of Kremenets, the community's dignitaries came to greet the holy man and pay him homage. However, he did not face them but looked through the window at the mountain at the foot of which the town sat.† One of those who came to greet him—who considered himself an esteemed Torah scholar and did not want his honor slighted—said impatiently, "Why is Your Honor gazing at the mountain? Have you never seen one?" The rabbi replied: "I look and wonder how a small lump of dirt got so haughty that it swelled into a large mountain."

---

* Avraham Malakh, a leader of the Shabbatai Hasidim.
† Mount Bona.

[271]

SUPPLEMENT

THIS IS HOW I SAW YOU, MY TOWN . . .

Miryam Bat (Afula)
English translation by Thia Persoff

The final year I spent in my town before I left it forever is embedded in my memory as if it is still alive: the promise of spring in the air and the snow melting even before Passover, its white brightness darkening. In the mountains around it, the snows melt and puddles of water overflow, running and flooding the alleys, sweeping bundles of straw, horse droppings, pieces of lumber, and an old, dilapidated shoe on their way .... On days like these, the children do not rush home from school, but run joyously in the puddles and slide on the remnants of ice. Who could refrain from such a pleasure? Even the adults are pulled more and more outdoors ....

In the large shop windows on Sheroka Street, snowdrops are seen, and right next to them are blue violets. The Poles are already ruling the town. Business and negotiation between the Jews and gentiles are thriving in anticipation of the coming Passover holiday. The market is humming. Jews carry bundles of onions on their shoulders and the best of the produce in their hands. Chickens and ducks raise Cain from inside the farmers' wagons. Groups of farmers' wives walk by the stores and buy assorted merchandise from the Jewish merchants: colorful cloth, decorated kerchiefs, pink dolls made of sugar, paper flowers, lovely toy roosters so lifelike you expect to hear them crowing "kookoorikoo" at any moment .... Day by day, the weather turns nicer, and nature all around is balm to the soul—everything green and sparkling in the light. Children roam the streets. The heart longs for the mountains, the fresh green of the budding gardens. Who can resist nature's charm? The white blooms of the acacia trees line the street, intoxicating the air with the aroma of spring.

This is the time of the Balfour Declaration. The Zionist organizations' work is flourishing, and Kremenets leads the activities for the entire area. Regards from the first pioneers are arriving from Israel, and the Zionist idea is increasingly taking hold in people's hearts. It is then that you sense that the hands of murderers hold all the charming beauty and abundance of nature, and one day our eyes open to see that there is no future for us here.

Very soon new names and expressions like orchard, vineyard, work brigade, kibbutz, and collective rapidly penetrate the town. The living link between the Kremenets community and the Land of Israel is strengthened.

[272]

[Blank]

פנקס קרמניץ

[274]

PINKAS KREMENETS

EDITORIAL BOARD

Mordekhay Otiker, Manus Goldenberg, Tovye Troshinski, Yitschak Rokhel

EDITOR

A. Sh. Shteyn

**Title page in Hebrew section drawn by Duvid Tushinski (Paris)
Other illustrations in Yiddish section by M. Kagan (Israel, Kibbutz Shamir)**

Published by the Organization of Kremenets Emigrants in Israel

1954 / 12 Years after the Disaster

[275]

PART TWO [YIDDISH]

Historical Overview
RYB"L
Between the Two World Wars
The Jewish Workers' Movement
Prominent Figures
Remembrances and Customs
Destruction and Holocaust
Kremenets in the World

[276]

The Old Market

[277-279]

INTRODUCTION

The Editors

> [**Translation Editor's Note:** For a translation of this article, see the translation of the introduction to the Hebrew section (page 7).]

[280]

View of the Town from the Top of Mount Vidomka

[281-287]

HISTORY OF JEWISH SETTLEMENT IN KREMENETS

Sh. Etinger and Ch. Shmeruk (Jerusalem)

> [**Translation Editor's Note:** This article is an abridged version of the article of the same name in the Hebrew section (page 9).]

[288]

R' YITSCHAK BER LEVINZON (RYB"L, 1788–1860)

THE BATTLES BEFORE THE ENLIGHTENMENT

Volf Shnayder (Detroit)

[289]

י. ב. לעווינזאהן (ריב"ל)

Y. B. levinzon (RYB"l)

[299]

RESTORING R' YITSCHAK BER LEVINZON'S HOUSE

Yisrael Margalit

What did we do, many years ago, to preserve Yitschak Ber Levinzon's memory?

In 1906, at the initiative of and with the cooperation of a group of community members —Dr. Litvak, Pinchas Ras, Rabbi B. Kunin, Leyb Shumski, and myself—an assembly was called of people interested in preserving our distinguished citizen Y. B. Levinzon's name and memory. About 70-80 persons attended—the community's intelligentsia and cultural workers—to discuss how we could preserve Y. B. Levinzon's memory in Kremenets.

After an exchange of opinions and ideas, it was decided to use the entire Jewish press in former Russia to publish an open appeal to the Jews, asking them to donate money to buy the little house where Yitschak Ber Levinzon had lived and worked, with the purpose of transforming it into a public library and reading room. We elected the following committee to carry out the decision: president, Rabbi B. Kunin; secretary, Dr. M. Litvak; treasurer, P. Ras, and two members, H. L. Shumski and the writer of these lines.

After the first call was published, money began pouring in from all parts of former Russia. An especially warm response came from the Lithuanian Jews and others who admired Levinzon and were thankful to those who had initiated the project. In the meantime, we contacted the authorities about the future reading hall's legal status— we had to wait for official authorization of the hall's status before we could buy back the little house where Levinzon had lived; at that time, the house was being used as a pub.

[300]

However, the czar's authorities maintained that libraries and especially reading rooms were harmful to the public, so they rejected our request. We then called an additional general assembly to discuss the problem and decide how we could in any case buy the house and remove the pub, since we thought it was a disgrace to run a pub in Levinzon's house.

It was decided to buy the house in the name of private individuals, not the community, and the following buyers were appointed: M. Litvak, Leyb Shumski, and the writer of these lines.

Indeed, we bought the house, closed the pub, and waited for better times, when we hoped to realize the plan. However, time passed and World War II broke out, and during the war we didn't have the time or motivation to pursue the matter. Most of the committee members passed away, and finally we, the three buyers, decided to transfer the rights of ownership to a legal organization. So we did, and we transferred the house to the only legal organization that possessed the right to buy and own property—ORT.

Y. B. Levinzon's house

BETWEEN THE TWO WORLD WARS

English translation by Yocheved Klausner

JEWISH KREMENETS

Yisrael Otiker (Na'an)

The following survey of social and economic life in Kremenets before 1931 is, in fact, characteristic of almost the entire period between the two world wars.

From *Kremenitser Shtime*, 22 Tevet 5692 [December 19, 1931]

ECONOMIC CIRCUMSTANCES

The Jewish population's economic circumstances, difficult as they were, continued deteriorating year after year. A large segment of the population was completely ruined and was forced to look for new ways to make a living. Many respected merchants and formerly well-to-do families became quite penniless. Some even became dependent on charitable institutions and would ask their support or beg for a loan of 60 zloty ... including some people who had donated large sums to charity in the past.

The situation was even worse for small businesses. Most kept their shops closed week after week because profits were so scarce. A significant number liquidated their businesses altogether and, as I said before, began looking for other means of making a living. For every job advertised by an institution, enterprise, etc., there were dozens of applicants, including many respected former homeowners. The incomes of the rest of the population sank as well; farmers became impoverished, and office employees' salaries fell drastically.

Craftsmen also experienced a very difficult year. Many crafts died out entirely, and many workers remained without work. A very few were given some work by surrounding estate owners or the few Jews who were not strongly affected by the crisis.

Also, Jewish teachers, office workers, and the like, whom small businessmen have always envied as "people with a secure living," have suffered greatly this year. Pensions and regular pay fell considerably.

The laborers' situation was no better. Unemployment and very low pay have brought hunger and need.

Other segments of the population shared the same difficult circumstances. Only a very few were able to hold onto their jobs. Unfortunately, many of them did not fulfill their duty toward their impoverished brothers, as required by the hard times.

[302]

Another factor in the difficult circumstances is the tax rate, which has not been lowered in spite of the crisis—on the contrary, taxes have been raised. This was a fatal blow to masses of merchants. Lack of credit added to the difficulty. The banks rejected requests for loans, and people kept their capital at home, afraid to trust even their best friends. Due to the difficult circumstances in America, support from relatives or townspeople in the U.S., to individuals as well as institutions, has become limited. The Jewish population now depends on self-support, which is limited as well.

THE TOWN ADMINISTRATION

Last year, the town administration also experienced financial difficulties, and regular financial assistance to Jewish institutions arrived irregularly.

By the end of the year, the City Council had allotted 2,000 zloty for shoes for needy children in the schools.

THE COMMUNITY

Only now has the community begun to emerge from the "verge of death." It is about to prepare next year's preliminary budget and is finally beginning to return to normal functioning.

There is almost nothing of note to say about last year's activities, except for the unsuccessful attempt to take possession of the cemetery, the establishment of the slaughterhouse (quite far from the town), the hiring of ritual slaughterers (a source of arguments, as usual), etc. Recently, the community took over management of the Home for the Aged.

Social institutions had a difficult year as well.

Panoramic View of Kremenets

[303]

ORT Society

ORT's circumstances were very sad indeed. Support from the central offices ceased almost entirely, and the school was in danger of closing. It was only thanks to the activity of a few devoted people and to ORT representative B. Eysurovitsh's participation that a rescue operation for the school began. A serious educational campaign was launched, and members of the Jewish community responded almost beyond their means. In a short time, $400 was collected, a sum that not even the activists themselves had expected. The school's situation was somewhat alleviated.

In general, during the past year, the women's wear workshop has expanded and now includes 40 students. The locksmith workshop numbers 35 students.

Tarbut Organization

This year, the Tarbut School opened all seven grades and is doing well. It has about 200 students, compared to 63 (in three grades) in 1928. Of the 200 students, 52 are entirely exempt from tuition, 46 pay tuition of less than 5 zloty a month, and 75 receive a reduction of 25-75%.

The Tarbut School curriculum is as follows: all general studies follow the state school curriculum—Polish studies in Polish and general studies in Hebrew; in addition, Hebrew and Jewish classes are offered to a great extent: Hebrew language and literature, Jewish history, Bible, Torah with Rashi's commentary, Mishna, prayers, and the geography of the Land of Israel.

The Tarbut School gives students not only instruction but education as well. The children absorb the spirit and importance of work and independence. They have organized committees in each grade, and in the higher grades, the committees are self-governing, with their own institutions. The main body is the Head Committee and the Peers' Judicial Committee. This self-governing society has so far put the following institutions into place: a Jewish National Fund committee, a cooperative, and a mutual aid society. The society has organized several study groups—recently, for example, it instituted a research circle for old Kremenets. It also issued a periodical, *Kehilatenu*, and decided to hold a get-together every Sabbath.

> [**Translator's Note:** *Kehilatenu* means *Our Community.*]

This year, the first nine students will graduate from the Tarbut School.

The social standing of the students' parents is as follows: small businessmen—30%, laborers—11%, craftsmen—20%, orphans—12%, clerks—7%, working intelligentsia—7%, and merchants 3%. Forty percent to 50% of the laborers, craftsmen, and clerks are unemployed.

The children receive breakfast at school every day.

[304]

CHARITY FUND

This loan fund was very important for impoverished small businessmen, craftsmen, and even formerly important merchants. The fund expanded over time and numbered 700 contributing members.

At a time when obtaining even the smallest loan in town was very difficult, this charitable fund was able to meet its members' needs and offer interest-free loans. Last year, the fund distributed 150 loans for a total of nearly 70,000 zloty. Loan amounts were 50-100 zloty. Before New Year's, merchants received a sum of 4,500 zloty.

This year, the fund experienced some difficulties due to the Joint's withdrawal of credit. In general, however, it managed to overcome these difficulties, and it became one of the most well-liked and respected institutions in town.

TOZ SOCIETY

The local TOZ Society numbered about 120 members. Children in private schools, cheder, and Talmud Torah, as well as an additional 60 children, are under doctors' supervision. Last summer, a "summer colony" for 115 children was organized. In winter, free cod-liver oil was distributed to needy children.

The material circumstances of other Jewish institutions—the Talmud Torah, the Home for the Aged, and the like—are difficult today, due to the crisis and reduced support from the population.

TOZ Management

Seated, from right: (1) Duvid Bakimer, (2) Malye Gornfeld, (3) ... (4) Moshe'ki Margalit. Standing: (1) Kapuzer, (2) Chayim Fishman, (3) Yosef Kroyt, (4) Nasi Shnayder, (5) Avraham Bitker.

[305]

ORPHAN AID SOCIETY

Last year, thanks to the devoted work of several active members, the orphanage was completed, and 22 children now live there. The Orphan Aid Society supervises 88 additional orphans who live in town.

The Circle of Independent Orphans has made progress as well: it runs a cultural center and drama group. Many of the older orphans are now independent, have learned a trade, and are working.

JEWISH HOSPITAL

Last year, the Jewish Hospital cared for 541 patients, including 95 with contagious diseases. Ambulatory cases numbered 10,031 patients last year.

The distribution of hospital patients was as follows: 120 through the town administration, 85 through TOZ, 49 free of charge, 287 paid.

The members' fee, collected more or less regularly, was significant, and it was important for the hospital budget's management and security.

Zionist Youth Activists, 1920

First row, right to left: (1) Pinchas Lemberg (Kfar Vitkin), (Avraham Biberman (Jerusalem), (3) Yente Verthaym (Tel Aviv), (4) Pesach Litvak (Tel Aviv). *Second row:* (1) Shlome Giterman, (2) Feyge Biberman (USSR), (3) Chane Fridman (perished in Kremenets), (4) Bunim Lemberg, (5) Risye Fishman, (6) Sime Raykhman (perished in Kremenets), (7) Chanokh Rokhel (Tel Yosef).

[306]

Group of Community Leaders, 1924

Seated, from right: (1) Aleksander Frishberg, (2) Dr. M. Litvak, (3) Yisrael Landsberg. *Standing, row 1:* (1) Eliyahu Shtern, (2) Azriel Kremenitski, (3) Dr. Zalman Sheynberg, (4) Moshe Gershteyn. *Row 2:* (1) Shmuel Feldman, (2) Chayim Suchodolg, (3) Mikhael Shumski, (4) Aharon Fridman, (5) Meir Goldring, (6) Ruven Goldenberg. *Row 3:* Moshe Eydis, (2) Yitschak Poltorak, (3) Avraham Vaynberg, (4) Arye Hindes, (5) Moshe Eydelman, (6) Zeydi Perlmuter, (7) Fishel Perlmuter, (8) Chayim Ovadies.

ZIONIST MOVEMENT

In the general Zionist party, for several years the custom was for the Central Committee to do the day-to-day work. Members would participate in the General Assembly once a year, go to Simchas Torah prayers, and the like.

However, it was different in the Zionist youth movements. In the years when immigration to the Land of Israel was not possible, the youth organizations underwent an internal consolidation. Pioneer and the other organizations run a regular cultural program. It should also be noted that Zionist organizations continued to expand last year, and the establishment of a revisionist faction attracted many members, mostly young people.

However, the Working Land of Israel parties, which obtained the most votes in the elections to the Zionist Congresses, held first place among the Zionist groups.

[307]

JEWISH NATIONAL FUND INCOME

Last year, the income of this important fund fell as well. The reason is, again, the population's difficult circumstances. Last Hanukah, the JNF held its yearly bazaar, but this year it was not possible.

The Foundation Fund's goal, on the other hand, was to reach the same number of **donors this year as last year.**

PROFESSIONAL ORGANIZATIONS

Last year, the professional unions ran a campaign to organize all the workers, and in most cases they succeeded. Cultural activity among members was noteworthy: the workers had their own sports club, Morningstar; their own library, which included several hundred books; a drama group; etc. The club has become a real home for members, who dropped in almost every evening.

CULTURAL SITUATION

The Zionist Organization library holds 3,000 books in Yiddish, Hebrew, Polish, and Russian, and 250 registered readers. It should be noted that many people canceled their registration due to the difficult times.

The greater Warsaw press has fewer readers today as well. *Haynt* [Today] has no more than 150 readers, and *Moment*, 120. On the other hand, cheaper newsletters and "tabloids" are selling better. People are not buying books outside the library these days.

It should be noted that even now, during these hard times, a new weekly, *Kremenitser Shtime,* was founded, while similar attempts in better times did not succeed.

In the first three months of its existence, *Kremenitser Shtime* aroused widespread interest, and it is being read by all sectors of the population.

ANTI-SEMITIC INCIDENTS

The wave of anti-Semitic disturbances that engulfed the whole country last October and November did not spare our town. On Sunday, November 22, high school students tried to attack Jews in the street, smash windows, and do other "good deeds." Only thanks to the brave reaction of Jewish youth and local police intervention were the riots stopped **immediately. The authorities have not allowed anti-Jewish activities since.**

BIRTHS, WEDDINGS, AND DEATHS

During the year, we had 121 births, 65 weddings, and 57 deaths.

[308]

THE COMMUNITY BUDGET

We feel it is necessary to reprint the Kremenets Jewish community budget for 1932-1933, which illustrates its leaders' worth and talent.

The publication of the community budget aroused criticism even before it was discussed in the community itself. It was talked about everywhere, and several articles were published on the subject, even in the Kremenets press. The Kremenets budget was compared to that of Volhynia, and the general demand was to take into account the general Jewish population's circumstances.

Community leaders made every effort to present a realistic budget that would not end in deficit. The community budget for 1935 was 71,304 zloty. Among its expense items were culture, Talmud Torah, the Jewish Hospital, a free loan fund, accommodation of guests, care of orphans, aid for winter fuel, matzos for Passover, immigration, the sports club, etc.—*Editorial Board*

INCOME

1. General income:

Documents, licenses etc.		200 zl.	200 zl.

2. The Rabbinate:

Certificates, etc.		1,500	1,500

3. Slaughtering:

400 oxen and cows	6.30 each	2,520	
1,700 young cows	3.20 each	5,440	
4,200 calves	1.35 each	5,670	
8,200 geese	0.65 each	5,330	
38,000 hens, ducks	0.40 each	15,200	
1500 young chickens	0.20 each	3,000	37,260

4. Cemetery:

Cemetery plots 10-400 zl.		4,000	
Licenses to erect tombstones		6,000	10,000

5. Receipts:

From 1,104 individuals		35,600	
Penalties and executions		1,780	37,380
			86,340

EXPENSES

1. Debts:

Bank and private	2,350	
Slaughterhouse construction in 1929-30	2,780	5,130

[309]

2. Administrative:

Local	800	
Heating	150	
Lights	100	
Local maintenance	50	
Furniture: 2 tables	50	
24 chairs at 3 zl.	72	
2 cupboards	100	
2 racks	20	
Installation of 20 lamps	150	
Telephone	200	
Writing utensils	25	

Office expenses

Writing material	300	
Printing	500	
Telephone subscription	200	
Telegraph	200	
Newspaper subscription	159	

Administrative expenses

Representation	200	
Court and trial expenses	300	
Travel costs	300	
Local taxes	300	
Secretary	2,600	

Personnel

Bookkeeper	1,500	
Treasurer	1,500	
Manager	1,200	
Health care fund & unemployment aid	16	11,392

3. Rabbinate

Community rabbi	3,000
Judge	1,500
R' Duvid Rog	600
Secretary, registry keeper	1,200
Cash box	102

Rabbi emeritus: Rabbi Bernshteyn	1,500	
Family of Rabbi Rapaport, of blessed memory	2,560	
Family of Rabbi Senderovits, of blessed memory	1,300	
Ballot box for the election of a rabbi and a judge	500	12,262

[310]

4. Slaughtering and *Kashrut*

1 slaughterer—4,160 zl.	4,160	
2 slaughterers—2,600 "	5,200	
2 slaughterers—1,560 "	3,200	
1 slaughterer—	1,200	
1 slaughterer—	800	
Kashrut supervisor	1,040	
Collector	1,000	
2 *Kashrut* workers	1,900	
Coaches for the rabbi and the supervisors	1,000	
Pension for the slaughterhouse treasurer	1,300	
Pension for the slaughterhouse manager	400	
Maintenance of the slaughterhouse building	200	
Health care fund	1,100	
Writing material for the slaughterhouse	400	22,820

5. Cemetery

Pensions: manager	1,200	
2 gravediggers	2,400	
2 helpers	1,200	
A tailor for preparing the burial shrouds	200	
Health care fund	206	
10 burial shrouds free for the poor at 20 zl.	200	
10 tombstones for the poor	350	
Maintenance & repair	500	6,256

6. Religious needs

Ritual bath preparation	500	
Eruv	100	
Eruv supervision	200	800

7. Home for the Aged

Maintenance, taking into account incomes, subsidies, etc.	3,000	
Great Synagogue	500	
Religious education for the young	5,000	
Hospital	8,000	
Accommodation of guests	600	

Free loan fund	1,500	
Free loan fund, D. Rog	200	
Orphanage	2,000	
Ice for the poor	300	
Wood for the poor	1,000	

[**Translation Editor's Note:** An *eruv* is a ritual enclosure around a community to enable the carrying of objects outdoors on the Jewish Sabbath, which would otherwise be forbidden by Torah law.]

[311]

Passover matzos for the poor	2000	
Hosting Jewish soldiers for Passover	300	
Hosting Jewish prisoners for Passover	300	
Single requests for increase in support	1,000	22,700
9. Debt Payments		
Printing & printed matter	100	
Distribution of printed matter	100	
Interest at 5%	1,780	1,980
Total		86,340

THE GREAT SYNAGOGUE

H. Gelernt (New York)

This was the synagogue that stood in the center of town; it was also called the Old Synagogue. According to our oral tradition, it was built during the first half of the 18th century. This can also be inferred from the synagogue's Gothic architecture: the windows in the high walls were narrow and tall, with an arch on top. The ceiling was arched as well, diagonally, and formed an ornate dome. Two windows appeared in the synagogue's eastern wall, and three each in the north and south walls. The building was about 55 meters long on the outside and about 35 inside, and 35 meters wide. Inside the building, an ornate stone railing ran along the entire length of the western wall—that was the gallery of the women's section.

Several hundred people prayed in the synagogue. We did not have shelves for the books. The main furniture consisted of the prayer stands, with only one long table and two benches standing in the north corner near the wall. These seats were for the poorest of "Your people." You entered the synagogue through white stone stairs. In the middle, several stairs led to the pulpit. In the east, there was a small depression, one step below the floor—the cantor's stand. This was the custom: the cantor would recite the prayers from a lower level in literal observance of the verse in Psalms 130:1: "Out of the depths I have cried to You, Lord." Above the cantor's stand hung a tall *shiviti*. The letters were written by an authorized scribe, and it was adorned by two lion figures leaning on diagonally painted, gilded columns. On both sides of the *shiviti* were various paintings. The frame was made of hand-carved mahogany. The bright colors coalesced majestically with light from two candles burning in two shining brass candlesticks and flickering candle flames in the big brass chandelier.

> [**Translator's Note:** A *shiviti* (literally, "I have set") is a meditative ornate plaque for contemplation of God's name. The name and concept are based on the verse in Psalms 16:8: "I have set the Lord always before me."]

Splendor also emanated from the tall ark holding the Torah scrolls, which was entirely hand carved. Two angels spread wings that reached to the domed ceiling.

[312]

The Ten Commandments soared into the air from the crown in the middle, the letters made of gilded wood. The green velvet curtain with golden trim, and light reflected from the lamp garlands, gave the inside of our synagogue a majestic appearance.

There were two entrances to the building from the cobblestone courtyard. The south entrance led to the women's section. Several tombstones stood half-sunk into the earth in a hidden corner not far from this entrance: tradition had it that these were the remains of an old special cemetery where two couples, both bride and groom, died during the plague and were buried on their wedding day.

Another small synagogue, the Tailors' Synagogue, was located in the vestibule. The southwestern corner was used for reciting Lamentations on the Ninth of Av. It was also used for the performance of the special, complicated "Removing" ceremony. At the beginning of the 20th century, Rabbi Hertsele performed one such ceremony one day before the afternoon prayer,

[**Translator's Note:** The Ninth of Av commemorates the destruction of the First and Second Temples. "Removing" (*Chalitsa* in Hebrew) is the ancient ceremony in which a woman removes the shoe of her deceased husband's brother, releasing him from marrying her, according to Levirate law. The full description of the ceremony has not been translated.]

The Great Synagogue

[313]

Each Sabbath afternoon in this same little prayer room, R' Avrahamtse the Teacher, the regular Torah reader, would study the portion of the week and the Alshikh commentary with the people. During the summer, he would study *Sayings of the Fathers* with them.

At the same time, Ite the ritual slaughterer's wife would read the weekly chapter of the women's book *Tsena Urena* to the women.

> [**Translation Editor's Note:** *Tsena Urena,* first published in the 16th century, contains Yiddish adaptations of portions of the Bible. The title comes from Song of Songs 3:11: *tse'ena ure'ena benot tsion* (Go forth and look, daughters of Zion).]

The synagogue courtyard was where the wedding canopy would be raised for every wedding in town. Every funeral procession would stop in the same place for the memorial prayer, "God, Full of Compassion." This was the tradition in Kremenets for generations—that both the living and the dead would be sanctified near the synagogue....

According to our tradition, there was no *mezuzah* on the synagogue doorpost, but the corner was black from the many hands that had touched the place, kissing the shape of the Hebrew letter *shin* that was there. This letter, the people said, would block the way of the souls of the dead who came every midnight to pray in the synagogue. Where did that story come from?

One Saturday night, in the cold winter of 1904, Jews' Street suddenly awoke to wild, frightened cries.

It was during the Russo-Japanese war, when many Jews had been drafted into the military and sent to the front, and there was no news from them for months. Everybody was certain that their bodies were deep in the ocean in Russian ships sunk

357

by the Japanese. Late that night, Rabbi Mendele the ritual slaughterer and his son, Leybele, were returning from the slaughterhouse. The street was empty, it was pitch black, and only the flickering Eternal Light could be seen through the synagogue windows, casting light and shadows. Leybele became very frightened, sure that he heard voices murmuring inside the synagogue—the voices of the dead coming for the midnight prayer. He fainted and fell onto the frozen snow, and his father's wild cries for help woke up the entire street.

But Leybele could not be calmed. The next morning, the entire town was in an uproar. R' Moshke'le, the grandson of R' Mordekhay'le the righteous, who lived in back of the synagogue, added to the excitement by saying, "This is not new; he had heard those voices every night...." So it was decided unanimously that that the dead must be pacified. Consequently, on Monday evening, a special minyan was assembled, and the ceremony began.

[314]

They studied portions of the Mishna in the vestibule until midnight, as was the custom, and at 12 o'clock they went to the synagogue door, knocked three times, and declared, "Dead souls, ten Jews are coming to appease you, please calm yourselves!" As they stepped in, they recited from psalms and various prayers, and said Kaddish. This was the end of the affair.

The synagogue attendant, Mendele the Short, kept the synagogue tidy and spotless. He would open the synagogue and close up after prayers, and when someone observed the anniversary of a death, he would provide the necessary brandy and egg cookies. Mendele had no fear of his synagogue's dead, since he was familiar with them, as was Leybish's wife (whose regular job was to lead the prayers in the women's section), who would go to the cemetery and discuss matters with "her" dead ....

The synagogue commanded respect from all passersby. The square nearby was the marketplace where peasants would come once a week with their horse-drawn wagons to sell their wares. They would never park their wagons too close to the building.

It was the only synagogue in town in which prayers were performed by a professional cantor accompanied by a choir.

The most respected people in town would pray there, and the official ceremony for Czar Nikolas's coronation day was performed there every year. We would hold large meetings there, and there we celebrated the czar's Constitutional Declaration after the 1905 revolution and demonstrated in the street, singing "Hatikva" and "The Oath." Binyamin Yaspe, the son of Tsadok the ritual slaughterer, led the procession and the songs.

***

There is no more synagogue, as there are no more Jews. Their souls have no one to visit, no one to pray for. The souls have turned to dust, as have the bodies that they once kept alive.

May their souls be bound up in the bond of eternal life.

THE ORPHANAGE

Bela Bernshteyn (Buenos Aires)

The story of orphan care in Kremenets is strongly connected with the name of Mrs. Sofia Isakovna Kremenetskaya—the longtime head of the orphanage, until the last moment of the tragic destruction. She rightly deserved to be called "mother of the orphans."

Sofia, who was born in Niezhin, went to school in Petersburg, where she met Azriel Kremenetski, a student from Kremenets. They married and came to live in our town.

During World War I, when heavy fighting was underway around Lake Ikva, many Jewish families from the towns and villages along the front lines fled to Kremenets. The refugees were poor, and they were robbed on the way. Sofia—then still a young woman—was the first to care for the refugee families. She visited them house by house and began rounding up help. She was particularly affected by the grim circumstances of the solitary refugee children, many of whom were orphans and half-orphans whose parents were killed on the various fronts or died wandering from place to place.

[315]

Flower Day for the Benefit of the Orphanage (1928)

359

Orphanage Children (1925); in the middle are A. Levinson and Sonye Kremenetski.

[316]

She devoted all her attention and effort to these children, and even before an official body was formed to care for the orphans, on her own initiative she registered all the children, took on the burden, and began her own support efforts. She collected food from acquaintances and well-to-do people, explained the cause, and succeeded in her endeavors. However, she came to the conclusion that such support was not enough; to really help these children, take care of their needs, and give them a good education, they would have to be removed from their problematic environment—the atmosphere of poverty and need—and given proper care.

At that time, the Joint had already begun relief efforts for the Jewish population. However, due to the special circumstances of Kremenets, which was a border crossing, the Joint had not reached it. Moreover, that institution was hardly known in Kremenets. The energetic and devoted Sofia organized a committee, which several young girls, including my sister Rive and me, immediately joined. We all began working for the war orphans as a volunteer team. In 1922, she rented a house near Dubno and established a summer camp for 60 orphans under Rive Bernshteyn's management and supervision. The situation was not an easy one: there was not enough food, but they managed to keep the camp functioning until the end of the summer. However, only then did the real problem arise: the camp had to be closed, but there was no place to send the children. After a great deal of effort, two rooms were rented on Beaupré Street: this was the beginning of the orphanage in Kremenets.

Now, they did manage to receive some support from the Joint, but it was not enough to maintain the place and care for the children, and certainly not enough to hire the personnel needed. Sofia herself began to work in the kitchen, cooking, cleaning, and performing all other necessary tasks. With love and devotion, she dedicated her time and health to the children. She sent the older children to the ORT School or private

360

workshops to learn a trade; she cared for each and every child as if she were his or her mother.

The Orphanage Committee's secretary and bookkeeper, Leybke Rozental, a dedicated volunteer for all civic activities in town, was one of Sofia's devoted helpers. He made every effort to find new funding sources for the orphan organization. He found addresses for townspeople in America and, with Sofia, asked them for support. In time, he established strong ties with the Kremenets Society in America; its representative, Buma Treger, of blessed memory (Roza Vaynberg's husband from Kremenets), managed to collect significant sums of money from the Kremenets Society and sent regular help for the orphans.

Thanks to this support, the children relocated to a more comfortable apartment, at Mrs. Boym's on Slovatski Street. It was also possible to buy a piano and hire a supervisor, Mrs. Manye Kotlar. As expenses increased continuously, Sofia organized a "tax collection" from almost every family in town, a street collection, collection days, and various other activities aimed at raising money.

[317]

Cornerstone Ceremony for the Orphanage Building (1928)

There was a strongly felt need for the orphans to have their own building. It was time to stop wandering from place to place. For a long time, this was only a dream, but finally it seemed that the dream could be realized. Azriel Kremenitski, a member of the City Council, lobbied for the cause. Finally, the council decided to donate a site on Slovatski Street, and a two-story building was built for the orphans. A festive and joyous housewarming party was held in April 1930. Mayor Beaupré was given the honor of cutting the ribbon, after which he kissed Mrs. Sofia on the forehead in recognition of her outstanding work. It was a grand civic celebration in Kremenets.

The orphanage already held 70 children. Time passed, and the children grew up, became men and women, and left the institution, and new children arrived. But Sofia never lost contact with her children, even when they became adults. She helped them find work, assisted them with deeds and advice, and remained forever their devoted guide.

Sofia had a family of her own—a husband and a child—but she still found time to care for the lonely and suffering. She was active in several institutions, such as ORT, OZE, the hospital, etc. She often visited poor families in town, helped when needed, offered encouragement, taught the mothers hygiene, and had a warm word for everyone. She generated an understanding for her work in people and received the support and assistance she needed from them.

> [**Translation Editor's Note:** OZE stands for *Obshchestvo okhraneniia zdorov'ia evreiskogo naseleniia* (Society for the Protection of the Health of the Jewish Population).]

She educated an entire generation of women who became active in social work in Kremenets; she was an important role model for them.

[318]

But she was mainly dedicated to "her" orphans with every beat of her big heart—until the murderous hand cut off her life and her life's work.

May my words remain as an eternal memorial for Sofia, her noble husband, and their only daughter, and the institution that bore the name "Kremenets Orphanage."

Orphanage Management with the Central Office Representative

NOTE FROM THE EDITORIAL BOARD

According to *Kremenitser Shtime*, the people involved in orphanage activities during the last few years were Ch. Grinberg, B. Feldman, Mrs. Landesberg, Naumik

Fingerhut, Mrs. Kremenetskaya, Pinchasovitsh, D. Vaynberg, B. Yaspe, Mrs. F. Baytler, M. Kapuzer, and Dr. Landesberg.

[319]

Children's Library in the Orphanage, 1939

Performance by the Orphanage Children

[320]

THE CIRCLE OF INDEPENDENT ORPHANS

L. Eler (*Kremenitser Shtime*)

The day when the first group of children became independent and left the building was a great holiday. They had finished their studies, and the trade they had learned helped them earn enough money to support themselves and not be dependent on outside help.

The faces of the self-supporting orphans were serious and thoughtful, because they were aware that the day represented an important step in their lives. From that day on, they knew, they must care for themselves, earn money to cover all their needs, and be responsible for whatever happened in their lives. For the educators, teachers, and organization members, this was a day of deep satisfaction and moral fulfillment. They remembered the children's condition on their arrival, how much effort and work they had invested in each child, how worried they were when a child was sick, or, on the other hand, how much joy they felt with every good grade the children brought back from school or evening courses. These were the thoughts that went through the heads of the teachers and "graduates" alike when they observed the younger children of the orphanage happy, singing, and dancing at the celebration that evening.

The next day, they took their things and went out to begin their independent lives, each according to his or her means.

At first, they came in often "to see how things were and what was new," and later they would come every Sabbath "to visit." In time, these visits naturally became rarer, since they were busy working and taking care of every little thing. However, spending so much time alone and being in the streets so much during their free time worried their former teachers, so they began to think of creating a place where the older children could gather and spend their free time.

Such a place was soon established—the Circle of Independent Orphans. Its aim was to hold literary evenings, establish a library, and so on.

Later, a drama group was also founded, which successfully performed *The Treasure,* a play by Shalom Aleichem—with the entire proceeds donated to the orphanage. The Circle members helped the Society with all its activities. Every evening, they would meet in the place rented for the "club," so old friendships formed in the orphanage days were kept alive.

It is to be hoped that the Circle will help keep this "family of children" together and that at least some of them will become "doers" who are always concerned with the welfare and development of the orphanage, where their little sisters and brothers are still being educated.

May the first fruits of our labor be blessed!

Long live the Circle of Independent Children!

[321]

A WORKING TOWN

B. Barshap (New York)

Kremenets was, to a certain extent, a town of labor and crafts, a town of Jewish hard workers. Beside the scholars and liberal professions, the town was home to many different trades and occupations, which supplied industrial necessities to the many smaller towns and villages that surrounded it.

Let us list the various occupations that existed and flourished in the town, thanks only to the Jews.

There were tailors—of two kinds: fine, high-quality tailors and poor tailors. They made men's wear, women's wear, and military uniforms. Our Yankel Shmukler is worth mentioning here: he was highly valued by high-ranking military types. He received orders for the most important uniforms, especially those with rank emblems woven or embroidered in gold thread; he worked on them by hand, one by one.

There were carpenters who made fine furniture and construction joiners; roof constructors and tile layers; lathe workers, who worked on two products: fine furniture decorations and cigarette holders—the latter exported to Russia; blacksmiths and tinsmiths; wagon-wheel makers, tile makers, coopers (barrelmakers), shoemakers, leather workers, tanners, potters, glaziers, cotton makers, purse makers, goldsmiths, watchmakers, road and bridge workers, grinders, brick makers, carriers, water carriers, butchers, barber-surgeons, cigarette makers, linen seamstresses, etc.

The transport business was in Jewish hands as well, whether delivery work or hauling wares between the neighboring villages. Of the carriage drivers, Shimele Poyker, the lively, beloved wagon owner, is worth mentioning. Every Sabbath afternoon, young boys and girls would gather at his house, and he would read to them from books he obtained ahead of time from Moshe Pakentreger ....

The Jewish people in Kremenets lived modestly, their livelihood based on their own toil. This was the way they managed their community activities as well. They did not make much noise, as others did.

Even the first strike—over the demand to have the nights of Jewish holidays free—was decided on a Saturday morning after prayers, during the Kiddush they held at the home of Etel, Manus's wife....

... And my ears would absorb scores of folk wisdom on winter days, when we would seek a little warmth behind the stove in the Butchers' Synagogue.

This is what we were when we came over here, to the free land of America, armed not only with working hands, but also with the heritage of the home where we were born. Here as well, we observed and cherished our fathers' simple, unsophisticated, and modest lifestyle.

[322]

THE TAILOR

S. Fingerut

In the little town of K, in the middle of Green Street
lived a tailor; his face is pale—it looks green as well.
In a little room, always too dark,

the tailor worked, deep in thought.
His room is full of dust, never very clean,
as was fitting for a beggar—it is easy to see ...
Children, little ones, half-naked and bare, roam around,
each wanting to eat, to put something in their mouth.
The poor, sickly father must work and toil,
sew and produce clothes for the smallest of pay.
His wife, she does not know what to do first:
cook the "warm meal" or sit by the sewing machine.
Poor thing, she wants to help and earn something, too,
so she cannot think about warm meals now.
The children cry: "Mommy, give us something to eat!"
The tailor, as well, cannot forget this cry.
His heart is weak, pulling him down to earth:
"Woe to the fate bestowed on me,
always toil, always hard labor, nothing of my own.
Still, this is God's little world, and there's nothing to say,
and whatever happens must be taken as good.
One must have complete faith in His mercy,
since He leads His world in splendor and beauty,
which we, little men, can never understand ....
Since He is the God, the only Creator,
we believe in Him and learn His Torah.
So the poor tailor must follow his fate,
and from his darkened nest strive and aspire—
while thousands of others are happy and full,
and never knew a bad day.
... At the end of Green Street, to the right,
that is where the tailor lives.
You know him very well ...

[323]

THE PORTER

HADASA RUBIN

Who needs strength?—I sell strength—
a back of iron, and hands, too.

One bag of coals, and ten bags of fire.
And the sun is facing me, burning ... only the sun is burning.

My eyes are fixed on the dusty sky.
The carrier's sky—the dusty bridge.

We carry the rich and noble their mirrored wardrobes,
And our luck is mirrored in the mirrors.

Hey, you, don't rush, watch the mirror, go slow!
The eyes are sweating, so are the forehead and body.

Faster, go faster, the children are waiting.
A mother is waiting, a sister, a wife.

I'm selling my days, my years and my strength
For a meager reward: only for bread, just a piece.

You who are full and tired from the abundance of food—give me the bundle,
I have a back, I have children, and hands, and a rope.

"Father, for weeks we don't have any flour—
Why is your jacket full of flour?"

Children should have rosy cheeks—
Why are you so yellow, my little son?

Nobleman, take me, I'm the healthiest,
But today I haven't earned anything yet.

Over the years I have carried many pounds of wheat on my back,
and—ha, ha, ha, I am still hungry.

Strength for sale! Who needs some strength?
Buy it from me, so I have less of it left.

Yes, I long for more heavy wardrobes and plush velvet sofas
to bring to fat gentlemen and fleshy ladies.

[324]

THE ORT SCHOOL

One of the most beautiful and important institutions owned by Kremenets was the ORT School, which during its existence educated Jewish young people and turned them into helpful and productive elements of society.

The ORT School was founded in 1922, thanks mainly to F. Perlmuter and Ovadies. At first, the school operated in a rented apartment and had two divisions: a locksmith's workshop and a lathe workshop. The school's first director was Eng. Dekalboym.

The ORT Central Office in Warsaw provided the school with the necessary tools. The school's high educational standards were of great interest among Jewish youth in Kremenets and vicinity.

In time, the school grew and relocated to a building of its own, and two new divisions were opened. The new director was Eng. Raykh.

The school's graduates worked in various craftsmen's workshops, while some of them remained in the school workshops and continued working and teaching there.

Exhibitions of products created in the ORT workshops gained recognition from the Jewish and non-Jewish population alike. The beautiful and trustworthy tailoring department, which always had orders for several months in advance, became especially famous.

The school's regular budget was covered mainly by the Central Office, but also by tuition, income from the sale of products created in the various workshops, etc. The financial situation was never too good, and the school had to overcome several crises.

[325]

ORT School Tailoring Department

368

Thanks to the teachers—including non-Jews as well—who almost never received the full pay they deserved, and to the devotion of a group of people headed by Ovadis, the ORT School managed to stay alive. From time to time, fundraising meetings were organized, and the public would respond warmly and generously. The students would organize theater performances and donation days—with all earnings going to the school. An effort was always made to cooperate with ORT Society members.

From time to time, a Central Office representative would come to Kremenets and help carry out various decisions for the school's benefit.

The town mayor assigned certain sums from the town budget to the school. The high school helped with building materials and wood for heating.

All this has helped expand craftsmanship and general education even to the poorest segments of the Jewish population.

In 1932, the school's principal and director was Eng. Avraham Rozin, and at that time the ORT School was recognized by the state as a State Craftsmanship School.

In 1936, ORT had 160 students. Seven classes had graduated by then, including 39 candidates for the tailor's assistant exam and 14 candidates for the locksmith's exam. There were also special seamstress courses for adult women, which have earned a very good reputation.

[326]

Under Soviet rule, the ORT School was converted into a school for tractor drivers.

Many of the graduates now live in Israel and are practicing their professions.

For many years, the ORT School in Kremenets enjoyed the help and support of the Relief Society in America. A testament to the ORT School's popularity and the respect felt by the Jewish population is the fact that Yitschak Ber Levinzon's place was registered under the ORT name—the only state-authorized institution with a permit to buy real estate.

Active supporters of ORT last year included Goldring Meir, Vaynshtok, Trakhtenberg M., Margalit Yisrael, Ovadies Chayim, Kroyt, and Eng. Rovin.

JEWISH THEATER LIFE

From time to time, a drama or theater group—Jewish, Polish, or Ukrainian—would come to Kremenets and give a performance. The performances were usually well received by the Jewish public, and attendance was very satisfactory.

However, Jewish young people were not content with that alone, and various organizations created drama circles. These circles organized performances as well, sometimes very successfully. To their credit, it must be said that even a failure would not discourage them, and the Jewish public would forgive them, because "they are our own people ... who are 'playing the theater,' and the artists are only amateurs."

Performances included plays by Perets Hirshbeyn, performed by the Professional Organization's drama circle and directed by Bluvshteyn; "The Haunted Inn," also by Hirshbeyn, performed by the Independent Orphans drama circle under the same direction; "The Vagabond," performed by the Zionist Organization Amateur Group and directed by Pinchasovitsh; "Kol Nidre" and "Bar Kokhba" by the same group, and many others.

Musical-artistic evenings were sometimes held at the Tarbut and ORT schools. These evenings were usually very successful, the subjects being poetry reading and singing, as well as short plays in either Hebrew or Yiddish. The audience consisted mainly of the children's parents, who received these evenings enthusiastically and supported them willingly.

Other organizations would arrange such evenings as well, and they offered very pleasant entertainment. Especially when a satiric-humorous evening was organized, and the "victims" were local active members and various organizations, the entire town was in an uproar.

[327]

THE CHARITY FUND

Kremenitser Shtime

One of the most popular institutions in town was the Charity Fund. It was established in 1927, and with the community's ruin, this beautiful enterprise was destroyed as well.

The founders and managing members made every effort to increase the fund's income. They organized Support Circles and a Charity Fund Month, advertised in the local press, asked for pledges on Simchas Torah, etc.

On the fund's fifth anniversary, a special booklet was issued as part of the festivities. The City Council and Jewish community both allocated sums of money to the fund.

The Joint helped as well and supervised the fund's activities. While the fund's only income came from philanthropic sources after appeals to people's goodwill, bookkeeping followed strict economic principles. The treasurer and accountants would see to it that loans were paid on time, no debts accumulated, and all past debts collected.

Before a holiday, when needs and, accordingly, loans increased, a good soul could always be found to donate several hundred zloty to the fund.

Loans were given to cart owners to buy a horse, to needy sick people to buy medicine, to poor families to help pay the rent, to small businessmen and craftsmen to help with yearly expenses, etc. The loans were always interest free and were paid back in weekly installments.

The Charity Fund has given a great deal of help to the Jewish masses. Thanks to the fund, many families were saved. The fund administrators were very careful not to let one zloty be lost. People who were too ashamed to ask openly for a loan would receive one secretly.

The local rabbi, Rabbi Mendiuk, would often mention the Charity Fund in his sermons; sometimes he devoted the entire sermon to the commandment to help the needy and the necessity of having a fund for this purpose. And the fund's main objective was, indeed, to make sure everyone who needed help would receive it.

The members of the fund's last administration were Moshe Gershteyn, Shlome Fingerut, Duvid Goldenberg, and Neta Shtern.

Our Charity Fund was a chapter of the central offices of the Charity Fund in Poland, and its representatives participated in the funds' general conferences.

[328]

One conference was held in Kremenets, with representatives from neighboring towns participating.

A special fund was organized in the Dubno district as well.

LEDGER OF THE "FREE LOAN" CHARITY FUND

M. Gershteyn
Kremenitser Shtime, **January 8, 1932**

According to the ledger that began in 5587 [1826–1827], the oldest Charity Fund in Kremenets was the Free Loan Society, which lent money to the needy against a guarantee. The ledger shows that this society was a carryover from another of the same name that had ceased to exist.

"These are the activities of Free Loan, duly recorded in this ledger," we read on the cover page of the 1827 ledger.

That year, several respected members of the community—educated people from Y. B. Levinson's time—got together with the aim of renewing the former Free Loan Society's activity. They compiled the following regulations:

1. Elections of society officers will take place once a year on Saturday night, not later than the Saturday when the Torah portion *Mishpatim* is read, the day the

society was founded. It is requested that the majority of society members participate in the elections.

2. At the election, the members draw lots, and the three who win are nominated as mediators. They have the right to decide whether the former officers continue to serve or whether they will take over the jobs themselves. None of the officers may be related up to the fourth degree, and if relatives are elected, they must draw lots to decide which one will step down.

3. All revenues and expenses must be duly registered in the books.

4. A trustee who serves as treasurer and keeps the sums of money and the guarantees must be elected by the entire society; the ledger will be kept by the head officer.

5. The elections must not be carried over to the next day; if the procedure cannot be completed the same night, the members must convene the next day and perform the entire procedure from the beginning. It must end the same day.

6. The trustee (treasurer) shall not issue a loan unless the head officer is present; if he does, the loan will be registered to his own account. (Note, added later in a different ink: the treasurer may indeed issue a small loan, but he must submit it for approval at the first executive meeting.)

7. No more than one and a half rubles may be given as a loan to one person; the guarantee received from the borrower must be at least twice the value of the loan.

8. If the borrower does not pay back the loan in three months, he will be sent a cautionary note, after which the guarantee may be sold.

9. The borrower may not be given another loan until he has returned the loan and redeemed the guarantee.

[329]

10. A person who registers as a member, not a borrower, must pay a one-ruble registration fee and then 10 groshen a month for membership.

11. If a member does not pay the monthly membership fee, he/she cannot take part in the elections.

12. A new member may become a candidate at the third election.

13. One member will be appointed collector of membership fees.

14. If there is a serious disagreement or conflict between a member and one of the officers, the three officers and seven respected society members must meet and resolve the conflict together.

15. On the Sabbath of the Torah portion *Mishpatim,* "lend money," the society shall convene a minyan for the additional prayer and the Torah reading, and all the officers and active members shall be called to the Torah and also given other honors during the service.

[**Translator's Note:** The Torah portion *Mishpatim* includes the words "lend money" (Exodus 22:24).]

16. Each year before the elections, the officers and trustee must update the ledger with all income and expenses, as well as the value of guarantees.

17. On Yom Kippur eve, the officers must sit by the collecting box in the Great Synagogue and Study Hall.

18. Three weeks after the election, the officers may spend three rubles on a festive meal to honor and strengthen the society. If, God forbid, the society desires a grand meal with warm dishes and various gourmet foods, which would require great expense, the expense <u>may not</u> be covered by the fund. Each member shall pay out of his own pocket according to his means.

The above regulations have been compiled and approved by the general assembly and officers of the society. Signed:

The scribe Moshe Shlome, son of our master and teacher, R' Yakov of Vladimir

As we can see from the minutes of meetings in the following years, the regulations changed over time. We find, for example, that the society's officers were elected by a majority of votes and not by drawing lots. The permitted loan amount increased to three rubles. The monthly membership fee was lowered, the loan repayment period was extended from three months to three years, the registration fee increased from three to six rubles, etc.

The number of borrowers can be assumed from the total amount of the loans issued. When the society was founded, the sum of the loans issued was 50 rubles, 52 years later it was 300 rubles, and in 1913 it reached 1,000 rubles.

Considering that the maximum amount loaned was 5 rubles in 1913, we can easily imagine the great number of borrowers and the fund's success in Kremenets Jewish population.

According to the minutes registered in the books, elections took place every year, no later than the week of *Mishpatim,* in a festive atmosphere. In time, at the formal meals organized by the chief officer, 13 courses were served; however, brandy was not allowed, only beer, which guests had pay for.

[330]

The members covered the rest of the cost of the meal. The leftovers were used by former and newly elected officers. The Free Loan Society never knew any conflict or disagreement.

In the ledger containing members' names, we find some most distinguished individuals, including great scholars, such as Chayim Landsberg and Dr. Arye Landsberg, the descendants and followers of Avraham Ber Landsberg, of blessed memory. They were relatives and friends of Y. B. Levinson. R' Avraham Ber Landsberg died on the 33rd day of the counting of the *omer* [May 1], 1831, during an epidemic. He was the father of Arye Leyb Landsberg, the well-known scholar and bibliophile, and Shlome Yeshaya Landsberg, *Hakarmel* contributor. The leaders also included Nachman Prilutski, father of *Moment* editor Tsvi Prilutski.

[**Translation Editor's Note:** *Hakarmel* was a Hebrew-language journal.]

A former leader's son told me that 45 years ago, the well-known community activist Dr. Hindes's membership was terminated because he came from the craftsman's class. It was rumored that he and his friend Tsvi Prilutski went to the officer and demanded to be shown where in the ledger it was stated that Hasidim and craftsmen could not be accepted as members.

Naturally, there was no such statement in the ledger. The fact was, however, that Hasidim and craftsmen were not accepted as society members.

At the outbreak of World War I, the fund's activity ceased, and it was only when the war ended that a general assembly was called and the members tried to renew activity. Finally, however, after several meetings and investigations, the decision was made to liquidate the society. Guarantees were returned to borrowers, and loans were canceled; some of the silverware that had been deposited as guarantees was donated to the local Home for the Aged, and the rest of the valuable guarantees were sold. The money was used to help renovate the public bath, which had been built 41 years before by a Jewish tailor named Malakhov, who had built the big New Study Hall as well. The income from the bath was supposed to fund the maintenance of the study hall.

In consideration of the community's needs, the remaining Free Loan Society members decided to donate the rest of the society's capital to the maintenance and renewal of the hospital, orphanage, and Home for the Aged. The renovated bath was turned over to the management of a homeless Jew in return for payment of a certain amount of interest.

The society owned two stores and used to add the rent to its budget. Since societies like the Free Loan Society were not registered during Russian rule, the stores were registered in the officer's name. In later years, the two stores were demolished, and an heir of the last officer sold the property to a Christian.

Thus ended the existence of this old Jewish charitable institution, and all that remained was its history, recorded in an old ledger ....

[331]

Tarbut Elementary School, 1922

[332]

THE "OTHER" KREMENETS

Kremenitser Shtime

Kremenets has become famous for its institutions, devoted community workers, beautiful youth, and energetic civic life. However, the truth must be told: there were negative aspects as well—disputes, betrayals, and even fights. To be sure, Kremenets was no exception to this.

There were intrigues and conspiracies, different "camps" formed, and arguments became conflicts .... Still, the sympathy of Jewish society in general was always with honest people.

A dispute might occur anywhere, even in the synagogue during prayer. It would begin with a simple discussion but would soon develop into a fight—sometimes a real fistfight—and more than once the affair would end up in court.

The local press held these fights in check, somewhat: people were ashamed "to be mentioned in the newspaper." On the other hand, some people found ways to overcome this problem: the paper was printed in Rovno, and an anonymous hand would mysteriously delay its arrival until after the Sabbath, when the news was already "old news" and readers had lost interest.

A burial society had existed for over 100 years, but another society, the Pallbearers, was created and soon received a license from the authorities. Fierce competition between the two caused the authorities to appoint a special "commissar" to investigate the matter, and some of the managers were arrested during the investigation.

Although the rabbi was usually elected by an enormous margin, there were some who tried to prevent him from taking the post by getting the authorities to intervene.

In the Hasidic Synagogue, a fierce argument broke out concerning the appointment of a cantor, and the same thing happened in the *Magid's* Synagogue.

One community leader did not come to meetings for an entire year and conducted a campaign against the community.

The greatest aggravation, however, was caused by an open attack on the community in 1931. The butchers went on strike, asking for a reduction in the fees they had to pay for slaughtering. Since their demands were not met, they took the animals to slaughterers in surrounding towns. This dispute grew into a huge, long fight: the butchers hired their own slaughterer from a neighboring town, the community confiscated the slaughtering knives, the butchers responded by snatching another slaughterer's knife, and so on.

[333]

The community secretary was even beaten, and a meeting to try and resolve the dispute ended in nothing but some broken teeth and a demand from the head of the community that he resign. Instead, he called the police. The police began an investigation.

The Union of Rabbis then sent the "obedient crown rabbi" from Rovno to aid the investigation and end the dispute.

Then a special committee was appointed, and according to its decision, the rabbis and several community leaders "toured" the Jewish butcher shops and asked customers not to buy meat slaughtered outside the town. This infuriated the butchers even more, and they gave the rabbi and his friends a good beating. A protest meeting was called; over 1,000 people came to the meeting and condemned the butchers' behavior. Finally, the authorities intervened again, and at long last the bitter conflict was liquidated. The final stage of the affair was played out in the local court, which recognized the Kremenets Jewish community's full rights in the slaughtering dispute. Since the community won the trial, its authority was strengthened, and the Jewish public could finally relax.

רעשטלען פון פעסטונג אויף דער באנא
שרידי המבצר על ה.בונא"

Fortress Ruins on the Bona River

[334]

Near the High School

[335]

THE JEWISH LABOR MOVEMENT

THE PROFESSIONAL MOVEMENT

Manus Goldenberg (Givat Hashlosha)
English translation by Yocheved Klausner

The first buds of a professional movement in Kremenets sprouted at the beginning of the 20th century. It was still somewhat chaotic in nature and was strongly connected to the Bund's underground activity in town. The first signs of life were revolutionary leaflets in Yiddish, which spread like a storm in the Jewish street, taking the place of the then-widespread "sensational novels." The booklets were gobbled up with great enthusiasm—they alleviated the misery of the unending hours of work and constant need, and they gave hope for a bright dawn in the future.

At the time, the word "Bund" was already casting a heavy shadow of fear over the lives of the well-to-do in Kremenets. The name was readily associated with conspiracy, prison, deportation to Siberia, and even hanging. And when spontaneous strikes began and tailors and carpenters came out with a demand for a 12-hour workday, employers were bitterly opposed. Often, quarrels and violent fights broke out in workplaces, and in many cases the czar's police had to intervene.

In this context, the following episode is worth mentioning. It happened right after 1905 (the year of the revolution). One summer afternoon, a Kremenets barber, an active member of the volunteer fire department, attacked two seamstresses who were taking a walk in the fresh air. He shouted at the top of his voice, "See, these snot-nosed tailor-maids want to overthrow Czar Nikolas!" ... A large crowd gathered—such an accusation could naturally cause very serious consequences. Soon all the laborers in town boycotted this devoted follower of the czar and threatened to ruin him. The barber was forced to ask for mercy and beg for the boycott to be lifted.

This type of incident, in which organized laborers showed solidarity, resulted in great respect for them. Almost all the workshops introduced a 12-hour workday.

[336]

Pressure from the labor activists forced employers to improve working conditions and raise wages. They also tried to organize non-Jewish workers.

But these early sprouts were flooded by waves of dark reaction, which smoldered until World War I. Handworkers and laborers in Kremenets were completely ruined and, little by little, any remnant of the workers' movement was wiped out.

Only after the 1917 Revolution did Kremenets workers reestablish strong professional associations and become involved in a wide range of professional and political activity.

They were organized, supported, and protected by the Bund and the Labor Zionist parties.

The strongest association was the Needleworkers Union, which included tailors, sewing-machine operators, gaiter manufacturers, etc., and had the strongest impact on the Jewish street. Driven by the intense revolutionary zeal of that period, over the course of only weeks, union members founded cultural institutions and various study classes, and organized a very successful election campaign. This was the first time the Kremenets community was run by a council with a large Labor majority.

With the German army's occupation of the region in autumn 1918, the persecution of all progressive organizations began. A large number of activists were arrested. The professional associations' activity was stopped entirely, and the left-wing political parties withdrew to the underground.

During the Civil War, any social activity was out of the question, as the government changed often (the longest lasting was the Petliura government). The slightest indication of the existence of a labor organization would immediately cause it to be labeled as a "Bolshevik-Communist danger," and the suspected organizers' lives were in danger.

The situation was no better at the beginning of the Polish occupation of 1920-1921.

Only in 1924, when the connection with the Polish administrative centers had stabilized and their cultural and economic influence increased, did younger members of the working circles resume party activity (a significant number of left-wing labor leaders of the older generation had followed the Bolsheviks to the East and remained in Russia). One of the first things they did was to strengthen the relationship with the professional unions in Krakow and Warsaw.

In Kremenets, as in the entire country, this was a period of "prosperity" in handicrafts and commerce. For the first time, a carpenters' union was formed, and soon afterward, office workers and commercial employees, tailors, bakers, barbers, print shop workers, and others formed unions. Their first meeting place was the courtyard of Aba Tsukerman's house, and later they met in an apartment located in Bernshteyn's courtyard, on Gorna Street.

[337]

Apart from the professional activity, diverse cultural activity was conducted as well. The Drama Group occupied a particularly important place, and it appeared in Kremenets and surrounding towns with great success. A workers' sports club, Morningstar, was founded. A number of books collected from several people formed the foundation of a workers' library, which in time developed and expanded, attracting a great number of young readers from all strata of society.

The cultural groups' leaders invested time and effort in various evening courses, where workers learned to read and write, and others completed their elementary or higher studies. Of particular importance were various training courses. Teachers and tutors came from the young intelligentsia of the left-wing movements, and very often lectures were given on political or other themes. In addition to local teachers, lecturers from Warsaw, Lvov, and other cities were invited.

All union and association activity was led by a central office, which included two representatives from each association. The Communist members naturally had the greatest influence in this office.

Group of Professional Association Members, 1927

[338]

However, this central office's main objective was to improve working conditions and raise salaries, and the greatest efforts were devoted to this goal. The most difficult struggle was with the workshop owners, who had been working long hours themselves and demanded the same from their employees. Long discussions and strenuous negotiations were held before any raise was approved, and sometimes a strike was inevitable. It must be admitted that a great number of the workers were former Bund members.

One of the central office's most difficult fights against the employers was the struggle with the carpenters, headed by one of the most distinguished Bund members.

The workers called a strike and held on stubbornly. The union had many members who had worked for many years under very poor conditions, in crowded workshops, and with the most primitive tools. This struggle was also an attempt to reach the goal of an eight-hour working day, and the carpenters' union was a pioneer in this area. The strike was accompanied by bloody fights with employers and strikebreakers. The strikers were supported financially by progressive groups in town, among them the left-wing Zionist groups. As the stubborn struggle became more and more severe, the authorities found it necessary to intervene. With the help of the Workers' Inspector, the mayor, a former PPS [Polish left-wing Socialist Party] member, exerted heavy pressure on the employers until they yielded to the workers' most important demand: an eight-hour workday. Following this victory, the other unions' demands were granted relatively easily.

This victory boosted the central office's status and authority. Feeling economically powerful, the office now turned to politics. The first elections to the City Council were then occurring in Kremenets. Two Jewish parties registered their candidates: the general Jewish party and the professional unions' party. The election campaign was materially supported by the workers themselves.

At the end of the elections, it was announced that two representatives from the workers' party and ten from the United Citizens Party had been elected. Despite their small number, the workers' representatives played an important role on the City Council, since they constituted the tiebreakers on many votes, particularly when the Jewish bloc stood in opposition to the Christian one. In these cases, the workers' bloc representatives were guided by the class standpoint in their decisions, and their position and vote always aroused great interest.

It often happened, however, that the Jewish workers voted with the Christians against the Jewish councilmembers when the issue was raising taxes for merchants and the well-to-do or raising the rent on town-owned public buildings.

[339]

When the question of subsidies for schools came up, the workers voted against supporting the Talmud Torah and Tarbut schools, asking instead for subsidies for the Yiddish cultural institutions, and often supported the Christian councilmembers.

However, in the discussion about support for the Jewish Hospital, the ORT School, or certain charitable institutions, the workers' representatives voted openly for Jewish causes, and their vote often tipped the scales in favor of the Jewish issue. The Ukrainian and Polish councilmen, whose anti-Semitic tendencies were quite strong, met bold opposition.

The professional associations' dynamic activity continued to expand, and "with food came the appetite," as the saying goes. They began energetic political public relations activity, organizing open lectures in Yiddish and Polish, literary evenings, political self-education, and so on.

At about that time, leadership policy in Poland began to shift quickly toward Fascism. Government representatives in Kremenets began looking around and inspecting the unions' activity. Persecution of labor leaders worsened, and two were arrested on the charge of Communist activity. The labor representatives led an energetic defense campaign, which echoed loudly among the entire Jewish population. Large amounts of money were collected, and the well-known attorney Pascholski and his assistants agreed to conduct the defense. As a result of all these efforts, the two were acquitted at the trial (the first political trial in Kremenets) and set free.

But this was only the beginning of the plan to suppress the labor movement and harass its leaders. Police investigation of professional activists and raids on assembly halls and libraries became frequent occurrences. The May 1 celebrations were closely watched by police agents. It also happened that police broke into the place the night before May 1 and tore down the furniture and decorations prepared for the festivities.

However, neither the persecutions nor the arrests deterred the activities of the responsible labor activists and young intelligentsia. Some were again charged with Communist activity, and a second trial took place. This time, they were all sentenced to many years in prison.

[340]

In February 1937, under central government directives, the Kremenets authorities arrested professional union members en masse, and 36 were accused of belonging to the Ukrainian Communist Party. This was clearly intended to be the deathblow to the labor movement in the East. Indeed, under the influence of terrible fear and panic, the unions' activity was interrupted, and their cultural work was entirely upset. Under the pressure of persecution and difficult economic conditions, some union members immigrated to South America.

The arrested members suffered terrible agony. Provocateurs mingled with them in their cells, and this resulted in more arrests. One of the inmates couldn't endure the suffering and died in prison in great pain.

Finally, there was a trial, which the authorities overstressed and exaggerated, and a grand "accusation ceremony" performance was prepared. The dozens of Jews and Ukrainians who had been arrested were charged with crimes, and, despite the brilliant defense by the attorney Landau and others, they were sentenced to many years in prison.

But none of them finished their prison terms. The Red Army, marching into Eastern Poland, opened the prison gates wide and liberated them all.

As often happens, the veteran political and labor activists found themselves facing an entirely new reality. Some remained loyal to their past, but others began to retreat, in view of the sharpness with which any reality differs from its dream.

THE BUND

Tovye Troshinski (Tel Aviv)
As told by Motye Kornits and others
English translation by Yocheved Klausner

The Jewish Socialist Labor Party "Bund" took its first steps in our town in 1904-1905, on the eve of the first Russian revolution. At about that time, the midwife Yampolskaya, known as Sore Moiseyevna, took up residence in Kremenets. An energetic woman and a very talented speaker, she began to spread Bundist ideas among workers and young members of the intelligentsia. Although most young people leaned toward Zionism in its various manifestations and parties, she managed to organize a small circle of young intellectuals who became engaged in assembling workers in town and teaching them the basics of socialism. It is worth noting that the language at the circle's meetings was Russian at first, because the circle included mostly the intellectuals among the young Jews, and it aimed to demonstrate "progress" and a break with "reactionary" Jewish tradition.

[341]

Only after the Bund had attained a strong position among the Jewish working masses did Yiddish replace Russian—and the Kremenets Bund thus became the stronghold of Yiddishism in town.

The Bund organization was illegal, and it conducted its activities in secret. The meetings took place in the forest or mountains around town, and the Committee met in Moiseyevna's apartment.

When the authorities finally became aware of the illegal activity, they arrested Comrade Yampolskaya and kept her in prison for eight months. When she was released, she left town, after nearly five years of activity.

During that time, a new generation of Bund members had grown up. Among them, we shall mention Yitschak Kremenetski, son of a rich textile merchant, who was arrested with Yampolskaya; Shlome Fingerhut, a conscientious socialist and devoted member of the professional union, who for many years was a City Council member; the two Manusevitsh brothers, dedicated workers in the area of Jewish-Yiddish culture, who helped assemble a collection of folklore during the An-Ski expedition in 1912, and thanks to their successful endeavor, interest in modern Jewish literature increased manifold (they now live in America); Chayim Gibelbank, a teacher, who founded a school where the classroom language was Yiddish, which functioned for a long time; Frants Eydis, Moshe Eydis's son, owner of a drugstore, one of the assimilated rich men in town, and an experienced member of the professional unions, who now lives in Russia; Chanokh Hokhgelernter, a former Zionist who later became a zealous Bundist and Yiddishist, famously knowledgeable in Jewish folklore, who now lives in America and is involved in the cultural activity of the Kremenets Association; Dr. Shklovin, formerly the only female doctor in the town's Children's Homes; and Yonye Grinberg, an attorney, one of the first Bundists in town.

Working with them were the following: the teacher Yitschak Charash was an intelligent and talented educator who was first a teacher of the Russian language, and later specialized in the teaching of Yiddish and was one of the most gifted teachers of that language; the student Gluzman was a Russian teacher; Dora Kimel, daughter of Yechezkel the carpenter, was known by the name Comrade Dvore; Duvid Roykhel, son of a rich merchant, an uncompromising fighter for Yiddish language and literature, moved to Vilna and Warsaw and was Kletskin's partner in his publishing house, authored a series of children's books (details in the *Lexicon* by Zalman Rayzin), later became an active Communist, and now lives in the USSR; Barukh Barshap, nicknamed Kashtan; and many others.

From the list of Bundist active members in various periods, it can be seen that the Bund's aim in Kremenets was to become involved with the townspeople; they were accepted in particular by young intellectuals from bourgeois families, most of them assimilated, who, captivated by the socialist ideals, adopted them and replanted them in Jewish soil.

[342]

Photocopy of a Document of Historical Value: The 1906 Budget Ledger of the Kremenets Bund Organization

[343]

They didn't intend to join the general Russian parties; instead, they preferred to work among their own people and create a Jewish socialist party in town. Through this work, they came in close contact with the Jewish masses and became accustomed to their way of life, and over the course of the years, they expanded their activity in educational and cultural fields as well as in the professional and political domain.

The years 1917-1922 were the blossoming years of the Bund organization in town. With the outbreak of the October Revolution, the Bund tried to win over the Jewish street to its cause, and its members succeeded in obtaining several important social positions. They found an attentive ear among most laborers, youth, and intelligentsia. Their representatives were elected to the Jewish community and City Council. The professional unions were under their influence for some time, until the Communists took control. While the Bund was a minority in the unions, they earned a respected place and played a significant role in the field of culture and popular education. During World War I, the Joint helped open schools for refugees and displaced persons; some of these schools were under the direct influence of the Bund and functioned until 1922. Other institutions in town were equally inspired by the Bund, such as some children's homes, the orphanage, the ORT School, and the Cultural League.

From 1922 on, the Bund began to lose power in Kremenets, its membership diminished, and a decline of its influence on the social and political life followed. The masses of laborers and youth joined the lines of the Zionist pioneer organizations, and union members and their leaders went over to the Communists. Only remnants of the proud Bund of long ago remained loyal to their party, and their activity was mainly cultural and educational.

NOTE FROM THE EDITORIAL BOARD

We have made every effort to obtain a detailed review of the Bund from party members who live in the United States and Argentina, but unfortunately without success. Consequently, we collected information from individuals in Israel who weren't members of the Bund. It is possible, therefore, that the above article is not exhaustive, and some important facts and details may be missing.

[344]

THE COMMUNIST MOVEMENT IN KREMENETS

Manus Goldenberg

In Kremenets, the bloody years of 1918-1920 resulted in a relatively small number of victims. But tension and dread of the day to follow were constantly present.

The few years of revolution inspired the young people of Kremenets with feelings of pride and national awareness. Unfortunately, however, they were not given the opportunity to turn these positive values into action.

Somewhere on the front, Jews were already fighting in the ranks of the Red Army against "White" pogrom armies and gangs of all kinds. Masses of Jewish workers, students, and high school youth volunteered for various Red Army units and soon achieved considerable recognition.

In the summer of 1919, the long-awaited opportunity reached Kremenets. One afternoon, the Jews, who had been watching the streets through attic windows and cracks in the shutters, saw Petliura's well-armed units fleeing in panic. After a short exchange of fire, the first soldiers of the attacking Tarastshanski people were seen arriving in town.

From every street and narrow lane, Jewish residents, young and old, flocked to the town's main street to meet the Red Army soldiers, dusty and full of battle smoke, with red flowers stuck in their caps and bayonets.

The next morning, after the Red Army had established itself in town, young people from all walks of life volunteered. Some of them were so young that the Command had to send them back home at their parents' demand. Many of the volunteers had been known as Communists. Others were members of the Labor Zionist and Bund organizations.

A great surprise for the entire community was the sudden news that Liubkin the Hebrew teacher, a tall young man with a blond beard, a regular member of the Hasidic synagogue, was an ardent follower of the Communists. At the very beginning of Bolshevik rule in town, he was appointed a member of the REVCOM (Revolutionary Committee). He would walk through town with a gun stuck in his belt and give fiery speeches in the same synagogue where in former years he had prayed with great devotion.

Another member of the REVCOM was his young friend Y. Shnayder (mentioned in the article "Alterman's Courtyard"). Among the volunteers in Kremenets was also high school student Tsivya Grinberg, a member of the Young Zionists, who led a circle of students in the study of Zionism and national problems and later joined the Red Army, working very diligently as a Communist Party political commissar.

[345]

Among the first Kremenetsers to join the Communist Party ranks was Bedzieski, son of Bedzieski the paper merchant, a leader of the Labor Zionist Left in Kremenets. He was a passionate speaker, with the qualities of a genius. He as well was rewarded with a high-ranking position in the Ukraine Justice Commissariat.

As we cite the names of some of the first Communists in Kremenets, it is important to mention Shimon Gletshteyn. As early as when he was a pupil in the Russian-Jewish Elementary School, the school principal, Goldfarb, predicted a brilliant future for him. At the age of 18, as a second-year student at the Biological Institute, he devoted himself with all his energy to acts of "agitation." With a group of followers from the Red Army, he traveled from town to town and village to village, giving fiery speeches calling on his listeners to support the revolution. He also organized the so-called Bezvozhniki movement (an antireligious movement during the militaristic Communism era).

After one of the assemblies, in the Great Synagogue in Vishnevets, he and his friends were attacked by an armed mob of incited farmers and cruelly murdered.

We shall mention here Mr. Barenboym as well, who was active in various army delegations after the February revolution. He would often give brilliant speeches at the military meetings that took place in the great piazza near the old market.

There were others, but unfortunately I don't remember their names. Dynamic, stormy characters in their formative years had found a place to unload their burning energy—the civil war battlefield. Very few returned. One of them, Avrasha Bernshteyn, returned a year later at the head of a Cossack unit. The town considered this a miracle of the Revolution: a brave Cossack officer, with a round, fur-trimmed cap, red bands on his trousers, a sword and whip on his side—and all this a Jew, our well-known Avrashke.

Some Kremenetsers, particularly young students, joined the ranks of the active revolution in faraway Russian university towns. The most prominent among them were the Ovadis brothers, two sons of the esteemed and talented Ovadis family. Entering their home, one had the feeling of a warm home and a hub of idealist doers.

[346]

This special atmosphere was created by the father of the family, a learned and liberal activist in the community, Chayim Ovadis, and his educated wife, Berish Perlmuter's daughter. The two sons were mentioned in the Russian press when, as young 15- and 16-year-old boys, they passed Kharkov Polytechnic University's "competition exams." They fought somewhere against Denikin's forces and never returned to Kremenets. There were rumors that one of them fell in battle and that the other became one of the most distinguished engineers in Ukraine.

At the end of summer 1919, the Red units and Communist administration retreated from Kremenets under the pressure of the peasant uprising in the region. Beyond the railroad station, tens of retreating Jewish Red Army soldiers from other regions found their final resting place in a mass grave dug by their own hands. They were surrounded by peasants at the station and were shot, along with some 20 Russian Bolsheviks. Among them were several young men from Kremenets, who were accidentally caught in the area.

In spring 1920, the Semyon Budyoni Riders attacked and invaded Kremenets. The Polish army arrived in a panic from Kiev, and what they managed to do was disarm the town's self-defense units, composed mainly of Jewish young men and discharged soldiers.

For several months, the Communists ruled in Kremenets. The official personnel grew daily, with many Jewish employees among them.

A certain number of school students were employed by the Budyoni army's various military offices, following the fighting units to Lvov. The Communist Youth Organization (Komsomol) was founded, and many students joined its ranks.

In autumn 1920, the era of Polish rule began. We had almost no news from Kremenetsers on the other side of the border. The Polish counterespionage organization, Defensiva, ruled high-handedly and arrested many progressive-thinking residents and other citizens. Even such Zionist leaders as B. Landesberg, Y. Shafir, and others were arrested on suspicion of Communism.

At the same time, strong "Polonization" activity took place. Over the course of several months, the Polish language was introduced as the language of instruction in the Russian schools. The already thin ranks of former Jewish-Russian intelligentsia became almost nonexistent. Some formed the first Pioneer organization and immigrated to the Land of Israel—the first immigrants of the Third Immigration. Others became leaders of Zionist youth organizations. Still others led the professional movements and the Communist organization. A considerable number sought to gain a personal career.

[347]

Soon a second generation grew up. As children, they had lived through the stormy days of the Revolution. Their language—for reading and writing—was Polish. Many young people filled the ranks of the organizations that bloomed in the 1920s: Youth Guard, Young Pioneer, Union, etc. The anti-Semitic activity of all Polish governments, the locked doors of higher education, and the almost total prohibition of immigration to the Land of Israel—all this served as a force that drove the youth of Kremenets, as of other places, toward the Left.

Soviet literature translated into Polish, enthusiastic books, and foreign newspaper reports about the success of huge Soviet construction enterprises excited and attracted young people. Many became devout followers of a group of local Communist leaders who carefully conducted underground propaganda activities.

The Kremenets Communist organization was in close contact with the Communist Party of Western Ukraine, whose main offices were in Lvov. At about that time, the International Society for the Aid of Revolutionaries began to operate in Kremenets. Many young people, who for various reasons had not joined the Communist movement, took part in this organization's activities.

Although it had almost no influence on the masses, Petliura's National Ukrainian Movement did manage to cause disturbances. With the authorities' help, the movement succeeded in winning over part of the peasant youth, especially from among the rich farmers. From the ranks of this movement came a great number of provocateurs, who often caused setbacks to the Communist Party. In general, the Communist Party's influence in rural areas was not very strong.

In contrast, the party managed to attract to active work a large number of gentile shoemakers who lived in the small towns in the vicinity of Kremenets. During the liberation movement in 1939, the Bolsheviks placed some of these shoemakers at the head of the municipal offices; one of them even became mayor.

Often, the Kremenets Communist Party was infiltrated by experienced provocateurs. It suffered a most severe letdown in 1934 at the hand of Trigova, the infamous provocateur.

[348]

During such difficult times, the party's activity centered mostly on self-education in groups of 4-5 people. The group would meet in a private home and study the Communist leaders' teachings. Most of the participants in this activity were the so-called "salon Communists." They were, however, absorbed little by little into the Communist Party mainstream.

The Kremenets police patiently investigated Communist Party activity in Kremenets. They knew the names of the members due to carelessness and unnecessary chatter; their aim was to liquidate the party's leaders.

The Western Ukraine Communist Party's activity assumed a serious and menacing character during the frequent peasant uprisings in Eastern Galicia, whose echoes were heard in the Kremenets region as well.

The police knew very well that the professional movement and widespread cultural activity in Kremenets were almost entirely under Communist Party influence (see "The Professional Movement in Kremenets"). However, since they did not have enough evidence against it, they began harassing the leaders of the professional movement. Finally, the police succeeded in obtaining statements from the weaker party members; based on these statements, several responsible leaders were arrested. The first prisoners were soon released for lack of evidence, but in time the police decided to devote all their energy to uprooting the Communist nest in Kremenets and vicinity.

As early as 1929, the police succeeded in bringing Tovye Tsinberg, a 12th-grade high school student, Hirshke Gun, and two others to trial. They were accused of collecting money for the Communist Party. Thanks to the brilliant defense of Paskhalski and Etinger, the famous lawyers from Warsaw, they were acquitted and released.

The huge expenses of the defense were covered in large part by Kremenets merchants.

A few years passed in relative calm. In 1932, however, the police decided to attack. They spread their net of provocateurs, and with their help, they completed the first stage of the liquidation of the Kremenets Communist Party.

[349]

They arrested Liora Gurevits, Chane Der, Rosye Rozenberg, and Roytberg. Their sentences were 2 to 5 years in prison. Chane Der was pregnant, and her child was born in prison. With great dignity and pride, she survived her suffering in captivity.

The party's second setback occurred in 1934. More than 60 people, Jews and Ukrainians, were accused of belonging to the Communist Party. Among the arrested were Yonye Bernshteyn (during the Nazi occupation, he was leader of the partisan unit in the Kremenets region), Freydiks, Misha Rabinovits, the Trostinetski brothers, and others. The trial lasted several days, and the entire town was in suspense. The stone building where the trial took place was surrounded by armed police.

Among others, the Polish engineer Shprung attracted general attention. He was employed by the Ministry of Agriculture in the Division of Economic Development. Since he was in close contact with the Communists in Kremenets, he served as mediator—he was a reserve officer, and he appeared in court wearing the highest decoration for bravery in the Polish army, which he had received during the Polish-Soviet war.

His appearance before the judges severely harmed the ruling Polish circles. With pride, he stepped forward and responded to the judge's accusations, stating that it was not worth fighting a war for the Poland that they had created. His dignified stand encouraged the other Communists and their stricken parents.

Almost all the accused were sentenced to long terms in prison. The terrible pain suffered by the accused during the investigation did not stop after the sentences were pronounced. One of the Trostinetski brothers, who suffered from heart disease, died in prison. During the Soviet rule in Kremenets in 1939, a street was named after them.

The last arrests in Kremenets were in 1936. Some of the Communist Party intelligentsia fell into the hands of the police, among them Sime Makagon, Misha Rabinovits (who had been acquitted in the previous trial), and Meir Pintshuk's wife. Pintshuk himself was arrested somewhere in the Vilna area. He had been a well-known underground activist in the Communist Party.

During Bolshevik rule in Kremenets, Pintshuk and his wife headed the high school.

[350]

These people who were accused and tried in 1936 were also sentenced to long terms in prison, 5 to 10 years. Others were sent to the concentration camp in Bereza Kartuska as administrative punishment. Among them were Avraham Rayz and Aynbinder. All imprisoned Communists were liberated by Soviet soldiers after the collapse of Poland.

A considerable number of Communist Party members fell in the battles of World War II. Some survived and, after the war ended, were scattered in Russia, Poland, and over the entire world. It is not known how many remained faithful to the ideals of their youth and how many became disenchanted.

In the Jewish and Polish press from that time, we can find traces of the sharp reaction of Polish progressive opinions against the pain that those accused of Communism had to suffer in the Kremenets, Lutsk, Lublin, and other prisons. This was a chapter of youth martyrology in which young Kremenetsers played a significant part.

Group of Youth Guard members in 1931

[351]

old-style house

[352]

[blank]

[353]

PROMINENT FIGURES

TSVI PRILUTSKI

English translation by Yocheved Klausner

From *Lexicon of Jewish Literature, Press, and Philology*, Zalman Rayzen, 1927, Vilna, B. Kletskin Publishers.

Tsvi Prilutski was born in Kremenets, Volhynia, to a rich merchant family. His father, a friend of the RYB"L, raised him in the spirit of the Enlightenment movement and let him study foreign languages—Russian, German, and French—in addition to Jewish studies. In 1880, he studied at Kiev University and later at the University of Berlin. In his youth, he was a correspondent for Hebrew periodicals, where he made his debut with the article "Return to Zion" in the periodical *Haboker Or* in 1880. He took an active part in the Love of Zion movement from the time it was established, and before the elections he traveled a great deal and campaigned for the idea of Jewish settlements in the Land of Israel. He was a member of the Sons of Moses Order, and in the 1890s he wrote a regular column, titled *Pinkas Katan*, in the *Hamelits* newspaper, where he wrote about the need to settle the Land of Israel. He argued with Moshe Leyb Lilienblum about Jewish labor in the Land of Israel, disputed Ahad Ha'am's impressions of his trip to the Land of Israel in a series of 100 articles, and participated in the newspaper *Hatsefira* when it was still against "Palestinism."

> [**Translator's Note:** *Haboker Or* means *Morning Light,* and *Pinkas Katan* means *Little Notebook.*]

In 1900, following a business failure, Prilutski left Kremenets and relocated to Petersburg, and from then on, he devoted himself entirely to journalism. Until 1903, he was a member of the *Hamelits* editorial board and was its political editor for a time. He wrote many articles under various names (Bar Galuta, Ben Terach, etc.) and anonymously. Later, he wrote for the Petersburg newspaper *Hazman* and the Russian-Yiddish weekly *Bodushtshnust,* and contributed to the Jewish anthology *Yevreyski Yezhegodnik,* published in 1902, writing articles about Y. L. Gordon and Dr. S. Pinsker, a review of the Zionist movement, etc.

> [**Translator's Note:** The titles of these three publications translate as *Time, The Future,* and *Jewish Yearbook,* respectively].

He wrote in Yiddish for the first time in Leon Rabinovitsh's *Pages from a Diary.* As early as 1902, he began lobbying for a permit to publish a Yiddish newspaper, but he did not receive the permit until the "political spring" in Russia. He founded a new newspaper in Warsaw; one of the editorial board members was the engineer Y. B. Ipa, who was dedicated to propagating culture among the Jewish people through the Yiddish language. On August 14, 1905, the first issue of the first Jewish newspaper in

Poland, *Der Weg,* appeared, with the collaboration of Dr. Eliashev, H. D. Namberg, Dr. Vartman, A. L. Yakobovitsh, L. Shapira, and Duvid Druk and with contributions from famous Jewish writers.

> [**Translator's Note:** *Der Weg* means *The Way.*]

[354]

As a result of internal frictions and other difficulties, the publisher, who had added 25,000 rubles from his own pocket to the expenses, withdrew from the enterprise, and *Der Weg* closed after two months of existence. It had opened again by the end of November, but it still encountered many problems. Prilutski tried to overcome them in various ways, such as by adding an evening edition, collaborating with the Hebrew daily *Hayom* (the newspaper run by Y. Ch. Zagaradski and partners Mikhel Veber and A. L. Yakobovitsh) and other means; however, the entire enterprise finally ended in 1906. About that time, S. Y. Yatskan began publishing the newly founded newspaper *Yiddishes Togeblatt.*

> [**Translator's Note:** *Hayom* means *Today,* and *Yiddishes Togeblatt* means *Jewish Daily.*]

As a means of dealing with competition from the first cooperative Yiddish newspaper, *Unzer Leben,* published beginning February 18, 1907, by M. Spektor and S. Hokhberg, Prilutski was hired as the main correspondent, and for four years he wrote general political reviews in his column, *Moment.* On November 18, 1910, his son, Noach Prilutski, succeeded in starting a new daily, which he titled *Moment,* with Prilutski as editor-in-chief. This newspaper underwent various changes, adapting to changes in the European world, and became the strongest Jewish newspaper in Poland. In July 1914, a noon edition, titled *Radio,* appeared as well. In 1921, *Almanac in Honor of the 10th Anniversary of* Moment appeared (Warsaw, 232 pp, with photographs of the newspaper staff). In it, Prilutski published an important work, "The Role of the Jewish Woman in Modern Jewish Civic Life."

> [**Translator's Note:** *Unzer Leben* means *Our Life.*]

MIKHEL BARSHAP

English translation by Yocheved Klausner

Mikhel Barshap, or "Mikhel the Lame," as he was called, was a unique type. Everybody knew him; if an "organization" was in any measure important, then Mikhel no doubt was its "guiding light."

Twenty-four hours a day, Mikhel Barshap made his room the center of discussions between parties, as was the custom in many cities and towns.

He came from a respected but impoverished family, was orphaned as a young boy, and was forced to leave the cheder before he even knew the prayers properly. He learned a trade—painting houses. Unfortunately, tragedy struck while he was working: he fell from a balcony, and although he recovered, he remained an invalid. While he lay in the hospital, he learned to read.

In 1904-1905, he sympathized with the Bund, but when the Labor Zionists were founded, he joined. He devoted most of his time, however, to working for the Jewish National Fund.

Since he was alone and an invalid, the community arranged a place for him in the Home for the Aged. There, too, he worked for the Jewish National Fund. The money he helped collect was used to register Yosef Rozenfeld of Berdichev, founder of the first Jewish Workers' Circle, and Yitschak Ber Levinzon in the Jewish National Fund Golden Book.

[355]

In time, his friends took him out of the Home and arranged work for him at the Zionist library, selling cookies and helping out as a watchman.

But for various reasons he was ruined again and returned to the Home for the Aged, nevertheless continuing his work for the Jewish National Fund. He died in 1936.

His funeral was arranged by the Zionist Organization, and his coffin was covered with the Zionist flag.

VOLF GORNFELD (1862-1940)

***Kremenitser Shtime*, 11.4.1930**
English translation by Yocheved Klausner

Volf Gornfeld was active in Jewish civic life. He was a founder of the ORT School and a member of its administration for many years. He was active in the community and Merchants' Union as well. He was president of the Burial Society and helped spread the idea of learning a useful trade among the Jews.

Three of his sons and their families were murdered by the Nazis. The other children survived, including a daughter, who is a music teacher in Haifa.

Volf Gornfeld

M. B. GOLDFARB

T.

M. B. Goldfarb was born in Ostrog in 1850. After graduating from the Rabbinical Seminary in Zhitomir, he was appointed teacher in Chernigov, where he worked for five years.

For the next 14 years, he was director of schools in Zaslav, Rovno, and Radzivilov, and then he was transferred to the Kremenets school, where he served for 26 years. In 1916, he retired with a lifetime pension.

In addition to his educational and pedagogic work, he contributed a great deal to civic life in the community.

In the 1880s, during and after the pogroms, he supported and helped desperate Jewish emigrants—who left their towns in masses and fled wherever they could—and tried, thanks to his good relations with high-ranking officials, to help them cross the Russian-Austrian border at Radzivilov.

[356]

In 1903, he helped establish the School of Commerce in Kremenets. He was a member of the City Council for several years.

Because of all his merits and activity, he was not forgotten in his old age. On the initiative of several of his students, a committee was formed to celebrate his 80th birthday. On March 8, 1930, all his former students gathered in the Zionist Organization hall to honor their great teacher.

*M. B. Goldfarb in Front of
the Jewish Primary School*

MEIR GOLDRING (1886–1942)

English translation by Steven Wien and by Rabbi and Mrs. Ben Zion Friedman

Meir Goldring

Meir Goldring, may his memory be blessed, was one of the most prominent community activists in Kremenets. For more than a quarter of a century, he held top leadership positions in the Jewish community and served the interests of the Jewish people. A man of character, he fought for his principles and influenced others. He was active in community institutions in all areas and was an active Zionist. The Jewish community treated him with honor and complete trust.

In his writings and speeches, Meir Goldring campaigned for the Jewish Community Council to encompass all branches of Jewish life and to become a truly uniting Jewish entity. As the first step toward accomplishing this, he sought to use the full rights allowed by the Community Council regulations, even though those rights were limited to religious activities. He campaigned for confirmation of the Community Council budget to ensure the needed funds and for its takeover of the cemetery.

The following words, with which he ended an article in the *Kremenitser Shtime* concerning Community Council queries, are characteristic of him. "... The Community Council is the kernel of our self-determination, just as the magistrate is, and if we pay taxes to the magistrate, we must pay taxes to the Jewish Community Council. We will then surely show an interest in how these taxes are being spent. We will also want to ensure that the Jewish Community Council budget does not exceed the present financial capabilities of the impoverished Jewish masses on whom we are depending to sustain the budget."

This was also Meir Goldring's approach to all branches of Jewish and Zionist community work. His concern, first and foremost, was for the Jewish common folk. He campaigned with energy on his views, and it is no wonder that there were unscrupulous people who fought a nasty battle against him. It came to a point that approximately 60 representatives from all the community-based institutions came together in the Community Council and decried these attacks. Special resolutions were then undertaken emphasizing complete loyalty to Meir Goldring, and these were publicized in all synagogues. Also, about 300 people from over 20 organizations participated in a special banquet held in his honor. This banquet was an expression of love and loyalty to Goldring, the honest and energetic community activist. His 50th birthday was also celebrated with great pomp.

Kremenitser Shtime, of which he was the founder and editor, was an important factor in the lives of Jewish Kremenets. This weekly reflected local character, informed readers about everything that happened in the town and province, and campaigned for Jewish interests. *Kremenitser Shtime* was a part of his life and the life of Kremenets.

Weekly, he worried about the uninterrupted production of the paper and wrote much of its contents, and he was the living spirit of the newspaper. For years, the newspaper was printed and honestly served the interests of the Jewish people. Meir Goldring died in the slaughter of Kremenets. He served the Jewish people honestly his whole life.

[357]

AVRAHAM YAKOV VAYNBERG

English translation by Steven Wien and Rabbi and Mrs. Ben Zion Friedman

In 1931, the first head of the newly established democratic Community Council of Kremenets, Avraham Yakov Vaynberg, passed away. He earned that position honestly and upheld it with honor until the Community Council dissolved for various reasons. This caused him great heartache and pain.

A. Y. Vaynberg was a Jew, a scholar of stature and fine character. He was tolerant and almost never reacted to the injustices against him in the Community Council.

An industrialist, he was the proprietor of the famous foundry off the highway near the Vishnevets town gate, in partnership with Chayim Ovadis and Fishel Perlmuter. A Jew who was an industrialist was uncommon in those days. He was quite knowledgeable about the technical side of production.

A Zionist in his heart and soul, he left all his assets, including his extensive library, to the Jewish National Fund. It is noteworthy that the Jewish Community Council owed him money, and as a result he suffered financially.

He was a fine role model of a Jewish community activist. In Kremenets, they greatly grieved his untimely passing.

CHAYKEL OF KREMENETS (CHAYKEL BERNSHTEYN)

Yitschak Vakman (New York)
English translation by Steven Wien and Rabbi and Mrs. Ben Zion Friedman

He was a model of a proper Jewish gentleman, full of respect, of medium height with a full beard. He lived in his apartment in Shmoler Street, close to Shimon Beker, on the second floor. His apartment had large rooms that overlooked the Potik. He was a Jew who gave charity anonymously with an open hand. His wife was Chane, Avraham Moshe's daughter. Whoever did not see this couple at a Purim feast has never seen a beautiful sight. The table was bedecked with all kinds of goodies, and all the children, cousins, and grandchildren were required to be at the feast. R' Chaykel had a large golden chain on his vest; Chane wore a silken frock and a string of pearls around her neck, and her kind eyes sparkled with happiness and joy.

[358]

One morning, after a sleepless night, as R' Chaykel Bernshteyn was sitting at the window and looking outside, he saw the woman who carried milk around to sell. She was pouring some water from the pond into the milk container. About an hour later, she reached R' Chaykel's house, and he said to her, smiling: Until now I never knew how you make the milk "kosher," but today I saw how you do it. Please, from now on, bring me the milk and the pond water separately, and I will "kosher" the milk myself....

R' Chaykel had two sons and three daughters. They and their children all perished. Only five grandchildren survived: Rive and Tsire Bernshteyn in Israel, Beyle Bernshteyn in Argentina, Yitschak Vinshtin in England, and Aharon German in Jerusalem.

ELI CHAYKEL'S (BERNSHTEYN)

Manus Goldenberg
English translation by Yocheved Klausner

Eli Chaykel's

From time to time, figures from my past float before my eyes, figures whose personalities were warmhearted and sparkled with good humor, Jews who spent their days and nights working for the good of the community without seeking any profit or honor. One of those people in our town was Eli Chaykel's (Bernshteyn).

Somehow, from the time I was a child, I felt especially close to this Jew, with his yellowish beard and shining eyes, and was always ready to forgive him the pinch he gave my cheek .... These feelings were no doubt at least in part because Eli Chaykel's was a forest dealer. With his furrowed neck and beard, he reminded me of an old tree somewhere in the woods, where he actually spent most of his years.

In my mind, he was entirely different from all the other Jews in that he earned his living not by studying Torah or selling things in a little store; he was a Jew who smelled of pine trees, and on stormy days as well as in the burning heat, he could be found somewhere between forest and field, under the free sky. He was also trusted and loved by the gentiles, with whom he had business dealings.

Whether in the company of peasants or Jews, he was always ready with a Jewish or Ukrainian saying or joke, which put everyone in a good mood.

Eli was firmly rooted in our town. He had absorbed the town's rich folklore, passed down to him through generations; he always quoted sayings from and told stories about Jews who had lived many years before. His many charitable acts were always accompanied by a joke or funny saying, which made the situation of the needy, on the receiving end, more pleasant and easier.

[359]

While he worked hard to make a living for his own family, he devoted a great deal of time to helping the poor in town, and he did so secretly so as not to embarrass them. He was the president of the organizations for accommodating guests, helping needy brides, and visiting the sick. He considered sitting up all night by a sick person's bed an important commandment, and every year, on Yom Kippur eve, he would eat the midday meal with the residents of the Home for the Aged. Often he was called to serve as an arbiter in disputes.

His work in distributing matzos for Passover fairly and justly to the needy is especially worth mentioning. To make sure the matzos were of good quality and ready on time, he took an important step: several months before Passover, he and some of his friends signed promissory notes for a great sum of money and bought a matzo-baking machine. In a short time, he opened a matzo bakery, so he was able to provide matzos to all the needy. Many nights, he would go without sleep and supervise the work in the bakery, and his joy was enormous when he saw porters with white baskets carrying matzos to the most remote and isolated corners of the town. Just like the well-to-do, the needy had matzos several weeks before Passover.

He took care of the children of the poor, too. He was like a father to them. Whenever he saw a child without shoes or proper clothing, he would not rest until the child was clothed and had shoes. When the yeshiva in Kremenets was active, he was a member of the management and devoted a great deal of energy to ensure its existence and proper functioning.

He belonged to every charity organization in town. More than once, he had to fight with his wife, who would argue, not without reason, that his limitless devotion to others prevented him from taking care of his own family.

The Kremenets Jews understood and appreciated his activities and helped his causes willingly. His devotion was catching.

But he, too, like all the others, did not survive the horrible suffering and destruction. His wife, Shifre, his son, Yitschak, and his youngest daughter, Pola, perished with him.

DR. ARYE LANDSBERG (?-1932)

English translation by Yocheved Klausner

The Landsberg family was famous in Kremenets. The golden chain of Zionism passed through three generations of the family. The first was Chayim, the father, who was part of the Enlightenment Movement and the early Zionist movement, Lovers of Zion.

The son, Arye, studied medicine and was a Zionist with all his heart and soul. As a Jewish doctor, he was devoted to the Jewish people, cherished the Jewish tradition, and contributed to Jewish causes, the first being the Jewish National Fund and the Foundation Fund. He made his contributions modestly, and even his closest friends did not know that in 1917 he donated 500 rubles to the Jewish National Fund to build houses for Yemenite immigrants in the Land of Israel.

[360]

He was an honorary member of the Odessa committee for Jewish settlement in the Land of Israel.

Professionally, he worked hard and was devoted to his patients. It was no wonder that everybody admired and respected him.

He was a delegate to the Eighth Zionist Congress in Basel, and from there he went on a trip to the Land of Israel. On his return, he inspired the entire Zionist movement in Kremenets and instilled in everyone the desire to work for Zionism.

In times when Zionist activity was forbidden, he would receive Zionist books and journals under the cover of medical literature and then distribute them among organization members, who worked illegally.

Dr. Arye Landsberg was one of the first to work for the Zionist Organization. His son, the talented lawyer Binyamin Landsberg, was the third in the family to follow this path and dedicate himself to the Zionist movement.

May his memory be forever honored.

DR. MEIR LITVAK (1861-1932)

English translation by Yocheved Klausner

Dr. Meir Litvak

One of the most beautiful personalities in Jewish Kremenets was Dr. Meir Litvak, of blessed memory.

He was born to poor parents, graduated from primary school, went to the Gymnasium in Zhitomir, and studied medicine. After becoming a doctor, he returned to his hometown and settled there. Everybody knew Dr. M. Litvak, who was always ready to help Jewish Kremenets. He was the first chairman of the Lovers of Zion group and took an active part in the founding of the School of Commerce, the reorganization of the Talmud Torah, and the establishment of the cooperatives, the ORT School, and the Hebrew Tarbut School—whenever the community planned to found a new institution, Dr. Litvak was the one to go to for assistance. His influence was a great help when the time came to buy a home for the Talmud Torah. When he was in America, he helped acquire the means to buy a building for the Society for Welcoming and Accommodating Guests. For a time, he was president of the Great Synagogue.

He was a founding member of TOZ, the Polish health and relief society, where he sometimes lectured on hygiene.

He was very active in the field of Zionism, and for many years he was chairman of the Zionist Organization. Here is a characteristic occurrence: in 1904, an illegal Zionist meeting was held, and suddenly some high official appeared and made a list of all those present.

[361]

Dr. Litvak had left the meeting earlier, but when he heard what had happened, he went to the authorities and asked to be added to the list of the persons who participated in the illegal meeting.

He was an upright and honest communal worker. At the end of his life, when he found that he could not fully agree with the new ways of the social work organization, he withdrew.

By profession he was a medical doctor, and everyone sought his help. No wonder, then, that in 1904, when he was drafted into the army as a military doctor during the Russian-Japanese war, the Jewish population in Kremenets was distressed and alarmed. He was given five days to get to Harbin. Until the day before his departure, he continued his regular daily work and also spent time with his family; he felt that it was his duty to take care of the sick who came to him up to the last minute.

Dr. Litvak at His Father's Grave

He left for Harbin and was assigned to a military hospital in Khabarovsk. He served there until October 11, 1905, when he was discharged and sent home.

It is difficult to describe the joy in Kremenets when Dr. M. Litvak returned. The joy of the Jewish population was mixed with pride when it was reported that he had been promoted to the rank of general as a reward for his devoted and professional medical work. The hearts of Kremenets Jews filled with happiness to see him in uniform with the insignia on his shoulders—and all this during the Czar's rule.

Dr. Litvak shortly returned to his professional life and community activities. For many more years, he cared for his patients, who trusted him completely, and served Jewish society and the Zionist movement with deeds and advice.

In later years, he participated in the local press as well, publishing articles on various subjects. He had the courage to fight all negative phenomena in society and demanded that they be addressed and that improvements be made.

He was an admirer of RYB"L and considered himself one of his students. He devoted his time to the preservation of his memory, and helped create the library in his name and preserve the house where he had lived. During his visit to America in 1928, he obtained funding for these purposes.

[362]

As mentioned above, Dr. Litvak was born to poor parents. His father, whose name was Aba, was a tailor who was proud of his profession. Dr. Litvak was called "Abatshe the tailor's son."

Dr. Litvak was trusted by Jews and Christians alike, and he was employed as the doctor of the Pravoslavic Religious Seminary. Every Simchat Torah, he would organize a special festive morning service for children.

He passed away at a ripe old age.

Dr. Litvak's Funeral and Monument

[363]

The entire town—young and old, rich and poor, Jews, Ukrainians, and Poles—walked behind his coffin and escorted him to his final resting place. Representatives from each of these three nations eulogized him, and all felt Kremenets' great loss. His name will always be cherished in the memories and hears of all who knew him or heard about him.

RABBI SHRAGA-ARYE MARDER

M. Sambirer, *Kremenitser Leben*
English translation by Yocheved Klausner

Last Thursday, 2 Shevat 5697 [January 14, 1937], Rabbi Shraga-Arye, of blessed memory, rabbi of the Dubno suburb, died at the age of 80 years. Rabbi Shraga-Arye was from the old school of rabbis, the former generation, who excelled in scholarship and Talmud knowledge. As a young man, he was already a Torah and Talmud teacher, and his students occupied important rabbinic posts, such as rabbi of Radzivilov and rabbi of Shumsk, of blessed memory.

Rabbi Fayvish Marder was famous for his great caution and strict judgment in the matter of religious Responsa, astuteness in study, and intelligence and capability when sitting in judgment in the religious court. He was involved in the community and had a great understanding of life and society, and he followed the path of Torah and piety with modesty and determination.

His funeral was on a Friday. In spite of the very cold winter day, a large crowd from the town and the Dubno suburb came to pay him their last respects. The local rabbi, M. Mendiuk, delivered an inspiring eulogy and described Rabbi Marder's personality and character. Addressing the deceased, he concluded with the following words: "You can rest in peace, rabbi of our town, because your Torah and good deeds will be with you in your eternal rest, and your work is carried on by your son-in-law, a Torah scholar, a worthy and talented man, who is appreciated and loved by all." After Rabbi Mendiuk, the head of the religious court delivered another eulogy.

SHIMON CHAYIM MOLIAR (KARSH)

Yitschak Vakman, New York
English translation by Yocheved Klausner

Shimon Chayim was a bricklayer, one of the very few Jews in the community who had this profession.

It was obvious that he would be a devoted Zionist. Somehow "Zionist" and "bricklayer," or "Land of Israel" and "builder," seemed to fit together naturally. He joined the movement early, during the period of the Lovers of Zion movement. The members of the Zionist Organization were proud of this productive man, who was a member and a friend.

He was always composed and in a good mood, except when the subject was the Land of Israel. Whenever somebody started a discussion or an argument on this matter, he became another person—unrecognizable. His bearded face would burst into flames, his hands would move up and down, and it was dangerous to be around him.

"Your tragedy is exactly this," he would argue. "You want to wait until the Messiah comes on his white horse! Until then, who knows what will become of us."

All week long he was seen in his working clothes, always busy at work.

[364]

He was an expert at putting up chimneys and ovens, and he always had the upper hand over his competitors, the Christian bricklayers. His ovens never smoked. And although his prices were higher, there was a long waiting list—sometimes months long—for his services. He would come with his helpers (his sons), and for few workdays they would bring a Zionist atmosphere to the house: words like shekels, Jewish National Fund, Baron Rothschild, Herzl, etc. filled the air.

At the beginning of World War I, Shimon Chayim was the only builder trustworthy enough to engage in building secret hiding places in houses, where young Jews could hide to avoid being sent to the battlefields. These places were built with such skill that the police very seldom discovered them. He carried out this work with special pleasure because of his limitless hatred for the czarist regime. When the Russian troops began retreating and soldiers were sometimes seen running along the streets, and the Austrian army was heard approaching, he could be seen dancing in the street. He was one of the first to call to the Jews to leave their hiding places and voluntarily join the army after the revolution.

During the Polish occupation, when a strong movement for immigration to the Land of Israel began, Shimon Chayim and his family started to think about immigrating. To begin the fulfillment of this idealist dream, he bought a goat and preached about working the land in the Land of Israel.

Not even one of his family members attained this goal.

MENDEL KARSH

Manus Goldenberg
English translation by Yocheved Klausner

Mendel Karsh

Looking back at the destroyed past, some personalities stand out, shedding a shining light on their surroundings. These were the communal workers, always busy and acting for the good of society, simple people about whom the biblical verse "He that has clean hands and a pure heart" (Psalms 24:4) is appropriate; they had a deep trust and belief in humanity and the human conscience, and devoted their time and effort to the benefit of others, ready to help their suffering brothers at any opportunity. As we do with rare treasures, we shall always safeguard their memory.

One of these personalities was Mendel Karsh, a "man of the people" in the best sense of the word. The friendly smile on his broad face expressed a warm heart and radiated friendship, trust, and determination. A thin veil of pride grew around him—the pride of distinction, but distinction of a special kind: he was proud of his excellence at his profession, which passed from father to son; he was a member of the only family of Jewish builders in the entire neighborhood.

[365]

His father, Shimon Chayim, would mention on any occasion his connection with "my Mendel." It was indeed true that Mendel brought his father great satisfaction and happiness during his short life. He was an excellent pupil in the cheder and Talmud Torah. But Shimon Chayim's sons were not born to be Torah scholars. None of them betrayed their father's profession: they did not replace the toolbox and the hammer with the yardstick and scales or with the scissors and iron.

Mendel left school in his early youth to help his father. However, he absorbed enough Jewish knowledge to be able to cite, on occasion, a verse from the Torah or a saying from the Talmud. In later years, he continued his self-education by reading and absorbed a great deal of Hebrew and Yiddish culture from the written media of the times.

By 1905, he was one of the most active members of the Labor Zionists in Kremenets. He was so devoted that he and the party were considered one. When the Labor Zionists were mentioned, Mendel Karsh came to mind, and the opposite was true as well: it was enough to mention the name Karsh and the Labor Zionist organization came to life.

Later, during the Polish occupation, when the Labor Zionists ceased to exist and its leading members followed the retreating Bolsheviks, Mendel joined the General Zionist party and was elected to various committees. There he represented the "left wing" of the party. He was particularly active in Jewish National Fund functions, where he was strongly supported by his friend Mekhel Barshap, who initiated many of the Jewish National Fund meetings.

When the first Pioneer groups were organized in Kremenets, it was clear to all that Mendel would be the best leader for the training groups. He employed some of the Pioneers in bricklaying and was himself a candidate for immigration in the second group, which was scheduled to go to the Land of Israel in 1921. Unfortunately, I cannot remember what prevented him from carrying out his decision. Perhaps it was family matters, money difficulties, or his illness.

He supported various charitable institutions with the same enthusiasm that he devoted to politics and party activity. When the Jewish Hospital's situation became difficult, Mendel was called on for help, and with his energy and skill, he was able to provide the necessary support. It was the same with other charitable societies—he would carry the heaviest burden. The people had the greatest respect for him, admired his honesty, integrity, and fine character, and valued his words. Even in the Burial Society, which was continuously plagued with disputes, Mendel's word was enough to help a decision along.

He died in 1931, at the age of 41, at the peak of his activity.

[366]

RABBI YECHIEL YITSCHAK RAPAPORT

K. R.
English translation by Yocheved Klausner

Rabbi Yechiel Yitschak Rapaport was born in Lodz in 5656 [1896] to poor parents. As a very young man, he was recognized as a prodigy and was ordained as a rabbi. His scholarship and erudition in Talmud and legal scholarship was admired. He was married at 17 and continued his Jewish as well as secular studies. He belonged to the Mizrachi Zionist party and helped disseminate the idea of religious Zionism. He was a brilliant speaker.

Rabbi Yechiel Yitschak Rapaport

His first position as rabbi was in Zychlin. He traveled to neighboring towns and villages, spoke about the importance of religious Zionism, and founded Mizrachi groups. At the age of 21, he was appointed chief rabbi in Lutsk. He visited Kremenets, among other towns, and established the Mizrachi organization, with the participation of the chief rabbi at that time, Rabbi Senderovits, of blessed memory.

In 1923, Rabbi Rapaport was a candidate to the Polish Parliament for the "National Bloc" and conducted an energetic election campaign.

In 1928, the position of chief rabbi in Kremenets was vacated, and he was appointed rabbi. The first year was quite distressing, since his opponents did not approve of his appointment, but their activity was not successful.

Rabbi Rapaport developed a very serious eye illness and was operated on, but his general health deteriorated. He began suffering from heart disease as well and died in the prime of his life—35 years of age—in 5691 [1931]. His death caused grief not only in Kremenets but in all the towns he had visited during his short life.

He had two aspirations in his life: that his son-in-law, Rabbi Mendiuk, would be appointed his successor and that a collection of his sermons and lectures, *Or Hayahadut*, would appear in print. Both his wishes were realized.

On his first memorial day, one year after his death, his gravestone was erected. Moving eulogies were held in the cemetery and in the synagogue. A special edition of *Kremenitser Shtime* was devoted to his memory, with articles by his son-in-law, Rabbi Y. M. Mendiuk; the head of the community, A. Perlmuter; L. Feldman; Dr. M. Litvak; M. Ditun; D. Levinton; and A. Sambarer.

His youngest daughter, her husband, and their child live in Israel.

REMEMBRANCES AND CUSTOMS

THE ANSKI "EXPEDITION" IN KREMENETS

Chanokh Gilernt (New York)
English translation by Yocheved Klausner

At the beginning of the 20th century in Kremenets, as in other provincial towns in czarist Russia, most young people lived a traditional religious life. Except for a small percentage of children—about several hundred—who studied at government or private schools, the great majority of children went to the cheder or Talmud Torah. Sometimes, a well-to-do family paid the tuition for children from poor families.

After graduating from the cheder, most middle-class children were given a taste of general knowledge by private teachers and "writers." In general, the children took on their parents' occupations. In addition to the many shopkeepers and religious communal workers, there were carpenters, shingle makers, tinsmiths, turners, coopers (barrelmakers), wheel makers, glaziers, shoemakers, leatherworkers, secondhand clothing dealers, furriers, tailors, seamstresses, grinders, watchmakers, jewelers, candle makers, brick makers, bakers, porters, etc. Butcher and water carrier were occupations that didn't attract our young people. Some, however, became clerks in various offices, pharmacy employees, and photographers.

Until 1905, there was no labor union in any form. Most young people were employed at home by their parents. The only products that reached the general market in Russia came from Hertse and Dvore Frishberg's shoe factory, which employed some 20 workers.

The beginning of the 20th century was marked by a significant increase in young people's and adolescents' aspirations for a more extended foreign education. These aspirations might have never been realized if not for the year 1905, which brought about a great change in their attitude toward Jewish life, based, as they hoped, on modern foundations.

The various Jewish political groups formed at the time, such as Zionism, Bundism, and Zionist territorialism, awakened young people's national-political and sociocultural consciousness. The former course of study, which was aimed at advancing one's personal career, suddenly changed, giving way to the aspiration to become a "Jewish national being."

Yiddish became important and replaced Russian. The Jewish worker, the "Folk's Man," suddenly acquired more weight in the young intelligentsia's eyes. Jewish newspapers and journals were found more and more often in Jewish homes: *Unserleben, Moment, Der Freind, Hazman, Hatsefira, Dos Yiddishe Folk, Leben un Wissenschaft, Der Weg*, and others. Jewish journals in Russian appeared as well. The monthly *Die Yiddishe Welt*, published by the Vilna Kletskin Publishing House, had immediate success, as did the illegal newspaper *Die Zeit*, published in Petersburg. Of the Jewish dailies in Russian, only two—both with a liberal orientation—were widespread, one in Kiev and the other in Petersburg. Even the Radzin Hasid R' Moshe from Berezhtsy would bring *Der Freind* to the synagogue and read it aloud between the afternoon and evening prayers. Binyamin Yaspe, Tsadok the ritual slaughterer's son, would translate when needed and explain the difficult passages. His house was full of newspapers and books, which the entire family read.

> [**Translator's Note:** The names of these periodicals are as follows: *Unserleben,* Our Life; *DerError! Bookmark not defined. Freind,* The Friend; *Hazman;* The Times], *Hatsefira,* The Siren; *Dos Yiddishe Folk,* The Jewish Nation; *Leben un Wissenschaft,* Life and Science; *Der Weg,* The Road; *Die Yiddishe Welt,* The Jewish World; *Die Zeit,* Time.]

Books published by Warsaw publishers Shimin and Central, and later by Vilna Kletskin, were read diligently. When salesman Y. Trivaus appeared with samples of book covers from the works of Mendele, Peretz, and Shalom Aleichem, his work was easy: all sets were ordered immediately. The self-appointed acquirer of any printed word, Duvid Roykhel, who came from a well-to-do religious family, was the king of the "Yiddishists" in Kremenets. During World War I, he lived in Vilna, where he translated children's stories from Russian and German. Later, during Polish rule, he translated Buchbinder's history of the Jewish labor movement from Russian into Yiddish. Working as a cashier in his father's large store, he often paid for entire shipments of Yiddish books, which he then distributed to Jewish homes and Jewish youth. Luckily, he was on friendly terms with the police, who agreed to "look the other way" when illegal Russian brochures from the Social Democrats were added to the shipments. These brochures were kept hidden by Aharon Hokhgelernter, Leybele the ritual slaughterer's son, until they were taken to the attic of a house to be bound and distributed. Other activists were Mekhel Barshap, the invalid, and Yashe Broytman, Shlome the baker's Zionist son, who was a popular lecturer on Zionism in Russian. Yeshayahu Belohuz, a wealthy family's only son, would take anything printed in all three languages.

After the Czernowitz Conference, Kremenets youth began spreading Jewish culture with renewed energy. They read thirstily, in particular scientific articles about Yiddish by N. Shtif and B. Borokhov.

[369]

At the same time, they established illegal courses for adolescents and illegal schools for children. The main supporters of the illegal schools were Duvid Roykhel; Yeshayahu Belohuz; Yashe Broytman; M. Biberman; the two seamstress sisters, Feyge and Mindel; Ch. Gilernt; Barukh Barshap; and Gutye Aksel, Fishel the porter's daughter. However, the school's existence became known after a short time, and they relocated to the kitchen of Avraham the butcher, Feyge and Mindel's father. Classes were held at night, when the parents were busy at the slaughterhouse. But Kalman, the police officer's helper ("Kalman with the 'marble' below his eye"), became interested in the two sisters and watched them, so he noticed the school and let them know he was aware of its existence. They were forced to wander again, this time to Moshe Kadushke the water carrier's attic. All this happened during the winter. In the summertime, they held classes in a little forest near the town. This was also the fate of the adults' evening courses and the library, which was generally managed by young Zionists.

These young "culture bearers" were busy at work, idealistically and passionately. In 1910, the merchant A. Litvin gave their enterprise a new turn. He was a collector of folklore, and thanks to his visit to Kremenets, folk songs became very popular.

The Anski Delegation in Kremenets (1913)

From right to left: Pikangore, Yakov Roytman (Yashke Ponimayesh), Sh. Anski, the composer Kiselhof, the photographer-painter Yudavin.

(Photograph provided by Dr. Y. Levinski—Ed.)

[370]

Intellectual, educated young people, in particular the Manusevitsh brothers, played folk music with Hasidic fervor, and Sender Rozental accompanied them on the mandolin; thanks to them, the young Jewish population of Kremenets became interested in Jewish folklore and literature. In P. Vaytser's house, they organized a "literary anniversary" in honor of Mendele Mokher Seforim.

A. Litvin's and later Noach Prilutski's visit to Kremenets carried our town's name to places as far away as Petersburg. Here, the great Jewish philanthropist and patron of the arts, Baron Gintsburg, founded and supported the Jewish Ethnographic Society and also established a high-level course in ethnography to educate and prepare a core group of collectors and researchers.

THE YOUTH OF KREMENETS WITH SH. ANSKI

M. Sternberg, a well-known researcher of the deportations to Siberia and later the director of the Asian Museum in Petersburg, was a strong supporter of the abovementioned Society and was involved in its activities. The Society, headed by Sh. Anski, published the first volume of the excellent series *Der Mentsh* [The Man] and then organized what was known as the Anski Expedition.

In July 1912, the young intelligentsia of Kremenets awakened to a brand-new version of folk culture. Yiddish, until then a symbol only of national politics, acquired a national-spiritual character as well. All habits and customs, stories, legends, charms against the "evil eye," throwing a stone when one met a Christian priest, customs related to protecting a woman in childbirth or calming down a frightened child—for Kremenets Jews, everything that was an integral part of daily life became a matter of high-value culture in the enthusiastic young people's minds. Jewish art and ornamentation, the letters of a book or the script on a Torah scroll, tombstone inscriptions, or the pictures on Hanukah playing cards also acquired a special national significance among educated, Russian-assimilated young people.

Sh. Anski came to Kremenets with his two companions: B. Kiselhof, a teacher in the Modern Talmud Torah in Petersburg (headed by Rabbi Dr. Moshe [Moisey] Ayzenshtadt, who died in New York in 1942), who collected Jewish musical instruments and recordings of folk songs, and Y. Yudavin, a relative of Anski's from Vitebsk and an artist who specialized in Jewish ornaments and liked to photograph everything. The guests stayed at Moshe Melamed's hotel, and through him Anski met Duvid Roykhel and Henekh Gelernt. Melamed was very impressed by the guests from Petersburg, who spoke to him in Yiddish.

"... Some strange Jews have arrived"—Melamed said to Gelernt—"and they registered at the hotel as coming from Petersburg. Even before they washed and refreshed themselves after such a long journey, they asked to see you." ... Since H. Gelernt didn't dare go by himself, suspecting that they were undercover agents, Melamed agreed to go with him.

[371]

As he entered the room, H. Gelernt realized that the man's face was familiar from a photograph he'd seen. Sh. Anski gave him a very warm welcome. Soon Duvid Roykhel arrived, too, and from the next room came Anski's two assistants, B. Kiselhof and Y. Yudavin. They joked about Anski's attire, which was modern, not Hasidic: on his head he wore a modern hat.... Brothers Asher and Sender Manusevitsh came as well, then Khinke Barshap. Anski began explaining the purpose of his visit, but he was interrupted by a knock on the door. The hotel owner announced that the court bailiff and some other officials had come to inquire about the guests. Panicked, he helped

Anski and the local people escape through the back door, and they returned only after all the officials had left the hotel.

Being immersed in discussion, they hardly noticed that it was Friday afternoon and that the Sabbath was approaching. Anski looked out the window and saw Jews dressed in their best outfits walking toward the synagogues. His face suddenly lit up, and he asked Yudavin to discard the cigarette.

The news about the mysterious Jewish "delegates, sent by the Petersburg minister himself," spread through town like wildfire. On Friday night, the streets were usually filled with young people; this time, they all gathered around the hotel and envied the group that was privileged to be inside. Meanwhile, Sender Rozental and Yashe Roytman, Shlome the baker's son, joined the group and were told by the hotel owner that Anski had expressed a wish to go to the Hasidic *kloyz* on Sabbath morning. The hotel owner himself went to the caretaker, Peysi the blind, to let him know. Anski asked for information about Hasidic customs in the synagogue and details about the Hasidim in town. He was quite astonished to hear that there was peace among the Hasidim in town and that the Hasidic sects—Trisk, Stolin, Ruzhin, Husiatyn, Chernobyl—everyone prayed in the same synagogue and in the same style. He was not surprised, however, by the fact that the Enlightened prayed with them. After a while, the young men took Kiselhof and Yudavin for a short walk to the "mountain." Anski didn't forget to greet them with "good Sabbath" and remind them to behave properly, meaning that they should not smoke or speak Russian ... in other words, behave in a Jewish manner.

AMONG THE HASIDIM

Anski spent that Sabbath with the Hasidim. Peysi the synagogue caretaker himself took him to the synagogue. All hands were extended to greet him. Nachman the cantor (he was also the scribe) had prepared a prayer shawl for him; he was seated by the honored eastern wall of the synagogue, between the rabbi from Petrikov, Rabbi Senderovitsh, and the great storyteller, Ben-Tsion Hofman. He was called to the reading of the Torah portion.

[372]

Before they finished the additional prayer, the caretaker went to the large hall and set the big table near the oven with a snow-white tablecloth on top of the green velvet one. Everyone was friendly and respectful except Shlome Elyankes, the old Torah teacher with the blind eye and the bass, angry voice, who would always lecture and scold everyone. He was certain—and he expressed it loudly—that the guest was none other than the devil in disguise.

That Sabbath was the beginning of a close relationship between Anski and the community's religious leaders. They were a great help in his research, providing treasures of folklore and music. No one even opposed the visitors' anthropological investigations and measurements. And, in addition, from the Great Synagogue beadle,

Anski received two very old brass candlesticks, which were added to the holdings of the Ethnographic Museum in Petersburg.

Anski spent long hours with the cantors. The Katerburg cantor sang a long set of Hasidic songs for him, Cantor Matus Kop sang his own pleasant pieces, and even the cantor from the Kozatske Study Hall presented two melodies ....

> [**Translation Editor's Note:** As of 2020, some of these recordings were available from the Vernadsky National Library of Ukraine, http://audio.ipri.kiev.ua/CD4.html and http://audio.ipri.kiev.ua/CD5.html, and .]

In the Great Synagogue, Anski held afternoon meetings around set tables, and during the meal he listened to stories and folktales told by Mendel the caretaker. In the Hasidic *kloyz*, the storyteller was Chayim Henekh (Fridman)'s son Yosl. He also heard stories about old graves and tombstones, as well as jokes aimed at the Hasidim in town.

While Anski was busy with his Hasidic meetings, the young people in town were otherwise occupied. They collected and made lists of folk songs, invited people to sing the songs, and recorded them on a phonograph. They also recorded folktales and filled many notebooks with the stories. At that time, the folk song had attained great importance, and Yiddish singing was respected and cultivated. Christian names, especially in the academic world, were "out."

IN THE OLD CEMETERY

After some discussion and delicate negotiations with the Jews in the Great Synagogue, Anski obtained permission to dig out old tombstones that had sunk over the years and were buried in the ground. The keeper of the Old Cemetery, Mordekhay Chayim Yos, welcomed the group, and they began looking for sunken tombstones. Anski himself was an expert at finding places where such tombstones were buried. Mordekhay led them over thick grass and thorny bushes, and suddenly Anski pointed to an area where there must be very old graves, he said. He stopped not far from Y. B. Levinzon's grave and gave instructions to dig out the tombstone.

[373]

Mordekhay lifted the shovel and prepared to start working, but Anski took it from his hands and showed him how to dig carefully so as not to harm the finds. Indeed, a miracle happened: they found the tombstone of Rabbi Shimshon, the MHR"L's brother, and three other stones. The inscription was beautifully preserved. Yudavin photographed the tombstones; he was enthusiastic about the ornaments on them. They found R' Shimshon's sister's tombstone as well.

At cemetery entrance, there was a small structure around Rabbi Mordekhay'le's tomb. Inside, the tomb was covered with *kvitlakh* placed there by the Jews while visiting their parents' graves. Nearby was another structure, where the deceased would be placed before burial. Both structures and all the tombstones in and around them were immediately photographed.

> [**Translator's Note:** *Kvitlakh* (little notes) are slips of paper on which visitors asked the rabbi for help in various matters.]

From that time on, the young people, who sometimes held their illegal meetings near Y. B. Levinzon's grave, were very careful not to step on the ground where the few stones were found and unearthed and not to sit on the steps leading to the structure. One of the witnesses to the destruction of Kremenets, B. Shvarts, told us that even Hitler's murderers were afraid to touch this small area when they liquidated the entire cemetery ....

JEWISH CARRIAGE DRIVERS COMPETE—EVERYONE WANTS TO BE ANSKI'S DRIVER

Anski had to overcome some difficulties in preparing for his visit to Vishnevets. He had planned to go himself, accompanied by the writer of these lines, to hire a carriage. His intention was to observe—and maybe photograph—the Jewish carriage owners, who always sat on the front steps of Duvid the watchmaker's house, waiting for clients.

So we found a carriage, and toward evening, when the day had cooled off a bit, we left town. The driver said to his horses, "Well, horses, it's time we started running ...."

Darkness began to fall. When we reached the end of the slope, we saw a lone house on the vast plain in the distance, at the edge of town. It was a little inn, and the horses hurried toward it. When we reached the inn, the driver jumped off his seat and yelled at the top of his lungs that he had just brought important visitors from Petersburg. It didn't take long until the whole town was there—men, women, and children. One of them, a short, stocky man, stepped out of the crowd and welcomed him. It was Berger, a teacher at the Crown School, who invited the guest to spend the night at his home. The entire procession, accompanying the important guests, first headed toward the school. Suddenly, the little teacher disappeared, but he soon came back holding a book. He showed Anski the open book, where everyone could see Anski's photograph, and he proudly explained that his class had studied the poem below the photograph.

The chat was interrupted by a tall, skinny Jew called Avrahamtse the Second Cantor. He welcomed the guest and invited him to the evening prayer in the Old Synagogue. Anski thanked him, and everyone went to the synagogue, which really looked old, like the town itself.

[374]

The creaky, heavy wooden door at the entrance breathed with antiquity, like the old castle gates from Count Wiśniowiecki's time. To enter the anteroom, you had to bend down, as if you were entering a cellar. The walls were bent as well, carrying the weight of the heavy roof, and only the eastern wall was upright. The smoke on the glass lampshades darkened the flickering little flames inside the lamps. The praying Jews' voices seemed like gloomy moans.

After prayers, Anski asked to see Avrahamtse in his room. Meanwhile, he observed the eastern wall closely: the townspeople had mentioned that years ago this wall had been rebuilt and an old, "holy" stone embedded in it. Later, during the "brandy and cookies" that he offered as refreshments after prayer, his talent as an excellent and experienced researcher would be clearly demonstrated.

FOLKTALES

In Berger's house, the tables were set and loaded with food; Anski honored the guests by pouring the tea from the samovar himself. Avrahamtse had brought the "town jester"—a happy, joking beggar—with him, and they all began to talk about Jewish life in town. At a signal from Anski, brandy and cookies were again served, a fresh full samovar was brought—and the stories began to flow: people talked, and Anski's assistant wrote everything down. These were fantastic and frightening tales about dark powers hovering around a bride and groom the night before their wedding; witches with long, dark, disheveled hair, whose impurity was cleaned and washed away in the ritual bath, where the groom must bathe before his wedding; and evil spirits and dark angels howling in the chimneys during the long winter nights, especially the day before a circumcision ceremony. But he also told his listeners about the special qualities of Rabbi Leyb Sore's spring, not far from town, where they would draw water to cure sick Jews, God help us. Once even the nobleman who owned all the land in the region asked the Jews to save his dying daughter ... the doctors couldn't help her; only the water from the spring saved her life. Anski's assistant, who took notes constantly, became truly horrified when Avrahamtse began telling a "true" story about a man who went to Kremenets to bring back an experienced circumciser for his newborn son. Although he knew the road to Kremenets like the palm of his hand, he got lost on the way back because he followed some strange voices that were steering the horses in the dark night .... When dawn came, he realized that he'd wandered around and around in circles in a corner of the forest where it was "known by tradition" that the devil himself roamed.

[375]

That same night, demons tried to snatch the newborn out of his young mother's arms, but various measures taken by the family apparently drove them away: the mother shrieked at the top of her lungs as she struggled with the demons; clean, white sheets were hung around her bed; chapters from the Book of Psalms were spread around; and 10 Jews sat in the room and studied all night. Finally, the young father and the circumciser arrived home, everybody greeted them with congratulations, and both hurried to the ritual bath to purify themselves and get ready for the important ceremony.

Avrahamtse told his stories with such skill that everyone in the room "could see the demons with their own eyes." He assured them that he had a witness—a woman who was over 100 years old, still living at the far end of town—who could verify all his stories. Anski asked to meet her, and the next day he was indeed taken to her.

After another round of refreshments, Avrahamtse began to maneuver the discussion away from "tall tales" and toward the synagogue and its eastern wall. He told Anski that the anteroom was the only part of the building that remained from the old synagogue, and the latter expressed his wish to check the anteroom walls. Indeed, the next morning Anski was accompanied to the synagogue. He checked the walls, and in one corner he discovered that he could feel some Hebrew letters through the plaster with his fingers. With great care, he managed to free the stone from the wall. According to Avrahamtse, there was another important stone built into the eastern wall, and Anski was eager to remove it as well. However, the community leaders were worried that the entire wall might collapse, and only after Anski promised that he would work with utmost care and pay for any damage was he granted permission to look for the stone. Like a miracle worker, Anski felt the wall with his hands, suddenly stopped, and said, here it is. He moved his screwdriver in straight lines along the wall, just as an experienced surgeon would move his scalpel, and soon the stone was in his hands. It was washed with a chemical solution, and the letters emerged. Anski made a nice donation to the synagogue and received the stones for the Petersburg Museum. He also bought two old copper candleholders standing on carved peacock legs for the museum.

For Anski, Avrahamtse was a real treasure. On their way to the cemetery, someone in the group asked Avrahamtse whether he knew about the grave of Yitschak Ber Levinzon's wife, who was from Kremenets. Avrahamtse became very irritated, since Levinzon was not religious, so Anski skillfully turned the discussion toward the cemetery again, which, he said, must be very old. Avrahamtse then calmed down and resumed his role.

[376]

"In the cemetery," he said, "there are graves of people who participated in the original Council of Four Lands assembly at the Jaroslaw fair." He obtained permission to dig out these graves, if they were found.

In the cemetery, Avrahamtse led the procession to the oldest part, where the gravestones were sunken and overgrown. However, they soon found a gravestone on which they could clearly read a poem written by Levinzon in honor of his wife. The ornaments included two hands blessing the Sabbath candles. Later that day, a photographer returned and took photos of all the old tombstones.

In conclusion, it is worth relating why Anski chose Vishnevets, of all the towns in the region.

This little town had been famous since the 18th century for its artistically built castles, erected by the Wiśniowiecki princes' family. Particularly famous was the castle of Jeremi Wiśniowiecki, who ruled over a great deal of land and owned slaves from various regions. He cruelly persecuted the Orthodox Church and Ukrainians, which led to the Chmielnitski uprising.

The Wiśniowiecki castle was packed with antiques, paintings, and other important examples of art. When the Tatars occupied Vishnevets, they spared the castle museum. However, the Turks, who occupied the town after them, destroyed the castle, which was later restored by Jan Sobieski.

HOW WE ONCE DISSEMINATED JEWISH LITERATURE (A PAGE OF MEMORIES)

Duvid Roykhel (Warsaw)
Kremenetser Shtime, **August 12, 1932**
English translation by Yocheved Klausner

It was summer 1909. I was in Kremenets on summer vacation from Odessa, where I was studying. In Odessa, I'd been a member of a small "group," and, returning to my hometown, I intended to accomplish several things.

At that time, I had good connections with friends who were studying in other towns in Podolia and Volhynia provinces, and as I came home, I got in touch with them to join forces and try to arouse interest in *Vestnik Znanya* circles, especially among the young workers.

> [**Translator's Note:** *Vestnik Znanya* is a popular science magazine.]

Making our first steps, we encountered unexpected difficulties. The members of our group were assimilated or half-assimilated, and we never thought that we'd have to do our work in Yiddish, not Russian, if we intended to work among the Jewish masses.

[377]

We acquired a large number of *Vestnik Znanya* brochures from the then-liquidated publishing house, as well as a number of books dedicated to the life and work of the various nations in Russia, which had appeared under Sh. Anski's editorship. With this literature collection, we planned to begin our activity. But the books and magazines we brought for people to take and read weren't taken .... Their answer was simple: We don't know Russian ....

We realized that we had to find a solution to this problem. I suggested contacting the Literary Society in Petersburg and requesting that they recommend a course of action. Some of our group members were of the opinion that it would be preferable to teach the workers Russian, but we finally decided, albeit with heavy hearts, to conduct our activities in Yiddish.

We soon received a reply from Petersburg recommending that we get in touch with the Yiddish periodical *Leben un Wissenshaft* in Vilna.

[**Translator's Note:** *Leben un Wissenshaft* means *Life and Science*.]

As a testimony to our distance from Yiddish literature and our lack of knowledge about it, the mere fact that a Yiddish journal named *Leben un Wissenshaft* existed—and, moreover, the similarity of its title to that of our own *Vestnik Znanya*—hit us like a bomb .... Without delay, we ordered a sample issue, and as soon as I received it, I went to my friend Hirsh Yashpe (he was later killed in the war) and asked him to read it to me. I was interested in his opinion of the journal. We also invited Shmerl Feldman, a member of the Labor Zionist movement (he committed suicide in 1910)—and, after a general review of the journal and after reading the editor's article and the "Conversation Hall" section, it was clear that we'd found what we needed. I put aside Russian literature and began, seriously and resolutely, to learn Yiddish and read Yiddish literature. I gathered several friends around me, and in no time, 34 copies of the journal *Leben un Wissenshaft* arrived in Kremenets. All the subscribers were workers, and they paid for a subscription at a rate of 10 kopeks a week. The journal was a success. It didn't take long for people to begin reading literature as well: the works of Mendele, Peretz, Shalom Aleichem, Sholem Asch, and others. We contacted the S. Schrebrek bookstore in Vilna and later the Central in Warsaw, and we received a 40% discount. The buyers in town received the same discount, naturally, and they continued paying their weekly rates in kopeks. We must mention that there was never any question of "not paying." It even happened that one of the subscribers left for America and continued to send us his payments regularly.

The basic fund for this enterprise was created by several well-to-do friends.

[378]

Sometimes we could even give a loan when it was needed.

All this activity had a very positive and encouraging effect, and in time almost every worker had assembled a small library of his own. The brothers Mikhel and Lemel Sherman (both tailors, now in Russia) excelled, and Mikhel "the lame" Barshap in particular. Later, others joined as well, including brothers Sender and Asher Manusovitsh (now in Chicago, both active in Jewish cultural affairs)—and our work developed and branched out.

The journal *Leben un Wissenshaft* was a teacher and guide for us. The thin brochures, which appeared very irregularly, provided us with appropriate material for our educational and instructional work. We hadn't been very interested in literature before those days. Articles like those by Blumshteyn and Rodnyanski on philosophy, Yiddish language problems, articles on Yiddish grammar and on using the Latin alphabet for Yiddish by Dr. L. L. Zamenhof (creator of the Esperanto language), simple and popular monographs by A. Litvin on A. Mapu, Y. B. Levinzon, A. M. Dik, and others, historical articles by Ch. Shvis and G. Horvits, discussions by S. Niger, reviews, the "Conversation Hall"—all this was new for us, and with our friends the workers, we learned and were educated by it.

It was therefore no wonder that this journal played such an important role in our lives. Unlike *Literarishe Monatshriften,* which wasn't intended for mass readers, *Leben un Wissenshaft* was exactly right, and appropriate for the aims we'd set for ourselves.

[**Translator's Note:** *Literarishe Monatshriften* means *Literary Monthly.*]

THE FUNERAL FOR A TORAH SCROLL

Chanokh Gilernt
English translation by Yocheved Klausner

It happened on a frosty winter day in the winter of 1909-1910.

The Bedrik *kloyz,* with its polished wooden interior and furniture, the entire Holy Ark, and its Torah scrolls all went up in flames. Jews risked their lives trying to save the scrolls, but they could salvage only small, scorched pieces from the flames, quenching them in the wet snow. Parts of prayer shawls were also taken out, and the blackened parchments were wrapped in them.

Aba Tsukerman, the caretaker, stood broken and shriveled. His usually deep voice was choking as he uttered the words, "Our crown has fallen." He cried bitterly. Jews from every part of town rushed to the place and stood silently around the burned holy objects, which were covered with a white sheet.

The rabbi's beadle brought large earthen containers for the "holy remnants."

[379]

In the rabbi's house were gathered R' Hertsele the religious court judge and the scholars Yosl Fridman (Chayim Henekh's son); Moshe Velis, the religious court trial arbitrator; Shlomele Ditun, the scholar from the Hasidic Synagogue; Leybele the ritual slaughterer, the rabbi's devoted adviser; and many others. From a mountain of books on the table, the rabbi and his advisers looked for an answer to the important question following the fire: how to put the scrolls to their eternal rest: through immediate burial or through *geniza* .... Suddenly, the room became silent. The rabbi, wearing his black caftan and a fur hat on his head, stood up and made his decision: the men who will take care of the scrolls and other holy objects must first go to the ritual bath. The earthen containers must be ritually submerged in water as well to purify them. The day of burial will be a fast day for the entire community. All shops and workshops will be closed. All schoolchildren will accompany the funeral procession to the Great Synagogue. The rabbi will eulogize by the *kloyz,* and the religious court judge, by the Great Synagogue. The *geniza* containers will be carried on a specially prepared wooden plank. The procession will stop at the House of Prayer, the New Study Hall, the Hasidic Synagogue, the *Magid*'s Synagogue, and the entrance to the Great Synagogue. At each stop, the local cantor will recite his eulogy. The containers will be carried to the burial place, and the Burial Society will prepare the grave in R' Mordekhay'le the Righteous' "burial tent," next to his grave.

[**Translator's Note:** A *geniza* (hiding place) is a storeroom in a synagogue where worn-out Hebrew books and papers on religious topics are kept before they can receive a proper cemetery burial, since it is forbidden to throw away writings containing God's name.]

On the day of the funeral, the entire town was in mourning. Non-Jewish neighbors remained in their homes out of fear. Sadness spread like a cloud over the town.

After the rabbi's eulogy, Matus the cantor recited the prayer "God, Full of Compassion" and verses from the Book of Lamentations. Tearful and pale, he moved around the burned Torah Ark, and it seemed that he was asking the scorched remnants to pray with him. When he burst into tears, the entire community cried with him.

After the ceremony, the wooden plank with the scrolls and earthen containers was carried to the cemetery. Every member of the community tried to take part in the commandment to carry the board, and chapters from the Book of Psalms were recited all the way to the cemetery.

[380]

MARKET DAY IN THE DUBNO SUBURB

Moshe Shnayder (Rechovot)
English translation by Yocheved Klausner

One autumn evening, when I was walking home, the entire Dubno suburb was sound asleep. Night had begun early, because the next day was market day, and everyone was expected to be up at dawn.

Feeling guilty for disturbing the peace, I knocked on our door, and my good mother opened it. Still, she couldn't resist a good-natured remark—didn't I know that tomorrow was market day?

It happened every Tuesday: that day, the entire neighborhood was one big commotion. Our father rose at daybreak and said his morning prayer quickly. Outside, our neighbor Brayne was already standing in front of her door, dressed in her market apron with the large pockets, holding her big bags and waiting for her gentile peasants. That day, I was excused from going to the synagogue, because we were expecting to see many acquaintances, and I had to help.

The sky was gray, and the air was foggy; we were worried about the weather, which could, God forbid, get in the way. However, the clouds moved on, and a few rays of sun could be seen through the fog. All the faces suddenly looked happier. The shops opened for business with wide-open doors.

The neighborhood was unrecognizable. Everything was out on the street: clothes, sewing notions, wagon wheels, furniture, and so on. There was an old woman sitting with her barrels full of black tar; in another corner, a man was welcoming every arriving cart; it had been less than an hour since sunrise, and along the street we could already see numerous carts full of grain, vegetables, geese, chickens, turkeys, pigs, and even horses, tied to the wagons with rope. Half an hour later, it was impossible to pass through the place.

Mountain of the Virgins. At left: the Dubno suburb.

[381]

The horse dealers had already begun their business: checking the horse from head to tail, opening its mouth and looking at the teeth, lifting its legs one by one and checking the hoofs with a knowledgeable look, bargaining—a zloty up, a zloty down—and finally, the deal was made. Everybody was buying and selling, from a pin to a pig.

On that day, it wasn't easy for the town's coach drivers to take their passengers through town to the train station, for example, and they had to go on side roads. But in the marketplace, everything went on as usual. The sacks of grain were heavy on the scales, and money passed from hand to hand. The day passed without incident and, moreover, without competition. Every Jew had his own gentile—most of them owing money—and there was a feeling of solidarity. After all, we were all neighbors, residents of the Dubno suburb. And on the Sabbath, we all had to enter the synagogue with a "clean face." ...

Finally, market day drew to an end. The street was now almost empty. A drunken peasant, who had spent a little too much time trading or chatting, was driving his horse and cart, hurrying home. The remaining merchandise was taken back to the shops and arranged back on the shelves, and the shopkeepers were busy counting their proceeds. Money was taken out of pockets, aprons, bags—and with content faces, people calculated the final profits.

Even the police were involved: policemen issued "tickets" for not cleaning up the street, and so the police also "shared" some of the profit ....

In every house, the family gathered around the table enjoying dinner, which served as both lunch and supper on this day, since there had been no time to prepare a meal at noon. Tired from the eventful day, everybody went to bed early to get a good rest and gather strength for the next day.

For us, the young people, it was a second evening at home, and we tried not to disturb the elders. The profits of the market day were our means for living for the entire week.

ON OLD CUSTOMS

Chanokh Gilernt
English translation by Yocheved Klausner

A. THE HOLIDAY OF SHAVUOT

With the arrival of May, the town became enchanted and full of delight. The green mountains around it, the aroma of the newly opened young blossoms carried by the mild spring breeze—all this lifted our spirits.

On Shavuot eve, Christian neighbors brought wagon upon wagon of greenery to the market; among other things, heaps of watercress were supplied to Jewish houses, and the housewives would spread it on the freshly scrubbed floors, ready for the holiday. Young boys would fold leaves and turn them into musical whistles, playing all kinds of songs. Young girls would hang colorful flowers on the walls. Fathers would decorate the clean, sparkling windowpanes with heart-shaped leaves. Flower garlands mixed with green branches hung from the ceiling.

[382]

The synagogues as well were decorated with green branches intertwined with colorful flowers, and the floors were covered with watercress. The newly whitewashed walls, the brass candelabras hanging from the ceiling, the *menorah* on the cantor's stand— everything was ready, sparkling clean.

Among the Hasidic Jews, R' Mendele the ritual slaughterer would act out the "Crossing of the Red Sea" before our people received the Torah. On the morning of the holiday, he placed a bucket of water right under the flowers decorating the ceiling and hung a bag on his shoulder (a symbol of the exodus from Egypt). Thus dressed, he circled the bucket of water several times, a commemoration of the crossing of the sea.

Children in particular felt like grownups during the two weeks before the holiday. Even life in the cheder was different. The teacher didn't take studying as seriously as always, and the pupils were not as frightened as before; the air in the cheder sang. With special joy, the pupils read the chapters of the Book of Ruth. They could feel the fresh smell of the stalks of grain that Ruth gathered in the field ....

As the Shavuot season arrived, Jewish Kremenets sang. Young people in the mountains, their parents and grandparents in the study hall, children in the cheder—houses and streets were singing.

B. LAG BA'OMER

This day was always full of excitement for the children, for an additional reason: the holiday usually fell during May, when the Czar's coronation was celebrated every year with great festivities: the main street was beautifully decorated with lights, and we had to light oil lamps on both sides of the front door of each house. This was the children's duty—they would fill the containers with oil and place them on the sidewalk by the door, prepare the wicks and light them when evening fell, and then watch the lamps the entire evening. That night was full of the joyous sound of children.

The day before Lag Ba'omer, mothers would prepare clay for the cheder children to shape into little balls, which served as candlesticks, or into little cups, which they filled with oil and placed a wick inside. The children would go from store to store and collect candles and oil. The collection was brought to the synagogues, and all the little lights, white candles or oil, were placed on the windows. Each child would take care of his father's house of prayer.

The next morning, the children would not leave their mothers—whether in the kitchen at home or in the store—until they received their hard-cooked eggs, string of bagels, and bottle of *kvass*. With special joy, they ran to the cheder, where the teacher's assistant waited for them, ready with a bow and arrow for everyone. The mothers accompanied the children to the cheder, paper bags holding the food in their hands, and waited until the children formed an orderly line, like little soldiers —the rabbi in front, the assistant behind him, ready to march toward the Vidomka.

[383]

There, everyone stretched out on the grass and took out his or her food. The rabbi told the story of Rabbi Shimon Bar Yochay. Right after he finished his story, the children woke up as from a dream and eagerly began to shoot their "weapons"....

C. TISH'A BE-AV

On Tish'a Be-Av, a feeling of hidden grief and sorrow would fill every Jewish home.

During the "nine days," the butchers and ritual slaughterers were out of work. The four Jewish tavern owners, whose Sunday earnings would suffice for the entire week, rested as well.

> [**Translator's Notes:** The ninth day of Av is a day of mourning day that commemorates the destruction of the First and the Second Temples in Jerusalem. On the nine days between 1 and 9 Av, Jews avoided eating meat, as a symbol of mourning.]

The feeling of mourning was carried mainly by the children. The entire week, they studied the Book of Lamentations, reading it in its particular melody. They played a special "war-game"—in Yiddish—called *shelach* [send]: they formed two opposite rows, or "camps," and one from each camp was proclaimed "king" and stood at the head of the line. The distance between the two "armies" was about 15 steps. The "generals" held sticks in their hands, and all the soldiers were ready for combat. The "senior officer" called toward his rival: Send!—meaning "you send your soldiers first!" —to which the reply was, "My soldiers are weaker than yours, so you are first!" and with that, the war began. Each side tried to break through "enemy" lines, and those who succeeded even took prisoners ... this is how war was played, all day long.

The teachers' assistants helped out and added to the atmosphere of merriment.

At the Entrance to the Jewish Cemetery

[384]

During the previous week, they, too, had worked hard and made little wooden swords for the children, and like real masters, they carved various images on the hilts.

The children played another game, too: they would collect little black nuts and thorny berries, tie them with a string, and throw them at someone's back with all their strength. It wasn't pleasant to get hit by a bunch of nuts and thorns, but the adults participated as well: they would find other thorny fruits and pay back the children ....

The afternoon meal on the eve of the fast day was almost as holy and ceremonious as the meal at on the eve of the Yom Kippur fast. Lights did not burn in the houses that night. Leather shoes were not worn, and men and women wore only simple clothes. Leybushekhe, who all year long would remind people about the anniversaries of deaths and visit the cemetery to "bring greetings from the living," would on this day walk from grave to grave, touch every tombstone with her stick, and beg forgiveness in the name of each family.

After the 1905 revolution, two worlds met in the cemetery: Jewish labor groups and intelligentsia groups would hold their forbidden meetings there.

The meetings took place around Yitschak Ber Levinzon's gravestone and that of Berish Feldman, who committed suicide after the 1905 revolution failed.

Since then, two generations have come together there.

D. SUKKOT AND SIMCHAT TORAH

The first thing we did when the Yom Kippur prayers ended was the Benediction of the Moon. After that, everybody went home and began to prepare for Sukkot. Those who had a room or hallway with an open roof would take the tree branches that were left from last year down from the attic, preparing them to serve as *skhakh*. Those who did not have a "built-in" sukkah would begin collecting wooden boards for walls and branches for the roof early in the morning in order to put up a sukkah in the courtyard. The neighbors, who would eat their meals in the sukkah during the holiday, helped out as well. The main "workers," though, were the children. Decorating the walls and ceiling was the special good deed of the girls in the family.

> [**Translator's Note:** *Skhakh* (covering) refers to the roofing of the sukkah, which is made from natural materials such as bamboo or palm branches.]

The Kremenets Christians were aware of everything the Jews needed for the various holidays, and before Sukkot they would bring carts full of green branches to town, as well as sacks of walnuts for the children to play with. The real joy and holiday feeling were spread throughout the town by the children. But it must be said that their joy and anticipation was directed much more to the sukkah and games than to the preparations for holiday prayers in the synagogue and the reading of the Book of Ecclesiastes ....

On Sukkot eve, the children were free from cheder. We decorated the sukkah with the most beautiful autumn flowers, and we hung pictures on the walls.

[385]

Women and girls would not eat in the sukkah. They performed the good deed of serving the meals and listening to the blessing over the wine recited by the father or husband. Their good deed also consisted of setting the table and cleaning after the meal.

During the "intermediate days" of the holiday as well, Jewish Kremenets would "breathe holiday." The craftsmen, who didn't work on these days and took long walks in town instead, felt this especially. In the evening, they would visit friends or take the children to see a movie at the Illusion Theater.

The cheder teachers were especially busy. They would go from house to house to collect their teaching salaries, registering the children for the coming semester, and accepting new pupils. Their assistants were busy preparing flags for Simchat Torah and teaching the children to weave the little rings for the *lulav* from the long strips of palm leaves. On the eve of the seventh day of Sukkot, Hoshana Rabba, everybody was busy preparing the tender little branches called *hoshanot,* which were used during the prayer the next day.

The Jews called the entire week of the Sukkot holiday "the week of rejoicing with the Torah." A special elation was in the air, very much as it was during the week of Passover. This was caused by the holiday's particular laws and customs as well as by the lighter activities. The Kremenets Jews, adults and children alike, enjoyed their Jewish heritage.

E. CELEBRATING A JEWISH WEDDING IN TOWN

A wedding was not just the ceremony under the wedding canopy and the customary recitals and blessings. Kremenets Jews called such a "simple" wedding "a gentile wedding." In a real Jewish wedding, the entire Jewish street, rich and poor, rejoiced for a week before and a week after the wedding canopy ceremony.

The week before the wedding, a festive atmosphere dominated the in-laws' houses. The tailor and seamstresses prepared the bride's and groom's attire, the cooks began their cooking and baking, and the house was full of guests—neighbors and friends. On the Sabbath before the wedding, everyone went to the groom's house and accompanied him to the synagogue for the morning prayer, when the groom would be honored and called to the Torah reading. The children were happy to participate as well: they carried boxes full of small hazelnuts and candies and placed them in the women's section of the synagogue, to be thrown at the groom after he finished reading the Torah portion, as was the custom.

After the Sabbath prayer, everyone went to the groom's house to wish him and his family congratulations and have the traditional "cake and brandy." In the more well-to-do families, an entire meal was served after the Sabbath ended, and the party would continue until late at night.

[386]

The Kozatski Synagogue and the Road to the Three Springs

In the courtyard of the bride's house, the beginning of the new week would be marked by a group of musicians, and the bride's girlfriends would sing and dance. The members of the klezmer band were Hersh the conductor and his three sons: Moshe on the violin, Yankel on the trumpet, and Mekhl on the contrabass. The musicians played, the girls danced, and the mothers would enjoy the scene and make a wish: "May we soon dance, with God's help, at our daughter's wedding ...."

During the week of the wedding, the doors of the bride's and groom's houses never closed. Everyone was devoted to preparing the feast. Hinde the caterer would supervise the cooking and baking from dawn to late at night. Much attention was given to the "golden soup"—the special chicken soup served to the bride and groom right after the ceremony, when they broke their fast.

On the wedding day, the houses were bursting with noise and expectation. After returning from the ritual bath, the bride retired to her room, and her friends helped her get ready and put on her wedding gown and veil. Hersh Klezmer and his band, reinforced with cymbals and drums, played the famous *sher* dance, the polka, and even the "quarrel dance." This time, the in-laws joined the dance as well. The dancing stopped only when the messenger announced that the groom was being led to the bride to cover her face with the veil, which marked the beginning of the ceremony. Hersh and his band hurried to follow him and play a special "groom's tune."

With measured steps, led by the two fathers, the groom approached his bride, pulled the veil over her eyes, and stepped back. That was the time to "cheer up" the bride, which was done by the "wedding jester." Accompanied by the fiddler, the jester began to sing before the bride, saying, "Cry, bride, cry," and the eyes of the women and girls around her filled with tears ....

[387]

This continued until the time came for the two mothers, holding big white candles in their hands, to lead the bride toward the wedding canopy to join the groom.

The main ceremony under the wedding canopy was always held in the Great Synagogue courtyard. The rabbi performed the ceremony, the bride and groom drank from the special wedding cup, and as soon as the groom stepped on the glass and shattered it, three loud shouts of "mazal tov" filled the air. Accompanied by the entire crowd, the couple was led through the street to the house, where the musicians received them with music and songs and one of the mothers stepped backward before them, dancing and leading the way, with a big challah in her hand. The bride and groom were shown into a special room to eat their soup after the long fast, and the guests continued the joyful dancing ....

A wedding canopy ceremony was never performed after sunset. When the wedding was on a Friday, the festive meal was held the next evening, when the Sabbath was over. It was necessary to have a quorum of 10 men at the meal in order to add the seven wedding blessings to the blessing after the meal. After each course, the young people danced, while the groom, who sat among the scholars and Hasidim, gave a scholarly talk.

After the meal and before the blessings, the jester performed his task in full: it was time to play out the "sermon presents" game. The jester loudly called each guest's name and announced what present he had brought—first the couple's parents, then the families, then the guests. The usual gifts were silver Judaica articles (wine cups, candlesticks, etc.) or home and kitchen articles.

Section of Sheroka Street

[388]

The festive meal would continue until late at night, the guests dancing in a circle or with the bride and groom until the couple disappeared. Only then did the guests begin to leave and start for home.

The entire week, the wedding was the main talk of the town. Each day, the Hasidim would have a special meal hosting the couple, with the seven wedding blessings added to the blessing after the meal.

The Christian neighbors would stand for hours outside the windows, watching with interest the special way that a Jewish wedding was celebrated.

PURIM (MEMORIES OF MY CHILDHOOD YEARS)

L. Rozental
English translation by Yocheved Klausner

The winter went on, sleepily. The short winter days followed the long nights. We, the cheder children, had already begun to count the days to the expected holidays—how many days to Purim, how many to Passover, and so on. We counted and counted, until one Friday morning, before dismissing us to go home for the Sabbath, our teacher announced that on Sunday morning we'd begin learning the Book of Esther in preparation for Purim. However, we, the children, weren't thinking about the Book of Esther; we were thinking about the noisemakers ....

In our cheder, we had two boys—the father of one and the brother of another—who were carpenters. Their noisemakers clearly shamed all other noisemakers. The richer families ordered wooden noisemakers for their children from these carpenters, while the other children had to be satisfied with tin noisemakers, bought for three kopeks from Lazil the tinsmith; and those who didn't have even those three kopeks were happy with a simple stick....The noisemaker trading went on, back and forth, for the entire week that our teacher, the rabbi, tried to teach us the Book of Esther.

On the Fast of Esther (the day before Purim), we were "free." Instead of going to the cheder, we jumped around in the mud puddles with our galoshes. At home, the preparations for the holiday were going on at high speed. The Purim challah was in the oven, and I was honored with grinding the poppy seeds for the *hamentaschen.*

On Purim eve, several hours before nightfall, all the boys gathered around the synagogue, armed with various noisemakers, sticks, pieces of wood, and other such "weapons." The synagogue caretaker, festively dressed, didn't let us in, but we knocked on the door, made a loud noise, and called him by his nickname until finally people began to arrive for the evening prayer and we managed to sneak in, one by one. When the caretaker, R' Betsalel, discovered us and tried to throw us out, we swore by our parents that we'd sit behind the stove and keep still. Every time one of us tried out his noisemaker, and when the caretaker came running, we had a ready answer: it wasn't me....

The evening prayer ended, and they began reading the Book of Esther. We, the children, appointed one of us to follow the reading and warn us when Haman's name was about to be mentioned so we could make the required noise with our noisemakers and "kill" Haman. The cantor tried to read those passages quickly to avoid the noise, but of course it didn't help.

[389]

Sometimes our zeal was so strong that we didn't wait for Haman, and we "killed" Mordekhay instead.... Even the sexton was angry at us, but we didn't care—and finally we returned home, victorious.

The big oven at home was already filled with challah, cookies, and *hamentaschen*. Several "goodies" were put aside for the gentile washerwoman, who, besides doing the heavy laundry, helped with other things at home.

The next morning, Purim day, during the reading of the Book of Esther in the synagogue, the noise wasn't as loud as the night before. At home, "charity collectors" were beginning to appear at the doors. At the market, near the leather merchants, the women displayed their merchandise: little "pillow cookies" sprinkled with colored poppy seeds, arranged in special containers, decorated with inscriptions: "Your best friend," "Dear groom," "Dear bride," and so on. For the children, they had little whistles, little dolls that could sing, little prayer books—all made of sugar. The best cookies and cakes were those made by "Big Hinde": in her little shop, you could find everything your heart desired, and all the wealthy ladies would do their shopping there.

In the afternoon, we began to prepare for the big Purim meal. The table was covered with a clean white tablecloth, with the two big challahs with saffron ready, the candlesticks sparkling. On the table in front of my father was a large bronze tray full of various coins—to be handed out later to every one of us.

Soon the "Purim gifts" began to arrive! The first was from the rabbi. It contained cake, cookies, a "bagel," and an orange. Father sent back a little silver basket, and the boy who brought the Purim gift received 5 kopeks.

Then came the presents from the cantor, the caretaker, and others, and each time, a present was sent back with the same messenger. Our aunts and uncles sent various gifts, among them material for a suit for my brother and a dress for my sister. Our grandmother sent a little prayer book for my little brother. What we children loved most were the oranges.

We stayed awake until late at night, busy with the problem of "what to send to whom." The joy of the Purim holiday was felt in the air.

Next day, we all wished all this would be repeated....But only the water carrier and the laundry woman came to receive their share of challah and *hamentaschen*.

WHAT HAPPENED ...

English translation by Yocheved Klausner

AN OATH BY THE LIGHT OF BLACK CANDLES IN THE SYNAGOGUE

In the Great Synagogue, Old Vishnevets resident Y. G., dressed in his robe, stood before black candles and took an oath concerning the following: he asked the peasant to return a loan of 1,300 zloty, while the peasant argued that he had borrowed only 300 zloty and deposited 1,000 zloty as a promissory note.

Present at the oath-taking event were judges, lawyers, the rabbi, and others.

During the deliberations, the Jew wept like a little child.

[390]

BECAUSE OF A BUS'S BIG WHEELS, A MATCH WAS DISSOLVED ...

A new bride from a small village was visiting her fiancé's family. As they were taking a walk through town, a big bus passed by. Astonished, the young fiancée cried out, "Look at those big wheels...." The man felt offended in that he had chosen such a "village girl" who had never seen a bus, and ... the match was called off immediately.

A CHRISTIAN WOMAN'S GOOD DEED

A Kremenets Christian woman had a sister who was a landowner in Belozirka. For several years, her estate manager was a Jew. When his wife died, he was left with small children, and his situation wasn't good. The Kremenets Christian woman was touched by his bad fortune, invited his 16-year-old daughter to live with her, and enrolled her in the ORT school, paying all expenses. She bought kosher food for the girl and bought new dishes, which she kept kosher according to Jewish law. Until adulthood, she raised the girl in the spirit of the Jewish religion.

FIRST SELL THE BUTTER, AND THEN BURY THE MOTHER

In the village M., not far from Shumsk and Kremenets, lived a Jewish peasant family. One Wednesday, the mother of the family, 95 years old, passed away. Since there was no Jewish cemetery in the village, the body had to be taken to Shumsk for burial. The family's oldest son thought that it wasn't feasible to take the cart and horses out solely for that purpose, so he decided that since he planned to go to Shumsk on the following Sunday to sell his butter, he would take his mother to the cemetery in the same trip to bury her properly "in a Jewish grave."

Said and done. On Sunday morning, the man harnessed his horses, placed the body on his cart, covered it with a sack, and on top of it he put the butter he had for sale— and away to Shumsk!

Being concerned that the burial would take a long time and that the customers probably wouldn't wait for him, the son first went to the market to sell the butter. When some of the customers tried to lift the sack and look for more merchandise, he declared, "This is not for sale!" Finally, after all the butter was sold, he drove the horses to the cemetery and gave his mother a proper Jewish burial.

EVEN THE HORSE RECEIVES A FEE FOR MATCHMAKING

A lady from Kremenets who was a matchmaker came to Belozirka and struck a deal with two local matchmakers, as follows: she would bring young men from Kremenets, and they would recommend young local girls, of which Belozirka had more than enough (may we be protected from the evil eye). To speed things up and save the young men money, the lady matchmaker bought a horse and wagon and, at her own expense, drove the prospective grooms to the village for their first date.

In this way, they succeeded in making several matches and creating new Jewish families. However, nothing could happen without an argument and a dispute—this time between the local matchmakers and the lady from Kremenets on the division of the matchmaking fees. The rabbi had to mediate, and he ruled that a certain sum be paid to the lady. However, she wasn't satisfied and forcefully demanded a "fee" for the horse as well. She didn't rest until the bride's father had paid her a dollar for the horse ....

It is interesting to note that when the Kremenets matchmaker stayed in Belozirka for the Sabbath, the mothers and fathers of the young women in the village would bring hay and oats for the horses, hoping they'd stay healthy and strong to be able to continue bringing young men to Belozirka ....

[391]

KREMENETS WIDOWS REMIND THE POCHAYEV RABBI TO FEAR GOD

At the election of Rabbi Mendiuk, the deceased Rabbi Rapaport's son-in-law, as rabbi of Kremenets on January 15, 1933, everybody was mobilized for the election campaign. There was also a lively exchange of letters between Rabbi Rapaport's widow and Rabbi M. Oretski of Pochayev, who planned to declare himself the challenger candidate for the position.

The culmination of this activity was the Kremenets widows' public protest against Rabbi Oretski's intention to submit his candidacy. The most interesting part was that the widows' call was published on the front page of *Kremenitser Shtime* and included the words "There is a God in this world, Who is the Father of orphans and the Judge of widows—fear Him, rabbi of Pochayev!"

The widows' public call helped—and the Pochayever rabbi withdrew his candidacy.

We present here the full text of this unique appeal, with all the widows' signatures.

The Kremenets Widows' Public Protest

Reading in the newspaper your letter, in which you announce that you are submitting your candidacy for the position of community rabbi in Kremenets, and considering that by this act you will add distress to the grieving and unhappy widow and children of our late Rabbi Rapaport, of blessed memory, who died so young—we see it as our duty to strongly protest against this action.

We, sorrowful widows, who more than anyone else can understand the bitter fate and feel the great pain of the widows and orphans punished by God with the most severe punishment —we all condemn your conduct, which was clearly directed against the fate of a widow with a family of little orphans.

It isn't appropriate for any Jew, particularly not for a rabbi, to undermine the life and livelihood of widows and children who have been struck by tragedy; a rabbi must serve as an example to the world through his integrity and compassion. In contrast, you have chosen to take such a dishonest and pitiless step, which no doubt would be a disgrace to the holy Torah and human consciousness. Where is your integrity? Where is your compassion? And where is the commandment in the Torah not to harm widows and orphans?

You'll stand accountable before God and before humanity and be denounced publicly if you submit your candidacy for the Kremenets rabbinate position! There can be no excuse!

The tears of many widows and orphans, who feel the sorrow and pain of the family of Rabbi Rapaport, of blessed memory, will turn against you and will certainly not be shed in vain!

[392]

There is a God in this world, Who is the Father of orphans and the Judge of widows—fear Him, Pochayever rabbi!

With great sorrow, the widows of Kremenets:

Tsipe Vaynberg, Nadi Shumski, Feyge Litvak, Ite Rozenfeld, Stisi Lemberg, Pesi Mandelkorn, Gitel Hokhberg, Miryam Zeltser, Mali Shepetin, Gitel Dolgoshey, Rivke Gornfeld, Rivke Boym, Feli Sheynberg, Beyle Borsht, Yente Sambirer, Rivke Shteynberg, Dvore Krivin, Pesi Reyts, Dantsi Gitelman, Chaye Fridkes, Pesi Fridman, Toyve Teper, Tsivye Shnayder, Beyle Pundik, Golde Barshap, Feyge Shtulberg, Pesi Katz, Beyle Doloshey, Ester Guz, Chayke Landa, M. Poyzner, Ester Oks, Sheyndel Poltorak, Idis Bielaguz, et al.

MY FIRST DAY IN CHEDER

Ester Laybel-Rubinshteyn (Tel Aviv)
English translation by Yocheved Klausner

One Saturday, when I was about five or six years old, my aunt, who raised me, told me that the next day, Sunday, we had to get up early because the teacher's assistant would come to take me to the cheder, run by the teacher Yoel Kishke. By then, I already knew the word "cheder" from my older brothers and sisters, but I had not really seen one.

I rose very early in the morning. My aunt dressed me in my best clothes, the Sabbath dress, and prepared some food for me: bread with plum jam and a piece of halvah.

The door opened, and in came a young man, his face full of pimples, with red eyes and a long nose, his body bent, his clothes dirty, wearing a too-small jacket with sleeves that were too short, shoes muddy, his whole appearance scary. Frightened, I hid under my mother's apron.

The assistant tried to calm me down, put me on a chair, and took me on his back. I had to put my little hands around his dirty neck, and in this way, he carried me to the cheder: a long room with one large window. A tall bench stood near the entrance, and on it was a heap of coats. One long table stood in the middle of the room, and on the sides were two benches for the children to sit on; some pupils my age were already sitting there. In the middle of the room, a beautiful big rooster "made the rounds."...

The assistant let me down near the door and left me there. I looked at the children, and they looked at me. Suddenly, a fat, dirty woman, the teacher's wife, appeared and ordered the assistant to find a seat for me among the other children. Soon a tall, handsome man with a long white beard came in; it was the teacher himself, Yoel Kishke. He sat down at the head of the table, the assistant next to him holding his big wooden stick, which served as a pointer, and the lesson began.

The teacher himself taught the older children, and the assistant taught the younger ones. The assistant would sometimes fall asleep and wouldn't notice how the pointer moved from one word to another. When the children became confused and inattentive, the teacher would show us his stick, which was always ready in his hand.

[393]

The minute the teacher cried out, "Well, bastards, go eat!" all was forgotten—fear of the assistant and the teacher's whip—and everyone rushed into the next room. The assistant stretched out on the long table and fell asleep right away.... The children began eating, and they played at the same time: who would get more plum jam (which every child had brought from home) on her face or other games, until everybody fell off the bench. The laughing and noise were impossible to imagine.

At that moment, the wife stormed in, holding a broom and yelling, "This is what you have in mind? Laughing? You'll soon laugh with the frogs outside!"

A deadly silence fell over the entire room.

OLD KREMENETS (LEAFING THROUGH THE "ALL KREMENETS" ALBUM)

Moshe Sorovski (New York)
English translation by Yocheved Klausner

A friend who had visited Kremenets brought me a present, "All Kremenets"—a photograph album from my hometown, where I spent my childhood and adolescence. With trembling hands, I opened it, and memories of the "good old days" were awakened, bringing back to life my memories of my forever lost home ....

THE TRAIN STATION

True—it isn't the same station I remember from when I left Kremenets, the station I watched being built with my own eyes. I was then a young boy, and in my cheder I heard that in the world there were wagons that ran on steam—and my young mind was very anxious to know how these wagons looked. The closest train station—before they built our own station—was in Rudnya, but I never had a chance to go there, a distance of about two miles through the forest. It was too far to walk, and I was afraid of robbers. Therefore, I waited patiently until the new train station was finished.

It was at the time of the Passover holiday when the first train was supposed to arrive from Dubno. It's hard to describe the excitement in Kremenets! People left their shops, women didn't feed their children, the schools were abandoned, old and young went to see the wonder .... Literally the entire town was at the station when the first train arrived in Kremenets.

I'll never forget the enormous impression made by the remarkable engine smokestack ... the pump where they filled the engine with water ... the marvelous way the engine maneuvered to the circular area, where one single man, just by turning a small wheel, caused the big engine to turn around 180 degrees ... miracle of miracles!!

[394]

The town breathed to the rhythm of the incoming train in the morning and the outgoing train in the evening. Young people suddenly had a new place to spend their free time, and on the Sabbath, the streets leading to the outskirts of town and the train station were full of people, an entire parade leading the gentile passengers to the station, and the Jews watching and enjoying the sight .... Today there isn't even one remnant of all this. During World War I, the station burned down, and in its place a very small station was built, which looks more like a tavern ....

THE GREAT SYNAGOGUE

Oh, the synagogue .... How many sweet memories are linked to this synagogue and the synagogue courtyard .... I spent almost half my childhood years here—for where else would Jewish children have free entrance and so much open space to play in? How many pairs of shoes, do you think, did I tear climbing and jumping around on the fenced lawn? Where else could we roll in the grass and feel at home? Where did I absorb so many Jewish melodies and prayers as they were sung by our cantors? Where else could we see such a magnificent, tall-to-the-ceiling Torah ark?

And we haven't yet mentioned the powerful impression made by the synagogue in general, with its tall, massive cornices, beautiful candelabra hanging from the tall ceiling, and wonderful acoustics. The wide, beautiful entrance from the anteroom, broad stairs, and large door to the synagogue seemed to have been built especially for us, the children, to have enough room to run in and out or to fight over a walnut or piece of candy thrown by the women, as was the custom, after honoring a bridegroom by calling him to the Torah reading ....

The synagogue builders had very good taste, no doubt. No better or more beautiful monument could have been erected, in which so much effort and so much money was invested. Generations have come, and generations will go, but such a synagogue will never again be built in Kremenets ....

SHIMELE'S PLACE

It's a big leap from the calm, beautiful synagogue to "Shimele Shepherd's place," but this picture as well is attached to my sweetest childhood memories. The place played an important role in the lives of the young people of Kremenets.

Where did I see real-life wild animals for the first time in my life? At Shimele's! A circus—whether under the open sky or in a huge tent—at Shimele's! A wild party for the peasants, where the main attraction was climbing on a rope dipped in soap—at Shimele's! Training on horses—at Shimele's! A fair—at Shimele's! Horse trading—at Shimele's! Everything at Shimele's ....

One Hanukah, I saved my Hanukah money, all six kopeks, and went to Shimele's to buy a colt for myself.... How I envied the peasants' young sons, who, sitting on their fathers' horses, looked down at us—the Jewish children—with such pride and contempt ....

[395]

THE PUBLIC BATHHOUSE

After Shimele's place, I think the best place to have a good time was, without any doubt, the bath .... We used to go to the bathhouse every Friday, since on Fridays we were free from cheder because the rabbi's wife was busy preparing for the Sabbath. I always loved the great hustle and bustle in the bathhouse. The room was full of hot steam, and it was almost impossible to see each other through the mist. It was fun to see the fathers looking for their children, trying to lure them up to the highest bench, where the most honored citizens were sitting and noisily hitting their bodies with branches or little brooms .... I remember that once we witnessed a real "show" near the bathhouse: It was Friday, and a Jew was coming "from the mountain," driving his cart full of sand, beautiful bronze sand that the women would buy to spread on their wooden floors. Suddenly, as the man drove his cart and horses over the bridge near the bathhouse—boom! The bridge collapsed, and the cart, horses, and driver fell into the small brook underneath. The entire town ran over to watch, and it certainly was the first time in the history of Kremenets that a horse took a bath in the local creek ....

THE CHURCH

In the very heart of Kremenets, I see the picture of the church, its domes, and its bells with their constant, almost deafening, sound. It's true that for us, the Jewish boys, it wasn't a very fitting place to roam, in spite of the broad stone sidewalk and the large beautiful plaza, where various parades took place.

On Sundays, the plaza outside the church would fill with life, and even Jews made a good profit, even though the shops were closed for half the day. So many gentiles would gather there that I'd always wonder where all those gentiles came from in such great numbers .... In general, however, the church and its surroundings left a bad taste in my **mouth ....**

THE RELIGIOUS SEMINARY

The seminary was almost a town of its own: large, tall, white gates, many windows, and a tall fence along the entire length and width of the mysterious building, where a Jewish soul could never enter. For us, the boys, it presented no attraction at all.

In one way, though, the Kremenets Jews enjoyed the seminary: through the big clock in the tall tower. There was no better entertainment on a summer night, when the moon shone and the stars were spread through the sky, than when people, exhausted from the unbearable heat during the day, would sit on their balconies or porch stairs because they couldn't sleep—and suddenly the seminary clock would begin to ring its bell, again and again, until it completed all 12 chimes ....

[396]

SHIRAKAYA ULITSA—BROAD STREET

This was the street where I lived. From our terrace, I saw many parades and processions, and I was quite familiar with music .... But the most beautiful music I ever heard on Broad Street, and it sounds in my ears to this day, was every Sabbath before dawn, around four in the morning, when in the stillness of the night I heard very clearly through the closed shutters the voice of the Jew who'd taken upon himself the task of calling the Jews to prayer and sang with a melody that came straight from his heart:

Children of Israel, the holy people,
rise, rise,
to the worship of the Creator,
for this is the reason of your being ....

The soft tones of the call, which I heard every Sabbath at dawn, are stored in my memory, stronger than anything else that I cherish.

THE LITTLE HILL BEHIND THE GREAT SYNAGOGUE

And now, I can see three pictures at once! The Hill was the place where we Jewish children most loved to pass our time, in particular when winter came, and with the first big snow, the special road for the sleighs was ready. Where in Kremenets would be the best and safest place to skate and go tobogganing, if not on the broad, aristocratic street behind the synagogue?

When the Holy Sabbath day arrived, the morning prayer was over, the meal and kugel were eaten, and the adults lay down to take a well-deserved nap after a long week of toil and worry, then the entire street filled with children .... How did Jewish children get hold of so many sleds? How come Jewish children knew how to use skates? And yet our noise and cries of joy filled the noble street and gave us indescribable happiness!

I'm looking at the photograph of my grandfather R' Iser Fingerhut's little house, with its garden and big oak tree, about 200 years old; oh, how dear this little house and the courtyard were to me .... In the yard was a little room that was mine during the summer, as soon as it was emptied of the firewood it contained during the winter. I'd transform the little room into a circus, where I was the acrobat, the ticket-taker, or even the owner himself .... There was enough room in the large courtyard to play "soldiers," and I liked to lie down in the shade of the oak tree with a book in my hand and philosophize with myself about what I was reading.

THE BOULEVARD

I see before my eyes the boulevard, with the gate that leads to the Bagayavlenski monastery. Several times I risked my life and crossed the long monastery courtyard and still came out alive ....

[397]

As far as I remember, no Jewish child ever entered the place, for fear of "the evil eye" .... Therefore, I enjoyed the guardhouse near the monastery very much: every Sunday afternoon, they played music on the square in front of the guardhouse, and there was no greater pleasure in the world than to listen to music.

All of Kremenets liked to listen to the performers. The girls would stand for hours at the windows listening to Chatskele Klezmer and his band .... Even one accordionist and his partner, who would set up four walls and present a puppet show, would attract a large crowd.

I'll never forget the melody played by the accordionist while his partner performed, showing the Christian youngster Gavrile kissing a girl while his rival hit him on the head and killed him. Soon the murderer tried to wake him and called out, weeping:

Gavrile Gavrile
Get up and drink some vodka

Then they covered him with a black cloth and gave him a funeral, and during the procession the main actor—to the crowd's merriment—cried:

Charity saves from death!
Give charity! Give charity!

For us, the children, watching the play was a rare pleasure. We always had a good laugh and, besides, the play took place outdoors under the blue sky and was free, so everybody could come.

THE CREEK

Kremenets Jews, as well as guests who came to visit—everyone made fun of our "river." ... True, the creek was so narrow and shallow that even chickens could cross it easily, and there was no question of swimming there, in any case. However, as young boys, we found a way. We worked as beavers do: we gathered straw, wood, and sand, rolled up our pants, and began working until a small "lake" was formed, in which we'd splash until the peasants noticed us and sent their ducklings to the lake, and we had to leave the premises ....

I remember that one summer a terrible summer storm broke out in Kremenets. In the course of some three hours, there was terrible thunder and lightning that roared and exploded—we thought a new flood was coming .... When it was over, the first thing we did was to run to our creek.

A rare picture unfolded before our eyes: the creek streamed and stormed like a real river, the water covered the hills all around, and the waves carried with them everything that was in their way—trees, wooden boards, logs. The rumor was that people even drowned in the river ....

[398]

TWO POEMS

Hadasa Rubin (Warsaw)
English translation by Yocheved Klausner

AN AUTUMN RAIN

(*Kremenitser Shtime*, October 9, 1931)

> The rain is pouring, it drenches all,
> Sands, paths, ponds, roads,
> It fills them,
> It kneads them,
> Just like sourdough for bread.
> In drops and streams,
> It strikes the roofs,
> Bores holes in all the ceilings,
> Soaks the poverty inside;
> Drop by drop it falls
> And fills little earthen dishes,
> Sometimes wets the little feet
> Of a small child.
> Blue little feet, lean arms,
> Old, cold and wet walls
> Bent by the wind.
>
> The rain is pouring, it drenches all,
> Sands, paths, ponds, roads,
> And shatters heaps
> Of rotten leaves,
> Mixing them with mud.
> Jets of water running fast,
> Drenching perforated shoes.
> Ripping, dragging in the stream
> Wooden boards and heaps of dirt.
> Streets and lanes become empty.
> The wind rushes over them
> Tearing from end to end, mocking
> The poor hungry dogs.

[399]

> The rain is pouring, it drenches all,
> Sands, paths, ponds, roads,
> It fills them,

It kneads them,
Just like sourdough for bread.
In drops and streams it strikes the roofs,
Bores holes in all the ceilings,
Soaks the poverty inside.

THE FIRST SNOW

(*Kremenitser Shtime*, January 15, 1932)

On a little hill stood a little house
An old little house, with an old fence.
In the little house there were many little children
But in the little house there was no bread at all.
There was a little grandmother, old as well,
Who could not bear any crying.
The little house and the little hill
Were all covered with snow.
Said the children: Oh, a little sleigh,
Oh a little sleigh on the snow!
Said the grandmother: Who needs the sleigh—
Clean your noses and go away!
The children lift their heads and stretch their tender necks
To reach the cold window-pane,
And the dear grandmother, so old
But not at all deaf ...
Through the window the children see
Only a white fence,
But soon they are bored and remember
That what they want is bread.
But the dear grandmother, old as she is,
Does not bear any crying.
Said she: It is still early, meanwhile look out the window
And see how the first snow is falling ...

[400]

KREMENETS NICKNAMES

Heynekh Kesler (New York)
English translation by Yocheved Klausner

A. THE "HERD"

Ayzik di Ki (cow)

Yankel di Shof (sheep)

Kive (Akiva) Leviten (whale

Fertel Of (quarter chicken)

444

Fayvish Kelvales (calf's)

Yuresh mit der Kie (with the cow)

Yankel Tsap (goat)

Shime'le Pastukh (shepherd)

Rachel fun di Genz (from the geese)

Mayzele (little mouse)

Avraham-Yoel Tshizshik (finch)

B. ADDITIONS TO THE FIRST NAME

R' Avraham Pipik (bellybutton)

Avraham Tsitske (understand)

Avraham Shpring-in-Bet (jump-in-bed)

Ayzik Pare (steam)

Ayizik Shlisale (middleman)

Idel Tsap (pigtail)

Aharon mit di Gleklakh (with the bells)

Berel Choygel

Basi di Moyd (girl)

Duvid'l Korol (coral)

Duvid Vas (what)

Duvid Parkh (scab)

Hersh Shkravalnik

Hersh-Mendel Amalek

Heynekh Kapota (coat)

Heynekh mit der Blat (with the paper)

Hinde di Sorvern (waitress)

Zelig Oder (vein)

Zalmenishke

Chaskel Balebos (homeowner)

Chayim Dzhinshik

Chaykel of Kremenits

Yoel Kishke (gut)

Yoel fun der Leyvent (linen seller)

Yosi Ditina (kid)

Yashke Ponimayesh (understand)

Yekl Shkalik (bottle)

Yankel der Langer (long)

Yankel Zaverekhe (snowstorm)

Yankel Bortsh

Yankel Plokht (twist)

Libe di Grobe (fat)

Leybenov Atiets (priest)

Leybish Spodek (tall fur hat)

Leyzer Draykop (head twister [swindler])

Leyzer der Gendreyter (crazy)

Mendel funem Plats (from the market)

Moti Kashe (porridge)

Muni Zhmenye (handful)

Moshe Hipsh (nice)

Moshe Shibeye (wheel)

Moshe Kadushke (barrel)

Moshe Kadoynik

Moshe Povitinye (spiderweb)

Moshe Kraf (lump; evil person)

Natan Soldat (soldier)

Pinye Pitsyatsye

Fishke General

Pesye Milkhike (dairy)

Kalman di Mame (mommy)

Shaye Tyutye

Shimelc Pastukh (shepherd)

Simche Gorgl (throat)

Shlome Sondi's

Shaul Kozeratske

C. VARIOUS NICKNAMES

Beztolk

Bizem Keshene (vest pocket)

Bashkeyer

Bilitshikhe

Tsherire Haroshi

Tap Teyglekh (pot dumplings)

Trentel

Tsherindik

Broyt mit Shmalts (bread with goose fat)

Groysekhe (bragger)

Der Malakh (the angel)

The Choymer

Di Terkinye (the Turkish woman)

Vizale

Varnitshke

Father Poish

Todi Bode

Tarashtshekhe

Malakh Hamavet (angel of death)

Spasiba za Torah (Thank You for Torah)

Pitsieritsye

Papalik

Pontshekhe (doughnut)

Tsikorye (chicory)

Koyolterlekhe

[401]

KREMENETS CHARACTERS

Motye Kornits (Jerusalem)
English translation by Yocheved Klausner

> Dedicated to the shining memory of my father- and mother-in law, Chayim and Feyge Bakimer. May their memory be bound in the bond of the living.

My townspeople were "all-year Jews," simple people, devoid of particular pretensions, who led quiet lives, earning their livelihood with difficulty—sometimes with more and sometimes with less success— through commerce, by selling groceries, or through simple labor or craftsmanship. Not ultra-fanatics but not unbelievers, God forbid— "give to Caesar what is Caesar's and to God what is God's" was their motto. They sent their children to "school" but also to the Talmud Torah or the cheder for Jewish studies. They experienced worries and joyful moments but were far from depressed or gloomy. On the contrary, they always liked a good joke or a clever saying and laughed with hope, not forgetting to mention "God willing"....

This was the majority, the mainstream of Jewish Kremenets.

Every one of them found his "equals," lived close to his peers in profession or livelihood, prayed in "his" synagogue, and lived in "his" neighborhood. The tailor who lived on the tailors' street prayed in the Tailors' Small Synagogue; the butcher, in the Butchers' Study Hall, and so on.

They were friends with one another, they knew "what was cooking in their neighbor's kitchen," and they called themselves by their occupations: Menashe Shuster (shoemaker), Chayim Gershon Shnayder (tailor), Leybtshe Katsav (butcher). Often, the occupation would become a nickname, which stuck to this or that person at random, following a slip of the tongue or a chance saying uttered by one friend or another. The individuals would accept that willingly and gladly, and would even stress it in their conversations with other people: "You can trust me, Ayzik Shlisale (middleman). I'll take care of that ..." or "I, Pinye Pitsyatse, am telling you ..." and so on and so forth.

The nickname actually lived longer than the real name and was inherited by the children and the children's children.

Here, I'd like to mention a few of those simple Jews who remain in my memory and describe some of the characters we all remember.

YIDEL SHUSTER (SHOEMAKER)

His name was Portnoy, which in Russian means tailor, but by occupation he was a shoemaker, and so he was called. He was a good craftsman and also active in community work. In particular, he helped with the soup kitchen, the Society for Visiting the Sick, and the Home for the Aged. He helped many poor people and had a good reputation.

The house where he lived belonged to him and his neighbor, Yosl the tailor, and contained two apartments. To avoid resentment and bad feelings, every year they'd exchange apartments. Such good neighbors are hard to find.

CHAYIM GERSHON SHNAYDER (TAILOR)

His surname was Nudel [needle], by occupation he was a tailor, as befit his name, and he was called "Chayim Gershon Shnayder," with a long, accented "a."

[402]

A skilled worker, he'd make festive suits for all the bridegrooms in town. His patriarchal demeanor commanded respect. Radiating importance, on Sabbath eve or a holiday eve he'd walk with measured steps, carrying newly finished clothes to his clients, self-confident and satisfied with his work: "I, Chayim Gershon the tailor, do my work perfectly; you won't find any flaws in my work ...."

MORDEKHAY SHNAYDER

Mordekhay was another tailor, but a ladies' tailor. I don't remember his real surname. A tall Jew, always in a hurry, he never had enough time, and he was very proud of the beautiful wedding gowns he'd make for brides. When the bride came for the fitting, her entire family was present, every member of the family expressing an opinion and giving advice. In short, the families were happy, and Mordekhay the tailor earned his good name honestly.

VIZALE

I forgot his real surname, but he was a ladies' tailor as well, and everybody called him Vizale, maybe because he was so short. He was not a first-class tailor, but he had his clients. When he had a non-Jewish client, it was a wonder how he managed to communicate with her, since he didn't know Russian. He talked with his hands and worked fast, and when the garment was finished, he rehearsed several times how much money he'd have to ask for his work.

YANKEL VASERTREGER (WATER CARRIER)

Yankel's surname was Kadushke [barrel], but everybody called him Yankel Water Carrier. He had two sons, Chayim Pinchas and Moshe. Father and sons earned their livelihood by carrying water.

The sons had their own "weaknesses": Chayim Pinchas loved watches. When he managed to save a little money from his meager income, he bought a watch, and he wore it all day. As soon as he could spare some money again, he bought a gold watch. On the Sabbath and holidays, he'd wear both watches, and when asked what time it was, he'd ask, on the Sabbath watch or the weekday watch? Finally, he acquired a third little watch, which he held in his vest pocket in case the other two stopped working ....

The other son, Moshe, liked to take a walk on the Sabbath wearing squeaky shoes, and this was his greatest pleasure ....

MOSHE HIPSH (NICE)

A simple Jew, he was a porter, and that was how he made his living. Even when he was already advanced in age, he'd carry a sack of flour on his back or even a barrel of herring, which was twice as heavy. In addition to that, our merchants would hire him as their "town crier": he'd walk the streets and loudly advertise their merchandise.

[403]

And this is what he'd proclaim: Fresh fish, come, ladies, nice ladies, buy fish for the Sabbath, nice fish, good fish, nice, nice!

And so he got his nickname, "Nice."

However, with all these occupations, he lived in great poverty, but he never complained and was a very honest man.

SHALOM PEYKE (PIPE)

He started as a turner and ended up as a porter. He was nicknamed Peyke, which meant pipe, because in his turner days he made himself a pipe and always smoked it.

When he was a turner, he was very poor and lived in a hole. In time, he managed to save 25 rubles and borrowed another 25 to return the loan at half a ruble a week, and he and Shimon Chayim the miller built themselves two little houses on the other side of the pond, near the town dump. They were good neighbors all their lives.

HINDE DI GROYSE (BIG) AND HINDE DI KLEYNE (LITTLE)

Both were named Hinde, and both were caterers. One was big and one was small, and therefore they were called Big Hinde and Little Hinde.

They were hired at weddings, and they'd prepare everything with great care, good taste, and a loving heart. Family and guests enjoyed the hospitality and the wonderful taste of the food.

HERSH KLEZMER

His real surname was Komediant [comedian]. His children were ashamed of this name, and they changed it to Commandant, but in town he was called Hersh Klezmer. All his family members were talented Jewish musicians, and they played at weddings and other Jewish happy occasions. The entire family was a wonderful orchestra—Hersh and his children: Moshe, Ayzik, Yosl, Sore, and Malke. Each played a different instrument, but the drummer was Tovye the water carrier, who wasn't even a relative. For three years they taught him where and how to beat the drum, yet more than once he disappointed them ....

[404]

MOSHE TATE (FATHER)

He was a teacher by profession, and he taught little boys and girls the prayers and weekly Torah portion. He was not a great scholar, and there was not too much he could teach his pupils. He lived a simple life and died at the ripe old age of 75.

He was a bachelor for his entire life, yet he was the one whom all the children in town called Father.

AYZIK SHLISELE (MIDDLEMAN)

I forgot his surname, although he was very popular in town. When a merchant in town needed a short-term loan, he'd go to Ayzik Shlisele, and soon he'd have the money. What was the exact source of the money? That was a secret, and Shlisele kept the secret stubbornly. It was known, though, that he'd procure money only when he knew it would be in safe hands, since the original fund was intended for a sacred purpose: it was mothers' savings for their daughters' dowry.

LEYBENOV ATIETS (PRIEST)

He was a wise Jew and lived "on air." ... Every time a priest or an estate owner would want to sell some object or another, he'd know about it and would immediately find a buyer and arrange the deal. The money he earned as mediator was his living for the next few months.

He acquired the name "Priest" through a mistake he'd made, but the nickname stuck and stayed with him his entire life.

MALKE DE LANGE (LONG)

Her name was Yadushliver, but everybody called her Malke the Long. She lived in the Vishnevets suburb across the pond, but she always was busy in town. People would ask her jokingly what she needed her apartment for and who was doing the cooking at home. She was in the mediating business and acted as an agent mainly in the grains trade—a clever Jewess who managed her business wisely.

BABTSYE FUN DER FISH (FROM THE FISH) AND BABTSYE FUN DER PUTER (FROM THE BUTTER)

We had two Babtsyes—one sold fish, and the other, dairy products. The Kremenets Jewish women enjoyed this situation and liked both of them. And, in truth, thanks "first to God and then to the Babtsyes," the town was provided with two main products: fish fresh out of the river for the Sabbath and holidays, and butter, sour cream, and cheese for weekdays.

Both were welcome guests in Jewish homes because they wouldn't wait for the customers to come to them, but would bring their wares to the customer's house, to everyone's kitchen. And when a needy woman didn't have enough money to pay, they'd say, "Well, eat it in good health, and when you have, you'll pay." And many poor women would leave it at that, eat in health, and thank "first God and next Babtsye, may she be blessed with the light of Heaven, amen ...."

RACHEL FUN DER GENZ (FROM THE GEESE)

Around the Hanukah holiday, it was time to begin preparing "goose fat" for Passover. The aroma of the cooking fat wafted through the entire neighborhood, and the children would wait impatiently for the tasty cracklings.

[405]

This was the "high season" for Rachel from the Geese, who would have the geese slaughtered and sell the raw fat and the clean, plucked geese separately. As with many others in our town, we didn't know her real name—and, actually, who needed to know it? Who didn't know Rachel from the Geese? She was a short, round woman, always wearing her long apron, two large baskets full of plucked geese in her hands, with the fine smell of goose fat announcing her arrival. That was how she lived her few years, and it was said that she made a very decent living.

PERL CHICORY

Her name was Perl Beznoska; she was dark, and this was the source of her nickname, Chicory. She was a short woman, and she sold very tasty egg cookies. Even the Russian officials would come to buy her cookies. Perl Chicory lived below the pond and was Shalom Peyke's neighbor.

R' SHLOME KOVAL (THE BLACKSMITH)

Yitschak Vakman (New York)
English translation by Yocheved Klausner

A white beard, blue eyes, always humming some melody and always looking absorbed in thoughts—so is his figure engraved in my memory.

He was a wise Jew. He rented an apartment in Shpigler's house, and he had his workshop there as well. There was nothing that R' Shlome couldn't fix—and he always did a good job. Yet earning a living wasn't very easy. During the week, he managed somehow—but how to provide for the Sabbath? And so R' Shlome would sit in his shop and watch for a customer—it was Wednesday, tomorrow would be Thursday, and what about the Sabbath?

Suddenly an acquaintance—a priest—came in, holding a small package wrapped in newspaper. A little icon of Jesus with a broken leg. "Can you mend it so it looks like new?" "Yes, Father," said Shlome—is there anything Shlome the Blacksmith can't do? "But it'll cost you a ruble, Father." "I'll give you a ruble and 50 kopeks," said the priest. And Shlome stood there and said to himself, "Master of the Universe, how dear and sweet You are! You break the arms and legs of their gods only to give Shlome the means to provide for the Sabbath ...."

[406]

Old Kremenets

[407]

DOCUMENTS

Echoes of the 1860s
Kremenitser Shtime, No. 8, November 20, 1931
English translation by Ite Toybe Doktorski

In *Raz-svyet* of 1860 (no. 35) we read, among other things, the following lines:

... "We can say with satisfaction that the Jews of Kremenets have for some time had a different point of view about life's interests in general and about education in particular: they are more or less permeated with the need to give their children a fine education in real life. And the women don't lag behind; modern education is important even when there are no boarding schools. You can find a first-class primary school there, but its success is not great, if we are to believe the rumors we hear. With satisfaction, we note that the girls speak good Russian, Polish, German, and French. They show a particular love for the latter. As for how they dress and behave, they are no less than the girls of main cities are. For that reason, the Jews of the neighboring villages call Kremenets a heretic town ...."

In this same article, the author tells us about the sad case of a 16-year-old girl from a well-respected Kremenets family. The girl was lured by a few fanatics to the local monastery for the purpose of converting her to Christianity. She suffered there for about a year. With great efforts, her unfortunate father succeeded in obtaining the child's freedom from the authorities. They freed her, but she paid a heavy price for staying a year in the monastery: she had lost her innocence .... And the author ends his article with one exclamation: "It would be very interesting to know how history judges a case such as this one, which could happen in the 19th century ...."

The article is signed by a certain Y. Rozental. Translated and sent for publication by Alexander Rozental.

[408]

THE DISRUPTED MEETING (AN EPISODE FROM WORKING LIFE IN KREMENETS)

L. Rozental, *Kremenitser Shtime*
English translation by Yocheved Klausner

The first strike, organized by the seamstresses ("tailor girls," as they were called), lasted three months. They had one single demand: to cut the working day from 16 to 10 hours.

The strike succeeded, and it brought them great satisfaction. As soon as the first workshop owner gave in, the others followed, one by one. What had a great effect was that the strike took place during the high season. Every evening at 8:00, the working girls would show up on the workshop street. Those who were detained at home were quickly called out. The bosses would become angry and even use foul language, but it didn't help.

Meanwhile, the strike leaders initiated another project: teach the girls to read and write. Almost none of the girls could write or even read. Only a very small number had ever studied anything. Some would go to the rabbi's wife during their lunch break, and for five kopeks a week she would teach them the prayers. You can imagine how much "learning" could take place at the rabbi's wife's house, as the entire lunch break, including eating, didn't last more than half an hour ....

In wintertime, during the long Friday evenings, the girls would gather in one of the houses, each bringing "seeds" (roasted sunflower or pumpkin seeds), and they would tell stories or dance a quadrille or a *sher*. In the summer, during the long Sabbath days or holidays, some would go for long walks in the park or the mountains. Others would go to Liskovski or elsewhere to play on the swings or drink *kvass* or milk fresh from the cow. This was how the young people would spend their time....

> [**Translator's Note:** A *sher* is a popular Jewish folkdance.]

A few weeks after the strike, the leaders assembled all the girls, divided them into groups of four or five, and assigned a teacher to each group, who taught them Russian and Yiddish reading and writing. This course lasted a year and a half, during which time other strikes were organized. Following the first strike, these strikes were much easier to carry out and considerably shorter.

At that time, the first workers' parties began to appear. In our town, a Labor Zionist chapter was established first. Several months later, a student from Odessa organized a "Bund" chapter. They had a series of gatherings, meetings, and discussions, each chapter attempting to win over members of the other. The main activities took place during the free summer Sabbath days and holidays. The Labor Zionists were the larger group, mostly intelligent people who contributed a great deal to the group as a whole.

Every Sabbath, some of the members would go to the mountains and look for a secluded valley or forest, where the entire group would meet.

[409]

Right after the Sabbath meal, the young people would go out into the street, and one of them would indicate to several others an address, where they would find another friend, who showed them the way further. The information thus passed from one to another, indicating four or five such "meeting points," where assemblies would be taking place. Each place had a "patrol" on guard, which through accepted signs would convey to the others when a suspicious person was noticed. This arrangement worked regularly, and meetings were held every Saturday. After the meeting, everybody went back to town for a leisurely walk through the Jewish streets.

On one summer Saturday, a new member was scheduled to speak at a Labor Zionist meeting. At the same time, the Bund had a meeting as well, and at that meeting, a Christian member was scheduled to speak. In his honor, the meeting was conducted in Russian. During his speech, a noise was suddenly heard, and the guard asked the listeners to leave the place quickly. One by one, the group members left, pale and frightened. One young lady fainted.

Soon one of the guards appeared and announced that nothing had happened; they could return to the meeting: a soldier had stopped near one of the guards and asked for directions—the road to a certain village in the area—and this looked suspicious to the other guard, who panicked. However, nobody returned to the meeting, and when the rumor about the "disrupted meeting" spread to the Bund assembly, they broke up their meeting as well and scattered in all directions.

It was a hot day, and everyone met finally in town, tired and sweaty, and had a good laugh about the entire affair ... the "frightened guard" could not show his face in public for a long time ... because of him, two important meetings had been disrupted.

PASSOVER FOR JEWISH SOLDIERS

***Kremenitser Lebn,* No. 16, April 17, 1936**
English translation by Yocheved Klausner

This year, the military units stationed in town included a large number of Jews. Sometime before Passover, the community leaders and the rabbi, Rabbi M. Mendiuk, got in touch with the authorities and made sure the Jewish soldiers would be free during the eight days of the holiday. Some of them received only the first and last days; some even received ten days of leave. The community arranged a special kitchen in a private home for them, and there they ate during the holiday, like all other Jews.

[410]

During the intermediate days of Passover, they received a special room with beautifully set tables in their barracks. Every day, the rabbi sat with them during meals and spent several hours with them. The military authorities acted with special consideration and exempted them from hard work. On the last day of Passover, during the prayer in memory of the dead, a special prayer was dedicated to Marshal Josef Pilsudski, with all Jewish soldiers from the local military unit participating as well as those from units in the surrounding towns.

PREPARING TO BUILD THE TARBUT SCHOOL

Kremenitser Lebn, **No. 19, June 10, 1938**
English translation by Ite Toybe Doktorski

After many interruptions, we have recently received the plan as validated by the district authorities. Undertaking to create the Tarbut School and its eventual high school is an enormous enterprise. On the acquired plot of land, we'll build a three-story building with the latest modern equipment. It is understood that this can only be achieved with the participation of the entire community, which will have to find the necessary means for its own school and also show great readiness for sacrifice. At the joint meeting of the Tarbut Committee and the Parents' Association president, a special construction committee was elected, which has already started working on its assignment. A select committee was also elected, with a restricted number of members. The Construction Committee members are Mrs. F. Baytler, M. Goldring, Ch. Grinberg, Y. Vayner, M. Zaytshik, N. Fiks, A. Pintshuk, A. Fayer, Y. Kop, and A. Shnayder. The elected president of the Select Committee is Mr. M. Goldring. The other Select Committee members are Messrs. Ch. Grinberg, A. Fayer, and A. Shnayder. Mr. Margolis was appointed to the Construction Committee. The committee has already started working on its assignment.

THE JEWISH NATIONAL FUND BAZAAR

Kremenitser Lebn, **No. 16, April 17, 1936**
English translation by Ite Toybe Doktorski

On Saturday of the intermediate days of Passover, on April 11 of this year, the Women's International Zionist Organization (WIZO) organized the opening of the bazaar for the benefit of the Jewish National Fund in the *Hashmonai* hall. All the participants admired the exhibition, which was arranged in an exemplary manner. Wares of varied nature were exhibited for sale in different kiosks: glassware, spices, toys, and much handicraft.

At exactly 10:00 in the evening, the president, Mrs. F. Baytler, opened the bazaar. In a short speech, she explained WIZO's aims and its role in the Zionist movement. Mr. M. Goldring, the president of the Zionist Organization, saluted WIZO in the name of all the Zionist associations and underscored the movement's praiseworthy activities.

After the opening greetings, a concert took place. The recently engaged cantor of the Great Synagogue, M. Shrager, accompanied by Mrs. K. Berman-Litvak, performed three pieces.

[411]

The pieces were performed professionally and in good taste. The audience applauded enthusiastically. Some of the audience had come to the bazaar opening especially to hear the cantor's performance.

After the cantor's concert, Mrs. Baytler invited Mrs. Kamenshon, Mr. Goldring, and Mr. Gofman to cut the ribbons of particular kiosks. Groups of people had assembled near the kiosks to buy different objects. At small tables, people feasted on Passover pastry from the buffet.

By organizing the bazaar, WIZO once again demonstrated the dedication and seriousness with which it carries out every assignment and task. WIZO fully deserves the praise bestowed on it. The gains from the bazaar—so it is said—will be beyond all their hopes.

In the same hall that same evening, the solemn handover of the Jewish National Fund Golden Book certificate, in which the Zionist Organization had inscribed the name of the deceased Dr. Arye Landsberg, also took place. Editor M. Goldring recalled Dr. Landsberg's great achievements and his big contributions to the movement. The doctor's son, Lawyer Landsberg, thanked the members and organizers in warm and emotional words for the honor bestowed on his deceased father. The certificate was handed to the Zionist Organization board, which put it up on the wall of its premises.

OPENING OF THE PIONEER FUND CAMPAIGN

Krementitser Lebn, **No. 17, April 24, 1936**
English translation by Ite Toybe Doktorski

On Sunday, the 19th of this month, a big public assembly took place in the women's premises next to the Great Synagogue over questions regarding pioneering youth and their collective farm training.

The speakers were the president and the central board of Pioneer in Poland, Messrs. Y. Otiker, Y. Sheynboym, and A. Vayner (from Warsaw). The speeches were received with great enthusiasm by the enormous assembly. There were more than 1,000 people on the very crowded premises, and many people couldn't get in because there was no room.

The gathering—which became an impressive demonstration in favor of pioneering thought and solidarity with pioneering youth—ended with the sounds of the "*Tehezakna.*"

> [**Translator's Note:** The poem *Birkat Am,* of which *Tehezakna* is the opening word, was written by Hebrew Chayim Nachman Bialik. It was put to music and became a popular anthem in Zionist circles.]

APPEAL BY THE PIONEER CHAPTER SPONSORS

Kremenitser Lebn, **No. 10, March 3, 1936**
English translation by Ite Toybe Doktorski

Due to the catastrophic situation in which the Kremenets Pioneer chapter finds itself, the supervising sponsors held an urgent meeting to examine the situation from every angle. It was decided to launch an appeal to all Jewish social institutions and private enterprises to hire only pioneers for any job.

[412]

It is really a crime that some don't want to see what's happening around us and don't want to understand that Jewish society has an obligation to pay the greatest attention to the builders of our future.

We know the warmth with which people relate to the Pioneer chapters in other cities, where they offer them work and where all Jewish enterprises employ only pioneers.

This isn't about asking for charity, and it isn't about philanthropy. We must give them work, and we ask that this work be carried out properly. Higher salaries are not requested; they make only the very important request that people hire only pioneers for any job be taken seriously. We are convinced that our appeal will not fall on deaf ears.

Sponsors' board members: M. Goldring, Lawyer Landsberg, M. Zaytshik, Ch. Krementshutski, Y. Blumenfeld.

MONTHLY KREMENETSER RELIEF SUPPORT HAS ARRIVED

Kremenitser Lebn, **No. 53, January 22, 1937**
English translation by Ite Toybe Doktorski

This week, a telegram arrived announcing that $136 has been sent for January. Of that sum, $100 is earmarked for institutions, and $36, for the Avraham Vaynberg Fund, to be distributed to poor families. Only the Fund committee members know what great deeds are accomplished with the Fund's monies, because they know the needs of those asking for help. This Fund's money is especially earmarked for impoverished, needy families that manage to receive public assistance. It is worth noting that the amounts the Fund is now distributing for the third time are greater than the usual amounts distributed as social help by the community. This Fund, named after the first head of the community, Mr. Avraham Vaynberg, of blessed memory, was founded by the directors of the Kremenetser Relief Organization in New York, our town's friends, who tirelessly devote time and energy to putting together the help promised to Kremenets. We know that only a few members of the directorate take this heavy task upon themselves: Messrs. Barshap and Shrayer. Given that not all those receiving the help are in a position to thank our fellow townspeople for their noble work, this newspaper is hereby doing it in their stead. We can assure our dear fellow townspeople that the whole town of Kremenets fully appreciates their warm relationship to their old home, which needs their help so much now, and considers it not only a material gesture on their part but also as moral support in times of great need. May the hands that do this holy work be blessed.

[413]

DESTRUCTION AND HOLOCAUST

A SHTETL BY THE POTIK, DESTROYED AND DESOLATE ...

Manus Goldenberg
From *Kremenitser Shtime,* 1932

English translation by Yocheved Klausner

> [**Translator's Note:** The following poem was published in *Kremenitser Shtime,* the Kremenets Jewish newspaper, in 1932. The grim situation described in the poem and the sad, depressing images must thus be attributed not to World War II and the Holocaust, but to the horrors of World War I and the Jews' terrible economic hardships, combined with cruel anti-Semitism, which prevailed in the 1920s in Eastern Europe.]

A gift for my little daughter Lili

A town by the river, destroyed and forgotten—
Full of beggars, as God created them,
Surrounded by mountains and many green fields
The "bridge" in the middle, then shops and more shops.

The windows are shining, bright lamps through the night
The war gave the owners much richness and might
Happy are their faces, proudly they walk
Who can bring us those old times back?

Poor was our town, God help us all,
Burned many times through summer and fall,
From Chmielnitski's time many houses stand
Who can afford to replace them with new ones?

Crooked little streets, dirty and flooded
Attics, porches—all crowded and locked,
Young boys and girls, old Jews with beards,
Clad like the farmers, backs bent to the ground.

And there was another street, muddy and full of children,
The street where the butchers' profession reigned,
The butchers—strong Jews with large bones like the bulls,
They would fight till they saw many rivers of blood.

[414]

Today they are beaten and humiliated,
Plagued by taxes, pursued and hurt.

Except on Friday night, when carrot stew and meat are on the table
And on the Sabbath, yawning on the porch and chewing Sosye's seeds.[11]

Way up the street were the shoemakers: Vanke and Sashke,
In the light from the small windows, in their working clothes
They were polishing boots, carefully sawing the leather.

The old little market, with so many carts
Dirty booths, broken roofs,
Jews who sell sawdust and tar that smelled,
Their livelihood worries sunken in darkness.

Smart and strong women crying, "Come here!
Hey, sir, what will you buy?
Boots made of the best leather!"
The shopkeepers grumble in the neglected market.

There are also quiet and clean streets, where the rich live,
Noblemen, officers, with royal demeanor,
And well-to-do Jews also living nearby,
But many of them destitute—selling their wives' jewelry …

A house with high fences, on one side and the other,
Grandpa and grandson are trading in grains;
Big, spacious houses, storehouses and courts,
Good neighbors to friendly rich farmers.

The carpenters still make beautiful things,
Unmatched in the entire region.
But their sons do not have work
And fathers toil and hardly win their bread.

[415]

The turners and their barefoot assistants
While working sing prayers like cantors.
Mountains of cigarette butts in the corner,
For the "Russians" to use and enjoy.

From the trade union members just a few remained,
All beaten and destroyed in the year 1914[2]
Only old furniture, antique broken tables—
That is all that remained from the turners' labors.

---

[1] Sosye sold pumpkin seeds in the market.
[2] The outbreak of World War I.

The cart owners, happy and in a good mood,
Dressed in colorful jackets, caps on their heads,
United in friendship with their colleagues
They have a drop of whiskey to warm their blood.

The policemen would hide in the corners
Who can stand a beating by a cart owner?
Hey, watch out! When the young men are merry
Even the czar's recruits hide behind the walls.

The old people tell stories, "Once upon a time,"
How they would wander in forests and valleys
On horses, like lions carrying their bones—
Not one remains from those old heroes.

The cemetery at the lake is desolate and neglected,
Little greenish stones stand alone
Jews came to rest from their hardships in life,
The tall mountains keep watch all around.

[416]

GHETTO MARTYROLOGY AND THE DESTRUCTION OF KREMENETS

B. Shvarts

I shall convey here, as a testimony, everything that is in my power to express, from memory and from feeling. Horrible pictures flutter in front of my eyes, and my ears are torn by the pitiful, moaning cries of the dying.

The question, the distressing riddle, surfaces again and again: how could that have been possible? I ask myself: was it at all possible that parents would knowingly abandon their children to blind fate; a brother—his sister, children—their parents? That masses of people would let themselves be driven like sheep to the slaughter, take off their clothes, and lie down in the death pits to be shot together with their children? Bitter fears squeeze our hearts: why haven't we, the survivors, lived to see a revenge on our hangmen?

The world has remained indifferent to our catastrophe. The spilled innocent blood demands revenge.

Dieburg-Hessen, March 10, 1948

In Memory

Of my beloved father and teacher Simche son of Yitschak Shvarts, my mother Rachel, daughter of Betsalel, my brother Yisrael, my sister Zisel, my wife Lusye-Male, her parents Fayvish and Leye Rozenblit, and my daughter Miryam Etel.

THE BEGINNING OF THE WAR

Immediately after the German-Polish war broke out, Kremenets suffered air raids. Most of the first 40 victims perished not because of bombs, but from machine-gun fire from low-flying airplanes, spreading death among passersby in the street. Fortunately, our region was not occupied by the Germans right away. According to the Stalin-Hitler agreement, part of Poland was given over to the Soviet Union; Kremenets was situated in that region.

The catastrophe began after war broke out with Russia. The fighting around town lasted 10 full days. Kremenets was in a strategic defense position. On Wednesday 2 July 1941, the 11th day of fighting, the first Germans soldiers entered the town. Some of the residents took refuge in the mountains; others left town and fled wherever they could. Thousands tried to follow the retreating Soviet army but were forced to return to town. There they found that a small group of Russian soldiers remained in town and took control of a bakery, intending to take bread and brandy "for the road." From inside, they shot at the German soldiers, the result being that many civilians were hit and wounded, among them the wife of Shlome Basis the blacksmith and his daughter, Golde. A German soldier was killed, and they buried him in Pinye Fridman's backyard.

[417]

A decree was issued stating that the Jews must take off their hats when they passed by that location. On this occasion, many were beaten and arrested.

THE FIRST POGROM

The next day, Thursday morning, a looting raid began. All the Jewish shops were robbed by the soldiers, with the cooperation of civilian gangs. Since war had begun unexpectedly, no one had had time to prepare food. Soon, there was a milk and bread shortage, and long lines formed in front of the bakeries. The members of the hastily organized Ukrainian militia also turned against the Jews, beating them and driving them away from the bread lines. With cries of "You have sucked our blood long enough!" the bandits began their killing spree. They caught everyone, old and young, arranged them in rows, and led them, beaten and bleeding, to the tower at the Rovno Gate. Elye Reznik managed to run away but lost his mind, Potikhe soon died, and Gun died before the eyes of his entire family. This first pogrom was carried out by Ukrainians and Poles, with the full cooperation of the German SS soldiers and the Gendarmerie.

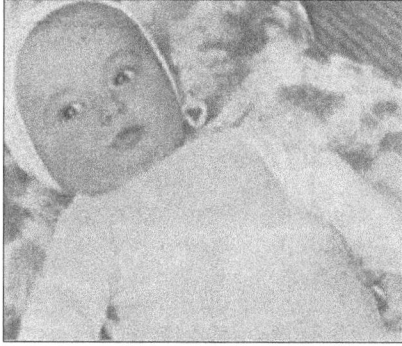

the author's daughter,
miryam etil, killed in the ghetto

During Russian rule, several people had been shot in the tower, and now the Jews were blamed. Under severe beatings, the Jews were forced to dig the corpses out with their bare hands and wash the bodies. They were beaten, and some died from the blows alone. Gangs of Ukrainian hooligans from the surrounding villages, armed with sticks, marched into town, pulled people out of their houses, and murdered them on the streets. Most residents of the Dubno road were killed and thrown into pits.

This bloodbath lasted throughout Thursday and Friday. It is impossible to describe the cruel tortures suffered by the people in the tower. One of them, my wife, crawled out from under the mountain of bodies that covered her and, under cover of night and through roundabout ways in the mountains, managed to reach our home. Others tried to run in several directions, but some were caught and tortured to death. Mr. Barshap's son was caught near Sapanuv village. He was tied to barbed wire and later thrown into the lake. Others perished by other horrible means. Women were raped. Dr. Groyzenberg's daughter lost her mind.

[418]

With gifts in their hands and fear in their hearts, a group of Jews approached the commander and asked him to stop the slaughter. The commander "was very surprised by the news ..." and ordered a stop to the murders. During those few days of the pogrom, about 800 Jews perished—men, women, and children. Some Jews who had remained hidden in their houses were pulled out after being exposed by Ukrainian informers, and they disappeared without a trace.

THE "JUDENRAT"

The Town Administration soon established a "Judenrat" [Jewish council]. Its members were esteemed Jews in town, joined by some refugees from Western Europe, who had a good command of the German language. The Judenrat offices were located in Roykhel's courtyard, on Slovatski Street. Catching people in the streets, beating them up and dragging them to work—this stopped. The Judenrat's duty was to provide the required number of slaves for forced labor and also to dispense bread to the workers and to poor families in town.

News began to arrive from the smaller towns and villages in the area that slaughter had reached those places as well. The majority of the Jewish residents of the nearby town of Vishnevets perished, and that was also the fate of the Jewish population of Ostrog, the MHRSh"A's town.

[**Translator's Note**: MHRSh"A stands for our teacher the rabbi R' Shmuel Eydels.]

It was difficult to estimate the number of Jews in Kremenets, after so many refugees from other towns rushed in to seek shelter. Before the Nazi plague, the Jewish population numbered over 20,000 souls. It is known that in the summer of 1942, 8,500 Jews were in the ghetto.

The author's family. Standing at left is B. Shvarts

[419]

"NO-MAN'S" JEWS, UNPROTECTED

A period of utter anarchy began. Ukrainian gangs, in full collaboration with the Germans, looted the Jewish houses. In addition, Jews were required to make various "contributions"; they tried to save their lives by complying, willingly or forcibly. Every Jew was required to wear a white band with a red Star of David on his right arm. Walking on the sidewalks was forbidden—if someone forgot, he was killed immediately. The Judenrat managed to obtain an annulment of this decree from the town administration, but the German and Ukrainian "street guards" continued to beat "trespassers" on the sidewalks. The Jews were outside the law. Chasing Jews out of their houses without allowing them to take any belongings became commonplace. The Jews were commanded to take off their hats every time they met a German—often the German so "honored" would beat up the poor Jew .... A Jewish child who went to the market place to buy food for his family would be forced by a Nazi to stand on the table and dance for the spectators around him, and then the murderers would spit on the table and force the child to lick it clean. The prohibition to buy not in the shops but only in the market enabled Ukrainian bandits to arrest some buyers. Often, these people disappeared altogether. This piece of news we heard from Nute Barshap, himself a victim of that inquisition; once a strong, physically powerful man, he became a broken man.

All this, however, seemed only a prologue to what was about to happen with the arrival of the Gestapo, who took power. Soon a series of arrests began. Also among those arrested were Poles and Russians who were considered "pro-Soviet elements."

The Judenrat was ordered to supply people of various occupations "for work." It is hard to say whether the Judenrat knew what bitter fate awaited these people. The fact is that after liberation, in summer 1945, a mass grave was found in the valley near the town, containing all the victims. Only one was identified, by his clothes—the engineer Rozen, an active member of the ORT organization. A Soviet Historical Committee investigating Nazi crimes discovered another row of mass graves near the tower and in old defense trenches on the road to Podlisets. People living in the neighborhood knew about the killings but kept silent. The Jewish population couldn't believe, or didn't want to believe, that such cruelties were taking place. In order to avoid panic, the Judenrat supported the story that those sent to work were safe and that nothing had happened to them. One Jew who was released from work and managed to return to town, however, related that the people had been murdered and that some of the victims had been torn to pieces by cruel dogs.

[420]

In this "action," the Gestapo murdered most of the Jewish intelligentsia and religious officials, such as rabbis, ritual slaughterers, judges, etc. It was a horrible moment when the victims' relatives and wives brought food for their family members. The Gestapo took the food and led the relatives to the place where they could "see" their beloved. None of them returned alive. Among those who perished was Sheyne Shklovin, B. Shnayder's wife, who had come from Argentina to visit just before the war broke out and remained there. The fact that she was an Argentinian citizen was of no help. She brought food for the veteran community worker, Eng. Ovadia. Her son died after terrible torture in the first action, poisoned by very slowly flowing gas. The Gestapo's first action took 800 lives—all this happened by the end of August 1941.

THE OLD GREAT SYNAGOGUE IN FLAMES

One night, all the Jews were awakened by a huge fire in town. At first, nobody knew what had happened. They thought that the light was coming from the Soviet side of the border—the Soviets preparing for attack; the feeling was that soon the town would be liberated.

[420]

On the wreckage of the great synagogue

[421]

But they realized the mistake very soon, when it became clear that flames had engulfed the Great Synagogue. They wept bitterly. The synagogue had thick walls, built out of large stones. The day before, the Gestapo had stolen all the valuable objects from the synagogue and placed barrels of gasoline inside the building and firefighters around it to make sure that the fire would not spread. All the wooden furnishings inside, including the beautiful Ark with the Torah scrolls, burned down. Only the walls remained. After the fire, the Gestapo came to the Judenrat "to investigate," thereby forcing it to sign a "protocol" stating that the Jews themselves had set the synagogue on fire.

A few days before, German soldiers set up an "inquisition-play" in the synagogue. They caught a Jew named Lipin and forced him to gather a *minyan* in the synagogue. The ten Jews were forced to put on their prayer shawls and pray. In fear and desperation, they covered themselves and prayed silently. But the German animals demanded that they pray in a loud voice. They turned over the prayerbook stands and forced Lipin to beat his friends and order them to dance around the stands. When Lipin's too-merciful beating was not enough for the soldiers, they killed the poor victims. After this devil's dance, all the Jews who had gathered there were chased away.

JEWS CROWDED INTO THE GHETTO

In spring 1942, an order was issued to lock all the Jews in a ghetto. The area allocated as living area was 1.5 square meters per person. The ghetto was situated in the western part of town, from the Jewish Hospital to Gogolevska Street; from there to the High School, down to Sheroka Street; then along the east to the fire station. This was about one mile in length and 100 meters wide—enough to be suffocated! Petitions and pleas to increase the area did not help. The ghetto was enclosed in a wooden fence three meters high. Although the Jews were permitted to take with them any belongings they required, they had to leave most of their things because of the lack of space. They sold what they could, and with the money they bought mostly food supplies. By December of that year, the ghetto had become even more crowded because of the stream of Jewish refugees from other towns. As could be expected, many disputes and quarrels broke out, and the Jewish police had to deal with and resolve them.

At about that time, Commissar Miler ordered the Jews to tear down the walls of the burned synagogue and plant grass over the area so that no trace of the synagogue would remain. However, all the Jews who were able to work were laboring for the military forces, and only the elderly, the weak, and the sick remained in the ghetto. Proper tools to tear down the thick walls were not to be found.

[422]

The Judenrat mobilized engineers and blacksmiths, but the stone walls were as strong as rocks, and they withstood all efforts to move them. Even the bricks were glued together, impossible to take apart. Meanwhile, the deadline for finishing the work approached. The Judenrat somehow managed to postpone the deadline, but even at that time half of the walls were still standing, and Miler the murderer warned "for the last time" and threatened to shoot if the work was not completed. Panic spread among everyone involved. The Judenrat ordered that children 14 years old and adults of 55 join the hard work. It was shocking to see how people swollen with hunger toiled with their last strength. They all went to work voluntarily, since the third deadline was approaching and the Jews felt the danger of death in the air. The Judenrat issued an order for the Jews who worked for the German army during the day to join the demolition teams at night. The engineers tried to use various means to accelerate the process, but with little success. It was also necessary to keep the bricks intact, since the Germans intended to use them to build a tobacco plant. After some time, the workers had an idea: they poured soft earth around the walls until it reached the upper level of the remaining walls so that no parts would stick out. On this earth they sowed grass. But this work cost lives. During the demolition of the walls, one wall collapsed and buried several people. The cries for help were horrible. This time Commissar Miler, riding on a white horse, allowed the firefighters to help dig out the victims, who had been injured so badly that they were unrecognizable. The only person who was identified was Moshe Milman's 17-year-old son, a handsome youth who had just returned from work at the army barracks.

CRACKS IN THE GHETTO

When the Judenrat was established, the first members were community leaders. They made every effort to help and very often risked their lives in the process. It was their responsibility to carry out the Germans' various orders, supply the number of workers demanded by the Germans, and distribute the rationed food. Often the Judenrat would intervene when robberies or beatings occurred. Among the members were Dr.

Bozi Landesberg and Dr. B. Katz—both Zionist leaders—and Dr. Lione Grinberg, a Bundist. In fulfilling their tasks, they suffered many difficulties.

From the first days of the Judenrat's establishment, the life of Dr. B. Landesberg, who struggled against the Nazis' cruel decrees and their continuous demand for "contributions," hung by a thin thread. He was treated murderously by the Germans, and one day he tried to take his own life with the help of a razor blade. He was saved by a miracle. His wife Sonye, Yitschak Poltorak's daughter, ran from house to house, begging the Jews to conform to the Nazi demands.

[423]

The same danger loomed over the heads of the other Judenrat members. B. Katz was arrested and kept hostage because some Jewish workers were late for work at the military barracks. Only thanks to the fact that other workers arrived soon was his life saved this time.

The Judenrat's duties became more difficult as a result of various new Nazi requests day by day. Some of the refugees from Western Europe who knew German joined the Judenrat. One of them, Dr. Mandel, organized the "Jewish Police." He chose the best people for this duty, but it turned out that two members of that "police force" behaved like German agents. I could tell a great deal about the others as well, but as a Jew from the ghetto who is trying to understand the psychological circumstances, I would rather keep silent. Two of them must be mentioned, however—the Czech Jew Bronfeld and Itsi Diamant from Lodz.

In the summer of 1942, Bronfeld became the chairman of the Judenrat. He compiled a list called "people for work." My brother-in-law Lemberger was also on the list, but he didn't go with the group. Actually, he told me that nobody wanted to go, since people never returned from "work." Bronfeld had taken money from the families, allegedly to help find their relatives, but he never found them.

Diamant tried to compete with him. He had an assistant, Nutin; both were connected to an international group of thieves. Nutin was more human than his associate was. That summer, the broken and tired-out Jews reached bottom and could barely stand on their feet. They simply could not go to work. Nutin understood the danger of that situation, so he began to hand out money to those who would agree to go to work, and thus saved the Jews from a catastrophe. What was the source of this money? Whether the Judenrat or another source—I don't know.

The refugees who knew German and were Judenrat members established relations with the Germans, even with the bestial Commissar Miler, who was bribed constantly. But the main "player" in the murders was the aforementioned Bronfeld. He was befriended not only with the commissar but also with the head of the gendarmes, Shuman. Those two supplied the men who were sent to death in the labor camp.

Bronfeld and Diamant figured as *Schutzjuden* ["protected Jews"] of the two rulers, Miler and Shuman. Diamant was Miler's Jew, and Bronfeld was Shuman's. They competed in loyalty to their masters, each showing exaggerated devotion.

[424]

In this strange competition, Bronfeld won. Searching Diamant's house, in the presence of the Jewish police, they found diamonds and other expensive stolen objects. Finally, he and his assistants were shot at the tower. The "competition" went on between the two German murderers as well, in the sense of "if you beat my Jews, then I'll beat your Jews." Reports on the happenings reached the higher German authorities, and Bronfeld and his helpers suffered the same fate as his friend. This rough playing with Jewish lives lasted from fall 1941 until summer 1942. After their death, the aforementioned Dr. Mandel from Krakow became Judenrat chairman. He served the Jewish population devotedly until the last day of the ghetto's destruction. In addition to the regular sections of the Judenrat—finances, food, work duty, and Jewish police—they established a soup kitchen in the firehouse.

By Commissar Miler's order, Jews had to change the "Star of David" band that they wore on their arm to a yellow patch, sewn to the back of their clothing, beneath the collar. With my own eyes, I saw a Christian neighbor weeping when he saw this mark of disgrace .... By the same order, Jews received a ration of 75 grams of barley bread a day. The death rate increased, to 10–12 people a day.

The murderer Miler kept issuing new decrees every day. Five hundred death sentences were executed on the prisoners in the tower, for various "crimes." For example, 10 young people who worked in the German camp were shot under the suspicion that they had stolen gasoline. Every week, another contribution was demanded: money, bedding, clothes, white winter coats for the army. In that way, the Jews were robbed of the last of their property. And if this was not enough, they suddenly asked for 25 tons of grain. The Jewish police, led by the Judenrat, broke into basements and bunkers and confiscated the provisions that had been hidden there. During this operation, heartbreaking cries, from fear of death by hunger, would be heard. Many contributions had to be bought outside the ghetto and exchanged for the remaining few hidden objects.

Men were not allowed to grow hair, and women had to keep their hair cut short.

Just like the synagogue, the Jewish cemetery was destroyed as well—and the work was done by Jews. The tombstones were uprooted and used as building materials, and so was the stone fence around the place. Only very few tombstones on the hilltop were left standing.

The sadistic desire to humiliate the Jew as long as he breathed went so far that the cruel Miler ordered the Judenrat to erect a "house of shame" for youths 16 to 19 years old.

[425]

Every youth was obliged to visit the "house" and show a certificate that he had actually been there. The only way to escape from that was to pay another "contribution" of money. It was rumored in the ghetto that the source of this devilish idea was the same Diamant.

Many Jewish houses outside the ghetto were demolished by the commissar, and the contents sold to the farmers in the surrounding villages. Some houses were given to local Christians.

In August 1941, again by the order of the murderer Miler, the Jews made a "contribution" of gold and silver: 11 kg of gold and tons of silver, including silver objects from the study halls and synagogues.

THE JEWISH POLICE

The Jewish police were organized by the Judenrat. Before the Jews were locked in the ghetto, the function of the police was to assign people to work and collect contributions. Every Jew was required to work three times a week. The police would go from house to house and take people to forced labor. Those who did not turn up on time were forced to work six times a week. This problem of trying to avoid work caused the Ukrainian police to join in the patrols through the houses, and then they had no choice but to go .... They were all assembled in one place. Their food consisted of half a liter soup and 250 grams of bread for the whole day. Hard work and such meager sustenance soon reduced their physical strength to a minimum, and they tried by every means to find a hiding place and thus evade work duty.

At first the Jews were not very anxious to join the Jewish police. This changed, however, when the Jewish population was forced to live in the ghetto, which was watched by the German gendarmerie and the Ukrainian militia. The situation turned much worse. The Jewish police were burdened with difficult tasks. The hungry population was devoid of any physical strength. People died of hunger in the streets. The corpses were thrown onto a wagon and taken away—no funeral and no grave. Diseases spread among the population, and in this situation, people were still forced to go to work. At the Judenrat's instructions, the Jewish police helped carry out these orders, as they did with other orders. True, the Judenrat believed that this way the Jews were saved from being shot on the spot, although in Rovno at that time, fall 1941, 17,000 Jews perished.

It was a miracle that in that crowded place where hunger ruled, an epidemic did not break out. This was certainly due to cleanliness and hygiene. We had three wells in the ghetto. Early every morning, a long line would form to get water for the day. Lines would form at the public toilets as well, but everything was kept clean, despite the water shortage.

[426]

The police, wearing yellow caps and shoulder straps, was very strict about keeping every place clean, including bakeries and grocery stores. After seven in the evening, no one was allowed on the street.

Naturally, among the police there were some brutal elements as well. They used drastic means to collect the contributions. The Judenrat "treasurer" decided how much every person or family was ordered to give; there were some that had nothing to give but their souls. On the Judenrat's instructions, the police conducted house-to-house searches and confiscated everything they could find. When there was not enough to meet all the demands, we would buy things outside the ghetto and carry them inside, often by bribing the guards; this way we could deliver the entire "contribution punishment."

The Jewish police took part in the cruelty, but objectively, it must be said that as long as the ghetto existed, we could at least breathe. We did indeed risk our lives by smuggling in food, but it was meant to sustain our lives. These smuggling operations took place at night, while the Jewish policeman would distract his German or Ukrainian colleague's attention, meanwhile fulfilling his own family's needs. However, when the order came to liquidate the ghetto, "contributions" or any other means of appeasing the enemy would be of no help.

DAYS OF ANGUISH IN THE GHETTO

Besides forced labor and the struggle to survive the day, our hearts would shrink from fear and anxiety that always loomed. Someone returned from his work duty outside the ghetto and told us the SS were advancing toward the town with machine guns; another said that he had heard from a German that he next day a new contribution would be imposed; still another brought the news that additional people would be taken to work, or that a new "action" was being prepared for sick people, children, and people unfit for work—and other similar "news." The atmosphere was depressing, the people's mood miserable. We thanked God for the arrival of night and asked for it to go on forever. This was "a day in the ghetto."

Early in the morning, people were on their feet, often accompanied by Judenrat or police, ready to lead them to work. But first they would hurry to the well to get a place in the line for water.

[427]

Then came street cleaning, meanwhile trying also to reach the kitchen to get a little soup and the distribution places for a piece of bread. Sometimes we left empty-handed. Sometimes there were arguments—and the police had to intervene. At the same time, the corpses lying in the streets—the people who had died during the night—were loaded on wagons and taken to be buried. No one was impressed any more ... on the contrary, some were envious, saying that this was a "deluxe" death.

Then the gathering at the ghetto gate began. Young people were taken to the workplaces. Our hearts trembled with worry about their fate. At the head of each group, a policeman led them out through the gate. Outside, German gendarmes and Ukrainians performed a search, and if they found something they liked, they took it away. Beating was added as well. But much worse was the search when they returned from work and were about to enter the gates. If they found an onion or an apple on someone, probably obtained through begging, everybody was beaten. A woman who dared hide an egg for her child was beaten murderously. It was a miracle that she was not arrested, which would have meant certain death. Sometimes one or two were "fortunate"—as the guard standing at the gate had some human feeling and would look away. Then people would say, "Today was a lucky day; we could bring something in to the ghetto." Those miracles, however, were rare. When it did happen, the Jewish police and a hospital employee would be at the gate, and part of the smuggled goods would be taken for the hospital patients. We did this wholeheartedly, because the hospital did not receive regular support to buy food or medicine. There were many cruel moments at that gate to hell—like murderous beatings for hiding a small piece of bread, but one would risk his life for the hope of sustaining that same life with a piece of bread.

There was an illegal market in the ghetto. The Jewish police would look the other way—since the policemen themselves would often purchase what they needed. But as soon as one felt even the faintest "smell" of a German, the entire market would disappear in a wink. When danger was over, everything resumed, as before.

On Y. B. Levinzon Street, near the *kloyz*, people were lying around, disfigured and swollen from hunger. They warmed themselves in the sun and waited for death to redeem them. They "lived" in the *kloyz* on two rows of wooden boards covered with straw. Dirt was all around and worms multiplied, and no disinfectant helped. They burned the straw, but the crawling insects returned. This was the place of poverty and despair in the ghetto.

[428]

Even in the former "Grand Hotel," the air was rotten and deadly. Like flickering candles before going out, people would become extinguished. These poor souls, together with the sick in the hospital, were the first to be taken in every action.

"GOOD GERMANS"

One day, a drunken German entered the ghetto and walked along Gorna Street. People became frightened and fled in every direction; only the children remained. The German began to hug and kiss them, handed out candies, and wept in a loud voice: "Poor Jewish children! Why does cursed Hitler pursue you?"

The Jews were horrified, thinking of what the results of such a scene could be if the authorities found out. It did happen sometimes that such a German, who had some form of heart, would wander into the ghetto and show human feeling toward the Jews.

We had a special "saying" for such Germans: "For a good German—a good death, for a bad German—a horrible death." By the way, every Jew in the ghetto paid a "per capita" tax of 20 rubles for the Germans.

Among the guards at the gate were some who would let a wagon or two loaded with food pass through the gate into the ghetto for a good bribe. Sometimes it was possible to smuggle in some meat. This was done during the night.

HIDING FROM DEATH

News about the extermination of Jews in other places began arriving in the ghetto. We feared that a "Jewish cleansing" action was in store for Kremenets as well. People began to plan for ways to avoid certain death. Some slipped out of the ghetto during the night, relying only on God in Heaven; some tried searching for a safer place, where the knife was not yet at their throat; some fell directly into the murderers' hands. The majority, however, remained in the ghetto and began digging underground hiding places and building bunkers. Naturally, the bunkers were very crowded, and not every ghetto resident could find room for a 14-square-meter area where 24 people, adults and children, would have to squeeze in. There were many who could not take it anymore and willingly surrendered to the murderers. There were some exceptions. A very few managed to build real shelters for themselves and their families, even with electricity and sanitary installations. However, it did not help in the end. The Nazis set fire to the ghetto, and there was no escape for anyone.

Crowding and shortages led to moral breakdown. We lost control of ourselves and over the children.

[429]

Young people felt that the end was near and behaved shamelessly. Although many decent people gathered into the ghetto from other places—among them intelligentsia, scholars, and the like, there was no lack of immoral and underworld elements. No one, even the leaders, had the strength or interest to lead the community on the path to normal human behavior. Life was sunken in the fear of death, and every person's desire was sharply pointed to one aim: escape, rescue.

The food situation worsened from day to day, and hunger spread. Smuggling food from the outside became almost impossible. The number of dead increased, and begging the Christians on the other side to sell a piece of bread was of no help. With no attention to danger, desperate people tried to crawl under the fence, only to be caught by the murderers. The watch around the ghetto was reinforced by adding Ukrainian guards. The Judenrat warned us against illegal trade, and the Jewish police made extra rounds. But the power of hunger was so strong that people were ready to risk anything.

A 16-year-old girl who could not bear it any more risked her life, with her parents' consent. With a basket in her hand, she was on her way toward the fence. As she began climbing, she was hit by two Ukrainian bullets and fell, landing on the outside. Somehow the Germans were moved by the beautiful face and punished the Ukrainian guards.

Among the Christians, with whom Jews had left some of their belongings in hope for better times, some would toss parcels containing food over the fence. Most, however, waited for the last execution, to become the heirs.

FORCED LABOR BECOMES MORE CRUEL

The Judenrat "work office" received greater and greater demands for workers. Exhausted people were driven to slave labor. Some of the seven overseers of the seven work details were good people, and they tried to help the beaten and the humiliated workers by paying ransom money from the more affluent elements. However, the work was so hard and so terrible that people simply wouldn't go, even though they risked their lives in doing so. The work office was aware of the danger and decided to investigate the situation. They found that the workplace was tobacco plantations, having a fixed—and very large—amount of produce that the workers were asked to deliver every day. Those who could not meet the demands were beaten murderously by the Ukrainian supervisors.

[430]

The head overseer, Tsiger, informed the German commandant, Hamershteyn, and as the latter realized the truth, he killed some of the Ukrainian guards and sent the rest to work in Germany.

For his "goodness," Hamershteyn was thanked by "gifts" bestowed on him by the cautious Tsiger. The same Hamershteyn conducted the action in Dubno, because he had not received such "gifts."

Although there was a demand for work in town outside the ghetto and many women were prepared to go, they were not accepted. Only through bribes could such work be "arranged." The women hoped that they would be able to smuggle some food into the ghetto as they returned from work. Every morning, a crowd of women would gather in front of the work office, demanding noisily to be included in the day's "working group." Many tried to sneak through the lines, but of no avail.

TO ROVNO, FOR WORK

After the first action in Rovno, a workforce shortage was felt in town, and Jewish work committees from neighboring places, including Kremenets, were asked to supply workers. However, no one would go voluntarily; the committee registered men who did not have families to care for, but they found hiding places and did not report to work. Finally, Hamershteyn ordered that people be caught wherever they could be found, and the German gendarmes, aided by the Ukrainian and Jewish police, conducted raids. People were caught and thrown on wagons. Women's and children's heartbreaking cries cut through the air, and we were certain that this was the beginning of the annihilation of the ghetto. Workers who had just returned from work, tired and broken, were taken again—which strengthened the feeling that this was the end. Christian residents outside the ghetto looked on, laughing happily; very few showed any sympathy. If someone jumped off the wagon and tried to run away, the Jewish police would catch them and bring them back, although, rarely, they looked the other way, and the poor Jew managed to escape. Running through fields and forests, the runaways finally returned to the ghetto.

Outside the ghetto, wagons loaded with people brought from surrounding towns were waiting to be taken to the train. There was a rumor that they had been "bought" by Tsiger from Hamershteyn, to be sent to Rovno for work—and the rumor turned out to be correct.

[431]

Another rumor said that they were fed properly. Following all these rumors, people were fighting to be included in the next transport to Rovno.

Soon, the fateful moment arrived for the heads of the Jewish Work Committee: Hamershteyn was transferred to Dubno, Tsiger lost his "protective power," and the murderer Miler took his place. On his new orders, even the dead were not allowed to be taken out of the ghetto for burial without his permission. Once they managed to smuggle out a dead man and tried to bury him, but Miler was informed and he gave an order to arrest Tsiger and his family, and they were all shot. This was how he took his revenge on Tsiger, who used to satisfy Hamershteyn with "gifts" ....

CATASTROPHE IS NEAR

In August 1941, news arrived about the Jews' extermination in several places. Refugees from Rovno related that the town had become "cleansed of Jews." Meanwhile, in our ghetto we continued to bear heavy hunger, went to work, paid "contributions"— but we also heard rumors, news picked up by the radios outside the ghetto, about German defeats and Russian victories on the battlefield. Jews sought consolation and hope, waiting for a miracle from heaven, dreaming that they would be saved. But the dreams and hopes were soon shattered.

One Sunday morning, a week before the "action," a call was heard in the entire ghetto, through megaphones mounted on cars that crossed every street in town: the population was called to kill the Jews. Sabbath, August 9, was their last Sabbath. That afternoon, the work committee received the order to send everyone those returning from work to the train station, to load grain. It was a cold, rainy day. The Jewish police waited near the ghetto gate, and as soon as a group of workers came back from work, tired and soaked by the rain, they were pushed into the wagons. Any Jew who tried to reach the ghetto gate was caught by the Ukrainians and pushed back. The Germans knew very well that it was the last day for the Jews, but they wanted to gain another night of slave labor from them. The poor, suffering workers returned to the ghetto only late at night. Just like the darkness of night, the fate that awaited them in the morning was also unknown to them.

A NIGHT OF DEADLY FRIGHT

In the middle of the night between August 9 and 10, the ghetto was shaken by gunshots all around. A deadly silence fell upon the ghetto, and a silent desire that the darkness would last forever.

[432]

The shots did not stop, however; they became stronger and closer, and bullets began to hit the ghetto. Loud screams were heard from Gorna Street and from around the synagogue. Soon the murderers tore down the gate and broke into the ghetto, found the hiding places, and took all the Jews away, constantly shooting in every direction. People fell dead all around. The deafening screams of children and adults filled the air. People ran like hunted animals, trying to find shelter, whether in a cellar or an attic. Children trembled in their mothers' hands, looking for protection from death. It was a night of horror, on the eve of annihilation.

The night came to an end, however, and a beautiful sunny day began to shine on the ghetto.

A rumor spread that 60 Nazi gendarmes, reinforced by the Ukrainian SS unit stationed in the neighboring town of Belaya Krinitsa, were about to storm into the ghetto, under the pretext that there was an uprising of the Jews. They ordered the Judenrat to bring all the "fit-to-work" to the gate, to be taken to work. The Judenrat appealed to everyone to obey the order, but very few appeared. The gendarmes and the SS decided then, according to certificates they had received from the work places, who would be taken away from the ghetto. During this selection process, almost the entire population of the ghetto, men, women, and children, gathered along the wall.

The victims were placed in two long lines—one from the Great Synagogue to Y. B. Levinzon Street and Tailors' Street, and the other along Gorna Street. The Ukrainians stood between the two lines. No shot was fired. The Jews could have easily disarmed them, but unfortunately no one dared. They were at the lowest stage of despair. They were also too weak to counter the cruel beatings. Everybody moved toward the gate, perhaps thinking that they would find a way to escape. Even the sick and the swollen from hunger crawled out of their beds and joined the crowd. Meanwhile the "selection" went on: the fortunate were led away from the gate and in groups of 400 were sent to Belaya Krinitsa. The few who tried to escape were pursued by the Ukrainians and shot, and their clothes were taken off. The Ukrainians warned that the same fate awaited anyone trying to escape. I looked at the Christian passers-by, and on some faces, I saw laughter. I saw Sonye Goldenberg-Shpigel-Gurevits being pushed by a policeman and beaten with the butt of his revolver. The child in her arms looked on with deadly horror ....

ON THE ROAD TO DEATH

On the Death Road, people tried to comfort one another. Some still believed that life would be given back to them; others said that they did not want to live without their families.

[433]

Deportation of the jews of kremenets

When we arrived at our destination, we were all crowded into stables, surrounded by a human chain of Ukrainian SS. We sat on the ground. Many of us cried bitterly, mourning their beloved.

Next to me sat the lawyer Lione Grinberg, his head in his hands, and he wept: "I am a criminal," he said to me. "I left my wife and my children in the ghetto; why did we behave like that?" Like a thorn stuck in the heart, the question remained in the air—without answer....

After the "selection" and after some of us were sent to Belaya Krinitsa, those who remained in the ghetto sought shelter in the bunkers. But there was not enough room for all of us. The first victims were the residents of the Grand Hotel and the hospital patients. The Ukrainians and the German gendarmes drove them to the synagogue yard, and from there they were driven, in wagons or on foot, to the old barracks outside the town, where the defense trenches dug during World War I were still intact. The victims were beaten and forced to undress; then they were forced into the trenches and shot by an SS murderer.

[434]

Those who were not hit by bullets were finished off by the Ukrainians, who were standing ready around the pits. The screams, especially those of women and children, reached to heaven. There were also many local Christian residents who came to enjoy the spectacle. Every row that fell into the grave was covered with earth and lime—

while some of the murdered were still moving, in death convulsions—and over them, a new row of people was shot. Some tried, naked, to escape, but the bullets caught them. The living were forced to throw them into the pits and then were thrown in after them. After this "operation" was finished, the Germans and Ukrainians began raiding the bunkers. The children's cries helped the murderers find the hiding places and take the people to their deaths. In some cases, parents covered their children's mouths, and they suffocated. In other cases, parents gave the children poison injections and after that killed themselves rather than fall into the murderers' hands. In the assembly place, Dr. Shklovina begged the Germans to kill her, and one of the Germans had mercy on her and did just that. Her three-year-old grandson was thrown alive into the pit.

The selection was carried out systematically: men fit for work separately, women and children separately. When a child was spotted among the rows of the men, he or she was cruelly pulled out.

Two children clung to their father. The older, a girl, begged the murderers to let her stay with her mother, but suddenly, deadly pale and deadly silent, she broke away and joined the children who were being loaded on the death wagon. The younger child clung with all his strength to his father, screaming, "Father, I don't want to go!" But he was snatched away by a kick of the murderer's boot and then thrown through the air from murderer to murderer until the last one threw him into the wagon.

MURDERERS' TRICKS

To make all the Jews come out of their hiding places, the Germans spread the rumor that those who were still alive would not be killed; they were asked to come out of the bunkers and help identify the possessions of the dead. Accompanied by Germans and Ukrainians, the Jews who did come out walked through the houses, calling: "Jews, come out; no harm will be done to you. You'll just have to go to work."

[435]

Many of the hidden, hearing the words in Yiddish, or even recognizing the voices of their acquaintances, fell for this ruse. As soon as they came out of their bunkers, they were caught and arrested. They were forced to collect the dead from the streets, and then they were all taken to the tower yard and killed there. Some bribed the watchmen to let them out of the ghetto, but they were shot at the gates anyway. One woman, with a small child in her arms, tried to jump over the fence near Gogol Street, and the guard shot her on the spot. The child was still whimpering when they threw them on the wagon.

A MOUNTAIN OF RUINS

The liquidation of the ghetto lasted two weeks. In spite of all the horrors, some did manage to remain alive in the bunkers. However, the murderers' final act was to set fire to the ghetto from all sides. All around the fence, on the outside, firefighters were stationed to make sure the fire didn't spread to the rest of the town. The fire forced the hidden Jews outside; most were murdered by Ukrainians or firefighters.

Then the Nazis spread another rumor: that the Jews themselves had set the ghetto on fire. This rumor, however, was not taken seriously even by the Christian residents, since they had seen with their own eyes how the Germans lit the fires all around and forbade anyone to extinguish it. They made sure that the ghetto would burn to the ground, with all the Jews who were still hidden in the bunkers.

After the fire, the Christians gathered the burned corpses lying among the heaps of ruins.

Sometime after the fire, the murderers discovered living Jews who had been hidden in the cellar of the Milshteyn house. Milshteyn was the *kvass* brewer. Jews were also discovered in the bunker under the Feld family's house, where soda water was produced. There was the entire Feld family, as well as Basis, Golde,* and Shlome the blacksmith's son, with their families and several children. All those remnants were taken out and killed after great agony. They were kept locked up until 100 victims were gathered. Weak and broken, suffering from hunger, they died a horrible death. The corpses were thrown in prepared pits and covered with earth; then the earth was plowed and a garden was planted, so that no person would know or remember their bones' final resting place.

Covering the mass graves
(after the investigation commission's visit, 1945)

[436]

Covering the mass graves
(after the investigation commission's visit, 1945)

[437]

In Veselivka village, near Belaya Krinitsa, old farmers caught fugitive Jews and pulled them back to jail. Others first agreed to hide some of the Jews, among them several young girls, and later betrayed them and delivered them to the Nazis. One of the partners of the Gofman-Yaspe firm transferred his property to a Christian neighbor. During the liquidation, he tried to seek refuge in that neighbor's house, but the latter took him out to the murderers. They beat him up so severely that he lost the appearance of a human being, and when he was brought to the jail, the jail doctor had mercy and put him out of his misery with a lethal injection.

The fateful hour for the jailed people was near. One of the hangmen announced that the day of judgment had come and that the Jews would not be able to "suck the blood of the Christians" any more. At the graves near the military barracks, one Jew dared to speak to his friends around him, saying that there would come a day of revenge for the innocent blood that had been spilled. The son-in-law of Leybele the ritual slaughterer, Hokhgelernter's brother-in-law, comforted everyone present, promising revenge for the murdered innocent victims.

On the eve of the war, a Jewish doctor named Meler took residence in Kremenets. One of the Germans was charmed by his daughter's beauty, and he was interested in keeping her alive. After the parents were killed, the child, who was still in jail, was under the watchman's close supervision. He tried to comfort her and would even walk with her in the garden sometimes. One day, he received an order to "finish off" the child. He took the girl for a walk, and while she played with the flowers, he shot her with his revolver.

In an old chronicle about the Chmielnitski massacres of 1648-49, we read,

> In Kremenets, the murderer took the ritual knife from the ritual slaughterer and killed several hundred Jewish children, asking his friend whether this would be kosher meat or not. His friend replied "not kosher," so he threw one little corpse to the dogs. Then he took another slaughtered child and carried it to the slaughterhouse, opened it, and asked again the same question. This time the friend answered "kosher," so he stuck it on a pole and carried it through the streets calling: Who wants to buy little lambs and little kids?

The author of the chronicle finishes this gruesome tale with the words: May God avenge their spilled blood.

[438]

From a Jewish community of 19,000 Jewish souls, only 13 people remained alive from Kremenets and 7 of the refugees from other places who sought shelter in our town. Another 20 Jews survived by hiding in Christian homes, 8 at a Christian woman's home and 4 in a man's home. This man was later murdered by the gang led by the bandit Bandara.

Kremenets, a mother town of the Hebrew nation, was cut off. The bulk of Jewish life, Jewish culture, Jewish work, and Jewish fruitful creativity was wiped out from the face of the earth. May you be damned, you and your murderers!

We shall forever cherish the memory of the murdered martyrs. Forever, forever they will remain etched in the memory of the nation.

THE LAST CHAPTER

English translation by Yocheved Klausner

Eliezer Barshap, Ramla (Israel), recounts:

On 16 July 1945, I returned to Kremenets. Only two or three Jewish families lived there at the time. I stayed with Duvid Rubin, who lived near the monastery; every day he awaited Kremenets survivors and gave them a place to sleep.

The first terrible shock was when I was shown the site where the Kremenets Jews were murdered. It was on the Dubno road near the coalmine, not far from the cotton factory. I met Sanya Kagan, and we both went to the site. A horrible picture unfolded before our eyes: three large pits where the Jews were murdered; scattered around were bones and heads with hair, bones of small children and torn pieces of clothing and shoes. Cows were grazing in the area.

I went to Kovalski and asked to build a fence around the place; he agreed at first, but he soon changed his mind because he feared the murderous gangs.

The Jewish ghetto extended from the Gindes pharmacy to the Geler house. The entire area was ruined. When cleaning up the ghetto, the workers found many gold coins. Was there anyone who hoped to return and find their money and houses?

Netanel (Sanya) Kagan recounts:

... Early the next morning, we stepped out onto the street. The town appeared before us, completely ruined. Nothing was left of the streets where the Jews had lived. The sites where the houses of learning, the Jewish Hospital, and Jewish houses had stood were now no more than mounds of broken bricks and stones, partly already overgrown with grass.

[439]

Beginning from the site of the high school, there was less destruction around, but the houses were unoccupied. The entire area was a dead wasteland.

We met many Ukrainian acquaintances, who stared at us and asked how and from where we had come. They had been certain that we were all dead. "In spite of our enemies, many young people have survived, and they will avenge the blood of their parents, brothers, and sisters"— this was what we told them; but deep in our hearts, we thought: how we wished it were true ....

We also met one of the eight Jews who had managed to hide and survive. He showed us his hiding place: a cellar with one small window.

We were told that a considerable number of Jews in the ghetto decided to commit suicide rather than die at the hands of the German murderers. One morning, they carried out this decision by blowing themselves up in the houses in which they were locked up. This ended the great chapter of Jewish life in Kremenets.

WITH REFUGEES IN ITALY

Yitschak Vakman (New York)
English translation by Yocheved Klausner

In 1947, being in Europe, I decided to visit Italy to meet the surviving Kremenetsers in the refugee camps. Our relief committee had received many letters from the camps, and we knew that some of the refugees had crossed the border from Austria to Italy, on their way to the Land of Israel.

It was a very cold winter when I arrived in Milan. The town was in ruins after the war. People in rags were begging in the streets. It was difficult to get a taxi at the train station. Despite the hardships, I managed to get to Turin, to the refugee camp. I wandered in the camp for over an hour, searching, until I finally found a few survivors: Mani Okun's son, Shlome Fingerhut's son, R' Tsadok the ritual slaughterer's grandson (his daughter's son), Ayzik Kutsher's son, and several other Kremenetsers whose parents I remembered, and some whom I had known from when they worked at R' Ayzik Shteyner's. From the camp, we went by train to Milan, where we spent the time talking and reminiscing about our old home. With luck, I managed to revive them a little, and I felt like a father who had found his lost children. I gave them some money from the committee, and I left with the decision that our duty was to continue to help them leave for the Land of Israel as soon as possible.

[440]

TO YOU ...

Tovye Troshinski (Tel Aviv)

English translation by Yocheved Klausner

On your threshold I fell, broken with despair,
Driven by a storm in a furious hour,
Suffering and scorned, lonely and tired—
Silently I knocked on your door seeking relief.
Night fell wildly .... Dark wild shadows lingered
Like a veil over the world, wasting, devastating....
Heavy clouds have hidden clear skies
A cold and angry wind extinguishing the last stars.
Silently I knocked on your door seeking rescue.
Only you can heal my wounds, only you can give me comfort.

My path of suffering has led me to your door—
With one last spark of belief: you know, you feel, you understand ....

It was not the dew that covered the field with pearls,
Only my tears, my hot tears—not the dew,
It was not the white clear waves flooding the valleys—
It was my bleeding wounds ....
It was not the wind of spring moaning at your window,
It was my sigh, my heavy anguish, that broke your sleep—
While not one ray of sun pierced the clouds.
My pain is sharp as steel, my anger is burning high!
It smothers my cursing, which is stronger than thunder,
Which is carried over all the worlds and asks for vengeance!
Listen, O listen to the call, hear the great pain,
My generation was cut down, my nation was ruined.

- -

Mourning in front of your door, I am awaiting my sentence,
Will my sun shine again when the day awakens?
Or, at your doorstep, will I suffer the dying pains
And silently breathe my last, in the windstorm of the night? ...

- -

Mourning in front of your door, I await my sentence. **Kermina (Uzbekistan) 1943**

[441]

KREMENETS IN THE WORLD

FORTY YEARS OF THE KREMENETS *LANDSMANSCHAFT* IN NEW YORK

Yitschak Vakman (New York)
(Memories conveyed by Binyamin Barshap)
English translation by Yocheved Klausner

Emigration from Kremenets to America began some 50-60 years ago. Among the first Kremenetsers who came to America were Yakov Kremenetski, Itshi Foks' three sons, Mendel Heker's son, the Benderski children, and others. At that time, the situation in America was difficult and challenging. The *landsleit* felt very lonely; therefore, they tried to stick together. Most of them lived in rented single rooms—very few had their own apartments. The *landsleit* meetings, where they discussed the possibilities of helping new arrivals, would take place on the flat roof of one of the houses. Help was always given willingly.

In 1900, the first Kremenets social organization in America was created, with the help of Mordekhay Shniter's son. However, due to internal disagreements, the organization was soon dissolved.

In 1904, another organization was founded under the name Independent Order of Beit Avraham. Every member was insured for $500 and obtained a life insurance policy. The money was paid to the family at death and was also used to pay burial expenses. Many members between the ages of 50 and 60 registered, and since a number of them died in a short time, the organization was forced to cut the policy to $250. However, this did not help financially, and this second organization was suspended as well.

Several years later, the Benderski children helped establish an organization called the Yosef Shalom Society—Yosef Shalom was apparently a member of the Benderski family. This society is active to this day but has very few members.

In 1914, at the outbreak of World War I, the Kremenets *landsleit* received bitter news about the material situation in their old home. The urgent need to send regular help arose.

[442]

Board of the Kremenets Landsmanschaft of New York

First row, seated (right to left): Harry Vayner, Binyamin Barshap, Yitschak Vakman, Henokh Kesler, Izidor Salmovitsh. *Second row:* Mrs. P. Veiner, Mrs. D. Goldman, Mrs. G. Berenson, Mrs. Guterman, Mrs. Sander, Mrs. Chaye Rapoport. *Third row:* Louis Sigal, L. Berenson, A. Hertsberg, Gordon, Landisberg, Mints.

gathering of kremenets natives in new york

[443]

After a meeting among Binyamin Barshap, Eli Mints, Goldenberg, Binshtok, and others, the Kremenets-Volhynia Benevolent Society of New York was founded. To found the Society, it was necessary to have at least seven American citizens as members. Mr. Kortman joined the committee and was elected president. After World War I, he was sent to Kremenets to dispense help and give support from the Society.

In 1916, the Society founded a relief committee. The members were Barshap, Dr. Marants-Shiedanski, Poltorak, and others. The young members would go every Saturday and Sunday to collect money—at that time, 25 cents was considered a lot of money. The *landsleit* always welcomed the relief messengers, and every week, money would be sent to Kremenets.

In 1916, and later in 1924, the Society bought sites for a cemetery. If the family of the deceased could pay for their plot, they did so; if not, they were exempt.

At about that time, R' Avraham Vaynberg's son-in-law came to New York. He devoted his heart and soul to the Kremenets *landsmanschaft*. In everything he did, he never forgot his hometown—and managed to collect large sums of money. Several times he went to Kremenets in person and distributed the relief money among the organizations: the Society for Visiting the Sick, the Talmud Torah, the Free Loan Society, the Home for the Aged, etc. He died two years ago of a heart attack.

In 1923, Dr. Meir Litvak came to America for a visit. He was welcomed with the greatest honor. On his return to Europe, he took with him a considerable sum of money for various purposes, in addition to money for the Society for Visiting the Sick and smaller sums for several individuals. The money was delivered in the original banknotes.

In 1943, the author of these lines came to America. We then established a new relief society. Excelling in their activities were Binyamin Barshap, Yudel Salmonovitsh, Henikh Kesler, Henikh Gelernt, Harry Vayner, Louis Sigal, and Landsberg. The relief activities continued during the war and particularly right after the war, when relief was so much needed for our brothers who were scattered in concentration camps in Germany, Austria, and Italy. Wherever it was possible to help, whether with money, food, medicine or other necessities, it was done. As with the other relief organizations, this was holy work.

The Kremenets *landsmanschaft* exists to this day. It is not growing, however, since no new members are joining and the old members are getting older; the activities, naturally, have slowed down.

[444]

Banquet for kremenets natives, New York, 1954

[445]

The members meet twice a month in a rented hall and discuss various matters: visiting the sick, helping the needy, supporting various American organizations, taking care of the cemetery, etc. Every new arrival from Kremenets is given $10-$200 to help with initial necessities. It can be said that, in general, brotherhood and devotion prevail among us, and we remember the old home with love and longing. The officers elected every year are the president, vice president, treasurer, and secretary.

I would like to mention here our brothers who have devoted their time and energy to the *landsmanschaft*'s prosperity: Eli Mints, one of the founders, who now lives in California; Yudel Salmonovitsh and his wife, always working diligently and energetically for the Society and its relief projects; Harry Vayner, who has not missed even one meeting; Henekh Kesler; Henekh Gelernt; the Landsberg-Segal brothers, and last but not least, Binyamin (Benny) Barshap, always in a good mood, a "man of the people," ready to help his fellow Jews. One of the founders of the *landsmanschaft*, he was elected president 11 times. At 70 years of age, he still works at his profession, artistic painting.

A Ladies Auxiliary exists as well, founded 18 years ago by Mrs. Rapoport (née Berezitser). The members of the Ladies Auxiliary were of great help in the Society's relief projects. She passed away two years ago. The Ladies Auxiliary, under the presidency of Mrs. Shpigelman (née Kveytil), does very important and useful work.

Mount Bona in Winter

[446]

A WORD ON CHAYE RAPOPORT

Duvid Rapoport (New York)
English translation by Yocheved Klausner

Merciless death has taken Chaye Rapoport—the tireless doer, the charitable lady, the heart of all the needy, the suffering, and the abandoned—away from us.

She stepped through God's little world with great modesty, always helping the unhappy, bringing hope to the hopeless, and alleviating the misery of the sick and desolate. Her satisfaction in life was helping her fellow man and woman. She fulfilled her mission with love.

To the needy, she gave not only material help, but also a warm and sympathetic heart, and shared their pain in time of distress. Her entire life was devoted to social work, always with heartfelt words and an outstretched hand, without seeking a reward.

She was weak physically but strong spiritually, and her life was filled with good deeds and charity. She never complained, and nothing was too difficult for her. Simplicity, modesty, and a quest for justice were her constant companions in life. She was a true righteous woman.

***

Through her activity, Chaye Rapoport symbolized all the goodness and brotherly feelings of our beautiful Jewish Kremenets, now ruined. She must have inherited her good qualities from her mother-in-law, Blume Rapoport.

I remember the old, gentle soul, Blume Rapoport, walking or running through the muddy streets in her old shoes, stopping by the houses of the well-to-do to collect challahs for the needy. When all the needy had been taken care of and were ready for the Sabbath, her own face would shine with satisfaction. She would do all this work secretly, so as not to humiliate or embarrass anyone ....

***

A young woman, a Holocaust survivor, related that Chaye was like a mother to her.

"When I came over, without relatives or acquaintances, I lived in the HIAS House. With a husband and a child, I felt alone and desperate, not seeing any possibility of improvement. Chaye found an apartment for the family, helped my husband find work, and even registered our child in the Talmud Torah school. Every week, she would visit us to see that all was well."

She was a true righteous woman. She brought light to the darkness.

[447]

KREMENETSERS IN ARGENTINA

Yehuda Koyfman (Buenos Aires)
English translation by Yocheved Klausner

The first Kremenets Jews who left their homes for Argentina landed on these shores almost 30 years ago; the horrible thought that they would have to write reminiscences about our beloved hometown surely never crossed their minds.

Every one of us carries his own pain in his heart; everyone recites his personal Kaddish for his beloved. However, something was missing: the collective painful cry of the surviving Kremenets *landsleit*, expressing our grief but at the same time being a memorial for the martyrs. We hope that this yizkor book, published in Israel, will be that memorial; with these lines, we want to add our little pebble on the tombstone of Kremenets.

***

Jewish immigration to Argentina began in the 1880s with the so-called Baron Hirsch immigration; its aim was to colonize Jews in Argentina. It included large numbers of Jews from Lithuania, Podolia, Bessarabia, and southern Russia, but Kremenets Jews were not among those colonists, as far as we know.

However, some Kremenetsers did go to Argentina on their own initiative long before World War I, but these were only a small number of families.

Immigration from Kremenets to Argentina, as such, must therefore be counted from 1923, when a few young Kremenets Jews touched Argentina's land. In 1924 and 1925, the immigration flow to Argentina increased a little, reaching 50 persons by the end of 1925. Most were young men and women; some were the representatives of their families.

Regardless of their social or cultural standing, the newly arrived Kremenetsers maintained strong ties with their fellow countrymen, united by the sentiment of *landsmanschaft*. Not knowing the language and feeling alone in the unfamiliar environment, they kept close and created their own world, helping each other economically and morally.

Soon, however, the few "greenhorn" years passed. As soon as individuals reached a more or less satisfactory economic position, they began thinking of bringing over the family. In later years, entire families from Kremenets began to immigrate to Argentina.

[448]

Until 1931, immigration to Argentina was not limited and posed no difficulties. The Kremenets *landsmanschaft* numbered about 60 families (300 persons). Beginning in 1931, the Argentinian authorities limited immigration, and the number of Kremenetsers joining their relatives in Argentina decreased considerably—until the outbreak of World War II.

The Holocaust catastrophe, in particular the ruin of Kremenets, brought the Kremenets *landsleit* even closer together. They had lost their most dear and beloved, and through friendship and close contact, they sought consolation from their grief. Soon after the fall of Germany, gruesome news from the survivors in the camps in Poland, Austria, and Italy began to reach them daily; the Kremenets *landsleit* fulfilled the holy duty of stretching out a brotherly helping hand to anyone who was in need.

During the years 1948, 1949, and 1950, survivors kept coming. With the help of their families and friends, most of them adapted to their new life in a warm and friendly environment

Every year on August 14, we remember the destruction of Kremenets. We assemble in the Buenos Aires Jewish cemetery at the symbolic grave of the six million martyrs and cry out for their pain and suffering.

Last year on this Memorial Day, at the initiative of our elder landsman Duvid Shukhman, it was decided to plant the "Kremenets Forest" in the Jewish National Fund Martyrs Forest in Israel.

group of former Kremenets residents in Buenos Aires, 1951

[449]

Today, the Kremenets *landsmanschaft* numbers 250 families (about 600 persons). Except for a very few families that live in the provincial areas, most live in the capital and nearby towns. Their economic situation is, in general, satisfactory. Most families raised a second generation born here, some families even a third.

Our *landsleit* have not been assimilated, at least not language-wise, using generally the Yiddish language. Most of them still cherish their Jewish cultural heritage and take part as much as possible in Jewish social and cultural life, everyone in his or her own way.

[450]

MY TOWN KREMENETS

Helene Vaynberg (New York)

English translation by Yocheved Klausner

> I am still longing for you,
> My beautiful, beloved town Kremenets!
> You are often with me in my dreams,
> Dreams and fantasies without end.
> You are always in my thoughts.
> Never for a moment can I forget you—
> When my heart beats so intensely for you,
> For each stone in the walls of the little house,
> For the little house where I first saw the light of day.
> Where are you now, my town, my home?
> Why have you been so cruelly wiped out?
> I seek all of you, my beloved,
> I live with you my entire life!
> Without you—what is the meaning
> Of my troubled world,
> Of my struggles and my hopes?
> There is no respite, I cannot rest,
> I cannot achieve happiness,
> Until the word is uncovered

That will eternalize the memory of your life.
Like the yearly revival of the beautiful, rich month of May,
So will awake in me every day anew
The memory of my beloved town with its little streets
Adorned with green, blooming trees.
For you, my bright little town,
I shall build a memorial.
As I shall live, I shall forever remember you,
Forever long for you, forever miss you.
For an eternity I shall feel the full sound
Of my little town's song!

SUPPLEMENT:

DEATH NOTICE FOR GALINA SOROCHINSKI

Galina Sorochinski is mentioned in *Pinkas Kremenets* on pages 253 and 262. On page 262, the writer notes (in error) that she died of typhus while serving in the Polish army. However, her daughter, who was nine years old at the time, received the death notice below while in an orphanage in Lublin:

> Regional Command of Supplements, Lublin City, L. Dz. 6946/L. 45. Lublin, 11 June 1945
>
> To: Citizen Natalia Soroczynska, Lublin, Domonikanska Street No. 5
>
> I hereby notify you that your mother, Ms. Halina Soroczynska, faithful to her military oath, exhibiting bravery and courage in the fight for the Fatherland, was wounded and died from wounds on 16 May 1945. She was buried with military honors in the city of Posen in the cemetery at 35 Ksiedza Skorupki Street, in tomb no. 14—20 meters from the main entrance.
>
> Regional Commander of Supplements, Lublin City, Lieutenant Colonel Putrament
>
> [Stamp: Polish Army, R.K.U. Lublin-City]

We thank Anna Brune, Galina Sorochinski's granddaughter, for the information about her grandmother, for translating the notice, and for allowing us to reprint it here.

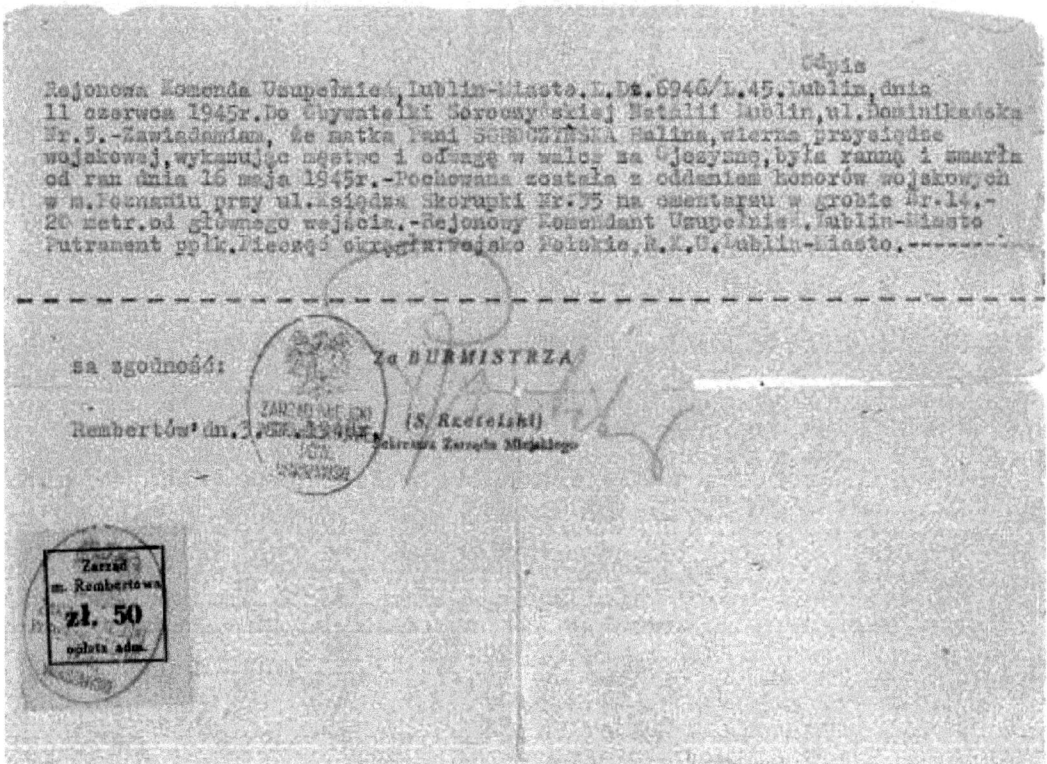

Death Notice for Galina Sorochinski

NAME INDEX

The page numbers in this index represent those in the original yizkor book, found in [brackets] in the text. An asterisk (*) after a surname indicates that is it a woman's married surname.

Ezra Podkaminer (from Podkamien), 159

F

Farber*, Mrs. (teacher), 140

Father Poish, 400

Faydel, Natan, Rabbi, note 53

Faydel, Shmuel Fayvish, R', note 53

Fayer, A., 410

Faygenberg, Rachel, 154, 156. *See also* Amari, Rachel

Fayngloz, Aharon, R' (ritual slaughterer), 181

Fayvish Kelvales (heifer), 159, 400

Fayvishis, 118

Fayvish-Leyb, Rabbi (rabbi of Kremenets), 181

Fayvush (son of Chaye-Rikel), 158

Feld (family), 249, 435

Feldman*, Rachel (née Otiker), 129 (photo), 143, 148, 187, 205

Feldman, Arye (Leybchik/Libchik; 1900-1942), 132, 143, 144, 148, 187, 200, 204-205

Feldman, Berish, 318, 384

Feldman, Fayvel, 92

Feldman, L., 366

Feldman, Malke (Maliusya), 143

Feldman, Rivke, 143

Feldman, Shmerl, 377

Feldman, Shmuel, 306 (photo)

Feliks (1560-1561, father of Yakov), 13

Fertel Of (quarter chicken), 400

Feyge (seamstress), 369

Fidel, Ester, 224

Fiks, N., 410

Fild (family), 249, 435

Fingerhut (singers), 87

Fingerhut, Babe, 103

Fingerhut, Iser, 396

Fingerhut, Naumik, 318

Fingerhut, Shlome (1888-1942), 63, 84, 105, 148, 149 (photo), 203 (photo), 203-204, 266, 322, 327, 341, 439

Fingerhut. *See also* Fingerut

Fingerut (cabinetmaker), 170

Fingerut, Mordekhay Leyb, R', 203

Fingerut, Shlome (1888-1942), 63, 84, 105, 148, 149 (photo), 203 (photo), 203-204, 266, 322, 327, 341, 439

Fingerut. *See also* Fingerut

Finkelshteyn (alias of Yosef Avidar), 221

Finkelshteyn, 137

Fisherman, Avraham, 109

Fisherman, Tsvi, 143

Fishil, R' (son of Leyb), 26

Fishman (family), 48

Fishman, Chayim, 102, 104, 304 (photo)

Fishman, Eli, 106

Fishman, Hinde, 218, 224 (photo), 224-225

Fishman, R., 138 (photo)

Fishman, Risye, 305 (photo)

Fishman, Shlome, 135

Fishman, Yeshayahu, 118

Flyer (Commander), 225

Fokner, Heinrich, 209

Foks, Itshi, 441

Forman, Dr., 153

Frenkel*, Vitye (née Karshun), 206

Frenkel, Moshe (Mishe; 1902-1944), 206, 206 (photo)

Frenkel, Shlome, R', 206

Frenkel, Yone, 130, 143

Freyde di Miltshnitshke (flour seller), 159

Freydiks, 349

Fridkes, Chaye, 392

Fridman, Aharon, 59, 108 (photo), 109, 306 (photo)

Fridman, Chane, 305 (photo)

Fridman, Chayim, 372, 379

Fridman, Henekh, 372, 379

Fridman, Pesi, 392

Fridman, Pini, 234, 416

Fridman, T., 103

Fridman, Yosl, 372, 379

Frishberg*, Dvore, 367

Frishberg (house), 177

TOWN LOCATOR

[**Translation Editor's Note:** This translation of *Pinkas Kremenets* uses common English names of well-known cities and towns (e.g., Haifa, Jerusalem, Moscow, New York, Petersburg, Warsaw). Names of other European cities and towns are the 1900 names as they appear in the JewishGen Gazetteer (https://www.jewishgen.org/Communities/LocTown.asp).]

Town Name	Probable Location and Distance from Kremenets (50°06' N 25°43' E)
Aleksinets	49°50' N 25°33' E, 19.8 miles SSW
Bar	49°04' N 27°40' E, 112.7 miles SE
Bazaliya	49°43' N 26°28' E, 42.6 miles SE
Bedzin	50°20' N 19°09' E, 290.5 miles W
Belaya Krinitsa	50°09' N 25°45' E, 3.8 miles NNE
Belozirka	49°46' N 26°11' E, 31.0 miles SE
Belz	50°23' N 24°01' E, 77.6 miles WNW
Bensheig	49°41' N 8°37' E, 759.6 miles W
Berestechko	50°21' N 25°07' E, 31.6 miles WNW
Bereza Kartuska	52°32' N 24°59' E, 171.0 miles N
Berezhtsy	50°06' N 25°37' E, 4.4 miles W
Bogo-Yablonskaya	52°44' N 40°43' E, 669.6 miles ENE
Boremel	50°28' N 25°12' E, 34.1 miles NW
Braslav	51°06' N 17°02' E, 386.5 miles WNW
Brest	52°06' N 23°42' E, 163.4 miles NNW
Brody	50°05' N 25°09' E, 25.1 miles W
Cheliabinsk	55°09' N 61°26' E, 1,519.0 miles ENE
Chelm	51°08' N 23°30' E, 120.5 miles NW
Chernigov	51°30' N 31°18' E, 262.0 miles ENE
Chernobyl	51°16' N 30°14' E, 213.3 miles ENE
Czestochowa	50°48' N 19°07' E, 294.1 miles WNW
Dorpat	58°22' N 26°44' E, 572.2 miles N
Dubno	50°25' N 25°45' E, 21.9 miles N
Dubrovitsa	51°34' N 26°34' E, 107.8 miles NNE
Feldefing	47°57' N 11°18' E, 668.3 miles W
Folwarki Wielkie	50°03' N 25°47' E, 5 mi. SE
Fulda	50°33' N 9°40' E, 706.8 miles W
Gorinka	49°59' N 25°47' E, 8.6 miles SSE
Gorodno	51°52' N 26°30' E, 126.6 miles NNE
Gorokhov	50°30' N 24°46' E, 50.2 miles NW
Gritsev	49°58' N 27°13' E, 67.2 miles E

Grodno	51°52' N 26°30' E, 126.6 miles NNE
Halicz	49°07' N 24°44' E, 80.9 miles SSW
Hanau	50°08' N 8°55' E, 742.2 miles W
Holgrad	48°42' N 25°51' E, 96.9 miles S
Jaroslaw	50°01' N 22°41' E, 134.6 miles W
Kalisz	51°45' N 18°05' E, 351.0 miles WNW
Kamenets Podolskiy	48°40' N 26°34' E, 106.1 miles SSE
Kamenitsa	50°21' N 25°42' E, 17.3 miles N
Katerburg	50°00' N 25°53' E, 10.1 miles SE
Kazan	55°45' N 49°08' E, 1,043.6 miles ENE
Kherson	46°38' N 32°36' E, 396.0 miles SE
Kishinev	47°00' N 28°51' E, 257.4 miles SE
Klesov	51°20' N 26°56' E, 100.5 miles NNE
Klusk	51°04' N 24°36' E, 82.8 miles NW
Kobi	43°30' N 46°15' E, 1,067.0 miles ESE
Korets	50°37' N 27°10' E, 73.2 miles ENE
Kornitsa	50°03' N 26°32' E, 36.4 miles E
Korsun	49°26' N 31°15' E, 251.0 miles E
Kotsi	?
Kovel	51°13' N 24°43' E, 88.7 miles NNW
Kozin	50°16' N 25°28' E, 16.0 miles NW
Krasilov	49°39' N 26°58' E, 63.7 miles ESE
Krupets	50°09' N 25°19' E, 18.0 miles W
Kulchiny	49°45' N 26°54' E, 57.9 miles ESE
Kunev	50°15' N 26°22' E, 30.6 miles ENE
Kurilovtsy	49°10' N 27°59' E, 120.1 miles ESE
Kuzmin	49°42' N 27°05' E, 66.8 miles ESE
Kuzmin	49°15' N 26°31' E, 68.7 miles SSE
Labun	50°01' N 27°22' E, 73.4 miles E
Lakhovtsy	50°00' N 26°25' E, 31.8 miles ESE
Lanovtsy	49°52' N 26°05' E, 22.9 miles SE
Lvov	49°50' N 24°00' E, 78.4 miles WSW
Leszniow	50°14' N 25°05' E, 29.5 miles WNW
Lokachi	50°44' N 24°39' E, 64.1 miles NW
Lublin	51°15' N 22°34' E, 159.0 miles WNW
Ludvipol	50°50' N 27°00' E, 75.8 miles NE
Lutsk	50°45' N 25°20' E, 47.9 miles NNW
Lyubar	49°55' N 27°45' E, 91.1 miles E
Lyuboml	51°14' N 24°02' E, 107.5 miles NW

Makow	52°52' N 21°06' E, 275.4 miles NW
Markisch Friedland	53°20' N 16°06' E, 467.5 miles WNW
Mezherichi	50°39' N 26°52' E, 63.3 miles NE
Namangan	41°00' N 71°40' E, 2270.0 miles E
Nemirov	50°07' N 23°27' E, 100.4 miles W
Nesvizh	50°38' N 25°06' E, 45.8 miles NW
Nezhny Novgorod	56°20' N 44°00' E, 866.1 miles NE
Niezhin	51°03' N 31°53' E
Nofketora	?
Novograd Volynskiy	50°36' N 27°37' E, 91.0 miles ENE
Ostrog	50°20' N 26°31' E, 38.8 miles ENE
Ostropol	49°48' N 27°34' E, 84.8 miles ESE
Ovruch	51°19' N 28°48' E, 158.8 miles ENE
Ozhigovtsy	49°38' N 26°14' E, 39.6 miles SE
Petrikov	49°32' N 25°35' E, 39.6 miles S
Pinczow	50°32' N 20°32' E, 230.4 miles W
Pishchatintsy	48°47' N 25°59' E, 91.7 miles S
Pochayev	50°01' N 25°29' E, 11.8 miles WSW
Podkamien	49°56' N 25°19' E, 21.2 miles WSW
Podlisets	50°00' N 26°49' E, 49.3 miles E
Polonnoye	50°07' N 27°31' E, 79.7 miles E
Polotsk	55°29' N 28°48' E, 393.5 miles NNE
Posen	52°25' N 16°58' E, 410.2 miles WNW
Potok	48°55' N 25°21' E, 83.9 miles SSW
Przemysl	49°47' N 22°47' E, 132.2 miles W
Przeworsk	50°04' N 22°30' E, 142.5 miles W
Pticha	50°18' N 25°37' E, 14.5 miles NNW
Radzivilov	50°08' N 25°15' E, 20.8 miles W
Reichenbach	50°43' N 16°39' E, 401.0 miles W
Rokhmanov	50°08' N 26°06' E, 17.1 miles E
Rokitno	51°17' N 27°13' E, 104.8 miles NE
Rovno	50°37' N 26°15' E, 42.7 miles NNE
Rozishche	50°55' N 25°16' E, 59.8 miles NNW
Rudnya	50°13' N 25°29' E, 13.1 miles NW
Sapanuv	50°09' N 25°41' E, 3.8 miles NNW
Sarny	51°20' N 26°36' E, 93.5 miles NNE
Semiatyche	52°27' N 22°53' E, 203.2 miles NW
Shavli	55°56' N 23°19' E, 414.9 miles NNW
Shchepetovka	50°11' N 27°04' E, 60.0 miles E

Shumsk	50°07' N 26°07' E, 17.8 miles E
Slavuta	50°18' N 26°52' E, 52.7 miles ENE
Starokonstantinov	49°45' N 27°13' E, 70.9 miles ESE
Stolin	51°53' N 26°51' E, 132.6 miles NNE
Sudilkov	50°10' N 27°08' E, 62.9 miles E
Szczebrzeszyn	50°42' N 22°58' E, 127.9 miles WNW
Tambov	52°44' N 41°26' E, 699.2 miles ENE
Tarnopol	49°33' N 25°35' E, 38.4 miles S
Teofipol	49°50' N 26°25' E, 36.1 miles ESE
Tetiev	49°23' N 29°40' E, 183.0 miles ESE
Tikhomel	49°58' N 26°15' E, 25.4 miles ESE
Trembowla	49°18' N 25°43' E, 55.2 miles S
Tulchin	48°41' N 28°52' E, 172.0 miles ESE
Tulichuv	51°00' N 24°39' E, 77.8 miles NW
Tykocin	53°12' N 22°47' E, 248.2 miles NNW
Uman	48°45' N 30°13' E, 222.7 miles ESE
Velikiy Kochurov	50°06' N 25°43' E, 131.5 miles S
Verba	50°17' N 25°37' E, 13.4 miles NNW
Veselivka	Near 50°13' N 25°77 E [page 249: "Veselivka near Belaya Krinitsa"]
Vilna	54°41' N 25°19' E, 316.9 miles N
Vinnitsa	49°14' N 28°29' E, 137.3 miles ESE
Vishnevets	49°54' N 25°45' E, 13.9 miles S
Vladimir	50°51' N 24°20' E, 79.9 miles NW
Volochisk	49°32' N 26°10' E, 44.0 miles SSE
Vyshgorodok	49°46' N 25°58' E, 25.6 miles SSE
Worms	49°38' N 8°22' E, 771.4 miles W
Yampol	49°58' N 26°15' E, 25.4 miles ESE
Yekaterinoslav	50°06' N 25°43' E, 432.4 miles ESE
Zaleszczyki	48°39' N 25°44' E, 100.5 miles S
Zalozce	49°47' N 25°22' E, 26.8 miles SW
Zaslav	50°07' N 26°48' E, 48.0 miles E
Zbarazh	49°40' N 25°47' E, 30.1 miles S
Zdolbunov	50°31' N 26°15' E, 37.2 miles NE
Zhitomir	50°15' N 28°40' E, 130.9 miles E
Zloczow	49°48' N 24°54' E, 41.8 miles WSW
Zolkiew	50°04' N 23°58' E, 77.6 miles W
Zurawica	49°49' N 22°48' E, 131.0 miles W
Zychlin	52°15' N 19°38' E, 302.2 miles WNW

THE KREMENETS SHTETL CO-OP

Coordinators: Ellen Garshick (KremenetsDRG@gmail.com), Ron Doctor (rddpdx@gmail.com) and Sheree Roth (ssroth@pacbell.net)

The Kremenets Shtetl CO-OP, and activity of the Kremenets District Research Group, is a worldwide group of people who trace their ancestors to Kremenets and the towns of the Kremenets District in present-day Ukraine. Ron Doctor and Sheree Roth formed the CO-OP in August 2000, following the International Association of Jewish Genealogical Societies (IAJGS) Conference in Salt Lake City. The CO-OP is part of Jewish Records Indexing—Poland (JRI-Poland) and a project of the Kremenets District Research Group.

The Kremenets Shtetl CO-OP translates records, Yizkor Books, cemetery gravestones, and many other documents. When a translation is completed, we add all personal names, town names, and source document information to our Indexed Concordance of Personal Names and Town Names. For more information on our projects and on resources for researching your Kremenets roots, see http://kehilalinks.jewishgen.org/Kremenets/web-pages/about-kremenets.html.

SUPPORT OUR PROJECTS

The CO-OP is volunteer-based, but we use paid professional translators to accelerate some translation projects. You can help make the project a success by donating time, money, or both. If you can read (or at least recognize) the Cyrillic and/or Hebrew alphabets and would like to help, please contact KremenetsDRG@gmail.com.

To contribute to the translation of records from Kremenets, please send your donation to JRI-Poland (a nonprofit 501(c)(3) organization), following the instructions at https://jri-poland.org/support.htm. Earmark your donations for Kremenets Towns.

To enable us to track contributions, please send an e-mail message to KremenetsDRG@gmail.com indicating the amount of your donation.

NAME INDEX

This is the Name Index for this English Translation

Gilman, 169, 503
Gilrant, 128, 166, 503
Gindes, 214, 248, 482, 503
Ginsberg, 39, 503
Ginsburg, 497
Gintsburg, 103, 124, 126, 503
Gitelman, 436, 503
Giterman, 349, 503
Gletshteyn, 388, 503
Gliklis, 125, 126, 503
Gluzman, 107, 149, 385, 503
Gofman, 309, 456, 503
Golander, 119, 503
Golberg, 503
Goldberg, 45, 124, 157, 168, 179, 312, 503
Goldenberg, 46, 56, 70, 85, 105, 114, 117, 122, 124, 126, 128, 153, 179, 198, 242, 246, 249, 261, 269, 275, 279, 280, 286, 339, 350, 371, 379, 387, 401, 408, 459, 486, 503
Goldenberg-Shpigel-Gurevits, 476
Goldenberg-Shpigl-Gurvits, 306, 503
Goldfarb, 161, 275, 388, 398, 503
Goldgart, 75, 76, 503
Goldman, 486, 503
Goldring, 63, 65, 73, 78, 103, 105, 128, 131, 133, 162, 169, 174, 178, 179, 183, 350, 369, 399, 400, 455, 456, 457, 503
Goldsher, 128, 503
Goldshteyn, 214, 503
Goltsman, 321, 503
Gordon, 170, 208, 244, 395, 486, 503
Goren, 79, 504
Gorengut, 63, 79, 86, 131, 139, 142, 143, 144, 166, 504
Gorinfeld, 123, 504
Gorinshteyn, 122, 124, 247, 504
Gornfeld, 348, 397, 436, 504
Gotlober, 45, 59, 87, 504
Greben, 259, 504
Grinberg, 115, 122, 124, 133, 149, 295, 306, 332, 335, 362, 384, 388, 455, 468, 477, 504
Grinboym, 182, 239, 504
Grinshpun, 155, 504
Groyzenberg, 291, 463, 504
Gun, 290, 391, 462, 504
Gurevits, 126, 148, 323, 391, 504
Gurvits, 279, 504
Guterman, 486, 504
Guthelf, 154, 504
Guz, 436, 504

H

Halperin, 18, 19, 20, 24, 25, 29, 31, 32, 33, 34, 35, 36, 37, 504
Handelman, 172, 504
Handelrafel, 259, 504
Hanover, 20, 23, 34, 504
Havis, 122, 127, 130, 135, 139, 145, 148, 151, 152, 153, 156, 175
Heftman, 230, 504
Heker, 485, 504
Heler, 18, 19, 70, 71, 218, 258, 504
Hertsberg, 486, 504
Heylprin, 283, 500, 504, 512
Hindes, 46, 59, 60, 128, 183, 233, 234, 235, 236, 237, 241, 264, 320, 350, 374, 504
Hipsh, 192, 223, 445, 448, 515
Hirschfeld, 193
Hirshfeld, 44, 504
Hofman, 80, 153, 154, 155, 173, 244, 252, 332, 415, 504, 505
Hokhberg, 114, 396, 436, 505
Hokhgelernter, 70, 219, 220, 309, 384, 412, 481, 503, 505, 508
Holander, 168, 229, 505
Holtsman, 128, 505
Horovits, 20, 37, 153, 172, 173, 179, 271, 503, 505
Horovits-Goldenberg, 171

I

Ikar, 72, 505
Ipa, 395, 505

K

Kadushke, 192, 223, 413, 445, 448, 505
Kagan, 2, 119, 124, 339, 482, 505
Kagarlitski, 321, 324, 326, 505, 506
Kahana, 128, 505
Kahaner, 256, 505
Kamenshon, 456, 505
Kaner, 321, 323, 505
Kaplan, 206, 321, 505
Kapuza, 103, 505
Kapuzer, 109, 113, 127, 150, 348, 363, 505
Karsh, 131, 166, 406, 408, 505
Karshun, 253, 502, 505
Katraborski, 128, 505
Katsav, 192, 446, 498, 508
Katsizne, 2, 204, 216, 505
Katsner, 166, 168, 505